Blackstone's Statutes
Criminal Justice & Sentencing

Blackstone's Statutes
Criminal Justice
& Sentencing

···

Third Edition

Edited by

Barry Mitchell

*Professor of Criminal Law and Criminal Justice
at Coventry University*

Salim Farrar

*Associate Professor at the International Islamic
University Malaysia*

OXFORD
UNIVERSITY PRESS

OXFORD

UNIVERSITY PRESS

Great Clarendon Street, Oxford OX2 6DP

Oxford University Press is a department of the University of Oxford.
It furthers the University's objective of excellence in research, scholarship,
and education by publishing worldwide in

Oxford New York

Auckland Cape Town Dar es Salaam Hong Kong Karachi
Kuala Lumpur Madrid Melbourne Mexico City Nairobi
New Delhi Shanghai Taipei Toronto

With offices in

Argentina Austria Brazil Chile Czech Republic France Greece
Guatemala Hungary Italy Japan Poland Portugal Singapore
South Korea Switzerland Thailand Turkey Ukraine Vietnam

Oxford is a registered trade mark of Oxford University Press
in the UK and in certain other countries

Published in the United States
by Oxford University Press Inc., New York

This selection © Barry Mitchell and Salim Farrar 2007

First edition 2002
Second edition 2004
Third edition 2007

British Library Cataloguing in Publication Data

Data available

Typeset by Newgen Imaging Systems (P) Ltd., Chennai, India
Printed in Great Britain
on acid-free paper by
CPI Bath

ISBN 0–19–928824–0   978–0–19–928824–3

1 3 5 7 9 10 8 6 4 2

EDITORS' PREFACE TO THE THIRD EDITION

In the two years since our last edition, the process of criminal justice reform has continued apace. With the exception of the restrictions on jury trial (ss 43–48), 'live links' (ss 51–54) and expedited appeals in relation to evidential rulings (ss 62–66), many of the changes introduced by the Criminal Justice Act 2003 are now in force and are incorporated in this current volume. In combination with the changes brought about by the Serious Organised Crime and Police Act 2005 (SOCPA), the Drugs Act 2005 and the Revised Codes of Practice (2005/6), these amendments have significantly expanded police powers and, to some extent, continued the process of restricting the rights and protections afforded to suspects and defendants.

The Criminal Justice Act 2003 extends police stop and search powers to offences under section 1 of the Criminal Damage Act 1971, through the insertion of a new section 1(e) to PACE 1984, and there is a further provision dealing with fireworks (inserted by SOCPA). There is also a new power to direct a person to leave a place who is in breach of a specific court order following a conviction (section 112 of SOCPA).

Powers of arrest and detention have also been amended and enhanced. SOCPA 2005 amends the arrest powers under section 24 of PACE and inserts a new section 24A, facilitating arrest, without warrant, by persons other than police officers. This offloading of police functions to other agencies is reflected in the Revised Codes of Practice[1] and the new Code G, in particular, which purports to guide and regulate their duties. Section 25 of PACE detailing General Arrest Conditions is now repealed. Under the new section 42(1) of PACE (amended by the Criminal Justice Act 2003), Superintendents can authorize detention of persons suspected of 'arrestable offences' for up to 36 hours. There is no longer a requirement that he be arrested for a 'serious arrestable offence'. Under the Drugs Act 2005, suspected drugs offenders now can be remanded in custody by a magistrate for up to 192 days (amending section 152 of the Criminal Justice Act 1988). The Drugs Act also amends section 55 of PACE 1984 and inserts a new section 55A providing for X-rays and ultrasound scans.

Fingerprints and non-intimate samples can all be obtained without consent from any suspect arrested for a recordable offence, irrespective of whether his fingerprint or sample is needed in the investigation of the offence (these amendments to ss 61 and 63 of PACE were introduced by the Criminal Justice Act 2003). Section 117 of SOCPA (amending section 61 of PACE) also allows fingerprints to be taken of persons whom a police officer is unable to ascertain their name through ordinary channels. Section 118 of SOCPA 2005 inserts a new section 61A into PACE, enabling footprint impressions to be taken with or without consent (in the specified circumstances). Other notable amendments to police powers and their regulation include the new provisions on staff custody officers (see sections 120–121 of SOCPA 2005) and the amendments to section 64A of PACE (the photographing of suspects) by section 116 of SOCPA.

Bail procedures have also been rationalized and tightened. Schedule 1 of the Bail Act 1976 has been amended (by the Criminal Justice Act 2003) to reduce the likelihood of persons absconding and committing offences whilst on bail (new paragraph 6 of Part 1).

As for matters relating to trial and appeal, the statutory rationalization of similar fact evidence and bad character evidence are now in force (sections 98–110 of the CJA 2003) and are included in this edition. We have also inserted the new procedures on a Prosecutor's Right to Appeal and to ask for a Retrial (sections 57–67 and 75–91 of the CJA 2003, respectively).

---

[1] The Revised Codes of Practice came into force after midnight on 31 December 2005. Many of the revisions of the existing codes also reflect changes brought about by SOCPA 2005 and the Drugs Act 2005.

For reasons of space, there are a number of texts related to the pre-trial and trial process that are not included in our text but are referred to in the website linked to this edition. These include relevant parts of the new Criminal Procedure Rules and the Code for Crown Prosecutors. In keeping with the editorial decision of the two previous editions, we have also decided not to include RIPA 2000 or the various pieces of anti-terrorism legislation as we feel they deserve specialist treatment elsewhere.

The greatest impact on sentencing since the last edition has been made by the implementation of further provisions of the CJA 2003, and yet more are due to be brought into effect in the foreseeable future. In this latter respect, it is important for readers to make regular checks to see when new provisions are brought into force. Hence this third edition includes new provisions, for example, on dangerous offenders and short terms of imprisonment, especially intermittent custody, whilst new provisions on deferment of sentencing and on suspended sentences of imprisonment have replaced the old law. A whole range of amendments have been made to community orders. The section on life sentences has also been expanded, and there are new provisions on concurrent and consecutive sentencing. An additional feature of the CJA 2003 is the identification of general sentencing guidelines, including the setting up of the Sentencing Guidelines Council, and these have been included in this latest edition.

Barry Mitchell and Salim Farrar
May 2006

EDITORS' PREFACE TO THE FIRST EDITION

There are numerous undergraduate and postgraduate courses in law and other disciplines such as criminology which include various aspects of criminal justice and sentencing. In the general sense at least, sentencing is an integral part of the criminal justice process, and it is arguable therefore that there is no need to identify sentencing separately. We have done so however simply because not all courses include it—some do not go beyond the point of conviction—and we obviously want to make it clear that this book encompasses important statutory provisions which apply across the whole gamut of the criminal justice system.

As most of us appreciate (if only through the media), there has been a constant stream of legislation, especially during the last fifteen years or so, which has affected all dimensions of criminal justice. Although this has precipitated a considerable number of statutory instruments, working guidelines and practice directions, this book confines itself to relevant statutory provisions (including the Codes of Practice under the Police and Criminal Evidence Act 1984). In an attempt to consolidate what had become an increasingly unmanageable mass of provisions on sentencing contained in several statutes, Parliament enacted the Powers of Criminal Courts (Sentencing) Act 2000. As is evident from the Contents pages at the start of this book, this has simplified the situation, but amendments have already been made to it (which we have incorporated) by, for example, the Criminal Justice and Court Services Act 2000. Furthermore, there are some sections of the Powers of Criminal Courts (Sentencing) Act 2000 which contain important changes to the law but which have not yet been brought into force. For example, sections 87 and 88 will replace section 67 of the Criminal Justice Act 1967 on time spent in custody on remand, and section 61 of the PCC(S)A 2000 will abolish detention in a young offender institution and thereby lower the eligibility for imprisonment from 21 to 18 years of age. At the time of writing, no dates have been fixed for implementing these changes but they have been included in italic type. Other amendments to the PCC(S)A 2000 include the introduction of exclusion orders, a new type of community order, but it is unknown when this amendment will be brought into effect and the relevant provisions have been omitted from this book.

One area in which Parliament has recently been active is surveillance and electronic searches. The statutes relating to these issues are the Police Act 1997 and the Regulation of Investigatory Powers Act 2000, but the subject is very complex and one which we feel merits separate consideration elsewhere.

There were various formats available to us for structuring the book. We suspect that most people will want to use it by reference to a particular topic—arrest and detention, bail, disclosure, etc.—and we have set the book out on that basis.

We should like to record our thanks to colleagues at Oxford University Press, especially to Barbara Laing and John Grandidge, for their support, assistance and patience. As ever, though, any errors remain our responsibility.

Barry Mitchell and Salim Farrar
August 2002

CONTENTS

Editors' Preface to the Third Edition   v
Editors' Preface to the First Edition   vii

PART I   **Criminal Justice**   1

(a) **Access to Justice**   1

   Right to legal representation   1

   European Convention on Human Rights,
      Article 6(3)(b) and (c)   1
   Access to Justice Act 1999, ss. 12–18   1

(b) **Police Powers and Issues During Investigation**   5

   Rights to liberty, security and privacy   5

   European Convention on Human Rights, Articles 5, 8   5

   Stop and search   6

   Police and Criminal Evidence Act 1984, ss. 1–3   6
   Codes of Practice, Code A, paras 1–5   9
   Criminal Justice and Public Order Act 1994, s. 60   23

   Intimate searches   25

   Police and Criminal Evidence Act 1984, ss. 55, 55A   25

   Exclusion zones   28

   Serious Organised Crime and Police Act 2005, s. 112   28

   **The power to take intimate and non-intimate
   body samples**   29

   Police and Criminal Evidence Act 1984,
      ss. 61–65   29
   Criminal Evidence (Amendment) Act 1997, ss. 1, 2   42

   Arrest   44

   Police and Criminal Evidence Act 1984,
      ss. 24, 24A, 27–30, 56   44
   Codes of Practice, Code C, para 3   48
   Codes of Practice, Code G, paras 2–4   52

   Detention   55

   Police and Criminal Evidence Act 1984, ss. 37–46A   55
   Codes of Practice, Code C, paras 2, 5, 6, 8, 9, 15, 16   69

   Identification   86

   Codes of Practice, Code D, paras 3–6   86

Questioning   115

Police and Criminal Evidence Act 1984, s. 58   115
Criminal Justice Act 2003, ss. 22–24   116
Codes of Practice, Code C, paras 10–14   116
Codes of Practice, Code E, paras 3–6   125
Codes of Practice, Code F, paras 2–6   130

Control of abuse of police powers   136

Police Reform Act 2002, ss. 9–24, 26–29   136

Prosecutorial review   154

Prosecution of Offences Act 1985, ss. 1–3, 10   154

Bail   157

Bail Act 1976, ss. 3–7, Schedule 1, Pt 1,
    paras 2–6, 8, 9   157
Criminal Justice and Public Order Act 1994, s. 25   168
Police and Criminal Evidence Act 1984, ss. 46A–47A   169
Bail (Amendment) Act 1993, s. 1   171
Children and Young Persons Act 1969, ss. 23–23AA   172

Mode of trial   176

European Convention on Human Rights, Article 6   176
Magistrates' Courts Act 1980, ss. 17–23, 25–26, Schedule 1   177

Trial by jury   183

Juries Act 1974, ss. 1, 3, 8–9A, 17, Schedule 1   183
Contempt of Court Act 1981, s. 8   187

(c) **Issues During Trial, Evidence and Procedure**   187

Disclosure   187

Criminal Procedure and Investigations Act 1996,
    ss. 1, 3–8, 10–18   187

Vulnerable witnesses   197

Criminal Justice Act 1988, ss. 32, 34   197
Youth Justice and Criminal Evidence Act 1999,
    ss. 16–30, 34–43   197

Right to silence/drawing inferences   212

Criminal Justice and Public Order Act 1994, ss. 34–37   212
Youth Justice and Criminal Evidence Act 1999, s. 59   215

Confessions   215

Police and Criminal Evidence Act 1984,
    ss. 76–78, 82(1) and (3)   215

Bad character evidence   217

Criminal Justice Act 2003, ss. 98–110, 118   217
Theft Act 1968, s. 27(3)   223

Appeals and reviews   224

Magistrates' Courts Act 1980, ss. 108, 111   224
Supreme Court Act 1981, s. 48   224
Criminal Appeal Act 1968, ss. 2, 7(1), 23, 23A, 33   225
Criminal Appeal Act 1995, ss. 8, 13   227

The prosecution's right to appeal   228

Criminal Justice Act 2003, ss. 57–61, 67   228

Re-trials   230

Criminal Justice Act 2003, ss. 75–79, 82, 84   230

PART II   **Sentencing**   234

(a) **Deferment and Postponement of Sentencing**   234

Powers of Criminal Courts (Sentencing) Act 2000   234
Deferment of sentence (ss. 1–1D)   234
Committal to Crown Court for sentence (ss. 3–7)   236
Remission for sentence: young offenders etc. (ss. 8–10)   241
Remand by magistrates' court for medical
examination (s. 11)   243

(b) **General Provisions about Sentencing**   243

Criminal Justice Act 2003, ss. 142, 144–146, 174   243

**Community sentences and discretionary
custodial sentences**   246

Criminal Justice Act 2003, ss. 147–150, 156–159   246

More general provisions   248

Criminal Justice Act 2003, ss. 196–213   248

(c) **Sentencing Guidelines**   255

Criminal Justice Act 2003, ss. 167, 169–172   255

(d) **Custodial Sentencing**   257

General provisions   257

Powers of Criminal Courts (Sentencing)
Act 2000, ss. 76, 77   257
Criminal Justice Act 2003, ss. 152, 153   257
Powers of Criminal Courts (Sentencing) Act 2000
ss. 83, 89–92, 99–107, 110, 111   258
Magistrates' Courts Act 1980, s. 32   264
Murder (Abolition of Death Penalty)
Act 1965 (as amended), s. 1   265

Prison sentences of less than 12 months   265

Criminal Justice Act 2003, ss. 181–186   265

Suspended sentences   268
Criminal Justice Act 2003, ss. 189–192   268

Consecutive or concurrent terms   270
Criminal Justice Act 2003, ss. 263–265   270

Release on licence   272
Criminal Justice Act 2003, ss. 237–240, 244, 246–258   272

(e) Dangerous Offenders   278
Criminal Justice Act 2003, ss. 224–229, 231–235   278

(f) Sex Offenders   281

Notification requirement for sex offenders   281
Sexual Offences Act 2003, ss. 80–92   281

(g) Life Sentences   289
Powers of Criminal Courts (Sentencing) Act 2000, s. 82A   289
Criminal Justice Act 2003, ss. 269, 270, Schedule 21   290

(h) Community Orders   292

Powers of Criminal Courts (Sentencing) Act 2000
  (as amended)   292
  General provisions (s. 33)   292
Criminal Justice Act 2003, ss. 177–179   293
Powers of Criminal Courts (Sentencing)
  Act 2000 (as amended), s. 36B   294
  Curfew orders (ss. 37, 39, 40)   294
  Attendance centre orders (s. 60, Schedule 5)   295
  Supervision orders (ss. 63–64A, Schedule 6, Schedule 7)   298
  Action plan orders (ss. 69–71)   304

(i) Financial Penalties and Orders   307

Fines   307
Criminal Justice Act 2003, ss. 162–166   307
Powers of Criminal Courts (Sentencing) Act 2000   308
  Compensation orders (ss. 130, 131, 133)   308
  Young offenders (ss. 135–138)   310
  Miscellaneous powers (ss. 139, 140)   312

Deprivation orders   314

Powers of Criminal Courts (Sentencing) Act 2000,
  ss. 143–145   314
Misuse of Drugs Act 1971, s. 27   315
Firearms Act 1968, s. 52   315
Prevention of Crime Act 1953, s. 1   316

(j) Restitution Orders   316

Powers of Criminal Courts (Sentencing) Act 2000,
  ss. 148, 149   316

(k) **Reparation Orders etc.**   317

Reparation orders   317
Powers of Criminal Courts (Sentencing) Act 2000,
  ss. 73, 74, Schedule 8   317

Referral of young offenders   319
Powers of Criminal Courts (Sentencing) Act 2000,
  ss. 16–27, 29, Schedule 1   319

Parenting orders   330
Crime and Disorder Act 1998, ss. 8, 9   330

Binding over to keep the peace   332
Justices of the Peace Act 1968, s. 1(7)   332
Magistrates' Courts Act 1980, s. 115   332

Binding over of parent or guardian   333
Powers of Criminal Courts (Sentencing) Act 2000, s. 150   333

Discharge   333
Powers of Criminal Courts (Sentencing)
  Act 2000, ss. 12–15   333

(l) **Confiscation Orders**   336
Proceeds of Crime Act 2002, ss. 6–14   336

(m) **Disqualification and Exclusion etc.**   340

Recommendation for deportation   340
Immigration Act 1971, ss. 6, 7, Schedule 3   340

Exclusion from licensed premises   342
Licensed Premises (Exclusion of Certain Persons)
  Act 1980, ss. 1, 2   342

Football banning orders   343
Football Spectators Act 1989 (as amended), ss. 14–14J   343

Disqualification of company directors   346
Company Directors Disqualification Act 1986, ss. 1, 2, 13   346

Disqualification from driving   347
Road Traffic Offenders Act 1988 (as amended),
  ss. 34–40, 42, 43   347
Powers of Criminal Courts (Sentencing) Act 2000, ss. 146, 147   354

(n) **Mentally Disorded Offenders**   355
Powers of Criminal Courts (Sentencing) Act 2000,
  Schedule 6   355
Mental Health Act 1983 (as amended),
  ss. 37–43, 45–45B, 47, 54   356

Criminal Procedure (Insanity) Act 1964 (as amended), s. 5   363

(o) **Human Rights**   **364**

Human Rights Act 1998, ss. 1–8, Schedule 1 (Articles 3, 5, 7)   364

(p) **Rehabilitation**   **369**

Rehabilitation of Offenders Act 1974 (as amended),
   ss. 1, 4–7   369

Index   **377**

ALPHABETICAL CONTENTS

A Access to Justice Act 1999, ss. 12–18...**1**

B Bail Act 1976, ss. 3–7, Schedule 1, Pt 1, paras 2–6, 8, 9 ...**157**

Bail (Amendment) Act 1993, s. 1...**171**

C Children and Young Persons Act 1969, ss. 23–23AA...**172**

Company Directors Disqualification Act 1986, ss. 1, 2, 13...**346**

Contempt of Court Act 1981, s. 8...**187**

Crime and Disorder Act 1998, ss. 8, 9...**330**

Criminal Appeal Act 1968, ss. 2, 7(1), 23, 23A, 33...**225**

Criminal Appeal Act 1995, ss. 8, 13...**227**

Criminal Evidence (Amendment) Act 1997, ss. 1–2...**42**

Criminal Justice Act 1988, ss. 32, 34...**197**

Criminal Justice Act 2003
ss. 22–24...**116**
ss. 57–61, 67...**228**
ss. 75–79, 82, 84...**230**
ss. 98–110, 118...**217**
ss. 142, 144–146, 174...**243**
ss. 147–150, 156–159...**246**
ss. 152, 153...**257**
ss. 162–166...**307**
ss. 167, 169–172...**255**
ss. 177–179...**293**
ss. 181–186...**265**
ss. 189–192...**268**
ss. 196–213...**248**
ss. 224–229, 231–235...**278**
ss. 237–240, 244, 246–258...**272**
ss. 263–265...**270**
ss. 269, 270, Schedule 21...**290**

Criminal Justice and Public Order Act 1994
s. 25...**168**
ss. 34–37...**212**
s. 60...**23**

Criminal Procedure and Investigations Act 1996, ss. 1, 3–8, 10–18...**187**

Criminal Procedure (Insanity) Act 1964, (as amended), s. 5...**363**

E European Convention on Human Rights
Articles 5, 8...**5**
Article 6...**176**
Article 6(3)(b) and (c)...**1**

F Firearms Act 1968, s. 52...**315**

Football Spectators Act 1989 (as amended), ss. 14–14J...**343**

H Human Rights Act 1998, ss. 1–8; Schedule 1 (Articles 3, 5, 7)...**364**

I Immigration Act 1971, ss. 6, 7, Schedule 3...**340**

J Juries Act 1974, ss. 1, 3, 8–9A, 17, Schedule 1...**183**

Justices of the Peace Act 1968, s. 1(7)...**332**

L Licensed Premises (Exclusion of Certain Persons) Act 1980, ss. 1, 2...**342**

M Magistrates' Courts Acts 1980,
ss. 17–23, 25–26, Schedule 1...**177**
s. 32...**264**
ss. 108, 111...**224**
s. 115...**332**

Mental Health Act 1983 (as amended), ss. 37–43, 45–45B, 47, 54...**356**

Misuse of Drugs Act 1971, s. 27...**315**

Murder (Abolition of Death Penalty) Act 1965 (as amended), s. 1...**265**

P Police and Criminal Evidence Act 1984
ss. 1–3...**6**
Codes of Practice,
Code A paras 1–5...**9**
ss. 24, 24A, 27–30, 56...**44**
Codes of Practice, Code C,
para 3...**48**
Codes of Practice, Code G,
paras 2–4...**52**
ss. 37–46A...**55**
Codes of Practice, Code C,
paras 2, 5, 6, 8, 9, 15, 16...**69**
ss. 46A–47A...**169**
ss. 55, 55A...**25**
s. 58...**115**
Codes of Practice, Code C,
paras 10–14...**116**
Codes of Practice, Code E,
paras 3–6...**125**

Codes of Practice, Code F,
paras 2–6 . . . **130**
ss. 61–65 . . . **29**
ss. 76–78, 82 . . . **215**
Codes of Practice, Code D,
paras 3–6 . . . **86**

Police Reform Act 2002,
ss. 9–24, 26–29 . . . **136**

Powers of Criminal Courts (Sentencing)
Act 2000 (as amended)
Action plan orders (ss. 69–71) . . . **304**
Attendance centre orders (s. 60,
Schedule 5) . . . **295**
Curfew orders (ss. 37, 39, 40) . . . **294**
General provisions (ss. 33) . . . **292**
Supervision orders (ss. 63–64A,
Schedule 6, Schedule 7) . . . **298**

Powers of Criminal Courts (Sentencing)
Act 2000
Committal to Crown Court for
sentence (ss. 3–7) . . . **236**
Deferment of sentence
(ss. 1–1D) . . . **234**
Remand by magistrates' court for
medical examination
(s. 11) . . . **243**
Remission for sentence: young
offenders etc. (ss. 8–10) . . . **241**

Powers of Criminal Courts (Sentencing)
Act 2000
Compensation orders (ss. 130, 131,
133) . . . **308**
Miscellaneous powers
(ss. 139, 140) . . . **312**
Young offenders (ss. 135–138) . . . **310**

Powers of Criminal Courts (Sentencing)
Act 2000
ss. 12–15 . . . **333**
ss. 16–27, 29, Schedule 1 . . . **319**

s. 36B . . . **294**
ss. 73, 74, Schedule 8 . . . **317**
ss. 76, 77 . . . **257**
s. 82A . . . **289**
ss. 83, 89–92, 99–107,
110, 111 . . . **258**
ss. 143–145 . . . **314**
ss. 146, 147 . . . **354**
ss. 148, 149 . . . **316**
s. 150 . . . **333**
Schedule 6 . . . **355**

Prevention of Crime Act 1953,
s. 1 . . . **316**

Proceeds of Crime Act 2002,
ss. 6–14 . . . **336**

Prosecution of Offences Act 1985,
ss. 1–3 and 10 . . . **154**

R Rehabilitation of Offenders
Act 1974 (as amended),
ss. 1, 4–7 . . . **369**

Road Traffic Offenders Act 1988
(as amended), ss. 34–40,
42, 43 . . . **347**

S Serious Organised Crime and Police
Act 2005, s. 112 . . . **28**

Sexual Offences Act 2003,
ss. 80–92 . . . **281**

Supreme Court Act 1981,
s. 48 . . . **224**

T Theft Act 1968,
s. 27(3) . . . **223**

Y Youth Justice and Criminal Evidence
Act 1999
ss. 16–30, 34–43 . . . **197**
s. 59 . . . **215**

CHRONOLOGICAL CONTENTS

1953   Prevention of Crime Act 1953,
        s. 1...**316**

1964   Criminal Procedure (Insanity)
        Act 1964 (as amended), s. 5...**363**

1965   Murder (Abolition of Death Penalty)
        Act 1965 (as amended), s. 1...**265**

1968   Criminal Appeal Act 1968, ss. 2, 7(1),
        23, 23A, 33...**225**

        Firearms Act 1968, s. 52...**315**

        Justice of the Peace Act 1968,
        s. 1(7)...**332**

        Theft Act 1968, s. 27(3)...**223**

1969   Children and Young Persons
        Act 1969, ss. 23–23AA...**172**

1971   Immigration Act 1971,
        ss. 6, 7, Schedule 3...**340**

        Misuse of Drugs Act 1971,
        s. 27...**315**

1974   Juries Act 1974, ss. 1, 3, 8–9A, 17,
        Schedule 1...**183**

        Rehabilitation of Offenders Act 1974
        (as amended), ss. 1, 4–7...**369**

1976   Bail Act 1976, ss. 3–7, Schedule 1,
        Pt 1, paras 2–6, 8, 9...**157**

1980   Licensed Premises (Exclusion of
        Certain Persons) Act 1980,
        ss. 1, 2...**342**

        Magistrates' Courts Acts 1980
        ss. 17–23, 25, 26, Schedule 1...**177**
        s. 32...**264**
        ss. 108, 111...**224**
        s. 115...**332**

1981   Contempt of Court Act 1981,
        s. 8...**187**

        Supreme Court Act 1981, s. 48...**224**

1983   Mental Health Act 1983,
        (as amended), ss. 37–43, 45–45B,
        47, 54...**356**

1984   Police and Criminal Evidence
        Act 1984
        ss. 1–3...**6**
        Codes of Practice, Code A,
        paras 1–5...**9**
        ss. 24, 24A, 27–30, 56...**44**
        Codes of Practice, Code C,
        para 3...**48**
        Codes of Practice, Code G,

        paras 2–4...**52**
        ss. 37–46A...**55**
        Codes of Practice, Code C,
        paras 2, 5, 6, 8, 9, 15, 16...**69**
        ss. 46A–47A...**169**
        ss. 55, 55A...**25**
        s. 58...**115**
        Codes of Practice, Code C,
        paras 10–14...**116**
        Codes of Practice, Code E,
        paras 3–6...**125**
        Codes of Practice, Code F,
        paras 2–6...**130**
        ss. 61–65...**29**
        ss. 76–78, 82...**215**
        Codes of Practice, Code D,
        paras 3–6...**86**

1985   Prosecution of Offences Act 1985,
        ss. 1–3, 10...**154**

1986   Company Directors
        Disqualification
        Act 1986, ss. 1, 2, 13...**346**

1988   Criminal Justice Act 1988,
        ss. 32, 34...**197**

        Road Traffic Offenders
        Act 1988 (as amended),
        ss. 34–40, 42, 43...**347**

1989   Football Spectators Act 1989
        (as amended), ss. 14–14J...**343**

1993   Bail (Amendment) Act 1993,
        s. 1...**171**

1994   Criminal Justice and Public
        Order Act 1994
        s. 25...**168**
        ss. 34–37...**212**
        s. 60...**23**

1995   Criminal Appeal Act 1995,
        ss. 8, 13...**227**

1996   Criminal Procedure and
        Investigations Act 1996,
        ss. 1, 3–8, 10–18...**187**

1997   Criminal Evidence (Amendment)
        Act 1997, ss. 1, 2...**42**

1998   Crime and Disorder Act 1998,
        ss. 8, 9...**330**

        Human Rights Act 1998, ss. 1–8,
        Schedule 1 (Articles 3, 5, 7)...**364**

        European Convention on Human
        Rights

Articles 5, 8...**5**
Article 6...**176**
Article 6(3)(b) and (c)...**1**

1999   Access to Justice Act 1999,
ss. 12–18...**1**

Youth Justice and Criminal Evidence
Act 1999,
ss. 16–30, 34–43...**197**
s. 59...**215**

2000   Powers of Criminal Courts
(Sentencing) Act 2000
(as amended)

Action plan orders (ss. 69–71)...**304**

Attendance centre orders
(s. 60, Schedule 5)...**295**
Curfew orders (ss. 37, 39,
40)...**294**
General provisions (s. 33)...**292**
General provisions (s. 36B)...**294**

Supervision orders (ss. 63–64A,
Schedule 6, Schedule 7)...**298**

Powers of Criminal Courts
(Sentencing) Act 2000
Committal to Crown Court for
sentence (ss. 3–7)...**236**
Deferment of sentence
(ss. 1–1D)...**234**
Remand by magistrates' court
for medical examination
(s. 11)...**243**
Remission for sentence: young
offenders etc. (ss. 8–10)...**241**

Powers of Criminal Courts
(Sentencing) Act 2000
Compensation orders (ss. 130,
131, 133)...**308**
Miscellaneous powers
(ss. 139, 140)...**312**
Young offenders
(ss. 135–138)...**310**

Powers of Criminal Courts
(Sentencing) Act 2000
ss. 12–15...**333**
ss. 16–27, 29, Schedule 1...**319**
ss. 73, 74, Schedule 8...**317**
ss. 76, 77...**257**
s. 82A...**289**
ss. 83, 89–92, 99–107,
110, 111...**258**
ss. 122–125...**000**
ss. 143–145...**314**
ss. 146, 147...**354**
ss. 148, 149...**316**
s. 150...**333**
Schedule 6...**355**

2002   Police Reform Act 2002,
ss. 9–24, 26–29...**136**

Proceeds of Crime Act 2002,
ss. 6–14...**336**

2003   Criminal Justice Act 2003
ss. 22–24...**116**
ss. 57–61, 67...**228**
ss. 75–79, 82, 84...**230**
ss. 98–110, 118...**217**
ss. 142, 144–146, 174...**243**
ss. 147–150, 156–159...**246**
ss. 152, 153...**257**
ss. 162–166...**307**
ss. 167, 169–172...**255**
ss. 177–179...**293**
ss. 181–186...**265**
ss. 189–192...**268**
ss. 196–213...**248**
ss. 224–229, 231–235...**278**
ss. 237–240, 244, 246–258...**272**
ss. 263–265...**270**
ss. 269, 270, Schedule 21...**290**

Sexual Offences Act 2003,
ss. 80–92...**281**

2005   Serious Organised Crime and
Police Act 2005, s. 112...**28**

PART I

Criminal Justice

(a) ACCESS TO JUSTICE

Right to legal representation

European Convention on Human Rights

Article 6 **Right to a fair trial**

3. Everyone charged with a criminal offence has the following minimum rights:

...

(b) to have adequate time and facilities for the preparation of his defence;

(c) to defend himself in person or through legal assistance of his own choosing or, if he has not sufficient means to pay for legal assistance, to be given it free when the interests of justice so require.

Access to Justice Act 1999

12 **Criminal Defence Service**

(1) The Commission shall establish, maintain and develop a service known as the Criminal Defence Service for the purpose of securing that individuals involved in criminal investigations or criminal proceedings have access to such advice, assistance and representation as the interests of justice require.

(2) In this Part 'criminal proceedings' means—

(a) proceedings before any court for dealing with an individual accused of an offence,

(b) proceedings before any court for dealing with an individual convicted of an offence (including proceedings in respect of a sentence or order),

(c) proceedings for dealing with an individual under the Extradition Act 2003,

(d) proceedings for binding an individual over to keep the peace or to be of good behaviour under section 115 of the Magistrates' Courts Act 1980 and for dealing with an individual who fails to comply with an order under that section,

(e) proceedings on an appeal brought by an individual under section 44A of the Criminal Appeal Act 1968,

(f) proceedings for contempt committed, or alleged to have been committed, by an individual in the face of a court, and

(g) such other proceedings concerning an individual, before any such court or other body, as may be prescribed.

(3) The Commission shall fund services as part of the Criminal Defence Service in accordance with sections 13 to 15.

(4) The Commission may accredit, or authorise others to accredit, persons or bodies providing services which may be funded by the Commission as part of the Criminal Defence

Service; and any system of accreditation shall include provision for the monitoring of the services provided by accredited persons and bodies and for the withdrawal of accreditation from any providing services of unsatisfactory quality.

(5) The Commission may charge—

    (a) for accreditation,

    (b) for monitoring the services provided by accredited persons and bodies, and

    (c) for authorising accreditation by others;

and persons or bodies authorised to accredit may charge for accreditation, and for such monitoring, in accordance with the terms of their authorisation.

(6) The Lord Chancellor may by order require the Commission to discharge the functions in subsections (4) and (5) in accordance with the order.

13   Advice and assistance

(1) The Commission shall fund such advice and assistance as it considers appropriate—

    (a) for individuals who are arrested and held in custody at a police station or other premises, and

    (b) in prescribed circumstances, for individuals who—

        (i)   are not within paragraph (a) but are involved in investigations which may lead to criminal proceedings,

        (ii)   are before a court or other body in such proceedings, or

        (iii) have been the subject of such proceedings;

and the assistance which the Commission may consider appropriate includes assistance in the form of advocacy.

(2) The Commission may comply with the duty imposed by subsection (1) by—

    (a) entering into contracts with persons or bodies for the provision of advice or assistance by them,

    (b) making payments to persons or bodies in respect of the provision of advice or assistance by them,

    (c) making grants or loans to persons or bodies to enable them to provide, or facilitate the provision of, advice or assistance,

    (d) establishing and maintaining bodies to provide, or facilitate the provision of, advice or assistance,

    (e) making grants to individuals to enable them to obtain advice or assistance,

    (f) employing persons to provide advice or assistance, or

    (g) doing anything else which it considers appropriate for funding advice and assistance.

(3) The Lord Chancellor may by order require the Commission to discharge the function in subsection (2) in accordance with the order.

(4) The Commission may fund advice and assistance by different means—

    (a) in different areas in England and Wales, and

    (b) in relation to different descriptions of cases.

14   Representation

(1) Schedule 3 (which makes provision about the grant of a right to representation in criminal proceedings) has effect; and the Commission shall fund representation to which an individual has been granted a right in accordance with that Schedule.

(2) Subject to the following provisions, the Commission may comply with the duty imposed by subsection (1) by—

    (a) entering into contracts with persons or bodies for the provision of representation by them,

    (b) making payments to persons or bodies in respect of the provision of representation by them,

    (c) making grants or loans to persons or bodies to enable them to provide, or facilitate the provision of, representation,

(d) establishing and maintaining bodies to provide, or facilitate the provision of, representation,

(e) making grants to individuals to enable them to obtain representation,

(f) employing persons to provide representation, or

(g) doing anything else which it considers appropriate for funding representation.

(3) The Lord Chancellor—

(a) shall by order make provision about the payments which may be made by the Commission in respect of any representation provided by non-contracted private practitioners, and

(b) may by order make any other provision requiring the Commission to discharge the function in subsection (2) in accordance with the order.

(4) For the purposes of subsection (3)(a) representation is provided by a non-contracted private practitioner if it is provided, otherwise than pursuant to a contract entered into by the Commission, by a person or body which is neither—

(a) a person or body in receipt of grants or loans made by the Commission as part of the Criminal Defence Service, nor

(b) the Commission itself or a body established or maintained by the Commission.

(5) The provision which the Lord Chancellor is required to make by order under subsection (3)(a) includes provision for reviews of, or appeals against, determinations required for the purposes of the order.

(6) The Commission may fund representation by different means—

(a) in different areas in England and Wales, and

(b) in relation to different descriptions of cases.

15 Selection of representative

(1) An individual who has been granted a right to representation in accordance with Schedule 3 may select any representative or representatives willing to act for him; and, where he does so, the Commission is to comply with the duty imposed by section 14(1) by funding representation by the selected representative or representatives.

(2) Regulations may provide that in prescribed circumstances—

(a) the right conferred by subsection (1) is not to apply in cases of prescribed descriptions,

(b) an individual who has been provided with advice or assistance funded by the Commission under section 13 by a person whom he chose to provide it for him is to be taken to have selected that person as his representative pursuant to that right,

(c) that right is not to include a right to select a representative of a prescribed description,

(d) that right is to select only a representative of a prescribed description,

(e) that right is to select not more than a prescribed number of representatives to act at any one time, and

(f) that right is not to include a right to select a representative in place of a representative previously selected.

(3) Regulations under subsection (2)(b) may prescribe circumstances in which an individual is to be taken to have chosen a person to provide advice or assistance for him.

(4) Regulations under subsection (2) may not provide that only a person employed by the Commission, or by a body established and maintained by the Commission, may be selected.

(5) Regulations may provide that in prescribed circumstances the Commission is not required to fund, or to continue to fund, representation for an individual by a particular representative (but such provision shall not prejudice any right of the individual to select another representative).

(6) The circumstances which may be prescribed by regulations under subsection (2) or (5) include that a determination has been made by a prescribed body or person.

16   Code of conduct

(1) The Commission shall prepare a code of conduct to be observed by employees of the Commission, and employees of any body established and maintained by the Commission, in the provision of services as part of the Criminal Defence Service.

(2) The code shall include—

   (a) duties to avoid discrimination,

   (b) duties to protect the interests of the individuals for whom services are provided,

   (c) duties to the court,

   (d) duties to avoid conflicts of interest, and

   (e) duties of confidentiality,

and duties on employees who are members of a professional body to comply with the rules of the body.

(3) The Commission may from time to time prepare a revised version of the code.

(4) Before preparing or revising the code the Commission shall consult the Law Society and the General Council of the Bar and such other bodies or persons as it considers appropriate.

(5) After preparing the code or a revised version of the code the Commission shall send a copy to the Lord Chancellor.

(6) If he approves it he shall lay it before each House of Parliament.

(7) The Commission shall publish—

   (a) the code as first approved by the Lord Chancellor, and

   (b) where he approves a revised version, either the revisions or the revised code as appropriate.

(8) The code, and any revised version of the code, shall not come into force until it has been approved by a resolution of each House of Parliament.

17   Terms of provision of funded services

(1) An individual for whom services are funded by the Commission as part of the Criminal Defence Service shall not be required to make any payment in respect of the services except where subsection (2) applies.

(2) Where representation for an individual in respect of criminal proceedings in any court other than a magistrates' court is funded by the Commission as part of the Criminal Defence Service, the court may, subject to regulations under subsection (3), make an order requiring him to pay some or all of the cost of any representation so funded for him (in proceedings in that or any other court).

(3) Regulations may make provision about—

   (a) the descriptions of individuals against whom an order under subsection (2) may be made,

   (b) the circumstances in which such an order may be made and the principles to be applied in deciding whether to make such an order and the amount to be paid,

   (c) the determination of the cost of representation for the purposes of the making of such an order,

   (d) the furnishing of information and evidence to the court or the Commission for the purpose of enabling the court to decide whether to make such an order and (if so) the amount to be paid,

   (e) prohibiting individuals who are required to furnish information or evidence from dealing with property until they have furnished the information or evidence or until a decision whether to make an order, or the amount to be paid, has been made,

   (f) the person or body to which, and manner in which, payments required by such an order must be made and what that person or body is to do with them, and

   (g) the enforcement of such an order (including provision for the imposition of charges in respect of unpaid amounts).

18 Funding

(1) The Secretary of State shall pay to the Commission such sums as are required to meet the costs of any advice, assistance and representation funded by the Commission as part of the Criminal Defence Service.

(2) The Secretary of State may—

(a) determine the manner in which and times at which the sums referred to in subsection (1) shall be paid to the Commission, and

(b) impose conditions on the payment of the sums.

(3) In funding services as part of the Criminal Defence Service the Commission shall aim to obtain the best possible value for money.

(b) POLICE POWERS AND ISSUES DURING INVESTIGATION

Rights to liberty, security and privacy

European Convention on Human Rights

Article 5 Right to liberty and security

1. Everyone has the right to liberty and security of person. No one shall be deprived of his liberty save in the following cases and in accordance with a procedure prescribed by law:

(a) the lawful detention of a person after conviction by a competent court;

(b) the lawful arrest or detention of a person for non-compliance with the lawful order of a court or in order to secure the fulfilment of any obligation prescribed by law;

(c) the lawful arrest or detention of a person effected for the purpose of bringing him before the competent legal authority on reasonable suspicion of having committed an offence or when it is reasonably considered necessary to prevent his committing an offence or fleeing after having done so;

(d) the detention of a minor by lawful order for the purpose of educational supervision or his lawful detention for the purpose of bringing him before the competent legal authority;

(e) the lawful detention of persons for the prevention of the spreading of infectious diseases, of persons of unsound mind, alcoholics or drug addicts or vagrants;

(f) the lawful arrest or detention of a person to prevent his effecting an unauthorised entry into the country or of a person against whom action is being taken with a view to deportation or extradition.

2. Everyone who is arrested shall be informed promptly, in a language which he understands, of the reasons for his arrest and of any charge against him.

3. Everyone arrested or detained in accordance with the provisions of paragraph 1.c of this article shall be brought promptly before a judge or other officer authorised by law to exercise judicial power and shall be entitled to trial within a reasonable time or to release pending trial. Release may be conditioned by guarantees to appear for trial.

4. Everyone who is deprived of his liberty by arrest or detention shall be entitled to take proceedings by which the lawfulness of his detention shall be decided speedily by a court and his release ordered if the detention is not lawful.

5. Everyone who has been the victim of arrest or detention in contravention of the provisions of this article shall have an enforceable right to compensation.

Article 8

1. Everyone has the right to respect for his private and family life, his home and his correspondence.

2. There shall be no interference by a public authority with the exercise of this right except such as is in accordance with the law and is necessary in a democratic society in the interests of national security, public safety or the economic well-being of the country, for the prevention of disorder or crime, for the protection of health or morals, or for the protection of the rights and freedoms of others.

Stop and search

Police and Criminal Evidence Act 1984

1 Power of constable to stop and search persons, vehicles etc.

(1) A constable may exercise any power conferred by this section—

    (a) in any place to which at the time when he proposes to exercise the power the public or any section of the public has access, on payment or otherwise, as of right or by virtue of express or implied permission; or

    (b) in any other place to which people have ready access at the time when he proposes to exercise the power but which is not a dwelling.

(2) Subject to subsection (3) to (5) below, a constable—

    (a) may search—

        (i)   any person or vehicle;

        (ii) anything which is in or on a vehicle,

        for stolen or prohibited articles, any article to which subsection (8A) below applies, or any firework to which subsection (8B) below applies; and

    (b) may detain a person or vehicle for the purpose of such a search.

(3) This section does not give a constable power to search a person or vehicle or anything in or on a vehicle unless he has reasonable grounds for suspecting that he will find stolen or prohibited articles or any article to which subsection (8A) below applies, or any firework to which subsection (8B) below applies,

(4) If a person is in a garden or yard occupied with and used for the purposes of a dwelling or on other land so occupied and used, a constable may not search him in the exercise of the power conferred by this section unless the constable has reasonable grounds for believing—

    (a) that he does not reside in the dwelling; and

    (b) that he is not in the place in question with the express or implied permission of a person who resides in the dwelling.

(5) If a vehicle is in a garden or yard occupied with and used for the purposes of a dwelling or on other land so occupied and used, a constable may not search the vehicle or anything in or on it in the exercise of the power conferred by this section unless he has reasonable grounds for believing—

    (a) that the person in charge of the vehicle does not reside in the dwelling; and

    (b) that the vehicle is not in the place in question with the express or implied permission of a person who resides in the dwelling.

(6) If in the course of such a search a constable discovers an article which he has reasonable grounds for suspecting to be a stolen or prohibited article or any article to which subsection (8A) below applies or a firework to which subsection (8B) below applies, he may seize it.

(7) An article is prohibited for the purposes of this Part of this Act if it is—

    (a) an offensive weapon; or

    (b) an article—

        (i)   made or adapted for use in the course of or in connection with an offence to which this sub-paragraph applies; or

        (ii) intended by the person having it with him for such use by him or by some other person.

(8) The offences to which subsection (7)(b)(i) above applies are—

    (a) burglary;

    (b) theft;

    (c) offences under section 12 of the Theft Act 1968 (taking motor vehicle or other conveyance without authority); and

    (d) offences under section 15 of that Act (obtaining property by deception).

    (e) offences under section 1 of the Criminal Damage Act 1971 (destroying or damaging property).

(8A) This subsection applies to any article in relation to which a person has committed, or is committing or is going to commit an offence under section 139 of the Criminal Justice Act 1988.

(8B) This subsection applies to any firework which a person possesses in contravention of a prohibition imposed by fireworks regulations.

(8C) In this section—

    (a) 'firework' shall be construed in accordance with the definition of 'fireworks' in section 1(1) of the Fireworks Act 2003; and

    (b) 'fireworks regulations' has the same meaning as in that Act.

(9) In this Part of this Act 'offensive weapon' means any article—

    (a) made or adapted for use for causing injury to persons; or

    (b) intended by the person having it with him for such use by him or by some other person.

2 Provisions relating to search under section 1 and other powers

(1) A constable who detains a person or vehicle in the exercise—

    (a) of the power conferred by section 1 above; or

    (b) of any other power—

        (i) to search a person without first arresting him; or

        (ii) to search a vehicle without making an arrest,

need not conduct a search if it appears to him subsequently—

        (i) that no search is required; or

        (ii) that a search is impracticable.

(2) If a constable contemplates a search, other than a search of an unattended vehicle, in the exercise—

    (a) of the power conferred by section 1 above; or

    (b) of any other power, except the power conferred by section 6 below and the power conferred by section 27(2) of the Aviation Security Act 1982—

        (i) to search a person without first arresting him; or

        (ii) to search a vehicle without making an arrest,

it shall be his duty, subject to subsection (4) below, to take reasonable steps before he commences the search to bring to the attention of the appropriate person—

        (i) if the constable is not in uniform, documentary evidence that he is a constable; and

        (ii) whether he is in uniform or not, the matters specified in subsection (3) below;

and the constable shall not commence the search until he has performed that duty.

(3) The matters referred to in subsection (2)(ii) above are—

    (a) the constable's name and the name of the police station to which he is attached;

    (b) the object of the proposed search;

    (c) the constable's grounds for proposing to make it; and

    (d) the effect of section 3(7) or (8) below, as may be appropriate.

(4) A constable need not bring the effect of section 3(7) or (8) below to the attention of the appropriate person if it appears to the constable that it will not be practicable to make the record in section 3(1) below.

(5) In this section 'the appropriate person' means—

(a) if the constable proposes to search a person, that person; and

(b) if he proposes to search a vehicle, or anything in or on a vehicle, the person in charge of the vehicle.

(6) On completing a search of an unattended vehicle or anything in or on such a vehicle in the exercise of any such power as is mentioned in subsection (2) above a constable shall leave a notice—

(a) stating that he has searched it;

(b) giving the name of the police station to which he is attached;

(c) stating that an application for compensation for any damage caused by the search may be made to that police station; and

(d) stating the effect of section 3(8) below.

(7) The constable shall leave the notice inside the vehicle unless it is not reasonably practicable to do so without damaging the vehicle.

(8) The time for which a person or vehicle may be detained for the purposes of such a search is such time as is reasonably required to permit a search to be carried out either at the place where the person or vehicle was first detained or nearby.

(9) Neither the power conferred by section 1 above nor any other power to detain and search a person without first arresting him or to detain and search a vehicle without making an arrest is to be construed—

(a) as authorising a constable to require a person to remove any of his clothing in public other than an outer coat, jacket or gloves; or

(b) as authorising a constable not in uniform to stop a vehicle.

(10) This section and section 1 above apply to vessels, aircraft and hovercraft as they apply to vehicles.

3   Duty to make records concerning searches

(1) Where a constable has carried out a search in the exercise of any such power as is mentioned in section 2(1) above, other than a search—

(a) under section 6 below; or

(b) under section 27(2) of the Aviation Security Act 1982, he shall make a record of it in writing unless it is not practicable to do so.

(2) If—

(a) a constable is required by subsection (1) above to make a record of a search; but

(b) it is not practicable to make the record on the spot, he shall make it as soon as practicable after the completion of the search.

(3) The record of a search of a person shall include a note of his name, if the constable knows it, but a constable may not detain a person to find out his name.

(4) If a constable does not know the name of a person whom he has searched, the record of the search shall include a note otherwise describing that person.

(5) The record of a search of a vehicle shall include a note describing the vehicle.

(6) The record of a search of a person or a vehicle—

(a) shall state—

(i)   the object of the search;

(ii) the grounds for making it;

(iii) the date and time when it was made;

(iv) the place where it was made;

(v)   whether anything, and if so what, was found;

(vi) whether any, and if so what, injury to a person or damage to property appears to the constable to have resulted from the search; and

(b) shall identify the constable making it.

(7) If a constable who conducted a search of a person made a record of it, the person who was searched shall be entitled to a copy of the record if he asks for one before the end of the period specified in subsection (9) below.

(8) If—
    (a) the owner of a vehicle which has been searched or the person who was in charge
    of the vehicle at the time when it was searched asks for a copy of the record of the
    search before the end of the period specified in subsection (9) below; and
    (b) the constable who conducted the search made a record of it,
the person who made the request shall be entitled to a copy.

(9) The period mentioned in subsections (7) and (8) above is the period of 12 months
beginning with the date on which the search was made.

(10) The requirements imposed by this section with regard to records of searches of
vehicles shall apply also to records of searches of vessels, aircraft and hovercraft.

A.   CODE OF PRACTICE FOR THE EXERCISE BY:

POLICE OFFICERS OF STATUTORY POWERS
OF STOP AND SEARCH

POLICE OFFICERS AND POLICE STAFF OF REQUIREMENTS
TO RECORD PUBLIC ENCOUNTERS

Commencement—transitional arrangements
This code applies to any search by a police officer and the requirement to record public
encounters taking place after midnight on 31 December 2005.

General
This code of practice must be readily available at all police stations for consultation by police
officers, police staff, detained persons and members of the public.

The notes for guidance included are not provisions of this code, but are guidance to
police officers and others about its application and interpretation. Provisions in the annexes
to the code are provisions of this code.

This code governs the exercise by police officers of statutory powers to search a person or
a vehicle without first making an arrest. The main stop and search powers to which this code
applies are set out in Annex A, but that list should not be regarded as definitive. [See Note 1]
In addition, it covers requirements on police officers and police staff to record encounters not
governed by statutory powers. This code does not apply to:
    (a) the powers of stop and search under;
      (i) Aviation Security Act 1982, section 27(2);
      (ii) Police and Criminal Evidence Act 1984, section 6(1) (which relates specifi-
      cally to powers of constables employed by statutory undertakers on the
      premises of the statutory undertakers).
    (b) searches carried out for the purposes of examination under Schedule 7 to the
    Terrorism Act 2000 and to which the Code of Practice issued under paragraph 6 of
    Schedule 14 to the Terrorism Act 2000 applies.

1   Principles governing stop and search
1.1 Powers to stop and search must be used fairly, responsibly, with respect for people
being searched and without unlawful discrimination. The Race Relations (Amendment) Act
2000 makes it unlawful for police officers to discriminate on the grounds of race, colour,
ethnic origin, nationality or national origins when using their powers.

1.2 The intrusion on the liberty of the person stopped or searched must be brief and
detention for the purposes of a search must take place at or near the location of the stop.

1.3 If these fundamental principles are not observed the use of powers to stop and search
may be drawn into question. Failure to use the powers in the proper manner reduces their

effectiveness. Stop and search can play an important role in the detection and prevention of crime, and using the powers fairly makes them more effective.

1.4 The primary purpose of stop and search powers is to enable officers to allay or confirm suspicions about individuals without exercising their power of arrest. Officers may be required to justify the use or authorisation of such powers, in relation both to individual searches and the overall pattern of their activity in this regard, to their supervisory officers or in court. Any misuse of the powers is likely to be harmful to policing and lead to mistrust of the police. Officers must also be able to explain their actions to the member of the public searched. The misuse of these powers can lead to disciplinary action.

1.5 An officer must not search a person, even with his or her consent, where no power to search is applicable. Even where a person is prepared to submit to a search voluntarily, the person must not be searched unless the necessary legal power exists, and the search must be in accordance with the relevant power and the provisions of this Code. The only exception, where an officer does not require a specific power, applies to searches of persons entering sports grounds or other premises carried out with their consent given as a condition of entry.

2   Explanation of powers to stop and search

2.1 This code applies to powers of stop and search as follows:
   (a) powers which require reasonable grounds for suspicion, before they may be exercised; that articles unlawfully obtained or possessed are being carried, or under Section 43 of the Terrorism Act 2000 that a person is a terrorist;
   (b) authorised under section 60 of the Criminal Justice and Public Order Act 1994, based upon a reasonable belief that incidents involving serious violence may take place or that people are carrying dangerous instruments or offensive weapons within any locality in the police area;
   (c) authorised under section 44(1) and (2) of the Terrorism Act 2000 based upon a consideration that the exercise of one or both powers is expedient for the prevention of acts of terrorism;
   (d) powers to search a person who has not been arrested in the exercise of a power to search premises (see Code B paragraph 2.4).

Searches requiring reasonable grounds for suspicion

2.2 Reasonable grounds for suspicion depend on the circumstances in each case. There must be an objective basis for that suspicion based on facts, information, and/or intelligence which are relevant to the likelihood of finding an article of a certain kind or, in the case of searches under section 43 of the Terrorism Act 2000, to the likelihood that the person is a terrorist. Reasonable suspicion can never be supported on the basis of personal factors alone without reliable supporting intelligence or information or some specific behaviour by the person concerned. For example, a person's race, age, appearance, or the fact that the person is known to have a previous conviction, cannot be used alone or in combination with each other as the reason for searching that person. Reasonable suspicion cannot be based on generalisations or stereotypical images of certain groups or categories of people as more likely to be involved in criminal activity. A person's religion cannot be considered as reasonable grounds for suspicion and should never be considered as a reason to stop or stop and search an individual.

2.3 Reasonable suspicion can sometimes exist without specific information or intelligence and on the basis of some level of generalisation stemming from the behaviour of a person. For example, if an officer encounters someone on the street at night who is obviously trying to hide something, the officer may (depending on the other surrounding circumstances) base such suspicion on the fact that this kind of behaviour is often linked to stolen or prohibited articles being carried. Similarly, for the purposes of section 43 of the Terrorism Act 2000, suspicion that a person is a terrorist may arise from the person's behaviour at or near a location which has been identified as a potential target for terrorists.

2.4 However, reasonable suspicion should normally be linked to accurate and current intelligence or information, such as information describing an article being carried, a suspected offender, or a person who has been seen carrying a type of article known to have been stolen recently from premises in the area. Searches based on accurate and current intelligence or information are more likely to be effective. Targeting searches in a particular area at specified crime problems increases their effectiveness and minimises inconvenience to law-abiding members of the public. It also helps in justifying the use of searches both to those who are searched and to the public. This does not however prevent stop and search powers being exercised in other locations where such powers may be exercised and reasonable suspicion exists.

2.5 Searches are more likely to be effective, legitimate, and secure public confidence when reasonable suspicion is based on a range of factors. The overall use of these powers is more likely to be effective when up to date and accurate intelligence or information is communicated to officers and they are well-informed about local crime patterns.

2.6 Where there is reliable information or intelligence that members of a group or gang habitually carry knives unlawfully or weapons or controlled drugs, and wear a distinctive item of clothing or other means of identification to indicate their membership of the group or gang, that distinctive item of clothing or other means of identification may provide reasonable grounds to stop and search a person. [See *Note 9*]

2.7 A police officer may have reasonable grounds to suspect that a person is in innocent possession of a stolen or prohibited article or other item for which he or she is empowered to search. In that case the officer may stop and search the person even though there would be no power of arrest.

2.8 Under section 43(1) of the Terrorism Act 2000 a constable may stop and search a person whom the officer reasonably suspects to be a terrorist to discover whether the person is in possession of anything which may constitute evidence that the person is a terrorist. These searches may only be carried out by an officer of the same sex as the person searched.

2.9 An officer who has reasonable grounds for suspicion may detain the person concerned in order to carry out a search. Before carrying out a search the officer may ask questions about the person's behaviour or presence in circumstances which gave rise to the suspicion. As a result of questioning the detained person, the reasonable grounds for suspicion necessary to detain that person may be confirmed or, because of a satisfactory explanation, be eliminated. [See *Notes 2* and *3*] Questioning may also reveal reasonable grounds to suspect the possession of a different kind of unlawful article from that originally suspected. Reasonable grounds for suspicion however cannot be provided retrospectively by such questioning during a person's detention or by refusal to answer any questions put.

2.10 If, as a result of questioning before a search, or other circumstances which come to the attention of the officer, there cease to be reasonable grounds for suspecting that an article is being carried of a kind for which there is a power to stop and search, no search may take place. [See *Note 3*] In the absence of any other lawful power to detain, the person is free to leave at will and must be so informed.

2.11 There is no power to stop or detain a person in order to find grounds for a search. Police officers have many encounters with members of the public which do not involve detaining people against their will. If reasonable grounds for suspicion emerge during such an encounter, the officer may search the person, even though no grounds existed when the encounter began. If an officer is detaining someone for the purpose of a search, he or she should inform the person as soon as detention begins.

Searches authorised under section 60 of the Criminal Justice and Public Order Act 1994

2.12 Authority for a constable in uniform to stop and search under section 60 of the Criminal Justice and Public Order Act 1994 may be given if the authorising officer reasonably believes:

    (a) that incidents involving serious violence may take place in any locality in the officer's police area, and it is expedient to use these powers to prevent their occurrence, or

(b) that persons are carrying dangerous instruments or offensive weapons without good reason in any locality in the officer's police area.

2.13 An authorisation under section 60 may only be given by an officer of the rank of inspector or above, in writing, specifying the grounds on which it was given, the locality in which the powers may be exercised and the period of time for which they are in force. The period authorised shall be no longer than appears reasonably necessary to prevent, or seek to prevent incidents of serious violence, or to deal with the problem of carrying dangerous instruments or offensive weapons. It may not exceed 24 hours. [See *Notes 10–13*]

2.14 If an inspector gives an authorisation, he or she must, as soon as practicable, inform an officer of or above the rank of superintendent. This officer may direct that the authorisation shall be extended for a further 24 hours, if violence or the carrying of dangerous instruments or offensive weapons has occurred, or is suspected to have occurred, and the continued use of the powers is considered necessary to prevent or deal with further such activity. That direction must also be given in writing at the time or as soon as practicable afterwards. [See *Note 12*]

Powers to require removal of face coverings

2.15 Section 60AA of the Criminal Justice and Public Order Act 1994 also provides a power to demand the removal of disguises. The officer exercising the power must reasonably believe that someone is wearing an item wholly or mainly for the purpose of concealing identity. There is also a power to seize such items where the officer believes that a person intends to wear them for this purpose. There is no power to stop and search for disguises. An officer may seize any such item which is discovered when exercising a power of search for something else, or which is being carried, and which the officer reasonably believes is intended to be used for concealing anyone's identity. This power can only be used if an authorisation under section 60 or an authorisation under section 60AA is in force.

2.16 Authority for a constable in uniform to require the removal of disguises and to seize them under section 60AA may be given if the authorising officer reasonably believes that activities may take place in any locality in the officer's police area that are likely to involve the commission of offences and it is expedient to use these powers to prevent or control these activities.

2.17 An authorisation under section 60AA may only be given by an officer of the rank of inspector or above, in writing, specifying the grounds on which it was given, the locality in which the powers may be exercised and the period of time for which they are in force. The period authorised shall be no longer than appears reasonably necessary to prevent, or seek to prevent the commission of offences. It may not exceed 24 hours. [See *Notes 10–13*]

2.18 If an inspector gives an authorisation, he or she must, as soon as practicable, inform an officer of or above the rank of superintendent. This officer may direct that the authorisation shall be extended for a further 24 hours, if crimes have been committed, or is suspected to have been committed, and the continued use of the powers is considered necessary to prevent or deal with further such activity. This direction must also be given in writing at the time or as soon as practicable afterwards. [See *Note 12*]

Searches authorised under section 44 of the Terrorism Act 2000

2.19 An officer of the rank of assistant chief constable (or equivalent) or above, may give authority for the following powers of stop and search under section 44 of the Terrorism Act 2000 to be exercised in the whole or part of his or her police area if the officer considers it is expedient for the prevention of acts of terrorism:

(a) under section 44(1) of the Terrorism Act 2000, to give a constable in uniform power to stop and search any vehicle, its driver, any passenger in the vehicle and anything in or on the vehicle or carried by the driver or any passenger; and

(b) under section 44(2) of the Terrorism Act 2000, to give a constable in uniform power to stop and search any pedestrian and anything carried by the pedestrian. An authorisation under section 44(1) may be combined with one under section 44(2).

2.20 If an authorisation is given orally at first, it must be confirmed in writing by the officer who gave it as soon as reasonably practicable.

2.21 When giving an authorisation, the officer must specify the geographical area in which the power may be used, and the time and date that the authorisation ends (up to a maximum of 28 days from the time the authorisation was given). [See *Notes 12* and *13*]

2.22 The officer giving an authorisation under section 44(1) or (2) must cause the Secretary of State to be informed, as soon as reasonably practicable, that such an author-isation has been given. An authorisation which is not confirmed by the Secretary of State within 48 hours of its having been given, shall have effect up until the end of that 48 hour period or the end of the period specified in the authorisation (whichever is the earlier). [See *Note 14*]

2.23 Following notification of the authorisation, the Secretary of State may:
(i) cancel the authorisation with immediate effect or with effect from such other time as he or she may direct;
(ii) confirm it but for a shorter period than that specified in the authorisation; or
(iii) confirm the authorisation as given.

2.24 When an authorisation under section 44 is given, a constable in uniform may exercise the powers:
(a) only for the purpose of searching for articles of a kind which could be used in connection with terrorism (see paragraph 2.25);
(b) whether or not there are any grounds for suspecting the presence of such articles.

2.24A When a Community Support Officer on duty and in uniform has been conferred powers under Section 44 of the Terrorism Act 2000 by a Chief Officer of their force, the exercise of this power must comply with the requirements of this Code of Practice, including the recording requirements.

2.25 The selection of persons stopped under section 44 of Terrorism Act 2000 should reflect an objective assessment of the threat posed by the various terrorist groups active in Great Britain. The powers must not be used to stop and search for reasons unconnected with terrorism. Officers must take particular care not to discriminate against members of minority ethnic groups in the exercise of these powers. There may be circumstances, however, where it is appropriate for officers to take account of a person's ethnic origin in selecting persons to be stopped in response to a specific terrorist threat (for example, some international terrorist groups are associated with particular ethnic identities). [See *Notes 12* and *13*]

2.26 The powers under sections 43 and 44 of the Terrorism Act 2000 allow a constable to search only for articles which could be used for terrorist purposes. However, this would not prevent a search being carried out under other powers if, in the course of exercising these powers, the officer formed reasonable grounds for suspicion.

Powers to search in the exercise of a power to search premises

2.27 The following powers to search premises also authorise the search of a person, not under arrest, who is found on the premises during the course of the search:
(a) section 139B of the Criminal Justice Act 1988 under which a constable may enter school premises and search the premises and any person on those premises for any bladed or pointed article or offensive weapon; and
(b) under a warrant issued under section s.23(3) of the Misuse of Drugs Act 1971 to search premises for drugs or documents but only if the warrant specifically authorises the search of persons found on the premises.

2.28 Before the power under section 139B of the Criminal Justice Act 1988 may be exercised, the constable must have reasonable grounds to believe that an offence under section 139A of the Criminal Justice Act 1988 (having a bladed or pointed article or offensive weapon on school premises) has been or is being committed. A warrant to search premises and persons found therein may be issued under section s.23(3) of the Misuse of Drugs Act 1971 if there are reasonable grounds to suspect that controlled drugs or certain documents are in the possession of a person on the premises.

2.29 The powers in paragraph 2.27(a) or (b) do not require prior specific grounds to suspect that the person to be searched is in possession of an item for which there is an existing power to search. However, it is still necessary to ensure that the selection and treatment of those searched under these powers is based upon objective factors connected with the search of the premises, and not upon personal prejudice.

3   Conduct of searches

3.1 All stops and searches must be carried out with courtesy, consideration and respect for the person concerned. This has a significant impact on public confidence in the police. Every reasonable effort must be made to minimise the embarrassment that a person being searched may experience. [See *Note 4*]

3.2 The co-operation of the person to be searched must be sought in every case, even if the person initially objects to the search. A forcible search may be made only if it has been established that the person is unwilling to co-operate or resists. Reasonable force may be used as a last resort if necessary to conduct a search or to detain a person or vehicle for the purposes of a search.

3.3 The length of time for which a person or vehicle may be detained must be reasonable and kept to a minimum. Where the exercise of the power requires reasonable suspicion, the thoroughness and extent of a search must depend on what is suspected of being carried, and by whom. If the suspicion relates to a particular article which is seen to be slipped into a person's pocket, then, in the absence of other grounds for suspicion or an opportunity for the article to be moved elsewhere, the search must be confined to that pocket. In the case of a small article which can readily be concealed, such as a drug, and which might be concealed anywhere on the person, a more extensive search may be necessary. In the case of searches mentioned in paragraph 2.1(b), (c), and (d), which do not require reasonable grounds for suspicion, officers may make any reasonable search to look for items for which they are empowered to search. [See *Note 5*]

3.4 The search must be carried out at or near the place where the person or vehicle was first detained. [See *Note 6*]

3.5 There is no power to require a person to remove any clothing in public other than an outer coat, jacket or gloves except under section 45(3) of the Terrorism Act 2000 (which empowers a constable conducting a search under section 44(1) or 44(2) of that Act to require a person to remove headgear and footwear in public) and under section 60AA of the Criminal Justice and Public Order Act 1994 (which empowers a constable to require a person to remove any item worn to conceal identity). [See *Notes 4* and *6*] A search in public of a person's clothing which has not been removed must be restricted to superficial examination of outer garments. This does not, however, prevent an officer from placing his or her hand inside the pockets of the outer clothing, or feeling round the inside of collars, socks and shoes if this is reasonably necessary in the circumstances to look for the object of the search or to remove and examine any item reasonably suspected to be the object of the search. For the same reasons, subject to the restrictions on the removal of headgear, a person's hair may also be searched in public (see paragraphs 3.1 and 3.3).

3.6 Where on reasonable grounds it is considered necessary to conduct a more thorough search (e.g. by requiring a person to take off a T-shirt), this must be done out of public view, for example, in a police van unless paragraph 3.7 applies, or police station if there is one nearby. [See *Note 6*] Any search involving the removal of more than an outer coat, jacket, gloves, headgear or footwear, or any other item concealing identity, may only be made by an officer of the same sex as the person searched and may not be made in the presence of anyone of the opposite sex unless the person being searched specifically requests it. [See *Notes 4, 7* and *8*]

3.7 Searches involving exposure of intimate parts of the body must not be conducted as a routine extension of a less thorough search, simply because nothing is found in the course of the initial search. Searches involving exposure of intimate parts of the body may be carried out only at a nearby police station or other nearby location which is out of public view (but not a police vehicle). These searches must be conducted in accordance with paragraph 11 of Annex A to Code C except that an intimate search mentioned in paragraph 11(f) of Annex A to Code C may not be authorised or carried out under any stop and search powers. The other provisions of Code C do not apply to the conduct and recording of searches of persons detained at police stations in the exercise of stop and search powers. [See *Note 7*]

Steps to be taken prior to a search

3.8 Before any search of a detained person or attended vehicle takes place the officer must take reasonable steps to give the person to be searched or in charge of the vehicle the following information:
- (a) that they are being detained for the purposes of a search
- (b) the officer's name (except in the case of enquiries linked to the investigation of terrorism, or otherwise where the officer reasonably believes that giving his or her name might put him or her in danger, in which case a warrant or other identification number shall be given) and the name of the police station to which the officer is attached;
- (c) the legal search power which is being exercised; and
- (d) a clear explanation of:
  - (i) the purpose of the search in terms of the article or articles for which there is a power to search; and
  - (ii) in the case of powers requiring reasonable suspicion (see paragraph 2.1(a)), the grounds for that suspicion; or
  - (iii) in the case of powers which do not require reasonable suspicion (see paragraph 2.1(b), and (c)), the nature of the power and of any necessary authorisation and the fact that it has been given.

3.9 Officers not in uniform must show their warrant cards. Stops and searches under the powers mentioned in paragraphs 2.1(b), and (c) may be undertaken only by a constable in uniform.

3.10 Before the search takes place the officer must inform the person (or the owner or person in charge of the vehicle that is to be searched) of his or her entitlement to a copy of the record of the search, including his entitlement to a record of the search if an application is made within 12 months, if it is wholly impracticable to make a record at the time. If a record is not made at the time the person should also be told how a copy can be obtained (see section 4). The person should also be given information about police powers to stop and search and the individual's rights in these circumstances.

3.11 If the person to be searched, or in charge of a vehicle to be searched, does not appear to understand what is being said, or there is any doubt about the person's ability to understand English, the officer must take reasonable steps to bring information regarding the person's rights and any relevant provisions of this Code to his or her attention. If the person is deaf or cannot understand English and is accompanied by someone, then the officer must try to establish whether that person can interpret or otherwise help the officer to give the required information.

4 Recording requirements

4.1 An officer who has carried out a search in the exercise of any power to which this Code applies, must make a record of it at the time, unless there are exceptional circumstances which would make this wholly impracticable (e.g. in situations involving public disorder or when the officer's presence is urgently required elsewhere). If a record is not made at the time, the officer must do so as soon as practicable afterwards. There may be situations in which it is not practicable to obtain the information necessary to complete a record, but the officer should make every reasonable effort to do so. [See *Note 21*.]

4.2 A copy of a record made at the time must be given immediately to the person who has been searched. The officer must ask for the name, address and date of birth of the person searched, but there is no obligation on a person to provide these details and no power of detention if the person is unwilling to do so.

4.3 The following information must always be included in the record of a search even if the person does not wish to provide any personal details:

- (i)   the name of the person searched, or (if it is withheld) a description;
- (ii)   a note of the person's self-defined ethnic background; [*See Note 18*]
- (iii)   when a vehicle is searched, its registration number; [*See Note 16*]
- (iv)   the date, time, and place that the person or vehicle was first detained;
- (v)   the date, time and place the person or vehicle was searched (if different from (iv));
- (vi)   the purpose of the search;
- (vii) the grounds for making it, or in the case of those searches mentioned in paragraph 2.1(b) and (c), the nature of the power and of any necessary authorisation and the fact that it has been given; [*See Note 17*]
- (viii) its outcome (e.g. arrest or no further action);
- (ix)   a note of any injury or damage to property resulting from it;
- (x)   subject to paragraph 3.8(b), the identity of the officer making the search. [*See Note 15*]

4.4 Nothing in paragraph 4.3 (x) or 4.10A requires the names of police officers to be shown on the search record or any other record required to be made under this code in the case of enquiries linked to the investigation of terrorism or otherwise where an officer reasonably believes that recording names might endanger the officers. In such cases the record must show the officers' warrant or other identification number and duty station.

4.5 A record is required for each person and each vehicle searched. However, if a person is in a vehicle and both are searched, and the object and grounds of the search are the same, only one record need be completed. If more than one person in a vehicle is searched, separate records for each search of a person must be made. If only a vehicle is searched, the name of the driver and his or her self-defined ethnic background must be recorded, unless the vehicle is unattended.

4.6 The record of the grounds for making a search must, briefly but informatively, explain the reason for suspecting the person concerned, by reference to the person's behaviour and/or other circumstances.

4.7 Where officers detain an individual with a view to performing a search, but the search is not carried out due to the grounds for suspicion being eliminated as a result of questioning the person detained, a record must still be made in accordance with the procedure outlined in Paragraph 4.12.

4.8 After searching an unattended vehicle, or anything in or on it, an officer must leave a notice in it (or on it, if things on it have been searched without opening it) recording the fact that it has been searched.

4.9 The notice must include the name of the police station to which the officer concerned is attached and state where a copy of the record of the search may be obtained and where any application for compensation should be directed.

4.10 The vehicle must if practicable be left secure.

4.10A When an officer makes a record of the stop electronically and is unable to produce a copy of the form at the time, the officer must explain how the person can obtain a full copy of the record of the stop or search and give the person a receipt which contains:

- a unique reference number and guidance on how to obtain a full copy of the stop or search;

- the name of the officer who carried out the stop or search (unless paragraph 4.4 applies); and
- the power used to stop and search them. [See Note 21]

Recording of encounters not governed by Statutory Powers

4.11 Not used.

4.12 When an officer requests a person in a public place to account for themselves, i.e. their actions, behaviour, presence in an area or possession of anything, a record of the encounter must be completed at the time and a copy given to the person who has been questioned. The record must identify the name of the officer who has made the stop and conducted the encounter. This does not apply under the exceptional circumstances outlined in paragraph 4.1 of this code.

4.13 This requirement does not apply to general conversations such as when giving directions to a place, or when seeking witnesses. It also does not include occasions on which an officer is seeking general information or questioning people to establish background to incidents which have required officers to intervene to keep the peace or resolve a dispute.

4.14 A separate record need not be completed when:
— stopping a person in a vehicle when an HORT/1 form, a Vehicle Defect Rectification Scheme Notice, or a Fixed Penalty Notice is issued. It also does not apply when a specimen of breath is required under Section 6 of the Road Traffic Act 1988.
— stopping a person when a Penalty Notice is issued for an offence.

4.15 Officers must inform the person of their entitlement to a copy of a record of the encounter.

4.16 The provisions of paragraph 4.4 of this code apply equally when the encounters described in 4.12 and 4.13 are recorded.

4.17 The following information must be included in the record
   (i)   the date, time and place of the encounter;
   (ii) if the person is in a vehicle, the registration number;
   (iii) the reason why the officer questioned that person; [See *Note 17*]
   (iv) a note of the person's self-defined ethnic background; [See *Note 18*]
   (v)   the outcome of the encounter.

4.18 There is no power to require the person questioned to provide personal details. If a person refuses to give their self-defined ethnic background, a form must still be completed, which includes a description of the person's ethnic background. [See Note 18]

4.19 A record of an encounter must always be made when the criteria set out in 4.12 have been met. If the criteria are not met but the person requests a record, the officer should provide a copy of the form but record on it that the encounter did not meet the criteria. The officer can refuse to issue the form if he or she reasonably believes that the purpose of the request is deliberately aimed at frustrating or delaying legitimate police activity. [See *Note 20*]

4.20 All references to officers in this section include police staff designated as Community Support Officers under section 38 of the Police Reform Act 2002.

5   Monitoring and supervising the use of stop and search powers

5.1 Supervising officers must monitor the use of stop and search powers and should consider in particular whether there is any evidence that they are being exercised on the basis of stereotyped images or inappropriate generalisations. Supervising officers should satisfy themselves that the practice of officers under their supervision in stopping, searching and recording is fully in accordance with this Code. Supervisors must also examine whether the records reveal any trends or patterns which give cause for concern, and if so take appropriate action to address this

5.2 Senior officers with area or force-wide responsibilities must also monitor the broader use of stop and search powers and, where necessary, take action at the relevant level.

5.3 Supervision and monitoring must be supported by the compilation of comprehensive statistical records of stops and searches at force, area and local level. Any apparently disproportionate use of the powers by particular officers or groups of officers or in relation to specific sections of the community should be identified and investigated.

5.4 In order to promote public confidence in the use of the powers, forces in consultation with police authorities must make arrangements for the records to be scrutinised by representatives of the community, and to explain the use of the powers at a local level. [See *Note 19*].

Notes for Guidance

Officers exercising stop and search powers

1 This code does not affect the ability of an officer to speak to or question a person in the ordinary course of the officer's duties without detaining the person or exercising any element of compulsion. It is not the purpose of the code to prohibit such encounters between the police and the community with the co-operation of the person concerned and neither does it affect the principle that all citizens have a duty to help police officers to prevent crime and discover offenders. This is a civic rather than a legal duty; but when a police officer is trying to discover whether, or by whom, an offence has been committed he or she may question any person from whom useful information might be obtained, subject to the restrictions imposed by Code C. A person's unwillingness to reply does not alter this entitlement, but in the absence of a power to arrest, or to detain in order to search, the person is free to leave at will and cannot be compelled to remain with the officer.

2 In some circumstances preparatory questioning may be unnecessary, but in general a brief conversation or exchange will be desirable not only as a means of avoiding unsuccessful searches, but to explain the grounds for the stop/search, to gain cooperation and reduce any tension there might be surrounding the stop/search.

3 Where a person is lawfully detained for the purpose of a search, but no search in the event takes place, the detention will not thereby have been rendered unlawful.

4 Many people customarily cover their heads or faces for religious reasons—for example, Muslim women, Sikh men, Sikh or Hindu women, or Rastarfarian men or women. A police officer cannot order the removal of a head or face covering except where there is reason to believe that the item is being worn by the individual wholly or mainly for the purpose of disguising identity, not simply because it disguises identity. Where there may be religious sensitivities about ordering the removal of such an item, the officer should permit the item to be removed out of public view. Where practicable, the item should be removed in the presence of an officer of the same sex as the person and out of sight of anyone of the opposite sex.

5 A search of a person in public should be completed as soon as possible.

6 A person may be detained under a stop and search power at a place other than where the person was first detained, only if that place, be it a police station or elsewhere, is nearby. Such a place should be located within a reasonable travelling distance using whatever mode of travel (on foot or by car) is appropriate. This applies to all searches under stop and search powers, whether or not they involve the removal of clothing or exposure of intimate parts of the body (see paragraphs 3.6 and 3.7) or take place in or out of public view. It means, for example, that a search under the stop and search power in section 23 of the Misuse of Drugs Act 1971 which involves the compulsory removal of more than a person's outer coat, jacket or gloves cannot be carried out unless a place which is both nearby the place they were first detained and out of public view, is available. If a search involves exposure of intimate parts of the body and a police station is not nearby, particular care must be taken to ensure that the location is suitable in that it enables the search to be conducted in accordance with the requirements of paragraph 11 of Annex A to Code C.

7 A search in the street itself should be regarded as being in public for the purposes of paragraphs 3.6 and 3.7 above, even though it may be empty at the time a search begins. Although there is no power to require a person to do so, there is nothing to prevent an officer from asking a person voluntarily to remove more than an outer coat, jacket or gloves (and headgear or footwear under section 45(3) of the Terrorism Act 2000) in public.

8 Where there may be religious sensitivities about asking someone to remove headgear using a power under section 45(3) of the Terrorism Act 2000, the police officer should offer to carry out the search out of public view (for example, in a police van or police station if there is one nearby).

9 Other means of identification might include jewellery, insignias, tattoos or other features which are known to identify members of the particular gang or group.

Authorising officers

10 The powers under section 60 are separate from and additional to the normal stop and search powers which require reasonable grounds to suspect an individual of carrying an offensive weapon (or other article). Their overall purpose is to prevent serious violence and the widespread carrying of weapons which might lead to persons being seriously injured by disarming potential offenders in circumstances where other powers would not be sufficient. They should not therefore be used to replace or circumvent the normal powers for dealing with routine crime problems. The purpose of the powers under section 60AA is to prevent those involved in intimidatory or violent protests using face coverings to disguise identity.

11 Authorisations under section 60 require a reasonable belief on the part of the authorising officer. This must have an objective basis, for example: intelligence or relevant information such as a history of antagonism and violence between particular groups; previous incidents of violence at, or connected with, particular events or locations; a significant increase in knife-point robberies in a limited area; reports that individuals are regularly carrying weapons in a particular locality; or in the case of section 60AA previous incidents of crimes being committed while wearing face coverings to conceal identity.

12 It is for the authorising officer to determine the period of time during which the powers mentioned in paragraph 2.1 (b) and (c) may be exercised. The officer should set the minimum period he or she considers necessary to deal with the risk of violence, the carrying of knives or offensive weapons, or terrorism. A direction to extend the period authorised under the powers mentioned in paragraph 2.1(b) may be given only once. Thereafter further use of the powers requires a new authorisation. There is no provision to extend an authorisation of the powers mentioned in paragraph 2.1(c); further use of the powers requires a new authorisation.

13 It is for the authorising officer to determine the geographical area in which the use of the powers is to be authorised. In doing so the officer may wish to take into account factors such as the nature and venue of the anticipated incident, the number of people who may be in the immediate area of any possible incident, their access to surrounding areas and the anticipated level of violence. The officer should not set a geographical area which is wider than that he or she believes necessary for the purpose of preventing anticipated violence, the carrying of knives or offensive weapons, acts of terrorism, or, in the case of section 60AA, the prevention of commission of offences. It is particularly important to ensure that constables exercising such powers are fully aware of where they may be used. If the area specified is smaller than the whole force area, the officer giving the authorisation should specify either the streets which form the boundary of the area or a divisional boundary within the force area. If the power is to be used in response to a threat or incident that straddles police force areas, an officer from each of the forces concerned will need to give an authorisation.

14 An officer who has authorised the use of powers under section 44 of the Terrorism Act 2000 must take immediate steps to send a copy of the authorisation to the National Joint Unit, Metropolitan Police Special Branch, who will forward it to the Secretary of State. The Secretary of State should be informed of the reasons for the authorisation. The National Joint Unit will inform the force concerned, within 48 hours of the authorisation being made, whether the Secretary of State has confirmed or cancelled or altered the authorisation.

Recording

15 Where a stop and search is conducted by more than one officer the identity of all the officers engaged in the search must be recorded on the record. Nothing prevents an officer who is present but not directly involved in searching from completing the record during the course of the encounter.

16 Where a vehicle has not been allocated a registration number (e.g. a rally car or a trials motorbike) that part of the requirement under 4.3(iii) does not apply.

17 It is important for monitoring purposes to specify whether the authority for exercising a stop and search power was given under section 60 of the Criminal Justice and Public Order Act 1994, or under section 44(1) or 44(2) of the Terrorism Act 2000.

18 Officers should record the self-defined ethnicity of every person stopped according to the categories used in the 2001 census question listed in Annex B. Respondents should be asked to select one of the five main categories representing broad ethnic groups and then a more specific cultural background from within this group. The ethnic classification should be coded for recording purposes using the coding system in Annex B. An additional 'Not stated' box is available but should not be offered to respondents explicitly. Officers should be aware and explain to members of the public, especially where concerns are raised, that this information is required to obtain a true picture of stop and search activity and to help improve ethnic monitoring, tackle discriminatory practice, and promote effective use of the powers. If the person gives what appears to the officer to be an 'incorrect' answer (e.g. a person who appears to be white states that they are black), the officer should record the response that has been given. Officers should also record their own perception of the ethnic background of every person stopped and this must be done by using the PNC/Phoenix classification system. If the 'Not stated' category is used the reason for this must be recorded on the form.

19 Arrangements for public scrutiny of records should take account of the right to confidentiality of those stopped and searched. Anonymised forms and/or statistics generated from records should be the focus of the examinations by members of the public.

20 Where an officer engages in conversation which is not pertinent to the actions or whereabouts of the individual (e.g. does not relate to why the person is there, what they are doing or where they have been or are going) then issuing a form would not meet the criteria set out in paragraph 4.12. Situations designed to impede police activity may arise, for example, in public order situations where individuals engage in dialogue with the officer but the officer does not initiate or engage in contact about the person's individual circumstances.

21 In situations where it is not practicable to provide a written record of the stop or stop and search at that time, the officer should consider providing the person with details of the station to which the person may attend for a record. This may take the form of a simple business card, adding the date of the stop or stop and search.

ANNEX A   SUMMARY OF MAIN STOP AND SEARCH POWERS

THIS TABLE RELATES TO STOP AND SEARCH POWERS ONLY. INDIVIDUAL STATUTES BELOW MAY CONTAIN OTHER POLICE POWERS OF ENTRY, SEARCH AND SEIZURE

Power	Object of Search	Extent of Search	Where Exercisable
Unlawful articles general			
1. Public Stores Act 1875, s6	HM Stores stolen or unlawfully obtained	Persons, vehicles and vessels	Anywhere where the constabulary powers are exercisable
2. Firearms Act 1968, s47	Firearms	Persons and vehicles	A public place, or anywhere in the case of reasonable suspicion of offences of carrying firearms with criminal intent or trespassing with firearms

Power	Object of Search	Extent of Search	Where Exercisable
3. Misuse of Drugs Act 1971, s23	Controlled drugs	Persons and vehicles	Anywhere
4. Customs and Excise Management Act 1979, s163	Goods: (a) on which duty has not been paid; (b) being unlawfully removed, imported or exported; (c) otherwise liable to forfeiture to HM Customs and Excise	Vehicles and vessels only	Anywhere
5. Aviation Security Act 1982, s27(1)	Stolen or unlawfully obtained goods	Airport employees and vehicles carrying airport employees or aircraft or any vehicle in a cargo area whether or not carrying an employee	Any designated airport
6. Police and Criminal Evidence Act 1984, s1	Stolen goods; articles for use in certain Theft Act offences; offensive weapons, including bladed or sharply-pointed articles (except folding pocket knives with a bladed cutting edge not exceeding 3 inches); prohibited possession of a category 4 (display grade) firework, any person under 18 in possession of an adult firework in a public place.	Persons and vehicles	Where there is public access
	Criminal Damage: Articles made, adapted or intended for use in destroying or damaging property	Persons and vehicles	Where there is public access
Police and Criminal Evidence Act 1984, s6(3) (by a constable of the United Kingdom Atomic Energy Authority Constabulary in respect of property owned or controlled by British Nuclear Fuels plc	HM Stores (in the form of goods and chattels belonging to British Nuclear Fuels plc)	Persons, vehicles and vessels	Anywhere where the constabulary powers are exercisable

Power	Object of Search	Extent of Search	Where Exercisable
7. Sporting events (Control of Alcohol etc.) Act 1985, s7	Intoxicating liquor	Persons, coaches and trains	Designated sports grounds or coaches and trains travelling to or from a designated sporting event
8. Crossbows Act 1987, s4	Crossbows or parts of crossbows (except crossbows with a draw weight of less than 1.4 kilograms)	Persons and vehicles	Anywhere except dwellings
9. Criminal Justice Act 1988 s139B	Offensive weapons, bladed or sharply pointed article	Persons	School premises

Evidence of game and wildlife offences

Power	Object of Search	Extent of Search	Where Exercisable
10. Poaching Prevention Act 1862, s2	Game or Poaching equipment	Persons and vehicles	A public place
11. Deer Act 1991, s12	Evidence of offences under the Act	Persons and vehicles	Anywhere except dwellings
12. Conservation of Seals Act 1970, s4	Seals or hunting equipment	Vehicles only	Anywhere
13. Badgers Act 1992, s11	Evidence of offences under the Act	Persons and vehicles	Anywhere
14. Wildlife and Countryside Act 1981, s19	Evidence of wildlife offences	Persons and vehicles	Anywhere except dwellings

Other

Power	Object of Search	Extent of Search	Where Exercisable
15. Terrorism Act 2000, s.43	*Evidence of liability to arrest under section 14 of the Act*	Persons	Anywhere
16. Terrorism Act 2000, s.44(1)	Articles which could be used for a purpose connected with the commission, preparation or instigation of acts of terrorism	*Vehicles, driver and passengers*	Anywhere within the area or locality authorised under subsection (1)
17. Terrorism Act 2000, s.44(2)	*Articles which could be used for a purpose connected with the commission, preparation or instigation of acts of terrorism*	*Pedestrians*	Anywhere within the area of locality authorised

Power	Object of Search	Extent of Search	Where Exercisable
18. Paragraphs 7 and 8 of Schedule 7 to the Terrorism Act 2000	*Anything relevant to determining if a person being examined falls within paragraph 2(1)(a) to (c) of Schedule 5*	Persons, vehicles, vessels etc.	*Ports and airports*
19. Section 60 Criminal Justice and Public Order Act 1994, *as amended by s.8 of the Knives Act 1997*	Offensive weapons or dangerous instruments to prevent incidents of serious violence or *to deal with the carrying of such items*	Persons and vehicles	Anywhere within a locality authorised under subsection (1)

ANNEX B   SELF-DEFINED ETHNIC CLASSIFICATION CATEGORIES

White   **W**

A. White—British   W1
B. White—Irish   W2
C. Any other White background   W9

Mixed   **M**
D. White and Black Caribbean   M1
E. White and Black African   M2
F. White and Asian   M3
G. Any other Mixed Background   M9

Asian/Asian—British   **A**
H. Asian—Indian   A1
I. Asian—Pakistani   A2
J. Asian—Bangladeshi   A3
K. Any other Asian background   A9

Black/Black—British   **B**
L. Black—Caribbean   B1
M. Black African   B2
N. Any other Black background   B9

Other   **O**
O. Chinese   O1
P. Any other   O9

Not Stated   **NS**

Criminal Justice and Public Order Act 1994

60   Powers to stop and search in anticipation of violence
   (1) If a police officer of or above the rank of inspector reasonably believes—

(a) that incidents involving serious violence may take place in any locality in his police area, and that it is expedient to give an authorisation under this section to prevent their occurrence, or

(b) that persons are carrying dangerous instruments or offensive weapons in any locality in his police area without good reason,

he may give an authorisation that the powers conferred by this section are to be exercisable at any place within that locality for a specified period not exceeding 24 hours.

(2) Repealed.

(3) If it appears to an officer of or above the rank of superintendent that it is expedient to do so, having regard to offences which have, or are reasonably suspected to have, been committed in connection with any activity falling within the authorisation, he may direct that the authorisation shall continue in being for a further 24 hours.

(3A) If an inspector gives an authorisation under subsection (1) he must, as soon as it is practicable to do so, cause an officer of or above the rank of superintendent to be informed.

(4) This section confers on any constable in uniform power—

(a) to stop any pedestrian and search him or anything carried by him for offensive weapons or dangerous instruments;

(b) to stop any vehicle and search the vehicle, its driver and any passenger for offensive weapons or dangerous instruments.

(4A) This section also confers on any constable in uniform power—

(a) to require any person to remove any item which the constable reasonably believes that person is wearing wholly or mainly for the purpose of concealing his identity;

(b) to seize any item which the constable reasonably believes any person intends to wear wholly or mainly for that purpose.

(5) A constable may, in the exercise of the powers conferred by subsection (4) above stop any person or vehicle and make any search he thinks fit whether or not he has any grounds for suspecting that the person or vehicle is carrying weapons or articles of that kind.

(6) If in the course of a search under this section a constable discovers a dangerous instrument or an article which he has reasonable grounds for suspecting to be an offensive weapon, he may seize it.

(7) This section applies (with the necessary modifications) to ships, aircraft and hovercraft as it applies to vehicles.

(8) A person who fails (a) to stop, or to stop the vehicle; or (b) to remove an item worn by him, when required to do so by a constable in the exercise of his powers under this section shall be liable on summary conviction to imprisonment for a term not exceeding one month or to a fine not exceeding level 3 on the standard scale or both.

(9) Any authorisation under this section shall be in writing signed by the officer giving it and shall specify the grounds on which it is given and the locality in which and the period during which the powers conferred by this section are exercisable and a direction under subsection (3) above shall also be given in writing or, where that is not practicable, recorded in writing as soon as it is practicable to do so.

(9A) The preceding provisions of this section, so far as they relate to an authorisation by a member of the British Transport Police Force (including one who for the time being has the same powers and privileges as a member of a police force for a police area), shall have effect as if the references to a locality in his police area were references to a place specified in section 31(1)(a) to (f) of the Railways and Transport Safety Act 2003.

(10) Where a vehicle is stopped by a constable under this section, the driver shall be entitled to obtain a written statement that the vehicle was stopped under the powers conferred by this section if he applies for such a statement not later than the end of the period of twelve months from the day on which the vehicle was stopped as respects a pedestrian who is stopped and searched under this section.

(10A) A person who is searched by a constable under this section shall be entitled to obtain a written statement that he was searched under the powers conferred by this section if he applies for such a statement not later than the end of the period of twelve months from the day on which he was searched.

(11) In this section—

'dangerous instruments' means instruments which have a blade or are sharply pointed;

'offensive weapon' has the meaning given by section 1(9) of the Police and Criminal Evidence Act 1984 or, in relation to Scotland, section 47(4) of the Criminal Law (Consolidation) (Scotland) Act 1995; and

'vehicle' includes a caravan as defined in section 29(1) of the Caravan Sites and Control of Development Act 1960.

(11A) For the purposes of this section, a person carries a dangerous instrument or an offensive weapon if he has it in his possession.

(12) The powers conferred by this section are in addition to and not in derogation of, any power otherwise conferred.

Intimate searches

Police and Criminal Evidence Act 1984

55   Intimate searches

(1) Subject to the following provisions of this section, if an officer of at least the rank of inspector has reasonable grounds for believing—

(a) that a person who has been arrested and is in police detention may have concealed on him anything which—

(i)   he could use to cause physical injury to himself or others; and

(ii) he might so use while he is in police detention or in the custody of a court; or

(b) that such a person—

(i)   may have a Class A drug concealed on him; and

(ii) was in possession of it with the appropriate criminal intent before his arrest, he may authorise an intimate search of that person.

(2) An officer may not authorise an intimate search of a person for anything unless he has reasonable grounds for believing that it cannot be found without his being intimately searched.

(3) An officer may give an authorisation under subsection (1) above orally or in writing but, if he gives it orally, he shall confirm it in writing as soon as is practicable.

(3A) A drug offence search shall not be carried out unless the appropriate consent has been given in writing.

(3B) Where it is proposed that a drug offence search be carried out, an appropriate officer shall inform the person who is to be subject to it—

(a) of the giving of the authorisation for it; and

(b) of the grounds for giving the authorisation.

(4) An intimate search which is only a drug offence search shall be by way of examination by a suitably qualified person.

(5) Except as provided by subsection (4) above, an intimate search shall be by way of examination by a suitably qualified person unless an officer of at least the rank of inspector considers that this is not practicable.

(6) An intimate search which is not carried out as mentioned in subsection (5) above shall be carried out by a constable.

(7) A constable may not carry out an intimate search of a person of the opposite sex.

(8) No intimate search may be carried out except—

    (a) at a police station;

    (b) at a hospital;

    (c) at a registered medical practitioner's surgery; or

    (d) at some other place used for medical purposes.

(9) An intimate search which is only a drug offence search may not be carried out at a police station.

(10) If an intimate search of a person is carried out, the custody record relating to him shall state—

    (a) which parts of his body were searched; and

    (b) why they were searched.

(10A) If the intimate search is a drug offence search, the custody record relating to that person shall also state—

    (a) the authorisation by virtue of which the search was carried out;

    (b) the grounds for giving the authorisation; and

    (c) the fact that the appropriate consent was given.

(11) The information required to be recorded by subsections (10) and (10A) above shall be recorded as soon as practicable after the completion of the search.

(12) The custody officer at a police station may seize and retain anything which is found on an intimate search of a person, or cause any such thing to be seized and retained—

    (a) if he believes that the person from whom it is seized may use it—

        (i)   to cause physical injury to himself or any other person;

        (ii) to damage property;

        (iii) to interfere with evidence; or

        (iv) to assist him to escape; or

    (b) if he has reasonable grounds for believing that it may be evidence relating to an offence.

(13) Where anything is seized under this section, the person from whom it is seized shall be told the reason for the seizure unless he is—

    (a) violent or likely to become violent; or

    (b) incapable of understanding what is said to him.

(13A) Where the appropriate consent to a drug offence search of any person was refused without good cause, in any proceedings against that person for an offence—

    (a) the court, in determining whether there is a case to answer;

    (b) a judge, in deciding whether to grant an application made by the accused under paragraph 2 of Schedule 3 to the Crime and Disorder Act 1998 (applications for dismissal); and

    (c) the court or jury, in determining whether that person is guilty of the offence charged, may draw such inferences from the refusal as appear proper.

(14) Every annual report—

    (a) under section 22 of the Police Act 1996; or

    (b) made by the Commissioner of Police of the Metropolis,

shall contain information about searches under this section which have been carried out in the area to which the report relates during the period to which it relates.

(15) The information about such searches shall include—

    (a) the total number of searches;

    (b) the number of searches conducted by way of examination by a suitably qualified person;

    (c) the number of searches not so conducted but conducted in the presence of such a person; and

    (d) the result of the searches carried out.

(16) The information shall also include, as separate items—

    (a) the total number of drug offence searches; and

    (b) the result of those searches.

(17) In this section—

'the appropriate criminal intent' means an intent to commit an offence under—

    (a) section 5(3) of the Misuse of Drugs Act 1971 (possession of controlled drug with intent to supply to another); or

    (b) section 68(2) of the Customs and Excise Management Act 1979 (exportation etc. with intent to evade a prohibition or restriction);

'appropriate officer' means—

    (a) a constable,

    (b) a person who is designated as a detention officer in pursuance of section 38 of the Police Reform Act 2002 if his designation applies paragraph 33D of Schedule 4 to that Act, or

    (c) a person who is designated as a staff custody officer in pursuance of section 38 of that Act if his designation applies paragraph 35C of Schedule 4 to that Act;

'Class A drug' has the meaning assigned to it by section 2(1)(b) of the Misuse of Drugs Act 1971;

'drug offence search' means an intimate search for a Class A drug which an officer has authorised by virtue of subsection (1)(b) above; and

'suitably qualified person' means—

    (a) a registered medical practitioner; or

    (b) a registered nurse.

55A X-rays and ultrasound scans

(1) If an officer of at least the rank of inspector has reasonable grounds for believing that a person who has been arrested for an offence and is in police detention—

    (a) may have swallowed a Class A drug, and

    (b) was in possession of it with the appropriate criminal intent before his arrest,

the officer may authorise that an x-ray is taken of the person or an ultrasound scan is carried out on the person (or both).

(2) An x-ray must not be taken of a person and an ultrasound scan must not be carried out on him unless the appropriate consent has been given in writing.

(3) If it is proposed that an x-ray is taken or an ultrasound scan is carried out, an appropriate officer must inform the person who is to be subject to it—

    (a) of the giving of the authorisation for it, and

    (b) of the grounds for giving the authorisation.

(4) An x-ray may be taken or an ultrasound scan carried out only by a suitably qualified person and only at—

    (a) a hospital,

    (b) a registered medical practitioner's surgery, or

    (c) some other place used for medical purposes.

(5) The custody record of the person must also state—

    (a) the authorisation by virtue of which the x-ray was taken or the ultrasound scan was carried out,

    (b) the grounds for giving the authorisation, and

    (c) the fact that the appropriate consent was given.

(6) The information required to be recorded by subsection (5) must be recorded as soon as practicable after the x-ray has been taken or ultrasound scan carried out (as the case may be).

(7) Every annual report—

    (a) under section 22 of the Police Act 1996, or

    (b) made by the Commissioner of Police of the Metropolis,

must contain information about x-rays which have been taken and ultrasound scans which have been carried out under this section in the area to which the report relates during the period to which it relates.

(8) The information about such x-rays and ultrasound scans must be presented separately and must include—

    (a) the total number of x-rays;

    (b) the total number of ultrasound scans;

    (c) the results of the x-rays;

    (d) the results of the ultrasound scans.

(9) If the appropriate consent to an x-ray or ultrasound scan of any person is refused without good cause, in any proceedings against that person for an offence—

    (a) the court, in determining whether there is a case to answer,

    (b) a judge, in deciding whether to grant an application made by the accused under paragraph 2 of Schedule 3 to the Crime and Disorder Act 1998 (applications for dismissal), and

    (c) the court or jury, in determining whether that person is guilty of the offence charged,

may draw such inferences from the refusal as appear proper.

(10) In this section 'the appropriate criminal intent', 'appropriate officer', 'Class A drug' and 'suitably qualified person' have the same meanings as in section 55 above.

Exclusion zones

Serious Organised Crime and Police Act 2005

112   Power to direct a person to leave a place

(1) A constable may direct a person to leave a place if he believes, on reasonable grounds, that the person is in the place at a time when he would be prohibited from entering it by virtue of—

    (a) an order to which subsection (2) applies, or

    (b) a condition to which subsection (3) applies.

(2) This subsection applies to an order which—

    (a) was made, by virtue of any enactment, following the person's conviction of an offence, and

    (b) prohibits the person from entering the place or from doing so during a period specified in the order.

(3) This subsection applies to a condition which—

    (a) was imposed, by virtue of any enactment, as a condition of the person's release from a prison in which he was serving a sentence of imprisonment following his conviction of an offence, and

    (b) prohibits the person from entering the place or from doing so during a period specified in the condition.

(4) A direction under this section may be given orally.

(5) Any person who knowingly contravenes a direction given to him under this section is guilty of an offence and liable on summary conviction to imprisonment for a term not exceeding 51 weeks or to a fine not exceeding level 4 on the standard scale, or to both.

    […]

(8) In subsection (3)(a)—

    (a) 'sentence of imprisonment' and 'prison' are to be construed in accordance with section 62(5) of the Criminal Justice and Court Services Act 2000 (c. 43);

    (b) the reference to a release from prison includes a reference to a temporary release.

(9) In this section, 'place' includes an area.

(10) This section applies whether or not the order or condition mentioned in subsection (1) was made or imposed before or after the commencement of this section.

The power to take intimate and non-intimate body samples

Police and Criminal Evidence Act 1984

61   Fingerprinting

(1) Except as provided by this section no person's fingerprints may be taken without the appropriate consent.

(2) Consent to the taking of a person's fingerprints must be in writing if it is given at a time when he is at a police station.

(3) The fingerprints of a person detained at a police station may be taken without the appropriate consent if—

    (a) he is detained in consequence of his arrest for a recordable offence; and

    (b) he has not had his fingerprints taken in the course of the investigation of the offence by the police.

(3A) Where a person mentioned in paragraph (a) of subsection (3) or (4) has already had his fingerprints taken in the course of the investigation of the offence by the police, that fact shall be disregarded for the purposes of that subsection if—

    (a) the fingerprints taken on the previous occasion do not constitute a complete set of his fingerprints; or

    (b) some or all of the fingerprints taken on the previous occasion are not of sufficient quality to allow satisfactory analysis, comparison or matching (whether in the case in question or generally).

(4) The fingerprints of a person detained at a police station may be taken without the appropriate consent if—

    (a) he has been charged with a recordable offence or informed that he will be reported for such an offence; and

    (b) he has not had his fingerprints taken in the course of the investigation of the offence by the police.'

(4A) The fingerprints of a person who has answered to bail at a court or police station may be taken without the appropriate consent at the court or station if—

    (a) the court, or

    (b) an officer of at least the rank of inspector,

authorises them to be taken.

(4B) A court or officer may only give an authorisation under subsection (4A) if—

    (a) the person who has answered to bail has answered to it for a person whose fingerprints were taken on a previous occasion and there are reasonable grounds for believing that he is not the same person; or

    (b) the person who has answered to bail claims to be a different person from a person whose fingerprints were taken on a previous occasion.

(5) An officer may give an authorisation under subsection (4A) above orally or in writing but, if he gives it orally, he shall confirm it in writing as soon as is practicable.

(6) Any person's fingerprints may be taken without the appropriate consent if—

    (a) he has been convicted of a recordable offence;

    (b) he has been given a caution in respect of a recordable offence which, at the time of the caution, he has admitted; or

    (c) he has been warned or reprimanded under section 65 of the Crime and Disorder Act 1998 (c. 37) for a recordable offence.

(7) In a case where by virtue of subsection (3), (4) or (6) above a person's fingerprints are taken without the appropriate consent—

    (a) he shall be told the reason before his fingerprints are taken; and

(b) the reason shall be recorded as soon as is practicable after the fingerprints are taken.

(7A) If a person's fingerprints are taken at a police station, whether with or without the appropriate consent—

(a) before the fingerprints are taken, an officer shall inform him that they may be the subject of a speculative search; and

(b) the fact that the person has been informed of this possibility shall be recorded as soon as is practicable after the fingerprints have been taken.

(8) If he is detained at a police station when the fingerprints are taken, the reason for taking them and, in the case falling within subsection (7A) above, the fact referred to in paragraph (b) of that subsection shall be recorded on his custody record.

(8B) The power to take the fingerprints of a person detained at a police station without the appropriate consent shall be exercisable by any constable.

(9) Nothing in this section—

(a) affects any power conferred by paragraph 18(2) of Schedule 2 to the Immigration Act 1971; or

(b) applies to a person arrested or detained under the terrorism provisions.

(10) Nothing in this section applies to a person arrested under an extradition arrest power.

61A Impressions of footwear

(1) Except as provided by this section, no impression of a person's footwear may be taken without the appropriate consent.

(2) Consent to the taking of an impression of a person's footwear must be in writing if it is given at a time when he is at a police station.

(3) Where a person is detained at a police station, an impression of his footwear may be taken without the appropriate consent if—

(a) he is detained in consequence of his arrest for a recordable offence, or has been charged with a recordable offence, or informed that he will be reported for a recordable offence; and

(b) he has not had an impression taken of his footwear in the course of the investigation of the offence by the police.

(4) Where a person mentioned in paragraph (a) of subsection (3) above has already had an impression taken of his footwear in the course of the investigation of the offence by the police, that fact shall be disregarded for the purposes of that subsection if the impression of his footwear taken previously is—

(a) incomplete; or

(b) is not of sufficient quality to allow satisfactory analysis, comparison or matching (whether in the case in question or generally).

(5) If an impression of a person's footwear is taken at a police station, whether with or without the appropriate consent—

(a) before it is taken, an officer shall inform him that it may be the subject of a speculative search; and

(b) the fact that the person has been informed of this possibility shall be recorded as soon as is practicable after the impression has been taken, and if he is detained at a police station, the record shall be made on his custody record.

(6) In a case where, by virtue of subsection (3) above, an impression of a person's footwear is taken without the appropriate consent—

(a) he shall be told the reason before it is taken; and

(b) the reason shall be recorded on his custody record as soon as is practicable after the impression is taken.

(7) The power to take an impression of the footwear of a person detained at a police station without the appropriate consent shall be exercisable by any constable.

(8) Nothing in this section applies to any person—

(a) arrested or detained under the terrorism provisions;

(b) arrested under an extradition arrest power.

62 Intimate samples

(1) Subject to section 63B below an intimate sample may be taken from a person in police detention only—

(a) if a police officer of at least the rank of inspector authorises it to be taken; and

(b) if the appropriate consent is given.

(1A) An intimate sample may be taken from a person who is not in police detention but from whom, in the course of the investigation of an offence, two or more non-intimate samples suitable for the same means of analysis have been taken which have proved insufficient—

(a) if a police officer of at least the rank of inspector authorises it to be taken; and

(b) if the appropriate consent is given.

(2) An officer may only give an authorisation under subsection (1) or (1A) above if he has reasonable grounds—

(a) for suspecting the involvement of the person from whom the sample is to be taken in a recordable offence; and

(b) for believing that the sample will tend to confirm or disprove his involvement.

(3) An officer may given an authorisation under subsection (1) or (1A) above orally or in writing but, if he gives it orally, he shall confirm it in writing as soon as is practicable.

(4) The appropriate consent must be given in writing.

(5) Where—

(a) an authorisation has been given; and

(b) it is proposed that an intimate sample shall be taken in pursuance of the authorisation,

an officer shall inform the person from whom the sample is to be taken—

(i) of the giving of the authorisation; and

(ii) of the grounds for giving it.

(6) The duty imposed by subsection (5)(ii) above includes a duty to state the nature of the offence in which it is suspected that the person from whom the sample is to be taken has been involved.

(7) If an intimate sample is taken from a person—

(a) the authorisation by virtue of which it was taken;

(b) the grounds for giving the authorisation; and

(c) the fact that the appropriate consent was given,

shall be recorded as soon as is practicable after the sample is taken.

(7A) If an intimate sample is taken from a person at a police station—

(a) before the sample is taken, an officer shall inform him that it may be the subject of a speculative search; and

(b) the fact that the person has been informed of this possibility shall be recorded as soon as practicable after the sample has been taken.

(8) If an intimate sample is taken from a person detained at a police station, the matters required to be recorded by subsection (7) or (7A) above shall be recorded in his custody record.

(9) In the case of an intimate sample which is a dental impression, the sample may be taken from a person only by a registered dentist.

(9A) In the case of any other form of intimate sample, except in the case of a sample of urine, the sample may be taken from a person only by—

(a) a registered medical practitioner; or

(b) a registered health care professional.

(10) Where the appropriate consent to the taking of an intimate sample from a person was refused without good cause, in any proceedings against that person for an offence—

(a) the court, in determining—
  (i) whether to commit that person for trial; or
  (ii) whether there is a case to answer; and
(aa) a judge, in deciding whether to grant an application made by the accused under paragraph 2 of Schedule 3 to the Crime and Disorder Act 1998 (applications for dismissal); and
(b) the court or jury, in determining whether that person is guilty of the offence charged, may draw such inferences from the refusal as appear proper.

(11) Nothing in this section applies to the falling of a specimen for the purposes of any provisions of sections 4 to 11 of the Road Traffic Act 1988 or of sections 26 to 38 of the Transport and Works Act 1992.

(12) Nothing in this section applies to a person arrested or detained under the terrorism provisions; and subsection (1A) shall not apply where the non-intimate samples mentioned in that subsection were taken under paragraph 10 of Schedule 8 to the Terrorism Act 2000.

63 Other samples

(1) Except as provided by this section, a non-intimate sample may not be taken from a person without the appropriate consent.

(2) Consent to the taking of a non-intimate sample must be given in writing.

(2A) A non-intimate sample may be taken from a person without the appropriate consent if two conditions are satisfied.

(2B) The first is that the person is in police detention in consequence of his arrest for a recordable offence.

(2C) The second is that—
(a) he has not had a non-intimate sample of the same type and from the same part of the body taken in the course of the investigation of the offence by the police, or
(b) he has had such a sample taken but it proved insufficient.

(3) A non-intimate sample may be taken from a person without the appropriate consent if—
(a) he is being held in custody by the police on the authority of a court; and
(b) an officer of at least the rank of inspector authorises it to be taken without the appropriate consent.

(3A) A non-intimate sample may be taken from a person (whether or not he is in police detention or held in custody by the police on the authority of a court without the appropriate consent if—
(a) he has been charged with a recordable offence or informed that he will be reported for such an offence; and
(b) either he has not had a non-intimate sample taken from him in the course of the investigation of the offence by the police or he has had a non-intimate sample taken from him but either it was not suitable for the same means of analysis or, though so suitable, the sample proved insufficient.

(3B) A non-intimate sample may be taken from a person without the appropriate consent if he has been convicted of a recordable offence.

(3C) A non-intimate sample may also be taken from a person without the appropriate consent if he is a person to whom section 2 of the Criminal Evidence (Amendment) Act 1997 applies (persons detained following acquittal on grounds of insanity or finding of unfitness to plead).

(4) An officer may only give an authorisation under subsection (3) above if he has reasonable grounds—
(a) for suspecting the involvement of the person from whom the sample is to be taken in a recordable offence; and
(b) for believing that the sample will tend to confirm or disprove his involvement.

(5) An officer may give an authorisation under subsection (3) above orally or in writing but, if he gives it orally, he shall confirm it in writing as soon as is practicable.

(5A) An officer shall not give an authorisation under subsection (3) above for the taking from any person of a non-intimate sample consisting of a skin impression if—
>   (a) a skin impression of the same part of the body has already been taken from that person in the course of the investigation of the offence; and
>   (b) the impression previously taken is not one that has proved insufficient.

(6) Where—
>   (a) an authorisation has been given; and
>   (b) it is proposed that a non-intimate sample shall be taken in pursuance of the authorisation,

an officer shall inform the person from whom the sample is to be taken—
>   (i)   of the giving of the authorisation; and
>   (ii) of the grounds for giving it.

(7) The duty imposed by subsection (6)(ii) above includes a duty to state the nature of the offence in which it is suspected that the person from whom the sample is to be taken has been involved.

(8) If a non-intimate sample is taken from a person by virtue of subsection (3) above—
>   (a) the authorisation by virtue of which it was taken; and
>   (b) the grounds for giving the authorisation,

shall be recorded as soon as is practicable after the sample is taken.

(8A) In a case where by virtue of subsection (2A), (3A), (3B) or (3C) above a sample is taken from a person without the appropriate consent—
>   (a) he shall be told the reason before the sample is taken; and
>   (b) the reason shall be recorded as soon as practicable after the sample is taken.

(8B) If a non-intimate sample is taken from a person at a police station, whether with or without the appropriate consent—
>   (a) before the sample is taken, an officer shall inform him that it may be the subject of a speculative search; and
>   (b) the fact that the person has been informed of this possibility shall be recorded as soon as practicable after the sample has been taken.

(9) If a non-intimate sample is taken from a person detained at a police station, the matters required to be recorded by subsection (8), (8A) or (8B) above shall be recorded in his custody record.

(9ZA) The power to take as non-intimate sample from a person without the appropriate consent shall be exercisable by any constable.

(9A) Subsection (3B) above shall not apply to any person convicted before 10th April 1995 unless he is a person to whom section 1 of the Criminal Evidence (Amendment) Act 1997 applies (persons imprisoned or detained by virtue of pre-existing conviction for sexual offence etc.).

(10) Nothing in this section applies to a person arrested or detained under the terrorism provisions.

(11) Nothing in this section applies to a person arrested under an extradition arrest power.

63A Fingerprints and samples: supplementary provisions

(1) Where a person has been arrested on suspicion of being involved in a recordable offence or has been charged with such an offence or has been informed that he will be reported for such an offence, fingerprints, impressions of footwear or samples or the information derived from samples taken under any power conferred by this Part of this Act from the person may be checked against—
>   (a) other fingerprints, impressions of footwear or samples to which the person seeking to check has access and which are held by or on behalf of any one or more relevant law-enforcement authorities or which are held in connection with or as a result of an investigation of an offence;

(b) information derived from other samples if the information is contained in records to which the person seeking to check has access and which are held as mentioned in paragraph (a) above.

(1A) In subsection (1) above 'relevant law-enforcement authority' means—

(a) a police force;

(b) the National Criminal Intelligence Service;

(c) the National Crime Squad;

(d) a public authority (not falling within paragraphs (a) to (c)) with functions in any part of the British Islands which consist of or include the investigation of crimes or the charging of offenders;

(e) any person with functions in any country or territory outside the United Kingdom which—

   (i) correspond to those of a police force; or

   (ii) otherwise consist of or include the investigation of conduct contrary to the law of that country or territory, or the apprehension of persons guilty of such conduct;

(f) any person with functions under any international agreement which consist of or include the investigation of conduct which is—

   (i)   unlawful under the law of one or more places,

   (ii) prohibited by such an agreement, or

   (iii) contrary to international law,

or the apprehension of persons guilty of such conduct.

(1B) The reference in subsection (1A) above to a police force is a reference to any of the following—

(a) any police force maintained under section 2 of the Police Act 1996 (c. 16) (police forces in England and Wales outside London);

(b) the metropolitan police force;

(c) the City of London police force;

(d) any police force maintained under or by virtue of section 1 of the Police (Scotland) Act 1967 (c. 77);

(e) the Police Service of Northern Ireland;

(f) the Police Service of Northern Ireland Reserve;

(g) the Ministry of Defence Police;

(h) the Royal Navy Regulating Branch;

(i) the Royal Military Police;

(j) the Royal Air Force Police;

(k) the Royal Marines Police;

(l) the British Transport Police;

(m) the States of Jersey Police Force;

(n) the salaried police force of the Island of Guernsey;

(o) the Isle of Man Constabulary.

(1C) Where—

(a) fingerprints, impressions of footwear or samples have been taken from any person in connection with the investigation of an offence but otherwise than in circumstances to which subsection (1) above applies, and

(b) that person has given his consent in writing to the use in a speculative search of the fingerprints, of the impressions of footwear or of the samples and of information derived from them, the fingerprints or, the impressions of footwear as the case may be, those samples and that information may be checked against any of the fingerprints, impressions of footwear, samples or information mentioned in paragraph (a) or (b) of that subsection.

(1D) A consent given for the purposes of subsection (IC) above shall not be capable of being withdrawn.

(2) Where a sample of hair other than pubic hair is to be taken the sample may be taken either by cutting hairs or by plucking hairs with their roots so long as no more are plucked than the person taking the sample reasonably considers to be necessary for a sufficient sample.

(3) Where any power to take a sample is exercisable in relation to a person the sample may be taken in a prison or other institution to which the Prison Act 1952 applies.

(3A) Where—

    (a) the power to take a non-intimate sample under section 63(3B) above is exercisable in relation to any person who is detained under Part III of the Mental Health Act 1983 in pursuance of—

        (i) a hospital order or interim hospital order made following his conviction for the recordable offence in question, or

        (ii) a transfer direction given at a time when he was detained in pursuance of any sentence or order imposed following that conviction, or

    (b) the power to take a non-intimate sample under section 63(3C) above is exercisable in relation to any person,

the sample may be taken in the hospital in which he is detained under that Part of that Act. Expressions used in this subsection and in the Mental Health Act 1983 have the same meaning as in that Act.

(3B) Where the power to take a non-intimate sample under section 63(3B) above is exercisable in relation to a person detained in pursuance of directions of the Secretary of State under section 92 of the Powers of Criminal Courts (Sentencing) Act 2000 the sample may be taken at the place where he is so detained.

(4) Any constable may, within the allowed period, require a person who is neither in police detention nor held in custody by the police on the authority of a court to attend a police station in order to have a sample taken where—

    (a) the person has been charged with a recordable offence or informed that he will be reported for such an offence and either he has not had a sample taken from him in the course of the investigation of the offence by the police or he has had a sample so taken from him but either it was not suitable for the same means of analysis or, though so suitable, the sample proved insufficient; or

    (b) the person has been convicted of a recordable offence and either he has not had a sample taken from him since the conviction or he has had a sample taken from him (before or after his conviction) but either it was not suitable for the same means of analysis or, though so suitable, the sample proved insufficient.

(5) The period allowed for requiring a person to attend a police station for the purpose specified in subsection (4) above is—

    (a) in the case of a person falling within paragraph (a), one month beginning with the date of the charge or of his being informed as mentioned in that paragraph or one month beginning with the date on which the appropriate officer is informed of the fact that the sample is not suitable for the same means of analysis or has proved insufficient, as the case may be;

    (b) in the case of a person falling within paragraph (b), one month beginning with the date of the conviction or one month beginning with the date on which the appropriate officer is informed of the fact that the sample is not suitable for the same means of analysis or has proved insufficient, as the case may be.

(6) A requirement under subsection (4) above—

    (a) shall give the person at least 7 days within which he must so attend; and

    (b) may direct him to attend at a specified time of day or between specified times of day.

(7) Any constable may arrest without a warrant a person who has failed to comply with a requirement under subsection (4) above.

(8) In this section 'the appropriate officer' is—

    (a) in the case of a person falling within subsection (4)(a), the officer investigating the offence with which that person has been charged or as to which he was informed that he would be reported;

    (b) in the case of a person falling within subsection (4)(b), the officer in charge of the police station from which the investigation of the offence of which he was convicted was conducted.

63B Testing for presence of Class A drugs

(1) A sample of urine or a non-intimate sample may be taken from a person in police detention for the purpose of ascertaining whether he has any specified Class A drug in his body if—

    (a) either the arrest condition or the charge condition is met;

    (b) both the age condition and the request condition are met; and

    (c) the notification condition is met in relation to the arrest condition, the charge condition or the age condition (as the case may be).

(1A) The arrest condition is that the person concerned has been arrested for an offence but has not been charged with that offence and either—

    (a) the offence is a trigger offence; or

    (b) a police officer of at least the rank of inspector has reasonable grounds for suspecting that the misuse by that person of a specified Class A drug caused or contributed to the offence and has authorised the sample to be taken.

(2) The charge condition is either—

    (a) that the person concerned has been charged with a trigger offence; or

    (b) that the person concerned has been charged with an offence and a police officer of at least the rank of inspector, who has reasonable grounds for suspecting that the misuse by that person of any specified Class A drug caused or contributed to the offence, has authorised the sample to be taken.

(3) The age condition is—

    (a) if the arrest condition is met, that the person concerned has attained the age of 18;

    (b) if the charge condition is met, that he has attained the age of 14.

(4) The request condition is that a police officer has requested the person concerned to give the sample.

(4A) The notification condition is that—

    (a) the relevant chief officer has been notified by the Secretary of State that appropriate arrangements have been made for the police area as a whole, or for the particular police station, in which the person is in police detention, and

    (b) the notice has not been withdrawn.

(4B) For the purposes of subsection (4A) above, appropriate arrangements are arrangements for the taking of samples under this section from whichever of the following is specified in the notification—

    (a) persons in respect of whom the arrest condition is met;

    (b) persons in respect of whom the charge condition is met;

    (c) persons who have not attained the age of 18.

(5) Before requesting the person concerned to give a sample, an officer must—

    (a) warn him that if, when so requested, he fails without good cause to do so he may be liable to prosecution, and

    (b) in a case within subsection (1A)(b) or (2)(b) above, inform him of the giving of the authorisation and of the grounds in question.

(5A) In the case of a person who has not attained the age of 17—

    (a) the making of the request under subsection (4) above;

    (b) the giving of the warning and (where applicable) the information under subsection (5) above; and

    (c) the taking of the sample,

may not take place except in the presence of an appropriate adult.

(5B) If a sample is taken under this section from a person in respect of whom the arrest condition is met no other sample may be taken from him under this section during the same continuous period of detention but—

   (a) if the charge condition is also met in respect of him at any time during that period, the sample must be treated as a sample taken by virtue of the fact that the charge condition is met;
   (b) the fact that the sample is to be so treated must be recorded in the person's custody record.

(5C) Despite subsection (1)(a) above, a sample may be taken from a person under this section if—

   (a) he was arrested for an offence (the first offence),
   (b) the arrest condition is met but the charge condition is not met,
   (c) before a sample is taken by virtue of subsection (1) above he would (but for his arrest as mentioned in paragraph (d) below) be required to be released from police detention,
   (d) he continues to be in police detention by virtue of his having been arrested for an offence not falling within subsection (1A) above, and
   (e) the sample is taken before the end of the period of 24 hours starting with the time when his detention by virtue of his arrest for the first offence began.

(5D) A sample must not be taken from a person under this section if he is detained in a police station unless he has been brought before the custody officer.

(6) A sample may be taken under this section only by a person prescribed by regulations made by the Secretary of State by statutory instrument.

No regulations shall be made under this subsection unless a draft has been laid before, and approved by resolution of, each House of Parliament.

(6A) The Secretary of State may by order made by statutory instrument amend—

   (a) paragraph (a) of subsection (3) above, by substituting for the age for the time being specified a different age specified in the order, or different ages so specified for different police areas so specified;
   (b) paragraph (b) of that subsection, by substituting for the age for the time being specified a different age specified in the order.

(6B) A statutory instrument containing an order under subsection (6A) above shall not be made unless a draft of the instrument has been laid before, and approved by a resolution of, each House of Parliament.

(7) Information obtained from a sample taken under this section may be disclosed—

   (a) for the purpose of informing any decision about granting bail in criminal proceedings (within the meaning of the Bail Act 1976) to the person concerned;
   (aa) for the purpose of informing any decision about the giving of a conditional caution under Part 3 of the Criminal Justice Act 2003 to the person concerned;
   (b) where the person concerned is in police detention or is remanded in or committed to custody by an order of a court or has been granted such bail, for the purpose of informing any decision about his supervision;
   (c) where the person concerned is convicted of an offence, for the purpose of informing any decision about the appropriate sentence to be passed by a court and any decision about his supervision or release;
   (ca) for the purpose of an assessment which the person concerned is required to attend by virtue of section 9(2) or 10(2) of the Drugs Act 2005;
   (cb) for the purpose of proceedings against the person concerned for an offence under section 12(3) or 14(3) of that Act;
   (d) for the purpose of ensuring that appropriate advice and treatment is made available to the person concerned.

(8) A person who fails without good cause to give any sample which may be taken from him under this section shall be guilty of an offence.

(10) In this section—

'appropriate adult', in relation to a person who has not attained the age of 17, means—

    (a) his parent or guardian or, if he is in the care of a local authority or voluntary organisation, a person representing that authority or organisation; or

    (b) a social worker of a local authority; or

    (c) if no person falling within paragraph (a) or (b) is available, any responsible person aged 18 or over who is not a police officer or a person employed by the police;

'relevant chief officer' means—

    (a) in relation to a police area, the chief officer of police of the police force for that police area; or

    (b) in relation to a police station, the chief officer of police of the police force for the police area in which the police station is situated.

63C Testing for presence of Class A drugs: supplementary

(1) A person guilty of an offence under section 63B above shall be liable on summary conviction to imprisonment for a term not exceeding 51 weeks, or to a fine not exceeding level 4 on the standard scale, or to both.

(2) A police officer may give an authorisation under section 63B above orally or in writing but, if he gives it orally, he shall confirm it in writing as soon as is practicable.

(3) If a sample is taken under section 63B above by virtue of an authorisation, the authorisation and the grounds for the suspicion shall be recorded as soon as is practicable after the sample is taken.

(4) If the sample is taken from a person detained at a police station, the matters required to be recorded by subsection (3) above shall be recorded in his custody record.

(5) Subsections (11) and (12) of section 62 above apply for the purposes of section 63B above as they do for the purposes of that section; and section 63B above does not prejudice the generality of sections 62 and 63 above.

(6) In section 63B above—

'Class A drug' and 'misuse' have the same meanings as in the Misuse of Drugs Act 1971;

'specified' (in relation to a Class A drug) and 'trigger offence' have the same meanings as in Part III of the Criminal Justice and Court Services Act 2000.

64 Destruction of fingerprints and samples

(1A) Where—

    (a) fingerprints, impressions of footwear or samples are taken from a person in connection with the investigation of an offence, and

    (b) subsection (3) below does not require them to be destroyed,

the fingerprints, impressions of footwear or samples may be retained after they have fulfilled the purposes for which they were taken but shall not be used by any person except for purposes related to the prevention or detection of crime, the investigation of an offence or the conduct of a prosecution, or the identification of a deceased person or of the person from whom a body part came.

(1B) In subsection (1A) above—

    (a) the reference to using a fingerprint or an impression of footwear includes a reference to allowing any check to be made against it under section 63A(1) or (1C) above and to disclosing it to any person;

    (b) the reference to using a sample includes a reference to allowing any check to be made under section 63A(1) or (1C) above against it or against information derived from it and to disclosing it or any such information to any person;

    (c) the reference to crime includes a reference to any conduct which—

(i) constitutes one or more criminal offences (whether under the law of a part of the United Kingdom or of a country or territory outside the United Kingdom); or

(ii) is, or corresponds to, any conduct which, if it all took place in any one part of the United Kingdom, would constitute one or more criminal offences; and

(d) the references to an investigation and to a prosecution include references, respectively, to any investigation outside the United Kingdom of any crime or suspected crime and to a prosecution brought in respect of any crime in a country or territory outside the United Kingdom.

(3) If—

(a) fingerprints, impressions of footwear or samples are taken from a person in connection with the investigation of an offence; and

(b) that person is not suspected of having committed the offence,

they must, except as provided in the following provisions of this section, be destroyed as soon as they have fulfilled the purpose for which they were taken.

(3AA) Samples, fingerprints and impressions of footwear are not required to be destroyed under subsection (3) above if—

(a) they were taken for the purposes of the investigation of an offence of which a person has been convicted; and

(b) a sample, fingerprint, or (as the case may be) an impression of footwear was also taken from the convicted person for the purposes of that investigation.

(3AB) Subject to subsection (3AC) below, where a person is entitled under subsection (3) above to the destruction of any fingerprint, impression of footwear or sample taken from him (or would be but for subsection (3AA) above), neither the fingerprint, nor the impression of footwear nor the sample, nor any information derived from the sample, shall be used—

(a) in evidence against the person who is or would be entitled to the destruction of that fingerprint, impression of footwear or sample; or

(b) for the purposes of the investigation of any offence;

and subsection (1B) above applies for the purposes of this subsection as it applies for the purposes of subsection (1A) above.

(3AC) Where a person from whom a fingerprint, impression of footwear or sample has been taken consents in writing to its retention—

(a) that sample need not be destroyed under subsection (3) above;

(b) subsection (3AB) above shall not restrict the use that may be made of the fingerprint impression of footwear or sample or, in the case of a sample, of any information derived from it; and

(c) that consent shall be treated as comprising a consent for the purposes of section 63A(1C) above;

and a consent given for the purpose of this subsection shall not be capable of being withdrawn.

(3AD) For the purposes of subsection (3AC) above it shall be immaterial whether the consent is given at, before or after the time when the entitlement to the destruction of the fingerprint, impressions of footwear or sample arises.

(5) If fingerprints or impressions of footwear are destroyed—

(a) any copies of the fingerprints or impressions of footwear shall also be destroyed; and

(b) any chief officer of police controlling access to computer data relating to the fingerprints or impressions of footwear shall make access to the data impossible, as soon as it is practicable to do so.

(6) A person who asks to be allowed to witness the destruction of his fingerprints or impression of footwear or copies of them shall have a right to witness it.

(6A) If—
  (a) subsection (5)(b) above falls to be complied with; and
  (b) the person to whose fingerprints or impressions of footwear the data relate asks
      for a certificate that it has been complied with,
such a certificate shall be issued to him, not later than the end of the period of three months
beginning with the day on which he asks for it, by the responsible chief officer of police or a
person authorised by him or on his behalf for the purposes of this section.
  (6B) In this section—
'the responsible chief officer of police' means the chief officer of police in whose police
area the computer data were put on to the computer.
  (7) Nothing in this section—
  (a) affects any power conferred by paragraph 18(2) of Schedule 2 to the Immigration
      Act 1971 or section 20 of the Immigration and Asylum Act 1999 (c. 33) (disclosure
      of police information to the Secretary of State for use for immigration
      purposes); or
  (b) applies to a person arrested or detained under the terrorism provisions.

64A   Photographing of suspects etc.
  (1) A person who is detained at a police station may be photographed—
  (a) with the appropriate consent; or
  (b) if the appropriate consent is withheld or it is not practicable to obtain it, without it.
  (1A) A person falling within subsection (1B) below may, on the occasion of the
relevant event referred to in subsection (1B), be photographed elsewhere than at a police
station—
  (a) with the appropriate consent; or
  (b) if the appropriate consent is withheld or it is not practicable to obtain it,
      without it.
  (1B) A person falls within this subsection if he has been—
  (a) arrested by a constable for an offence;
  (b) taken into custody by a constable after being arrested for an offence by a person
      other than a constable;
  (c) made subject to a requirement to wait with a community support officer under
      paragraph 2(3) or (3B) of Schedule 4 to the Police Reform Act 2002 ('the 2002
      Act');
  (d) given a penalty notice by a constable in uniform under Chapter 1 of Part 1 of the
      Criminal Justice and Police Act 2001, a penalty notice by a constable under sec-
      tion 444A of the Education Act 1996, or a fixed penalty notice by a constable in
      uniform under section 54 of the Road Traffic Offenders Act 1988;
  (e) given a notice in relation to a relevant fixed penalty offence (within the meaning
      of paragraph 1 of Schedule 4 to the 2002 Act) by a community support officer by
      virtue of a designation applying that paragraph to him; or
  (f) given a notice in relation to a relevant fixed penalty offence (within the meaning
      of paragraph 1 of Schedule 5 to the 2002 Act) by an accredited person by virtue of
      accreditation specifying that that paragraph applies to him.
  (2) A person proposing to take a photograph of any person under this section—
  (a) may, for the purpose of doing so, require the removal of any item or substance
      worn on or over the whole or any part of the head or face of the person to be
      photographed; and
  (b) if the requirement is not complied with, may remove the item or substance
      himself.
  (3) Where a photograph may be taken under this section, the only persons entitled to
take the photograph are constables

(4) A photograph taken under this section—

    (a) may be used by, or disclosed to, any person for any purpose related to the prevention or detection of crime, the investigation of an offence or the conduct of a prosecution or to the enforcement of a sentence; and

    (b) after being so used or disclosed, may be retained but may not be used or disclosed except for a purpose so related.

(5) In subsection (4)—

    (a) the reference to crime includes a reference to any conduct which—

        (i) constitutes one or more criminal offences (whether under the law of a part of the United Kingdom or of a country or territory outside the United Kingdom); or

        (ii) is, or corresponds to, any conduct which, if it all took place in any one part of the United Kingdom, would constitute one or more criminal offences; and

    (b) the references to an investigation and to a prosecution include references, respectively, to any investigation outside the United Kingdom of any crime or suspected crime and to a prosecution brought in respect of any crime in a country or territory outside the United Kingdom; and

    (c) 'sentence' includes any order made by a court in England and Wales when dealing with an offender in respect of his offence.

(6) References in this section to taking a photograph include references to using any process by means of which a visual image may be produced; and references to photographing a person shall be construed accordingly.

(6A) In this section, a 'photograph' includes a moving image, and corresponding expressions shall be construed accordingly.

(7) Nothing in this section applies to a person arrested under an extradition arrest power.

65 Part V—supplementary

(1) In this Part of this Act—

'analysis' in relation to a skin impression, includes comparison and matching;

'appropriate consent' means—

    (a) in relation to a person who has attained the age of 17 years, the consent of that person;

    (b) in relation to a person who has not attained that age but has attained the age of 14 years, the consent of that person and his parent or guardian; and

    (c) in relation to a person who has not attained the age of 14 years, the consent of his parent or guardian;

'extradition arrest power' means any of the following—

    (a) a Part 1 warrant (within the meaning given by the Extradition Act 2003) in respect of which a certificate under section 2 of that Act has been issued;

    (b) section 5 of that Act;

    (c) a warrant issued under section 71 of that Act;

    (d) a provisional warrant (within the meaning given by that Act).

'fingerprints', in relation to any person, means a record (in any form and produced by any method) of the skin pattern and other physical characteristics or features of—

    (a) any of that person's fingers; or

    (b) either of his palms;

'intimate sample' means—

    (a) a sample of blood, semen or any other tissue fluid, urine or pubic hair;

    (b) a dental impression;

    (c) a swab taken from a person's body orifice other than the mouth;

'intimate search' means a search which consists of the physical examination of a person's body orifices other than the mouth;

'non-intimate sample' means—

    (a) a sample of hair other than pubic hair;

(b) a sample taken from a nail on from under a nail;

(c) a swab taken from any part of a person's body other than a part from which a swab taken would be an intimate sample.

(d) saliva;

(e) a skin impression;

'registered dentist' has the same meaning as in the Dentists Act 1984;

'registered health care professional' means a person (other than a medical practitioner) who is:—

(a) a registered nurse; or

(b) a registered member of a health care profession which is designated for the purposes of this paragraph by an order made by the Secretary of State;

'skin impression', in relation to any person, means any record (other than a fingerprint) which is a record (in any form and produced by any method) of the skin pattern and other physical characteristics or features of the whole or any part of his foot or of any other part of his body;

'speculative search', in relation to a person's fingerprints or samples, means such a check against other fingerprints or samples or against information derived from other samples as is referred to in section 63A(1) above;

'sufficient' and 'insufficient', in relation to a sample, means (subject to subsection (2) below) sufficient or insufficient (in point of quantity or quality) for the purpose of enabling information to be produced by the means of analysis used or to be used in relation to the sample;

'the terrorism provisions' means section 41 of the Terrorism Act 2000, and any provision of Schedule 7 to that Act conferring a power of detention; and

'terrorism' has the meaning given in section 1 of that Act.

(1A) A health care profession is any profession mentioned in section 60(2) of the Health Act 1999 (c. 8) other than the profession of practising medicine and the profession of nursing.

(1B) An order under subsection (1) shall be made by statutory instrument and shall be subject to annulment in pursuance of a resolution of either House of Parliament.

(2) References in this Part of this Act to a sample's proving insufficient include references to where, as a consequence of—

(a) the loss, destruction or contamination of the whole or any part of the sample,

(b) any damage to the whole or a part of the sample, or

(c) the use of the whole or a part of the sample for an analysis which produced no results or which produced results some or all of which must be regarded, in the circumstances, as unreliable,

the sample has become unavailable or insufficient for the purpose of enabling information, or information of a particular description, to be obtained by means of analysis of the sample.

Criminal Evidence (Amendment) Act 1997

Extension of power to take non-intimate body samples without consent

1 Persons imprisoned or detained by virtue of pre-existing conviction for sexual offence etc

(1) This section has effect for removing, in relation to persons to whom this section applies, the restriction on the operation of section 63(3B) of the Police and Criminal Evidence Act 1984 (power to take non-intimate samples without the appropriate consent from persons convicted of recordable offences)—

(a) which is imposed by the subsection (10) inserted in section 63 by section 55(6) of the Criminal Justice and Public Order Act 1994, and

(b) by virtue of which section 63(3B) does not apply to persons convicted before 10th April 1995.

(2) —

(3) This section applies to a person who was convicted of a recordable offence before 10th April 1995 if—

    (a) that offence was one of the offences listed in Schedule 1 to this Act (which lists certain sexual, violent and other offences), and

    (b) at the relevant time he is serving a sentence of imprisonment in respect of that offence.

(4) This section also applies to a person who was convicted of a recordable offence before 10th April 1995 if—

    (a) that offence was one of the offences listed in Schedule 1 to this Act, and

    (b) at the relevant time he is detained under Part III of the Mental Health Act 1983 in pursuance of—

        (i) a hospital order or interim hospital order made following that conviction, or

        (ii) a transfer direction given at a time when he was serving a sentence of imprisonment in respect of that offence.

Expressions used in this subsection and in the Mental Health Act 1983 have the same meaning as in that Act.

(5) Where a person convicted of a recordable offence before 10th April 1995 was, following his conviction for that and any other offence or offences, sentenced to two or more terms of imprisonment (whether taking effect consecutively or concurrently), he shall be treated for the purposes of this section as serving a sentence of imprisonment in respect of that offence at any time when serving any of those terms.

(6) For the purposes of this section, references to a person serving a sentence of imprisonment include references—

    (a) to his being detained in any institution to which the Prison Act 1952 applies in pursuance of any other sentence or order for detention imposed by a court in criminal proceedings, or

    (b) to his being detained (otherwise than in any such institution) in pursuance of directions of the Secretary of State under section 92 of the Powers of Criminal Courts (Sentencing) Act 2000,

and any reference to a term of imprisonment shall be construed accordingly.

2 Persons detained following acquittal on grounds of insanity or finding of unfitness to plead

(1) This section has effect for enabling non-intimate samples to be taken from persons under section 63 of the 1984 Act without the appropriate consent where they are persons to whom this section applies.

(2) —

(3) This section applies to a person if—

    (a) at the relevant time he is detained under Part III of the Mental Health Act 1983 in pursuance of an order made under—

        (i) section 5(2)(a) of the Criminal Procedure (Insanity) Act 1964 or section 6 or 14 of the Criminal Appeal Act 1968 (findings of insanity or unfitness to plead), or

        (ii) section 37(3) of the Mental Health Act 1983 (power of magistrates' court to make hospital order without convicting accused); and

    (b) that order was made on or after the date of the passing of this Act in respect of a recordable offence.

(4) This section also applies to a person if—

    (a) at the relevant time he is detained under Part III of the Mental Health Act 1983 in pursuance of an order made under—

(i)   any of the provisions mentioned in subsection (3)(a), or

(ii) section 5(1) of the Criminal Procedure (Insanity) Act 1964 as originally enacted; and

(b) that order was made before the date of the passing of this Act in respect of any offence listed in Schedule 1 to this Act.

(5) Subsection (4)(a)(i) does not apply to any order made under section 14(2) of the Criminal Appeal Act 1968 as originally enacted.

(6) For the purposes of this section an order falling within subsection (3) or (4) shall be treated as having been made in respect of an offence of a particular description—

(a) if, where the order was made following—

(i)   a finding of not guilty by reason of insanity, or

(ii) a finding that the person in question was under a disability and did the act or made the omission charged against him, or

(iii) a finding for the purposes of section 37(3) of the Mental Health Act 1983 that the person in question did the act or made the omission charged against him, or

(iv) (in the case of an order made under section 5(1) of the Criminal Procedure (Insanity) Act 1964 as originally enacted) a finding that he was under a disability,

that finding was recorded in respect of an offence of that description; or

(b) if, where the order was made following the Court of Appeal forming such opinion as is mentioned in section 6(1) or 14(1) of the Criminal Appeal Act 1968, that opinion was formed on an appeal brought in respect of an offence of that description.

(7) In this section any reference to an Act 'as originally enacted' is a reference to that Act as it had effect without any of the amendments made by the Criminal Procedure (Insanity and Unfitness to Plead) Act 1991.

Arrest

Police and Criminal Evidence Act 1984

24   Arrest without warrant: constables

(1) A constable may arrest without a warrant—

(a) anyone who is about to commit an offence;

(b) anyone who is in the act of committing an offence;

(c) anyone whom he has reasonable grounds for suspecting to be about to commit an offence;

(d) anyone whom he has reasonable grounds for suspecting to be committing an offence.

(2) If a constable has reasonable grounds for suspecting that an offence has been committed, he may arrest without a warrant anyone whom he has reasonable grounds to suspect of being guilty of it.

(3) If an offence has been committed, a constable may arrest without a warrant—

(a) anyone who is guilty of the offence;

(b) anyone whom he has reasonable grounds for suspecting to be guilty of it.

(4) But the power of summary arrest conferred by subsection (1), (2) or (3) is exercisable only if the constable has reasonable grounds for believing that for any of the reasons mentioned in subsection (5) it is necessary to arrest the person in question.

(5) The reasons are—

(a) to enable the name of the person in question to be ascertained (in the case where the constable does not know, and cannot readily ascertain, the person's name, or

has reasonable grounds for doubting whether a name given by the person as his name is his real name);
(b) correspondingly as regards the person's address;
(c) to prevent the person in question—
   (i)   causing physical injury to himself or any other person;
   (ii) suffering physical injury;
   (iii) causing loss of or damage to property;
   (iv) committing an offence against public decency (subject to subsection (6)); or
   (v)   causing an unlawful obstruction of the highway;
(d) to protect a child or other vulnerable person from the person in question;
(e) to allow the prompt and effective investigation of the offence or of the conduct of the person in question;
(f) to prevent any prosecution for the offence from being hindered by the disappearance of the person in question.

(6) Subsection (5)(c)(iv) applies only where members of the public going about their normal business cannot reasonably be expected to avoid the person in question.

24A   Arrest without warrant: other persons

(1) A person other than a constable may arrest without a warrant—
(a) anyone who is in the act of committing an indictable offence;
(b) anyone whom he has reasonable grounds for suspecting to be committing an indictable offence.

(2) Where an indictable offence has been committed, a person other than a constable may arrest without a warrant—
(a) anyone who is guilty of the offence;
(b) anyone whom he has reasonable grounds for suspecting to be guilty of it.

(3) But the power of summary arrest conferred by subsection (1) or (2) is exercisable only if—
(a) the person making the arrest has reasonable grounds for believing that for any of the reasons mentioned in subsection (4) it is necessary to arrest the person in question; and
(b) it appears to the person making the arrest that it is not reasonably practicable for a constable to make it instead.

(4) The reasons are to prevent the person in question—
(a) causing physical injury to himself or any other person;
(b) suffering physical injury;
(c) causing loss of or damage to property; or
(d) making off before a constable can assume responsibility for him.

27   Fingerprinting of certain offenders

(1) If a person—
(a) has been convicted of a recordable offence;
(b) has not at any time been in police detention for the offence; and
(c) has not had his fingerprints taken—
   (i) in the course of the investigation of the offence by the police; or
   (ii) since the conviction,
any constable may at any time not later than one month after the date of the conviction require him to attend a police station in order that his fingerprints may be taken.

(1A) Where a person convicted of a recordable offence has already had his fingerprints taken as mentioned in paragraph (c) of subsection (1) above, that fact (together with any time when he has been in police detention for the offence) shall be disregarded for the purposes of that subsection if—
(a) the fingerprints taken on the previous occasion do not constitute a complete set of his fingerprints; or

    (b) some or all of the fingerprints taken on the previous occasion are not of sufficient quality to allow satisfactory analysis, comparison or matching.

(1B) Subsections (1) and (1A) above apply—

    (a) where a person has been given a caution in respect of a recordable offence which, at the time of the caution, he has admitted, or

    (b) where a person has been warned or reprimanded under section 65 of the Crime and Disorder Act 1998 (c. 37) for a recordable offence,

as they apply where a person has been convicted of an offence, and references in this section to a conviction shall be construed accordingly.

(2) A requirement under subsection (1) above—

    (a) shall give the person a period of at least 7 days within which he must so attend; and

    (b) may direct him to so attend at a specified time of day or between specified times of day.

(3) Any constable may arrest without warrant a person who has failed to comply with a requirement under subsection (1) above.

(4) The Secretary of State may by regulations make provision for recording in national police records convictions for such offences as are specified in the regulations.

(5) Regulations under this section shall be made by statutory instrument and shall be subject to annulment in pursuance of a resolution of either House of Parliament.

28   Information to be given on arrest

(1) Subject to subsection (5) below, where a person is arrested, otherwise than by being informed that he is under arrest the arrest is not lawful unless the person arrested is informed that he is under arrest as soon as is practicable after his arrest.

(2) Where a person is arrested by a constable, subsection (1) above applies regardless of whether the fact of the arrest is obvious.

(3) Subject to subsection (5) below, no arrest is lawful unless the person arrested is informed of the ground for the arrest at the time of, or as soon as is practicable after, the arrest.

(4) Where a person is arrested by a constable, subsection (3) above applies regardless of whether the ground for the arrest is obvious.

(5) Nothing in this section is to be taken to require a person to be informed—

    (a) that he is under arrest; or

    (b) of the ground for the arrest,

if it was not reasonably practicable for him to be so informed by reason of his having escaped from arrest before the information could be given.

29   Voluntary attendance at police station etc.

Where for the purpose of assisting with an investigation a person attends voluntarily at a police station or at any other place where a constable is present or accompanies a constable to a police station or any such other place without having been arrested—

    (a) he shall be entitled to leave at will unless he is placed under arrest;

    (b) he shall be informed at once that he is under arrest if a decision is taken by a constable to prevent him from leaving at will.

30   Arrest elsewhere than at police station

(1) Subsection (1A) applies where a person is, at any place other than a police station—

    (a) arrested by a constable for an offence, or

    (b) taken into custody by a constable after being arrested for an offence by a person other than a constable.

(1A) The person must be taken by a constable to a police station as soon as practicable after the arrest.

(1B) Subsection (1A) has effect subject to section 30A (release on bail) and subsection (7) (release without bail).

(2) Subject to subsections (3) and (5) below, the police station to which an arrested person is taken under subsection (1A) above shall be a designated police station.

(3) A constable to whom this subsection applies may take an arrested person to any police station unless it appears to the constable that it may be necessary to keep the arrested person in police detention for more than six hours.

(4) Subsection (3) above applies—

   (a) to a constable who is working in a locality covered by a police station which is not a designated police station; and

   (b) to a constable belonging to a body of constables maintained by an authority other than a police authority.

(5) Any constable may take an arrested person to any police station if—

   (a) either of the following conditions is satisfied—

      (i) the constable has arrested him without the assistance of any other constable and no other constable is available to assist him;

      (ii) the constable has taken him into custody from a person other than a constable without the assistance of any other constable and no other constable is available to assist him; and

   (b) it appears to the constable that he will be unable to take the arrested person to a designated police station without the arrested person injuring himself, the constable or some other person.

(6) If the first police station to which an arrested person is taken after his arrest is not a designated police station, he shall be taken to a designated police station not more than six hours after his arrival at the first police station unless he is released previously.

(7) A person arrested by a constable at any place other than a police station must be released without bail if the condition in subsection (7A) is satisfied.

(7A) The condition is that, at any time before the person arrested reaches a police station, a constable is satisfied that there are no grounds for keeping him under arrest or releasing him on bail under section 30A.

(8) A constable who releases a person under subsection (7) above shall record the fact that he has done so.

(9) The constable shall make the record as soon as is practicable after the release.

(10) Nothing in subsection (1A) or in section 30A prevents a constable delaying taking a person to a police station or releasing him on bail if the condition in subsection (10A) is satisfied.

(10A) The condition is that the presence of the person at a place (other than a police station) is necessary in order to carry out such investigations as it is reasonable to carry out immediately.

(11) Where there is any such delay the reasons for the delay must be recorded when the person first arrives at the police station or (as the case may be) is released on bail.

(12) Nothing in subsection (1A) or section 30A above shall be taken to affect—

   (a) paragraphs 16(3) or 18(1) of Schedule 2 to the Immigration Act 1971;

   (b) section 34(1) of the Criminal Justice Act 1972; or

   (c) any provision of the Terrorism Act 2000.

(13) Nothing in subsection (10) above shall be taken to affect paragraph 18(3) of Schedule 2 to the Immigration Act 1971.

56 Right to have someone informed when arrested

(1) Where a person has been arrested and is being held in custody in a police station or other premises, he shall be entitled, if he so requests, to have one friend or relative or other person who is known to him or who is likely to take an interest in his welfare told, as soon as is practicable except to the extent that delay is permitted by this section, that he has been arrested and is being detained there.

(2) Delay is only permitted—

   (a) in the case of a person who is in police detention for an indictable offence; and

   (b) if an officer of at least the rank of inspector authorises it.

(3) In any case the person in custody must be permitted to exercise the right conferred by subsection (1) above within 36 hours from the relevant time, as defined in section 41(2) above.

(4) An officer may give an authorisation under subsection (2) above orally or in writing but, if he gives it orally, he shall confirm it in writing as soon as is practicable.

(5) Subject to sub-section (5A) below an officer may only authorise delay where he has reasonable grounds for believing that telling the named person of the arrest—

(a) will lead to interference with or harm to evidence connected with an indictable offence or interference with or physical injury to other persons; or

(b) will lead to the alerting of other persons suspected of having committed such an offence but not yet arrested for it; or

(c) will hinder the recovery of any property obtained as a result of such an offence.

(5A) An officer may also authorise delay where he has reasonable grounds for believing that—

(a) the person detained for the indictable offence has benefited from his criminal conduct, and

(b) the recovery of the value of the property constituting the benefit will be hindered by telling the named person of the arrest.

(5B) For the purposes of subsection (5A) above the question whether a person has benefited from his criminal conduct is to be decided in accordance with Part 2 of the Proceeds of Crime Act 2002.

(6) If a delay is authorised—

(a) the detained person shall be told the reason for it; and

(b) the reason shall be noted on his custody record.

(7) The duties imposed by subsection (6) above shall be performed as soon as is practicable.

(8) The rights conferred by this section on a person detained at a police station or other premises are exercisable whenever he is transferred from one place to another; and this section applies to each subsequent occasion on which they are exercisable as it applies to the first such occasion.

(9) There may be no further delay in permitting the exercise of the right conferred by subsection (1) above once the reason for authorising delay ceases to subsist.

(10) Nothing in this section applies to a person arrested or detained under the terrorism provisions.

CODES OF PRACTICE, CODE C

3 Initial action

(a) Detained persons—normal procedure

3.1 When a person is brought to a police station under arrest or arrested at the station having gone there voluntarily, the custody officer must make sure the person is told clearly about the following continuing rights which may be exercised at any stage during the period in custody:

(i)   the right to have someone informed of their arrest as in *section 5*;

(ii) the right to consult privately with a solicitor and that free independent legal advice is available;

(iii) the right to consult these Codes of Practice. See *Note 3D*

3.2 The detainee must also be given:

- a written notice setting out:
  - the above three rights;
  - the arrangements for obtaining legal advice;
  - the right to a copy of the custody record as in *paragraph 2.4A;*
  - the caution in the terms prescribed in *section 10.*
- an additional written notice briefly setting out their entitlements while in custody, see *Notes 3A* and *3B.*

Note: The detainee shall be asked to sign the custody record to acknowledge receipt of these notices. Any refusal must be recorded on the custody record.

3.3 A citizen of an independent Commonwealth country or a national of a foreign country, including the Republic of Ireland, must be informed as soon as practicable about their rights of communication with their High Commission, Embassy or Consulate. See *section 7*

3.4 The custody officer shall:
- record the offence(s) that the detainee has been arrested for and the reason(s) for the arrest on the custody record. See paragraph 10.3 and Code G paragraphs 2.2 and 4.3.
- note on the custody record any comment the detainee makes in relation to the arresting officer's account but shall not invite comment. If the arresting officer is not physically present when the detainee is brought to a police station, the arresting officer's account must be made available to the custody officer remotely or by a third party on the arresting officer's behalf. If the custody officer authorises a person's detention the detainee must be informed of the grounds as soon as practicable and before they are questioned about any offence;
- note any comment the detainee makes in respect of the decision to detain them but shall not invite comment;
- not put specific questions to the detainee regarding their involvement in any offence, nor in respect of any comments they may make in response to the arresting officer's account or the decision to place them in detention. Such an exchange is likely to constitute an interview as in *paragraph 11.1A* and require the associated safeguards in *section 11*.

See *paragraph 11.13* in respect of unsolicited comments.

3.5 The custody officer shall:
(a) ask the detainee, whether at this time, they:
　(i)　would like legal advice, see *paragraph 6.5*;
　(ii)　want someone informed of their detention, see *section 5*;
(b) ask the detainee to sign the custody record to confirm their decisions in respect of (*a*);
(c) determine whether the detainee:
　(i)　is, or might be, in need of medical treatment or attention, see *section 9*;
　(ii)　requires:
　　- an appropriate adult;
　　- help to check documentation;
　　- an interpreter;
(d) record the decision in respect of (*c*).

3.6 When determining these needs the custody officer is responsible for initiating an assessment to consider whether the detainee is likely to present specific risks to custody staff or themselves. Such assessments should always include a check on the Police National Computer, to be carried out as soon as practicable, to identify any risks highlighted in relation to the detainee. Although such assessments are primarily the custody officer's responsibility, it may be necessary for them to consult and involve others, e.g. the arresting officer or an appropriate health care professional, see *paragraph 9.13*. Reasons for delaying the initiation or completion of the assessment must be recorded.

3.7 Chief Officers should ensure that arrangements for proper and effective risk assessments required by *paragraph 3.6* are implemented in respect of all detainees at police stations in their area.

3.8 Risk assessments must follow a structured process which clearly defines the categories of risk to be considered and the results must be incorporated in the detainee's custody record. The custody officer is responsible for making sure those responsible for the detainee's custody are appropriately briefed about the risks. If no specific risks are identified by the assessment, that should be noted in the custody record. See *Note 3E* and *paragraph 9.14*

3.9 The custody officer is responsible for implementing the response to any specific risk assessment, e.g.:

- reducing opportunities for self harm;
- calling a health care professional;
- increasing levels of monitoring or observation.

3.10 Risk assessment is an ongoing process and assessments must always be subject to review if circumstances change.

3.11 If video cameras are installed in the custody area, notices shall be prominently displayed showing cameras are in use. Any request to have video cameras switched off shall be refused.

(b) Detained persons—special groups

3.12 If the detainee appears deaf or there is doubt about their hearing or speaking ability or ability to understand English, and the custody officer cannot establish effective communication, the custody officer must, as soon as practicable, call an interpreter for assistance in the action under *paragraphs 3.1–3.5*. See *section 13*

3.13 If the detainee is a juvenile, the custody officer must, if it is practicable, ascertain the identity of a person responsible for their welfare. That person:

- may be:
  - the parent or guardian;
  - if the juvenile is in local authority or voluntary organisation care, or is otherwise being looked after under the Children Act 1989, a person appointed by that authority or organisation to have responsibility for the juvenile's welfare;
  - any other person who has, for the time being, assumed responsibility for the juvenile's welfare.
- must be informed as soon as practicable that the juvenile has been arrested, why they have been arrested and where they are detained. This right is in addition to the juvenile's right in *section 5* not to be held incommunicado. See *Note 3C*

3.14 If a juvenile is known to be subject to a court order under which a person or organisation is given any degree of statutory responsibility to supervise or otherwise monitor them, reasonable steps must also be taken to notify that person or organisation (the 'responsible officer'). The responsible officer will normally be a member of a Youth Offending Team, except for a curfew order which involves electronic monitoring when the contractor providing the monitoring will normally be the responsible officer.

3.15 If the detainee is a juvenile, mentally disordered or otherwise mentally vulnerable, the custody officer must, as soon as practicable:

- inform the appropriate adult, who in the case of a juvenile may or may not be a person responsible for their welfare, as in *paragraph 3.13*, of:
  - the grounds for their detention;
  - their whereabouts.
- ask the adult to come to the police station to see the detainee.

3.16 It is imperative that a mentally disordered or otherwise mentally vulnerable person, detained under the Mental Health Act 1983, section 136, be assessed as soon as possible. If that assessment is to take place at the police station, an approved social worker and a registered medical practitioner shall be called to the station as soon as possible in order to interview and examine the detainee. Once the detainee has been interviewed, examined and suitable arrangements made for their treatment or care, they can no longer be detained under section 136. A detainee must be immediately discharged from detention under section 136 if a registered medical practitioner, having examined them, concludes they are not mentally disordered within the meaning of the Act.

3.17 If the appropriate adult is:

- already at the police station, the provisions of *paragraphs 3.1* to *3.5* must be complied with in the appropriate adult's presence;
- not at the station when these provisions are complied with, they must be complied with again in the presence of the appropriate adult when they arrive.

3.18 The detainee shall be advised that:

- the duties of the appropriate adult include giving advice and assistance;
- they can consult privately with the appropriate adult at any time.

3.19 If the detainee, or appropriate adult on the detainee's behalf, asks for a solicitor to be called to give legal advice, the provisions of *section 6* apply.

3.20 If the detainee is blind, seriously visually impaired or unable to read, the custody officer shall make sure their solicitor, relative, appropriate adult or some other person likely to take an interest in them and not involved in the investigation is available to help check any documentation. When this Code requires written consent or signing the person assisting may be asked to sign instead, if the detainee prefers. This paragraph does not require an appropriate adult to be called solely to assist in checking and signing documentation for a person who is not a juvenile, or mentally disordered or otherwise mentally vulnerable (see *paragraph 3.15*).

(c) Persons attending a police station voluntarily

3.21 Anybody attending a police station voluntarily to assist with an investigation may leave at will unless arrested. See *Note 1K*. If it is decided they shall not be allowed to leave, they must be informed at once that they are under arrest and brought before the custody officer, who is responsible for making sure they are notified of their rights in the same way as other detainees. If they are not arrested but are cautioned as in *section 10*, the person who gives the caution must, at the same time, inform them they are not under arrest, they are not obliged to remain at the station but if they remain at the station they may obtain free and independent legal advice if they want. They shall be told the right to legal advice includes the right to speak with a solicitor on the telephone and be asked if they want to do so.

3.22 If a person attending the police station voluntarily asks about their entitlement to legal advice, they shall be given a copy of the notice explaining the arrangements for obtaining legal advice. See *paragraph 3.2*

(d) Documentation

3.23 The grounds for a person's detention shall be recorded, in the person's presence if practicable.

3.24 Action taken under *paragraphs 3.12* to *3.20* shall be recorded.

(e) Persons answering street bail

3.25 When a person is answering street bail, the custody officer should link any documentation held in relation to arrest with the custody record. Any further action shall be recorded on the custody record in accordance with *paragraphs 3.23* and *3.24* above.

Notes for guidance

1K   This Code does not affect the principle that all citizens have a duty to help police officers to prevent crime and discover offenders. This is a civic rather than a legal duty; but when a police officer is trying to discover whether, or by whom, an offence has been committed he is entitled to question any person from whom he thinks useful information can be obtained, subject to the restrictions imposed by this Code. A person's declaration that he is unwilling to reply does not alter this entitlement

3A The notice of entitlements should:

- *list the entitlements in this Code, including:*
  - *— visits and contact with outside parties, including special provisions for Common-wealth citizens and foreign nationals;*
  - *— reasonable standards of physical comfort;*
  - *— adequate food and drink;*
  - *— access to toilets and washing facilities, clothing, medical attention, and exercise when practicable.*
- *mention the:*
  - *— provisions relating to the conduct of interviews;*
  - *— circumstances in which an appropriate adult should be available to assist the detainee and their statutory rights to make representation whenever the period of their detention is reviewed.*

3B In addition to notices in English, translations should be available in Welsh, the main minority ethnic languages and the principal European languages, whenever they are likely to be helpful. Audio versions of the notice should also be made available.

3C If the juvenile is in local authority or voluntary organisation care but living with their parents or other adults responsible for their welfare, although there is no legal obligation to inform them, they should normally be contacted, as well as the authority or organisation unless suspected of involve-ment in the offence concerned. Even if the juvenile is not living with their parents, consideration should be given to informing them.

3D The right to consult the Codes of Practice does not entitle the person concerned to delay unreasonably any necessary investigative or administrative action whilst they do so. Examples of action which need not be delayed unreasonably include:

- *procedures requiring the provision of breath, blood or urine specimens under the Road Traffic Act 1988 or the Transport and Works Act 1992*
- *searching detainees at the police station*
- *taking fingerprints, footwear impressions or non-intimate samples without consent for evidential purposes*

3E Home Office Circular 32/2000 provides more detailed guidance on risk assessments and identifies key risk areas which should always be considered.

CODES OF PRACTICE, CODE G

2 Elements of Arrest under section 24 PACE

2.1 A lawful arrest requires two elements:

A person's involvement or suspected involvement or attempted involvement in the com-mission of a criminal offence;

AND

Reasonable grounds for believing that the person's arrest is necessary.

2.2 Arresting officers are required to inform the person arrested that they have been arrested, even if this fact is obvious, and of the relevant circumstances of the arrest in relation to both elements and to inform the custody officer of these on arrival at the police station. See Code C paragraph 3.4.

Involvement in the commission of an offence

2.3 A constable may arrest without warrant in relation to any offence, except for the single exception listed in Note for Guidance 1. A constable may arrest anyone:

- who is about to commit an offence or is in the act of committing an offence
- whom the officer has reasonable grounds for suspecting is about to commit an offence or to be committing an offence

- whom the officer has reasonable grounds to suspect of being guilty of an offence which he or she has reasonable grounds for suspecting has been committed
- anyone who is guilty of an offence which has been committed or anyone whom the officer has reasonable grounds for suspecting to be guilty of that offence.

Necessity criteria

2.4 The power of arrest is only exercisable if the constable has reasonable grounds for believing that it is necessary to arrest the person. The criteria for what may constitute necessity are set out in paragraph 2.9. It remains an operational decision at the discretion of the arresting officer as to:

- what action he or she may take at the point of contact with the individual;
- the necessity criterion or criteria (if any) which applies to the individual; and
- whether to arrest, report for summons, grant street bail, issue a fixed penalty notice or take any other action that is open to the officer.

2.5 In applying the criteria, the arresting officer has to be satisfied that at least one of the reasons supporting the need for arrest is satisfied.

2.6 Extending the power of arrest to all offences provides a constable with the ability to use that power to deal with any situation. However applying the necessity criteria requires the constable to examine and justify the reason or reasons why a person needs to be taken to a police station for the custody officer to decide whether the person should be placed in police detention.

2.7 The criteria below are set out in section 24 of PACE as substituted by section 110 of the Serious Organised Crime and Police Act 2005. The criteria are exhaustive. However, the circumstances that may satisfy those criteria remain a matter for the operational discretion of individual officers. Some examples are given below of what those circumstances may be.

2.8 In considering the individual circumstances, the constable must take into account the situation of the victim, the nature of the offence, the circumstances of the suspect and the needs of the investigative process.

2.9 The criteria are that the arrest is necessary:

(a) to enable the name of the person in question to be ascertained (in the case where the constable does not know, and cannot readily ascertain, the person's name, or has reasonable grounds for doubting whether a name given by the person as his name is his real name)

(b) correspondingly as regards the person's address an address is a satisfactory address for service of summons if the person will be at it for a sufficiently long period for it to be possible to serve him or her with a summons; or, that some other person at that address specified by the person will accept service of the summons on their behalf.

(c) to prevent the person in question—
   (i) causing physical injury to himself or any other person;
   (ii) suffering physical injury ;
   (iii) causing loss or damage to property;
   (iv) committing an offence against public decency (only applies where members of the public going about their normal business cannot reasonably be expected to avoid the person in question); or
   (v) causing an unlawful obstruction of the highway;

(d) to protect a child or other vulnerable person from the person in question

(e) to allow the prompt and effective investigation of the offence or of the conduct of the person in question.
   This may include cases such as:
   (i) Where there are reasonable grounds to believe that the person:

- has made false statements;
- has made statements which cannot be readily verified;
- has presented false evidence;
- may steal or destroy evidence;
- may make contact with co-suspects or conspirators;
- may intimidate or threaten or make contact with witnesses;
- where it is necessary to obtain evidence by questioning; or

(ii) when considering arrest in connection with an indictable offence, there is a need to:

- enter and search any premises occupied or controlled by a person
- search the person
- prevent contact with others
- take fingerprints, footwear impressions, samples or photographs of the suspect

(iii) ensuring compliance with statutory drug testing requirements.

(f) to prevent any prosecution for the offence from being hindered by the disappearance of the person in question.

This may arise if there are reasonable grounds for believing that

- if the person is not arrested he or she will fail to attend court
- street bail after arrest would be insufficient to deter the suspect from trying to evade prosecution

3   Information to be given on arrest

(a) Cautions–when a caution must be given (taken from Code C section 10)

3.1 A person whom there are grounds to suspect of an offence (see Note 2) must be cautioned before any questions about an offence, or further questions if the answers provide the grounds for suspicion, are put to them if either the suspect's answers or silence, (i.e. failure or refusal to answer or answer satisfactorily) may be given in evidence to a court in a prosecution. A person need not be cautioned if questions are for other necessary purposes e.g.:

(a) solely to establish their identity or ownership of any vehicle;

(b) to obtain information in accordance with any relevant statutory requirement;

(c) in furtherance of the proper and effective conduct of a search, e.g. to determine the need to search in the exercise of powers of stop and search or to seek cooperation while carrying out a search;

(d) to seek verification of a written record as in *Code C paragraph 11.13*;

(e) when examining a person in accordance with the Terrorism Act 2000, Schedule 7 and the Code of Practice for Examining Officers issued under that Act, Schedule 14, paragraph 6.

3.2 Whenever a person not under arrest is initially cautioned, or reminded they are under caution, that person must at the same time be told they are not under arrest and are free to leave if they want to.

3.3 A person who is arrested, or further arrested, must be informed at the time, or as soon as practicable thereafter, that they are under arrest and the grounds for their arrest, see *Note 3*.

3.4 A person who is arrested, or further arrested, must also be cautioned unless:

(a) it is impracticable to do so by reason of their condition or behaviour at the time;

(b) they have already been cautioned immediately prior to arrest as in *paragraph 3.1*.

(c) Terms of the caution (Taken from Code C section 10)

3.5 The caution, which must be given on arrest, should be in the following terms:

'You do not have to say anything. But it may harm your defence if you do not mention when questioned something which you later rely on in Court. Anything you do say may be given in evidence.'

See *Note 5*

3.6 Minor deviations from the words of any caution given in accordance with this Code do not constitute a breach of this Code, provided the sense of the relevant caution is preserved. See *Note 6*

3.7 When, despite being cautioned, a person fails to co-operate or to answer particular questions which may affect their immediate treatment, the person should be informed of any relevant consequences and that those consequences are not affected by the caution. Examples are when a person's refusal to provide:

- their name and address when charged may make them liable to detention;
- particulars and information in accordance with a statutory requirement, e.g. under the Road Traffic Act 1988, may amount to an offence or may make the person liable to a further arrest.

4   Records of Arrest

(a) General

4.1 The arresting officer is required to record in his pocket book or by other methods used for recording information:

- the nature and circumstances of the offence leading to the arrest
- the reason or reasons why arrest was necessary
- the giving of the caution
- anything said by the person at the time of arrest

4.2 Such a record should be made at the time of the arrest unless impracticable to do. If not made at that time, the record should then be completed as soon as possible thereafter.

4.3 On arrival at the police station, the custody officer shall open the custody record (see paragraph 1.1A and section 2 of Code C). The information given by the arresting officer on the circumstances and reason or reasons for arrest shall be recorded as part of the custody record. Alternatively, a copy of the record made by the officer in accordance with paragraph 4.1 above shall be attached as part of the custody record.

See *paragraph 2.2* and *Code C paragraphs 3.4 and 10.3.*

4.4 The custody record will serve as a record of the arrest. Copies of the custody record will be provided in accordance with paragraphs 2.4 and 2.4A of Code C and access for inspection of the original record in accordance with paragraph 2.5 of Code C.

(b) Interviews and arrests

4.5 Records of interview, significant statements or silences will be treated in the same way as set out in sections 10 and 11 of Code C and in Code E (tape recording of interviews).

Notes for guidance

1 The powers of arrest for offences under sections 4(1) and 5(1) of the Criminal Law Act 1967 require that the offences to which they relate must carry a sentence fixed by law or one in which a first time offender aged 18 or over could be sentenced to 5 years or more imprisonment

---

Detention

Police and Criminal Evidence Act 1984

37   Duties of custody officer before charge

(1) Where—
  (a) a person is arrested for an offence—
      (i)   without a warrant; or
      (ii) under a warrant not endorsed for bail,
      the custody officer at each police station where he is detained after his arrest shall determine whether he has before him sufficient evidence to charge that person with the offence for which he was arrested and may detain him at the police station for such period as is necessary to enable him to do so.

(2) If the custody officer determines that he does not have such evidence before him, the person arrested shall be released either on bail or without bail, unless the custody officer has reasonable grounds for believing that his detention without being charged is necessary to secure or preserve evidence relating to an offence for which he is under arrest or to obtain such evidence by questioning him.

(3) If the custody officer has reasonable grounds for so believing, he may authorise the person arrested to be kept in police detention.

(4) Where a custody officer authorises a person who has not been charged to be kept in police detention, he shall, as soon as is practicable, make a written record of the grounds for the detention.

(5) Subject to subsection (6) below, the written record shall be made in the presence of the person arrested who shall at that time be informed by the custody officer of the grounds for his detention.

(6) Subsection (5) above shall not apply where the person arrested is, at the time when the written record is made—

(a) incapable of understanding what is said to him;

(b) violent or likely to become violent; or

(c) in urgent need of medical attention.

(7) Subject to section 41(7) below, if the custody officer determines that he has before him sufficient evidence to charge the person arrested with the offence for which he was arrested, the person arrested—

(a) shall be released without charge and on bail for the purpose of enabling the Director of Public Prosecutions to make a decision under section 37B below,

(b) shall be released without charge and on bail but not for that purpose,

(c) shall be released without charge and without bail, or

(d) shall be charged.

(7A) The decision as to how a person is to be dealt with under subsection (7) above shall be that of the custody officer.

(7B) Where a person is released under subsection (7)(a) above, it shall be the duty of the custody officer to inform him that he is being released to enable the Director of Public Prosecutions to make a decision under section 37B below.

(8) Where—

(a) a person is released under subsection (7)(b) or (c) above; and

(b) at the time of his release a decision whether he should be prosecuted for the offence for which he was arrested has not been taken, it shall be the duty of the custody officer so to inform him.

(8A) Subsection (8B) applies if the offence for which the person is arrested is one in relation to which a sample could be taken under section 63B below and the custody officer—

(a) is required in pursuance of subsection (2) above to release the person arrested and decides to release him on bail, or

(b) decides in pursuance of subsection (7)(a) or (b) above to release the person without charge and on bail.

(8B) The detention of the person may be continued to enable a sample to be taken under section 63B, but this subsection does not permit a person to be detained for a period of more than 24 hours after the relevant time.

(9) If the person arrested is not in a fit state to be dealt with under subsection (7) above, he may be kept in police detention until he is.

(10) The duty imposed on the custody officer under subsection (1) above shall be carried out by him as soon as practicable after the person arrested arrives at the police station or, in the case of a person arrested at the police station, as soon as practicable after the arrest.

(15) In this Part of this Act—

'arrested juvenile' means a person arrested with or without a warrant who appears to be under the age of 17;

'endorsed for bail' means endorsed with a direction for bail in accordance with section 117(2) of the Magistrates' Courts Act 1980.

37A   Guidance

(1) The Director of Public Prosecutions may issue guidance—

    (a) for the purpose of enabling custody officers to decide how persons should be dealt with under section 37(7) above or 37C(2) below, and

    (b) as to the information to be sent to the Director of Public Prosecutions under section 37B(1) below.

(2) The Director of Public Prosecutions may from time to time revise guidance issued under this section.

(3) Custody officers are to have regard to guidance under this section in deciding how persons should be dealt with under section 37(7) above or 37C(2) below.

(4) A report under section 9 of the Prosecution of Offences Act 1985 (report by DPP to Attorney General) must set out the provisions of any guidance issued, and any revisions to guidance made, in the year to which the report relates.

(5) The Director of Public Prosecutions must publish in such manner as he thinks fit—

    (a) any guidance issued under this section, and

    (b) any revisions made to such guidance.

(6) Guidance under this section may make different provision for different cases, circumstances or areas.

37B   Consultation with the Director of Public Prosecutions

(1) Where a person is released on bail under section 37(7)(a) above, an officer involved in the investigation of the offence shall, as soon as is practicable, send to the Director of Public Prosecutions such information as may be specified in guidance under section 37A above.

(2) The Director of Public Prosecutions shall decide whether there is sufficient evidence to charge the person with an offence.

(3) If he decides that there is sufficient evidence to charge the person with an offence, he shall decide—

    (a) whether or not the person should be charged and, if so, the offence with which he should be charged, and

    (b) whether or not the person should be given a caution and, if so, the offence in respect of which he should be given a caution.

(4) The Director of Public Prosecutions shall give written notice of his decision to an officer involved in the investigation of the offence.

(5) If his decision is—

    (a) that there is not sufficient evidence to charge the person with an offence, or

    (b) that there is sufficient evidence to charge the person with an offence but that the person should not be charged with an offence or given a caution in respect of an offence,

a custody officer shall give the person notice in writing that he is not to be prosecuted.

(6) If the decision of the Director of Public Prosecutions is that the person should be charged with an offence, or given a caution in respect of an offence, the person shall be charged or cautioned accordingly.

(7) But if his decision is that the person should be given a caution in respect of the offence and it proves not to be possible to give the person such a caution, he shall instead be charged with the offence.

(9) In this section 'caution' includes—

    (a) a conditional caution within the meaning of Part 3 of the Criminal Justice Act 2003; and

    (b) a warning or reprimand under section 65 of the Crime and Disorder Act 1998.[1]

37C   Breach of bail following release under section 37(7)(a)

(1) This section applies where—

    (a) a person released on bail under section 37(7)(a) above or subsection (2)(b) below is arrested under section 46A below in respect of that bail, and

---

[1] Subsections (8) and (9)(a) are not yet in force.

(b) at the time of his detention following that arrest at the police station mentioned in section 46A(2) below, notice under section 37B(4) above has not been given.

(2) The person arrested—

(a) shall be charged, or

(b) shall be released without charge, either on bail or without bail.

(3) The decision as to how a person is to be dealt with under subsection (2) above shall be that of a custody officer.

(4) A person released on bail under subsection (2)(b) above shall be released on bail subject to the same conditions (if any) which applied immediately before his arrest.

37D   Release under section 37(7)(a): further provision

(1) Where a person is released on bail under section 37(7)(a) or section 37C(2)(b) above, a custody officer may subsequently appoint a different time, or an additional time, at which the person is to attend at the police station to answer bail.

(2) The custody officer shall give the person notice in writing of the exercise of the power under subsection (1).

(3) The exercise of the power under subsection (1) shall not affect the conditions (if any) to which bail is subject.

(4) Where a person released on bail under section 37(7)(a) or 37C(2)(b) above returns to a police station to answer bail or is otherwise in police detention at a police station, he may be kept in police detention to enable him to be dealt with in accordance with section 37B or 37C above or to enable the power under subsection (1) above to be exercised.

(5) If the person is not in a fit state to enable him to be so dealt with or to enable that power to be exercised, he may be kept in police detention until he is.

(6) Where a person is kept in police detention by virtue of subsection (4) or (5) above, section 37(1) to (3) and (7) above (and section 40(8) below so far as it relates to section 37(1) to (3)) shall not apply to the offence in connection with which he was released on bail under section 37(7)(a) or 37C(2)(b) above.

38   Duties of custody officer after charge

(1) Where a person arrested for an offence otherwise than under a warrant endorsed for bail is charged with an offence, the custody officer shall, subject to section 25 of the Criminal Justice and Public Order Act 1994, order his release from police detention, either on bail or without bail, unless—

(a) if the person arrested is not an arrested juvenile—

(i)   his name or address cannot be ascertained or the custody officer has reasonable grounds for doubting whether a name or address furnished by him as his name or address is his real name or address;

(ii)   the custody officer has reasonable grounds for believing that the person arrested will fail to appear in court to answer to bail;

(iii)   in the case of a person arrested for an imprisonable offence, the custody officer has reasonable grounds for believing that the detention of the person arrested is necessary to prevent him from committing an offence;

(iiia)   in a case where a sample may be taken from the person under section 63B below, the custody officer has reasonable grounds for believing that the detention of the person is necessary to enable the sample to be taken from him;

(iv)   in the case of a person arrested for an offence which is not an imprisonable offence, the custody officer has reasonable grounds for believing that the detention of the person arrested is necessary to prevent him from causing physical injury to any other person or from causing loss of or damage to property;

(v)   the custody officer has reasonable grounds for believing that the detention of the person arrested is necessary to prevent him from interfering with the administration of justice or with the investigation of offences or of a particular offence; or

      (vi) the custody officer has reasonable grounds for believing that the detention of the person arrested is necessary for his own protection;

    (b) if he is an arrested juvenile—

      (i) any of the requirements of paragraph (a) above is satisfied (but, in the case of paragraph (a)(iiia) above, only if the arrested juvenile has attained the minimum age); or

      (ii) the custody officer has reasonable grounds for believing that he ought to be detained in his own interests.

(2) If the release of a person arrested is not required by subsection (1) above, the custody officer may authorise him to be kept in police detention but may not authorise a person to be kept in police detention by virtue of subsection (1)(a)(iiia) after the end of the period of six hours beginning when he was charged with the offence.

(2A) The custody officer, in taking the decisions required by subsection (1)(a) and (b) above (except (a)(i) and (vi) and (b)(ii)), shall have regard to the same considerations as those which a court is required to have regard to in taking the corresponding decisions under paragraph 2(1) of Part I of Schedule 1 to the Bail Act 1976 (disregarding paragraph 2(2) of that Part).

(3) Where a custody officer authorises a person who has been charged to be kept in police detention, he shall, as soon as practicable, make a written record of the grounds for the detention.

(4) Subject to subsection (5) below, the written record shall be made in the presence of the person charged who shall at that time be informed by the custody officer of the grounds for his detention.

(5) Subsection (4) above shall not apply where the person charged is, at the time when the written record is made—

    (a) incapable of understanding what is said to him;

    (b) violent or likely to become violent; or

    (c) in urgent need of medical attention.

(6) Where a custody officer authorises an arrested juvenile to be kept in police detention under subsection (1) above, the custody officer shall, unless he certifies—

    (a) that, by reason of such circumstances as are specified in the certificate, it is impracticable for him to do so; or

    (b) in the case of an arrested juvenile who has attained the age of 12 years, that no secure accommodation is available and that keeping him in other local authority accommodation would not be adequate to protect the public from serious harm from him, secure that the arrested juvenile is moved to local authority accommodation.

(6A) In this section—

'local authority accommodation' means accommodation provided by or on behalf of a local authority (within the meaning of the Children Act 1989);

['minimum age' means the age specified in section 63B(3)(b) below];

'secure accommodation' means accommodation provided for the purpose of restricting liberty;

'sexual offence' means an offence specified in Part 2 of Schedule 15 to the Criminal Justice Act 2003;

'violent offence' means murder or an offence specified in Part 1 of that Schedule;

and any reference, in relation to an arrested juvenile charged with a violent or sexual offence, to protecting the public from serious harm from him shall be construed as a reference to protecting members of the public from death or serious personal injury, whether physical or psychological, occasioned by further such offences committed by him.

(6B) Where an arrested juvenile is moved to local authority accommodation under subsection (6) above, it shall be lawful for any person acting on behalf of the authority to detain him.

(7) A certificate made under subsection (6) above in respect of an arrested juvenile shall be produced to the court before which he is first brought thereafter.

(7A) In this section 'imprisonable offence' has the same meaning as in Schedule 1 to the Bail Act 1976.

(8) In this Part of this Act 'local authority' has the same meaning as in the Children and Young Persons Act 1969.

39   Responsibilities in relation to persons detained

(1) Subject to subsections (2) and (4) below, it shall be the duty of the custody officer at a police station to ensure—

    (a) that all persons in police detention at that station are treated in accordance with this Act and any code of practice issued under it and relating to the treatment of persons in police detention; and

    (b) that all matters relating to such persons which are required by this Act or by such codes of practice to be recorded are recorded in the custody records relating to such persons.

(2) If the custody officer, in accordance with any code of practice issued under this Act, transfers or permits the transfer of a person in police detention—

    (a) to the custody of a police officer investigating an offence for which that person is in police detention; or

    (b) to the custody of an officer who has charge of that person outside the police station,

the custody officer shall cease in relation to that person to be subject to the duty imposed on him by subsection (1)(a) above; and it shall be the duty of the officer to whom the transfer is made to ensure that he is treated in accordance with the provisions of this Act and of any such codes of practice as are mentioned in subsection (1) above.

(3) If the person detained is subsequently returned to the custody of the custody officer, it shall be the duty of the officer investigating the offence to report to the custody officer as to the manner in which this section and the codes of practice have been complied with while that person was in his custody.

(4) If an arrested juvenile is transferred to the care of a local authority in pursuance of arrangements made under section 38(6) above, the custody officer shall cease in relation to that person to be subject to the duty imposed on him by subsection (1) above.

(6) Where—

    (a) an officer of higher rank than the custody officer gives directions relating to a person in police detention; and

    (b) the directions are at variance—

        (i) with any decision made or action taken by the custody officer in the performance of a duty imposed on him under this Part of this Act; or

        (ii) with any decision or action which would but for the directions have been made or taken by him in the performance of such a duty,

the custody officer shall refer the matter at once to an officer of the rank of superintendent or above who is responsible for the police station for which the custody officer is acting as custody officer.

40   Review of police detention

(1) Reviews of the detention of each person in police detention in connection with the investigation of an offence shall be carried out periodically in accordance with the following provisions of this section—

    (a) in the case of a person who has been arrested and charged, by the custody officer; and

    (b) in the case of a person who has been arrested but not charged, by an officer of at least the rank of inspector who has not been directly involved in the investigation.

(2) The officer to whom it falls to carry out a review is referred to in this section as a 'review officer'.

(3) Subject to subsection (4) below—
  (a) the first review shall be not later than six hours after the detention was first authorised;
  (b) the second review shall be not later than nine hours after the first;
  (c) subsequent reviews shall be at intervals of not more than nine hours.
(4) A review may be postponed—
  (a) if, having regard to all the circumstances prevailing at the latest time for it specified in subsection (3) above, it is not practicable to carry out the review at that time;
  (b) without prejudice to the generality of paragraph (a) above—
    (i) if at that time the person in detention is being questioned by a police officer and the review officer is satisfied that an interruption of the questioning for the purpose of carrying out the review would prejudice the investigation in connection with which he is being questioned; or
    (ii) if at that time no review officer is readily available.
(5) If a review is postponed under subsection (4) above it shall be carried out as soon as practicable after the latest time specified for it in subsection (3) above.
(6) If a review is carried out after postponement under subsection (4) above, the fact that it was so carried out shall not affect any requirement of this section as to the time at which any subsequent review is to be carried out.
(7) The review officer shall record the reasons for any postponement of a review in the custody record.
(8) Subject to subsection (9) below, where the person whose detention is under review has not been charged before the time of the review, section 37(1) to (6) above shall have effect in relation to him, but with the modifications specified in subsection (8A).
  (8A) The modifications are—
  (a) the substitution of references to the person whose detention is under review for references to the person arrested;
  (b) the substitution of references to the review officer for references to the custody officer; and
  (c) in subsection (6), the insertion of the following paragraph after paragraph (a)— '(aa) asleep;'.
(9) Where a person has been kept in police detention by virtue of section 37(9) above, section 37(1) to (6) shall not have effect in relation to him but it shall be the duty of the review officer to determine whether he is yet in a fit state.
(10) Where the person whose detention is under review has been charged before the time of the review, section 38(1) to (6B) above shall have effect in relation to him, but with the modifications specified in subsection (10A).
  (10A) The modifications are—
  (a) the substitution of a reference to the person whose detention is under review for any reference to the person arrested or to the person charged; and
  (b) in subsection (5), the insertion of the following paragraph after paragraph (a)— '(aa) asleep;'.
(11) Where—
  (a) an officer of higher rank than the review officer gives directions relating to a person in police detention; and
  (b) the directions are at variance—
    (i) with any decision made or action taken by the review officer in the performance of a duty imposed on him under this Part of this Act; or
    (ii) with any decision or action which would but for the directions have been made or taken by him in the performance of such a duty,
the review officer shall refer the matter at once to an officer of the rank of superintendent or above who is responsible for the police station for which the review officer is acting as review officer in connection with the detention.

(12) Before determining whether to authorise a person's continued detention the review officer shall give—

(a) that person (unless he is asleep); or

(b) any solicitor representing him who is available at the time of the review,

an opportunity to make representations to him about the detention.

(13) Subject to subsection (14) below, the person whose detention is under review or his solicitor may make representations under subsection (12) above either orally or in writing.

(14) The review officer may refuse to hear oral representations from the person whose detention is under review if he considers that he is unfit to make such representations by reason of his condition or behaviour.

40A   Use of telephone for review under s. 40

(1) A review under section 40(1)(b) may be carried out by means of a discussion, conducted by telephone, with one or more persons at the police station where the arrested person is held.

(2) But subsection (1) does not apply if—

(a) the review is of a kind authorised by regulations under section 45A to be carried out using video-conferencing facilities; and

(b) it is reasonably practicable to carry it out in accordance with those regulations.

(3) Where any review is carried out under this section by an officer who is not present at the station where the arrested person is held—

(a) any obligation of that officer to make a record in connection with the carrying out of the review shall have effect as an obligation to cause another officer to make the record;

(b) any requirement for the record to be made in the presence of the arrested person shall apply to the making of that record by that other officer; and

(c) the requirements under section 40(12) and (13) above for—

(i)   the arrested person, or

(ii) a solicitor representing him,

to be given any opportunity to make representations (whether in writing or orally) to that officer shall have effect as a requirement for that person, or such a solicitor, to be given an opportunity to make representations in a manner authorised by subsection (4) below.

(4) Representations are made in a manner authorised by this subsection—

(a) in a case where facilities exist for the immediate transmission of written representations to the officer carrying out the review, if they are made either—

(i)   orally by telephone to that officer; or

(ii) in writing to that officer by means of those facilities;

and

(b) in any other case, if they are made orally by telephone to that officer.

(5) In this section 'video-conferencing facilities' has the same meaning as in section 45A below.

41   Limits on period of detention without charge

(1) Subject to the following provisions of this section and to section 42 and 43 below, a person shall not be kept in police detention for more than 24 hours without being charged.

(2) The time from which the period of detention of a person is to be calculated (in this Act referred to as 'the relevant time')—

(a) in the case of a person to whom this paragraph applies, shall be—

(i)   the time at which that person arrives at the relevant police station; or

(ii) the time 24 hours after the time of that person's arrest,

whichever is the earlier;

(b) in the case of a person arrested outside England and Wales, shall be—

(i)   the time at which that person arrives at the first police station to which he is taken in the police area in England or Wales in which the offence for which he was arrested is being investigated; or

(ii) the time 24 hours after the time of that person's entry into England and Wales,

whichever is the earlier;

(c) in the case of a person who—

(i)　attends voluntarily at a police station; or

(ii)　accompanies a constable to a police station without having been arrested, and is arrested at the police station, the time of his arrest;

(ca) in the case of a person who attends a police station to answer bail granted under section 30A, the time when he arrives at the police station;

(d) in any other case, except where subsection (5) below applies, shall be the time at which the person arrested arrives at the first police station to which he is taken after his arrest.

(3) Subsection (2)(a) above applies to a person if—

(a)　his arrest is sought in one police area in England and Wales;

(b)　he is arrested in another police area; and

(c)　he is not questioned in the area in which he is arrested in order to obtain evidence in relation to an offence for which he is arrested;

and in sub-paragraph (i) of that paragraph 'the relevant police station' means the first police station to which he is taken in the police area in which his arrest was sought.

(4) Subsection (2) above shall have effect in relation to a person arrested under section 31 above as if every reference in it to his arrest or his being arrested were a reference to his arrest or his being arrested for the offence for which he was originally arrested.

(5) If—

(a)　a person is in police detention in a police area in England and Wales ('the first area'); and

(b)　his arrest for an offence is sought in some other police area in England and Wales ('the second area'); and

(c)　he is taken to the second area for the purposes of investigating that offence, without being questioned in the first area in order to obtain evidence in relation to it,

the relevant time shall be—

(i)　the time 24 hours after he leaves the place where he is detained in the first area; or

(ii)　the time at which he arrives at the first police station to which he is taken in the second area,

whichever is the earlier.

(6) When a person who is in police detention is removed to hospital because he is in need of medical treatment, any time during which he is being questioned in hospital or on the way there or back by a police officer for the purpose of obtaining evidence relating to an offence shall be included in any period which falls to be calculated for the purposes of this Part of this Act, but any other time while he is in hospital or on his way there or back shall not be so included.

(7) Subject to subsection (8) below, a person who at the expiry of 24 hours after the relevant time is in police detention and has not been charged shall be released at that time either on bail or without bail.

(8) Subsection (7) above does not apply to a person whose detention for more than 24 hours after the relevant time has been authorised or is otherwise permitted in accordance with section 42 or 43 below.

(9) A person released under subsection (7) above shall not be re-arrested without a warrant for the offence for which he was previously arrested unless new evidence justifying a further arrest has come to light since his release; but this subsection does not prevent an arrest under section 46A below.

42　Authorisation of continued detention

(1) Where a police officer of the rank of superintendent or above who is responsible for the police station at which a person is detained has reasonable grounds for believing that—

    (a) the detention of that person without charge is necessary to secure or preserve evidence relating to an offence for which he is under arrest or to obtain such evidence by questioning him;

    (b) an offence for which he is under arrest is an [indictable] offence; and

    (c) the investigation is being conducted diligently and expeditiously,

he may authorise the keeping of that person in police detention for a period expiring at or before 36 hours after the relevant time.

(2) Where an officer such as is mentioned in subsection (1) above has authorised the keeping of a person in police detention for a period expiring less than 36 hours after the relevant time, such an officer may authorise the keeping of that person in police detention for a further period expiring not more than 36 hours after that time if the conditions specified in subsection (1) above are still satisfied when he gives the authorisation.

(3) If it is proposed to transfer a person in police detention to another police area, the officer determining whether or not to authorise keeping him in detention under subsection (1) above shall have regard to the distance and the time the journey would take.

(4) No authorisation under subsection (1) above shall be given in respect of any person—

    (a) more than 24 hours after the relevant time; or

    (b) before the second review of his detention under section 40 above has been carried out.

(5) Where an officer authorises the keeping of a person in police detention under subsection (1) above, it shall be his duty—

    (a) to inform that person of the grounds for his continued detention; and

    (b) to record the grounds in that person's custody record.

(6) Before determining whether to authorise the keeping of a person in detention under subsection (1) or (2) above, an officer shall give—

    (a) that person; or

    (b) any solicitor representing him who is available at the time when it falls to the officer to determine whether to give the authorisation,

an opportunity to make representations to him about the detention.

(7) Subject to subsection (8) below, the person in detention or his solicitor may make representations under subsection (6) above either orally or in writing.

(8) The officer to whom it falls to determine whether to give the authorisation may refuse to hear oral representations from the person in detention if he considers that he is unfit to make such representations by reason of his condition or behaviour.

(9) Where—

    (a) an officer authorises the keeping of a person in detention under subsection (1) above; and

    (b) at the time of the authorisation he has not yet exercised a right conferred on him by section 56 or 58 below,

the officer—

    (i)   shall inform him of that right;

    (ii) shall decide whether he should be permitted to exercise it;

    (iii) shall record the decision in his custody record; and

    (iv) if the decision is to refuse to permit the exercise of the right, shall also record the grounds for the decision in that record.

(10) Where an officer has authorised the keeping of a person who has not been charged in detention under subsection (1) or (2) above, he shall be released from detention, either on bail or without bail, not later than 36 hours after the relevant time, unless—

    (a) he has been charged with an offence; or

    (b) his continued detention is authorised or otherwise permitted in accordance with section 43 below.

(11) A person released under subsection (10) above shall not be re-arrested without a warrant for the offence for which he was previously arrested unless new evidence justifying a

further arrest has come to light since his release; but this subsection does not prevent an arrest under section 46A below.

43   Warrants of further detention

(1) Where, on an application on oath made by a constable and supported by an information, a magistrates' court is satisfied that there are reasonable grounds for believing that the further detention of the person to whom the application relates is justified, it may issue a warrant of further detention authorising the keeping of that person in police detention.

(2) A court may not hear an application for a warrant of further detention unless the person to whom the application relates—

    (a) has been furnished with a copy of the information; and

    (b) has been brought before the court for the hearing.

(3) The person to whom the application relates shall be entitled to be legally represented at the hearing and, if he is not so represented but wishes to be so represented—

    (a) the court shall adjourn the hearing to enable him to obtain representation; and

    (b) he may be kept in police detention during the adjournment.

(4) A person's further detention is only justified for the purposes of this section or section 44 below if—

    (a) his detention without charge is necessary to secure or preserve evidence relating to an offence for which he is under arrest or to obtain such evidence by questioning him;

    (b) an offence for which he is under arrest is an indictable offence; and

    (c) the investigation is being conducted diligently and expeditiously.

(5) Subject to subsection (7) below, an application for a warrant of further detention may be made—

    (a) at any time before the expiry of 36 hours after the relevant time; or

    (b) in a case where—

        (i) it is not practicable for the magistrates' court to which the application will be made to sit at the expiry of 36 hours after the relevant time; but

        (ii) the court will sit during the 6 hours following the end of that period,

    at any time before the expiry of the said 6 hours.

(6) In a case to which subsection (5)(b) above applies—

    (a) the person to whom the application relates may be kept in police detention until the application is heard; and

    (b) the custody officer shall make a note in that person's custody record—

        (i) of the fact that he was kept in police detention for more than 36 hours after the relevant time; and

        (ii) of the reason why he was so kept.

(7) If—

    (a) an application for a warrant of further detention is made after the expiry of 36 hours after the relevant time; and

    (b) it appears to the magistrates' court that it would have been reasonable for the police to make it before the expiry of that period,

the court shall dismiss the application.

(8) Where on an application such as is mentioned in subsection (1) above a magistrates' court is not satisfied that there are reasonable grounds for believing that the further detention of the person to whom the application relates is justified, it shall be its duty—

    (a) to refuse the application; or

    (b) to adjourn the hearing of it until a time not later than 36 hours after the relevant time.

(9) The person to whom the application relates may be kept in police detention during the adjournment.

(10) A warrant of further detention shall—
   (a) state the time at which it is issued;
   (b) authorise the keeping in police detention of the person to whom it relates for the period stated in it.

(11) Subject to subsection (12) below, the period stated in a warrant of further detention shall be such period as the magistrates' court thinks fit, having regard to the evidence before it.

(12) The period shall not be longer than 36 hours.

(13) If it is proposed to transfer a person in police detention to a police area other than that in which he is detained when the application for a warrant of further detention is made, the court hearing the application shall have regard to the distance and the time the journey would take.

(14) Any information submitted in support of an application under this section shall state—
   (a) the nature of the offence for which the person to whom the application relates has been arrested;
   (b) the general nature of the evidence on which that person was arrested;
   (c) what inquiries relating to the offence have been made by the police and what further inquiries are proposed by them;
   (d) the reasons for believing the continued detention of that person to be necessary for the purposes of such further inquiries.

(15) Where an application under this section is refused, the person to whom the application relates shall forthwith be charged or, subject to subsection (16) below, released, either on bail or without bail.

(16) A person need not be released under subsection (15) above—
   (a) before the expiry of 24 hours after the relevant time; or
   (b) before the expiry of any longer period for which his continued detention is or has been authorised under section 42 above.

(17) Where an application under this section is refused, no further application shall be made under this section in respect of the person to whom the refusal relates, unless supported by evidence which has come to light since the refusal.

(18) Where a warrant of further detention is issued, the person to whom it relates shall be released from police detention, either on bail or without bail, upon or before the expiry of the warrant unless he is charged.

(19) A person released under subsection (18) above shall not be re-arrested without a warrant for the offence for which he was previously arrested unless new evidence justifying a further arrest has come to light since his release; but this subsection does not prevent an arrest under section 46A below.

44   Extension of warrants of further detention

(1) On an application on oath made by a constable and supported by an information a magistrates' court may extend a warrant of further detention issued under section 43 above if it is satisfied that there are reasonable grounds for believing that the further detention of the person to whom the application relates is justified.

(2) Subject to subsection (3) below, the period for which a warrant of further detention may be extended shall be such period as the court thinks fit, having regard to the evidence before it.

(3) The period shall not—
   (a) be longer than 36 hours; or
   (b) end later than 96 hours after the relevant time.

(4) Where a warrant of further detention has been extended under subsection (1) above, or further extended under this subsection, for a period ending before 96 hours after the relevant time, on an application such as is mentioned in that subsection a magistrates' court

may further extend the warrant if it is satisfied as there mentioned; and subsections (2) and (3) above apply to such further extensions as they apply to extensions under subsection (1) above.

(5) A warrant of further detention shall, if extended or further extended under this section, be endorsed with a note of the period of the extension.

(6) Subsections (2), (3) and (14) of section 43 above shall apply to an application made under this section as they apply to an application made under that section.

(7) Where an application under this section is refused, the person to whom the application relates shall forthwith be charged or, subject to subsection (8) below, released, either on bail or without bail.

(8) A person need not be released under subsection (7) above before the expiry of any period for which a warrant of further detention issued in relation to him has been extended or further extended on an earlier application made under this section.

45 Detention before charge—supplementary

(1) In sections 43 and 44 of this Act 'magistrates' court' means a court consisting of two or more justices of the peace sitting otherwise than in open court.

(2) Any reference in this Part of this Act to a period of time or a time of day is to be treated as approximate only.

45A Use of video-conferencing facilities for decisions about detention

(1) Subject to the following provisions of this section, the Secretary of State may by regulations provide that, in the case of an arrested person who is held in a police station, some or all of the functions mentioned in subsection (2) may be performed (notwithstanding anything in the preceding provisions of this Part) by an officer who—

(a) is not present in that police station; but
(b) has access to the use of video-conferencing facilities that enable him to communicate with persons in that station.

(2) Those functions are—

(a) the functions in relation to an arrested person taken to, or answering to bail at a police station that is not a designated police station which, in the case of an arrested person taken to a station that is a designated police station, are functions of a custody officer under section 37, 38 or 40 above; and
(b) the function of carrying out a review under section 40 (1)(b) above (review, by an officer of at least the rank of inspector, of the detention of person arrested but not charged).

(3) Regulations under this section shall specify the use to be made in the performance of the functions mentioned in subsection (2) above of the facilities mentioned in subsection (1) above.

(4) Regulations under this section shall not authorise the performance of any of the functions mentioned in subsection (2) (a) above by such an officer as is mentioned in subsection (1) above unless he is a custody officer for a designated police station.

(5) Where any functions mentioned in subsection (2) above are performed in a manner authorised by regulations under this section—

(a) any obligation of the officer performing those functions to make a record in connection with the performance of those functions shall have effect as an obligation to cause another officer to make the record; and
(b) any requirement for the record to be made in the presence of the arrested person shall apply to the making of that record by that other officer.

(6) Where the functions mentioned in subsection (2)(b) are performed in a manner authorised by regulations under this section, the requirements under section 40(12) and (13) above for—

(a) the arrested person, or
(b) a solicitor representing him,

to be given any opportunity to make representations (whether in writing or orally) to the person performing those functions shall have effect as a requirement for that person, or such a solicitor, to be given an opportunity to make representations in a manner authorised by subsection (7) below.

(7) Representations are made in a manner authorised by this subsection—

    (a) in a case where facilities exist for the immediate transmission of written representations to the officer performing the functions, if they are made either—

        (i) orally to that officer by means of the video-conferencing facilities used by him for performing those functions; or

        (ii) in writing to that officer by means of the facilities available for the immediate transmission of the representations;

    and

    (b) in any other case if they are made orally to that officer by means of the video-conferencing facilities used by him for performing the functions.

(8) Regulations under this section may make different provision for different cases and may be made so as to have effect in relation only to the police stations specified or described in the regulations.

(9) Regulations under this section shall be made by statutory instrument and shall be subject to annulment in pursuance of a resolution of either House of Parliament.

(10) Any reference in this section to video-conferencing facilities, in relation to any functions, is a reference to any facilities (whether a live television link or other facilities) by means of which the functions may be performed with the officer performing them, the person in relation to whom they are performed and any legal representative of that person all able to both see and to hear each other.

46[2]   Detention after charge

(1) Where a person—

    (a) is charged with an offence; and

    (b) after being charged—

        (i) is kept in police detention; or

        (ii) is detained by a local authority in pursuance of arrangements made under section 38(6) above,

he shall be brought before a magistrates' court in accordance with the provisions of this section.

(2) If he is to be brought before a magistrates' court in the local justice area in which the police station at which he was charged is situated, he shall be brought before such a court as soon as is practicable and in any event not later than the first sitting after he is charged with the offence.

(3) If no magistrates' court for that area is due to sit either on the day on which he is charged or on the next day, the custody officer for the police station at which he was charged shall inform the designated officer for the area that there is a person in the area to whom subsection (2) above applies.

(4) If the person charged is to be brought before a magistrates' court in a local justice area other than that in which the police station at which he was charged is situated, he shall be removed to that area as soon as is practicable and brought before such a court as soon as is practicable after his arrival in the area and in any event not later than the first sitting of a magistrates' court for that area after his arrival in the area.

(5) If no magistrates' court for that area is due to sit either on the day on which he arrives in the area or on the next day—

    (a) he shall be taken to a police station in the area; and

    (b) the custody officer at that station shall inform the designated officer in that area that there is a person in the area to whom subsection (4) applies.

---

[2] Various words and phrases in subsections (2) to (8) will be amended when section 109(1) and Schedule 8, para 282 of the Courts Act 2003 comes into force.

(6) Subject to subsection (8) below, where the designated officer for a local justice area has been informed—

    (a) under subsection (3) above that there is a person in the area to whom subsection (2) above applies; or

    (b) under subsection (5) above that there is a person in the area to whom subsection (4) above applies,

the designated officer shall arrange for a magistrates' court to sit not later than the day next following the relevant day.

(7) In this section 'the relevant day'—

    (a) in relation to a person who is to be brought before a magistrates' court in the local justice area in which the police station at which he was charged is situated, means the day on which he was charged; and

    (b) in relation to a person who is to be brought before a magistrates' court in any other local justice area, means the day on which he arrives in the area.

(8) Where the day next following the relevant day is Christmas Day, Good Friday or a Sunday, the duty of the justices' chief executive under subsection (6) above is a duty to arrange for a magistrates' court to sit not later than the first day after the relevant day which is not one of those days.

(9) Nothing in this section requires a person who is in hospital to be brought before a court if he is not well enough.

46A   Power of arrest for failure to answer to police bail.

(1) A constable may arrest without a warrant any person who, having been released on bail under this Part of this Act subject to a duty to attend at a police station, fails to attend at that police station at the time appointed for him to do so.

(1A) A person who has been released on bail under section 37(7)(a) or 37C(2)(b) above may be arrested without warrant by a constable if the constable has reasonable grounds for suspecting that the person has broken any of the conditions of bail.

(2) A person who is arrested under this section shall be taken to the police station appointed as the place at which he is to surrender to custody as soon as practicable after the arrest.

(3) For the purposes of—

    (a) section 30 above (subject to the obligation in subsection (2) above), and

    (b) section 31 above,

an arrest under this section shall be treated as an arrest for an offence.

CODES OF PRACTICE, CODE C

2   Custody records

2.1A When a person is brought to a police station:

- under arrest;
- is arrested at the police station having attended there voluntarily; or
- attends a police station to answer bail they should be brought before the custody officer as soon as practicable after their arrival at the station or, if appropriate, following arrest after attending the police station voluntarily. This applies to designated and non-designated police stations. A person is deemed to be 'at a police station' for these purposes if they are within the boundary of any building or enclosed yard which forms part of that police station.

2.1 A separate custody record must be opened as soon as practicable for each person brought to a police station under arrest or arrested at the station having gone there voluntarily or attending a police station in answer to street bail. All information recorded under this Code must be recorded as soon as practicable in the custody record unless otherwise specified. Any audio or video recording made in the custody area is not part of the custody record.

2.2 If any action requires the authority of an officer of a specified rank, subject to *paragraph 2.6A*, their name and rank must be noted in the custody record.

2.3 The custody officer is responsible for the custody record's accuracy and completeness and for making sure the record or copy of the record accompanies a detainee if they are transferred to another police station. The record shall show the:
- time and reason for transfer;
- time a person is released from detention.

2.4 A solicitor or appropriate adult must be permitted to consult a detainee's custody record as soon as practicable after their arrival at the station and at any other time whilst the person is detained. Arrangements for this access must be agreed with the custody officer and may not unreasonably interfere with the custody officer's duties.

2.4A When a detainee leaves police detention or is taken before a court they, their legal representative or appropriate adult shall be given, on request, a copy of the custody record as soon as practicable. This entitlement lasts for 12 months after release.

2.5 The detainee, appropriate adult or legal representative shall be permitted to inspect the original custody record after the detainee has left police detention provided they give reasonable notice of their request. Any such inspection shall be noted in the custody record.

2.6 Subject to *paragraph 2.6A*, all entries in custody records must be timed and signed by the maker. Records entered on computer shall be timed and contain the operator's identification.

2.6A Nothing in this Code requires the identity of officers or other police staff to be recorded or disclosed:
- (a) in the case of enquiries linked to the investigation of terrorism; or
- (b) if the officer or police staff reasonably believe recording or disclosing their name might put them in danger.

In these cases, they shall use their warrant or other identification numbers and the name of their police station. See *Note 2A*

2.7 The fact and time of any detainee's refusal to sign a custody record, when asked in accordance with this Code, must be recorded.

Note for guidance

2A The purpose of paragraph 2.6A(b) is to protect those involved in serious organised crime investigations or arrests of particularly violent suspects when there is reliable information that those arrested or their associates may threaten or cause harm to those involved. In cases of doubt, an officer of inspector rank or above should be consulted.

5   Right not to be held incommunicado
(a) Action

5.1 Any person arrested and held in custody at a police station or other premises may, on request, have one person known to them or likely to take an interest in their welfare informed at public expense of their whereabouts as soon as practicable. If the person cannot be contacted the detainee may choose up to two alternatives. If they cannot be contacted, the person in charge of detention or the investigation has discretion to allow further attempts until the information has been conveyed. See *Notes 5C* and *5D*

5.2 The exercise of the above right in respect of each person nominated may be delayed only in accordance with *Annex B*.

5.3 The above right may be exercised each time a detainee is taken to another police station.

5.4 The detainee may receive visits at the custody officer's discretion. See *Note 5B*

5.5 If a friend, relative or person with an interest in the detainee's welfare enquires about their whereabouts, this information shall be given if the suspect agrees and *Annex B* does not apply. See *Note 5D*

5.6 The detainee shall be given writing materials, on request, and allowed to telephone one person for a reasonable time, see *Notes 5A* and *5E*. Either or both these privileges may be denied or delayed if an officer of inspector rank or above considers sending a letter or making a telephone call may result in any of the consequences in:

 (a) *Annex B paragraphs 1* and *2* and the person is detained in connection with an indictable offence; or

 (b) *Annex B paragraphs 8* and *9* and the person is detained under the Terrorism Act 2000, Schedule 7 or section 41

Nothing in this paragraph permits the restriction or denial of the rights in *paragraphs 5.1* and *6.1*.

5.7 Before any letter or message is sent, or telephone call made, the detainee shall be informed that what they say in any letter, call or message (other than in a communication to a solicitor) may be read or listened to and may be given in evidence. A telephone call may be terminated if it is being abused. The costs can be at public expense at the custody officer's discretion.

5.7A Any delay or denial of the rights in this section should be proportionate and should last no longer than necessary.

(b) Documentation

5.8 A record must be kept of any:

 (a) request made under this section and the action taken;

 (b) letters, messages or telephone calls made or received or visit received;

 (c) refusal by the detainee to have information about them given to an outside enquirer. The detainee must be asked to countersign the record accordingly and any refusal recorded.

Notes for guidance

 5A A person may request an interpreter to interpret a telephone call or translate a letter.

 5B At the custody officer's discretion, visits should be allowed when possible, subject to having sufficient personnel to supervise a visit and any possible hindrance to the investigation.

 5C If the detainee does not know anyone to contact for advice or support or cannot contact a friend or relative, the custody officer should bear in mind any local voluntary bodies or other organisations who might be able to help. Paragraph 6.1 applies if legal advice is required.

 5D In some circumstances it may not be appropriate to use the telephone to disclose information under paragraphs 5.1 and 5.5.

 5E The telephone call at paragraph 5.6 is in addition to any communication under paragraphs 5.1 and 6.1.

6 Right to legal advice

(a) Action

6.1 Unless *Annex B* applies, all detainees must be informed that they may at any time consult and communicate privately with a solicitor, whether in person, in writing or by telephone, and that free independent legal advice is available from the duty solicitor. See *paragraph 3.1, Note 6B* and *Note 6J*

6.2 Not Used

6.3 A poster advertising the right to legal advice must be prominently displayed in the charging area of every police station. See *Note 6H*

6.4 No police officer should, at any time, do or say anything with the intention of dissuading a detainee from obtaining legal advice.

6.5 The exercise of the right of access to legal advice may be delayed only as in *Annex B*. Whenever legal advice is requested, and unless *Annex B* applies, the custody officer must act without delay to secure the provision of such advice. If, on being informed or reminded of this right, the detainee declines to speak to a solicitor in person, the officer should point out that the right includes the right to speak with a solicitor on the telephone. If the detainee continues to waive this right the officer should ask them why and any reasons should be recorded on the custody record or the interview record as appropriate. Reminders of the right to legal advice must be given as in *paragraphs 3.5, 11.2, 15.4, 16.4, 2B of Annex A, 3 of Annex K* and *16.5* and Code D, *paragraphs 3.17(ii)* and *6.3*. Once it is clear a detainee does not want to speak to a solicitor in person or by telephone they should cease to be asked their reasons. See *Note 6K*

6.5A In the case of a juvenile, an appropriate adult should consider whether legal advice from a solicitor is required. If the juvenile indicates that they do not want legal advice, the appropriate adult has the right to ask for a solicitor to attend if this would be in the best interests of the person. However, the detained person cannot be forced to see the solicitor if he is adamant that he does not wish to do so.

6.6 A detainee who wants legal advice may not be interviewed or continue to be interviewed until they have received such advice unless:

(a) *Annex B* applies, when the restriction on drawing adverse inferences from silence in *Annex C* will apply because the detainee is not allowed an opportunity to consult a solicitor; or

(b) an officer of superintendent rank or above has reasonable grounds for believing that:

   (i) the consequent delay might:

       • lead to interference with, or harm to, evidence connected with an offence;

       • lead to interference with, or physical harm to, other people;

       • lead to serious loss of, or damage to, property;

       • lead to alerting other people suspected of having committed an offence but not yet arrested for it;

       • hinder the recovery of property obtained in consequence of the commission of an offence.

   (ii) when a solicitor, including a duty solicitor, has been contacted and has agreed to attend, awaiting their arrival would cause unreasonable delay to the process of investigation.

Note: In these cases the restriction on drawing adverse inferences from silence in *Annex C* will apply because the detainee is not allowed an opportunity to consult a solicitor;

(c) the solicitor the detainee has nominated or selected from a list:

   (i) cannot be contacted;

   (ii) has previously indicated they do not wish to be contacted; or

   (iii) having been contacted, has declined to attend; and

the detainee has been advised of the Duty Solicitor Scheme but has declined to ask for the duty solicitor.

In these circumstances the interview may be started or continued without further delay provided an officer of inspector rank or above has agreed to the interview proceeding.

Note: The restriction on drawing adverse inferences from silence in *Annex C* will not apply because the detainee is allowed an opportunity to consult the duty solicitor;

(d) the detainee changes their mind, about wanting legal advice.

In these circumstances the interview may be started or continued without delay provided that:

   (i) the detainee agrees to do so, in writing or on the interview record made in accordance with Code E or F; and

   (ii) an officer of inspector rank or above has inquired about the detainee's reasons for their change of mind and gives authority for the interview to proceed.

Confirmation of the detainee's agreement, their change of mind, the reasons for it if given and, subject to *paragraph 2.6A*, the name of the authorising officer shall be recorded in the written interview record or the interview record made in accordance with Code E or F. See *Note 6I*.

Note: In these circumstances the restriction on drawing adverse inferences from silence in *Annex C* will not apply because the detainee is allowed an opportunity to consult a solicitor if they wish.

6.7 If *paragraph 6.6(b)(i)* applies, once sufficient information has been obtained to avert the risk, questioning must cease until the detainee has received legal advice unless *paragraph 6.6(a), (b)(ii), (c)* or *(d)* applies.

6.8 A detainee who has been permitted to consult a solicitor shall be entitled on request to have the solicitor present when they are interviewed unless one of the exceptions in *paragraph 6.6* applies.

6.9 The solicitor may only be required to leave the interview if their conduct is such that the interviewer is unable properly to put questions to the suspect. See *Notes 6D and 6E*

6.10 If the interviewer considers a solicitor is acting in such a way, they will stop the interview and consult an officer not below superintendent rank, if one is readily available, and otherwise an officer not below inspector rank not connected with the investigation. After speaking to the solicitor, the officer consulted will decide if the interview should continue in the presence of that solicitor. If they decide it should not, the suspect will be given the opportunity to consult another solicitor before the interview continues and that solicitor given an opportunity to be present at the interview. *See Note 6E*

6.11 The removal of a solicitor from an interview is a serious step and, if it occurs, the officer of superintendent rank or above who took the decision will consider if the incident should be reported to the Law Society. If the decision to remove the solicitor has been taken by an officer below superintendent rank, the facts must be reported to an officer of super-intendent rank or above who will similarly consider whether a report to the Law Society would be appropriate. When the solicitor concerned is a duty solicitor, the report should be both to the Law Society and to the Legal Services Commission.

6.12 'Solicitor' in this Code means:
- a solicitor who holds a current practising certificate
- an accredited or probationary representative included on the register of repre-sentatives maintained by the Legal Services Commission.

6.12A An accredited or probationary representative sent to provide advice by, and on behalf of, a solicitor shall be admitted to the police station for this purpose unless an officer of inspector rank or above considers such a visit will hinder the investigation and directs otherwise. Hindering the investigation does not include giving proper legal advice to a detainee as in *Note 6D*. Once admitted to the police station, *paragraphs 6.6 to 6.10* apply.

6.13 In exercising their discretion under *paragraph 6.12A*, the officer should take into account in particular:
- whether:
  - the identity and status of an accredited or probationary representative have been satisfactorily established;
  - they are of suitable character to provide legal advice, e.g. a person with a criminal record is unlikely to be suitable unless the conviction was for a minor offence and not recent.
- any other matters in any written letter of authorisation provided by the solicitor on whose behalf the person is attending the police station. See *Note 6F*

6.14 If the inspector refuses access to an accredited or probationary representative or a decision is taken that such a person should not be permitted to remain at an interview, the inspector must notify the solicitor on whose behalf the representative was acting and give them an opportunity to make alternative arrangements. The detainee must be informed and the custody record noted.

6.15 If a solicitor arrives at the station to see a particular person, that person must, unless *Annex B* applies, be so informed whether or not they are being interviewed and asked if they would like to see the solicitor. This applies even if the detainee has declined legal advice or, having requested it, subsequently agreed to be interviewed without receiving advice. The solicitor's attendance and the detainee's decision must be noted in the custody record.

(b) Documentation

6.16 Any request for legal advice and the action taken shall be recorded.

6.17 A record shall be made in the interview record if a detainee asks for legal advice and an interview is begun either in the absence of a solicitor or their representative, or they have been required to leave an interview.

Notes for guidance

6A In considering if paragraph 6.6(b) applies, the officer should, if practicable, ask the solicitor for an estimate of how long it will take to come to the station and relate this to the time detention is permitted, the time of day (i.e. whether the rest period under paragraph 12.2 is imminent) and the requirements of other investigations. If the solicitor is on their way or is to set off immediately, it will not normally be appropriate to begin an interview before they arrive. If it appears necessary to begin an interview before the solicitor's arrival, they should be given an indication of how long the police would be able to wait before 6.6(b) applies so there is an opportunity to make arrangements for someone else to provide legal advice.

6B A detainee who asks for legal advice should be given an opportunity to consult a specific solicitor or another solicitor from that solicitor's firm or the duty solicitor. If advice is not available by these means, or they do not want to consult the duty solicitor, the detainee should be given an opportunity to choose a solicitor from a list of those willing to provide legal advice. If this solicitor is unavailable, they may choose up to two alternatives. If these attempts are unsuccessful, the custody officer has discretion to allow further attempts until a solicitor has been contacted and agrees to provide legal advice. Apart from carrying out these duties, an officer must not advise the suspect about any particular firm of solicitors.

6C Not Used

6D A detainee has a right to free legal advice and to be represented by a solicitor. The solicitor's only role in the police station is to protect and advance the legal rights of their client. On occasions this may require the solicitor to give advice which has the effect of the client avoiding giving evidence which strengthens a prosecution case. The solicitor may intervene in order to seek clarification, challenge an improper question to their client or the manner in which it is put, advise their client not to reply to particular questions, or if they wish to give their client further legal advice. Paragraph 6.9 only applies if the solicitor's approach or conduct prevents or unreasonably obstructs proper questions being put to the suspect or the suspect's response being recorded. Examples of unacceptable conduct include answering questions on a suspect's behalf or providing written replies for the suspect to quote.

6E An officer who takes the decision to exclude a solicitor must be in a position to satisfy the court the decision was properly made. In order to do this they may need to witness what is happening.

6F If an officer of at least inspector rank considers a particular solicitor or firm of solicitors is persistently sending probationary representatives who are unsuited to provide legal advice, they should inform an officer of at least superintendent rank, who may wish to take the matter up with the Law Society.

6G Subject to the constraints of Annex B, a solicitor may advise more than one client in an investigation if they wish. Any question of a conflict of interest is for the solicitor under their professional code of conduct. If, however, waiting for a solicitor to give advice to one client may lead to unreasonable delay to the interview with another, the provisions of paragraph 6.6(b) may apply.

6H In addition to a poster in English, a poster or posters containing translations into Welsh, the main minority ethnic languages and the principal European languages should be displayed wherever they are likely to be helpful and it is practicable to do so.

6I Paragraph 6.6(d) requires the authorisation of an officer of inspector rank or above to the continuation of an interview when a detainee who wanted legal advice changes their mind. It is permissible for such authorisation to be given over the telephone, if the authorising officer is able to satisfy themselves about the reason for the detainee's change of mind and is satisfied it is proper to continue the interview in those circumstances.

6J Whenever a detainee exercises their right to legal advice by consulting or communicating with a solicitor, they must be allowed to do so in private. This right to consult or communicate in private is fundamental. Except as allowed by the Terrorism Act 2000, Schedule 8, paragraph 9, if the requirement for privacy is compromised because what is said or written by the detainee or solicitor for the purpose of giving and receiving legal advice is overheard, listened to, or read by others without the informed consent of the detainee, the right will effectively have been denied. When a detainee chooses to speak to a solicitor on the telephone, they should be allowed to do so in private unless this is impractical because of the design and layout of the custody area or the location of telephones. However, the normal expectation should be that facilities will be available, unless they are being used, at all police stations to enable detainees to speak in private to a solicitor either face to face or over the telephone.

6K A detainee is not obliged to give reasons for declining legal advice and should not be pressed to do so.

8 Conditions of detention

(a) Action

8.1 So far as it is practicable, not more than one detainee should be detained in each cell.

8.2 Cells in use must be adequately heated, cleaned and ventilated. They must be adequately lit, subject to such dimming as is compatible with safety and security to allow people detained overnight to sleep. No additional restraints shall be used within a locked cell unless absolutely necessary and then only restraint equipment, approved for use in that force by the Chief Officer, which is reasonable and necessary in the circumstances having regard to the detainee's demeanour and with a view to ensuring their safety and the safety of others. If a detainee is deaf, mentally disordered or otherwise mentally vulnerable, particular care must be taken when deciding whether to use any form of approved restraints.

8.3 Blankets, mattresses, pillows and other bedding supplied shall be of a reasonable standard and in a clean and sanitary condition. See *Note 8A*

8.4 Access to toilet and washing facilities must be provided.

8.5 If it is necessary to remove a detainee's clothes for the purposes of investigation, for hygiene, health reasons or cleaning, replacement clothing of a reasonable standard of comfort and cleanliness shall be provided. A detainee may not be interviewed unless adequate clothing has been offered.

8.6 At least two light meals and one main meal should be offered in any 24 hour period. See *Note 8B*. Drinks should be provided at meal times and upon reasonable request between meals. Whenever necessary, advice shall be sought from the appropriate health care professional, see *Note 9A*, on medical and dietary matters. As far as practicable, meals provided shall offer a varied diet and meet any specific dietary needs or religious beliefs the detainee may have. The detainee may, at the custody officer's discretion, have meals supplied by their family or friends at their expense. See *Note 8A*

8.7 Brief outdoor exercise shall be offered daily if practicable.

8.8 A juvenile shall not be placed in a police cell unless no other secure accommodation is available and the custody officer considers it is not practicable to supervise them if they are not placed in a cell or that a cell provides more comfortable accommodation than other secure accommodation in the station. A juvenile may not be placed in a cell with a detained adult.

(b) Documentation

8.9 A record must be kept of replacement clothing and meals offered.

8.10 If a juvenile is placed in a cell, the reason must be recorded.

8.11 The use of any restraints on a detainee whilst in a cell, the reasons for it and, if appropriate, the arrangements for enhanced supervision of the detainee whilst so restrained, shall be recorded. See *paragraph 3.9*

Notes for guidance

8A The provisions in paragraph 8.3 and 8.6 respectively are of particular importance in the case of a person detained under the Terrorism Act 2000, immigration detainees and others likely to be detained for an extended period. In deciding whether to allow meals to be supplied by family or friends, the custody officer is entitled to take account of the risk of items being concealed in any food or package and the officer's duties and responsibilities under food handling legislation.

8B Meals should, so far as practicable, be offered at recognised meal times, or at other times that take account of when the detainee last had a meal.

9 Care and treatment of detained persons

(a) General

9.1 Nothing in this section prevents the police from calling the police surgeon or, if appropriate, some other health care professional, to examine a detainee for the purposes of obtaining evidence relating to any offence in which the detainee is suspected of being involved. See *Note 9A*

9.2 If a complaint is made by, or on behalf of, a detainee about their treatment since their arrest, or it comes to notice that a detainee may have been treated improperly, a report must be made as soon as practicable to an officer of inspector rank or above not connected with the investigation. If the matter concerns a possible assault or the possibility of the unnecessary or unreasonable use of force, an appropriate health care professional must also be called as soon as practicable.

9.3 Detainees should be visited at least every hour. If no reasonably foreseeable risk was identified in a risk assessment, see *paragraphs 3.6–3.10*, there is no need to wake a sleeping detainee. Those suspected of being intoxicated through drink or drugs or having swallowed drugs, see *Note 9CA*, or whose level of consciousness causes concern must, subject to any clinical directions given by the appropriate health care professional, see *paragraph 9.13*:

- be visited and roused at least every half hour
- have their condition assessed as in *Annex H*
- and clinical treatment arranged if appropriate

See *Notes 9B, 9C* and *9H*

9.4 When arrangements are made to secure clinical attention for a detainee, the custody officer must make sure all relevant information which might assist in the treatment of the detainee's condition is made available to the responsible health care professional. This applies whether or not the health care professional asks for such information. Any officer or police staff with relevant information must inform the custody officer as soon as practicable.

(b) Clinical treatment and attention

9.5 The custody officer must make sure a detainee receives appropriate clinical attention as soon as reasonably practicable if the person:

(a) appears to be suffering from physical illness; or
(b) is injured; or
(c) appears to be suffering from a mental disorder;
(d) appears to need clinical attention.

9.5A This applies even if the detainee makes no request for clinical attention and whether or not they have already received clinical attention elsewhere. If the need for attention appears urgent, e.g. when indicated as in *Annex H*, the nearest available health care professional or an ambulance must be called immediately.

9.5B The custody officer must also consider the need for clinical attention as set out in Note for Guidance 9C in relation to those suffering the effects of alcohol or drugs.

9.6 *Paragraph 9.5* is not meant to prevent or delay the transfer to a hospital if necessary of a person detained under the Mental Health Act 1983, section 136. See *Note 9D*. When an assessment under that Act takes place at a police station, see *paragraph 3.16*, the custody officer must consider whether an appropriate health care professional should be called to conduct an initial clinical check on the detainee. This applies particularly when there is likely to be any significant delay in the arrival of a suitably qualified medical practitioner.

9.7 If it appears to the custody officer, or they are told, that a person brought to a station under arrest may be suffering from an infectious disease or condition, the custody officer must take reasonable steps to safeguard the health of the detainee and others at the station. In deciding what action to take, advice must be sought from an appropriate health care professional. See *Note 9E*. The custody officer has discretion to isolate the person and their property until clinical directions have been obtained.

9.8 If a detainee requests a clinical examination, an appropriate health care professional must be called as soon as practicable to assess the detainee's clinical needs. If a safe and appropriate care plan cannot be provided, the police surgeon's advice must be sought. The detainee may also be examined by a medical practitioner of their choice at their expense.

9.9 If a detainee is required to take or apply any medication in compliance with clinical directions prescribed before their detention, the custody officer must consult the appropriate health care professional before the use of the medication. Subject to the restrictions in *paragraph 9.10*, the custody officer is responsible for the safekeeping of any medication and for making sure the detainee is given the opportunity to take or apply prescribed or approved medication. Any such consultation and its outcome shall be noted in the custody record.

9.10 No police officer may administer or supervise the self-administration of medically prescribed controlled drugs of the types and forms listed in the Misuse of Drugs Regulations 2001, Schedule 2 or 3. A detainee may only self-administer such drugs under the personal supervision of the registered medical practitioner authorising their use. Drugs listed in Schedule 4 or 5 may be distributed by the custody officer for self administration if they have consulted the registered medical practitioner authorizing their use, this may be done by telephone, and both parties are satisfied self administration will not expose the detainee, police officers or anyone else to the risk of harm or injury.

9.11 When appropriate health care professionals administer drugs or other medications, or supervise their self-administration, it must be within current medicines legislation and the scope of practice as determined by their relevant professional body.

9.12 If a detainee has in their possession, or claims to need, medication relating to a heart condition, diabetes, epilepsy or a condition of comparable potential seriousness then, even though *paragraph 9.5* may not apply, the advice of the appropriate health care professional must be obtained.

9.13 Whenever the appropriate health care professional is called in accordance with this section to examine or treat a detainee, the custody officer shall ask for their opinion about:

- any risks or problems which police need to take into account when making decisions about the detainee's continued detention;
- when to carry out an interview if applicable; and
- the need for safeguards.

9.14 When clinical directions are given by the appropriate health care professional, whether orally or in writing, and the custody officer has any doubts or is in any way uncertain about any aspect of the directions, the custody officer shall ask for clarification. It is particularly important that directions concerning the frequency of visits are clear, precise and capable of being implemented. See *Note 9F*.

(c) Documentation

9.15 A record must be made in the custody record of:
   (a) the arrangements made for an examination by an appropriate health care professional under *paragraph 9.2* and of any complaint reported under that paragraph together with any relevant remarks by the custody officer;

   (b) any arrangements made in accordance with *paragraph 9.5*;
   (c) any request for a clinical examination under *paragraph 9.8* and any arrangements
       made in response;
   (d) the injury, ailment, condition or other reason which made it necessary to make
       the arrangements in (*a*) to (*c*), see *Note 9G*;
   (e) any clinical directions and advice, including any further clarifications, given to
       police by a health care professional concerning the care and treatment of the
       detainee in connection with any of the arrangements made in (*a*) to (*c*), see *Note
       9F*;
   (f) if applicable, the responses received when attempting to rouse a person using the
       procedure in *Annex H, see Note 9H*.

9.16 If a health care professional does not record their clinical findings in the custody record,
the record must show where they are recorded. See *Note 9G*. However, information which is
necessary to custody staff to ensure the effective ongoing care and well being of the detainee must
be recorded openly in the custody record, see *paragraph 3.8* and *Annex G, paragraph 7*.

9.17 Subject to the requirements of *Section 4*, the custody record shall include:

* a record of all medication a detainee has in their possession on arrival at the police
  station;
* a note of any such medication they claim to need but do not have with them.

Notes for guidance

*9A A 'health care professional' means a clinically qualified person working within the scope of
practice as determined by their relevant professional body. Whether a health care professional is
'appropriate' depends on the circumstances of the duties they carry out at the time.*

*9B Whenever possible juveniles and mentally vulnerable detainees should be visited more fre-
quently.*

*9C A detainee who appears drunk or behaves abnormally may be suffering from illness, the
effects of drugs or may have sustained injury, particularly a head injury which is not apparent. A
detainee needing or dependent on certain drugs, including alcohol, may experience harmful effects
within a short time of being deprived of their supply. In these circumstances, when there is any doubt,
police should always act urgently to call an appropriate health care professional or an ambulance.
Paragraph 9.5 does not apply to minor ailments or injuries which do not need attention. However, all
such ailments or injuries must be recorded in the custody record and any doubt must be resolved in
favour of calling the appropriate health care professional.*

*9CA Paragraph 9.3 would apply to a person in police custody by order of a magistrates' court
under the Criminal Justice Act 1988, section 152 (as amended by the Drugs Act 2005, section 8) to
facilitate the recovery of evidence after being charged with drug possession or drug trafficking and
suspected of having swallowed drugs. In the case of the healthcare needs of a person who has
swallowed drugs, the custody officer subject to any clinical directions, should consider the necessity for
rousing every half hour. This does not negate the need for regular visiting of the suspect in the cell.*

*9D Whenever practicable, arrangements should be made for persons detained for assessment
under the Mental Health Act 1983, section 136 to be taken to a hospital. There is no power under that
Act to transfer a person detained under section 136 from one place of safety to another place of safety
for assessment.*

*9E It is important to respect a person's right to privacy and information about their health must
be kept confidential and only disclosed with their consent or in accordance with clinical advice when it
is necessary to protect the detainee's health or that of others who come into contact with them.*

*9F The custody officer should always seek to clarify directions that the detainee requires constant
observation or supervision and should ask the appropriate health care professional to explain precisely
what action needs to be taken to implement such directions.*

*9G Paragraphs 9.15 and 9.16 do not require any information about the cause of any injury, ailment
or condition to be recorded on the custody record if it appears capable of providing evidence of an offence.*

9H The purpose of recording a person's responses when attempting to rouse them using the procedure in Annex H is to enable any change in the individual's consciousness level to be noted and clinical treatment arranged if appropriate.

15   Reviews and extensions of detention

(a) Persons detained under PACE

15.1 The review officer is responsible under PACE, section 40 for periodically determining if a person's detention, before or after charge, continues to be necessary. This requirement continues throughout the detention period and except as in *paragraph 15.10*, the review officer must be present at the police station holding the detainee. See *Notes 15A* and *15B*

15.2 Under PACE, section 42, an officer of superintendent rank or above who is responsible for the station holding the detainee may give authority any time after the second review to extend the maximum period the person may be detained without charge by up to 12 hours. Further detention without charge may be authorised only by a magistrates' court in accordance with PACE, sections 43 and 44. See *Notes 15C, 15D* and *15E*

15.2A Section 42(1) of PACE as amended extends the maximum period of detention for indictable offences from 24 hours to 36 hours. Detaining a juvenile or mentally vulnerable person for longer than 24 hours will be dependent on the circumstances of the case and with regard to the person's:

    (a) special vulnerability;

    (b) the legal obligation to provide an opportunity for representations to be made prior to a decision about extending detention;

    (c) the need to consult and consider the views of any appropriate adult; and

    (d) any alternatives to police custody.

15.3 Before deciding whether to authorise continued detention the officer responsible under *paragraphs 15.1* or *15.2* shall give an opportunity to make representations about the detention to:

    (a) the detainee, unless in the case of a review as in *paragraph 15.1*, the detainee is asleep;

    (b) the detainee's solicitor if available at the time; and

    (c) the appropriate adult if available at the time.

15.3A Other people having an interest in the detainee's welfare may also make representations at the authorising officer's discretion.

15.3B Subject to *paragraph 15.10*, the representations may be made orally in person or by telephone or in writing. The authorising officer may, however, refuse to hear oral representations from the detainee if the officer considers them unfit to make representations because of their condition or behaviour. See *Note 15C*

15.3C The decision on whether the review takes place in person or by telephone or by video conferencing (see Note 15G) is a matter for the review officer. In determining the form the review may take, the review officer must always take full account of the needs of the person in custody. The benefits of carrying out a review in person should always be considered, based on the individual circumstances of each case with specific additional consideration if the person is:

    (a) a juvenile (and the age of the juvenile); or

    (b) mentally vulnerable; or

    (c) has been subject to medical attention for other than routine minor ailments; or

    (d) there are presentational or community issues around the person's detention.

15.4 Before conducting a review or determining whether to extend the maximum period of detention without charge, the officer responsible must make sure the detainee is reminded of their entitlement to free legal advice, see *paragraph 6.5*, unless in the case of a review the person is asleep.

15.5 If, after considering any representations, the officer decides to keep the detainee in detention or extend the maximum period they may be detained without charge, any comment made by the detainee shall be recorded. If applicable, the officer responsible under *paragraph 15.1* or *15.2* shall be informed of the comment as soon as practicable. See also *paragraphs 11.4* and *11.13*

15.6 No officer shall put specific questions to the detainee:
- regarding their involvement in any offence; or
- in respect of any comments they may make:
  — when given the opportunity to make representations; or
  — in response to a decision to keep them in detention or extend the maximum period of detention.

Such an exchange could constitute an interview as in *paragraph 11.1A* and would be subject to the associated safeguards in *section 11* and, in respect of a person who has been charged, *paragraph 16.5*. See also *paragraph 11.13*

15.7 A detainee who is asleep at a review, see *paragraph 15.1*, and whose continued detention is authorised must be informed about the decision and reason as soon as practicable after waking.

(b) Persons detained under the Terrorism Act 2000

15.8 In terrorism cases:
(a) the powers and duties of the review officer are in the Terrorism Act 2000, Schedule 8, Part II;
(b) a police officer of at least superintendent rank may apply to a judicial authority for a warrant of further detention under the Terrorism Act 2000, Schedule 8, Part III.

(c) Telephone review of detention

15.9 PACE, section 40A provides that the officer responsible under section 40 for reviewing the detention of a person who has not been charged, need not attend the police station holding the detainee and may carry out the review by telephone.

15.9A PACE, section 45A(2) provides that the officer responsible under section 40 for reviewing the detention of a person who has not been charged, need not attend the police station holding the detainee and may carry out the review by video conferencing facilities (See Note 15G).

15.9B A telephone review is not permitted where facilities for review by video conferencing exist and it is practicable to use them.

15.9C The review officer can decide at any stage that a telephone review or review by video conferencing should be terminated and that the review will be conducted in person. The reasons for doing so should be noted in the custody record. See *Note 15F*

15.10 When a telephone review is carried out, an officer at the station holding the detainee shall be required by the review officer to fulfil that officer's obligations under PACE section 40 or this Code by:
(a) making any record connected with the review in the detainee's custody record;
(b) if applicable, making a record in (*a*) in the presence of the detainee; and
(c) giving the detainee information about the review.

15.11 When a telephone review is carried out, the requirement in *paragraph 15.3* will be satisfied:
(a) if facilities exist for the immediate transmission of written representations to the review officer, e.g. fax or email message, by giving the detainee an opportunity to make representations:
(i) orally by telephone; or
(ii) in writing using those facilities; and

(b) in all other cases, by giving the detainee an opportunity to make their representations orally by telephone.

(d) Documentation

15.12 It is the officer's responsibility to make sure all reminders given under *paragraph 15.4* are noted in the custody record.

15.13 The grounds for, and extent of, any delay in conducting a review shall be recorded.

15.14 When a telephone review is carried out, a record shall be made of:
   (a) the reason the review officer did not attend the station holding the detainee;
   (b) the place the review officer was;
   (c) the method representations, oral or written, were made to the review officer, see *paragraph 15.11.*

15.15 Any written representations shall be retained.

15.16 A record shall be made as soon as practicable about the outcome of each review or determination whether to extend the maximum detention period without charge or an application for a warrant of further detention or its extension. If *paragraph 15.7* applies, a record shall also be made of when the person was informed and by whom. If an authorisation is given under PACE, section 42, the record shall state the number of hours and minutes by which the detention period is extended or further extended. If a warrant for further detention, or extension, is granted under section 43 or 44, the record shall state the detention period authorised by the warrant and the date and time it was granted.

Notes for guidance

15A *Review officer for the purposes of:*
   • *PACE, sections 40 and 40A means, in the case of a person arrested but not charged, an officer of at least inspector rank not directly involved in the investigation and, if a person has been arrested and charged, the custody officer;*
   • *the Terrorism Act 2000, means an officer not directly involved in the investigation connected with the detention and of at least inspector rank, for reviews within 24 hours of the detainee's arrest or superintendent for all other reviews.*

15B *The detention of persons in police custody not subject to the statutory review requirement in paragraph 15.1 should still be reviewed periodically as a matter of good practice. Such reviews can be carried out by an officer of the rank of sergeant or above. The purpose of such reviews is to check the particular power under which a detainee is held continues to apply, any associated conditions are complied with and to make sure appropriate action is taken to deal with any changes. This includes the detainee's prompt release when the power no longer applies, or their transfer if the power requires the detainee be taken elsewhere as soon as the necessary arrangements are made. Examples include persons:*
   (a) *arrested on warrant because they failed to answer bail to appear at court;*
   (b) *arrested under the Bail Act 1976, section 7(3) for breaching a condition of bail granted after charge;*
   (c) *in police custody for specific purposes and periods under the Crime (Sentences) Act 1997, Schedule 1;*
   (d) *convicted, or remand prisoners, held in police stations on behalf of the Prison Service under the Imprisonment (Temporary Provisions) Act 1980, section 6;*
   (e) *being detained to prevent them causing a breach of the peace;*
   (f) *detained at police stations on behalf of the Immigration Service.*
   (g) *detained by order of a magistrates' court under the Criminal Justice Act 1988, section 152 (as amended by the Drugs Act 2005, section 8) to facilitate the recovery of evidence after being charged with drug possession or drug trafficking and suspected of having swallowed drugs.*

The detention of persons remanded into police detention by order of a court under the Magistrates' Courts Act 1980, section 128 is subject to a statutory requirement to review that detention. This is to make sure the detainee is taken back to court no later than the end of the period authorised by the court or when the need for their detention by police ceases, whichever is the sooner.

15C In the case of a review of detention, but not an extension, the detainee need not be woken for the review. However, if the detainee is likely to be asleep, e.g. during a period of rest allowed as in paragraph 12.2, at the latest time a review or authorisation to extend detention may take place, the officer should, if the legal obligations and time constraints permit, bring forward the procedure to allow the detainee to make representations. A detainee not asleep during the review must be present when the grounds for their continued detention are recorded and must at the same time be informed of those grounds unless the review officer considers the person is incapable of understanding what is said, violent or likely to become violent or in urgent need of medical attention.

15D An application to a Magistrates' Court under PACE, sections 43 or 44 for a warrant of further detention or its extension should be made between 10am and 9pm, and if possible during normal court hours. It will not usually be practicable to arrange for a court to sit specially outside the hours of 10am to 9pm. If it appears a special sitting may be needed outside normal court hours but between 10am and 9pm, the clerk to the justices should be given notice and informed of this possibility, while the court is sitting if possible.

15E In paragraph 15.2, the officer responsible for the station holding the detainee includes a superintendent or above who, in accordance with their force operational policy or police regulations, is given that responsibility on a temporary basis whilst the appointed long-term holder is off duty or otherwise unavailable.

15F The provisions of PACE, section 40A allowing telephone reviews do not apply to reviews of detention after charge by the custody officer or to reviews under the Terrorism Act 2000, Schedule 8, Part II in terrorism cases. When video conferencing is not required, they allow the use of a telephone to carry out a review of detention before charge. The procedure under PACE, section 42 must be done in person.

15G The use of video conferencing facilities for decisions about detention under section 45A of PACE is subject to the introduction of regulations by the Secretary of State.

16 Charging detained persons

(a) Action

16.1 When the officer in charge of the investigation reasonably believes there is sufficient evidence to provide a realistic prospect of conviction for the offence *(see paragraph 11.6)*, they shall without delay, and subject to the following qualification, inform the custody officer who will be responsible for considering whether the detainee should be charged. *See Notes 11B and 16A.* When a person is detained in respect of more than one offence it is permissible to delay informing the custody officer until the above conditions are satisfied in respect of all the offences, but *see paragraph 11.6*. If the detainee is a juvenile, mentally disordered or otherwise mentally vulnerable, any resulting action shall be taken in the presence of the appropriate adult if they are present at the time. *See Notes 16B and 16C.*

16.1A Where guidance issued by the Director of Public Prosecutions under section 37A is in force the custody officer must comply with that Guidance in deciding how to act in dealing with the detainee. See *Notes 16AA and 16AB.*

16.1B Where in compliance with the DPP's Guidance the custody officer decides that the case should be immediately referred to the CPS to make the charging decision, consultation should take place with a Crown Prosecutor as soon as is reasonably practicable. Where the Crown Prosecutor is unable to make the charging decision on the information available at that time, the detainee may be released without charge and on bail (with conditions if necessary) under section 37(7)(a). In such circumstances, the detainee should be informed that they are being released to enable the Director of Public Prosecutions to make a decision under section 37B.

16.2 When a detainee is charged with or informed they may be prosecuted for an offence, see *Note 16B*, they shall, unless the restriction on drawing adverse inferences from silence applies, see *Annex C*, be cautioned as follows:

'*You do not have to say anything. But it may harm your defence if you do not mention now something which you later rely on in court. Anything you do say may be given in evidence.*'

Annex C, paragraph 2 sets out the alternative terms of the caution to be used when the restriction on drawing adverse inferences from silence applies.

16.3 When a detainee is charged they shall be given a written notice showing particulars of the offence and, subject to *paragraph 2.6A*, the officer's name and the case reference number. As far as possible the particulars of the charge shall be stated in simple terms, but they shall also show the precise offence in law with which the detainee is charged. The notice shall begin:

'*You are charged with the offence(s) shown below.*' Followed by the caution.

If the detainee is a juvenile, mentally disordered or otherwise mentally vulnerable, the notice should be given to the appropriate adult.

16.4 If, after a detainee has been charged with or informed they may be prosecuted for an offence, an officer wants to tell them about any written statement or interview with another person relating to such an offence, the detainee shall either be handed a true copy of the written statement or the content of the interview record brought to their attention. Nothing shall be done to invite any reply or comment except to:

    (a) caution the detainee, '*You do not have to say anything, but anything you do say may be given in evidence.*'; and

    (b) remind the detainee about their right to legal advice.

16.4A If the detainee:

- cannot read, the document may be read to them
- is a juvenile, mentally disordered or otherwise mentally vulnerable, the appropriate adult shall also be given a copy, or the interview record shall be brought to their attention

16.5 A detainee may not be interviewed about an offence after they have been charged with, or informed they may be prosecuted for it, unless the interview is necessary:

- to prevent or minimise harm or loss to some other person, or the public
- to clear up an ambiguity in a previous answer or statement
- in the interests of justice for the detainee to have put to them, and have an opportunity to comment on, information concerning the offence which has come to light since they were charged or informed they might be prosecuted

Before any such interview, the interviewer shall:

    (a) caution the detainee, '*You do not have to say anything, but anything you do say may be given in evidence.*';

    (b) remind the detainee about their right to legal advice.

See *Note 16B*

16.6 The provisions of *paragraphs 16.2* to *16.5* must be complied with in the appropriate adult's presence if they are already at the police station. If they are not at the police station then these provisions must be complied with again in their presence when they arrive unless the detainee has been released. See *Note 16C*

16.7 When a juvenile is charged with an offence and the custody officer authorises their continued detention after charge, the custody officer must try to make arrangements for the juvenile to be taken into the care of a local authority to be detained pending appearance in court unless the custody officer certifies it is impracticable to do so or, in the case of a juvenile of at least 12 years old, no secure accommodation is available and there is a risk to the public of serious harm from that juvenile, in accordance with PACE, section 38(6). See *Note 16D*

(b) Documentation

16.8 A record shall be made of anything a detainee says when charged.

16.9 Any questions put in an interview after charge and answers given relating to the offence shall be recorded in full during the interview on forms for that purpose and the record signed by the detainee or, if they refuse, by the interviewer and any third parties present. If the questions are audibly recorded or visually recorded the arrangements in Code E or F apply.

16.10 If it is not practicable to make arrangements for a juvenile's transfer into local authority care as in *paragraph 16.7*, the custody officer must record the reasons and complete a certificate to be produced before the court with the juvenile. See *Note 16D*

Notes for guidance

16A The custody officer must take into account alternatives to prosecution under the Crime and Disorder Act 1998, reprimands and warning applicable to persons under 18, and in national guidance on the cautioning of offenders, for persons aged 18 and over.

16AA When a person is arrested under the provisions of the Criminal Justice Act 2003 which allow a person to be re-tried after being acquitted of a serious offence which is a qualifying offence specified in Schedule 5 to that Act and not precluded from further prosecution by virtue of section 75(3) of that Act the detention provisions of PACE are modified and make an officer of the rank of superintendent or above who has not been directly involved in the investigation responsible for determining whether the evidence is sufficient to charge.

16AB Where Guidance issued by the Director of Public Prosecutions under section 37B is in force, a custody officer who determines in accordance with that Guidance that there is sufficient evidence to charge the detainee, may detain that person for no longer than is reasonably necessary to decide how that person is to be dealt with under PACE, section 37(7)(a) to (d), including, where appropriate, consultation with the Duty Prosecutor. The period is subject to the maximum period of detention before charge determined by PACE, sections 41 to 44. Where in accordance with the Guidance the case is referred to the CPS for decision, the custody officer should ensure that an officer involved in the investigation sends to the CPS such information as is specified in the Guidance.

16B The giving of a warning or the service of the Notice of Intended Prosecution required by the Road Traffic Offenders Act 1988, section 1 does not amount to informing a detainee they may be prosecuted for an offence and so does not preclude further questioning in relation to that offence.

16C There is no power under PACE to detain a person and delay action under paragraphs 16.2 to 16.5 solely to await the arrival of the appropriate adult. After charge, bail cannot be refused, or release on bail delayed, simply because an appropriate adult is not available, unless the absence of that adult provides the custody officer with the necessary grounds to authorise detention after charge under PACE, section 38.

16D Except as in paragraph 16.7, neither a juvenile's behaviour nor the nature of the offence provides grounds for the custody officer to decide it is impracticable to arrange the juvenile's transfer to local authority care. Similarly, the lack of secure local authority accommodation does not make it impracticable to transfer the juvenile. The availability of secure accommodation is only a factor in relation to a juvenile aged 12 or over when the local authority accommodation would not be adequate to protect the public from serious harm from them. The obligation to transfer a juvenile to local authority accommodation applies as much to a juvenile charged during the daytime as to a juvenile to be held overnight, subject to a requirement to bring the juvenile before a court under PACE, section 46.

ANNEX B   DELAY IN NOTIFYING ARREST OR ALLOWING ACCESS TO LEGAL ADVICE

A Persons detained under PACE

1. The exercise of the rights in *Section 5* or *Section 6*, or both, may be delayed if the person is in police detention, as in PACE, section 118(2), in connection with an indictable offence, has not yet been charged with an offence and an officer of superintendent rank or above, or inspector rank or above only for the rights in Section 5, has reasonable grounds for

believing their exercise will:

    (i) lead to:

- interference with, or harm to, evidence connected with an indictable offence; or
- interference with, or physical harm to, other people; or

    (ii) lead to alerting other people suspected of having committed an indictable offence but not yet arrested for it; or

    (iii) hinder the recovery of property obtained in consequence of the commission of such an offence.

2. These rights may also be delayed if the officer has reasonable grounds to believe that:

    (i) the person detained for an indictable offence has benefited from their criminal conduct (decided in accordance with Part 2 of the Proceeds of Crime Act 2002); and

    (ii) the recovery of the value of the property constituting that benefit will be hindered by the exercise of either right.

3. Authority to delay a detainee's right to consult privately with a solicitor may be given only if the authorising officer has reasonable grounds to believe the solicitor the detainee wants to consult will, inadvertently or otherwise, pass on a message from the detainee or act in some other way which will have any of the consequences specified under *paragraphs 1 or 2*. In these circumstances the detainee must be allowed to choose another solicitor. See *Note B3*

4. If the detainee wishes to see a solicitor, access to that solicitor may not be delayed on the grounds they might advise the detainee not to answer questions or the solicitor was initially asked to attend the police station by someone else. In the latter case the detainee must be told the solicitor has come to the police station at another person's request, and must be asked to sign the custody record to signify whether they want to see the solicitor.

5. The fact the grounds for delaying notification of arrest may be satisfied does not automatically mean the grounds for delaying access to legal advice will also be satisfied.

6. These rights may be delayed only for as long as grounds exist and in no case beyond 36 hours after the relevant time as in PACE, section 41. If the grounds cease to apply within this time, the detainee must, as soon as practicable, be asked if they want to exercise either right, the custody record must be noted accordingly, and action taken in accordance with the relevant section of the Code.

7. A detained person must be permitted to consult a solicitor for a reasonable time before any court hearing.

B Persons detained under the Terrorism Act 2000

8. The rights as in *sections 5 or 6*, may be delayed if the person is detained under the Terrorism Act 2000, section 41 or Schedule 7, has not yet been charged with an offence and an officer of superintendent rank or above has reasonable grounds for believing the exercise of either right will:

    (i) lead to:

- interference with, or harm to, evidence connected with an indictable offence;
- interference with, or physical harm to, other people; or

    (ii) lead to the alerting of other people suspected of having committed an indictable offence but not yet arrested for it; or

    (iii) hinder the recovery of property:

- obtained in consequence of the commission of such an offence; or
- in respect of which a forfeiture order could be made under that Act, section 23;

    (iv) lead to interference with the gathering of information about the commission, preparation or instigation of acts of terrorism; or

    (v) by alerting any person, make it more difficult to prevent an act of terrorism or secure the apprehension, prosecution or conviction of any person in connection with the commission, preparation or instigation of an act of terrorism.

9. These rights may also be delayed if the officer has reasonable grounds for believing that:

    (i) the person detained has benefited from their criminal conduct (decided in accordance with Part 2 of the Proceeds of Crime Act 2002), and

(ii) the recovery of the value of the property constituting that benefit will be hindered by the exercise of either right.

10. In these cases *paragraphs 3 (with regards to the consequences specified at paragraphs 8 and 9), 4* and *5* apply.

11. These rights may be delayed only for as long as is necessary but not beyond 48 hours from the time of arrest if arrested under section 41, or if detained under the Terrorism Act 2000, Schedule 7 when arrested under section 41, from the beginning of their examination. If the above grounds cease to apply within this time the detainee must as soon as practicable be asked if they wish to exercise either right, the custody record noted accordingly, and action taken in accordance with the relevant section of this Code.

12. In this case *paragraph 7* applies.

C   Documentation

13. The grounds for action under this Annex shall be recorded and the detainee informed of them as soon as practicable.

14. Any reply given by a detainee under *paragraphs 6* or *11* must be recorded and the detainee asked to endorse the record in relation to whether they want to receive legal advice at this point.

D   Cautions and special warnings

When a suspect detained at a police station is interviewed during any period for which access to legal advice has been delayed under this Annex, the court or jury may not draw adverse inferences from their silence.

Notes for guidance

B1 Even if Annex B applies in the case of a juvenile, or a person who is mentally disordered or otherwise mentally vulnerable, action to inform the appropriate adult and the person responsible for a juvenile's welfare if that is a different person, must nevertheless be taken as in paragraph 3.13 and 3.15.

B2 In the case of Commonwealth citizens and foreign nationals, see Note 7A.

B3 A decision to delay access to a specific solicitor is likely to be a rare occurrence and only when it can be shown the suspect is capable of misleading that particular solicitor and there is more than a substantial risk that the suspect will succeed in causing information to be conveyed which will lead to one or more of the specified consequences.

Identification

CODES OF PRACTICE, CODE D

3   Identification by witnesses

3.1 A record shall be made of the suspect's description as first given by a potential witness. This record must:

(a) be made and kept in a form which enables details of that description to be accurately produced from it, in a visible and legible form, which can be given to the suspect or the suspect's solicitor in accordance with this Code; and

(b) unless otherwise specified, be made before the witness takes part in any identification procedures under *paragraphs 3.5* to *3.10, 3.21* or *3.23*.

A copy of the record shall where practicable, be given to the suspect or their solicitor before any procedures under *paragraphs 3.5* to *3.10, 3.21* or *3.23* are carried out. See *Note 3E*

(a) Cases when the suspect's identity is not known

3.2 In cases when the suspect's identity is not known, a witness may be taken to a particular neighbourhood or place to see whether they can identify the person they saw. Although the number, age, sex, race, general description and style of clothing of other people present at the location and the way in which any identification is made cannot be controlled, the principles applicable to the formal procedures under *paragraphs 3.5* to *3.10* shall be followed as far as practicable. For example:

(a) where it is practicable to do so, a record should be made of the witness' description of the suspect, as in paragraph 3.1(a), before asking the witness to make an identification;

(b) care must be taken not to direct the witness' attention to any individual unless, taking into account all the circumstances, this cannot be avoided. However, this does not prevent a witness being asked to look carefully at the people around at the time or to look towards a group or in a particular direction, if this appears necessary to make sure that the witness does not overlook a possible suspect simply because the witness is looking in the opposite direction and also to enable the witness to make comparisons between any suspect and others who are in the area; See *Note 3F*

(c) where there is more than one witness, every effort should be made to keep them separate and witnesses should be taken to see whether they can identify a person independently;

(d) once there is sufficient information to justify the arrest of a particular individual for suspected involvement in the offence, e.g., after a witness makes a positive identification, the provisions set out from paragraph 3.4 onwards shall apply for any other witnesses in relation to that individual. Subject to *paragraphs 3.12* and *3.13*, it is not necessary for the witness who makes such a positive identification to take part in a further procedure;

(e) the officer or police staff accompanying the witness must record, in their pocket book, the action taken as soon as, and in as much detail, as possible. The record should include: the date, time and place of the relevant occasion the witness claims to have previously seen the suspect; where any identification was made; how it was made and the conditions at the time (e.g., the distance the witness was from the suspect, the weather and light); if the witness's attention was drawn to the suspect; the reason for this; and anything said by the witness or the suspect about the identification or the conduct of the procedure.

3.3 A witness must not be shown photographs, computerised or artist's composite likenesses or similar likenesses or pictures (including 'E-fit' images) if the identity of the suspect is known to the police and the suspect is available to take part in a video identification, an identification parade or a group identification. If the suspect's identity is not known, the showing of such images to a witness to obtain identification evidence must be done in accordance with *Annex E.*

(b) Cases when the suspect is known and available

3.4 If the suspect's identity is known to the police and they are available, the identification procedures set out in paragraphs 3.5 to 3.10 may be used. References in this section to a suspect being 'known' mean there is sufficient information known to the police to justify the arrest of a particular person for suspected involvement in the offence. A suspect being 'available' means they are immediately available or will be within a reasonably short time and willing to take an effective part in at least one of the following which it is practicable to arrange:

- video identification;
- identification parade; or
- group identification.

Video identification

3.5 Change to: 'A 'video identification' is when the witness is shown moving images of a known suspect, together with similar images of others who resemble the suspect.

Moving images must be used unless:
- the suspect is known but not available (see *paragraph 3.21* of this Code); or
- in accordance with *paragraph 2A of Annex A* of this Code, the identification officer does not consider that replication of a physical feature can be achieved or that it is not possible to conceal the location of the feature on the image of the suspect.

The identification officer may then decide to make use of video identification but using still images.

3.6 Video identifications must be carried out in accordance with *Annex A*.

Identification parade

3.7 An 'identification parade' is when the witness sees the suspect in a line of others who resemble the suspect.

3.8 Identification parades must be carried out in accordance with *Annex B*.

Group identification

3.9 A 'group identification' is when the witness sees the suspect in an informal group of people.

3.10 Group identifications must be carried out in accordance with *Annex C*.

Arranging identification procedures

3.11 Except for the provisions in *paragraph 3.19*, the arrangements for, and conduct of, the identification procedures in paragraphs 3.5 to 3.10 and circumstances in which an identification procedure must be held shall be the responsibility of an officer not below inspector rank who is not involved with the investigation, 'the identification officer'.

Unless otherwise specified, the identification officer may allow another officer or police staff, see *paragraph 2.21*, to make arrangements for, and conduct, any of these identification procedures. In delegating these procedures, the identification officer must be able to supervise effectively and either intervene or be contacted for advice.

No officer or any other person involved with the investigation of the case against the suspect, beyond the extent required by these procedures, may take any part in these procedures or act as the identification officer. This does not prevent the identification officer from consulting the officer in charge of the investigation to determine which procedure to use. When an identification procedure is required, in the interest of fairness to suspects and witnesses, it must be held as soon as practicable.

Circumstances in which an identification procedure must be held

3.12 Whenever:
  (i) a witness has identified a suspect or purported to have identified them prior to any identification procedure set out in paragraphs 3.5 to 3.10 having been held; or
  (ii) there is a witness available, who expresses an ability to identify the suspect, or where there is a reasonable chance of the witness being able to do so, and they have not been given an opportunity to identify the suspect in any of the procedures set out in paragraphs 3.5 to 3.10,

and the suspect disputes being the person the witness claims to have seen, an identification procedure shall be held unless it is not practicable or it would serve no useful purpose in proving or disproving whether the suspect was involved in committing the offence. For example, when it is not disputed that the suspect is already well known to the witness who claims to have seen them commit the crime.

3.13 Such a procedure may also be held if the officer in charge of the investigation considers it would be useful.

Selecting an identification procedure

3.14 If, because of paragraph 3.12, an identification procedure is to be held, the suspect shall initially be offered a video identification unless:
  a) a video identification is not practicable; or

b) an identification parade is both practicable and more suitable than a video identification; or

c) paragraph 3.16 applies.

The identification officer and the officer in charge of the investigation shall consult each other to determine which option is to be offered. An identification parade may not be practicable because of factors relating to the witnesses, such as their number, state of health, availability and travelling requirements. A video identification would normally be more suitable if it could be arranged and completed sooner than an identification parade.

3.15 A suspect who refuses the identification procedure first offered shall be asked to state their reason for refusing and may get advice from their solicitor and/or if present, their appropriate adult. The suspect, solicitor and/or appropriate adult shall be allowed to make representations about why another procedure should be used. A record should be made of the reasons for refusal and any representations made. After considering any reasons given, and representations made, the identification officer shall, if appropriate, arrange for the suspect to be offered an alternative which the officer considers suitable and practicable. If the officer decides it is not suitable and practicable to offer an alternative identification procedure, the reasons for that decision shall be recorded.

3.16 A group identification may initially be offered if the officer in charge of the investigation considers it is more suitable than a video identification or an identification parade and the identification officer considers it practicable to arrange.

Notice to suspect

3.17 Unless *paragraph 3.20* applies, before a video identification, an identification parade or group identification is arranged, the following shall be explained to the suspect:

(i)   the purposes of the video identification, identification parade or group identification;

(ii)   their entitlement to free legal advice; see Code C, paragraph 6.5;

(iii)   the procedures for holding it, including their right to have a solicitor or friend present;

(iv)   that they do not have to consent to or co-operate in a video identification, identification parade or group identification;

(v)   that if they do not consent to, and co-operate in, a video identification, identification parade or group identification, their refusal may be given in evidence in any subsequent trial and police may proceed covertly without their consent or make other arrangements to test whether a witness can identify them, see *paragraph 3.21;*

(vi)   whether, for the purposes of the video identification procedure, images of them have previously been obtained, see *paragraph 3.20*, and if so, that they may co-operate in providing further, suitable images to be used instead;

(vii)   if appropriate, the special arrangements for juveniles;

(viii)   if appropriate, the special arrangements for mentally disordered or otherwise mentally vulnerable people;

(ix)   that if they significantly alter their appearance between being offered an identification procedure and any attempt to hold an identification procedure, this may be given in evidence if the case comes to trial, and the identification officer may then consider other forms of identification, see *paragraph 3.21* and *Note 3C;*

(x)   that a moving image or photograph may be taken of them when they attend for any identification procedure;

(xi)   whether, before their identity became known, the witness was shown photographs, a computerised or artist's composite likeness or similar likeness or image by the police, see *Note 3B;*

(xii)   that if they change their appearance before an identification parade, it may not be practicable to arrange one on the day or subsequently and, because of the appearance change, the identification officer may consider alternative methods of identification, see *Note 3C;*

(xiii) that they or their solicitor will be provided with details of the description of the suspect as first given by any witnesses who are to attend the video identification, identification parade, group identification or confrontation, see *paragraph 3.1.*

3.18 This information must also be recorded in a written notice handed to the suspect. The suspect must be given a reasonable opportunity to read the notice, after which, they should be asked to sign a second copy to indicate if they are willing to co-operate with the making of a video or take part in the identification parade or group identification.
The signed copy shall be retained by the identification officer.

3.19 The duties of the identification officer under *paragraphs 3.17* and *3.18* may be performed by the custody officer or other officer not involved in the investigation if:

(a) it is proposed to release the suspect in order that an identification procedure can be arranged and carried out and an inspector is not available to act as the identification officer, see *paragraph 3.11*, before the suspect leaves the station; or

(b) it is proposed to keep the suspect in police detention whilst the procedure is arranged and carried out and waiting for an inspector to act as the identification officer, see *paragraph 3.11*, would cause unreasonable delay to the investigation.

The officer concerned shall inform the identification officer of the action taken and give them the signed copy of the notice. See *Note 3C*

3.20 If the identification officer and officer in charge of the investigation suspect, on reasonable grounds that if the suspect was given the information and notice as in *paragraphs 3.17* and *3.18*, they would then take steps to avoid being seen by a witness in any identification procedure, the identification officer may arrange for images of the suspect suitable for use in a video identification procedure to be obtained before giving the information and notice. If suspect's images are obtained in these circumstances, the suspect may, for the purposes of a video identification procedure, co-operate in providing new images which if suitable, would be used instead, see *paragraph 3.17(vi)*.

(c) Cases when the suspect is known but not available

3.21 When a known suspect is not available or has ceased to be available, see *paragraph 3.4*, the identification officer may make arrangements for a video identification (see Annex A). If necessary, the identification officer may follow the video identification procedures but using still images. Any suitable moving or still images may be used and these may be obtained covertly if necessary. Alternatively, the identification officer may make arrangements for a group identification. See *Note 3D*. These provisions may also be applied to juveniles where the consent of their parent or guardian is either refused or reasonable efforts to obtain that consent have failed (see *paragraph 2.12*).

3.22 Any covert activity should be strictly limited to that necessary to test the ability of the witness to identify the suspect.

3.23 The identification officer may arrange for the suspect to be confronted by the witness if none of the options referred to in paragraphs 3.5 to 3.10 or 3.21 are practicable. A 'confrontation' is when the suspect is directly confronted by the witness. A confrontation does not require the suspect's consent. Confrontations must be carried out in accordance with Annex D.

3.24 Requirements for information to be given to, or sought from, a suspect or for the suspect to be given an opportunity to view images before they are shown to a witness, do not apply if the suspect's lack of co-operation prevents the necessary action.

(d) Documentation

3.25 A record shall be made of the video identification, identification parade, group identification or confrontation on forms provided for the purpose.

3.26 If the identification officer considers it is not practicable to hold a video identification or identification parade requested by the suspect, the reasons shall be recorded and explained to the suspect.

3.27 A record shall be made of a person's failure or refusal to co-operate in a video identification, identification parade or group identification and, if applicable, of the grounds for obtaining images in accordance with *paragraph 3.20*.

(e) Showing films and photographs of incidents and information released to the media

3.28 Nothing in this Code inhibits showing films or photographs to the public through the national or local media, or to police officers for the purposes of recognition and tracing suspects. However, when such material is shown to potential witnesses, including police officers, see *Note 3A*, to obtain identification evidence, it shall be shown on an individual basis to avoid any possibility of collusion, and, as far as possible, the showing shall follow the principles for video identification if the suspect is known, see *Annex A*, or identification by photographs if the suspect is not known, see *Annex E*.

3.29 When a broadcast or publication is made, see *paragraph 3.28*, a copy of the relevant material released to the media for the purposes of recognising or tracing the suspect, shall be kept. The suspect or their solicitor shall be allowed to view such material before any procedures under *paragraphs 3.5* to *3.10, 3.21* or *3.23* are carried out, provided it is practicable and would not unreasonably delay the investigation. Each witness involved in the procedure shall be asked, after they have taken part, whether they have seen any broadcast or published films or photographs relating to the offence or any description of the suspect and their replies shall be recorded. This paragraph does not affect any separate requirement under the Criminal Procedure and Investigations Act 1996 to retain material in connection with criminal investigations.

(f) Destruction and retention of photographs taken or used in identification procedures

3.30 PACE, section 64A, see *paragraph 5.12*, provides powers to take photographs of suspects and allows these photographs to be used or disclosed only for purposes related to the prevention or detection of crime, the investigation of offences or the conduct of prosecutions by, or on behalf of, police or other law enforcement and prosecuting authorities inside and outside the United Kingdom or the enforcement of a sentence. After being so used or disclosed, they may be retained but can only be used or disclosed for the same purposes.

3.31 Subject to *paragraph 3.33*, the photographs (and all negatives and copies), of suspects not taken in accordance with the provisions in *paragraph 5.12* which are taken for the purposes of, or in connection with, the identification procedures in *paragraphs 3.5* to *3.10, 3.21* or *3.23* must be destroyed unless the suspect:

(a) is charged with, or informed they may be prosecuted for, a recordable offence;
(b) is prosecuted for a recordable offence;
(c) is cautioned for a recordable offence or given a warning or reprimand in accordance with the Crime and Disorder Act 1998 for a recordable offence; or
(d) gives informed consent, in writing, for the photograph or images to be retained for purposes described in *paragraph 3.30*.

3.32 When *paragraph 3.31* requires the destruction of any photograph, the person must be given an opportunity to witness the destruction or to have a certificate confirming the destruction if they request one within five days of being informed that the destruction is required.

3.33 Nothing in *paragraph 3.31* affects any separate requirement under the Criminal Procedure and Investigations Act 1996 to retain material in connection with criminal investigations.

Notes for guidance

3A *Except for the provisions of Annex E, paragraph 1, a police officer who is a witness for the purposes of this part of the Code is subject to the same principles and procedures as a civilian witness.*

3B *When a witness attending an identification procedure has previously been shown photographs, or been shown or provided with computerised or artist's composite likenesses, or similar likenesses or pictures, it is the officer in charge of the investigation's responsibility to make the identification officer aware of this.*

3C *The purpose of paragraph 3.19 is to avoid or reduce delay in arranging identification procedures by enabling the required information and warnings, see sub-paragraphs 3.17(ix) and 3.17(xii), to be given at the earliest opportunity.*

3D *Paragraph 3.21 would apply when a known suspect deliberately makes themself 'unavailable' in order to delay or frustrate arrangements for obtaining identification evidence. It also applies when a suspect refuses or fails to take part in a video identification, an identification parade or a group identification, or refuses or fails to take part in the only practicable options from that list. It enables any suitable images of the suspect, moving or still, which are available or can be obtained, to be used in an identification procedure. Examples include images from custody and other CCTV systems and from visually recorded interview records, see Code F Note for Guidance 2D.*

3E *When it is proposed to show photographs to a witness in accordance with Annex E, it is the responsibility of the officer in charge of the investigation to confirm to the officer responsible for supervising and directing the showing, that the first description of the suspect given by that witness has been recorded. If this description has not been recorded, the procedure under Annex E must be postponed. See Annex E paragraph 2*

3F *The admissibility and value of identification evidence obtained when carrying out the procedure under paragraph 3.2 may be compromised if:*

   (*a*) before a person is identified, the witness' attention is specifically drawn to that person; or

   (*b*) the suspect's identity becomes known before the procedure.

4   Identification by fingerprints and footwear impressions

(A) Taking fingerprints in connection with a criminal investigation

(a) General

4.1 References to 'fingerprints' means any record, produced by any method, of the skin pattern and other physical characteristics or features of a person's:

   (i)   fingers; or
   (ii) palms.

(b) Action

4.2 A person's fingerprints may be taken in connection with the investigation of an offence only with their consent or if *paragraph 4.3* applies. If the person is at a police station consent must be in writing.

4.3 PACE, section 61, provides powers to take fingerprints without consent from any person over the age of ten years:

   (a) under section 61(3), from a person detained at a police station in consequence of being arrested for a recordable offence, see Note 4A, if they have not had their fingerprints taken in the course of the investigation of the offence unless those previously taken fingerprints are not a complete set or some or all of those fingerprints are not of sufficient quality to allow satisfactory analysis, comparison or matching.

   (b) under section 61(4), from a person detained at a police station who has been charged with a recordable offence, see Note 4A, or informed they will be reported for such an offence if they have not had their fingerprints taken in the course of the investigation of the offence unless those previously taken fingerprints are not a complete set or some or all of those fingerprints are not of sufficient quality to allow satisfactory analysis, comparison or matching.

(c) under section 61(4A), from a person who has been bailed to appear at a court or police station if the person:

   (i)   has answered to bail for a person whose fingerprints were taken previously and there are reasonable grounds for believing they are not the same person; or

   (ii) who has answered to bail claims to be a different person from a person whose fingerprints were previously taken;

and in either case, the court or an officer of inspector rank or above, authorises the fingerprints to be taken at the court or police station;

(d) under section 61(6), from a person who has been:

   (i)   convicted of a recordable offence;

   (ii) given a caution in respect of a recordable offence which, at the time of the caution, the person admitted; or

   (iii) warned or reprimanded under the Crime and Disorder Act 1998, section 65, for a recordable offence.

4.4 PACE, section 27, provides power to:

(a) require the person as in *paragraph 4.3(d)* to attend a police station to have their fingerprints taken if the:

   (i)   person has not been in police detention for the offence and has not had their fingerprints taken in the course of the investigation of that offence; or

   (ii) fingerprints that were taken from the person in the course of the investigation of that offence, do not constitute a complete set or some, or all, of the fingerprints are not of sufficient quality to allow satisfactory analysis, comparison or matching; and

(b) arrest, without warrant, a person who fails to comply with the requirement.

Note: The requirement must be made within one month of the date the person is convicted, cautioned, warned or reprimanded and the person must be given a period of at least 7 days within which to attend. This 7 day period need not fall during the month allowed for making the requirement.

4.5 A person's fingerprints may be taken, as above, electronically.

4.6 Reasonable force may be used, if necessary, to take a person's fingerprints without their consent under the powers as in *paragraphs 4.3* and *4.4*.

4.7 Before any fingerprints are taken with, or without, consent as above, the person must be informed:

(a) of the reason their fingerprints are to be taken;

(b) of the grounds on which the relevant authority has been given if the power mentioned in *paragraph 4.3 (c) applies;*

(c) that their fingerprints may be retained and may be subject of a speculative search against other fingerprints, see *Note 4B*, unless destruction of the fingerprints is required in accordance with *Annex F, Part (a)*; and

(d) that if their fingerprints are required to be destroyed, they may witness their destruction as provided for in *Annex F, Part (a)*.

(c) Documentation

4.8 A record must be made as soon as possible, of the reason for taking a person's fingerprints without consent. If force is used, a record shall be made of the circumstances and those present.

4.9 A record shall be made when a person has been informed under the terms of *paragraph 4.7(c)*, of the possibility that their fingerprints may be subject of a speculative search.

(B) Taking fingerprints in connection with immigration enquiries Action

4.10 A person's fingerprints may be taken for the purposes of Immigration Service enquiries in accordance with powers and procedures other than under PACE and for which the Immigration Service (not the police) are responsible, only with the person's consent in writing or if *paragraph 4.11* applies.

4.11 Powers to take fingerprints for these purposes without consent are given to police and immigration officers under the:

    (a) Immigration Act 1971, Schedule 2, paragraph 18(2), when it is reasonably necessary for the purposes of identifying a person detained under the Immigration Act 1971, Schedule 2, paragraph 16 (Detention of person liable to examination or removal);

    (b) Immigration and Asylum Act 1999, section 141(7)(a), from a person who fails to produce, on arrival, a valid passport with a photograph or some other document satisfactorily establishing their identity and nationality if an immigration officer does not consider the person has a reasonable excuse for the failure;

    (c) Immigration and Asylum Act 1999, section 141(7)(b), from a person who has been refused entry to the UK but has been temporarily admitted if an immigration officer reasonably suspects the person might break a condition imposed on them relating to residence or reporting to a police or immigration officer, and their decision is confirmed by a chief immigration officer;

    (d) Immigration and Asylum Act 1999, section 141(7)(c), when directions are given to remove a person:

        • as an illegal entrant,

        • liable to removal under the Immigration and Asylum Act 1999, section 10,

        • who is the subject of a deportation order from the UK;

    (e) Immigration and Asylum Act 1999, section 141(7)(d), from a person arrested under UK immigration laws under the Immigration Act 1971, Schedule 2, paragraph 17;

    (f) Immigration and Asylum Act 1999, section 141(7)(e), from a person who has made a claim:

        • for asylum

        • under Article 3 of the European Convention on Human Rights; or

    (g) Immigration and Asylum Act 1999, section 141(7)(f), from a person who is a dependant of someone who falls into (b) to (f) above.

4.12 The Immigration and Asylum Act 1999, section 142(3), gives a police and immigration officer power to arrest, without warrant, a person who fails to comply with a requirement imposed by the Secretary of State to attend a specified place for fingerprinting.

4.13 Before any fingerprints are taken, with or without consent, the person must be informed:

    (a) of the reason their fingerprints are to be taken;

    (b) the fingerprints, and all copies of them, will be destroyed in accordance with *Annex F, Part B*.

4.14 Reasonable force may be used, if necessary, to take a person's fingerprints without their consent under powers as in *paragraph 4.11*.

4.15 *Paragraphs 4.1* and *4.8* apply.

(C) Taking footwear impressions in connection with a criminal investigation

(a) Action

4.16 Impressions of a person's footwear may be taken in connection with the investigation of an offence only with their consent or if *paragraph 4.17* applies. If the person is at a police station consent must be in writing.

4.17 PACE, section 61A, provides power for a police officer to take footwear impressions without consent from any person over the age of ten years who is detained at a police station:

(a) in consequence of being arrested for a recordable offence, see *Note 4A*; or if the detainee has been charged with a recordable offence, or informed they will be reported for such an offence; and

(b) the detainee has not had an impression of their footwear taken in the course of the investigation of the offence unless the previously taken impression is not complete or is not of sufficient quality to allow satisfactory analysis, comparison or matching (whether in the case in question or generally).

4.18 Reasonable force may be used, if necessary, to take a footwear impression from a detainee without consent under the power in *paragraph 4.17*.

4.19 Before any footwear impression is taken with, or without, consent as above, the person must be informed:

(a) of the reason the impression is to be taken;

(b) that the impression may be retained and may be subject of a speculative search against other impressions, see *Note 4B*, unless destruction of the impression is required in accordance with *Annex F, Part (a)*; and

(c) that if their footwear impressions are required to be destroyed, they may witness their destruction as provided for in *Annex F, Part (a)*.

(b) Documentation

4.20 A record must be made as soon as possible, of the reason for taking a person's footwear impressions without consent. If force is used, a record shall be made of the circumstances and those present.

4.21 A record shall be made when a person has been informed under the terms of *paragraph 4.19(b)*, of the possibility that their footwear impressions may be subject of a speculative search.

Notes for guidance

4A References to 'recordable offences' in this Code relate to those offences for which convictions, cautions, reprimands and warnings may be recorded in national police records. See PACE, section 27(4). The recordable offences current at the time when this Code was prepared, are any offences which carry a sentence of imprisonment on conviction (irrespective of the period, or the age of the offender or actual sentence passed) as well as the non-imprisonable offences under the Vagrancy Act 1824 sections 3 and 4 (begging and persistent begging), the Street Offences Act 1959, section 1 (loitering or soliciting for purposes of prostitution), the Road Traffic Act 1988, section 25 (tampering with motor vehicles), the Criminal Justice and Public Order Act 1994, section 167 (touting for hire car services) and others listed in the National Police Records (Recordable Offences) Regulations 2000 as amended.

4B Fingerprints, footwear impressions or a DNA sample (and the information derived from it) taken from a person arrested on suspicion of being involved in a recordable offence, or charged with such an offence, or informed they will be reported for such an offence, may be subject of a speculative search. This means the fingerprints, footwear impressions or DNA sample may be checked against other fingerprints, footwear impressions and DNA records held by, or on behalf of, the police and other law enforcement authorities in, or outside, the UK, or held in connection with, or as a result of, an investigation of an offence inside or outside the UK. Fingerprints, footwear impressions and samples taken from a person suspected of committing a recordable offence but not arrested, charged or informed they will be reported for it, may be subject to a speculative search only if the person consents in writing. The following is an example of a basic form of words:

'I consent to my fingerprints, footwear impressions and DNA sample and information derived from it being retained and used only for purposes related to the prevention and detection of a crime, the investigation of an offence or the conduct of a prosecution either nationally or internationally.

I understand that my fingerprints, footwear impressions or DNA sample may be checked against other fingerprint, footwear impressions and DNA records held by or on behalf of relevant law enforcement authorities, either nationally or internationally.

I understand that once I have given my consent for my fingerprints, footwear impressions or DNA sample to be retained and used I cannot withdraw this consent.'

See Annex F regarding the retention and use of fingerprints and footwear impressions taken with consent for elimination purposes.

5   Examinations to establish identity and the taking of photographs

(A) Detainees at police stations

(a) Searching or examination of detainees at police stations

5.1   PACE, section 54A (1), allows a detainee at a police station to be searched or examined or both, to establish:

> (a) whether they have any marks, features or injuries that would tend to identify them as a person involved in the commission of an offence and to photograph any identifying marks, see *paragraph 5.5*; or
>
> (b) their identity, see *Note 5A*.

A person detained at a police station to be searched under a stop and search power, see Code A, is not a detainee for the purposes of these powers.

5.2   A search and/or examination to find marks under section 54A (1) (a) may be carried out without the detainee's consent, see *paragraph 2.12*, only if authorised by an officer of at least inspector rank when consent has been withheld or it is not practicable to obtain consent, see *Note 5D*.

5.3   A search or examination to establish a suspect's identity under section 54A (1)(b) may be carried out without the detainee's consent, see *paragraph 2.12*, only if authorised by an officer of at least inspector rank when the detainee has refused to identify themselves or the authorising officer has reasonable grounds for suspecting the person is not who they claim to be.

5.4   Any marks that assist in establishing the detainee's identity, or their identification as a person involved in the commission of an offence, are identifying marks. Such marks may be photographed with the detainee's consent, see *paragraph 2.12*; or without their consent if it is withheld or it is not practicable to obtain it, see *Note 5D*.

5.5   A detainee may only be searched, examined and photographed under section 54A, by a police officer of the same sex.

5.6   Any photographs of identifying marks, taken under section 54A, may be used or disclosed only for purposes related to the prevention or detection of crime, the investigation of offences or the conduct of prosecutions by, or on behalf of, police or other law enforcement and prosecuting authorities inside, and outside, the UK. After being so used or disclosed, the photograph may be retained but must not be used or disclosed except for these purposes, see *Note 5B*.

5.7   The powers, as in *paragraph 5.1*, do not affect any separate requirement under the Criminal Procedure and Investigations Act 1996 to retain material in connection with criminal investigations.

5.8   Authority for the search and/or examination for the purposes of *paragraphs 5.2* and *5.3* may be given orally or in writing. If given orally, the authorising officer must confirm it in writing as soon as practicable. A separate authority is required for each purpose which applies.

5.9   If it is established a person is unwilling to co-operate sufficiently to enable a search and/or examination to take place or a suitable photograph to be taken, an officer may use reasonable force to:

> (a) search and/or examine a detainee without their consent; and
>
> (b) photograph any identifying marks without their consent.

5.10   The thoroughness and extent of any search or examination carried out in accordance with the powers in section 54A must be no more than the officer considers necessary to achieve the required purpose. Any search or examination which involves the removal of more than the person's outer clothing shall be conducted in accordance with Code C, Annex A, paragraph 11.

5.11 An intimate search may not be carried out under the powers in section 54A.

(b) Photographing detainees at police stations and other persons elsewhere than at a police station

5.12 Under PACE, section 64A, an officer may photograph :
  (a) any person whilst they are detained at a police station; and
  (b) any person who is elsewhere than at a police station and who has been:—
    (i)   arrested by a constable for an offence;
    (ii) taken into custody by a constable after being arrested for an offence by a person other than a constable;
    (iii) made subject to a requirement to wait with a community support officer under *paragraph 2(3) or (3B)* of Schedule 4 to the Police Reform Act 2002;
    (iv) given a penalty notice by a constable in uniform under Chapter 1 of Part 1 of the Criminal Justice and Police Act 2001, a penalty notice by a constable under section 444A of the Education Act 1996, or a fixed penalty notice by a constable in uniform under section 54 of the Road Traffic Offenders Act 1988;
    (v)   given a notice in relation to a relevant fixed penalty offence (within the meaning of paragraph 1 of Schedule 4 to the Police Reform Act 2002) by a community support officer by virtue of a designation applying that paragraph to him; or
    (vi) given a notice in relation to a relevant fixed penalty offence (within the meaning of paragraph 1 of Schedule 5 to the Police Reform Act 2002) by an accredited person by virtue of accreditation specifying that that paragraph applies to him.

5.12A Photographs taken under PACE, section 64A:
  (a) may be taken with the person's consent, or without their consent if consent is withheld or it is not practicable to obtain their consent, see *Note 5E*; and
  (b) may be used or disclosed only for purposes related to the prevention or detection of crime, the investigation of offences or the conduct of prosecutions by, or on behalf of, police or other law enforcement and prosecuting authorities inside and outside the United Kingdom or the enforcement of any sentence or order made by a court when dealing with an offence. After being so used or disclosed, they may be retained but can only be used or disclosed for the same purposes. See *Note 5B*.

5.13 The officer proposing to take a detainee's photograph may, for this purpose, require the person to remove any item or substance worn on, or over, all, or any part of, their head or face. If they do not comply with such a requirement, the officer may remove the item or substance.

5.14 If it is established the detainee is unwilling to co-operate sufficiently to enable a suitable photograph to be taken and it is not reasonably practicable to take the photograph covertly, an officer may use reasonable force, see *Note 5F*.
  (a) to take their photograph without their consent; and
  (b) for the purpose of taking the photograph, remove any item or substance worn on, or over, all, or any part of, the person's head or face which they have failed to remove when asked.

5.15 For the purposes of this Code, a photograph may be obtained without the person's consent by making a copy of an image of them taken at any time on a camera system installed anywhere in the police station.

(c) Information to be given

5.16 When a person is searched, examined or photographed under the provisions as in *paragraph 5.1* and *5.12*, or their photograph obtained as in *paragraph 5.15*, they must be informed of the:

(a) purpose of the search, examination or photograph;

(b) grounds on which the relevant authority, if applicable, has been given; and

(c) purposes for which the photograph may be used, disclosed or retained.

This information must be given before the search or examination commences or the photograph is taken, except if the photograph is:

(i) to be taken covertly;

(ii) obtained as in *paragraph 5.15*, in which case the person must be informed as soon as practicable after the photograph is taken or obtained.

(d) Documentation

5.17 A record must be made when a detainee is searched, examined, or a photograph of the person, or any identifying marks found on them, are taken. The record must include the:

(a) identity, subject to paragraph 2.18, of the officer carrying out the search, examination or taking the photograph;

(b) purpose of the search, examination or photograph and the outcome;

(c) detainee's consent to the search, examination or photograph, or the reason the person was searched, examined or photographed without consent;

(d) giving of any authority as in *paragraphs 5.2* and *5.3*, the grounds for giving it and the authorising officer.

5.18 If force is used when searching, examining or taking a photograph in accordance with this section, a record shall be made of the circumstances and those present.

(B) Persons at police stations not detained

5.19 When there are reasonable grounds for suspecting the involvement of a person in a criminal offence, but that person is at a police station voluntarily and not detained, the provisions of *paragraphs 5.1* to *5.18* should apply, subject to the modifications in the following paragraphs.

5.20 References to the 'person being detained' and to the powers mentioned in *paragraph 5.1* which apply only to detainees at police stations shall be omitted.

5.21 Force may not be used to:

(a) search and/or examine the person to:

(i) discover whether they have any marks that would tend to identify them as a person involved in the commission of an offence; or

(ii) establish their identity, see *Note 5A*;

(b) take photographs of any identifying marks, see *paragraph 5.4*; or

(c) take a photograph of the person.

5.22 Subject to *paragraph 5.24*, the photographs of persons or of their identifying marks which are not taken in accordance with the provisions mentioned in *paragraphs 5.1* or *5.12*, must be destroyed (together with any negatives and copies) unless the person:

(a) is charged with, or informed they may be prosecuted for, a recordable offence;

(b) is prosecuted for a recordable offence;

(c) is cautioned for a recordable offence or given a warning or reprimand in accordance with the Crime and Disorder Act 1998 for a recordable offence; or

(d) gives informed consent, in writing, for the photograph or image to be retained as in *paragraph 5.6*.

5.23 When *paragraph 5.22* requires the destruction of any photograph, the person must be given an opportunity to witness the destruction or to have a certificate confirming the destruction provided they so request the certificate within five days of being informed the destruction is required.

5.24 Nothing in *paragraph 5.22* affects any separate requirement under the Criminal Procedure and Investigations Act 1996 to retain material in connection with criminal investigations.

Notes for guidance

5A The conditions under which fingerprints may be taken to assist in establishing a person's identity, are described in Section 4.

5B Examples of purposes related to the prevention or detection of crime, the investigation of offences or the conduct of prosecutions include:

    (*a*) *checking the photograph against other photographs held in records or in connection with, or as a result of, an investigation of an offence to establish whether the person is liable to arrest for other offences;*

    (*b*) *when the person is arrested at the same time as other people, or at a time when it is likely that other people will be arrested, using the photograph to help establish who was arrested, at what time and where;*

    (*c*) *when the real identity of the person is not known and cannot be readily ascertained or there are reasonable grounds for doubting a name and other personal details given by the person, are their real name and personal details. In these circumstances, using or disclosing the photograph to help to establish or verify their real identity or determine whether they are liable to arrest for some other offence, e.g. by checking it against other photographs held in records or in connection with, or as a result of, an investigation of an offence;*

    (*d*) *when it appears any identification procedure in section 3 may need to be arranged for which the person's photograph would assist;*

    (*e*) *when the person's release without charge may be required, and if the release is:*

        (i) *on bail to appear at a police station, using the photograph to help verify the person's identity when they answer their bail and if the person does not answer their bail, to assist in arresting them; or*

        (ii) *without bail, using the photograph to help verify their identity or assist in locating them for the purposes of serving them with a summons to appear at court in criminal proceedings;*

    (*f*) *when the person has answered to bail at a police station and there are reasonable grounds for doubting they are the person who was previously granted bail, using the photograph to help establish or verify their identity;*

    (*g*) *when the person arrested on a warrant claims to be a different person from the person named on the warrant and a photograph would help to confirm or disprove their claim;*

    (*h*) *when the person has been charged with, reported for, or convicted of, a recordable offence and their photograph is not already on record as a result of (a) to (f) or their photograph is on record but their appearance has changed since it was taken and the person has not yet been released or brought before a court.*

5C There is no power to arrest a person convicted of a recordable offence solely to take their photograph. The power to take photographs in this section applies only where the person is in custody as a result of the exercise of another power, e.g. arrest for fingerprinting under PACE, section 27.

5D Examples of when it would not be practicable to obtain a detainee's consent, see paragraph 2.12, to a search, examination or the taking of a photograph of an identifying mark include:

    (*a*) *when the person is drunk or otherwise unfit to give consent;*

    (*b*) *when there are reasonable grounds to suspect that if the person became aware a search or examination was to take place or an identifying mark was to be photographed, they would take steps to prevent this happening, e.g. by violently resisting, covering or concealing the mark etc and it would not otherwise be possible to carry out the search or examination or to photograph any identifying mark;*

    (*c*) *in the case of a juvenile, if the parent or guardian cannot be contacted in sufficient time to allow the search or examination to be carried out or the photograph to be taken.*

5E Examples of when it would not be practicable to obtain the person's consent, see paragraph 2.12, to a photograph being taken include:

(a) *when the person is drunk or otherwise unfit to give consent;*

(b) *when there are reasonable grounds to suspect that if the person became aware a photograph, suitable to be used or disclosed for the use and disclosure described in paragraph 5.6, was to be taken, they would take steps to prevent it being taken, e.g. by violently resisting, covering or distorting their face etc, and it would not otherwise be possible to take a suitable photograph;*

(c) *when, in order to obtain a suitable photograph, it is necessary to take it covertly; and*

(d) *in the case of a juvenile, if the parent or guardian cannot be contacted in sufficient time to allow the photograph to be taken.*

5F The use of reasonable force to take the photograph of a suspect elsewhere than at a police station must be carefully considered. In order to obtain a suspect's consent and co-operation to remove an item of religious headwear to take their photograph, a constable should consider whether in the circumstances of the situation the removal of the headwear and the taking of the photograph should be by an officer of the same sex as the person. It would be appropriate for these actions to be conducted out of public view.

6   Identification by body samples and impressions

(A) General

6.1 References to:

(a) an 'intimate sample' mean a dental impression or sample of blood, semen or any other tissue fluid, urine, or pubic hair, or a swab taken from any part of a person's genitals or from a person's body orifice other than the mouth;

(b) a 'non-intimate sample' means:

(i)   a sample of hair, other than pubic hair, which includes hair plucked with the root, see *Note 6A*;

(ii) a sample taken from a nail or from under a nail;

(iii) a swab taken from any part of a person's body other than a part from which a swab taken would be an intimate sample;

(iv) saliva;

(v) a skin impression which means any record, other than a fingerprint, which is a record, in any form and produced by any method, of the skin pattern and other physical characteristics or features of the whole, or any part of, a person's foot or of any other part of their body. 167

(B) Action

(a) Intimate samples

6.2 PACE, section 62, provides that intimate samples may be taken under:

(a) section 62(1), from a person in police detention only:

(i)   if a police officer of inspector rank or above has reasonable grounds to believe such an impression or sample will tend to confirm or disprove the suspect's involvement in a recordable offence, see *Note 4A*, and gives authorisation for a sample to be taken; and

(ii) with the suspect's written consent;

(b) section 62(1A), from a person not in police detention but from whom two or more non-intimate samples have been taken in the course of an investigation of an offence and the samples, though suitable, have proved insufficient if:

(i)   a police officer of inspector rank or above authorises it to be taken; and

(ii) the person concerned gives their written consent. See *Notes 6B* and *6C*

6.3 Before a suspect is asked to provide an intimate sample, they must be warned that if they refuse without good cause, their refusal may harm their case if it comes to trial, see *Note 6D*. If the suspect is in police detention and not legally represented, they must also be reminded of their entitlement to have free legal advice, see Code C, *paragraph 6.5*, and the reminder noted in the custody record. If *paragraph 6.2(b)* applies and the person is attending a station voluntarily, their entitlement to free legal advice as in Code C, *paragraph 3.21* shall be explained to them.

6.4 Dental impressions may only be taken by a registered dentist. Other intimate samples, except for samples of urine, may only be taken by a registered medical practitioner or registered nurse or registered paramedic.

(b) Non-intimate samples

6.5 A non-intimate sample may be taken from a detainee only with their written consent or if *paragraph 6.6* applies.

6.6 (a)   under section 63, a non-intimate sample may not be taken from a person without consent and the consent must be in writing

(aa) A non-intimate sample may be taken from a person without the appropriate consent in the following circumstances:

(i)   under section 63(2A) where the person is in police detention as a consequence of his arrest for a recordable offence and he has not had a non-intimate sample of the same type and from the same part of the body taken in the course of the investigation of the offence by the police or he has had such a sample taken but it proved insufficient.

(ii) Under section 63(3) (a) where he is being held in custody by the police on the authority of a court and an officer of at least the rank of inspector authorises it to be taken.

(b) under section 63(3A), from a person charged with a recordable offence or informed they will be reported for such an offence: and

(i)   that person has not had a non-intimate sample taken from them in the course of the investigation; or

(ii) if they have had a sample taken, it proved unsuitable or insufficient for the same form of analysis, see *Note 6B*; or

(c) under section 63(3B), from a person convicted of a recordable offence after the date on which that provision came into effect. PACE, section 63A, describes the circumstances in which a police officer may require a person convicted of a recordable offence to attend a police station for a non-intimate sample to be taken.

6.7 Reasonable force may be used, if necessary, to take a non-intimate sample from a person without their consent under the powers mentioned in *paragraph 6.6*.

6.8 Before any intimate sample is taken with consent or non-intimate sample is taken with, or without, consent, the person must be informed:

(a) of the reason for taking the sample;

(b) of the grounds on which the relevant authority has been given;

(c) that the sample or information derived from the sample may be retained and subject of a speculative search, see *Note 6E*, unless their destruction is required as in *Annex F*, Part A.

6.9 When clothing needs to be removed in circumstances likely to cause embarrassment to the person, no person of the opposite sex who is not a registered medical practitioner or registered health care professional shall be present, (unless in the case of a juvenile, mentally disordered or mentally vulnerable person, that person specifically requests the presence of an appropriate adult of the opposite sex who is readily available) nor shall anyone whose presence is unnecessary. However, in the case of a juvenile, this is subject to the overriding proviso that such a removal of clothing may take place in the absence of the appropriate adult only if the juvenile signifies, in their presence, that they prefer the adult's absence and they agree.

(c) Documentation

6.10 A record of the reasons for taking a sample or impression and, if applicable, of its destruction must be made as soon as practicable. If force is used, a record shall be made of the circumstances and those present. If written consent is given to the taking of a sample or impression, the fact must be recorded in writing.

6.11 A record must be made of a warning given as required by *paragraph 6.3*.

6.12 A record shall be made of the fact that a person has been informed as in *paragraph 6.8(c)* that samples may be subject of a speculative search.

Notes for guidance

6A When hair samples are taken for the purpose of DNA analysis (rather than for other purposes such as making a visual match), the suspect should be permitted a reasonable choice as to what part of the body the hairs are taken from. When hairs are plucked, they should be plucked individually, unless the suspect prefers otherwise and no more should be plucked than the person taking them reasonably considers necessary for a sufficient sample.

6B (a) An insufficient sample is one which is not sufficient either in quantity or quality to provide information for a particular form of analysis, such as DNA analysis. A sample may also be insufficient if enough information cannot be obtained from it by analysis because of loss, destruction, damage or contamination of the sample or as a result of an earlier, unsuccessful attempt at analysis.

(b) An unsuitable sample is one which, by its nature, is not suitable for a particular form of analysis.

6C Nothing in paragraph 6.2 prevents intimate samples being taken for elimination purposes with the consent of the person concerned but the provisions of paragraph 2.12 relating to the role of the appropriate adult, should be applied. Paragraph 6.2(b) does not, however, apply where the non-intimate samples were previously taken under the Terrorism Act 2000, Schedule 8, paragraph 10.

6D In warning a person who is asked to provide an intimate sample as in paragraph 6.3, the following form of words may be used:

'You do not have to provide this sample/allow this swab or impression to be taken, but I must warn you that if you refuse without good cause, your refusal may harm your case if it comes to trial.'

6E Fingerprints or a DNA sample and the information derived from it taken from a person arrested on suspicion of being involved in a recordable offence, or charged with such an offence, or informed they will be reported for such an offence, may be subject of a speculative search. This means they may be checked against other fingerprints and DNA records held by, or on behalf of, the police and other law enforcement authorities in or outside the UK or held in connection with, or as a result of, an investigation of an offence inside or outside the UK. Fingerprints and samples taken from any other person, e.g. a person suspected of committing a recordable offence but who has not been arrested, charged or informed they will be reported for it, may be subject to a speculative search only if the person consents in writing to their fingerprints being subject of such a search. The following is an example of a basic form of words:

'I consent to my fingerprints/DNA sample and information derived from it being retained and used only for purposes related to the prevention and detection of a crime, the investigation of an offence or the conduct of a prosecution either nationally or internationally.

I understand that this sample may be checked against other fingerprint/DNA records held by or on behalf of relevant law enforcement authorities, either nationally or internationally.

I understand that once I have given my consent for the sample to be retained and used I cannot withdraw this consent.'

See Annex F regarding the retention and use of fingerprints and samples taken with consent for elimination purposes.

6F Samples of urine and non-intimate samples taken in accordance with sections 63B and 63C of PACE may not be used for identification purposes in accordance with this Code. See Code C note for guidance 17D.

ANNEX A   VIDEO IDENTIFICATION

(a) General

1. The arrangements for obtaining and ensuring the availability of a suitable set of images to be used in a video identification must be the responsibility of an identification officer, who has no direct involvement with the case.

2. The set of images must include the suspect and at least eight other people who, so far as possible, resemble the suspect in age, general appearance and position in life. Only one suspect shall appear in any set unless there are two suspects of roughly similar appearance, in which case they may be shown together with at least twelve other people.

2A If the suspect has an unusual physical feature, e.g., a facial scar, tattoo or distinctive hairstyle or hair colour which does not appear on the images of the other people that are available to be used, steps may be taken to:

(a) conceal the location of the feature on the images of the suspect and the other people; or

(b) replicate that feature on the images of the other people.

For these purposes, the feature may be concealed or replicated electronically or by any other method which it is practicable to use to ensure that the images of the suspect and other people resemble each other. The identification officer has discretion to choose whether to conceal or replicate the feature and the method to be used. If an unusual physical feature has been described by the witness, the identification officer should, if practicable, have that feature replicated. If it has not been described, concealment may be more appropriate.

2B If the identification officer decides that a feature should be concealed or replicated, the reason for the decision and whether the feature was concealed or replicated in the images shown to any witness shall be recorded.

2C If the witness requests to view an image where an unusual physical feature has been concealed or replicated without the feature being concealed or replicated, the witness may be allowed to do so.

3. The images used to conduct a video identification shall, as far as possible, show the suspect and other people in the same positions or carrying out the same sequence of movements. They shall also show the suspect and other people under identical conditions unless the identification officer reasonably believes:

(a) because of the suspect's failure or refusal to co-operate or other reasons, it is not practicable for the conditions to be identical; and

(b) any difference in the conditions would not direct a witness' attention to any individual image.

4. The reasons identical conditions are not practicable shall be recorded on forms provided for the purpose.

5. Provision must be made for each person shown to be identified by number.

6. If police officers are shown, any numerals or other identifying badges must be concealed. If a prison inmate is shown, either as a suspect or not, then either all, or none, of the people shown should be in prison clothing.

7. The suspect or their solicitor, friend, or appropriate adult must be given a reasonable opportunity to see the complete set of images before it is shown to any witness. If the suspect has a reasonable objection to the set of images or any of the participants, the suspect shall be

asked to state the reasons for the objection. Steps shall, if practicable, be taken to remove the grounds for objection. If this is not practicable, the suspect and/or their representative shall be told why their objections cannot be met and the objection, the reason given for it and why it cannot be met shall be recorded on forms provided for the purpose.

8. Before the images are shown in accordance with *paragraph 7*, the suspect or their solicitor shall be provided with details of the first description of the suspect by any witnesses who are to attend the video identification. When a broadcast or publication is made, as in *paragraph 3.28*, the suspect or their solicitor must also be allowed to view any material released to the media by the police for the purpose of recognising or tracing the suspect, provided it is practicable and would not unreasonably delay the investigation.

9. The suspect's solicitor, if practicable, shall be given reasonable notification of the time and place the video identification is to be conducted so a representative may attend on behalf of the suspect. If a solicitor has not been instructed, this information shall be given to the suspect. The suspect may not be present when the images are shown to the witness(es). In the absence of the suspect's representative, the viewing itself shall be recorded on video. No unauthorised people may be present.

(b) Conducting the video identification

10. The identification officer is responsible for making the appropriate arrangements to make sure, before they see the set of images, witnesses are not able to communicate with each other about the case, see any of the images which are to be shown, see, or be reminded of, any photograph or description of the suspect or be given any other indication as to the suspect's identity, or overhear a witness who has already seen the material. There must be no discussion with the witness about the composition of the set of images and they must not be told whether a previous witness has made any identification.

11. Only one witness may see the set of images at a time. Immediately before the images are shown, the witness shall be told that the person they saw on a specified earlier occasion may, or may not, appear in the images they are shown and that if they cannot make a positive identification, they should say so. The witness shall be advised that at any point, they may ask to see a particular part of the set of images or to have a particular image frozen for them to study. Furthermore, it should be pointed out to the witness that there is no limit on how many times they can view the whole set of images or any part of them. However, they should be asked not to make any decision as to whether the person they saw is on the set of images until they have seen the whole set at least twice.

12. Once the witness has seen the whole set of images at least twice and has indicated that they do not want to view the images, or any part of them, again, the witness shall be asked to say whether the individual they saw in person on a specified earlier occasion has been shown and, if so, to identify them by number of the image. The witness will then be shown that image to confirm the identification, see *paragraph 17*.

13. Care must be taken not to direct the witness' attention to any one individual image or give any indication of the suspect's identity. Where a witness has previously made an identification by photographs, or a computerised or artist's composite or similar likeness, the witness must not be reminded of such a photograph or composite likeness once a suspect is available for identification by other means in accordance with this Code. Nor must the witness be reminded of any description of the suspect.

14. After the procedure, each witness shall be asked whether they have seen any broadcast or published films or photographs, or any descriptions of suspects relating to the offence and their reply shall be recorded.

(c) Image security and destruction

15. Arrangements shall be made for all relevant material containing sets of images used for specific identification procedures to be kept securely and their movements accounted for.

In particular, no-one involved in the investigation shall be permitted to view the material prior to it being shown to any witness.

16. As appropriate, *paragraph 3.30* or *3.31* applies to the destruction or retention of relevant sets of images.

(d) Documentation

17. A record must be made of all those participating in, or seeing, the set of images whose names are known to the police.

18. A record of the conduct of the video identification must be made on forms provided for the purpose. This shall include anything said by the witness about any identifications or the conduct of the procedure and any reasons it was not practicable to comply with any of the provisions of this Code governing the conduct of video identifications.

ANNEX B   IDENTIFICATION PARADES

(a) General

1. A suspect must be given a reasonable opportunity to have a solicitor or friend present, and the suspect shall be asked to indicate on a second copy of the notice whether or not they wish to do so.

2. An identification parade may take place either in a normal room or one equipped with a screen permitting witnesses to see members of the identification parade without being seen. The procedures for the composition and conduct of the identification parade are the same in both cases, subject to *paragraph 8* (except that an identification parade involving a screen may take place only when the suspect's solicitor, friend or appropriate adult is present or the identification parade is recorded on video).

3. Before the identification parade takes place, the suspect or their solicitor shall be provided with details of the first description of the suspect by any witnesses who are attending the identification parade. When a broadcast or publication is made as in *paragraph 3.28*, the suspect or their solicitor should also be allowed to view any material released to the media by the police for the purpose of recognising or tracing the suspect, provided it is practicable to do so and would not unreasonably delay the investigation.

(b) Identification parades involving prison inmates

4. If a prison inmate is required for identification, and there are no security problems about the person leaving the establishment, they may be asked to participate in an identification parade or video identification.

5. An identification parade may be held in a Prison Department establishment but shall be conducted, as far as practicable under normal identification parade rules. Members of the public shall make up the identification parade unless there are serious security, or control, objections to their admission to the establishment. In such cases, or if a group or video identification is arranged within the establishment, other inmates may participate. If an inmate is the suspect, they are not required to wear prison clothing for the identification parade unless the other people taking part are other inmates in similar clothing, or are members of the public who are prepared to wear prison clothing for the occasion.

(c) Conduct of the identification parade

6. Immediately before the identification parade, the suspect must be reminded of the procedures governing its conduct and cautioned in the terms of Code C, paragraphs 10.5 or 10.6, as appropriate.

7. All unauthorised people must be excluded from the place where the identification parade is held.

8. Once the identification parade has been formed, everything afterwards, in respect of it, shall take place in the presence and hearing of the suspect and any interpreter, solicitor, friend or appropriate adult who is present (unless the identification parade involves a screen, in which case everything said to, or by, any witness at the place where the identification parade is held, must be said in the hearing and presence of the suspect's solicitor, friend or appropriate adult or be recorded on video).

9. The identification parade shall consist of at least eight people (in addition to the suspect) who, so far as possible, resemble the suspect in age, height, general appearance and position in life. Only one suspect shall be included in an identification parade unless there are two suspects of roughly similar appearance, in which case they may be paraded together with at least twelve other people. In no circumstances shall more than two suspects be included in one identification parade and where there are separate identification parades, they shall be made up of different people.

10. If the suspect has an unusual physical feature, e.g., a facial scar, tattoo or distinctive hairstyle or hair colour which cannot be replicated on other members of the identification parade, steps may be taken to conceal the location of that feature on the suspect and the other members of the identification parade if the suspect and their solicitor, or appropriate adult, agree. For example, by use of a plaster or a hat, so that all members of the identification parade resemble each other in general appearance.

11. When all members of a similar group are possible suspects, separate identification parades shall be held for each unless there are two suspects of similar appearance when they may appear on the same identification parade with at least twelve other members of the group who are not suspects. When police officers in uniform form an identification parade any numerals or other identifying badges shall be concealed.

12. When the suspect is brought to the place where the identification parade is to be held, they shall be asked if they have any objection to the arrangements for the identification parade or to any of the other participants in it and to state the reasons for the objection. The suspect may obtain advice from their solicitor or friend, if present, before the identification parade proceeds. If the suspect has a reasonable objection to the arrangements or any of the participants, steps shall, if practicable, be taken to remove the grounds for objection. When it is not practicable to do so, the suspect shall be told why their objections cannot be met and the objection, the reason given for it and why it cannot be met, shall be recorded on forms provided for the purpose.

13. The suspect may select their own position in the line, but may not otherwise interfere with the order of the people forming the line. When there is more than one witness, the suspect must be told, after each witness has left the room, that they can, if they wish, change position in the line. Each position in the line must be clearly numbered, whether by means of a number laid on the floor in front of each identification parade member or by other means.

14. Appropriate arrangements must be made to make sure, before witnesses attend the identification parade, they are not able to:
(i)   communicate with each other about the case or overhear a witness who has already seen the identification parade;
(ii) see any member of the identification parade;
(iii) see, or be reminded of, any photograph or description of the suspect or be given any other indication as to the suspect's identity; or
(iv) see the suspect before or after the identification parade.

15. The person conducting a witness to an identification parade must not discuss with them the composition of the identification parade and, in particular, must not disclose whether a previous witness has made any identification.

16. Witnesses shall be brought in one at a time. Immediately before the witness inspects the identification parade, they shall be told the person they saw on a specified earlier

occasion may, or may not, be present and if they cannot make a positive identification, they should say so. The witness must also be told they should not make any decision about whether the person they saw is on the identification parade until they have looked at each member at least twice.

17. When the officer or police staff (see paragraph 3.11) conducting the identification procedure is satisfied the witness has properly looked at each member of the identification parade, they shall ask the witness whether the person they saw on a specified earlier occasion is on the identification parade and, if so, to indicate the number of the person concerned, see *paragraph 28*.

18. If the witness wishes to hear any identification parade member speak, adopt any specified posture or move, they shall first be asked whether they can identify any person(s) on the identification parade on the basis of appearance only. When the request is to hear members of the identification parade speak, the witness shall be reminded that the participants in the identification parade have been chosen on the basis of physical appearance only. Members of the identification parade may then be asked to comply with the witness' request to hear them speak, see them move or adopt any specified posture.

19. If the witness requests that the person they have indicated remove anything used for the purposes of *paragraph 10* to conceal the location of an unusual physical feature, that person may be asked to remove it.

20. If the witness makes an identification after the identification parade has ended, the suspect and, if present, their solicitor, interpreter or friend shall be informed. When this occurs, consideration should be given to allowing the witness a second opportunity to identify the suspect.

21. After the procedure, each witness shall be asked whether they have seen any broadcast or published films or photographs or any descriptions of suspects relating to the offence and their reply shall be recorded.

22. When the last witness has left, the suspect shall be asked whether they wish to make any comments on the conduct of the identification parade.

(d) Documentation

23. A video recording must normally be taken of the identification parade. If that is impracticable, a colour photograph must be taken. A copy of the video recording or photograph shall be supplied, on request, to the suspect or their solicitor within a reasonable time.

24. As appropriate, *paragraph 3.30* or *3.31*, should apply to any photograph or video taken as in *paragraph 23*.

25. If any person is asked to leave an identification parade because they are interfering with its conduct, the circumstances shall be recorded.

26. A record must be made of all those present at an identification parade whose names are known to the police.

27. If prison inmates make up an identification parade, the circumstances must be recorded.

28. A record of the conduct of any identification parade must be made on forms provided for the purpose. This shall include anything said by the witness or the suspect about any identifications or the conduct of the procedure, and any reasons it was not practicable to comply with any of this Code's provisions.

ANNEX C   GROUP IDENTIFICATION

(a) General

1. The purpose of this Annex is to make sure, as far as possible, group identifications follow the principles and procedures for identification parades so the conditions are fair to the suspect in the way they test the witness' ability to make an identification.

2. Group identifications may take place either with the suspect's consent and cooperation or covertly without their consent.

3. The location of the group identification is a matter for the identification officer, although the officer may take into account any representations made by the suspect, appropriate adult, their solicitor or friend.

4. The place where the group identification is held should be one where other people are either passing by or waiting around informally, in groups such that the suspect is able to join them and be capable of being seen by the witness at the same time as others in the group. For example people leaving an escalator, pedestrians walking through a shopping centre, passengers on railway and bus stations, waiting in queues or groups or where people are standing or sitting in groups in other public places.

5. If the group identification is to be held covertly, the choice of locations will be limited by the places where the suspect can be found and the number of other people present at that time. In these cases, suitable locations might be along regular routes travelled by the suspect, including buses or trains or public places frequented by the suspect.

6. Although the number, age, sex, race and general description and style of clothing of other people present at the location cannot be controlled by the identification officer, in selecting the location the officer must consider the general appearance and numbers of people likely to be present. In particular, the officer must reasonably expect that over the period the witness observes the group, they will be able to see, from time to time, a number of others whose appearance is broadly similar to that of the suspect.

7. A group identification need not be held if the identification officer believes, because of the unusual appearance of the suspect, none of the locations it would be practicable to use satisfy the requirements of *paragraph 6* necessary to make the identification fair.

8. Immediately after a group identification procedure has taken place (with or without the suspect's consent), a colour photograph or video should be taken of the general scene, if practicable, to give a general impression of the scene and the number of people present. Alternatively, if it is practicable, the group identification may be video recorded.

9. If it is not practicable to take the photograph or video in accordance with *paragraph 8*, a photograph or film of the scene should be taken later at a time determined by the identification officer if the officer considers it practicable to do so.

10. An identification carried out in accordance with this Code remains a group identification even though, at the time of being seen by the witness, the suspect was on their own rather than in a group.

11. Before the group identification takes place, the suspect or their solicitor shall be provided with details of the first description of the suspect by any witnesses who are to attend the identification. When a broadcast or publication is made, as in *paragraph 3.28*, the suspect or their solicitor should also be allowed to view any material released by the police to the media for the purposes of recognising or tracing the suspect, provided that it is practicable and would not unreasonably delay the investigation.

12. After the procedure, each witness shall be asked whether they have seen any broadcast or published films or photographs or any descriptions of suspects relating to the offence and their reply recorded.

(b) Identification with the consent of the suspect

13. A suspect must be given a reasonable opportunity to have a solicitor or friend present. They shall be asked to indicate on a second copy of the notice whether or not they wish to do so.

14. The witness, the person carrying out the procedure and the suspect's solicitor, appropriate adult, friend or any interpreter for the witness, may be concealed from the sight of the individuals in the group they are observing, if the person carrying out the procedure considers this assists the conduct of the identification.

15. The person conducting a witness to a group identification must not discuss with them the forthcoming group identification and, in particular, must not disclose whether a previous witness has made any identification.

16. Anything said to, or by, the witness during the procedure about the identification should be said in the presence and hearing of those present at the procedure.

17. Appropriate arrangements must be made to make sure, before witnesses attend the group identification, they are not able to:

    (i)   communicate with each other about the case or overhear a witness who has already been given an opportunity to see the suspect in the group;

    (ii) see the suspect; or

    (iii) see, or be reminded of, any photographs or description of the suspect or be given any other indication of the suspect's identity.

18. Witnesses shall be brought one at a time to the place where they are to observe the group. Immediately before the witness is asked to look at the group, the person conducting the procedure shall tell them that the person they saw may, or may not, be in the group and that if they cannot make a positive identification, they should say so. The witness shall be asked to observe the group in which the suspect is to appear.

The way in which the witness should do this will depend on whether the group is moving or stationary.

Moving group

19. When the group in which the suspect is to appear is moving, e.g. leaving an escalator, the provisions of *paragraphs 20 to 24* should be followed.

20. If two or more suspects consent to a group identification, each should be the subject of separate identification procedures. These may be conducted consecutively on the same occasion.

21. The person conducting the procedure shall tell the witness to observe the group and ask them to point out any person they think they saw on the specified earlier occasion.

22. Once the witness has been informed as in *paragraph 21* the suspect should be allowed to take whatever position in the group they wish.

23. When the witness points out a person as in *paragraph 21* they shall, if practicable, be asked to take a closer look at the person to confirm the identification. If this is not practicable, or they cannot confirm the identification, they shall be asked how sure they are that the person they have indicated is the relevant person.

24. The witness should continue to observe the group for the period which the person conducting the procedure reasonably believes is necessary in the circumstances for them to be able to make comparisons between the suspect and other individuals of broadly similar appearance to the suspect as in *paragraph 6*.

Stationary groups

25. When the group in which the suspect is to appear is stationary, e.g. people waiting in a queue, the provisions of *paragraphs 26 to 29* should be followed.

26. If two or more suspects consent to a group identification, each should be subject to separate identification procedures unless they are of broadly similar appearance when they may appear in the same group. When separate group identifications are held, the groups must be made up of different people.

27. The suspect may take whatever position in the group they wish. If there is more than one witness, the suspect must be told, out of the sight and hearing of any witness, that they can, if they wish, change their position in the group.

28. The witness shall be asked to pass along, or amongst, the group and to look at each person in the group at least twice, taking as much care and time as possible according to the circumstances, before making an identification. Once the witness has done this, they shall be asked whether the person they saw on the specified earlier occasion is in the group and to

indicate any such person by whatever means the person conducting the procedure considers appropriate in the circumstances. If this is not practicable, the witness shall be asked to point out any person they think they saw on the earlier occasion.

29. When the witness makes an indication as in *paragraph 28*, arrangements shall be made, if practicable, for the witness to take a closer look at the person to confirm the identification. If this is not practicable, or the witness is unable to confirm the identification, they shall be asked how sure they are that the person they have indicated is the relevant person.

All cases

30. If the suspect unreasonably delays joining the group, or having joined the group, deliberately conceals themselves from the sight of the witness, this may be treated as a refusal to co-operate in a group identification.

31. If the witness identifies a person other than the suspect, that person should be informed what has happened and asked if they are prepared to give their name and address. There is no obligation upon any member of the public to give these details.

There shall be no duty to record any details of any other member of the public present in the group or at the place where the procedure is conducted.

32. When the group identification has been completed, the suspect shall be asked whether they wish to make any comments on the conduct of the procedure.

33. If the suspect has not been previously informed, they shall be told of any identifications made by the witnesses.

(c) Identification without the suspect's consent

34. Group identifications held covertly without the suspect's consent should, as far as practicable, follow the rules for conduct of group identification by consent.

35. A suspect has no right to have a solicitor, appropriate adult or friend present as the identification will take place without the knowledge of the suspect.

36. Any number of suspects may be identified at the same time.

(d) Identifications in police stations

37. Group identifications should only take place in police stations for reasons of safety, security or because it is not practicable to hold them elsewhere.

38. The group identification may take place either in a room equipped with a screen permitting witnesses to see members of the group without being seen, or anywhere else in the police station that the identification officer considers appropriate.

39. Any of the additional safeguards applicable to identification parades should be followed if the identification officer considers it is practicable to do so in the circumstances.

(e) Identifications involving prison inmates

40. A group identification involving a prison inmate may only be arranged in the prison or at a police station.

41. When a group identification takes place involving a prison inmate, whether in a prison or in a police station, the arrangements should follow those in *paragraphs 37 to 39*. If a group identification takes place within a prison, other inmates may participate. If an inmate is the suspect, they do not have to wear prison clothing for the group identification unless the other participants are wearing the same clothing.

(f) Documentation

42. When a photograph or video is taken as in *paragraph 8 or 9*, a copy of the photograph or video shall be supplied on request to the suspect or their solicitor within a reasonable time.

43. *Paragraph 3.30* or *3.31*, as appropriate, shall apply when the photograph or film taken in accordance with *paragraph 8* or *9* includes the suspect.

44. A record of the conduct of any group identification must be made on forms provided for the purpose. This shall include anything said by the witness or suspect about any identifications or the conduct of the procedure and any reasons why it was not practicable to comply with any of the provisions of this Code governing the conduct of group identifications.

ANNEX D   CONFRONTATION BY A WITNESS

1. Before the confrontation takes place, the witness must be told that the person they saw may, or may not, be the person they are to confront and that if they are not that person, then the witness should say so.

2. Before the confrontation takes place the suspect or their solicitor shall be provided with details of the first description of the suspect given by any witness who is to attend. When a broadcast or publication is made, as in *paragraph 3.28*, the suspect or their solicitor should also be allowed to view any material released to the media for the purposes of recognising or tracing the suspect, provided it is practicable to do so and would not unreasonably delay the investigation.

3. Force may not be used to make the suspect's face visible to the witness.

4. Confrontation must take place in the presence of the suspect's solicitor, interpreter or friend unless this would cause unreasonable delay.

5. The suspect shall be confronted independently by each witness, who shall be asked 'Is this the person?'. If the witness identifies the person but is unable to confirm the identification, they shall be asked how sure they are that the person is the one they saw on the earlier occasion.

6. The confrontation should normally take place in the police station, either in a normal room or one equipped with a screen permitting a witness to see the suspect without being seen. In both cases, the procedures are the same except that a room equipped with a screen may be used only when the suspect's solicitor, friend or appropriate adult is present or the confrontation is recorded on video.

7. After the procedure, each witness shall be asked whether they have seen any broadcast or published films or photographs or any descriptions of suspects relating to the offence and their reply shall be recorded.

ANNEX E   SHOWING PHOTOGRAPHS

(a) Action

1. An officer of sergeant rank or above shall be responsible for supervising and directing the showing of photographs. The actual showing may be done by another officer or police staff, see *paragraph 3.11*.

2. The supervising officer must confirm the first description of the suspect given by the witness has been recorded before they are shown the photographs. If the supervising officer is unable to confirm the description has been recorded they shall postpone showing the photographs.

3. Only one witness shall be shown photographs at any one time. Each witness shall be given as much privacy as practicable and shall not be allowed to communicate with any other witness in the case.

4. The witness shall be shown not less than twelve photographs at a time, which shall, as far as possible, all be of a similar type.

5. When the witness is shown the photographs, they shall be told the photograph of the person they saw may, or may not, be amongst them and if they cannot make a positive

identification, they should say so. The witness shall also be told they should not make a decision until they have viewed at least twelve photographs. The witness shall not be prompted or guided in any way but shall be left to make any selection without help.

6. If a witness makes a positive identification from photographs, unless the person identified is otherwise eliminated from enquiries or is not available, other witnesses shall not be shown photographs. But both they, and the witness who has made the identification, shall be asked to attend a video identification, an identification parade or group identification unless there is no dispute about the suspect's identification.

7. If the witness makes a selection but is unable to confirm the identification, the person showing the photographs shall ask them how sure they are that the photograph they have indicated is the person they saw on the specified earlier occasion.

8. When the use of a computerised or artist's composite or similar likeness has led to there being a known suspect who can be asked to participate in a video identification, appear on an identification parade or participate in a group identification, that likeness shall not be shown to other potential witnesses.

9. When a witness attending a video identification, an identification parade or group identification has previously been shown photographs or computerised or artist's composite or similar likeness (and it is the responsibility of the officer in charge of the investigation to make the identification officer aware that this is the case), the suspect and their solicitor must be informed of this fact before the identification procedure takes place.

10. None of the photographs shown shall be destroyed, whether or not an identification is made, since they may be required for production in court. The photographs shall be numbered and a separate photograph taken of the frame or part of the album from which the witness made an identification as an aid to reconstituting it.

(b) Documentation

11. Whether or not an identification is made, a record shall be kept of the showing of photographs on forms provided for the purpose. This shall include anything said by the witness about any identification or the conduct of the procedure, any reasons it was not practicable to comply with any of the provisions of this Code governing the showing of photographs and the name and rank of the supervising officer.

12. The supervising officer shall inspect and sign the record as soon as practicable.

ANNEX F   FINGERPRINTS, FOOTWEAR IMPRESSIONS AND SAMPLES — DESTRUCTION AND SPECULATIVE SEARCHES

(a) Fingerprints, footwear impressions and samples taken in connection with a criminal investigation

1. When fingerprints, footwear impressions or DNA samples are taken from a person in connection with an investigation and the person is not suspected of having committed the offence, see *Note F1*, they must be destroyed as soon as they have fulfilled the purpose for which they were taken unless:

    (a) they were taken for the purposes of an investigation of an offence for which a person has been convicted; and

    (b) fingerprints, footwear impressions or samples were also taken from the convicted person for the purposes of that investigation.

However, subject to *paragraph 2*, the fingerprints, footwear impressions and samples, and the information derived from samples, may not be used in the investigation of any offence or in evidence against the person who is, or would be, entitled to the destruction of the fingerprints, footwear impressions and samples, see *Note F2*.

2. The requirement to destroy fingerprints, footwear impressions and DNA samples, and information derived from samples, and restrictions on their retention and use in paragraph 1

do not apply if the person gives their written consent for their fingerprints, footwear impressions or sample to be retained and used after they have fulfilled the purpose for which they were taken, see *Note F1*.

3 When a person's fingerprints, footwear impressions or sample are to be destroyed:
  (a) any copies of the fingerprints and footwear impressions must also be destroyed;
  (b) the person may witness the destruction of their fingerprints, footwear impressions or copies if they ask to do so within five days of being informed destruction is required;
  (c) access to relevant computer fingerprint data shall be made impossible as soon as it is practicable to do so and the person shall be given a certificate to this effect within three months of asking; and
  (d) neither the fingerprints, footwear impressions, the sample, or any information derived from the sample, may be used in the investigation of any offence or in evidence against the person who is, or would be, entitled to its destruction.

4. Fingerprints, footwear impressions or samples, and the information derived from samples, taken in connection with the investigation of an offence which are not required to be destroyed, may be retained after they have fulfilled the purposes for which they were taken but may be used only for purposes related to the prevention or detection of crime, the investigation of an offence or the conduct of a prosecution in, as well as outside, the UK and may also be subject to a speculative search. This includes checking them against other fingerprints, footwear impressions and DNA records held by, or on behalf of, the police and other law enforcement authorities in, as well as outside, the UK.

(b) Fingerprints taken in connection with Immigration Service enquiries

5. Fingerprints taken for Immigration Service enquiries in accordance with powers and procedures other than under PACE and for which the Immigration Service, not the police, are responsible, must be destroyed as follows:
  (a) fingerprints and all copies must be destroyed as soon as practicable if the person from whom they were taken proves they are a British or Commonwealth citizen who has the right of abode in the UK under the Immigration Act 1971, section 2(1)(b);
  (b) fingerprints taken under the power as in *paragraph 4.11(g)* from a dependant of a person in *4.11 (b)* to *(f)* must be destroyed when that person's fingerprints are to be destroyed;
  (c) fingerprints taken from a person under any power as in *paragraph 4.11* or with the person's consent which have not already been destroyed as above, must be destroyed within ten years of being taken or within such period specified by the Secretary of State under the Immigration and Asylum Act 1999, section 143(5).

Notes for guidance

F1 Fingerprints, footwear impressions and samples given voluntarily for the purposes of elimination play an important part in many police investigations. It is, therefore, important to make sure innocent volunteers are not deterred from participating and their consent to their fingerprints, footwear impressions and DNA being used for the purposes of a specific investigation is fully informed and voluntary. If the police or volunteer seek to have the fingerprints, footwear impressions or samples retained for use after the specific investigation ends, it is important the volunteer's consent to this is also fully informed and voluntary.
Examples of consent for:
  - *DNA/fingerprints/footwear impressions–to be used only for the purposes of a specific investigation;*
  - *DNA/fingerprints/footwear impressions–to be used in the specific investigation* **and** *retained by the police for future use.*

*To minimise the risk of confusion, each consent should be physically separate and the volunteer should be asked to sign **each consent.***

   (a) *DNA:*

      (i) *DNA sample taken for the purposes of elimination or as part of an intelligence-led screening and to be used only for the purposes of that investigation and destroyed afterwards:*

         '*I consent to my DNA/mouth swab being taken for forensic analysis. I understand that the sample will be destroyed at the end of the case and that my profile will only be compared to the crime stain profile from this enquiry. I have been advised that the person taking the sample may be required to give evidence and/or provide a written statement to the police in relation to the taking of it'.*

      (ii) *DNA sample to be retained on the National DNA database and used in the future:*

         '*I consent to my DNA sample and information derived from it being retained and used only for purposes related to the prevention and detection of a crime, the investigation of an offence or the conduct of a prosecution either nationally or internationally.'*

         '*I understand that this sample may be checked against other DNA records held by, or on behalf of, relevant law enforcement authorities, either nationally or internationally'.*

         '*I understand that once I have given my consent for the sample to be retained and used I cannot withdraw this consent.'*

   (b) *Fingerprints:*

      (i) *Fingerprints taken for the purposes of elimination or as part of an intelligence-led screening and to be used only for the purposes of that investigation and destroyed afterwards:*

         '*I consent to my fingerprints being taken for elimination purposes. I understand that the fingerprints will be destroyed at the end of the case and that my fingerprints will only be compared to the fingerprints from this enquiry. I have been advised that the person taking the fingerprints may be required to give evidence and/or provide a written statement to the police in relation to the taking of it.'*

      (ii) *Fingerprints to be retained for future use:*

         '*I consent to my fingerprints being retained and used only for purposes related to the prevention and detection of a crime, the investigation of an offence or the conduct of a prosecution either nationally or internationally'.*

         '*I understand that my fingerprints may be checked against other records held by, or on behalf of, relevant law enforcement authorities, either nationally or internationally.'*

         '*I understand that once I have given my consent for my fingerprints to be retained and used I cannot withdraw this consent.'*

   (c) *Footwear impressions:*

      (i) *Footwear impressions taken for the purposes of elimination or as part of an intelligence-led screening and to be used only for the purposes of that investigation and destroyed afterwards:*

         '*I consent to my footwear impressions being taken for elimination purposes. I understand that the footwear impressions will be destroyed at the end of the case and that my footwear impressions will only be compared to the footwear impressions from this enquiry. I have been advised that the person taking the footwear impressions may be required to give evidence and/or provide a written statement to the police in relation to the taking of it.'*

      (ii) *Footwear impressions to be retained for future use:*

         '*I consent to my footwear impressions being retained and used only for purposes related to the prevention and detection of a crime, the investigation of an offence or the conduct of a prosecution, either nationally or internationally'.*

         '*I understand that my footwear impressions may be checked against other records held by, or on behalf of, relevant law enforcement authorities, either nationally or internationally.'*

'I understand that once I have given my consent for my footwear impressions to be retained and used I cannot withdraw this consent.'

F2 *The provisions for the retention of fingerprints, footwear impressions and samples in paragraph 1 allow for all fingerprints, footwear impressions and samples in a case to be available for any subsequent miscarriage of justice investigation.*

Questioning

Police and Criminal Evidence Act 1984

58 Access to legal advice

(1) A person arrested and held in custody in a police station or other premises shall be entitled, if he so requests, to consult a solicitor privately at any time.

(2) Subject to subsection (3) below, a request under subsection (1) above and the time at which it was made shall be recorded in the custody record.

(3) Such a request need not be recorded in the custody record of a person who makes it at a time while he is at a court after being charged with an offence.

(4) If a person makes such a request, he must be permitted to consult a solicitor as soon as is practicable except to the extent that delay is permitted by this section.

(5) In any case he must be permitted to consult a solicitor within 36 hours from the relevant time, as defined in section 41(2) above.

(6) Delay in compliance with a request is only permitted—

    (a) in the case of a person who is in police detention for an indictable offence; and

    (b) if an officer of at least the rank of superintendent authorises it.

(7) An officer may give an authorisation under subsection (6) above orally or in writing but, if he gives it orally, he shall confirm it in writing as soon as is practicable.

(8) Subject to sub-section (8A) below an officer may only authorise delay where he has reasonable grounds for believing that the exercise of the right conferred by subsection (1) above at the time when the person detained desires to exercise it—

    (a) will lead to interference with or harm to evidence connected with an indictable offence or interference with or physical injury to other persons; or

    (b) will lead to the alerting of other persons suspected of having committed such an offence but not yet arrested for it; or

    (c) will hinder the recovery of any property obtained as a result of such an offence.

(8A) An officer may also authorise delay where he has reasonable grounds for believing that—

    (a) the person detained for [the indictable offence] has benefited from his criminal conduct, and

    (b) the recovery of the value of the property constituting the benefit will be hindered by the exercise of the right conferred by subsection (1) above.

(8B) For the purposes of subsection (8A) above the question whether a person has benefited from his criminal conduct is to be decided in accordance with Part 2 of the Proceeds of Crime Act 2002.

(9) If delay is authorised—

    (a) the detained person shall be told the reason for it; and

    (b) the reason shall be noted on his custody record.

(10) The duties imposed by subsection (9) above shall be performed as soon as is practicable.

(11) There may be no further delay in permitting the exercise of the right conferred by subsection (1) above once the reason for authorising delay ceases to subsist.

(12) Nothing in this section applies to a person arrested or detained under the terrorism provisions.

Criminal Justice Act 2003

22   Conditional cautions

(1) An authorised person may give a conditional caution to a person aged 18 or over ('the offender') if each of the five requirements in section 23 is satisfied.

(2) In this Part 'conditional caution' means a caution which is given in respect of an offence committed by the offender and which has conditions attached to it with which the offender must comply.

(3) The conditions which may be attached to such a caution are those which have either or both of the following objects—

    (a) facilitating the rehabilitation of the offender,

    (b) ensuring that he makes reparation for the offence.

(4) In this Part 'authorised person' means—

    (a) a constable,

    (b) an investigating officer, or

    (c) a person authorised by a relevant prosecutor for the purposes of this section.

23   The five requirements

(1) The first requirement is that the authorised person has evidence that the offender has committed an offence.

(2) The second requirement is that a relevant prosecutor decides—

    (a) that there is sufficient evidence to charge the offender with the offence, and

    (b) that a conditional caution should be given to the offender in respect of the offence.

(3) The third requirement is that the offender admits to the authorised person that he committed the offence.

(4) The fourth requirement is that the authorised person explains the effect of the conditional caution to the offender and warns him that failure to comply with any of the conditions attached to the caution may result in his being prosecuted for the offence.

(5) The fifth requirement is that the offender signs a document which contains—

    (a) details of the offence,

    (b) an admission by him that he committed the offence,

    (c) his consent to being given the conditional caution, and

    (d) the conditions attached to the caution.

24   Failure to comply with conditions

(1) If the offender fails, without reasonable excuse, to comply with any of the conditions attached to the conditional caution, criminal proceedings may be instituted against the person for the offence in question.

(2) The document mentioned in section 23(5) is to be admissible in such proceedings.

(3) Where such proceedings are instituted, the conditional caution is to cease to have effect.

CODES OF PRACTICE, CODE C

10   Cautions

(a) When a caution must be given

10.1 A person whom there are grounds to suspect of an offence, see *Note 10A*, must be cautioned before any questions about an offence, or further questions if the answers provide the grounds for suspicion, are put to them if either the suspect's answers or silence, (i.e. failure or refusal to answer or answer satisfactorily) may be given in evidence to a court in a prosecution. A person need not be cautioned if questions are for other necessary purposes, e.g.:

    (a) solely to establish their identity or ownership of any vehicle;

    (b) to obtain information in accordance with any relevant statutory requirement, see
       paragraph 10.9;

(c) in furtherance of the proper and effective conduct of a search, e.g. to determine the need to search in the exercise of powers of stop and search or to seek cooperation while carrying out a search;

(d) to seek verification of a written record as in *paragraph 11.13*;

(e) when examining a person in accordance with the Terrorism Act 2000, Schedule 7 and the Code of Practice for Examining Officers issued under that Act, Schedule 14, paragraph 6.

10.2 Whenever a person not under arrest is initially cautioned, or reminded they are under caution, that person must at the same time be told they are not under arrest and are free to leave if they want to. See *Note 10C*

10.3 A person who is arrested, or further arrested, must be informed at the time, or as soon as practicable thereafter, that they are under arrest and the grounds for their arrest, see *paragraph 3.4, Note 10B* and *Code G, paragraphs 2.2* and *4.3*.

10.4 As per *Code G, section 3*, a person who is arrested, or further arrested, must also be cautioned unless:

(a) it is impracticable to do so by reason of their condition or behaviour at the time;

(b) they have already been cautioned immediately prior to arrest as in *paragraph 10.1*.

(b) Terms of the cautions

10.5 The caution which must be given on:

(a) arrest;

(b) all other occasions before a person is charged or informed they may be prosecuted, see *section 16*,

should, unless the restriction on drawing adverse inferences from silence applies, see *Annex C*, be in the following terms:

'You do not have to say anything. But it may harm your defence if you do not mention when questioned something which you later rely on in Court. Anything you do say may be given in evidence.'

See *Note 10G*

10.6 *Annex C, paragraph 2* sets out the alternative terms of the caution to be used when the restriction on drawing adverse inferences from silence applies.

10.7 Minor deviations from the words of any caution given in accordance with this Code do not constitute a breach of this Code, provided the sense of the relevant caution is preserved. See *Note 10D*

10.8 After any break in questioning under caution, the person being questioned must be made aware they remain under caution. If there is any doubt the relevant caution should be given again in full when the interview resumes. See *Note 10E*

10.9 When, despite being cautioned, a person fails to co-operate or to answer particular questions which may affect their immediate treatment, the person should be informed of any relevant consequences and that those consequences are not affected by the caution. Examples are when a person's refusal to provide:

• their name and address when charged may make them liable to detention;

• particulars and information in accordance with a statutory requirement, e.g. under the Road Traffic Act 1988, may amount to an offence or may make the person liable to a further arrest.

(c) Special warnings under the Criminal Justice and Public Order Act 1994, sections 36 and 37

10.10 When a suspect interviewed at a police station or authorised place of detention after arrest fails or refuses to answer certain questions, or to answer satisfactorily, after due warning, see *Note 10F*, a court or jury may draw such inferences as appear proper under the Criminal Justice and Public Order Act 1994, sections 36 and 37. Such inferences may only be drawn when:

    (a) the restriction on drawing adverse inferences from silence, see *Annex C*, does not apply; and

    (b) the suspect is arrested by a constable and fails or refuses to account for any objects, marks or substances, or marks on such objects found:

- on their person;
- in or on their clothing or footwear;
- otherwise in their possession; or
- in the place they were arrested;

    (c) the arrested suspect was found by a constable at a place at or about the time the offence for which that officer has arrested them is alleged to have been committed, and the suspect fails or refuses to account for their presence there.

When the restriction on drawing adverse inferences from silence applies, the suspect may still be asked to account for any of the matters in (*b*) or (*c*) but the special warning described in *paragraph 10.11* will not apply and must not be given.

10.11 For an inference to be drawn when a suspect fails or refuses to answer a question about one of these matters or to answer it satisfactorily, the suspect must first be told in ordinary language:

    (a) what offence is being investigated;

    (b) what fact they are being asked to account for;

    (c) this fact may be due to them taking part in the commission of the offence;

    (d) a court may draw a proper inference if they fail or refuse to account for this fact;

    (e) a record is being made of the interview and it may be given in evidence if they are brought to trial.

(d) Juveniles and persons who are mentally disordered or otherwise mentally vulnerable

10.12 If a juvenile or a person who is mentally disordered or otherwise mentally vulnerable is cautioned in the absence of the appropriate adult, the caution must be repeated in the adult's presence.

(e) Documentation

10.13 A record shall be made when a caution is given under this section, either in the interviewer's pocket book or in the interview record.

Notes for guidance

10A There must be some reasonable, objective grounds for the suspicion, based on known facts or information which are relevant to the likelihood the offence has been committed and the person to be questioned committed it.

10B An arrested person must be given sufficient information to enable them to understand that they have been deprived of their liberty and the reason they have been arrested, e.g. when a person is arrested on suspicion of committing an offence they must be informed of the suspected offence's nature, when and where it was committed. The suspect must also be informed of the reason or reasons why the arrest is considered necessary. Vague or technical language should be avoided.

10C The restriction on drawing inferences from silence, see Annex C, paragraph 1, does not apply to a person who has not been detained and who therefore cannot be prevented from seeking legal advice if they want, see paragraph 3.21.

10D If it appears a person does not understand the caution, the person giving it should explain it in their own words.

10E It may be necessary to show to the court that nothing occurred during an interview break or between interviews which influenced the suspect's recorded evidence. After a break in an interview or at the beginning of a subsequent interview, the interviewing officer should summarise the reason for the break and confirm this with the suspect.

10F The Criminal Justice and Public Order Act 1994, sections 36 and 37 apply only to suspects who have been arrested by a constable or Customs and Excise officer and are given the relevant warning by the police or customs officer who made the arrest or who is investigating the offence. They do not apply to any interviews with suspects who have not been arrested.

10G Nothing in this Code requires a caution to be given or repeated when informing a person not under arrest they may be prosecuted for an offence. However, a court will not be able to draw any inferences under the Criminal Justice and Public Order Act 1994, section 34, if the person was not cautioned.

11 Interviews—general

(a) Action

11.1A An interview is the questioning of a person regarding their involvement or suspected involvement in a criminal offence or offences which, under *paragraph 10.1*, must be carried out under caution. Whenever a person is interviewed they must be informed of the nature of the offence, or further offence. Procedures under the Road Traffic Act 1988, section 7 or the Transport and Works Act 1992, section 31 do not constitute interviewing for the purpose of this Code.

11.1 Following a decision to arrest a suspect, they must not be interviewed about the relevant offence except at a police station or other authorised place of detention, unless the consequent delay would be likely to:

    (a) lead to:
- interference with, or harm to, evidence connected with an offence;
- interference with, or physical harm to, other people; or
- serious loss of, or damage to, property;

    (b) lead to alerting other people suspected of committing an offence but not yet arrested for it; or

    (c) hinder the recovery of property obtained in consequence of the commission of an offence.

Interviewing in any of these circumstances shall cease once the relevant risk has been averted or the necessary questions have been put in order to attempt to avert that risk.

11.2 Immediately prior to the commencement or re-commencement of any interview at a police station or other authorised place of detention, the interviewer should remind the suspect of their entitlement to free legal advice and that the interview can be delayed for legal advice to be obtained, unless one of the exceptions in *paragraph 6.6* applies. It is the interviewer's responsibility to make sure all reminders are recorded in the interview record.

11.3 Not Used

11.4 At the beginning of an interview the interviewer, after cautioning the suspect, see *section 10*, shall put to them any significant statement or silence which occurred in the presence and hearing of a police officer or other police staff before the start of the interview and which have not been put to the suspect in the course of a previous interview. See *Note 11A*. The interviewer shall ask the suspect whether they confirm or deny that earlier statement or silence and if they want to add anything.

11.4A A significant statement is one which appears capable of being used in evidence against the suspect, in particular a direct admission of guilt. A significant silence is a failure or refusal to answer a question or answer satisfactorily when under caution, which might, allowing for the restriction on drawing adverse inferences from silence, see *Annex C*, give rise to an inference under the Criminal Justice and Public Order Act 1994, Part III,

11.5 No interviewer may try to obtain answers or elicit a statement by the use of oppression. Except as in *paragraph 10.9*, no interviewer shall indicate, except to answer a direct question, what action will be taken by the police if the person being questioned answers questions, makes a statement or refuses to do either. If the person asks directly what action will be taken if they answer questions, make a statement or refuse to do either, the interviewer may inform them what action the police propose to take provided that action is itself proper and warranted.

11.6 The interview or further interview of a person about an offence with which that person has not been charged or for which they have not been informed they may be prosecuted, must cease when:

(a) the officer in charge of the investigation is satisfied all the questions they consider relevant to obtaining accurate and reliable information about the offence have been put to the suspect, this includes allowing the suspect an opportunity to give an innocent explanation and asking questions to test if the explanation is accurate and reliable, e.g. to clear up ambiguities or clarify what the suspect said;

(b) the officer in charge of the investigation has taken account of any other available evidence; and

(c) the officer in charge of the investigation, or in the case of a detained suspect, the custody officer, see paragraph 16.1, reasonably believes there is sufficient evidence to provide a realistic prospect of conviction for that offence. See Note 11B

This paragraph does not prevent officers in revenue cases or acting under the confiscation provisions of the Criminal Justice Act 1988 or the Drug Trafficking Act 1994 from inviting suspects to complete a formal question and answer record after the interview is concluded.

(b) Interview records

11.7 (a) An accurate record must be made of each interview, whether or not the interview takes place at a police station;

(b) The record must state the place of interview, the time it begins and ends, any interview breaks and, subject to *paragraph 2.6A*, the names of all those present; and must be made on the forms provided for this purpose or in the interviewer's pocket book or in accordance with the Codes of Practice E or F;

(c) Any written record must be made and completed during the interview, unless this would not be practicable or would interfere with the conduct of the interview, and must constitute either a verbatim record of what has been said or, failing this, an account of the interview which adequately and accurately summarises it.

11.8 If a written record is not made during the interview it must be made as soon as practicable after its completion.

11.9 Written interview records must be timed and signed by the maker.

11.10 If a written record is not completed during the interview the reason must be recorded in the interview record.

11.11 Unless it is impracticable, the person interviewed shall be given the opportunity to read the interview record and to sign it as correct or to indicate how they consider it inaccurate. If the person interviewed cannot read or refuses to read the record or sign it, the senior interviewer present shall read it to them and ask whether they would like to sign it as correct or make their mark or to indicate how they consider it inaccurate.

The interviewer shall certify on the interview record itself what has occurred. See *Note 11E*

11.12 If the appropriate adult or the person's solicitor is present during the interview, they should also be given an opportunity to read and sign the interview record or any written statement taken down during the interview.

11.13 A written record shall be made of any comments made by a suspect, including unsolicited comments, which are outside the context of an interview but which might be relevant to the offence. Any such record must be timed and signed by the maker.

When practicable the suspect shall be given the opportunity to read that record and to sign it as correct or to indicate how they consider it inaccurate. See *Note 11E*

11.14 Any refusal by a person to sign an interview record when asked in accordance with this Code must itself be recorded.

(c) Juveniles and mentally disordered or otherwise mentally vulnerable people

11.15 A juvenile or person who is mentally disordered or otherwise mentally vulnerable must not be interviewed regarding their involvement or suspected involvement in a criminal offence or offences, or asked to provide or sign a written statement under caution or record of interview, in the absence of the appropriate adult unless *paragraphs 11.1, 11.18 to 11.20* apply. See *Note 11C*

11.16 Juveniles may only be interviewed at their place of education in exceptional circumstances and only when the principal or their nominee agrees. Every effort should be made to notify the parent(s) or other person responsible for the juvenile's welfare and the appropriate adult, if this is a different person, that the police want to interview the juvenile and reasonable time should be allowed to enable the appropriate adult to be present at the interview. If awaiting the appropriate adult would cause unreasonable delay, and unless the juvenile is suspected of an offence against the educational establishment, the principal or their nominee can act as the appropriate adult for the purposes of the interview.

11.17 If an appropriate adult is present at an interview, they shall be informed:
- they are not expected to act simply as an observer; and
- the purpose of their presence is to:
  - — advise the person being interviewed;
  - — observe whether the interview is being conducted properly and fairly;
  - — facilitate communication with the person being interviewed.

(d) Vulnerable suspects—urgent interviews at police stations

11.18. The following persons may not be interviewed unless an officer of superintendent rank or above considers delay will lead to the consequences in *paragraph 11.1(a) to (c)*, and is satisfied the interview would not significantly harm the person's physical or mental state (see Annex G):
- (a) a juvenile or person who is mentally disordered or otherwise mentally vulnerable if at the time of the interview the appropriate adult is not present;
- (b) anyone other than in (*a*) who at the time of the interview appears unable to:
  - appreciate the significance of questions and their answers; or
  - understand what is happening because of the effects of drink, drugs or any illness, ailment or condition;
- (c) a person who has difficulty understanding English or has a hearing disability, if at the time of the interview an interpreter is not present.

11.19 These interviews may not continue once sufficient information has been obtained to avert the consequences in *paragraph 11.1(a) to (c)*.

11.20 A record shall be made of the grounds for any decision to interview a person under *paragraph 11.18*.

Notes for guidance

11A Paragraph 11.4 does not prevent the interviewer from putting significant statements and silences to a suspect again at a later stage or a further interview.

11B The Criminal Procedure and Investigations Act 1996 Code of Practice, paragraph 3.4 states 'In conducting an investigation, the investigator should pursue all reasonable lines of enquiry, whether these point towards or away from the suspect. What is reasonable will depend on the particular circumstances.' Interviewers should keep this in mind when deciding what questions to ask in an interview.

11C Although juveniles or people who are mentally disordered or otherwise mentally vulnerable are often capable of providing reliable evidence, they may, without knowing or wishing to do so, be particularly prone in certain circumstances to provide information that may be unreliable, misleading or self-incriminating. Special care should always be taken when questioning such a person, and the appropriate adult should be involved if there is any doubt about a person's age, mental state or capacity. Because of the risk of unreliable evidence it is also important to obtain corroboration of any facts admitted whenever possible.

11D Juveniles should not be arrested at their place of education unless this is unavoidable. When a juvenile is arrested at their place of education, the principal or their nominee must be informed.

11E Significant statements described in paragraph 11.4 will always be relevant to the offence and must be recorded. When a suspect agrees to read records of interviews and other comments and sign them as correct, they should be asked to endorse the record with, e.g. 'I agree that this is a correct record of what was said' and add their signature. If the suspect does not agree with the record, the interviewer should record the details of any disagreement and ask the suspect to read these details and sign them to the effect that they accurately reflect their disagreement. Any refusal to sign should be recorded.

12 Interviews in police stations

(a) Action

12.1 If a police officer wants to interview or conduct enquiries which require the presence of a detainee, the custody officer is responsible for deciding whether to deliver the detainee into the officer's custody.

12.2 Except as below, in any period of 24 hours a detainee must be allowed a continuous period of at least 8 hours for rest, free from questioning, travel or any interruption in connection with the investigation concerned. This period should normally be at night or other appropriate time which takes account of when the detainee last slept or rested. If a detainee is arrested at a police station after going there voluntarily, the period of 24 hours runs from the time of their arrest and not the time of arrival at the police station. The period may not be interrupted or delayed, except:

    (a) when there are reasonable grounds for believing not delaying or interrupting the period would:

        (i)   involve a risk of harm to people or serious loss of, or damage to, property;

        (ii) delay unnecessarily the person's release from custody;

        (iii) otherwise prejudice the outcome of the investigation;

    (b) at the request of the detainee, their appropriate adult or legal representative;

    (c) when a delay or interruption is necessary in order to:

        (i)   comply with the legal obligations and duties arising under *section 15*;

        (ii) to take action required under *section 9* or in accordance with medical advice.

If the period is interrupted in accordance with *(a)*, a fresh period must be allowed. Interruptions under *(b)* and *(c)*, do not require a fresh period to be allowed.

12.3 Before a detainee is interviewed the custody officer, in consultation with the officer in charge of the investigation and appropriate health care professionals as necessary, shall assess whether the detainee is fit enough to be interviewed. This means determining and considering the risks to the detainee's physical and mental state if the interview took place and determining what safeguards are needed to allow the interview to take place. See *Annex G*. The custody officer shall not allow a detainee to be interviewed if the custody officer considers it would cause significant harm to the detainee's physical or mental state. Vulnerable suspects listed at *paragraph 11.18* shall be treated as always being at some risk during an interview and these persons may not be interviewed except in accordance with *paragraphs 11.18 to 11.20*.

12.4 As far as practicable interviews shall take place in interview rooms which are adequately heated, lit and ventilated.

12.5 A suspect whose detention without charge has been authorised under PACE, because the detention is necessary for an interview to obtain evidence of the offence for which they have been arrested, may choose not to answer questions but police do not require the suspect's consent or agreement to interview them for this purpose. If a suspect takes steps to prevent themselves being questioned or further questioned, e.g. by refusing to leave their cell to go to a suitable interview room or by trying to leave the interview room, they shall be advised their consent or agreement to interview is not required. The suspect shall be cautioned as in *section 10*, and informed if they fail or refuse to co-operate, the interview may take place in the cell and that their failure or refusal to co-operate may be given in evidence. The suspect shall then be invited to co-operate and go into the interview room.

12.6 People being questioned or making statements shall not be required to stand.

12.7 Before the interview commences each interviewer shall, subject to *paragraph 2.6A*, identify themselves and any other persons present to the interviewee.

12.8 Breaks from interviewing should be made at recognised meal times or at other times that take account of when an interviewee last had a meal. Short refreshment breaks shall be provided at approximately two hour intervals, subject to the interviewer's discretion to delay a break if there are reasonable grounds for believing it would:

    (i)   involve a:
- risk of harm to people;
- serious loss of, or damage to, property;

    (ii) unnecessarily delay the detainee's release;

    (iii) otherwise prejudice the outcome of the investigation.

See *Note 12B*

12.9 If during the interview a complaint is made by or on behalf of the interviewee concerning the provisions of this Code, the interviewer should:

    (i)   record it in the interview record;

    (ii) inform the custody officer, who is then responsible for dealing with it as in *section 9*.

(b) Documentation

12.10 A record must be made of the:
- time a detainee is not in the custody of the custody officer, and why
- reason for any refusal to deliver the detainee out of that custody

12.11 A record shall be made of:

    (a) the reasons it was not practicable to use an interview room; and

    (b) any action taken as in *paragraph 12.5*.

The record shall be made on the custody record or in the interview record for action taken whilst an interview record is being kept, with a brief reference to this effect in the custody record.

12.12 Any decision to delay a break in an interview must be recorded, with reasons, in the interview record.

12.13 All written statements made at police stations under caution shall be written on forms provided for the purpose.

12.14 All written statements made under caution shall be taken in accordance with *Annex D*. Before a person makes a written statement under caution at a police station they shall be reminded about the right to legal advice. See *Note 12A*

Notes for guidance

12A It is not normally necessary to ask for a written statement if the interview was recorded in writing and the record signed in accordance with paragraph 11.11 or audibly or visually recorded in accordance with Code E or F. Statements under caution should normally be taken in these circumstances only at the person's express wish. A person may however be asked if they want to make such a statement.

12B Meal breaks should normally last at least 45 minutes and shorter breaks after two hours should last at least 15 minutes. If the interviewer delays a break in accordance with paragraph 12.8 and prolongs the interview, a longer break should be provided. If there is a short interview, and another short interview is contemplated, the length of the break may be reduced if there are reasonable grounds to believe this is necessary to avoid any of the consequences in paragraph 12.8(i) to (iii).

13   Interpreters

(a) General

13.1 Chief officers are responsible for making sure appropriate arrangements are in place for provision of suitably qualified interpreters for people who:
- are deaf;
- do not understand English.

Whenever possible, interpreters should be drawn from the National Register of Public Service Interpreters (NRPSI) or the Council for the Advancement of Communication with Deaf People (CADCP) Directory of British Sign Language/English Interpreters.

(b) Foreign languages

13.2 Unless *paragraphs 11.1, 11.18 to 11.20* apply, a person must not be interviewed in the absence of a person capable of interpreting if:
(a) they have difficulty understanding English;
(b) the interviewer cannot speak the person's own language;
(c) the person wants an interpreter present.

13.3 The interviewer shall make sure the interpreter makes a note of the interview at the time in the person's language for use in the event of the interpreter being called to give evidence, and certifies its accuracy. The interviewer should allow sufficient time for the interpreter to note each question and answer after each is put, given and interpreted. The person should be allowed to read the record or have it read to them and sign it as correct or indicate the respects in which they consider it inaccurate. If the interview is audibly recorded or visually recorded, the arrangements in Code E or F apply.

13.4 In the case of a person making a statement to a police officer or other police staff other than in English:
(a) the interpreter shall record the statement in the language it is made;
(b) the person shall be invited to sign it;
(c) an official English translation shall be made in due course.

(c) Deaf people and people with speech difficulties

13.5 If a person appears to be deaf or there is doubt about their hearing or speaking ability, they must not be interviewed in the absence of an interpreter unless they agree in writing to being interviewed without one or *paragraphs 11.1, 11.18 to 11.20* apply.

13.6 An interpreter should also be called if a juvenile is interviewed and the parent or guardian present as the appropriate adult appears to be deaf or there is doubt about their hearing or speaking ability, unless they agree in writing to the interview proceeding without one or *paragraphs 11.1, 11.18 to 11.20* apply.

13.7 The interviewer shall make sure the interpreter is allowed to read the interview record and certify its accuracy in the event of the interpreter being called to give evidence. If the interview is audibly recorded or visually recorded, the arrangements in Code E or F apply.

(d) Additional rules for detained persons

13.8 All reasonable attempts should be made to make the detainee understand that interpreters will be provided at public expense.

13.9 If *paragraph 6.1* applies and the detainee cannot communicate with the solicitor because of language, hearing or speech difficulties, an interpreter must be called.

The interpreter may not be a police officer or any other police staff when interpretation is needed for the purposes of obtaining legal advice. In all other cases a police officer or other police staff may only interpret if the detainee and the appropriate adult, if applicable, give their agreement in writing or if the interview is audibly recorded or visually recorded as in Code E or F.

13.10 When the custody officer cannot establish effective communication with a person charged with an offence who appears deaf or there is doubt about their ability to hear, speak or to understand English, arrangements must be made as soon as practicable for an interpreter to explain the offence and any other information given by the custody officer.

(e) Documentation

13.11 Action taken to call an interpreter under this section and any agreement to be interviewed in the absence of an interpreter must be recorded.

14 Questioning—special restrictions

14.1 If a person is arrested by one police force on behalf of another and the lawful period of detention in respect of that offence has not yet commenced in accordance with PACE, section 41 no questions may be put to them about the offence while they are in transit between the forces except to clarify any voluntary statement they make.

14.2 If a person is in police detention at a hospital they may not be questioned without the agreement of a responsible doctor. See *Note 14A*

Note for guidance

14A If questioning takes place at a hospital under paragraph 14.2, or on the way to or from a hospital, the period of questioning concerned counts towards the total period of detention permitted.

CODES OF PRACTICE, CODE E
ON TAPE RECORDING OF INTERVIEWS WITH SUSPECTS

3 Interviews to be audio recorded

3.1 Subject to *paragraphs 3.3* and *3.4*, audio recording shall be used at police stations for any interview:

(a) with a person cautioned under Code C, *section 10* in respect of any indictable offence, including an offence triable either way; see *Note 3A*

(b) which takes place as a result of an interviewer exceptionally putting further questions to a suspect about an offence described in *paragraph 3.1(a)* after they have been charged with, or told they may be prosecuted for, that offence, see Code C, *paragraph 16.5*

(c) when an interviewer wants to tell a person, after they have been charged with, or informed they may be prosecuted for, an offence described in *paragraph 3.1(a)*, about any written statement or interview with another person, see Code C, *paragraph 16.4.*

3.2 The Terrorism Act 2000 makes separate provision for a Code of Practice for the audio recording of interviews of those arrested under Section 41 or detained under Schedule 7 of the Act. The provisions of this Code do not apply to such interviews.

3.3 The custody officer may authorise the interviewer not to audio record the interview when it is:

(a) not reasonably practicable because of equipment failure or the unavailability of a suitable interview room or recorder and the authorising officer considers, on reasonable grounds, that the interview should not be delayed; or

(b) clear from the outset there will not be a prosecution.

Note: In these cases the interview should be recorded in writing in accordance with Code C, *section 11.* In all cases the custody officer shall record the specific reasons for not audio recording. See *Note 3B*

3.4 If a person refuses to go into or remain in a suitable interview room, see Code C *paragraph 12.5*, and the custody officer considers, on reasonable grounds, that the interview should not be delayed the interview may, at the custody officer's discretion, be conducted in a cell using portable recording equipment or, if none is available, recorded in writing as in Code C, *section 11*. The reasons for this shall be recorded.

3.5 The whole of each interview shall be audio recorded, including the taking and reading back of any statement.

Notes for guidance

3A Nothing in this Code is intended to preclude audio recording at police discretion of interviews at police stations with people cautioned in respect of offences not covered by paragraph 3.1, or responses made by persons after they have been charged with, or told they may be prosecuted for, an offence, provided this Code is complied with.

3B A decision not to audio record an interview for any reason may be the subject of comment in court. The authorising officer should be prepared to justify that decision.

4 The interview

(a) General

4.1 The provisions of Code C:
- *sections 10 and 11*, and the applicable *Notes for Guidance* apply to the conduct of interviews to which this Code applies
- *paragraphs 11.7 to 11.14* apply only when a written record is needed.

4.2 Code C, *paragraphs 10.10, 10.11* and Annex C describe the restriction on drawing adverse inferences from a suspect's failure or refusal to say anything about their involvement in the offence when interviewed or after being charged or informed they may be prosecuted, and how it affects the terms of the caution and determines if and by whom a special warning under sections 36 and 37 can be given.

(b) Commencement of interviews

4.3 When the suspect is brought into the interview room the interviewer shall, without delay but in the suspect's sight, load the recorder with new recording media and set it to record. The recording media must be unwrapped or opened in the suspect's presence.

4.4 The interviewer should tell the suspect about the recording process. The interviewer shall:
- (a) say the interview is being audibly recorded
- (b) subject to *paragraph 2.3*, give their name and rank and that of any other interviewer present
- (c) ask the suspect and any other party present, e.g. a solicitor, to identify themselves
- (d) state the date, time of commencement and place of the interview
- (e) state the suspect will be given a notice about what will happen to the copies of the recording.

See Note 4A

4.5 The interviewer shall:
- caution the suspect, see Code C, *section 10*
- remind the suspect of their entitlement to free legal advice, see Code C, *paragraph 11.2*.

4.6 The interviewer shall put to the suspect any significant statement or silence; see Code C, *paragraph 11.4*.

(c) Interviews with deaf persons

4.7 If the suspect is deaf or is suspected of having impaired hearing, the interviewer shall make a written note of the interview in accordance with Code C, at the same time as audio recording it in accordance with this Code. See *Notes 4B* and *4C*

(d) Objections and complaints by the suspect

4.8 If the suspect objects to the interview being audibly recorded at the outset, during the interview or during a break, the interviewer shall explain that the interview is being audibly recorded and that this Code requires the suspect's objections to be recorded on the audio recording. When any objections have been audibly recorded or the suspect has refused to have their objections recorded, the interviewer shall say they are turning off the recorder, give their reasons and turn it off. The interviewer shall then make a written record of the interview as in Code C, *section 11*. If, however, the interviewer reasonably considers they may proceed to question the suspect with the audio recording still on, the interviewer may do so. This procedure also applies in cases where the suspect has previously objected to the interview being visually recorded, see *Code F 4.8*, and the investigating officer has decided to audibly record the interview. See *Note 4D*

4.9 If in the course of an interview a complaint is made by or on behalf of the person being questioned concerning the provisions of this Code or Code C, the interviewer shall act as in Code C, *paragraph 12.9*. See *Notes 4E* and *4F*

4.10 If the suspect indicates they want to tell the interviewer about matters not directly connected with the offence and they are unwilling for these matters to be audio recorded, the suspect should be given the opportunity to tell the interviewer at the end of the formal interview.

(e) Changing recording media

4.11 When the recorder shows the recording media only has a short time left, the interviewer shall tell the suspect the recording media are coming to an end and round off that part of the interview. If the interviewer leaves the room for a second set of recording media, the suspect shall not be left unattended. The interviewer will remove the recording media from the recorder and insert the new recording media which shall be unwrapped or opened in the suspect's presence. The recorder should be set to record on the new media. To avoid confusion between the recording media, the interviewer shall mark the media with an identification number immediately after they are removed from the recorder.

(f) Taking a break during interview

4.12 When a break is taken, the fact that a break is to be taken, the reason for it and the time shall be recorded on the audio recording.

4.12A When the break is taken and the interview room vacated by the suspect, the recording media shall be removed from the recorder and the procedures for the conclusion of an interview followed, see *paragraph 4.18*.

4.13 When a break is a short one and both the suspect and an interviewer remain in the interview room, the recording may be stopped. There is no need to remove the recording media and when the interview recommences the recording should continue on the same recording media. The time the interview recommences shall be recorded on the audio recording.

4.14 After any break in the interview the interviewer must, before resuming the interview, remind the person being questioned that they remain under caution or, if there is any doubt, give the caution in full again. See *Note 4G*

(g) Failure of recording equipment

4.15 If there is an equipment failure which can be rectified quickly, e.g. by inserting new recording media, the interviewer shall follow the appropriate procedures as in *paragraph 4.11*. When the recording is resumed the interviewer shall explain what happened and record the time the interview recommences. If, however, it will not be possible to continue recording on that recorder and no replacement recorder is readily available, the interview may continue without being audibly recorded. If this happens, the interviewer shall seek the custody officer's authority as in *paragraph 3.3*. See *Note 4H*

(h) Removing recording media from the recorder

4.16 When recording media is removed from the recorder during the interview, they shall be retained and the procedures in *paragraph 4.18* followed.

(i) Conclusion of interview

4.17 At the conclusion of the interview, the suspect shall be offered the opportunity to clarify anything he or she has said and asked if there is anything they want to add.

4.18 At the conclusion of the interview, including the taking and reading back of any written statement, the time shall be recorded and the recording shall be stopped. The interviewer shall seal the master recording with a master recording label and treat it as an exhibit in accordance with force standing orders. The interviewer shall sign the label and ask the suspect and any third party present during the interview to sign it. If the suspect or third party refuse to sign the label an officer of at least inspector rank, or if not available the custody officer, shall be called into the interview room and asked, subject to *paragraph 2.3*, to sign it.

4.19 The suspect shall be handed a notice which explains:

- how the audio recording will be used
- the arrangements for access to it
- that if the person is charged or informed they will be prosecuted, a copy of the audio recording will be supplied as soon as practicable or as otherwise agreed between the suspect and the police.

Notes for guidance

4A For the purpose of voice identification the interviewer should ask the suspect and any other people present to identify themselves.

4B This provision is to give a person who is deaf or has impaired hearing equivalent rights of access to the full interview record as far as this is possible using audio recording.

4C The provisions of Code C, section 13 on interpreters for deaf persons or for interviews with suspects who have difficulty understanding English continue to apply. However, in an audibly recorded interview the requirement on the interviewer to make sure the interpreter makes a separate note of the interview applies only to paragraph 4.7 (interviews with deaf persons).

4D The interviewer should remember that a decision to continue recording against the wishes of the suspect may be the subject of comment in court.

4E If the custody officer is called to deal with the complaint, the recorder should, if possible, be left on until the custody officer has entered the room and spoken to the person being interviewed. Continuation or termination of the interview should be at the interviewer's discretion pending action by an inspector under Code C, paragraph 9.2.

4F If the complaint is about a matter not connected with this Code or Code C, the decision to continue is at the interviewer's discretion. When the interviewer decides to continue the interview, they shall tell the suspect the complaint will be brought to the custody officer's attention at the conclusion of the interview. When the interview is concluded the interviewer must, as soon as practicable, inform the custody officer about the existence and nature of the complaint made.

4G The interviewer should remember that it may be necessary to show to the court that nothing occurred during a break or between interviews which influenced the suspect's recorded evidence. After a break or at the beginning of a subsequent interview, the interviewer should consider summarising on the record the reason for the break and confirming this with the suspect.

4H Where the interview is being recorded and the media or the recording equipment fails the officer conducting the interview should stop the interview immediately. Where part of the interview is unaffected by the error and is still accessible on the media, that media shall be copied and sealed in the suspect's presence and the interview recommenced using new equipment/media as required. Where the content of the interview has been lost in its entirety the media should be sealed in the suspect's presence and the interview begun again. If the recording equipment cannot be fixed or no replacement is immediately available the interview should be recorded in accordance with Code C, section 11.

5 After the interview

5.1 The interviewer shall make a note in their pocket book that the interview has taken place, was audibly recorded, its time, duration and date and the master recording's identification number.

5.2 If no proceedings follow in respect of the person whose interview was recorded, the recording media must be kept securely as in *paragraph 6.1* and *Note 6A*.

Note for guidance

5A Any written record of an audibly recorded interview should be made in accordance with national guidelines approved by the Secretary of State.

6 Media security

6.1 The officer in charge of each police station at which interviews with suspects are recorded shall make arrangements for master recordings to be kept securely and their movements accounted for on the same basis as material which may be used for evidential purposes, in accordance with force standing orders. See *Note 6A*

6.2 A police officer has no authority to break the seal on a master recording required for criminal trial or appeal proceedings. If it is necessary to gain access to the master recording, the police officer shall arrange for its seal to be broken in the presence of a representative of the Crown Prosecution Service. The defendant or their legal adviser should be informed and given a reasonable opportunity to be present. If the defendant or their legal representative is present they shall be invited to reseal and sign the master recording. If either refuses or neither is present this should be done by the representative of the Crown Prosecution Service. See *Notes 6B* and *6C*

6.3 If no criminal proceedings result or the criminal trial and, if applicable, appeal proceedings to which the interview relates have been concluded, the chief officer of police is responsible for establishing arrangements for breaking the seal on the master recording, if necessary.

6.4 When the master recording seal is broken, a record must be made of the procedure followed, including the date, time, place and persons present.

Notes for guidance

6A This section is concerned with the security of the master recording sealed at the conclusion of the interview. Care must be taken of working copies of recordings because their loss or destruction may lead to the need to access master recordings.

6B If the recording has been delivered to the crown court for their keeping after committal for trial the crown prosecutor will apply to the chief clerk of the crown court centre for the release of the recording for unsealing by the crown prosecutor.

6C Reference to the Crown Prosecution Service or to the crown prosecutor in this part of the Code should be taken to include any other body or person with a statutory responsibility for prosecution for whom the police conduct any audibly recorded interviews.

CODES OF PRACTICE, CODE F
ON VISUAL RECORDING WITH SOUND OF
INTERVIEWS WITH SUSPECTS

2 Recording and sealing of master tapes

2.1 The visual recording of interviews shall be carried out openly to instil confidence in its reliability as an impartial and accurate record of the interview. [See *Note 2A*].

2.2 The camera(s) shall be placed in the interview room so as to ensure coverage of as much of the room as is practicably possible whilst the interviews are taking place.

2.3 The certified recording medium will be of a high quality, new and previously unused. When the certified recording medium is placed in the recorder and switched on to record, the correct date and time, in hours, minutes and seconds, will be superimposed automatically, second by second, during the whole recording. [See *Note 2B*].

2.4 One copy of the certified recording medium, referred to in this code as the master copy, will be sealed before it leaves the presence of the suspect. A second copy will be used as a working copy. [See *Note 2C and 2D*].

2.5 Nothing in this code requires the identity of an officer to be recorded or disclosed if:
- (a) the interview or record relates to a person detained under the Terrorism Act 2000; or
- (b) otherwise where the officer reasonably believes that recording or disclosing their name might put them in danger.

In these cases, the officer will have their back to the camera and shall use their warrant or other identification number and the name of the police station to which they are attached. Such instances and the reasons for them shall be recorded in the custody record. [See *Note 2E*]

Notes for Guidance

2A Interviewing officers will wish to arrange that, as far as possible, visual recording arrangements are unobtrusive. It must be clear to the suspect, however, that there is no opportunity to interfere with the recording equipment or the recording media.

2B In this context, the certified recording media will be of either a VHS or digital CD format and should be capable of having an image of the date and time superimposed upon them as they record the interview.

2C The purpose of sealing the master copy before it leaves the presence of the suspect is to establish their confidence that the integrity of the copy is preserved.

2D The recording of the interview may be used for identification procedures in accordance with paragraph 3.21 or Annex E of Code D.

2E The purpose of the paragraph 2.5 is to protect police officers and others involved in the investigation of serious organised crime or the arrest of particularly violent suspects when there is reliable information that those arrested or their associates may threaten or cause harm to the officers, their families or their personal property.

3 Interviews to be visually recorded

3.1 Subject to paragraph 3.2 below, if an interviewing officer decides to make a visual recording these are the areas where it might be appropriate:
- (a) with a suspect in respect of an indictable offence (including an offence triable either way) [see *Notes 3A and 3B*];
- (b) which takes place as a result of an interviewer exceptionally putting further questions to a suspect about an offence described in sub-paragraph (a) above after they have been charged with, or informed they may be prosecuted for, that offence [see *Note 3C*];
- (c) in which an interviewer wishes to bring to the notice of a person, after that person has been charged with, or informed they may be prosecuted for an offence described in sub-paragraph (a) above, any written statement made by another person, or the content of an interview with another person [see *Note 3D*]
- (d) with, or in the presence of, a deaf or deaf/blind or speech impaired person who uses sign language to communicate;

    (e) with, or in the presence of anyone who requires an 'appropriate adult'; or

    (f) in any case where the suspect or their representative requests that the interview be recorded visually.

3.2 The Terrorism Act 2000 makes separate provision for a code of practice for the video recording of interviews in a police station of those detained under Schedule 7 or section 41 of the Act. The provisions of this code do not therefore apply to such interviews [see *Note 3E*].

3.3 The custody officer may authorise the interviewing officer not to record the interview visually:

    (a) where it is not reasonably practicable to do so because of failure of the equipment, or the non-availability of a suitable interview room, or recorder, and the authorising officer considers on reasonable grounds that the interview should not be delayed until the failure has been rectified or a suitable room or recorder becomes available. In such cases the custody officer may authorise the interviewing officer to audio record the interview in accordance with the guidance set out in Code E;

    (b) where it is clear from the outset that no prosecution will ensue; or

    (c) where it is not practicable to do so because at the time the person resists being taken to a suitable interview room or other location which would enable the interview to be recorded, or otherwise fails or refuses to go into such a room or location, and the authorising officer considers on reasonable grounds that the interview should not be delayed until these conditions cease to apply.

In all cases the custody officer shall make a note in the custody records of the reasons for not taking a visual record. [See *Note 3F*].

3.4 When a person who is voluntarily attending the police station is required to be cautioned in accordance with Code C prior to being interviewed, the subsequent interview shall be recorded, unless the custody officer gives authority in accordance with the provisions of paragraph 3.3 above for the interview not to be so recorded.

3.5 The whole of each interview shall be recorded visually, including the taking and reading back of any statement.

3.6 A visible illuminated sign or indicator will light and remain on at all times when the recording equipment is activated or capable of recording or transmitting any signal or information.

Notes for Guidance

3A Nothing in the code is intended to preclude visual recording at police discretion of interviews at police stations with people cautioned in respect of offences not covered by paragraph 3.1, or responses made by interviewees after they have been charged with, or informed they may be prosecuted for, an offence, provided that this code is complied with.

3B Attention is drawn to the provisions set out in Code C about the matters to be considered when deciding whether a detained person is fit to be interviewed.

3C Code C sets out the circumstances in which a suspect may be questioned about an offence after being charged with it.

3D Code C sets out the procedures to be followed when a person's attention is drawn after charge, to a statement made by another person. One method of bringing the content of an interview with another person to the notice of a suspect may be to play him a recording of that interview.

3E When it only becomes clear during the course of an interview which is being visually recorded that the interviewee may have committed an offence to which paragraph 3.2 applies, the interviewing officer should turn off the recording equipment and the interview should continue in accordance with the provisions of the Terrorism Act 2000.

3F A decision not to record an interview visually for any reason may be the subject of comment in court. The authorising officer should therefore be prepared to justify their decision in each case.

4 The Interview

(a) General

4.1 The provisions of Code C in relation to cautions and interviews and the Notes for Guidance applicable to those provisions shall apply to the conduct of interviews to which this Code applies.

4.2 Particular attention is drawn to those parts of Code C that describe the restrictions on drawing adverse inferences from a suspect's failure or refusal to say anything about their involvement in the offence when interviewed, or after being charged or informed they may be prosecuted and how those restrictions affect the terms of the caution and determine whether a special warning under Sections 36 and 37 of the Criminal Justice and Public Order Act 1994 can be given.

(b) Commencement of interviews

4.3 When the suspect is brought into the interview room the interviewer shall without delay, but in sight of the suspect, load the recording equipment and set it to record.

The recording media must be unwrapped or otherwise opened in the presence of the suspect. [See *Note 4A*]

4.4 The interviewer shall then tell the suspect formally about the visual recording. The interviewer shall:
    (a) explain the interview is being visually recorded;
    (b) subject to paragraph 2.5, give his or her name and rank, and that of any other interviewer present;
    (c) ask the suspect and any other party present (e.g. his solicitor) to identify themselves.
    (d) state the date, time of commencement and place of the interview; and
    (e) state that the suspect will be given a notice about what will happen to the recording.

4.5 The interviewer shall then caution the suspect, which should follow that set out in Code C, and remind the suspect of their entitlement to free and independent legal advice and that they can speak to a solicitor on the telephone.

4.6 The interviewer shall then put to the suspect any significant statement or silence (i.e. failure or refusal to answer a question or to answer it satisfactorily) which occurred before the start of the interview, and shall ask the suspect whether they wish to confirm or deny that earlier statement or silence or whether they wish to add anything.

The definition of a 'significant' statement or silence is the same as that set out in Code C.

(c) Interviews with the deaf

4.7 If the suspect is deaf or there is doubt about their hearing ability, the provisions of Code C on interpreters for the deaf or for interviews with suspects who have difficulty in understanding English continue to apply.

(d) Objections and complaints by the suspect

4.8 If the suspect raises objections to the interview being visually recorded either at the outset or during the interview or during a break in the interview, the interviewer shall explain the fact that the interview is being visually recorded and that the provisions of this code require that the suspect's objections shall be recorded on the visual recording. When any objections have been visually recorded or the suspect has refused to have their objections recorded, the interviewer shall say that they are turning off the recording equipment, give their reasons and turn it off. If a separate audio recording is being maintained, the officer shall ask the person to record the reasons for refusing to agree to visual recording of the interview. Paragraph 4.8 of Code E will apply if the person objects to audio recording of the interview. The officer shall then make a written record of the interview. If the interviewer reasonably considers they may proceed to question the suspect with the visual recording still on, the interviewer may do so. See *Note 4G.*

4.9 If in the course of an interview a complaint is made by the person being questioned, or on their behalf, concerning the provisions of this code or of Code C, then the interviewer shall act in accordance with Code C, record it in the interview record and inform the custody officer. [See *4B and 4C*].

4.10 If the suspect indicates that they wish to tell the interviewer about matters not directly connected with the offence of which they are suspected and that they are unwilling for these matters to be recorded, the suspect shall be given the opportunity to tell the interviewer about these matters after the conclusion of the formal interview.

(e) Changing the recording media

4.11 In instances where the recording medium is not of sufficient length to record all of the interview with the suspect, further certified recording medium will be used. When the recording equipment indicates that the recording medium has only a short time left to run, the interviewer shall advise the suspect and round off that part of the interview.

If the interviewer wishes to continue the interview but does not already have further certified recording media with him, they shall obtain a set. The suspect should not be left unattended in the interview room. The interviewer will remove the recording media from the recording equipment and insert the new ones which have been unwrapped or otherwise opened in the suspect's presence. The recording equipment shall then be set to record. Care must be taken, particularly when a number of sets of recording media have been used, to ensure that there is no confusion between them. This could be achieved by marking the sets of recording media with consecutive identification numbers.

(f) Taking a break during the interview

4.12 When a break is to be taken during the course of an interview and the interview room is to be vacated by the suspect, the fact that a break is to be taken, the reason for it and the time shall be recorded. The recording equipment must be turned off and the recording media removed. The procedures for the conclusion of an interview set out in paragraph 4.19, below, should be followed.

4.13 When a break is to be a short one, and both the suspect and a police officer are to remain in the interview room, the fact that a break is to be taken, the reasons for it and the time shall be recorded on the recording media. The recording equipment may be turned off, but there is no need to remove the recording media. When the interview is recommenced the recording shall continue on the same recording media and the time at which the interview recommences shall be recorded.

4.14 When there is a break in questioning under caution, the interviewing officer must ensure that the person being questioned is aware that they remain under caution. If there is any doubt, the caution must be given again in full when the interview resumes. [See *Notes 4D and 4E*].

(g) Failure of recording equipment

4.15 If there is a failure of equipment which can be rectified quickly, the appropriate procedures set out in paragraph 4.12 shall be followed. When the recording is resumed the interviewer shall explain what has happened and record the time the interview recommences. If, however, it is not possible to continue recording on that particular recorder and no alternative equipment is readily available, the interview may continue without being recorded visually. In such circumstances, the procedures set out in paragraph 3.3 of this code for seeking the authority of the custody officer will be followed. [See *Note 4F*].

(h) Removing used recording media from recording equipment

4.16 Where used recording media are removed from the recording equipment during the course of an interview, they shall be retained and the procedures set out in paragraph 4.18 below followed.

(i) Conclusion of interview

4.17 Before the conclusion of the interview, the suspect shall be offered the opportunity to clarify anything he or she has said and asked if there is anything that they wish to add.

4.18 At the conclusion of the interview, including the taking and reading back of any written statement, the time shall be recorded and the recording equipment switched off. The master tape or CD shall be removed from the recording equipment, sealed with a master copy label and treated as an exhibit in accordance with the force standing orders. The interviewer shall sign the label and also ask the suspect and any appropriate adults or other third party present during the interview to sign it. If the suspect or third party refuses to sign the label, an officer of at least the rank of inspector, or if one is not available, the custody officer, shall be called into the interview room and asked to sign it.

4.19 The suspect shall be handed a notice which explains the use which will be made of the recording and the arrangements for access to it. The notice will also advise the suspect that a copy of the tape shall be supplied as soon as practicable if the person is charged or informed that he will be prosecuted.

Notes for Guidance

4A *The interviewer should attempt to estimate the likely length of the interview and ensure that an appropriate quantity of certified recording media and labels with which to seal the master copies are available in the interview room.*

4B *Where the custody officer is called immediately to deal with the complaint, wherever possible the recording equipment should be left to run until the custody officer has entered the interview room and spoken to the person being interviewed. Continuation or termination of the interview should be at the discretion of the interviewing officer pending action by an inspector as set out in Code C.*

4C *Where the complaint is about a matter not connected with this code of practice or Code C, the decision to continue with the interview is at the discretion of the interviewing officer. Where the interviewing officer decides to continue with the interview, the person being interviewed shall be told that the complaint will be brought to the attention of the custody officer at the conclusion of the interview. When the interview is concluded, the interviewing officer must, as soon as practicable, inform the custody officer of the existence and nature of the complaint made.*

4D *In considering whether to caution again after a break, the officer should bear in mind that he may have to satisfy a court that the person understood that he was still under caution when the interview resumed.*

4E *The officer should bear in mind that it may be necessary to satisfy the court that nothing occurred during a break in an interview or between interviews which influenced the suspect's recorded evidence. On the re-commencement of an interview, the officer should consider summarising on the tape or CD the reason for the break and confirming this with the suspect.*

4F *If any part of the recording media breaks or is otherwise damaged during the interview, it should be sealed as a master copy in the presence of the suspect and the interview resumed where it left off. The undamaged part should be copied and the original sealed as a master tape in the suspect's presence, if necessary after the interview. If equipment for copying is not readily available, both parts should be sealed in the suspect's presence and the interview begun again.*

4G *The interviewer should be aware that a decision to continue recording against the wishes of the suspect may be the subject of comment in court.*

5 After the Interview

5.1 The interviewer shall make a note in his or her pocket book of the fact that the interview has taken place and has been recorded, its time, duration and date and the identification number of the master copy of the recording media.

5.2 Where no proceedings follow in respect of the person whose interview was recorded, the recording media must nevertheless be kept securely in accordance with paragraph 6.1 and Note 6A.

Note for Guidance

5A Any written record of a recorded interview shall be made in accordance with national guidelines approved by the Secretary of State, and with regard to the advice contained in the Manual of Guidance for the preparation, processing and submission of files.

6 Master Copy Security

(a) General

6.1 The officer in charge of the police station at which interviews with suspects are recorded shall make arrangements for the master copies to be kept securely and their movements accounted for on the same basis as other material which may be used for evidential purposes, in accordance with force standing orders [See *Note 6A*].

(b) Breaking master copy seal for criminal proceedings

6.2 A police officer has no authority to break the seal on a master copy which is required for criminal trial or appeal proceedings. If it is necessary to gain access to the master copy, the police officer shall arrange for its seal to be broken in the presence of a representative of the Crown Prosecution Service. The defendant or their legal adviser shall be informed and given a reasonable opportunity to be present. If the defendant or their legal representative is present they shall be invited to reseal and sign the master copy. If either refuses or neither is present, this shall be done by the representative of the Crown Prosecution Service. [See *Notes 6B and 6C*].

(c) Breaking master copy seal: other cases

6.3 The chief officer of police is responsible for establishing arrangements for breaking the seal of the master copy where no criminal proceedings result, or the criminal proceedings, to which the interview relates, have been concluded and it becomes necessary to break the seal. These arrangements should be those which the chief officer considers are reasonably necessary to demonstrate to the person interviewed and any other party who may wish to use or refer to the interview record that the master copy has not been tampered with and that the interview record remains accurate. [See *Note 6D*]

6.4 Subject to paragraph 6.6, a representative of each party must be given a reasonable opportunity to be present when the seal is broken, the master copy copied and resealed.

6.5 If one or more of the parties is not present when the master copy seal is broken because they cannot be contacted or refuse to attend or paragraph 6.6 applies, arrangements should be made for an independent person such as a custody visitor, to be present. Alternatively, or as an additional safeguard, arrangement should be made for a film or photographs to be taken of the procedure.

6.6 Paragraph 6.5 does not require a person to be given an opportunity to be present when:

    (a) it is necessary to break the master copy seal for the proper and effective further investigation of the original offence or the investigation of some other offence; and

(b) the officer in charge of the investigation has reasonable grounds to suspect that allowing an opportunity might prejudice any such an investigation or criminal proceedings which may be brought as a result or endanger any person. [See *Note 6E*]

(d) Documentation

6.7 When the master copy seal is broken, copied and re-sealed, a record must be made of the procedure followed, including the date time and place and persons present.

Notes for Guidance

6A This section is concerned with the security of the master copy which will have been sealed at the conclusion of the interview. Care should, however, be taken of working copies since their loss or destruction may lead unnecessarily to the need to have access to master copies.

6B If the master copy has been delivered to the Crown Court for their keeping after committal for trial the Crown Prosecutor will apply to the Chief Clerk of the Crown Court Centre for its release for unsealing by the Crown Prosecutor.

6C Reference to the Crown Prosecution Service or to the Crown Prosecutor in this part of the code shall be taken to include any other body or person with a statutory responsibility for prosecution for whom the police conduct any recorded interviews.

6D The most common reasons for needing access to master copies that are not required for criminal proceedings arise from civil actions and complaints against police and civil actions between individuals arising out of allegations of crime investigated by police.

6E Paragraph 6.6 could apply, for example, when one or more of the outcomes or likely outcomes of the investigation might be: (i) the prosecution of one or more of the original suspects, (ii) the prosecution of someone previously not suspected, including someone who was originally a witness; and (iii) any original suspect being treated as a prosecution witness and when premature disclosure of any police action, particularly through contact with any parties involved, could lead to a real risk of compromising the investigation and endangering witnesses.

Control of abuse of police powers

Police Reform Act 2002

9   The Independent Police Complaints Commission

(1) There shall be a body corporate to be known as the Independent Police Complaints Commission (in this Part referred to as 'the Commission').

(2) The Commission shall consist of—

(a) a chairman appointed by Her Majesty; and

(b) not less than ten other members appointed by the Secretary of State.

(3) A person shall not be appointed as the chairman of the Commission, or as another member of the Commission, if—

(a) he holds or has held office as a constable in any part of the United Kingdom;

(b) he is or has been under the direction and control of a chief officer or of any person holding an equivalent office in Scotland or Northern Ireland;

(c) he is a person in relation to whom a designation under section 39 is or has been in force;

(d) he is a person in relation to whom an accreditation under section 41 is or has been in force;

(da) he is or has been the chairman or a member of, or a member of the staff of, the Serious Organised Crime Agency;

(e) he is or has been a member of the National Criminal Intelligence Service or the National Crime Squad; or

(f) he is or has at any time been a member of a body of constables which at the time of his membership is or was a body of constables in relation to which any procedures are or were in force by virtue of an agreement or order under—

(i) section 26 of this Act; or

(ii) section 78 of the 1996 Act or section 96 of the 1984 Act (which made provision corresponding to that made by section 26 of this Act).

(4) An appointment made in contravention of subsection (3) shall have no effect.

(5) The Commission shall not—

(a) be regarded as the servant or agent of the Crown; or

(b) enjoy any status, privilege or immunity of the Crown;

and the Commission's property shall not be regarded as property of, or property held on behalf of, the Crown.

(6) Schedule 2 (which makes further provision in relation to the Commission) shall have effect.

(7) The Police Complaints Authority shall cease to exist on such day as the Secretary of State may by order appoint.

10   General functions of the Commission

(1) The functions of the Commission shall be—

(a) to secure the maintenance by the Commission itself, and by police authorities and chief officers, of suitable arrangements with respect to the matters mentioned in subsection (2);

(b) to keep under review all arrangements maintained with respect to those matters;

(c) to secure that arrangements maintained with respect to those matters comply with the requirements of the following provisions of this Part, are efficient and effective and contain and manifest an appropriate degree of independence;

(d) to secure that public confidence is established and maintained in the existence of suitable arrangements with respect to those matters and with the operation of the arrangements that are in fact maintained with respect to those matters;

(e) to make such recommendations, and to give such advice, for the modification of the arrangements maintained with respect to those matters, and also of police practice in relation to other matters, as appear, from the carrying out by the Commission of its other functions, to be necessary or desirable;

(f) to such extent as it may be required to do so by regulations made by the Secretary of State, to carry out functions in relation to bodies of constables maintained otherwise than by police authorities which broadly correspond to those conferred on the Commission in relation to police forces by the preceding paragraphs of this subsection; and

(g) to carry out functions in relation to the Serious Organised Crime Agency which correspond to those conferred on the Commission in relation to police forces by paragraph (e) of this subsection.

(2) Those matters are—

(a) the handling of complaints made about the conduct of persons serving with the police;

(b) the recording of matters from which it appears that there may have been conduct by such persons which constitutes or involves the commission of a criminal offence or behaviour justifying disciplinary proceedings;

(ba) the recording of matters from which it appears that a person has died or suffered serious injury during, or following, contact with a person serving with the police;

(c) the manner in which any such complaints or any such matters as are mentioned in paragraph (b) or (ba) are investigated or otherwise handled and dealt with.

(3) The Commission shall also have the functions which are conferred on it by—

    (b) any agreement or order under section 26 of this Act (other bodies of constables);

    (ba) any agreement under section 26A of this Act (Serious Organised Crime Agency);

    (c) any regulations under section 39 of this Act (police powers for contracted-out staff); or

    (d) any regulations or arrangements relating to disciplinary or similar proceedings against persons serving with the police, or against members of any body of constables maintained otherwise than by a police authority.

(4) It shall be the duty of the Commission—

    (a) to exercise the powers and perform the duties conferred on it by the following provisions of this Part in the manner that it considers best calculated for the purpose of securing the proper carrying out of its functions under subsections (1) and (3); and

    (b) to secure that arrangements exist which are conducive to, and facilitate, the reporting of misconduct by persons in relation to whose conduct the Commission has functions.

(5) It shall also be the duty of the Commission—

    (a) to enter into arrangements with the chief inspector of constabulary for the purpose of securing co-operation, in the carrying out of their respective functions, between the Commission and the inspectors of constabulary; and

    (b) to provide those inspectors with all such assistance and co-operation as may be required by those arrangements, or as otherwise appears to the Commission to be appropriate, for facilitating the carrying out by those inspectors of their functions.

(6) Subject to the other provisions of this Part, the Commission may do anything which appears to it to be calculated to facilitate, or is incidental or conducive to, the carrying out of its functions.

(7) The Commission may, in connection with the making of any recommendation or the giving of any advice to any person for the purpose of carrying out—

    (a) its function under subsection (1)(e),

    (b) any corresponding function conferred on it by virtue of subsection (1)(f), or

    (c) its function under subsection (1)(g), impose any such charge on that person for anything done by the Commission for the purposes of, or in connection with the carrying out of that function as it thinks fit.

(8) Nothing in this Part shall confer any function on the Commission in relation to so much of any complaint or conduct matter as relates to the direction and control of a police force by—

    (a) the chief officer of police of that force; or

    (b) a person for the time being carrying out the functions of the chief officer of police of that force.

11   Reports to the Secretary of State

(1) As soon as practicable after the end of each of its financial years, the Commission shall make a report to the Secretary of State on the carrying out of its functions during that year.

(2) The Commission shall also make such reports to the Secretary of State about matters relating generally to the carrying out of its functions as he may, from time to time, require.

(3) The Commission may, from time to time, make such other reports to the Secretary of State as it considers appropriate for drawing his attention to matters which—

    (a) have come to the Commission's notice; and

    (b) are matters that it considers should be drawn to his attention by reason of their gravity or of other exceptional circumstances.

(4) The Commission shall prepare such reports containing advice and recommendations as it thinks appropriate for the purpose of carrying out—

    (a) its function under subsection (1)(e) of section 10; or

    (b) any corresponding function conferred on it by virtue of subsection (1)(f) of that section.

(5) Where the Secretary of State receives any report under this section, he shall—
 (a) in the case of every annual report under subsection (1), and
 (b) in the case of any other report, if and to the extent that he considers it appropriate to do so,
lay a copy of the report before Parliament and cause the report to be published.
 (6) The Commission shall send a copy of every annual report under subsection (1)—
 (a) to every police authority;
 (b) to the Serious Organised Crime Agency; and
 (d) to every authority that is maintaining a body of constables in relation to which any procedures are for the time being in force by virtue of any agreement or order under section 26 or by virtue of subsection (9) of that section.
 (7) The Commission shall send a copy of every report under subsection (3)—
 (a) to any police authority that appears to the Commission to be concerned; and
 (b) to the chief officer of police of any police force that appears to it to be concerned.
 (8) Where a report under subsection (3) relates to the Serious Organised Crime Agency, the Commission shall send a copy of that report—
 (a) to the Service Authority for that Service or Squad; and
 (b) to its Director General.
 (9) Where a report under subsection (3) relates to a body of constables maintained by an authority other than a police authority, the Commission shall send a copy of that report—
 (a) to that authority; and
 (b) to the person having the direction and control of that body of constables.
 (10) The Commission shall send a copy of every report under subsection (4) to—
 (a) the Secretary of State;
 (b) every police authority;
 (c) every chief officer;
 (d) the Serious Organised Crime Agency;
 (f) every authority that is maintaining a body of constables in relation to which any procedures are for the time being in force by virtue of any agreement or order under section 26 or by virtue of subsection (9) of that section; and
 (g) every person who has the direction and control of such a body of constables.
 (11) The Commission shall send a copy of every report made or prepared by it under subsection (3) or (4) to such of the persons (in addition to those specified in the preceding subsections) who—
 (a) are referred to in the report, or
 (b) appear to the Commission otherwise to have a particular interest in its contents, as the Commission thinks fit.

Application of Part 2

12 Complaints, matters and persons to which Part 2 applies
 (1) In this Part references to a complaint are references (subject to the following provisions of this section) to any complaint about the conduct of a person serving with the police which is made (whether in writing or otherwise) by—
 (a) a member of the public who claims to be the person in relation to whom the conduct took place;
 (b) a member of the public not falling within paragraph (a) who claims to have been adversely affected by the conduct;
 (c) a member of the public who claims to have witnessed the conduct;
 (d) a person acting on behalf of a person falling within any of paragraphs (a) to (c).
 (2) In this Part 'conduct matter' means (subject to the following provisions of this section, paragraph 2(4) of Schedule 3 and any regulations made by virtue of section 23(2)(d)) any matter which is not and has not been the subject of a complaint but in the case of which

there is an indication (whether from the circumstances or otherwise) that a person serving with the police may have—

    (a) committed a criminal offence; or

    (b) behaved in a manner which would justify the bringing of disciplinary proceedings.

(2A) In this Part 'death or serious injury matter' (or 'DSI matter' for short) means any circumstances (other than those which are or have been the subject of a complaint or which amount to a conduct matter)—

    (a) in or in consequence of which a person has died or has sustained serious injury; and

    (b) in relation to which the requirements of either subsection (2B) or subsection (2C) are satisfied.

(2B) The requirements of this subsection are that at the time of the death or serious injury the person—

    (a) had been arrested by a person serving with the police and had not been released from that arrest; or

    (b) was otherwise detained in the custody of a person serving with the police.

(2C) The requirements of this subsection are that—

    (a) at or before the time of the death or serious injury the person had contact (of whatever kind, and whether direct or indirect) with a person serving with the police who was acting in the execution of his duties; and

    (b) there is an indication that the contact may have caused (whether directly or indirectly) or contributed to the death or serious injury.

(2D) In subsection (2A) the reference to a person includes a person serving with the police, but in relation to such a person 'contact' in subsection (2C) does not include contact that he has whilst acting in the execution of his duties.

(3) The complaints that are complaints for the purposes of this Part by virtue of subsection (1)(b) do not, except in a case falling within subsection (4), include any made by or on behalf of a person who claims to have been adversely affected as a consequence only of having seen or heard the conduct, or any of the alleged effects of the conduct.

(4) A case falls within this subsection if—

    (a) it was only because the person in question was physically present, or sufficiently nearby, when the conduct took place or the effects occurred that he was able to see or hear the conduct or its effects; or

    (b) the adverse effect is attributable to, or was aggravated by, the fact that the person in relation to whom the conduct took place was already known to the person claiming to have suffered the adverse effect.

(5) For the purposes of this section a person shall be taken to have witnessed conduct if, and only if—

    (a) he acquired his knowledge of that conduct in a manner which would make him a competent witness capable of giving admissible evidence of that conduct in criminal proceedings; or

    (b) he has in his possession or under his control anything which would in any such proceedings constitute admissible evidence of that conduct.

(6) For the purposes of this Part a person falling within subsection 1(a) to (c) to shall not be taken to have authorised another person to act on his behalf unless—

    (a) that other person is for the time being designated for the purposes of this Part by the Commission as a person through whom complaints may be made, or he is of a description of persons so designated; or

    (b) the other person has been given, and is able to produce, the written consent to his so acting of the person on whose behalf he acts.

(7) For the purposes of this Part, a person is serving with the police if—

    (a) he is a member of a police force;

    (b) he is an employee of a police authority who is under the direction and control of a chief officer; or

    (c) he is a special constable who is under the direction and control of a chief officer.

Handling of complaints and conduct matters etc.

13 Handling of complaints and conduct matters etc.

Schedule 3 (which makes provision for the handling of complaints and conduct matters and DSI matters, and for the carrying out of investigations) shall have effect subject to section 14(1).

14 Direction and control matters

    (1) Nothing in Schedule 3 shall have effect with respect to so much of any complaint as relates to the direction and control of a police force by—

    (a) the chief officer of police of that force; or

    (b) a person for the time being carrying out the functions of the chief officer of police of that force.

    (2) The Secretary of State may issue guidance to chief officers and to police authorities about the handling of so much of any complaint as relates to the direction and control of a police force by such a person as is mentioned in subsection (1).

    (3) It shall be the duty of a chief officer and of a police authority when handling any complaint relating to such a matter to have regard to any guidance issued under subsection (2).

Co-operation, assistance and information

15 General duties of police authorities, chief officers and inspectors

    (1) It shall be the duty of—

    (a) every police authority maintaining a police force,

    (b) the chief officer of police of every police force, and

    (c) every inspector of constabulary carrying out any of his functions in relation to a police force,

to ensure that it or he is kept informed, in relation to that force, about all matters falling within subsection (2).

    (1A) It shall be the duty of the Serious Organised Crime Agency to ensure that it is kept informed, in relation to the agency, about all matters falling within subsection (2).

    (2) Those matters are—

    (a) matters with respect to which any provision of this Part has effect;

    (b) anything which is done under or for the purposes of any such provision; and

    (c) any obligations to act or refrain from acting that have arisen by or under this Part but have not yet been complied with, or have been contravened.

    (3) Where—

    (a) a police authority maintaining any police force requires the chief officer of that force or of any other force to provide a member of his force for appointment under paragraph 16, 17 or 18 of Schedule 3,

    (b) the chief officer of police of any police force requires the chief officer of police of any other police force to provide a member of that other force for appointment under any of those paragraphs, or

    (c) a police authority or chief officer requires the Director General of the Serious Organised Crime Agency to provide a member of that Agency for appointment under any of those paragraphs,

it shall be the duty of the chief officer or Director General to whom the requirement is addressed to comply with it.

    (4) It shall be the duty of—

    (a) every police authority maintaining a police force,

    (b) the chief officer of police of every police force, and

    (c) the Serious Organised Crime Agency,

to provide the Commission and every member of the Commission's staff with all such assistance as the Commission or that member of staff may reasonably require for the purposes of, or in connection with, the carrying out of any investigation by the Commission under this Part.

(5) It shall be the duty of—

(a) every police authority maintaining a police force,

(b) the chief officer of every police force, and

(c) the Serious Organised Crime Agency

to ensure that a person appointed under paragraph 16, 17 or 18 of Schedule 3 to carry out an investigation is given all such assistance and co-operation in the carrying out of that investigation as that person may reasonably require

(6) The duties imposed by subsections (4) and (5) on a police authority maintaining a police force and on the chief officer of such a force and on the Serious Organised Crime Agency have effect—

(a) irrespective of whether the investigation relates to the conduct of a person who is or has been a member of that force or a member of the staff of the Agency; and

(b) irrespective of who has the person appointed to carry out the investigation under his direction and control;

but a chief officer of a third force may be required to give assistance and co-operation under subsection (5) only with the approval of the chief officer of the force to which the person who requires it belongs.

(7) In subsection (6) 'third force', in relation to an investigation, means a police force other than—

(a) the force to which the person carrying out the investigation belongs; or

(b) the force to which the person whose conduct is under investigation belonged at the time of the conduct;

and where the person whose conduct is under investigation was a member of the staff of the Serious Organised Crime Agency at the time of his conduct, 'third force' means any police force other than the force to which the person carrying out the investigation belongs.

(8) Where the person who requires assistance and co-operation under subsection (5) is a member of the staff of the Serious Organised Crime Agency, a chief officer of a third force may be required to give that assistance and co-operation only with the approval of the Director General of the Agency.

In this subsection, 'third force', in relation to an investigation, means any police force other than the force to which the person whose conduct is under investigation belonged at the time of the conduct.

(9) Where—

(a) the person carrying out an investigation is not a member of the staff of the Serious Organised Crime Agency; and

(b) the person whose conduct is under investigation was not a member of the staff of the Agency at the time of the conduct,

the Director General of the Agency may be required to give assistance and co-operation under subsection (5) only with the approval of the chief officer of the force to which the person requiring it belongs.

16 Payment for assistance with investigations

(1) This section applies where—

(a) one police force is required to provide assistance to another in connection with an investigation under this Part; or

(b) a police force is required to provide assistance in such a connection to the Commission.

(2) For the purposes of this section—

(a) assistance is required to be provided by one police force to another in connection with an investigation under this Part if the chief officer of the first force ('the assisting force') complies with a requirement under section 15(3) or (5) that is made in connection with

(i) an investigation relating to the conduct of a person who, at the time of the conduct, was a member of the other force, or

(ii) an investigation of a DSI matter in relation to which the relevant officer was, at the time of the death or serious injury, a member of the other force; and

(b) assistance is required to be provided in such a connection by a police force ('the assisting force') to the Commission if the chief officer of that force complies with a requirement under section 15(4) that is made in connection with

(i) an investigation relating to the conduct of a person who, at the time of the conduct, was not a member of that force, or

(ii) an investigation of a DSI matter in relation to which the relevant officer was, at the time of the death or serious injury, not a member of that force.

(3) Where the assistance is required to be provided by one police force to another, the police authority maintaining that other police force shall pay to the police authority maintaining the assisting force such contribution (if any) towards the costs of the assistance—

(a) as may be agreed between them; or

(b) in the absence of an agreement, as may be determined in accordance with any arrangements which—

(i) have been agreed to by police authorities generally; and

(ii) are for the time being in force with respect to the making of contributions towards the costs of assistance provided, in connection with investigations under this Part, by one police force to another; or

(c) in the absence of any such arrangements, as may be determined by the Secretary of State.

(4) Where the assistance is required to be provided by a police force to the Commission, the Commission shall pay to the police authority maintaining the assisting force such contribution (if any) towards the costs of the assistance—

(a) as may be agreed between the Commission and that authority; or

(b) in the absence of an agreement, as may be determined in accordance with any arrangements which—

(i) have been agreed to by police authorities generally and by the Commission; and

(ii) are for the time being in force with respect to the making of contributions towards the costs of assistance provided, in connection with investigations under this Part, to the Commission; or

(c) in the absence of any such arrangements, as may be determined by the Secretary of State.

(5) In this section (subject to subsection (6))—

(a) references to a police and to a police authority maintaining a police force include references to the Serious Organised Crime Agency; and

(b) in relation to that Agency, references to the chief officer are references to the Director General.

(6) This section shall have effect in relation to cases in which assistance is required to be provided by the Serious Organised Crime Agency as if—

(a) the reference in subsection (3)(b) to police authorities generally included a reference to the Agency; and

(b) the reference in subsection (4)(b) to police authorities generally were a reference to the Agency.

(7) This section is without prejudice to the application of section 24 of the 1996 Act (assistance given voluntarily by one force to another) in a case in which assistance is provided, otherwise than in pursuance of any duty imposed by section 15 of this Act, in connection with an investigation under this Part.

17 Provision of information to the Commission

(1) It shall be the duty of—

(a) every police authority, and

(b) every chief officer,

at such times, in such circumstances and in accordance with such other requirements as may be set out in regulations made by the Secretary of State, to provide the Commission with all such information and documents as may be specified or described in regulations so made.

(2) It shall also be the duty of every police authority and of every chief officer—

(a) to provide the Commission with all such other information and documents specified or described in a notification given by the Commission to that authority or chief officer, and

(b) to produce or deliver up to the Commission all such evidence and other things so specified or described,

as appear to the Commission to be required by it for the purposes of the carrying out of any of its functions.

(3) Anything falling to be provided, produced or delivered up by any person in pursuance of a requirement imposed under subsection (2) must be provided, produced or delivered up in such form, in such manner and within such period as may be specified in—

(a) the notification imposing the requirement; or

(b) in any subsequent notification given by the Commission to that person for the purposes of this subsection.

(4) Nothing in this section shall require a police authority or chief officer—

(a) to provide the Commission with any information or document, or to produce or deliver up any other thing, before the earliest time at which it is practicable for that authority or chief officer to do so; or

(b) to provide, produce or deliver up anything at all in a case in which it never becomes practicable for that authority or chief officer to do so.

(5) A requirement imposed by any regulations or notification under this section may authorise or require information or documents to which it relates to be provided to the Commission electronically.

18 Inspections of police premises on behalf of the Commission

(1) Where—

(a) the Commission requires—

(i) a police authority maintaining any police force, or

(ii) the chief officer of police of any such force,

to allow a person nominated for the purpose by the Commission to have access to any premises occupied for the purposes of that force and to documents and other things on those premises, and

(b) the requirement is imposed for any of the purposes mentioned in subsection (2),

it shall be the duty of the authority or, as the case may be, of the chief officer to secure that the required access is allowed to the nominated person.

(2) Those purposes are—

(a) the purposes of any examination by the Commission of the efficiency and effectiveness of the arrangements made by the force in question for handling complaints or dealing with recordable conduct matters or DSI matters;

(b) the purposes of any investigation by the Commission under this Part or of any investigation carried out under its supervision or management.

(3) A requirement imposed under this section for the purposes mentioned in subsection (2)(a) must be notified to the authority or chief officer at least 48 hours before the time at which access is required.

(4) Where—

(a) a requirement imposed under this section for the purposes mentioned in sub-section (2)(a) requires access to any premises, document or thing to be allowed to any person, but

(b) there are reasonable grounds for not allowing that person to have the required access at the time at which he seeks to have it,

the obligation to secure that the required access is allowed shall have effect as an obligation to secure that the access is allowed to that person at the earliest practicable time after there cease to be any such grounds as that person may specify.

(5) The provisions of this section are in addition to, and without prejudice to—

(a) the rights of entry, search and seizure that are or may be conferred on—

(i) a person designated for the purposes of paragraph 19 of Schedule 3, or

(ii) any person who otherwise acts on behalf of the Commission,

in his capacity as a constable or as a person with the powers and privileges of a constable; or

(b) the obligations of police authorities and chief officers under sections 15 and 17.

19   Use of investigatory powers by or on behalf of the Commission

(1) The Secretary of State may by order make such provision as he thinks appropriate for the purpose of authorising—

(a) the use of directed and intrusive surveillance, and

(b) the conduct and use of covert human intelligence sources,

for the purposes of, or for purposes connected with, the carrying out of the Commission's functions.

(2) An order under this section may, for the purposes of or in connection with any such provision as is mentioned in subsection (1), provide for—

(a) Parts 2 and 4 the Regulation of Investigatory Powers Act 2000 (c. 23) (surveillance and covert human intelligence sources and scrutiny of investigatory powers), and

(b) Part 3 of the 1997 Act (authorisations in respect of property), to have effect with such modifications as may be specified in the order.

(3) The Secretary of State shall not make an order containing (with or without any other provision) any provision authorised by this section unless a draft of that order has been laid before Parliament and approved by a resolution of each House.

(4) Expressions used in this section and in Part 2 of the Regulation of Investigatory Powers Act 2000 have the same meanings in this section as in that Part.

20   Duty to keep the complainant informed

(1) In any case in which there is an investigation of a complaint in accordance with the provisions of Schedule 3—

(a) by the Commission, or

(b) under its management,

it shall be the duty of the Commission to provide the complainant with all such information as will keep him properly informed, while the investigation is being carried out and sub-sequently, of all the matters mentioned in subsection (4).

(2) In any case in which there is an investigation of a complaint in accordance with the provisions of Schedule 3—

(a) by the appropriate authority on its own behalf, or

(b) under the supervision of the Commission,

it shall be the duty of the appropriate authority to provide the complainant with all such information as will keep him properly informed, while the investigation is being carried out and subsequently, of all the matters mentioned in subsection (4).

(3) Where subsection (2) applies, it shall be the duty of the Commission to give the appropriate authority all such directions as it considers appropriate for securing that that authority complies with its duty under that subsection; and it shall be the duty of the appropriate authority to comply with any direction given to it under this subsection.

(4) The matters of which the complainant must be kept properly informed are—
  (a) the progress of the investigation;
  (b) any provisional findings of the person carrying out the investigation;
  (c) whether any report has been submitted under paragraph 22 of Schedule 3;
  (d) the action (if any) that is taken in respect of the matters dealt with in any such report; and
  (e) the outcome of any such action.

(5) The duties imposed by this section on the Commission and the appropriate authority in relation to any complaint shall be performed in such manner, and shall have effect subject to such exceptions, as may be provided for by regulations made by the Secretary of State.

(6) The Secretary of State shall not by regulations provide for any exceptions from the duties imposed by this section except so far as he considers it necessary to do so for the purpose of—
  (a) preventing the premature or inappropriate disclosure of information that is relevant to, or may be used in, any actual or prospective criminal proceedings;
  (b) preventing the disclosure of information in any circumstances in which it has been determined in accordance with the regulations that its non-disclosure—
    (i)   is in the interests of national security;
    (ii) is for the purposes of the prevention or detection of crime, or the apprehension or prosecution of offenders;
    (iii) is required on proportionality grounds; or
    (iv) is otherwise necessary in the public interest.

(7) The non-disclosure of information is required on proportionality grounds if its disclosure would cause, directly or indirectly, an adverse effect which would be disproportionate to the benefits arising from its disclosure.

(8) Regulations under this section may include provision framed by reference to the opinion of, or a determination by, the Commission or any police authority or chief officer.

(9) It shall be the duty of a person appointed to carry out an investigation under this Part to provide the Commission or, as the case may be, the appropriate authority with all such information as the Commission or that authority may reasonably require for the purpose of performing its duty under this section.

21 Duty to provide information for other persons

(1) A person has an interest in being kept properly informed about the handling of a complaint, recordable conduct matter or DSI matter if—
  (a) it appears to the Commission or to an appropriate authority that he is a person falling within subsection (2) or 2A; and
  (b) that person has indicated that he consents to the provision of information to him in accordance with this section and that consent has not been withdrawn.

(2) A person falls within this subsection if—
  (a) he is a relative of a person whose death is the alleged result from the conduct complained of or to which the recordable conduct matter relates;
  (b) he is a relative of a person whose serious injury is the alleged result from that conduct and that person is incapable of making a complaint;
  (c) he himself has suffered serious injury as the alleged result of that conduct.

(2A) A person falls within this subsection if (in the case of a DSI matter)—
  (a) he is a relative of the person who has died;
  (b) he is a relative of the person who has suffered serious injury and that person is incapable of making a complaint;
  (c) he himself is the person who has suffered serious injury.

(3) A person who does not fall within subsection (2) has an interest in being kept properly informed about the handling of a complaint, recordable conduct matter or DSI matter if—

(a) the Commission or an appropriate authority considers that he has an interest in the handling of the complaint, recordable conduct matter or DSI matter which is sufficient to make it appropriate for information to be provided to him in accordance with this section; and

(b) he has indicated that he consents to the provision of information to him in accordance with this section.

(4) In relation to a complaint, this section confers no rights on the complainant.

(5) A person who has an interest in being kept properly informed about the handling of a complaint, conduct matter or DSI matter is referred to in this section as an 'interested person'.

(6) In any case in which there is an investigation of the complaint, recordable conduct matter or DSI matter in accordance with the provisions of Schedule 3—

(a) by the Commission, or

(b) under its management,

it shall be the duty of the Commission to provide the interested person with all such information as will keep him properly informed, while the investigation is being carried out and subsequently, of all the matters mentioned in subsection (9).

(7) In any case in which there is an investigation of the complaint, recordable conduct matter or DSI matter in accordance with the provisions of Schedule 3—

(a) by the appropriate authority on its own behalf, or

(b) under the supervision of the Commission,

it shall be the duty of the appropriate authority to provide the interested person with all such information as will keep him properly informed, while the investigation is being carried out and subsequently, of all the matters mentioned in subsection (9).

(8) Where subsection (7) applies, it shall be the duty of the Commission to give the appropriate authority all such directions as it considers appropriate for securing that that authority complies with its duty under that subsection; and it shall be the duty of the appropriate authority to comply with any direction given to it under this subsection.

(9) The matters of which the interested person must be kept properly informed are—

(a) the progress of the investigation;

(b) any provisional findings of the person carrying out the investigation;

(ba) whether the Commission or the appropriate authority has made a determination under paragraph 21A of Schedule 3;

(c) whether any report has been submitted under paragraph 22 of Schedule 3 or 24A of Schedule 3;

(d) the action (if any) that is taken in respect of the matters dealt with in any such report; and

(e) the outcome of any such action.

(10) The duties imposed by this section on the Commission and the appropriate authority in relation to any complaint, recordable conduct matter or DSI matter shall be performed in such manner, and shall have effect subject to such exceptions, as may be provided for by regulations made by the Secretary of State.

(11) Subsections (6) to (9) of section 20 apply for the purposes of this section as they apply for the purposes of that section.

(12) In this section 'relative' means a person of a description prescribed in regulations made by the Secretary of State.

Guidance and regulations

22 Power of the Commission to issue guidance

(1) The Commission may issue guidance—

(a) to police authorities,

(b) to chief officers, and

(c) to persons who are serving with the police otherwise than as chief officers, concerning the exercise or performance, by the persons to whom the guidance is issued, of any of the powers or duties specified in subsection (2).

(2) Those powers and duties are—

(a) those that are conferred or imposed by or under this Part; and

(b) those that are otherwise conferred or imposed but relate to—

(i) the handling of complaints;

(ii) the means by which recordable conduct matters or DSI matters are dealt with; or

(iii) the detection or deterrence of misconduct by persons serving with the police.

(3) Before issuing any guidance under this section, the Commission shall consult with—

(a) persons whom it considers to represent the interests of police authorities;

(b) persons whom it considers to represent the interests of chief officers of police; and

(c) such other persons as it thinks fit.

(4) The approval of the Secretary of State shall be required for the issue by the Commission of any guidance under this section.

(5) Without prejudice to the generality of the preceding provisions of this section, the guidance that may be issued under this section includes—

(a) guidance about the handling of complaints which have not yet been recorded and about dealing with recordable conduct matters or DSI matters that have not been recorded;

(b) guidance about the procedure to be followed by the appropriate authority when recording a complaint or any recordable conduct matter or DSI matter;

(c) guidance about—

(i) how to decide whether a complaint is suitable for being subjected to local resolution; and

(ii) about the information to be provided to a person before his consent to such resolution is given;

(d) guidance about how to protect the scene of an incident or alleged incident which—

(i) is or may become the subject-matter of a complaint; or

(ii) is or may involve a recordable conduct matter or DSI matter;

(e) guidance about the circumstances in which it is appropriate (where it is lawful to do so)—

(i) to disclose to any person, or to publish, any information about an investigation of a complaint, conduct matter or DSI matter;

(ii) to provide any person with, or to publish, any report or other document relating to such an investigation;

(f) guidance about the matters to be included in a memorandum under paragraph 23 or 25 of Schedule 3 and about the manner in which, and the place at which, such a memorandum is to be delivered to the Commission.

(6) Nothing in this section shall authorise the issuing of any guidance about a particular case.

(7) It shall be the duty of every person to whom any guidance under this section is issued to have regard to that guidance in exercising or performing the powers and duties to which the guidance relates.

(8) A failure by a person to whom guidance under this section is issued to have regard to the guidance shall be admissible in evidence in any disciplinary proceedings or on any appeal from a decision taken in any such proceedings.

23   Regulations

(1) The Secretary of State may make regulations as to the procedure to be followed under any provision of this Part.

(2) Without prejudice to the generality of the power conferred by subsection (1) or of any other power to make regulations conferred by any provision of this Part, the Secretary of State may also by regulations provide—

(a) for the appropriate authority, in the case of a complaint against any person, to be required, in accordance with procedures provided for in the regulations—
   (i) to supply the person complained against with a copy of the complaint; and
   (ii) to supply the complainant with a copy of the record made of that complaint;
(b) for the matters to be taken into account in making any determination as to which procedure to adopt for handling complaints and dealing with recordable conduct matters and DSI matters;
(c) for any procedure for the purposes of this Part to be discontinued where—
   (i)   a complaint is withdrawn;
   (ii) the complainant indicates that he does not wish any further steps to be taken; or
   (iii) the whole or part of the investigation of the complaint has been postponed until the conclusion of criminal proceedings and the complainant fails to indicate after the conclusion of those proceedings that he wishes the investigation to be resumed;
   and for the manner in which any such withdrawal or indication is to be effected or given, and for the circumstances in which it is to be taken as effected or given;
(d) for requiring the subject-matter of a complaint that has been withdrawn to be treated for the purposes of this Part, in the cases and to the extent specified in the regulations, as a recordable conduct matter;
(e) for the manner in which any procedure for the purposes of this Part is to be discontinued in a case where it is discontinued in accordance with the regulations, and for the consequences of any such discontinuance;
(f) for the circumstances in which any investigation or other procedure under this Part may be or must be suspended to allow any other investigation or proceedings to continue, and for the consequences of such a suspension;
(g) for the regulation of the appointment of persons to carry out investigations under this Part or to assist with the carrying out of such investigations, for limiting the persons who may be appointed and for the regulation of the carrying out of any such investigation;
(h) for combining into a single investigation the investigation of any complaint, conduct matter or DSI matter with the investigation or investigations of any one or more, or any combination, of the following—
   (i)   complaints (whether relating to the same or different conduct),
   (ii) conduct matters; or
   (iii) DSI matters,
   and for splitting a single investigation into two or more separate investigations;
(i) for the procedure to be followed in cases in which the Commission relinquishes the supervision or management of any investigation and for the consequences of its doing so;
(j) for the manner in which any reference of a complaint, conduct matter or DSI matter to the Commission is to be made;
(k) for applying the provisions of this Part with such modifications as the Secretary of State thinks fit in cases where a complaint or recordable conduct matter relates to the conduct of a person who has ceased to be a person serving with the police since the time of the conduct;
(l) for applying the provisions of this Part with such modifications as the Secretary of State thinks fit in cases where a complaint or conduct matter relates to the conduct of a person—
   (i)   whose identity is unascertained at the time at which a complaint is made or a conduct matter is recorded;

(ii) whose identity is not ascertained during, or subsequent to, the investigation of a complaint or recordable conduct matter;

(m) for the Commission—

(i) to be required to notify actions and decisions it takes in consequence of the receipt of a memorandum under paragraph 23 or 25 of Schedule 3; and

(ii) to be authorised to provide information in relation to the matters notified;

(n) for the records to be kept by police authorities and chief officers—

(i) with respect to complaints and purported complaints;

(ii) with respect to recordable conduct matters or DSI matters; and

(iii) with respect to the exercise and performance of their powers and duties under this Part;

(o) for the Commission to be required to establish and maintain a register of such information provided to it in accordance with this Part as may be of a description specified in the regulations and for regulating the extent to which information stored on that register, may be published or otherwise disclosed to any person by the Commission;

(p) for chief officers to have power to delegate the exercise or performance of powers and duties conferred or imposed on them by or under this Part;

(q) for the manner in which any notification for the purposes of any provision of this Part is to be given and the time at which, or period within which, any such notification must be given.

24 Consultation on regulations

Before making any regulations under this Part, the Secretary of State shall consult with—

(a) the Commission;

(b) persons whom he considers to represent the interests of police authorities;

(c) persons whom he considers to represent the interests of chief officers of police; and

(d) such other persons as he thinks fit.

Conduct of persons in other forms of police service

26 Forces maintained otherwise than by police authorities

(1) Notwithstanding any provision made by or under any enactment passed or made before this Act—

(a) the Commission, and

(b) an authority other than a police authority which maintains a body of constables,

shall each have power to enter into an agreement with the other for the establishment and maintenance in relation to that body of constables of procedures corresponding or similar to any of those provided for by or under this Part.

(2) If it appears to the Secretary of State appropriate to do so in relation to any body of constables maintained otherwise than by a police authority to establish any such corresponding or similar procedures, he may by order—

(a) provide for the establishment and maintenance of such procedures in relation to that body of constables; and

(b) in a case in which procedures in relation to that body of constables have effect by virtue of subsection (9) or have previously been established by virtue of this section—

(i) provide for those procedures to be superseded by the provision made by the order; and

(ii) make transitional provision in connection with the replacement of the superseded procedures.

(3) It shall be the duty of the Secretary of State to secure that procedures are established and maintained under subsection (2) in relation to each of the following—

(a) the Ministry of Defence Police; and

(b) the British Transport Police Force.

(4) An agreement under this section shall not be made, varied or terminated except with the approval of the Secretary of State.

(5) An agreement or order under this section in relation to any body of constables may contain provision for enabling the Commission to bring and conduct, or otherwise participate or intervene in, any proceedings which are identified by the agreement or order as disciplinary proceedings in relation to members of that body of constables.

(6) An agreement or order under this section in relation to any body of constables may provide for the application of procedures in relation to persons who are not themselves constables but are employed for the purposes of that body of constables and in relation to the conduct of such persons, as well as in relation to members of that body of constables and their conduct.

(7) Before making an order under this section the Secretary of State shall consult with both—
    (a) the Commission; and
    (b) the authority maintaining the body of constables to whom the order relates.

(8) Procedures established in accordance with any agreement or order under this section shall have no effect in relation to anything done outside England and Wales by any constable or any person employed for the purposes of a body of constables.

(9) Where, immediately before the coming into force of this section, any procedures have effect in relation to any body of constables by virtue of—
    (a) section 78 of the 1996 Act (which made provisions similar to that made by this section), or
    (b) paragraph 13 of Schedule 8 to that Act (transitional provisions),
those procedures shall continue to have effect thereafter (notwithstanding the repeal by this Act of Chapter 1 of Part 4 of the 1996 Act and of that paragraph) until superseded by procedures established by virtue of any agreement or order under this section.

(10) Subsection (9) has effect subject to the provisions of any order made under section 28.

27 Conduct of the Commission's staff

(1) The Secretary of State shall by regulations make provision for the manner in which the following cases are to be handled or dealt with—
    (a) cases in which allegations of misconduct are made against members of the Commission's staff; and
    (b) cases in which there is otherwise an indication that there may have been misconduct by a member of the Commission's staff.

(2) Regulations under this section may apply, with such modifications as the Secretary of State thinks fit, any provision made by or under this Part.

(3) Regulations under this section may provide for it to be the duty of any person on whom functions are conferred by the regulations to have regard, in the carrying out of those functions, to any guidance given by such persons and in such manner as may be specified in the regulations.

(4) Before making any regulations under this section the Secretary of State shall consult with the Commission.

Transitional provisions

28 Transitional arrangements connected with establishing the Commission etc.

(1) The Secretary of State may, in connection with the coming into force of any provision of this Part, by order make such transitional provision and savings (including provision modifying this Part) as he thinks fit.

(2) The Secretary of State may, for the purpose of facilitating the carrying out by the Commission of its functions, or in connection with the coming into force of any provision of this Part, by order make such provision as he thinks fit—
    (a) for the transfer and apportionment of property; and
    (b) for the transfer, apportionment and creation of rights and liabilities.

(3) The provision that may be made by an order under this section shall include provision that—

    (a) pending the coming into force of any repeal by this Act of an enactment contained in Chapter 1 of Part 4 of the 1996 Act (complaints), or

    (b) for transitional purposes connected with the coming into force of any such repeal,

the functions of the Police Complaints Authority under an enactment so contained are to be carried out by the Commission.

(4) The provision that may be made by an order under this section shall also include transitional provision in connection with the repeal by this Act of the reference to the Police Complaints Authority in Schedule 1 to the Superannuation Act 1972 (c. 11).

(5) An order under this section may—

    (a) provide for the Secretary of State, or any other person nominated by or in accordance with the order, to determine any matter requiring determination under or in consequence of the order; and

    (b) make provision as to the payment of fees charged, or expenses incurred, by any person nominated to determine any matter by virtue of paragraph (a).

(6) Where a person—

    (a) ceases to be a member of the Police Complaints Authority by reason of its abolition, and

    (b) does not become a member of the Commission,

the Secretary of State may make a payment to that person of such amount as the Secretary of State may, with the consent of the Treasury, determine.

Interpretation of Part 2

29 Interpretation of Part 2

(1) In this Part—

'the appropriate authority'—

    (a) in relation to a person serving with the police or in relation to any complaint, conduct matter or investigation relating to the conduct of such a person, means—

        (i) if that person is a senior officer, the police authority for the area of the police force of which he is a member; and

        (ii) if he is not a senior officer, the chief officer under whose direction and control he is; and

    (b) in relation to a death or serious injury matter, means—

        (i) if the relevant officer is a senior officer, the police authority for the area of the police force of which he is a member; and

        (ii) if he is not a senior officer, the chief officer under whose direction and control he is;

'chief officer' means the chief officer of police of any police force;

'the Commission' has the meaning given by section 9(1);

'complainant' shall be construed in accordance with subsection (2);

'complaint' has the meaning given by section 12;

'conduct' includes acts, omissions and statements (whether actual, alleged or inferred);

'conduct matter' has the meaning given by section 12;

'death or serious injury matter' and 'DSI matter' have the meaning given by section 12;

'disciplinary proceedings' means—

    (a) in relation to a member of a police force or a special constable, proceedings under any regulations made by virtue of section 50 or 51 of the 1996 Act and identified as disciplinary proceedings by those regulations; and

    (b) in relation to a person serving with the police who is not a member of a police force or a special constable, proceedings identified as such by regulations made by the Secretary of State for the purposes of this Part;

'document' means anything in which information of any description is recorded;

'information' includes estimates and projections, and statistical analyses;

'local resolution', in relation to a complaint, means the handling of that complaint in accordance with a procedure which—

(a) does not involve a formal investigation; and

(b) is laid down by regulations under paragraph 8 of Schedule 3 for complaints which it has been decided, in accordance with paragraph 6 of that Schedule, to subject to local resolution;

'person complained against', in relation to a complaint, means the person whose conduct is the subject-matter of the complaint;

'recordable conduct matter' means (subject to any regulations under section 23(2)(d))—

(a) a conduct matter that is required to be recorded by the appropriate authority under paragraph 10 or 11 of Schedule 3 or has been so recorded; or

(b) except in sub-paragraph (4) of paragraph 2 of Schedule 3, any matter brought to the attention of the appropriate authority under that sub-paragraph;

'relevant force', in relation to the appropriate authority, means—

(a) if that authority is a police authority, the police force maintained by it; and

(b) if that authority is the chief officer of police of a police force, his force;

'senior officer' means a member of a police force holding a rank above that of chief superintendent;

'serious injury' means a fracture, a deep cut, a deep laceration or an injury causing damage to an internal organ or the impairment of any bodily function;

'serving with the police', in relation to any person, shall be construed in accordance with section 12(7).

(1A) In this Part 'the relevant officer', in relation to a DSI matter, means the person serving with the police (within the meaning of section 12(7))—

(a) who arrested the person who has died or suffered serious injury,

(b) in whose custody that person was at the time of the death or serious injury, or

(c) with whom that person had the contact in question;

and where there is more than one such person it means, subject to subsection (1B), the one who so dealt with him last before the death or serious injury occurred.

(1B) Where it cannot be determined which of two or more persons serving with the police dealt with a person last before a death or serious injury occurred, the relevant officer is the most senior of them.

(2) References in this Part, in relation to anything which is or purports to be a complaint, to the complainant are references—

(a) except in the case of anything which is or purports to be a complaint falling within section 12(1)(d), to the person by whom the complaint or purported complaint was made; and

(b) in that case, to the person on whose behalf the complaint or purported complaint was made;

but where any person is acting on another's behalf for the purposes of any complaint or purported complaint, anything that is to be or may be done under this Part by or in relation to the complainant may be done, instead, by or in relation to the person acting on the complainant's behalf.

(3) Subject to subsection (4), references in this Part, in relation to any conduct or anything purporting to be a complaint about any conduct, to a member of the public include references to any person falling within any of the following paragraphs (whether at the time of the conduct or at any subsequent time)—

(a) a person serving with the police;

(b) a member of the staff of the Serious Organised Crime Agency;

(c) a member of the staff of the Central Police Training and Development Authority; or

(d) a person engaged on relevant service, within the meaning of section 97(1)(a), (cc) or (d) of the 1996 Act (temporary service of various kinds).

(4) In this Part references, in relation to any conduct or to anything purporting to be a complaint about any conduct, to a member of the public do not include references to—

(a) a person who, at the time when the conduct is supposed to have taken place, was under the direction and control of the same chief officer as the person whose conduct it was; or

(b) a person who—

(i) at the time when the conduct is supposed to have taken place, in relation to him, or

(ii) at the time when he is supposed to have been adversely affected by it, or to have witnessed it,

was on duty in his capacity as a person falling within subsection (3)(a) to (d).

(5) For the purposes of this Part a person is adversely affected if he suffers any form of loss or damage, distress or inconvenience, if he is put in danger or if he is otherwise unduly put at risk of being adversely affected.

(6) References in this Part to the investigation of any complaint or matter by the appropriate authority on its own behalf, under the supervision of the Commission, under the management of the Commission or by the Commission itself shall be construed as references to its investigation in accordance with paragraph 16, 17, 18 or, as the case may be, 19 of Schedule 3.

(7) The Commissioner of Police for the City of London shall be treated for the purposes of this Part as if he were a member of the City of London police force.

Prosecutorial review

Prosecution of Offences Act 1985

1   The Crown Prosecution Service

(1) There shall be a prosecuting service for England and Wales (to be known as the 'Crown Prosecution Service') consisting of—

(a) the Director of Public Prosecutions, who shall be head of the Service;

(b) the Chief Crown Prosecutors, designated under subsection (4) below, each of whom shall be the member of the Service responsible to the Director for supervising the operation of the Service in his area; and

(c) the other staff appointed by the Director under this section.

(2) The Director shall appoint such staff for the Service as, with the approval of the Treasury as to numbers, remuneration and other terms and conditions of service, he considers necessary for the discharge of his functions.

(3) The Director may designate any member of the Service who has a general qualification within the meaning of section 71 of the Courts and Legal Services Act 1990 for the purposes of this subsection, and any person so designated shall be known as a Crown Prosecutor.

(4) The Director shall divide England and Wales into areas and, for each of those areas, designate a Crown Prosecutor for the purposes of this subsection and any person so designated shall be known as a Chief Crown Prosecutor.

(5) The Director may, from time to time, vary the division of England and Wales made for the purposes of subsection (4) above.

(6) Without prejudice to any functions which may have been assigned to him in his capacity as a member of the Service, every Crown Prosecutor shall have all the powers of the

Director as to the institution and conduct of proceedings but shall exercise those powers under the direction of the Director.

(7) Where any enactment (whenever passed)—

(a) prevents any step from being taken without the consent of the Director or without his consent or the consent of another; or

(b) requires any step to be taken by or in relation to the Director;

any consent given by or, as the case may be, step taken by or in relation to, a Crown Prosecutor shall be treated, for the purposes of that enactment, as given by or, as the case may be, taken by or in relation to the Director.

2   The Director of Public Prosecutions

(1) The Director of Public Prosecutions shall be appointed by the Attorney General.

(2) The Director must be a person who has a 10 year general qualification within the meaning of section 71 of the Courts and Legal Services Act 1990.

(3) There shall be paid to the Director such remuneration as the Attorney General may, with the approval of the Treasury, determine.

3   Functions of the director

(1) The Director shall discharge his functions under this or any other enactment under the superintendence of the Attorney General.

(2) It shall be the duty of the Director, subject to any provisions contained in the Criminal Justice Act 1987—

(a) to take over the conduct of all criminal proceedings, other than specified proceedings, instituted on behalf of a police force (whether by a member of that force or by any other person);

(aa) to take over the conduct of any criminal proceedings instituted by an immigration officer (as defined for the purposes of the Immigration Act 1971) acting in his capacity as such an officer,

(b) to institute and have the conduct of criminal proceedings in any case where it appears to him that—

(i)   the importance or difficulty of the case makes it appropriate that proceedings should be instituted by him; or

(ii) it is otherwise appropriate for proceedings to be instituted by him;

(ba) to institute and have the conduct of any criminal proceedings in any case where the proceedings relate to the subject-matter of a report a copy of which has been sent to him under paragraph 23 or 24 of Schedule 3 of the Police Reform Act 2002 (c. 30) (reports an investigations into conduct of persons serving with the police);

(c) to take over the conduct of all binding over proceedings instituted on behalf of a police force (whether by a member of that force or by any other person);

(d) to take over the conduct of all proceedings begun by summons issued under section 3 of the Obscene Publications Act 1959 (forfeiture of obscene articles);

(e) to give, to such extent as he considers appropriate, advice to police forces on all matters relating to criminal offences;

(ea) to have the conduct of any extradition proceedings;

(eb) to give, to such extent as he considers appropriate, and to such persons as he considers appropriate, advice on any matters relating to extradition proceedings or proposed extradition proceedings;'

(f)   to appear for the prosecution, when directed by the court to do so, on any appeal under—

(i)   section 1 of the Administration of Justice Act 1960 (appeal from the High Court in criminal cases):

(ii) Part I or Part II of the Criminal Appeal Act 1968 (appeals from the Crown Court to the criminal division of the Court of Appeal and thence to the House of Lords); or

(iii) section 108 of the Magistrates' Courts Act 1980 (right of appeal to Crown Court) as it applies, by virtue of subsection (5) of section 12 of the Contempt of Court Act 1981, to orders made under section 12 (contempt of magistrates' courts);

(fa) to have the conduct of applications for orders under section 1C of the Crime and Disorder Act 1998 (orders made on conviction of certain offences) and section 14A of the Football Spectators Act 1989 (banning orders made on conviction of certain offences);

(fb) where it appears to him appropriate to do so, to have the conduct of applications under section 1CA(3) of the Crime and Disorder Act 1998 for the variation or discharge of orders made under section 1C of that Act;

(fc) where it appears to him appropriate to do so, to appear on any application under section 1CA of that Act made by a person subject to an order under section 1C of that Act for the variation or discharge of the order.

(g) to discharge such other functions as may from time to time be assigned to him by the Attorney General in pursuance of this paragraph.

(2A) Subsection (2)(ea) above does not require the Director to have the conduct of any extradition proceedings in respect of a person if he has received a request not to do so and—

(a) in a case where the proceedings are under Part 1 of the Extradition Act 2003, the request is made by the authority which issued the Part 1 warrant in respect of the person;

(b) in a case where the proceedings are under Part 2 of that Act, the request is made on behalf of the territory to which the person's extradition has been requested.

(3) In this section—

'the court' means—

(a) in the case of an appeal to or from the criminal division of the Court of Appeal, that division;

(b) in the case of an appeal from a Divisional Court of the Queen's Bench Division, the Divisional Court; and

(c) in the case of an appeal against an order of a magistrates' court, the Crown Court;

'police force' means any police force maintained by a police authority under the Police Act 1996, and any other body of constables for the time being specified by order made by the Secretary of State for the purposes of this section; and

'specified proceedings' means proceedings which fall within any category for the time being specified by order made by the Attorney General for the purposes of this section.

(4) The power to make orders under subsection (3) above shall be exercisable by statutory instrument subject to annulment in pursuance of a resolution of either House of Parliament.

10 Guidelines for Crown Prosecutors

(1) The Director shall issue a Code for Crown Prosecutors giving guidance on general principles to be applied by them—

(a) in determining, in any case—

(i) whether proceedings for an offence should be instituted or, where proceedings have been instituted, whether they should be discontinued; or

(ii) what charges should be preferred; and

(b) in considering, in any case, representations to be made by them to any magistrates' court about the mode of trial suitable for that case.

(2) The Director may from time to time make alterations in the Code.

(3) The provisions of the Code shall be set out in the Director's report under section 9 of this Act for the year in which the Code is issued; and any alteration in the Code shall be set out in his report under that section for the year in which the alteration is made.

Bail

Bail Act 1976

Incidents of bail in criminal proceedings

3 General provisions

(1) A person granted bail in criminal proceedings shall be under a duty to surrender to custody, and that duty is enforceable in accordance with section 6 of this Act.

(2) No recognizance for his surrender to custody shall be taken from him.

(3) Except as provided by this section—

(a) no security for his surrender to custody shall be taken from him.

(b) he shall not be required to provide a surety or sureties for his surrender to custody, and

(c) no other requirement shall be imposed on him as a condition of bail.

(4) He may be required, before release on bail, to provide a surety or sureties to secure his surrender to custody.

(5) He may be required, before release on bail, to give security for his surrender to custody.

The security may be given by him or on his behalf.

(6) He may be required to comply, before release on bail or later, with such requirements as appear to the court to be necessary—

(a) to secure that he surrenders to custody.

(b) to secure that he does not commit an offence while on bail,

(c) to secure that he does not interfere with witnesses or otherwise obstruct the course of justice whether in relation to himself or any other person,

(ca) for his own protection or, if he is a child or young person, for his own welfare, or in his own interests,

(d) to secure that he makes himself available for the purpose of enabling inquiries or a report to be made to assist the court in dealing with him for the offence.

(e) to secure that before the time appointed for him to surrender to custody, he attends an interview with an authorised advocate or authorised litigator, as defined by section 119(1) of the Courts and Legal Services Act 1990;

and, in any Act, 'the normal powers to impose conditions of bail' means the powers to impose conditions under paragraph (a), (b), (c) or (ca) above.

(6ZAA) Subject to section 3AA below, if he is a child or young person he may be required to comply with requirements imposed for the purpose of securing the electronic monitoring of his compliance with any other requirement imposed on him as a condition of bail.

(6ZA) Where he is required under subsection (6) above to reside in a bail hostel or probation hostel, he may also be required to comply with the rules of the hostel.

(6A) In the case of a person accused of murder the court granting bail shall, unless it considers that satisfactory reports on his mental condition have already been obtained, impose as conditions of bail—

(a) a requirement that the accused shall undergo examination by two medical practitioners, for the purpose of enabling such reports to be prepared; and

(b) a requirement that he shall for that purpose attend such an institution or place as the court directs and comply with any other directions which may be given to him for that purpose by either of those practitioners.

(6B) Of the medical practitioners referred to in subsection (6A) above at least one shall be practitioner approved for the purposes of section 12 of the Mental Health Act 1983.

(6C) Subsection (6D) below applies where—

 (a) the court has been notified by the Secretary of State that arrangements for conducting a relevant assessment or, as the case may be, providing relevant follow-up have been made for the petty sessions area in which it appears to the court that the person referred to in subsection (6D) would reside if granted bail; and

 (b) the notice has not been withdrawn.

(6D) In the case of a person ('P')—

 (a) in relation to whom paragraphs (a) to (c) of paragraph 6B(1) of Part 1 of Schedule 1 to this Act apply;

 (b) who, after analysis of the sample referred to in paragraph (b) of that paragraph, has been offered a relevant assessment or, if a relevant assessment has been carried out, has had relevant follow-up proposed to him; and

 (c) who has agreed to undergo the relevant assessment or, as the case may be, to participate in the relevant follow-up,

the court, if it grants bail, shall impose as a condition of bail that P both undergo the relevant assessment and participate in any relevant follow-up proposed to him or, if a relevant assessment has been carried out, that P participate in the relevant follow-up.

(6E) In subsections (6C) and (6D) above—

 (a) 'relevant assessment' means an assessment conducted by a suitably qualified person of whether P is dependent upon or has a propensity to misuse any specified Class A drugs;

 (b) 'relevant follow-up' means, in a case where the person who conducted the relevant assessment believes P to have such a dependency or propensity, such further assessment, and such assistance or treatment (or both) in connection with the dependency or propensity, as the person who conducted the relevant assessment (or conducts any later assessment) considers to be appropriate in P's case,

and in paragraph (a) above 'Class A drug' and 'misuse' have the same meaning as in the Misuse of Drugs Act 1971, and 'specified' (in relation to a Class A drug) has the same meaning as in Part 3 of the Criminal Justice and Court Services Act 2000.

(6F) In subsection (6E)(a) above, 'suitably qualified person' means a person who has such qualifications or experience as are from time to time specified by the Secretary of State for the purposes of this subsection.

Subsections (6C) to (6F) presently apply only where courts have been notified separately by the Secretary of State.

(7) If a parent or guardian of a child or young person consents to be surety for the child or young person for the purposes of this subsection, the parent or guardian may be required to secure that the child or young person complies with any requirement imposed on him by virtue of subsection (6), (6ZAA) or (6A) above, but—

 (a) no requirement shall be imposed on the parent or the guardian of a young person by virtue of this subsection where it appears that the young person will attain the age of seventeen before the time to be appointed for him to surrender to custody; and

 (b) the parent or guardian shall not be required to secure compliance with any requirement to which his consent does not extend and shall not, in respect of those requirements to which his consent does extend, be bound in a sum greater than £50.

(8) Where a court has granted bail in criminal proceedings that court or, where that court has sent a person on bail to the Crown Court for trial or to be sentenced or otherwise dealt with, that court or the Crown Court may on application—

 (a) by or on behalf of the person to whom bail was granted, or

 (b) by the prosecutor or a constable,

vary the conditions of bail or impose conditions in respect of bail which it has granted unconditionally.

(8A) Where a notice of transfer is given under a relevant transfer provision, subsection (8) above shall have effect in relation to a person in relation to whose case the notice is given as if he has been committed on bail on the Crown Court for trial.

(8B) Subsection (8) above applies where a court has sent a person on bail to the Crown Court for trial under section 51 of the Crime and Disorder Act 1998 as it applies where a court has committed a person on bail to the Crown Court for trial.

(9) This section is subject to subsection (3) of section 11 of the Powers of Criminal Courts (Sentencing) Act 2000 (conditions of bail on remand for medical examination).

(10) This section is subject, in its application to bail granted by a constable, to section 3A of this Act.

(10A) In subsection (8A) above 'relevant transfer provision' means—

    (a) section 4 of the Criminal Justice Act 1987, or

    (b) section 53 of the Criminal Justice Act 1991.

3A Conditions of bail in case of police bail

(1) Section 3 of this Act applies, in relation to bail granted by a custody officer under Part IV of the Police and Criminal Evidence Act 1984 in cases where the normal powers to impose conditions of bail are available to him, subject to the following modifications.

(2) Subsection (6) does not authorise the imposition of a requirement to reside in a bail hostel or any requirement under paragraph (d) or (e).

(3) Subsections (6ZAA), (6ZA) and (6A) to (6F) shall be omitted.

(4) For subsection (8), substitute the following—

'(8) Where a custody officer has granted bail in criminal proceedings he or another custody officer serving at the same police station may, at the request of the person to whom it was granted, vary the conditions of bail; and in doing so he may impose conditions or more onerous conditions.'.

(5) Where a constable grants bail to a person no conditions shall be imposed under subsections (4), (5), (6) or (7) of section 3 of this Act unless it appears to the constable that it is necessary to do so—

    (a) for the purpose of preventing that person from failing to surrender to custody, or

    (b) for the purpose of preventing that person from committing an offence while on bail, or

    (c) for the purpose of preventing that person from interfering with witnesses or otherwise obstructing the course of justice, whether in relation to himself or any other person, or

    (d) for that person's own protection or, if he is a child or young person, for his own welfare or in his own interests.

(6) Subsection (5) above also applies on any request to a custody officer under subsection (8) of section 3 of this Act to vary the conditions of bail.

3AA Electronic monitoring of compliance with bail conditions

(1) A court shall not impose on a child or young person a requirement under section 3 (6ZAA) above (an 'electronic monitoring requirement') unless each of the following conditions is satisfied.

(2) The first condition is that the child or young person has attained the age of twelve years.

(3) The second condition is that—

    (a) the child or young person is charged with or has been convicted of a violent or sexual offence, or an offence punishable in the case of an adult with imprisonment for a term of fourteen years or more; or

    (b) he is charged with or has been convicted of one or more imprisonable offences which, together with any other imprisonable offences of which he has been convicted in any proceedings—

        (i) amount, or

      (ii) would, if he were convicted of the offences with which he is charged, amount, to a recent history of repeatedly committing imprisonable offences while remanded on bail or to local authority accommodation.

(4) The third condition is that the court—

      (a) has been notified by the Secretary of State that electronic monitoring arrangements are available in each petty sessions area which is a relevant area; and

      (b) is satisfied that the necessary provision can be made under those arrangements.

(5) The fourth condition is that a youth offending team has informed the court that in its opinion the imposition of such a requirement will be suitable in the case of the child or young person.

(6) Where a court imposes an electronic monitoring requirement, the requirement shall include provision for making a person responsible for the monitoring; and a person who is made so responsible shall be of a description specified in an order made by the Secretary of State.

(7) The Secretary of State may make rules for regulating—

      (a) the electronic monitoring of compliance with requirements imposed on a child or young person as a condition of bail; and

      (b) without prejudice to the generality of paragraph (a) above, the functions of persons made responsible for securing the electronic monitoring of compliance with such requirements.

(8) Rules under this section may make different provision for different cases.

(9) Any power of the Secretary of State to make an order or rules under this section shall be exercisable by statutory instrument.

(10) A statutory instrument containing rules made under this section shall be subject to annulment in pursuance of a resolution of either House of Parliament.

(11) In this section 'local authority accommodation' has the same meaning as in the Children and Young Persons Act 1969 (c. 54).

(12) For the purposes of this section a petty sessions area is a relevant area in relation to a proposed electronic monitoring requirement if the court considers that it will not be practicable to secure the electronic monitoring in question unless electronic monitoring arrangements are available in that area.

Bail for accused persons and others

4   General right to bail of accused persons and others

(1) A person to whom this section applies shall be granted bail except as provided in Schedule 1 to this Act.

(2) This section applies to a person who is accused of an offence when—

      (a) he appears or is brought before a magistrates' court or the Crown Court in the course of or in connection with proceedings for the offence, or

      (b) he applies to a court for bail or for a variation of the conditions of bail in connection with the proceedings.

This subsection does not apply as respects proceedings on or against a person's conviction of the offence.

(2A) This section also applies to a person whose extradition is sought in respect of an offence, when—

      (a) he appears or is brought before a court in the course of or in connection with extradition proceedings in respect of the offence, or

      (b) he applies to a court for bail or for a variation of the conditions of bail in connection with the proceedings.

(2B) But subsection (2A) above does not apply if the person is alleged to be unlawfully at large after conviction of the offence.

(3) This section also applies to a person who, having been convicted of an offence, appears or is brought before a magistrates' court or the Crown Court to be dealt with under—

(a) Part 2 of Schedule 3 to the Powers of Criminal Courts (Sentencing) Act 2000 (breach of certain youth community orders), or

(b) Part 2 of Schedule 8 to the Criminal Justice Act 2003 (breach of requirement of community order).

(4) This section also applies to a person who has been convicted of an offence of enabling inquiries or a report to be made for the purpose of enabling inquiries or a report to be made to assist the court in dealing with him for the offence.

(5) Schedule 1 to this Act also has effect as respects conditions of bail for a person to whom this section applies.

(6) In Schedule 1 to this Act 'the defendant' means a person to whom this section applies and any reference to a defendant whose case is adjourned for inquiries or a report is a reference to a person to whom this section applies by virtue of subsection (4) above.

(7) This section is subject to section 41 of the Magistrates' Courts Act 1980 (restriction of bail by magistrates' court in cases of treason).

(8) This section is subject to section 25 of the Criminal Justice and Public Order Act 1994 (exclusion of bail in cases of homicide and rape).

(9) In taking any decisions required by Part I or II of Schedule 1 to this Act, the considerations to which the court is to have regard include, so far as relevant, any misuse of controlled drugs by the defendant ('controlled drugs' and 'misuse' having the same meanings as in the Misuse of Drugs Act 1971).

5 Supplementary provisions about decisions on bail

(1) Subject to subsection (2) below, where—

(a) a court or constable grants bail in criminal proceedings, or

(b) a court withholds bail in criminal proceedings from a person to whom section 4 of this Act applies, or

(c) a court, officer of a court or constable appoints a time or place or a court or officer of a court appoints a different time or place for a person granted bail in criminal proceedings to surrender to custody, or

(d) a court or constable varies any conditions of bail or imposes conditions in respect of bail in criminal proceedings,

that court, officer or constable shall make a record of the decision in the prescribed manner and containing the prescribed particulars and, if requested to do so by the person in relation to whom the decision was taken, shall cause him to be given a copy of the record of the decision as soon as practicable after the record is made.

(2) Where bail in criminal proceedings is granted by endorsing a warrant of arrest for bail the constable who releases on bail the person arrested shall make the record required by subsection (1) above instead of the judge or justice who issued the warrant.

(2A) Where a magistrates' court or the Crown Court grants bail in criminal proceedings to a person to whom section 4 of this Act applies after hearing representations from the prosecutor in favour of withholding bail, then the court shall give reasons for granting bail.

(2B) A court which is by virtue of subsection (2A) above required to give reasons for its decision shall include a note of those reasons in the record of its decision and, if requested to do so by the prosecutor, shall cause the prosecutor to be given a copy of the record of the decision as soon as practicable after the record is made.

(3) Where a magistrates' court or the Crown Court—

(a) withholds bail in criminal proceedings, or

(b) imposes conditions in granting bail in criminal proceedings, or

(c) varies any conditions of bail or imposes conditions in respect of bail in criminal proceedings,

and does so in relation to a person to whom section 4 of this Act applies, then the court shall, with a view to enabling him to consider making an application in the matter to another court, give reasons for withholding bail or for imposing or varying the conditions.

(4) A court which is by virtue of subsection (3) above required to give reasons for its decision shall include a note of those reasons in the record of its decision and shall (except in a case where, by virtue of subsection (5) below, this need not be done) give a copy of that note to the person in relation to whom the decision was taken.

(5) The Crown Court need not give a copy of the note of the reasons for its decision to the person in relation to whom the decision was taken where that person is represented by counsel or a solicitor unless his counsel or solicitor requests the court to do so.

(6) Where a magistrates' court withholds bail in criminal proceedings from a person who is not represented by counsel or a solicitor, the court shall—

(a) if it is sending him for trial to the Crown Court, or if it issues a certificate under subsection (6A) below, inform him that he may apply to the Crown Court to be granted bail.

(6A) Where in criminal proceedings—

(a) a magistrates' court remands a person in custody under section 52(5) of the Crime and Disorder Act 1998, section 11 of the Powers of Criminal Courts (Sentencing) Act 2000 (remand for medical examination) or any of the following provisions of the Magistrates' Courts Act 1980—
   (i)   section 5 (adjournment of inquiry into offence);
   (ii) section 10 (adjournment of trial); or
   (iii) section 18 (initial procedure on information against adult for offence triable either way),

after hearing full argument on an application for bail from him; and

(b) either—
   (i) it has not previously heard such argument on an application for bail from him in those proceedings; or
   (ii) it has previously heard full argument from him on such an application but it is satisfied that there has been a change in his circumstances or that new considerations have been placed before it,

it shall be the duty of the court to issue a certificate in the prescribed form that they heard full argument on his application for bail before they refused the application.

(6B) Where the court issues a certificate under subsection (6A) above in a case to which paragraph (b)(ii) of that subsection applies, it shall state in the certificate the nature of the change of circumstances or the new considerations which caused it to hear a further fully argued bail application.

(6C) Where a court issues a certificate under subsection (6A) above it shall cause the person to whom it refuses bail to be given a copy of the certificate.

(7) Where a person has given security in pursuance of section 3(5) above and a court is satisfied that he failed to surrender to custody then, unless it appears that he had reasonable cause for his failure, the court may order the forfeiture of the security.

(8) If a court orders the forfeiture of a security under subsection (7) above, the court may declare that the forfeiture extends to such amount less than the full value of the security as it thinks fit to order.

(8A) An order under subsection (7) above shall, unless previously revoked, have effect at the end of twenty-one days beginning with the day on which it is made.

(8B) A court which has ordered the forfeiture of a security under subsection (7) above may, if satisfied on an application made by or on behalf of the person who gave it that he did after all have reasonable cause for his failure to surrender to custody, by order remit the forfeiture or declare that it extends to such amount less than the full value of the security as it thinks fit to order.

(8C) An application under subsection (8B) above may be made before or after the order for forfeiture has taken effect, but shall not be entertained unless the court is satisfied that the prosecution was given reasonable notice of the applicant's intention to make it.

(9) A security which has been ordered to be forfeited by a court under subsection (7) above shall, to the extent of the forfeiture—

(a) if it consists of money, be accounted for and paid in the same manner as a fine imposed by that court would be;

(b) if it does not consist of money, be enforced by such magistrates' court as may be specified in the order.

(9A) Where an order is made under subsection (8B) above after the order for forfeiture of the security in question has taken effect, any money which would have fallen to be repaid or paid over to the person who gave the security if the order under subsection (8B) had been made before the order for forfeiture took effect shall be repaid or paid over to him.

(10) In this section 'prescribed' means, in relation to the decision of a court or an officer of a court, prescribed by Supreme Court rules. Courts-Martial Appeal rules, Crown Court rules or magistrates' courts rules, as the case requires or, in relation to a decision of a constable, prescribed by direction of the Secretary of State.

(11) This section is subject, in its application to bail granted by a constable, to section 5A of this Act.

5A Supplementary provisions in cases of police bail

(1) Section 5 of this Act applies, in relation to bail granted by a custody officer under Part IV of the Police and Criminal Evidence Act 1984 in cases where the normal powers to impose conditions of bail are available to him, subject to the following modifications.

(1A) Subsections (2A) and (2B) shall be omitted.

(2) For subsection (3) substitute the following—

(3) Where a custody officer, in relation to any person,—

(a) imposes conditions in granting bail in criminal proceedings, or

(b) varies any conditions of bail or imposes conditions in respect of bail in criminal proceedings, the custody officer shall, with a view to enabling that person to consider requesting him or another custody officer, or making an application to a magistrates' court, to vary the conditions, give reasons for imposing or varying the conditions.

(3) For subsection (4) substitute the following—

(4) A custody officer who is by virtue of subsection (3) above required to give reasons for his decision shall include a note of those reasons in the custody record and shall give a copy of that note to the person in relation to whom the decision was taken.

(4) Subsections (5) and (6) shall be omitted.

5B Reconsideration of decisions granting bail

(A1) This section applies in any of these cases—

(a) a magistrates' court has granted bail in criminal proceedings in connection with an offence to which this section applies or proceedings for such an offence;

(b) a constable has granted bail in criminal proceedings in connection with proceedings for such an offence;

(c) a magistrates' court or a constable has granted bail in connection with extradition proceedings.

(1) The court of the appropriate court in relation to the constable may, on application by the prosecutor for the decision to be reconsidered—

(a) vary the conditions of bail,

(b) impose conditions in respect of bail which has been granted unconditionally, or

(c) withhold bail.

(2) The offences to which this section applies are offences triable on indictment and offences triable either way.

(3) No application for the reconsideration of a decision under this section shall be made unless it is based on information which was not available to the court or constable when the decision was taken.

(4) Whether or not the person to whom the application relates appears before it, the magistrates' court shall take the decision in accordance with section 4(1) (and Schedule 1) of this Act.

(5) Where the decision of the court on a reconsideration under this section is to withhold bail from the person to whom it was originally granted the court shall—

>   (a) if that person is before the court, remand him in custody, and
>   (b) if that person is not before the court, order him to surrender himself forthwith into the custody of the court.

(6) Where a person surrenders himself into the custody of the court in compliance with an order under subsection (5) above, the court shall remand him in custody.

(7) A person who has been ordered to surrender to custody under subsection (5) above may be arrested without warrant by a constable if he fails without reasonable cause to surrender to custody in accordance with the order.

(8) A person arrested in pursuance of subsection (7) above shall be brought as soon as practicable, and in any event within 24 hours after his arrest, before a justice of the peace and the justice shall remand him in custody.

In reckoning for the purposes of this subsection any period of 24 hours, no account shall be taken of Christmas Day, Good Friday or any Sunday.

(8A) Where the court, on a reconsideration under this section, refuses to withhold bail from a relevant person after hearing representations from the prosecutor in favour of withholding bail, then the court shall give reasons for refusing to withhold bail.

(8B) In subsection (8A) above, 'relevant person' means a person to whom section 4(1) (and Schedule 1) of this Act is applicable in accordance with subsection (4) above.

(8C) A court which is by virtue of subsection (8A) above required to give reasons for its decision shall include a note of those reasons in any record of its decision and, if requested to do so by the prosecutor, shall cause the prosecutor to be given a copy of any such record as soon as practicable after the record is made.

(9) Magistrates' court rules shall include provision—

>   (a) requiring notice of an application under this section and of the grounds for it to be given to the person affected, including notice of the powers available to the court under it;
>   (b) for securing that any representations made by the person affected (whether in writing or orally) are considered by the court before making its decision; and
>   (c) designating the court which is the appropriate court in relation to the decision of any constable to grant bail.

6   Offence of absconding by person released on bail

(1) If a person who has been released on bail in criminal proceedings fails without reasonable cause to surrender to custody he shall be guilty of an offence.

(2) If a person who—

>   (a) has been released on bail in criminal proceedings, and
>   (b) having reasonable cause therefor, has failed to surrender to custody,

fails to surrender to custody at the appointed place as soon after the appointed time as is reasonably practicable he shall be guilty of an offence.

(3) It shall be for the accused to prove that he had reasonable cause for his failure to surrender to custody.

(4) A failure to give to a person granted bail in criminal proceedings a copy of the record of the decision shall not constitute a reasonable cause for that person's failure to surrender to custody.

(5) An offence under subsection (1) or (2) above shall be punishable either on summary conviction or as if it were a criminal contempt of court.

(6) Where a magistrates' court convicts a person of an offence under subsection (1) or (2) above the court may, if it thinks—

(a) that the circumstances of the offence are such that greater punishment should be inflicted for that offence than the court has power to inflict, or

(b) in a case where it sends that person for trial to the Crown Court for another offence, that it would be appropriate for him to be dealt with for the offence under subsection (1) or (2) above by the court before which he is tried for the other offence,

commit him in custody or on bail to the Crown Court for sentence.

(7) A person who is convicted summarily of an offence under subsection (1) or (2) above and is committed to the Crown Court for sentence shall be liable to imprisonment for a term not exceeding 3 months or to a fine not exceeding level 5 on the standard scale or to both and a person who is so committed for sentence or is dealt with as for such a contempt shall be liable to imprisonment for a term not exceeding 12 months or to a fine or to both.

(8) In any proceedings for an offence under subsection (1) or (2) above a document purporting to be a copy of the part of the prescribed record which relates to the time and place appointed for the person specified in the record to surrender to custody and to be duly certified to be a true copy of that part of the record shall be evidence of the time and place appointed for that person to surrender to custody.

(9) For the purposes of subsection (8) above—

(a) 'the prescribed record' means the record of the decision of the court, officer or constable made in pursuance of section 5(1) of this Act:

(b) the copy of the prescribed record is duly certified if it is certified by the appropriate officer of the court or, as the case may be, by the constable who took the decision or a constable designated for the purpose by the officer in charge of the police station from which the person to whom the record relates was released;

(c) 'the appropriate officer' of the court is—

(i) in the case of a magistrates' court, the justices' chief executive or such other officer as may be authorised by him to act for the purpose;

(ii) in the case of the Crown Court, such officer as may be designated for the purpose in accordance with arrangements made by the Lord Chancellor;

(iii) in the case of the High Court, such officer as may be designated for the purpose in accordance with arrangements made by the Lord Chancellor;

(iv) in the case of the Court of Appeal, the registrar of criminal appeals or such other officer as may be authorised by him to act for the purpose;

(v) in the case of the Courts-Martial Appeal Court, the registrar or such other officer as may be authorised by him to act for the purpose.

(10) Section 127 of the Magistrates' Courts Act 1980 shall not apply in relation to an offence under subsection (1) or (2) above.

(11) Where a person has been released on bail in criminal proceedings and that bail was granted by a constable, a magistrates' court shall not try that person for an offence under subsection (1) or (2) above in relation to that bail (the 'relevant offence') unless either or both of subsections (12) and (13) below applies.

(12) This subsection applies if an information is laid for the relevant offence within 6 months from the time of the commission of the relevant offence.

(13) This subsection applies if an information is laid for the relevant offence no later than 3 months from the time of the occurrence of the first of the events mentioned in subsection (14) below to occur after the commission of the relevant offence.

(14) Those events are—

(a) the person surrenders to custody at the appointed place;

(b) the person is arrested, or attends at a police station, in connection with the relevant offence or the offence for which he was granted bail;

(c) the person appears or is brought before a court in connection with the relevant offence or the offence for which he was granted bail.

7 Liability to arrest for absconding or breaking conditions of bail

(1) If a person who has been released on bail in criminal proceedings and is under a duty to surrender into the custody of a court fails to surrender to custody at the time appointed for him to do so the court may issue a warrant for his arrest.

(1A) Subsection (1B) applies if—

(a) a person has been released on bail in connection with extradition proceedings,

(b) the person is under a duty to surrender into the custody of a constable, and

(c) the person fails to surrender to custody at the time appointed for him to do so.

(1B) A magistrates' court may issue a warrant for the person's arrest.

(2) If a person who has been released on bail in criminal proceedings absents himself from the court at any time after he has surrendered into the custody of the court and before the court is ready to begin or to resume the hearing of the proceedings, the court may issue a warrant for his arrest; but no warrant shall be issued under this subsection where that person is absent in accordance with leave given to him by or on behalf of the court.

(3) A person who has been released on bail in criminal proceedings and is under a duty to surrender into the custody of a court may be arrested without warrant by a constable—

(a) if the constable has reasonable grounds for believing that that person is not likely to surrender to custody;

(b) if the constable has reasonable grounds for believing that that person is likely to break any of the conditions of his bail or has reasonable grounds for suspecting that that person has broken any of those conditions; or

(c) in a case where that person was released on bail with one or more surety or sureties, if a surety notifies a constable in writing that that person is unlikely to surrender to custody and that for that reason the surety wishes to be relieved of his obligations as a surety.

(4) A person arrested in pursuance of subsection (3) above—

(a) shall, except where he was arrested within 24 hours of the time appointed for him to surrender to custody, be brought as soon as practicable and in any event within 24 hours after his arrest before a justice of the peace; and

(b) in the said excepted case shall be brought before the court at which he was to have surrendered to custody.

(4A) A person who has been released on bail in connection with extradition proceedings and is under a duty to surrender into the custody of a constable may be arrested without warrant on any of the grounds set out in paragraphs (a) to (c) of subsection (3).

(4B) A person arrested in pursuance of subsection (4A) above shall be brought as soon as practicable and in any event within 24 hours after his arrest before a justice of the peace for the petty sessions area in which he was arrested.'

(5) A justice of the peace before whom a person is brought under subsection (4) or (4B) above may, subject to subsection (6) below, if of the opinion that that person—

(a) is not likely to surrender to custody, or

(b) has broken or is likely to break any condition of his bail,

remand him in custody or commit him to custody, as the case may require, or alternatively, grant him bail subject to the same or to different conditions, but if not of that opinion shall grant him bail subject to the same conditions (if any) as were originally imposed.

(6) Where the person so brought before the justice is a child or young person and the justice does not grant him bail, subsection (5) above shall have effect subject to the provisions of section 23 of the Children and Young Persons Act 1969 (remands to the care of local authorities).

(7) In reckoning for the purposes of this section any period of 24 hours, no account shall be taken of Christmas Day, Good Friday or any Sunday.

SCHEDULE 1

PERSONS ENTITLED TO BAIL: SUPPLEMENTARY PROVISIONS

PART I   DEFENDANTS ACCUSED OR CONVICTED OF IMPRISONABLE OFFENCES

Exceptions to right to bail

2(1) The defendant need not be granted bail if the court is satisfied that there are substantial grounds for believing that the defendant, if released on bail (whether subject to conditions or not) would—

    (a) fail to surrender to custody, or

    (b) commit an offence while on bail, or

    (c) interfere with witnesses or otherwise obstruct the course of justice, whether in relation to himself or any other person.

(2) Where the defendant falls within one or more of paragraphs 2A, 6 and 6B of this Part of this Schedule, this paragraph shall not apply unless—

    (a) where the defendant falls within paragraph 2A, the court is satisfied as mentioned in sub-paragraph (1) of that paragraph;

    (b) where the defendant falls within paragraph 6, the court is satisfied as mentioned in sub-paragraph (1) of that paragraph;

    (c) where the defendant falls within paragraph 6B, the court is satisfied as mentioned in paragraph 6A of this Part of this Schedule or paragraph 6A does not apply by virtue of paragraph 6C of this Part of this Schedule.

2A[1] The defendant need not be granted bail if—

    (a) the offence is an indictable offence or an offence triable either way; and

    (b) it appears to the court that he was on bail in criminal proceedings on the date of the offence.

2B The defendant need not to be granted bail in connection with extradition proceedings if—

    (a) the conduct constituting the offence would, if carried out by the defendant in England or Wales, constitute an indictable offence or an offence triable either way; and

    (b) it appears to the court that the defendant was on bail on the date of the offence.

3 The defendant need not be granted bail if the court is satisfied that the defendant should be kept in custody for his own protection or, if he is a child or young person, for his own welfare.

4 The defendant need not be granted bail if he is in custody in pursuance of the sentence of a court or of any authority acting under any of the Services Acts.

5 The defendant need not be granted bail where the court is satisfied that it has not been practicable to obtain sufficient information for the purpose of taking the decisions required by this Part of this Schedule for want of time since the institution of the proceedings against him.

6[2] The defendant need not be granted bail if, having been released on bail in or in connection with the proceedings for the offence or the extradition proceedings, he has been arrested in pursuance of section 7 of this Act.

Paragraphs 6A and 6B (exception applicable to certain drug-users) apply only where courts separately notified by Secretary of State.

---

[1] Paragraph 2A is due to be substituted when section 14 of the Criminal Justice Act 2003 comes into force.

[2] Paragraph 6 is due to be substituted when section 15(1) of the Criminal Justice Act 2003 comes into force.

Restrictions of conditions of bail

8 (1) Subject to sub-paragraph (3) below, where the defendant is granted bail, no conditions shall be imposed under subsections (4) to (6B) or (7) (except subsection (6)(d) or (e)) of section 3 of this Act unless it appears to the court that it is necessary to do so—

    (a) for the purpose of preventing the occurrence of any of the events mentioned in paragraph 2(1) of this Part of the Schedule, or (b) for the defendant's own protection or, if he is a child or young person, for his own welfare or in his own interests.

(1A) No condition shall be imposed under section 3(6)(d) of this Act unless it appears to be necessary to do so for the purpose of enabling inquiries or a report to be made.

(2) Sub-paragraphs (1) and (1A) above also apply on any application to the court to vary the conditions of bail or to impose conditions in respect of bail which has been granted unconditionally.

(3) The restriction imposed by sub-paragraph (1A) above shall not apply to the conditions required to be imposed under section 3(6A) of this Act or operate to override the direction in section 11(3) of the Powers of Criminal Courts (Sentencing) Act 2000 to a magistrates' court to impose conditions of bail under section 3(6)(d) of this Act of the description specified in [the said section 11(3) in the circumstances so specified].

9 In taking the decisions required by paragraph 2(1) or in deciding whether it is satisfied as mentioned in paragraph 2A(1), 6(1) or 6A, of this Part of this Schedule, the court shall have regard to such of the following considerations as appear to it to be relevant, that is to say—

    (a) the nature and seriousness of the offence or default (and the probable method of dealing with the defendant for it),

    (b) the character, antecedents, associations and community ties of the defendant,

    (c) the defendant's record as respects the fulfilment of his obligations under previous grants of bail in criminal proceedings,

    (d) except in the case of a defendant whose case is adjourned for inquiries or a report, the strength of the evidence of his having committed the offence or having defaulted,

as well as to any others which appear to be relevant.

Criminal Justice and Public Order Act 1994

25 **No bail for defendants charged with or convicted of homicide or rape after previous conviction of such offences**

(1) A person who in any proceedings has been charged with or convicted of an offence to which this section applies in circumstances to which it applies shall be granted bail in those proceedings only if the court or, as the case may be, the constable considering the grant of bail is satisfied that there are exceptional circumstances which justify it.

(2) This section applies, subject to subsection (3) below, to the following offences, that is to say—

    (a) murder;

    (b) attempted murder;

    (c) manslaughter;

    (d) rape under the law of Scotland or Northern Ireland;

    (e) an offence under section 1 of the Sexual Offences Act 1956 (rape);

    (f) an offence under section 1 of the Sexual Offences Act 2003 (rape);

    (g) an offence under section 2 of that Act (assault by penetration);

(h) an offence under section 4 of that Act (causing a person to engage in sexual activity without consent), where the activity caused involved penetration within subsection (4)(a) to (d) of that section;

(i) an offence under section 5 of that Act (rape of a child under 13);

(j) an offence under section 6 of that Act (assault of a child under 13 by penetration);

(k) an offence under section 8 of that Act (causing or inciting a child under 13 to engage in sexual activity), where an activity involving penetration within sub-section (3)(a) to (d) of that section was caused;

(l) an offence under section 30 of that Act (sexual activity with a person with a mental disorder impeding choice), where the touching involved penetration within subsection (3)(a) to (d) of that section;

(m) an offence under section 31 of that Act (causing or inciting a person, with a mental disorder impeding choice, to engage in sexual activity), where an activity involving penetration within subsection (3)(a) to (d) of that section was caused;

(n) an attempt to commit an offence within any of paragraphs (d) to (m).

(3) This section applies to a person charged with or convicted of any such offence only if he has been previously convicted by or before a court in any part of the United Kingdom of any such offence or of culpable homicide and, in the case of a previous conviction of manslaughter or of culpable homicide, if he was then sentenced to imprisonment or, if he was then a child or young person, to long-term detention under any of the relevant enactments.

(4) This section applies whether or not an appeal is pending against conviction or sentence.

(5) In this section—

'conviction' includes—

(a) a finding that a person is not guilty by reason of insanity;

(b) a finding under section 4A(3) of the Criminal Procedure (Insanity) Act 1964 (cases of unfitness to plead) that a person did the act or made the omission charged against him; and

(c) a conviction of an offence for which an order is made discharging the offender absolutely or conditionally;

and 'convicted' shall be construed accordingly; and

'the relevant enactments' means—

(a) as respects England and Wales, section 91 of the Powers of Criminal Courts (Sentencing) Act 2000;

(b) as respects Scotland, sections 205(1) to (3) and 208 of the Criminal Procedure (Scotland) Act 1995;

(c) as respects Northern Ireland, section 73(2) of the Children and Young Persons Act (Northern Ireland) 1968.

(6) This section does not apply in relation to proceedings instituted before its commencement.

Police and Criminal Evidence Act 1984

46A Power of arrest for failure to answer to police bail

(1) A constable may arrest without a warrant any person who, having been released on bail under this Part of this Act subject to a duty to attend at a police station, fails to attend at that police station at the time appointed for him to do so.

(1A) A person who has been released on bail under section 37(7)(a) or 37C(2)(b) above may be arrested without warrant by a constable if the constable has reasonable grounds for suspecting that the person has broken any of the conditions of bail.

(2) A person who is arrested under this section shall be taken to the police station appointed as the place at which he is to surrender to custody as soon as practicable after the arrest.

(3) For the purposes of—

(a) section 30 above (subject to the obligation in subsection (2) above), and

(b) section 31 above,

an arrest under this section shall be treated as an arrest for an offence.

47 Bail after arrest

(1) Subject to the following provisions of this section, a release on bail of a person under this Part of this Act shall be a release on bail granted in accordance with sections 3, 3A, 5 and 5A of the Bail Act 1976 as they apply to bail granted by a constable.

(1A) The normal powers to impose conditions of bail shall be available to him where a custody officer releases a person on bail under section 37(7)(A) above or section 38(1) above (including that subsection as applied by section 40(10) above) but not in any other cases.

In this subsection, 'the normal powers to impose conditions of bail' has the meaning given in section 3(6) of the Bail Act 1976.

(1B) No application may be made under section 5B of the Bail Act 1976 if a person is released on bail under section 37(7)(a) or 37C(2)(b) above.

(1C) Subsection (ID) to (IF) below apply where a person released on bail under section 37(7)(a) or 37C(2)(b) above is on bail subject to conditions.

(1D) The person shall not be entitled to make an application under section 43B of the Magistrates' Courts Act 1980.

(1E) A magistrates' court may, on an application by or on behalf of the person, vary the conditions of bail; and in this subsection 'vary' has the same meaning as in the Bail Act 1976.

(1F) Where a magistrates' court varies the conditions of bail under subsection (1E) above, that bail shall not lapse but shall continue subject to the conditions as so varied.

(2) Nothing in the Bail Act 1976 shall prevent the re-arrest without warrant of a person released on bail subject to a duty to attend at a police station if new evidence justifying a further arrest has come to light since his release.

(3) Subject to subsections (3A) and (4) below, in this Part of this Act references to 'bail' are references to bail subject to a duty—

(a) to appear before a magistrates' court at such time and such place; or

(b) to attend at such police station at such time, as the custody officer may appoint.

(3A) Where a custody officer grants bail to a person subject to a duty to appear before a magistrates' court, he shall appoint for the appearance—

(a) a date which is not later than the first sitting of the court after the person is charged with the offence; or

(b) where he is informed by the designated officer for the relevant local justice area that the appearance cannot be accommodated until a later date, that later date.

(4) Where a custody officer has granted bail to a person subject to a duty to appear at a police station, the custody officer may give notice in writing to that person that his attendance at the police station is not required.

(6) Where a person who has been granted bail under this Part and either has attended at the police station in accordance with the grant of bail or has been arrested under section 46A above is detained at a police station, any time during which he was in police detention prior to being granted bail shall be included as part of any period which falls to be calculated under this Part of this Act.

(7) Where a person who was released on bail under this Part subject to a duty to attend at a police station is re-arrested, the provisions of this Part of this Act shall apply to him as they apply to a person arrested for the first time; but this subsection does not apply to a person who is arrested under section 46A above or has attended a police station in accordance with the grant of bail (and who accordingly is deemed by section 34(7) above to have been arrested for an offence).

47A   Early administrative hearings conducted by justices' clerks

Where a person has been charged with an offence at a police station, any requirement imposed under this Part for the person to appear or be brought before a magistrates' court shall be taken to be satisfied if the person appears or is brought before a justice's clerk in order for the clerk to conduct a hearing under section 50 of the Crime and Disorder Act 1998 (early administrative hearings).

Bail (Amendment) Act 1993

1   Prosecution right of appeal

(1) Where a magistrates' court grants bail to a person who is charged with, or convicted of, an offence punishable by imprisonment, the prosecution may appeal to a judge of the Crown Court against the granting of bail.

(1A) Where a magistrates' court grants bail to a person in connection with extradition proceedings, the prosecution may appeal to a judge of the Crown Court against the granting of bail.

(2) Subsection (1) above applies only where the prosecution is conducted—

    (a) by or on behalf of the Director of Public Prosecutions; or

    (b) by a person who falls within such class or description of person as may be prescribed for the purposes of this section by order made by the Secretary of State.

(3) An appeal under subsection (1) or (1A) may be made only if—

    (a) the prosecution made representations that bail should not be granted; and

    (b) the representations were made before it was granted.

(4) In the event of the prosecution wishing to exercise the right of appeal set out in subsection (1) or (1A) above, oral notice of appeal shall be given to the court which has granted bail at the conclusion of the proceedings in which bail has been granted and before the release from custody of the person concerned.

(5) Written notice of appeal shall thereafter be served on the court which has granted bail and the person concerned within two hours of the conclusion of such proceedings.

(6) Upon receipt from the prosecution of oral notice of appeal from its decision to grant bail the court which has granted bail shall remand in custody the person concerned, until the appeal is determined or otherwise disposed of.

(7) Where the prosecution fails, within the period of two hours mentioned in subsection (5) above, to serve one or both of the notices required by that subsection, the appeal shall be deemed to have been disposed of.

(8) The hearing of an appeal under subsection (1) or (1A) above against a decision of the court to grant bail shall be commenced within forty-eight hours, excluding weekends and any public holiday (that is to say, Christmas Day, Good Friday or a bank holiday), from the date on which oral notice of appeal is given.

(9) At the hearing of any appeal by the prosecution under this section, such appeal shall be by way of re-hearing, and the judge hearing any such appeal may remand the person concerned in custody or may grant bail subject to such conditions (if any) as he thinks fit.

(10) In relation to a child or young person (within the meaning of the Children and Young Persons Act 1969)—

    (a) the reference in subsection (1) above to an offence punishable by imprisonment is to be read as a reference to an offence which would be so punishable in the case of an adult; and

    (b) the references in subsections (6) and (9) above to remand in custody are to be read subject to the provisions of section 23 of the Act of 1969 (remands to local authority accommodation).

(11) The power to make an order under subsection (2) above shall be exercisable by statutory instrument and any instrument shall be subject to annulment in pursuance of a resolution of either House of Parliament.

(12) 'Extradition proceedings' means proceedings under the Extradition Act 2003; 'magistrates' court' and 'court' in relation to extradition proceedings means a District Judge (Magistrates' Courts) designated in accordance with section 67 or section 139 of the Extradition Act 2003.

'prosecution' in relation to extradition proceedings means the person acting on behalf of the territory to which extradition is sought.

Children and Young Persons Act 1969

23 Remands and committals to local authority accommodation
(1) Where—
  (a) a court remands a child or young person charged with or convicted of one or more offences or commits him for trial or sentence; and
  (b) he is not released on bail,
the remand or committal shall be to local authority accommodation; and in the following provisions of this section (except subsection (1A)), any reference (however expressed) to a remand shall be construed as including a reference to a committal.

(1A) Where a court remands a child or young person in connection with extradition proceedings and he is not released on bail the remand shall be to local authority accommodation.

(2) A court remanding a person to local authority accommodation shall designate the local authority who are to receive him; and that authority shall be—
  (a) in the case of a person who is being looked after by a local authority, that authority; and
  (b) in any other case, the local authority in whose area it appears to the court that he resides or the offence or one of the offences was committed.

(3) Where a person is remanded to local authority accommodation, it shall be lawful for any person acting on behalf of the designated authority to detain him.

(4) Subject to subsections (5), (5ZA) and (5A) below, a court remanding a person to local authority accommodation may, after consultation with the designated authority, require that authority to comply with a security requirement, that is to say, a requirement that the person in question be placed and kept in secure accommodation.

(5) A court shall not impose a security requirement in relation to a person remanded in accordance with subsection (1) above except in respect of a child who has attained the age of twelve, or a young person, who (in either case) is of a prescribed description, and then only if—
  (a) he is charged with or has been convicted of a violent or sexual offence, or an offence punishable in the case of an adult with imprisonment for a term of fourteen years or more; or
  (b) he is charged with or has been convicted of one or more imprisonable offences which, together with any other imprisonable offences of which he has been convicted in any proceedings—
    (i) amount, or
    (ii) would, if he were convicted of the offences with which he is charged, amount, to a recent history of repeatedly committing imprisonable offences while remanded on bail or to local authority accommodation,
  and (in either case) the condition set out in subsection (5AA) below is satisfied.

(5ZA) A court shall not impose a security requirement in relation to a person remanded in accordance with subsection (1A) above unless—

(a) he has attained the age of twelve and is of a prescribed description;

(b) one or both of the conditions set out in subsection (5ZB) below is satisfied; and

(c) the condition set out in subsection (5AA) below is satisfied.

(5ZB) The conditions mentioned in subsection (5ZA)(b) above are—

(a) that the conduct constituting the offence to which the extradition proceedings relate would if committed in the United Kingdom constitute an offence punishable in the case of an adult with imprisonment for a term of fourteen years or more;

(b) that the person has previously absconded from the extradition proceedings or from proceedings in the United kingdom or the requesting territory which relate to the conduct constituting the offence to which the extradition proceedings relate.

(5ZC) For the purposes of subsection (5ZB) above a person has absconded from proceedings if in relation to those proceedings—

(a) he has been released subject to a requirement to surrender to custody at a particular time and he has failed to surrender to custody at that time, or

(b) he has surrendered into the custody of a court and he has at any time absented himself from the court without its leave.

(5AA) The condition mentioned in subsections (5) and (5ZA) above is that the court is of the opinion, after considering all the options for the remand of the person, that only remanding him to local authority accommodation with a security requirement would be adequate—

(a) to protect the public from serious harm from him; or

(b) to prevent the commission by him of imprisonable offences.

(5A) A court shall not impose a security requirement in respect of a child or young person who is not legally represented in the court unless—

(a) he was granted a right to representation funded by the Legal Services Commission as part of the Criminal Defence Service but the right was withdrawn because of his conduct; or

(b) having been informed of his right to apply for such representation and had the opportunity to do so, he refused or failed to apply.

(6) Where a court imposes a security requirement in respect of a person, it shall be its duty—

(a) to state in open court that it is of such opinion as is mentioned in subsection (5AA) above; and

(b) to explain to him in open court and in ordinary language why it is of that opinion; and a magistrates' court shall cause a reason stated by it under paragraph (b) above to be specified in the warrant of commitment and to be entered in the register.

(7) Subject to section 23AA below, a court remanding a person to local authority accommodation without imposing a security requirement may, after consultation with the designated authority, require that person to comply with

(a) any such conditions as could be imposed under section 3(6) of the Bail Act 1976 (c. 63) if he were then being granted bail; and

(b) any conditions imposed for the purpose of securing the electronic monitoring of his compliance with any other condition imposed under this subsection.

(7A) Where a person is remanded to local authority accommodation and a security requirement is imposed in respect of him—

(a) the designated local authority may, with the consent of the Secretary of State, arrange for the person to be detained, for the whole or any part of the period of the remand or committal, in a secure training centre; and

(b) his detention there pursuant to the arrangements shall be lawful.

(7B) Arrangements under subsection (7A) above may include provision for payments to be made by the authority to the Secretary of State.

(8) Where a court imposes on a person any such conditions as are mentioned in subsection (7) above, it shall be its duty to explain to him in open court and in ordinary language why it is imposing those conditions; and a magistrates' court shall cause a reason stated by it under this subsection to be specified in the warrant of commitment and to be entered in the register.

(9) A court remanding a person to local authority accommodation without imposing a security requirement may, after consultation with the designated authority, impose on that authority requirements—

  (a) for securing compliance with any conditions imposed on that person under subsection (7) above; or

  (b) stipulating that he shall not be placed with a named person.

(10) Where a person is remanded to local authority accommodation, a relevant court—

  (a) may, on the application of the designated authority, impose on that person any such conditions as could be imposed under subsection (7) above if the court were then remanding him to such accommodation; and

  (b) where it does so, may impose on that authority any requirements for securing compliance with the conditions so imposed.

(11) Where a person is remanded to local authority accommodation, a relevant court may, on the application of the designated authority or that person, vary or revoke any conditions or requirements imposed under subsection (7), (9) or (10) above.

(12) In this section—

'children's home' has the same meaning as in the Care Standards Act 2000;

'court' and 'magistrates' court' include a justice;

'extradition proceedings' means proceedings under the Extradition Act 2003;

'imprisonable offence' means an offence punishable in the case of an adult with imprisonment;

'prescribed description' means a description prescribed by reference to age or sex or both by an order of the Secretary of State;

'relevant court—

  (a) in relation to a person remanded to local authority accommodation under subsection (1) above, means the court by which he was so remanded, or any magistrates' court having jurisdiction in the place where he is for the time being;

  (b) in relation to a person remanded to local authority accommodation under subsection (1A), above, means the court by which he was so remanded.

'requesting territory' means the territory to which a person's extradition is sought in extradition proceedings;

'secure accommodation' means accommodation which is provided in a children's home in respect of which a person is registered under Part II of the Care Standards Act 2000 for the purpose of restricting liberty, and is approved for that purpose by the Secretary of State or the National Assembly for Wales;

'sexual offence' means an offence specified in Part 2 of Schedule 15 to the Criminal Justice Act 2003;

'violent offence' means murder or an offence specified in Part 1 of Schedule 15 to the Criminal Justice Act 2003;

'young person' means a person who has attained the age of fourteen years and is under the age of seventeen years.

but, for purposes of the definition of 'secure accommodation', 'local authority accommodation' includes any accommodation falling within section 61(2) of the Criminal Justice Act 1991.

(13) In this section—

  (a) any reference to a person who is being looked after by a local authority shall be construed in accordance with section 22 of the Children Act 1989;

(b) any reference to consultation shall be construed as a reference to such consultation (if any) as is reasonably practicable in all the circumstances of the case; and

(c) any reference, in relation to a person charged with or convicted of a violent or sexual offence, to protecting the public from serious harm from him shall be construed as a reference to protecting members of the public from death or serious personal injury, whether physical or psychological, occasioned by further such offences committed by him.

(14) This section has effect subject to—

(b) section 128(7) of that Act (remands to the custody of a constable for periods of not more than three days), but section 128(7) shall have effect in relation to a child or young person as if for the reference to three clear days there were substituted a reference to twenty-four hours.

23A Liability to arrest for breaking conditions of remand

(1) A person who has been remanded or committed to local authority accommodation and in respect of whom conditions under subsection (7) or (10) of section 23 of this Act have been imposed may be arrested without warrant by a constable if the constable has reasonable grounds for suspecting that that person has broken any of those conditions.

(2) A person arrested under subsection (1) above—

(a) shall, except where he was arrested within 24 hours of the time appointed for him to appear before the court in pursuance of the remand or committal, be brought as soon as practicable and in any event within 24 hours after his arrest before a justice of the peace; and

(b) in the said excepted case shall be brought before the court before which he was to have appeared.

In reckoning for the purposes of this subsection any period of 24 hours, no account shall be taken of Christmas Day, Good Friday or any Sunday.

(3) A justice of the peace before whom a person is brought under subsection (2) above—

(a) if of the opinion that that person has broken any condition imposed on him under subsection (7) or (10) of section 23 of this Act shall remand him; and that section shall apply as if he was then charged with or convicted of the offence for which he had been remanded or committed;

(b) if not of that opinion shall remand him to the place to which he had been remanded or committed at the time of his arrest subject to the same conditions as those which had been imposed on him at that time.

23AA Electronic monitoring of conditions of remand

(1) A court shall not impose a condition on a person under section 23(7)(b) above (an 'electronic monitoring condition') unless each of the following requirements is fulfilled.

(2) The first requirement is that the person has attained the age of twelve years.

(3) The second requirement is that—

(a) the person is charged with or has been convicted of a violent or sexual offence, or an offence punishable in the case of an adult with imprisonment for a term of fourteen years or more; or

(b) he is charged with or has been convicted of one or more imprisonable offences which, together with any other imprisonable offences of which he has been convicted in any proceedings—

(i) amount, or

(ii) would, if he were convicted of the offences with which he is charged, amount, to a recent history of repeatedly committing imprisonable offences while remanded on bail or to local authority accommodation.

(4) The third requirement is that the court—

(a) has been notified by the Secretary of State that electronic monitoring arrangements are available in each petty sessions area which is a relevant area; and

(b) is satisfied that the necessary provision can be made under those arrangements.

(5) The fourth requirement is that a youth offending team has informed the court that in its opinion the imposition of such a condition will be suitable in the person's case.

(6) Where a court imposes an electronic monitoring condition, the condition shall include provision for making a person responsible for the monitoring; and a person who is made so responsible shall be of a description specified in an order made by the Secretary of State.

(7) The Secretary of State may make rules for regulating—

    (a) the electronic monitoring of compliance with conditions imposed under section 23(7)(a) above, and

    (b) without prejudice to the generality of paragraph (a) above, the functions of persons made responsible for securing the electronic monitoring of compliance with such conditions.

(8) Subsection (8) to (10) of section 3AA of the Bail Act 1976 (c. 63) (provision about rules and orders under that section) shall apply in relation to this section as they apply in relation to that section.

(9) For the purposes of this section a local justice area is a relevant area in relation to a proposed electronic monitoring condition if the court considers that it will not be practicable to secure the electronic monitoring in question unless electronic monitoring arrangements are available in that area.

Mode of trial

European Convention on Human Rights

Article 6 **Right to a fair trial**

1. In the determination of his civil rights and obligations or of any criminal charge against him, everyone is entitled to a fair and public hearing within a reasonable time by an independent and impartial tribunal established by law. Judgment shall be pronounced publicly but the press and public may be excluded from all or part of the trial in the interests of morals, public order or national security in a democratic society, where the interests of juveniles or the protection of the private life of the parties so require, or to the extent strictly necessary in the opinion of the court in special circumstances where publicity would prejudice the interests of justice.

2. Everyone charged with a criminal offence shall be presumed innocent until proved guilty according to law.

3. Everyone charged with a criminal offence has the following minimum rights:

    (a) to be informed promptly, in a language which he understands and in detail, of the nature and cause of the accusation against him;

    (b) to have adequate time and facilities for the preparation of his defence;

    (c) to defend himself in person or through legal assistance of his own choosing or, if he has not sufficient means to pay for legal assistance, to be given it free when the interests of justice so require;

    (d) to examine or have examined witnesses against him and to obtain the attendance and examination of witnesses on his behalf under the same conditions as witnesses against him;

    (e) to have the free assistance of an interpreter if he cannot understand or speak the language used in court.

Magistrates' Courts Act 1980

17 Certain offences triable either way

(1) The offences listed in Schedule 1 to this Act shall be triable either way.

(2) Subsection (1) above is without prejudice to any other enactment by virtue of which any offence is triable either way.

17A Initial procedure: accused to indicate intention as to plea

(1) This section shall have effect where a person who has attained the age of 18 years appears or is brought before a magistrates' court on an information charging him with an offence triable either way.

(2) Everything that the court is required to do under the following provisions of this section must be done with the accused present in court.

(3) The court shall cause the charge to be written down, if this has not already been done, and to be read to the accused.

(4) The court shall then explain to the accused in ordinary language that he may indicate whether (if the offence were to proceed to trial) he would plead guilty or not guilty, and that if he indicates that he would plead guilty—

    (a) the court must proceed as mentioned in subsection (6) below; and

    (b) he may be committed for sentence to the Crown Court under [section 3 of the Powers of Criminal Courts (Sentencing) Act 2000] below if the court is of such opinion as is mentioned in subsection (2) of that section.

(5) The court shall then ask the accused whether (if the offence were to proceed to trial) he would plead guilty or not guilty.

(6) If the accused indicates that he would plead guilty the court shall proceed as if—

    (a) the proceedings constituted from the beginning the summary trial of the information; and

    (b) section 9(1) above was complied with and he pleaded guilty under it.

(7) If the accused indicates that he would plead not guilty section 18(1) below shall apply.

(8) If the accused in fact fails to indicate how he would plead, for the purposes of this section and section 18(1) below he shall be taken to indicate that he would plead not guilty.

(9) Subject to subsection (6) above, the following shall not for any purpose be taken to constitute the taking of a plea—

    (a) asking the accused under this section whether (if the offence were to proceed to trial) he would plead guilty or not guilty;

    (b) an indication by the accused under this section of how he would plead.

17B Intention as to plea: absence of accused

(1) This section shall have effect where—

    (a) a person who has attained the age of 18 years appears or is brought before a magistrates' court on an information charging him with an offence triable either way.

    (b) the accused is represented by a legal representative,

    (c) the court considers that by reason of the accused's disorderly conduct before the court it is not practicable for proceedings under section 17A above to be conducted in his presence, and

    (d) the court considers that it should proceed in the absence of the accused.

(2) In such a case—

    (a) the court shall cause the charge to be written down, if this has not already been done, and to be read to the representative;

    (b) the court shall ask the representative whether (if the offence were to proceed to trial) the accused would plead guilty or not guilty;

    (c) if the representative indicates that the accused would plead guilty the court shall proceed as if the proceedings constituted from the beginning the summary trial of the information, and as if section 9(1) above was complied with and the accused pleaded guilty under it;

(d) if the representative indicates that the accused would plead not guilty section 18(1) below shall apply.

(3) If the representative in fact fails to indicate how the accused would plead, for the purposes of this section and section 18(1) below he shall be taken to indicate that the accused would plead not guilty.

(4) Subject to subsection (2)(c) above, the following shall not for any purpose be taken to constitute the taking of a plea—

(a) asking the representative under this section whether (if the offence were to proceed to trial) the accused would plead guilty or not guilty;

(b) an indication by the representative under this section of how the accused would plead.

17C   Intention as to plea adjournment

A magistrates' court proceeding under section 17A or 17B above may adjourn the proceedings at any time, and on doing so on any occasion when the accused is present may remand the accused, and shall remand him if—

(a) on the occasion on which he first appeared, or was brought, before the court to answer to the information he was in custody or, having been released on bail, surrendered to the custody of the court; or

(b) he has been remanded at any time in the course of proceedings on the information;

and where the court remands the accused, the time fixed for the resumption of proceedings shall be that at which he is required to appear or be brought before the court in pursuance of the remand or would be required to be brought before the court but for section 128(3A) below.

18   Initial procedure on information against adult for offence triable either way

(1) Sections 19 to 23 below shall have effect where a person who has attained the age of 18 years appears or is brought before a magistrates' court on an information charging him with an offence triable either way and—

(a) he indicates under section 17A above that (if the offence were to proceed to trial) he would plead not guilty, or

(b) his representative indicates under section 17B above that (if the offence were to proceed to trial) he would plead not guilty.

(2) Without prejudice to section 11(1) above, everything that the court is required to do under sections 19 to 22 below must be done before any evidence is called and, subject to subsection (3) below and section 23 below, with the accused present in court.

(3) The court may proceed in the absence of the accused in accordance with such of the provisions of sections 19 to 22 below as are applicable in the circumstances if the court considers that by reason of his disorderly conduct before the court it is not practicable for the proceedings to be conducted in his presence; and subsections (3) to (5) of section 23 below, so far as applicable, shall have effect in relation to proceedings conducted in the absence of the accused by virtue of this subsection (references in those subsections to the person representing the accused being for this purpose read as references to the person, if any, representing him).

(4) A magistrates' court proceeding under sections 19 to 23 below may adjourn the proceedings at any time, and on doing so on any occasion when the accused is present may remand the accused, and shall remand him if—

(a) on the occasion on which he first appeared, or was brought, before the court to answer to the information he was in custody or, having been released on bail, surrendered to the custody of the court; or

(b) he has been remanded at any time in the course of proceedings on the information;

and where the court remands the accused, the time fixed for the resumption of the proceedings shall be that at which he is required to appear or be brought before the court in pursuance of the remand or would be required to be brought before the court but for section 128(3A) below.

(5) The functions of a magistrates' court under sections 19 to 23 below may be discharged by a single justice, but the foregoing provision shall not be taken to authorise the summary trial of an information by a magistrates' court composed of less than two justices.

19 Court to begin by considering which mode of trial appears more suitable

(1) The court shall consider whether, having regard to the matters mentioned in subsection (3) below and any representations made by the prosecutor or the accused, the offence appears to the court more suitable for summary trial or for trial on indictment.

(2) Before so considering, the court—

[ ]

(b) shall afford first the prosecutor and then the accused an opportunity to make representations as to which mode of trial would be more suitable.

(3) The matters to which the court is to have regard under subsection (1) above are the nature of the case; whether the circumstances make the offence one of serious character; whether the punishment which a magistrates' court would have power to inflict for it would be adequate; and any other circumstances which appear to the court to make it more suitable for the offence to be tried in one way rather than the other.

(4) If the prosecution is being carried on by the Attorney General, the Solicitor General or the Director of Public Prosecutions and he applies for the offence to be tried on indictment, the preceding provisions of this section and sections 20 and 21 below shall not apply, and the court shall proceed to inquire into the information as examining justices.

(5) The power of the Director of Public Prosecutions under subsection (4) above to apply for an offence to be tried on indictment shall not be exercised except with the consent of the Attorney General.

20 Procedure where summary trial appears more suitable

(1) If, where the court has considered as required by section 19(1) above, it appears to the court that the offence is more suitable for summary trial, the following provisions of this section shall apply (unless excluded by section 23 below).

(2) The court shall explain to the accused in ordinary language—

(a) that it appears to the court more suitable for him to be tried summarily for the offence, and that he can either consent to be so tried or, if he wishes, be tried by a jury; and

(b) that if he is tried summarily and is convicted by the court, he may be committed for sentence to the Crown Court under [section 3 of the Powers of Criminal Courts (Sentencing) Act 2000] if the convicting court, is of such opinion as is mentioned in subsection (2) of that section.

(3) After explaining to the accused as provided by subsection (2) above the court shall ask him whether he consents to be tried summarily or wishes to be tried by a jury, and—

(a) if he consents to be tried summarily, shall proceed to the summary trial of the information;

(b) if he does not so consent, shall proceed to inquire into the information as examining justices.

21 Procedure where trial on indictment appears more suitable

If, where the court has considered as required by section 19(1) above, it appears to the court that the offence is more suitable for trial on indictment, the court shall tell the accused that the court has decided that it is more suitable for him to be tried for the offence by a jury, and shall proceed to inquire into the information as examining justices.

22 Certain offences triable either way to be tried summarily if value involved is small

(1) If the offence charged by the information is one of those mentioned in the first column of Schedule 2 to this Act (in this section referred to as 'scheduled offences') then, the court shall, before proceeding in accordance with section 19 above, consider whether, having regard to any representations made by the prosecutor or the accused, the value involved (as defined in subsection (10) below) appears to the court to exceed the relevant sum.

For the purposes of this section the relevant sum is £5,000.

(2) If, where subsection (1) above applies, it appears to the court clear that, for the offence charged, the value involved does not exceed the relevant sum, the court shall proceed as if the offence were triable only summarily, and sections 19 to 21 above shall not apply.

(3) If, where subsection (1) above applies, it appears to the court clear that, for the offence charged, the value involved exceeds the relevant sum, the court shall thereupon proceed in accordance with section 19 above in the ordinary way without further regard to the provisions of this section.

(4) If, where subsection (1) above applies, it appears to the court for any reason not clear whether, for the offence charged, the value involved does or does not exceed the relevant sum, the provisions of subsections (5) and (6) below shall apply.

(5) The court shall cause the charge to be written down, if this has not already been done, and read to the accused, and shall explain to him in ordinary language—

    (a) that he can, if he wishes, consent to be tried summarily for the offence and that if he consents to be so tried, he will definitely be tried in that way; and

    (b) that if he is tried summarily and is convicted by the court, his liability to imprisonment or a fine will be limited as provided in section 33 below.

(6) After explaining to the accused as provided by subsection (5) above the court shall ask him whether he consents to be tried summarily and—

    (a) if he so consents, shall proceed in accordance with subsection (2) above as if that subsection applied;

    (b) if he does not so consent, shall proceed in accordance with subsection (3) above as if that subsection applied.

(8) Where a person is convicted by a magistrates' court of a scheduled offence, it shall not be open to him to appeal to the Crown Court against the conviction on the ground that the convicting court's decision as to the value involved was mistaken.

(9) If, where subsection (1) above applies, the offence charged is one with which the accused is charged jointly with a person who has not attained the age of 18 years, the reference in that subsection to any representations made by the accused shall be read as including any representations made by the person under 18.

(10) In this section 'the value involved', in relation to any scheduled offence, means the value indicated in the second column of Schedule 2 to this Act, measured as indicated in the third column of that Schedule; and in that Schedule 'the material time' means the time of the alleged offence.

(11) Where—

    (a) the accused is charged on the same occasion with two or more scheduled offences and it appears to the court that they constitute or form part of a series of two or more offences of the same or a similar character; or

    (b) the offence charged consists in incitement to commit two or more scheduled offences,

this section shall have effect as if any reference in it to the value involved were a reference to the aggregate of the values involved.

(12) Subsection (8) of section 12A of the Theft Act 1968 (which determines when a vehicle is recovered) shall apply for the purposes of paragraph 3 of Schedule 2 to this Act as it applies for the purposes of that section.

23 Power of court, with consent of legally represented accused, to proceed in his absence

(1) Where—

    (a) the accused is represented by a legal representative who in his absence signifies to the court the accused's consent to the proceedings for determining how he is to be tried for the offence being conducted in his absence; and

    (b) the court is satisfied that there is good reason for proceeding in the absence of the accused,

the following provisions of this section shall apply.

(2) Subject to the following provisions of this section, the court may proceed in the absence of the accused in accordance with such of the provisions of sections 19 to 22 above as are applicable in the circumstances.

(3) If, in a case where subsection (1) of section 22 above applies, it appears to the court as mentioned in subsection (4) of that section, subsections (5) and (6) of that section shall not apply and the court—

    (a) if the accused's consent to be tried summarily has been or is signified by the person representing him, shall proceed in accordance with subsection (2) of that section as if that subsection applied; or

    (b) if that consent has not been and is not so signified, shall proceed in accordance with subsection (3) of that section as if that subsection applied.

(4) If, where the court has considered as required by section 19(1) above, it appears to the court that the offence is more suitable for summary trial then—

    (a) if the accused's consent to be tried summarily has been or is signified by the person representing him, section 20 above shall not apply, and the court shall proceed to the summary trial of the information; or

    (b) if that consent has not been and is not so signified, section 20 above shall not apply and the court shall proceed to inquire into the information as examining justices and may adjourn the hearing without remanding the accused.

(5) If, where the court has considered as required by section 19(1) above, it appears to the court that the offence is more suitable for trial on indictment, section 21 above shall not apply, and the court shall proceed to inquire into the information as examining justices and may adjourn the hearing without remanding the accused.

25 Power to change from summary trial to committal proceedings, and vice versa

(1) Subsections (2) to (4) below shall have effect where a person who has attained the age of 18 years appears or is brought before a magistrates' court on an information charging him with an offence triable either way.

(2) Where the court has (otherwise than in pursuance of section 22(2) above) begun to try the information summarily, the court may, at any time before the conclusion of the evidence for the prosecution, discontinue the summary trial and proceed to inquire into the information as examining justices and, on doing so, shall adjourn the hearing.

(3) Where the court has begun to inquire into the information as examining justices, then, if at any time during the inquiry it appears to the court, having regard to any representations made in the presence of the accused by the prosecutor, or made by the accused, and to the nature of the case, that the offence is after all more suitable for summary trial, the court may, after doing as provided in subsection (4) below, ask the accused whether he consents to be tried summarily and, if he so consents, may subject to subsection (3A) below proceed to try the information summarily;

(3A) Where the prosecution is being carried on by the Attorney General or the Solicitor General, the court shall not exercise the power conferred by subsection (3) above without his consent and, where the prosecution is being carried on by the Director of Public Prosecutions, shall not exercise that power if the Attorney General directs that it should not be exercised.

(4) Before asking the accused under subsection (3) above whether he consents to be tried summarily, the court shall in ordinary language—

(a) explain to him that it appears to the court more suitable for him to be tried summarily for the offence, but that this can only be done if he consents to be so tried; and

(b) unless it has already done so, explain to him, as provided in section 20(2)(b) above, about the court's power to commit to the Crown Court for sentence.

(5) Where a person under the age of 18 years appears or is brought before a magistrates' court on an information charging him with an indictable offence other than one falling within section 24(1B) above,[1] and the court—

(a) has begun to try the information summarily on the footing that the case does not fall within paragraph (a) or (b) of section 24(1) above and must therefore be tried summarily, as required by the said section 24(1); or

(b) has begun to inquire into the case as examining justices on the footing that the case does so fall, subsection (6) or (7) below, as the case may be, shall have effect.

(6) If, in a case falling within subsection (5)(a) above, it appears to the court at any time before the conclusion of the evidence for the prosecution that the case is after all one which under the said section 24(1) ought not to be tried summarily, the court may discontinue the summary trial and proceed to inquire into the information as examining justices and, on doing so, shall adjourn the hearing.

(7) If, in a case falling within subsection (5)(b) above, it appears to the court at any time during the inquiry that the case is after all one which under the said section 24(1) ought to be tried summarily, the court may proceed to try the information summarily.

(8) If the court adjourns the hearing under subsection (2) or (6) above it may (if it thinks fit) do so without remanding the accused.

26   Power to issue summons to accused in certain circumstances

(1) Where—

(a) in the circumstances mentioned in section 23(1)(a) above the court is not satisfied that there is good reason for proceeding in the absence of the accused; or

(b) subsection (4)(b) or (5) of section 23 or subsection (2) or (6) of section 25 above applies, and the court adjourns the hearing in pursuance of that subsection without remanding the accused, the justice or any of the justices of which the court is composed may issue a summons directed to the accused requiring his presence before the court.

(2) If the accused is not present at the time and place appointed—

(a) in a case within subsection (1)(a) above, for the proceedings under section 19(1) or 22(1) above, as the case may be; or

(b) in a case within subsection (1)(b) above, for the resumption of the hearing, the court may issue a warrant for his arrest.

SCHEDULE 1

(5) Offences under the following provisions of the Offences against the Person Act 1861—

(a) section 16 (threats to kill);

(b) section 20 (inflicting bodily injury, with or without a weapon);

(c) section 26 (not providing apprentices or servants with food etc.);

(d) section 27 (abandoning or exposing child);

(e) section 34 (doing or omitting to do anything so as to endanger railway passengers);

(f) section 36 (assaulting a clergyman at a place of worship etc);

---

[1] This refers to homicide or to an offence under section 51A(1) of the Firearms Act 1968.

(g) section 38 (assault with intent to resist apprehension);

(h) section 47 (assault occasioning bodily harm [...]);

(i) section 57 (bigamy);

(j) section 60 (concealing the birth of a child).

(6) Offences under section 20 of the Telegraph Act 1868 (disclosing or intercepting messages).

(19) Offences under section 36 of the Criminal Justice Act 1925 (forgery of passports etc.).

(26) The following offences under the Criminal Law Act 1967—

(a) offences under section 4(1) (assisting offenders); and

(b) offences under section 5(1) (concealing arrestable offences and giving false information),

where the offence to which they relate is triable either way.

(28) All indictable offences under the Theft Act 1968 except:—

(a) robbery, aggravated burglary, blackmail and assault with intent to rob;

(b) burglary comprising the commission of, or an intention to commit, an offence which is triable only on indictment;

(c) burglary in a dwelling if any person in the dwelling was subjected to violence or the threat of violence.

(29) Offences under the following provisions of the Criminal Damage Act 1971—

(a) section 1(1) (destroying or damaging property);

(b) section 1(1) and (3) (arson);

(c) section 2 (threats to destroy or damage property);

(d) section 3 (possessing anything with intent to destroy or damage property).

(33) Aiding, abetting, counselling or procuring the commission of any offence listed in the preceding paragraphs of this Schedule except paragraph 26.

(35) Any offence consisting in the incitement to commit an offence triable either way except an offence mentioned in paragraph 33 above.

Trial by jury

Juries Act 1974

1 Qualification for jury service

(1) Subject to the provisions of this Act, every person shall be qualified to serve as a juror in the Crown Court, the High Court and county courts and be liable accordingly to attend for jury service when summoned under this Act if—

(a) he is for the time being registered as a parliamentary or local government elector and is not less than eighteen nor more than seventy years of age;

(b) he has been ordinarily resident in the United Kingdom, the Channel Islands or the Isle of Man for any period of at least five years since attaining the age of thirteen;

(c) he is not a mentally disordered person; and

(d) he is not disqualified for jury service.

(2) In subsection (1) above 'mentally disordered person' means any person listed in Part 1 of Schedule 1 to this Act.

(3) The persons who are disqualified for jury service are those listed in Part 2 of that Schedule.

3   Electoral register as basis of jury selection

(1) Every electoral registration officer under the Representation of the People Act 1983 shall as soon as practicable after the publication of any register of electors for his area deliver to such officer as the Lord Chancellor may designate such number of copies of the register as the designated officer may require for the purpose of summoning jurors, and on each copy there shall be indicated those persons on the register whom the registration officer has ascertained to be, or to have been on a date also indicated on the copy, less than eighteen or more than seventy years of age.

(2) The reference in subsection (1) above to a register of electors does not include a ward list within the meaning of section 4(1) of the City of London (Various Powers) Act 1957.

8   Excusal for previous jury service

(1) If a person summoned under this Act shows to the satisfaction of the appropriate officer, or of the court (or any of the courts) to which he is summoned—

   (a) that he has served on a jury, or duly attended to serve on a jury, in the prescribed period ending with the service of the summons on him, or

   (b) that the Crown Court or any other court has excused him from jury service for a period which has not terminated,

the officer or court shall excuse him from attending, or further attending, in pursuance of the summons.

(2) In subsection (1) above 'the prescribed period' means two years or such longer period as the Lord Chancellor may prescribe by order made by statutory instrument subject to annulment in pursuance of a resolution of either House of Parliament, and any such order may be varied or revoked by a subsequent order under this subsection.

(3) Records of persons summoned under this Act, and of persons included in panels, shall be kept in such manner as the Lord Chancellor may direct, and the Lord Chancellor may, if he thinks fit, make arrangements for allowing inspection of the records so kept by members of the public in such circumstances and subject to such conditions as he may prescribe.

(4) A person duly attending in compliance with a summons under this Act shall be entitled on application to the appropriate officer to a certificate recording that he has so attended.

(5) In subsection (1) above the words 'served on a jury' refer to service on a jury in any court, including any court of assize or other court abolished by the Courts Act 1971, but excluding service on a jury in a coroner's court.

9   Excusal for certain persons and discretionary excusal

(2) If any person summoned under this Act shows to the satisfaction of the appropriate officer that there is good reason why he should be excused from attending in pursuance of the summons, the appropriate officer may, subject to section 9A(1A) of this Act, excuse him from so attending.

(2A) Without prejudice to subsection (2) above, the appropriate officer shall excuse a full-time serving member of Her Majesty's naval, military or air forces from attending in pursuance of a summons if—

   (a) that member's commanding officer certifies to the appropriate officer that it would be prejudicial to the efficiency of the service if that member were to be required to be absent from duty, and

   (b) subsection (2A) or (2B) of section 9A of this Act applies.

(2B) Subsection (2A) above does not affect the application of subsection (2) above to a full-time serving member of Her Majesty's naval, military or air forces in a case where he is not entitled to be excused under subsection (2A).

(3) Criminal Procedure Rules[2] shall provide a right of appeal to the court (or one of the courts) before [or any failure by the appropriate officer to excuse him as required by

___

[2] See further the internet linked site accompanying this text.

subsection (2A) above] which the person is summoned to attend against any refusal of the appropriate officer to excuse him under subsection (2) above.

(4) Without prejudice to the preceding provisions of this section, the court (or any of the courts) before which a person is summoned to attend under this Act may excuse that person from so attending.

9A   Discretionary deferral

(1) If any person summoned under this Act shows to the satisfaction of the appropriate officer that there is good reason why his attendance in pursuance of the summons should be deferred, the appropriate officer may, subject to subsection (2) below, defer his attendance, and, if he does so, he shall very the days on which that person is summoned to attend and the summons shall have effect accordingly.

(1A) Without prejudice to subsection (1) above and subject to subsection (2) below, the appropriate officer—

(a) shall defer the attendance of a full-time serving member of Her Majesty's naval, military or air forces in pursuance of a summons if subsection (1B) below applies, and

(b) for this purpose, shall vary the dates upon which that member is summoned to attend and the summons shall have effect accordingly.

(1B) This subsection applies if that member's commanding officer certifies to the appropriate officer that it would be prejudicial to the efficiency of the service if that member were to be required to be absent from duty.

(1C) Nothing in subsection (1A) or (1B) above shall affect the application of subsection (1) above to a full-time serving member of Her Majesty's naval, military or air forces in a case where subsection (1B) does not apply.

(2) The attendance of a person in pursuance of a summons shall not be deferred under subsection (1) or (1A) above if subsection (2A) or (2B) below applies.

(2A) This subsection applies where a deferral of the attendance of the person in pursuance of the summons has previously been made or refused under subsection (1) above or has previously been made under subsection (1A) above.

(2B) This subsection applies where—

(a) the person is a full-time serving member of Her Majesty's naval, military or air forces, and

(b) in addition to certifying to the appropriate officer that it would be prejudicial to the efficiency of the service if that member were to be required to be absent from duty, that member's commanding officer certifies that this position is likely to remain for any period specified for the purpose of this subsection in guidance issued under section 9AA of this Act.

(3) Criminal Procedure Rules shall provide a right of appeal to the court (or one of the courts) before which the person is summoned to attend against any refusal of the appropriate officer to defer his attendance under subsection (1) above [or any failure by the appropriate officer to defer his attendance as required by subsection (1A) above].

(4) Without prejudice to the preceding provisions of this section, the court (or any of the courts) before which a person is summoned to attend under this Act may defer his attendance.

17   Majority verdicts

(1) Subject to subsections (3) and (4) below, the verdict of a jury in proceedings in the Crown Court or the High Court need not be unanimous if—

(a) in a case where there are not less than eleven jurors, ten of them agree on the verdict; and

(b) in a case where there are ten jurors, nine of them agree on the verdict.

(2) Subject to subsection (4) below, the verdict of a jury (that is to say a complete jury of eight) in proceedings in a county court need not be unanimous if seven of them agree on the verdict.

(3) The Crown Court shall not accept a verdict of guilty by virtue of subsection (1) above unless the foreman of the jury has stated in open court the number of jurors who respectively agreed to and dissented from the verdict.

(4) No court shall accept a verdict by virtue of subsection (1) or (2) above unless it appears to the court that the jury have had such period of time for deliberation as the court thinks reasonable having regard to the nature and complexity of the case; and the Crown Court shall in any event not accept such a verdict unless it appears to the court that the jury have had at least two hours for deliberation.

(5) This section is without prejudice to any practice in civil proceedings by which a court may accept a majority verdict with the consent of the parties, or by which the parties may agree to proceed in any case with an incomplete jury.

SCHEDULE 1   MENTALLY DISORDERED PERSONS AND PERSONS DISQUALIFIED FOR JURY SERVICE

PART 1   MENTALLY DISORDERED PERSONS

1 A person who suffers or has suffered from mental illness, psychopathic disorder, mental handicap or severe mental handicap and on account of that condition either—
>   (a) is resident in a hospital or similar institution; or
>   (b) regularly attends for treatment by a medical practitioner.

2 A person for the time being under guardianship under section 7 of the Mental Health Act 1983.

3 A person who, under Part 7 of that Act, has been determined by a judge to be incapable, by reason of mental disorder, of managing and administering his property and affairs.

4 (1) In this Part of this Schedule—
>   (a) 'mental handicap' means a state of arrested or incomplete development of mind (not amounting to severe mental handicap) which includes significant impairment of intelligence and social functioning;
>   (b) 'severe mental handicap' means a state of arrested or incomplete development of mind which includes severe impairment of intelligence and social functioning;
>   (c) other expressions are to be construed in accordance with the Mental Health Act 1983.

(2) For the purposes of this Part a person is to be treated as being under guardianship under section 7 of the Mental Health Act 1983 at any time while he is subject to guardianship pursuant to an order under section 116A(2)(b) of the Army Act 1955, section 116A(2)(b) of the Air Force Act 1955 or section 63A(2)(b) of the Naval Discipline Act 1957.

PART 2   PERSONS DISQUALIFIED

5 A person who is on bail in criminal proceedings (within the meaning of the Bail Act 1976).

6 A person who has at any time been sentenced in the United Kingdom, the Channel Islands or the Isle of Man—
>   (a) to imprisonment for life, detention for life or custody for life,
>   (b) to detention during her Majesty's pleasure or during the pleasure of the Secretary of State,
>   (c) to imprisonment for public protection or detention for public protection,
>   (d) to an extended sentence under section 227 or 228 of the Criminal Justice Act 2003 or section 210A of the Criminal Procedure (Scotland) Act 1995, or
>   (e) to a term of imprisonment of five years or more or a term of detention of five years or more.

7 A person who at any time in the last ten years has—
    (a) in the United Kingdom, the Channel Islands or the Isle of Man—
        (i)   served any part of a sentence of imprisonment or a sentence of detention, or
        (ii) had passed on him a suspended sentence of imprisonment or had made in respect of him a suspended order for detention,
    (b) in England and Wales, had made in respect of him a community order under section 177 of the Criminal Justice Act 2003, a community rehabilitation order, a community punishment order, a community punishment and rehabilitation order, a drug treatment and testing order or a drug abstinence order, or
    (c) had made in respect of him any corresponding order under the law of Scotland, Northern Ireland, the Isle of Man or any of the Channel Islands.
8 For the purposes of this Part of this Schedule—
    (a) a sentence passed by a court-martial is to be treated as having been passed in the United Kingdom, and
    (b) a person is sentenced to a term of detention if, but only if—
        (i)   a court passes on him, or makes in respect of him on conviction, any sentence or order which requires him to be detained in custody for any period, and
        (ii) the sentence or order is available only in respect of offenders below a certain age,
and any reference to serving a sentence of detention is to be construed accordingly.

Contempt of Court Act 1981

8 Confidentiality of jury's deliberations
(1) Subject to subsection (2) below, it is a contempt of court to obtain, disclose or solicit any particulars of statements made, opinions expressed, arguments advanced or votes cast by members of a jury in the course of their deliberations in any legal proceedings.
(2) This section does not apply to any disclosure of any particulars—
    (a) in the proceedings in question for the purpose of enabling the jury to arrive at their verdict, or in connection with the delivery of that verdict, or
    (b) in evidence in any subsequent proceedings for an offence alleged to have been committed in relation to the jury in the first mentioned proceedings,
or to the publication of any particulars so disclosed.
(3) Proceedings for a contempt of court under this section (other than Scottish proceedings) shall not be instituted except by or with the consent of the Attorney General or on the motion of a court having jurisdiction to deal with it.

(c) ISSUES DURING TRIAL, EVIDENCE AND PROCEDURE

Disclosure

Criminal Procedure and Investigations Act 1996

1 Application of this Part
(1) This Part applies where—
    (a) a person is charged with a summary offence in respect of which a court proceeds to summary trial and in respect of which he pleads not guilty,

(b) a person who has attained the age of 18 is charged with an offence which is triable either way, in respect of which a court proceeds to summary trial and in respect of which he pleads not guilty, or

(c) a person under the age of 18 is charged with an indictable offence in respect of which a court proceeds to summary trial and in respect of which he pleads not guilty.

(2) This Part also applies where—

(a) a person is charged with an indictable offence and he is committed for trial for the offence concerned,

(b) a person is charged with an indictable offence and proceedings for the trial of the person on the charge concerned are transferred to the Crown Court by virtue of a notice of transfer given under section 4 of the Criminal Justice Act 1987 (serious or complex fraud),

(c) a person is charged with an indictable offence and proceedings for the trial of the person on the charge concerned are transferred to the Crown Court by virtue of a notice of transfer served on a magistrates' court under section 53 of the Criminal Justice Act 1991 (certain cases involving children),

(cc) a person is charged with an offence for which he is sent for trial; or

(d) a count charging a person with a summary offence is included in an indictment under the authority of section 40 of the Criminal Justice Act 1988 (common assault etc.), or

(e) a bill of indictment charging a person with an indictable offence is preferred under the authority of section 2(2)(b) of the Administration of Justice (Miscellaneous Provisions) Act 1933 (bill preferred by direction of Court of Appeal, or by direction or with consent of a judge), or

(f) a bill of indictment charging a person with an indictable offence is preferred under section 22B(3)(a) of the Prosecution of Offences Act 1985.

(3) This Part applies in relation to alleged offences into which no criminal investigation has begun before the appointed day.

(4) For the purposes of this section a criminal investigation is an investigation which police officers or other persons have a duty to conduct with a view to it being ascertained—

(a) whether a person should be charged with an offence, or

(b) whether a person charged with an offence is guilty of it.

(5) The reference in subsection (3) to the appointed day is to such day as is appointed for the purposes of this Part by the Secretary of State by order.

3 Primary disclosure by prosecutor

(1) The prosecutor must—

(a) disclose to the accused any prosecution material which has not previously been disclosed to the accused and which might reasonably be considered capable of undermining the case for the prosecution against the accused, or

(b) give to the accused a written statement that there is no material of a description mentioned in paragraph (a).

(2) For the purposes of this section prosecution material is material—

(a) which is in the prosecutor's possession, and came into his possession in connection with the case for the prosecution against the accused, or

(b) which, in pursuance of a code operative under Part II, he has inspected in connection with the case for the prosecution against the accused.

(3) Where material consists of information which has been recorded in any form the prosecutor discloses it for the purposes of this section—

(a) by securing that a copy is made of it and that the copy is given to the accused, or

(b) if in the prosecutor's opinion that is not practicable or not desirable, by allowing the accused to inspect it at a reasonable time and a reasonable place or by taking steps to secure that he is allowed to do so;

and a copy may be in such form as the prosecutor thinks fit and need not be in the same form as that in which the information has already been recorded.

(4) Where material consists of information which has not been recorded the prosecutor discloses it for the purposes of this section by securing that it is recorded in such form as he thinks fit and—

    (a) by securing that a copy is made of it and that the copy is given to the accused, or

    (b) if in the prosecutor's opinion that is not practicable or not desirable, by allowing the accused to inspect it at a reasonable time and a reasonable place or by taking steps to secure that he is allowed to do so.

(5) Where material does not consist of information the prosecutor discloses it for the purposes of this section by allowing the accused to inspect it at a reasonable time and a reasonable place or by taking steps to secure that he is allowed to do so.

(6) Material must not be disclosed under this section to the extent that the court, on an application by the prosecutor, concludes it is not in the public interest to disclose it and orders accordingly.

(7) Material must not be disclosed under this section to the extent that it is material the disclosure of which is prohibited by section 17 of the Regulation of Investigatory Powers Act 2000.

(8) The prosecutor must act under this section during the period which, by virtue of section 12, is the relevant period for this section.

4   Initial duty to disclose

    (1) This section applies where—

        (a) the prosecutor acts under section 3, and

        (b) before so doing he was given a document in pursuance of provision included, by virtue of section 24(3), in a code operative under Part II.

    (2) In such a case the prosecutor must give the document to the accused at the same time as the prosecutor acts under section 3.

5   Compulsory disclosure by accused

    (1) Subject to subsections (2) to (4), this section applies where—

        (a) this Part applies by virtue of section 1(2), and

        (b) the prosecutor complies with section 3 or purports to comply with it.

    (2) Where this Part applies by virtue of section 1(2)(b), this section does not apply unless—

        (a) a copy of the notice of transfer, and

        (b) copies of the documents containing the evidence,

have been given to the accused under regulations made under section 5(9) of the Criminal Justice Act 1987.

    (3) Where this Part applies by virtue of section 1(2)(c), this section does not apply unless—

        (a) a copy of the notice of transfer, and

        (b) copies of the documents containing the evidence,

have been given to the accused under regulations made under paragraph 4 of Schedule 6 to the Criminal Justice Act 1991.

    (3A) Where this Part applies by virtue of section 1(2)(cc), this section does not apply unless—

        (a) copies of the documents containing the evidence have been served on the accused under regulations made under paragraph 1 of Schedule 3 to the Crime and Disorder Act 1998; and

        (b) a copy of the notice under subsection (1) of section 51D of that Act has been served on him under that subsection.

    (4) Where this Part applies by virtue of section 1(2)(e), this section does not apply unless the prosecutor has served on the accused a copy of the indictment and a copy of the set of documents containing the evidence which is the basis of the charge.

(5) Where this section applies, the accused must give a defence statement to the court and the prosecutor.

6   Voluntary disclosure by accused

(1) This section applies where—
   (a) this Part applies by virtue of section 1(1), and
   (b) the prosecutor complies with section 3 or purports to comply with it.

(2) The accused—
   (a) may give a defence statement to the prosecutor, and
   (b) if he does so, must also give such a statement to the court.

(4) If the accused gives a defence statement under this section he must give it during the period which, by virtue of section 12, is the relevant period for this section.

6A   Contents of defence statement

(1) For the purposes of this Part a defence statement is a written statement—
   (a) setting out the nature of the accused's defence, including any particular defences on which he intends to rely,
   (b) indicating the matters of fact on which he takes issue with the prosecution,
   (c) setting out, in the case of each such matter, why he takes issue with the prose-cution, and
   (d) indicating any point of law (including any point as to the admissibility of evid-ence or an abuse of process) which he wishes to take, and any authority on which he intends to rely for that purpose.

(2) A defence statement that discloses an alibi must give particulars of it, including—
   (a) the name, address and date of birth of any witness the accused believes is able to give evidence in support of the alibi, or as many of those details as are known to the accused when the statement is given;
   (b) any information in the accused's possession which might be of material assist-ance in identifying or finding any such witness in whose case any of the details mentioned in paragraph (a) are not known to the accused when the statement is given.

(3) For the purposes of this section evidence in support of an alibi is evidence tending to show that by reason of the presence of the accused at a particular place or in a particular area at a particular time he was not, or was unlikely to have been, at the place where the offence is alleged to have been committed at the time of its alleged commission.

(4) The Secretary of State may by regulations make provision as to the details of the matters that, by virtue of subsection (1), are to be included in defence statements.

6E   Disclosure by accused: further provisions

(1) Where an accused's solicitor purports to give on behalf of the accused—
   (a) a defence statement under section 5, 6 or 6B, or
   (b) a statement of the kind mentioned in section 6B(4),
the statement shall, unless the contrary is proved, be deemed to be given with the authority of the accused.

(2) If it appears to the judge at a pre-trial hearing that an accused has failed to comply fully with section 5, 6B or 6C, so that there is a possibility of comment being made or inferences drawn under section 11(5), he shall warn the accused accordingly.

(3) In subsection (2) 'pre-trial hearing' has the same meaning as in Part 4 (see section 39).

(4) The judge in a trial before a judge and jury—
   (a) may direct that the jury be given a copy of any defence statement, and
   (b) if he does so, may direct that it be edited so as not to include references to matters evidence of which would be inadmissible.

(5) A direction under subsection (4)—
   (a) may be made either of the judge's own motion or on the application of any party;

(b) may be made only if the judge is of the opinion that seeing a copy of the defence statement would help the jury to understand the case or to resolve any issue in the case.

(6) The reference in subsection (4) to a defence statement is a reference—

(a) where the accused has given only an initial defence statement (that is, a defence statement given under section 5 or 6), to that statement;

(b) where he has given both an initial defence statement and an updated defence statement (that is, a defence statement given under section 6B), to the updated defence statement;

(c) where he has given both an initial defence statement and a statement of the kind mentioned in section 6B(4), to the initial defence statement.

7A   Continuing duty of prosecutor to disclose

(1) This section applies at all times—

(a) after the prosecutor has complied with section 3 or purported to comply with it, and

(b) before the accused is acquitted or convicted or the prosecutor decides not to proceed with the case concerned.

(2) The prosecutor must keep under review the question whether at any given time (and, in particular, following the giving of a defence statement) there is prosecution material which—

(a) might reasonably be considered capable of undermining the case for the prosecution against the accused or of assisting the case for the accused, and

(b) has not been disclosed to the accused.

(3) If at any time there is any such material as is mentioned in subsection (2) the prosecutor must disclose it to the accused as soon as is reasonably practicable (or within the period mentioned in subsection (5)(a), where that applies).

(4) In applying subsection (2) by reference to any given time the state of affairs at that time (including the case for the prosecution as it stands at that time) must be taken into account.

(5) Where the accused gives a defence statement under section 5, 6 or 6B—

(a) if as a result of that statement the prosecutor is required by this section to make any disclosure, or further disclosure, he must do so during the period which, by virtue of section 12, is the relevant period for this section;

(b) if the prosecutor considers that he is not so required, he must during that period give to the accused a written statement to that effect.

(6) For the purposes of this section prosecution material is material—

(a) which is in the prosecutor's possession and came into his possession in connection with the case for the prosecution against the accused, or

(b) which, in pursuance of a code operative under Part 2, he has inspected in connection with the case for the prosecution against the accused.

(7) Subsections (3) to (5) of section 3 (method by which prosecutor discloses) apply for the purposes of this section as they apply for the purposes of that.

(8) Material must not be disclosed under this section to the extent that the court, on an application by the prosecutor, concludes it is not in the public interest to disclose it and orders accordingly.

(9) Material must not be disclosed under this section to the extent that it is material the disclosure of which is prohibited by section 17 of the Regulation of Investigatory Powers Act 2000 (c. 23).

8   Application by accused for disclosure

(1) This section applies where the accused has given a defence statement under section 5 or 6 and the prosecutor has complied with section 7A(5) or has purported to comply with it or has failed to comply with it.

(2) If the accused has at any time reasonable cause to believe that there is prosecution material which is required by section 7A to be disclosed to him and has not been, the accused may apply to the court for an order requiring the prosecutor to disclose it to him.

(3) For the purposes of this section prosecution material is material—

  (a) which is in the prosecutor's possession and came into his possession in connection with the case for the prosecution against the accused,

  (b) which, in pursuance of a code operative under Part II, he has inspected in connection with the case for the prosecution against the accused, or

  (c) which falls within subsection (4).

(4) Material falls within this subsection if in pursuance of a code operative under Part II the prosecutor must, if he asks for the material, be given a copy of it or be allowed to inspect it in connection with the case for the prosecution against the accused.

(5) Material must not be disclosed under this section to the extent that the court, on an application by the prosecutor, concludes it is not in the public interest to disclose it and orders accordingly.

(6) Material must not be disclosed under this section to the extent that it is material the disclosure of which is prohibited by section 17 of the Regulation of Investigatory Powers Act 2000.

10   Prosecutor's failure to observe time limits

(1) This section applies if the prosecutor—

  (a) purports to act under section 3 after the end of the period which, by virtue of section 12, is the relevant period for section 3, or

  (b) purports to act under section 7A(5) after the end of the period which, by virtue of section 12, is the relevant period for section 7A.

(2) Subject to subsection (3), the failure to act during the period concerned does not on its own constitute grounds for staying the proceedings for abuse of process.

(3) Subsection (2) does not prevent the failure constituting such grounds if it involves such delay by the prosecutor that the accused is denied a fair trial.

11   Faults in disclosure by accused

(1) This section applies in the three cases set out in subsections (2), (3) and (4).

(2) The first case is where section 5 applies and the accused—

  (a) fails to give an initial defence statement,

  (b) gives an initial defence statement but does so after the end of the period which, by virtue of section 12, is the relevant period for section 5,

  (c) is required by section 6B to give either an updated defence statement or a statement of the kind mentioned in subsection (4) of that section but fails to do so,

  (d) gives an updated defence statement or a statement of the kind mentioned in section 6B(4) but does so after the end of the period which, by virtue of section 12, is the relevant period for section 6B,

  (e) sets out inconsistent defences in his defence statement, or

  (f) at his trial—

    (i) puts forward a defence which was not mentioned in his defence statement or is different from any defence set out in that statement,

    (ii) relies on a matter which, in breach of the requirements imposed by or under section 6A, was not mentioned in his defence statement,

    (iii) adduces evidence in support of an alibi without having given particulars of the alibi in his defence statement, or

    (iv) calls a witness to give evidence in support of an alibi without having complied with section 6A(2)(a) or (b) as regards the witness in his defence statement.

(3) The second case is where section 6 applies, the accused gives an initial defence statement, and the accused—

    (a) gives the initial defence statement after the end of the period which, by virtue of section 12, is the relevant period for section 6, or

    (b) does any of the things mentioned in paragraphs (c) to (f) of subsection (2).

(5) Where this section applies—

    (a) the court or any other party may make such comment as appears appropriate;

    (b) the court or jury may draw such inferences as appear proper in deciding whether the accused is guilty of the offence concerned.

(6) Where—

    (a) this section applies by virtue of subsection (2)(f)(ii) (including that provision as it applies by virtue of subsection (3)(b)), and

    (b) the matter which was not mentioned is a point of law (including any point as to the admissibility of evidence or an abuse of process) or an authority,

comment by another party under subsection (5)(a) may be made only with the leave of the court.

(8) Where the accused puts forward a defence which is different from any defence set out in his defence statement, in doing anything under subsection (5) or in deciding whether to do anything under it the court shall have regard—

    (a) to the extent of the differences in the defences, and

    (b) to whether there is any justification for it.

(9) Where the accused calls a witness whom he has failed to include, or to identify adequately, in a witness notice, in doing anything under subsection (5) or in deciding whether to do anything under it the court shall have regard to whether there is any justification for the failure.

(10) A person shall not be convicted of an offence solely on an inference drawn under subsection (5).

(12) In this section—

    (a) 'initial defence statement' means a defence statement given under section 5 or 6;

    (b) 'updated defence statement' means a defence statement given under section 6B;

    (c) a reference simply to an accused's 'defence statement' is a reference—

        (i) where he has given only an initial defence statement, to that statement;

        (ii) where he has given both an initial and an updated defence statement, to the updated defence statement;

        (iii) where he has given both an initial defence statement and a statement of the kind mentioned in section 6B(4), to the initial defence statement;

    (d) a reference to evidence in support of an alibi shall be construed in accordance with section 6A(3);

    (e) 'witness notice' means a notice given under section 6C.

12   Time limits

(1) This section has effect for the purpose of determining the relevant period for sections 3, 5, 6, 6B, 6C and 7AC51.

(2) Subject to subsection (3), the relevant period is a period beginning and ending with such days as the Secretary of State prescribes by regulations for the purposes of the section concerned.

(3) The regulations may do one or more of the following—

    (a) provide that the relevant period for any section shall if the court so orders be extended (or further extended) by so many days as the court specifies;

    (b) provide that the court may only make such an order if an application is made by a prescribed person and if any other prescribed conditions are fulfilled;

    (c) provide that an application may only be made if prescribed conditions are fulfilled;

(d) provide that the number of days by which a period may be extended shall be entirely at the court's discretion;

(e) provide that the number of days by which a period may be extended shall not exceed a prescribed number;

(f) provide that there shall be no limit on the number of applications that may be made to extend a period;

(g) provide that no more than a prescribed number of applications may be made to extend a period;

and references to the relevant period for a section shall be construed accordingly.

(4) Conditions mentioned in subsection (3) may be framed by reference to such factors as the Secretary of State thinks fit.

(5) Without prejudice to the generality of subsection (4), so far as the relevant period for section 3 or 7A(5) is concerned—

(a) conditions may be framed by reference to the nature or volume of the material concerned;

(b) the nature of material may be defined by reference to the prosecutor's belief that the question of non-disclosure on grounds of public interest may arise.

(6) In subsection (3) 'prescribed' means prescribed by regulations under this section.

13 Time limits: transitional

(1) As regards a case in relation to which no regulations under section 12 have come into force for the purposes of section 3, section 3(8) shall have effect as if it read—

'(8) The prosecutor must act under this section as soon as is reasonably practicable after—

(a) the accused pleads not guilty (where this Part applies by virtue of section 1(1)),

(b) the accused is committed for trial (where this Part applies by virtue of section 1(2)(a)),

(c) the proceedings are transferred (where this Part applies by virtue of section 1(2)(b) or (c)),

(ca) copies of the documents containing the evidence on which the charge or charges are based are served on the accused (where this Part applies by virtue of section 1(2)(cc)).

(d) the count is included in the indictment (where this Part applies by virtue of section 1(2)(d)), or

(e) the bill of indictment is preferred (where this Part applies by virtue of section 1(2)(e)).'

(2) As regards a case in relation to which no regulations under section 12 have come into force for the purposes of section 7A, section 7A(5) shall have effect as if—

(a) in paragraph (a) for the words 'during the period' to the end, and

(b) in paragraph (b) for 'during that period', there were substituted 'as soon as reasonably practicable after the accused gives the statement in question.'

14 Public interest: review for summary trials

(1) This section applies where this Part applies by virtue of section 1(1).

(2) At any time—

(a) after a court makes an order under section 3(6), 7A(8) or 8(5), and

(b) before the accused is acquitted or convicted or the prosecutor decides not to proceed with the case concerned,

the accused may apply to the court for a review of the question whether it is still not in the public interest to disclose material affected by its order.

(3) In such a case the court must review that question, and if it concludes that it is in the public interest to disclose material to any extent—

(a) it shall so order, and

(b) it shall take such steps as are reasonable to inform the prosecutor of its order.

(4) Where the prosecutor is informed of an order made under subsection (3) he must act accordingly having regard to the provisions of this Part (unless he decides not to proceed with the case concerned).

15   Public interest: review in other cases
   (1) This section applies where this Part applies by virtue of section 1(2).
   (2) This section applies at all times—
      (a) after a court makes an order under section 3(6), 7A(8) or 8(5), and
      (b) before the accused is acquitted or convicted or the prosecutor decides not to proceed with the case concerned.
   (3) The court must keep under review the question whether at any given time it is still not in the public interest to disclose material affected by its order.
   (4) The court must keep the question mentioned in subsection (3) under review without the need for an application; but the accused may apply to the court for a review of that question.
   (5) If the court at any time concludes that it is in the public interest to disclose material to any extent—
      (a) it shall so order, and
      (b) it shall take such steps as are reasonable to inform the prosecutor of its order.
   (6) Where the prosecutor is informed of an order made under subsection (5) he must act accordingly having regard to the provisions of this Part (unless he decides not to proceed with the case concerned).

16   Applications: opportunity to be heard
Where—
      (a) an application is made under section 3(6), 7A(8), 8(5), 14(2) or 15(4),
      (b) a person claiming to have an interest in the material applies to be heard by the court, and
      (c) he shows that he was involved (whether alone or with others and whether directly or indirectly) in the prosecutor's attention being brought to the material,
the court must not make an order under section 3(6), 7A(8), 8(5), 14(3) or 15(5) (as the case may be) unless the person applying under paragraph (b) has been given an opportunity to be heard.

17   Confidentiality of disclosed information
   (1) If the accused is given or allowed to inspect a document or other object under—
      (a) section 3, 4, 7A, 14 or 15, or
      (b) an order under section 8,
then, subject to subsections (2) to (4), he must not use or disclose it or any information recorded in it.
   (2) The accused may use or disclose the object or information—
      (a) in connection with the proceedings for whose purposes he was given the object or allowed to inspect it,
      (b) with a view to the taking of further criminal proceedings (for instance, by way of appeal) with regard to the matter giving rise to the proceedings mentioned in paragraph (a), or
      (c) in connection with the proceedings first mentioned in paragraph (b).
   (3) The accused may use or disclose—
      (a) the object to the extent that it has been displayed to the public in open court, or
      (b) the information to the extent that it has been communicated to the public in open court;
but the preceding provisions of this subsection do not apply if the object is displayed or the information is communicated in proceedings to deal with a contempt of court under section 18.

(4) If—

    (a) the accused applies to the court for an order granting permission to use or disclose the object or information, and

    (b) the court makes such an order,

the accused may use or disclose the object or information for the purpose and to the extent specified by the court.

(5) An application under subsection (4) may be made and dealt with at any time, and in particular after the accused has been acquitted or convicted or the prosecutor has decided not to proceed with the case concerned; but this is subject to rules made by virtue of section 19(2).

(6) Where—

    (a) an application is made under subsection (4), and

    (b) the prosecutor or a person claiming to have an interest in the object or information applies to be heard by the court,

the court must not make an order granting permission unless the person applying under paragraph (b) has been given an opportunity to be heard.

(7) References in this section to the court are to—

    (a) a magistrates' court, where this Part applies by virtue of section 1(1);

    (b) the Crown Court, where this Part applies by virtue of section 1(2).

(8) Nothing in this section affects any other restriction or prohibition on the use or disclosure of an object or information, whether the restriction or prohibition arises under an enactment (whenever passed) or otherwise.

18   Confidentiality: contravention

(1) It is a contempt of court for a person knowingly to use or disclose an object or information recorded in it if the use or disclosure is in contravention of section 17.

(2) The following courts have jurisdiction to deal with a person who is guilty of a contempt under this section—

    (a) a magistrates' court, where this Part applies by virtue of section 1(1);

    (b) the Crown Court, where this Part applies by virtue of section 1(2).

(3) A person who is guilty of a contempt under this section may be dealt with as follows—

    (a) a magistrates' court may commit him to custody for a specified period not exceeding six months or impose on him a fine not exceeding £5,000 or both;

    (b) the Crown Court may commit him to custody for a specified period not exceeding two years or impose a fine on him or both.

(4) If—

    (a) a person is guilty of a contempt under this section, and

    (b) the object concerned is in his possession,

the court finding him guilty may order that the object shall be forfeited and dealt with in such manner as the court may order.

(5) The power of the court under subsection (4) includes power to order the object to be destroyed or to be given to the prosecutor or to be placed in his custody for such period as the court may specify.

(6) If—

    (a) the court proposes to make an order under subsection (4), and

    (b) the person found guilty, or any other person claiming to have an interest in the object, applies to be heard by the court,

the court must not make the order unless the applicant has been given an opportunity to be heard.

(7) If—

    (a) a person is guilty of a contempt under this section, and

    (b) a copy of the object concerned is in his possession,

the court finding him guilty may order that the copy shall be forfeited and dealt with in such manner as the court may order.

(8) Subsections (5) and (6) apply for the purposes of subsection (7) as they apply for the purposes of subsection (4), but as if references to the object were references to the copy.

(9) An object or information shall be inadmissible as evidence in civil proceedings if to adduce it would in the opinion of the court be likely to constitute a contempt under this section; and 'the court' here means the court before which the civil proceedings are being taken.

(10) The powers of a magistrates' court under this section may be exercised either of the court's own motion or by order on complaint.

Vulnerable witnesses

Criminal Justice Act 1988

32 Evidence through television links

(1) A person other than the accused may give evidence through a live television link in proceedings to which subsection (1A) below applies if–
  (a) the witness is outside the United Kingdom;
but evidence may not be so given without the leave of the court.
  (1A) This subsection applies—
  (a) to trials on indictment, appeals to the criminal division of the Court of Appeal and hearings of references under section 9 of the Criminal Appeal Act 1995; and
  (b) to proceedings in youth courts and appeals to the Crown Court arising out of such proceedings, and hearings of references under section 11 of the Criminal Appeal Act 1995 so arising.

(3) A statement made on oath by a witness outside the United Kingdom and given in evidence through a link by virtue of this section shall be treated for the purposes of section 1 of the Perjury Act 1911 as having been made in the proceedings in which it is given in evidence.

(4) Without prejudice to the generality of any enactment conferring power to make Criminal Procedure Rules, such rules may make such provision as appears to the Criminal Procedure Rule Committee to be necessary or expedient for the purposes of this section.

34 Abolition of requirement of corroboration for unsworn evidence of children

(2) Any requirement whereby at a trial on indictment it is obligatory for the court to give the jury a warning about convicting the accused on the uncorroborated evidence of a child is abrogated.

(3) Unsworn evidence admitted by virtue of [section 56 of the Youth Justice and Criminal Evidence Act 1999] may corroborate evidence (sworn or unsworn) given by any other person.

Youth Justice and Criminal Evidence Act 1999

PART II   SPECIAL MEASURES DIRECTIONS
IN CASE OF VULNERABLE AND
INTIMIDATED WITNESSES

16 Witnesses eligible for assistance on grounds of age or incapacity

(1) For the purposes of this Chapter a witness in criminal proceedings (other than the accused) is eligible for assistance by virtue of this section—
  (a) if under the age of 17 at the time of the hearing; or

    (b) if the court considers that the quality of evidence given by the witness is likely to be diminished by reason of any circumstances falling within subsection (2).

(2) The circumstances falling within this subsection are—

    (a) that the witness—

        (i)   suffers from mental disorder within the meaning of the Mental Health Act 1983, or

        (ii) otherwise has a significant impairment of intelligence and social functioning;

    (b) that the witness has a physical disability or is suffering from a physical disorder.

(3) In subsection (1)(a) 'the time of the hearing', in relation to a witness, means the time when it falls to the court to make a determination for the purposes of section 19(2) in relation to the witness.

(4) In determining whether a witness falls within subsection (1)(b) the court must consider any views expressed by the witness.

(5) In this Chapter references to the quality of a witness's evidence are to its quality in terms of completeness, coherence and accuracy; and for this purpose 'coherence' refers to a witness's ability in giving evidence to give answers which address the questions put to the witness and can be understood both individually and collectively.

17 **Witnesses eligible for assistance on grounds of fear or distress about testifying**

(1) For the purposes of this Chapter a witness in criminal proceedings (other than the accused) is eligible for assistance by virtue of this subsection if the court is satisfied that the quality of evidence given by the witness is likely to be diminished by reason of fear or distress on the part of the witness in connection with testifying in the proceedings.

(2) In determining whether a witness falls within subsection (1) the court must take into account, in particular—

    (a) the nature and alleged circumstances of the offence to which the proceedings relate;

    (b) the age of the witness;

    (c) such of the following matters as appear to the court to be relevant, namely—

        (i)   the social and cultural background and ethnic origins of the witness,

        (ii) the domestic and employment circumstances of the witness, and

        (iii) any religious beliefs or political opinions of the witness;

    (d) any behaviour towards the witness on the part of—

        (i)   the accused,

        (ii) members of the family or associates of the accused, or

        (iii) any other person who is likely to be an accused or a witness in the proceedings.

(3) In determining that question the court must in addition consider any views expressed by the witness.

(4) Where the complainant in respect of a sexual offence is a witness in proceedings relating to that offence (or to that offence and any other offences), the witness is eligible for assistance in relation to those proceedings by virtue of this subsection unless the witness has informed the court of the witness' wish not to be so eligible by virtue of this subsection.

18 **Special measures available to eligible witnesses**

(1) For the purposes of this Chapter—

    (a) the provision which may be made by a special measures direction by virtue of each of sections 23 to 30 is a special measure available in relation to a witness eligible for assistance by virtue of section 16; and

    (b) the provision which may be made by such a direction by virtue of each of sections 23 to 28 is a special measure available in relation to a witness eligible for assistance by virtue of section 17;

but this subsection has effect subject to subsection (2).

(2) Where (apart from this subsection) a special measure would, in accordance with subsection (1)(a) or (b), be available in relation to a witness in any proceedings, it shall not be taken by a court to be available in relation to the witness unless—

    (a) the court has been notified by the Secretary of State that relevant arrangements may be made available in the area in which it appears to the court that the proceedings will take place, and

    (b) the notice has not been withdrawn.

(3) In subsection (2) 'relevant arrangements' means arrangements for implementing the measure in question which cover the witness and the proceedings in question.

(4) The withdrawal of a notice under that subsection relating to a special measure shall not affect the availability of that measure in relation to a witness if a special measures direction providing for that measure to apply to the witness's evidence has been made by the court before the notice is withdrawn.

(5) The Secretary of State may by order make such amendments of this Chapter as he considers appropriate for altering the special measures which, in accordance with subsection (1)(a) or (b), are available in relation to a witness eligible for assistance by virtue of section 16 or (as the case may be) section 17, whether—

    (a) by modifying the provisions relating to any measure for the time being available in relation to such a witness,

    (b) by the addition—

        (i) (with or without modifications) of any measure which is for the time being available in relation to a witness eligible for assistance by virtue of the other of those sections, or

        (ii) of any new measure, or

    (c) by the removal of any measure.

19 Special measures direction relating to eligible witness

(1) This section applies where in any criminal proceedings—

    (a) a party to the proceedings makes an application for the court to give a direction under this section in relation to a witness in the proceedings other than the accused, or

    (b) the court of its own motion raises the issue whether such a direction should be given.

(2) Where the court determines that the witness is eligible for assistance by virtue of section 16 or 17, the court must then—

    (a) determine whether any of the special measures available in relation to the witness (or any combination of them) would, in its opinion, be likely to improve the quality of evidence given by the witness; and

    (b) if so—

        (i) determine which of those measures (or combination of them) would, in its opinion, be likely to maximise so far as practicable the quality of such evidence; and

        (ii) give a direction under this section providing for the measure or measures so determined to apply to evidence given by the witness.

(3) In determining for the purposes of this Chapter whether any special measure or measures would or would not be likely to improve, or to maximise so far as practicable, the quality of evidence given by the witness, the court must consider all the circumstances of the case, including in particular—

    (a) any views expressed by the witness; and

    (b) whether the measure or measures might tend to inhibit such evidence being effectively tested by a party to the proceedings.

(4) A special measures direction must specify particulars of the provision made by the direction in respect of each special measure which is to apply to the witness's evidence.

(5) In this Chapter 'special measures direction' means a direction under this section.

(6) Nothing in this Chapter is to be regarded as affecting any power of a court to make an order or give leave of any description (in the exercise of its inherent jurisdiction or otherwise)—

(a) in relation to a witness who is not an eligible witness, or

(b) in relation to an eligible witness where (as, for example, in a case where a foreign language interpreter is to be provided) the order is made or the leave is given otherwise than by reason of the fact that the witness is an eligible witness.

20 Further provisions about directions: general

(1) Subject to subsection (2) and section 21(8), a special measures direction has binding effect from the time it is made until the proceedings for the purposes of which it is made are either—

(a) determined (by acquittal, conviction or otherwise), or

(b) abandoned,

in relation to the accused or (if there is more than one) in relation to each of the accused.

(2) The court may discharge or vary (or further vary) a special measures direction if it appears to the court to be in the interests of justice to do so, and may do so either—

(a) on an application made by a party to the proceedings, if there has been a material change of circumstances since the relevant time, or

(b) of its own motion.

(3) In subsection (2) 'the relevant time' means—

(a) the time when the direction was given, or

(b) if a previous application has been made under that subsection, the time when the application (or last application) was made.

(4) Nothing in section 24(2) and (3), 27(4) to (7) or 28(4) to (6) is to be regarded as affecting the power of the court to vary or discharge a special measures direction under subsection (2).

(5) The court must state in open court its reasons for—

(a) giving or varying,

(b) refusing an application for, or for the variation or discharge of, or

(c) discharging,

a special measures direction and, if it is a magistrates' court, must cause them to be entered in the register of its proceedings.

(6) Criminal Procedure Rules may make provision—

(a) for uncontested applications to be determined by the court without a hearing;

(b) for preventing the renewal of an unsuccessful application for a special measures direction except where there has been a material change of circumstances;

(c) for expert evidence to be given in connection with an application for, or for varying or discharging, such a direction;

(d) for the manner in which confidential or sensitive information is to be treated in connection with such an application and in particular as to its being disclosed to, or withheld from, a party to the proceedings.

21 Special provisions relating to child witnesses

(1) For the purposes of this section—

(a) a witness in criminal proceedings is a 'child witness' if he is an eligible witness by reason of section 16(1)(a) (whether or not he is an eligible witness by reason of any other provision of section 16 or 17);

(b) a child witness is 'in need of special protection' if the offence (or any of the offences) to which the proceedings relate is—

(i) an offence falling within section 35(3)(a) (sexual offences etc.), or

(ii) an offence falling within section 35(3)(b), (c) or (d) (kidnapping, assaults etc.);

and

    (c) a 'relevant recording', in relation to a child witness, is a video recording of an interview of the witness made with a view to its admission as evidence in chief of the witness.

(2) Where the court, in making a determination for the purposes of section 19(2), determines that a witness in criminal proceedings is a child witness, the court must—

    (a) first have regard to subsections (3) to (7) below; and

    (b) then have regard to section 19(2);

and for the purposes of section 19(2), as it then applies to the witness, any special measures required to be applied in relation to him by virtue of this section shall be treated as if they were measures determined by the court, pursuant to section 19(2)(a) and (b)(i), to be ones that (whether on their own or with any other special measures) would be likely to maximise, so far as practicable, the quality of his evidence.

(3) The primary rule in the case of a child witness is that the court must give a special measures direction in relation to the witness which complies with the following requirements—

    (a) it must provide for any relevant recording to be admitted under section 27 (video recorded evidence in chief); and

    (b) it must provide for any evidence given by the witness in the proceedings which is not given by means of a video recording (whether in chief or otherwise) to be given by means of a live link in accordance with section 24.

(4) The primary rule is subject to the following limitations—

    (a) the requirement contained in subsection (3)(a) or (b) has effect subject to the availability (within the meaning of section 18(2)) of the special measure in question in relation to the witness;

    (b) the requirement contained in subsection (3)(a) also has effect subject to section 27(2); and

    (c) the rule does not apply to the extent that the court is satisfied that compliance with it would not be likely to maximise the quality of the witness's evidence so far as practicable (whether because the application to that evidence of one or more other special measures available in relation to the witness would have that result or for any other reason).

(5) However, subsection (4)(c) does not apply in relation to a child witness in need of special protection.

(6) Where a child witness is in need of special protection by virtue of subsection (1)(b)(i), any special measures direction given by the court which complies with the requirement contained in subsection (3)(a) must in addition provide for the special measure available under section 28 (video recorded cross-examination or re-examination) to apply in relation to—

    (a) any cross-examination of the witness otherwise than by the accused in person, and

    (b) any subsequent re-examination.

(7) The requirement contained in subsection (6) has effect subject to the following limitations—

    (a) it has effect subject to the availability (within the meaning of section 18(2)) of that special measure in relation to the witness; and

    (b) it does not apply if the witness has informed the court that he does not want that special measure to apply in relation to him.

(8) Where a special measures direction is given in relation to a child witness who is an eligible witness by reason only of section 16(1)(a), then—

    (a) subject to subsection (9) below, and

    (b) except where the witness has already begun to give evidence in the proceedings,

the direction shall cease to have effect at the time when the witness attains the age of 17.

(9) Where a special measures direction is given in relation to a child witness who is an eligible witness by reason only of section 16(1)(a) and—

    (a) the direction provides—

        (i) for any relevant recording to be admitted under section 27 as evidence in chief of the witness, or

        (ii) for the special measure available under section 28 to apply in relation to the witness, and

    (b) if it provides for that special measure to so apply, the witness is still under the age of 17 when the video recording is made for the purposes of section 28,

then, so far as it provides as mentioned in paragraph (a)(i) or (ii) above, the direction shall continue to have effect in accordance with section 20(1) even though the witness subsequently attains that age.

22   Extension of provisions of section 21 to certain witnesses over 17

(1) For the purposes of this section—

    (a) a witness in criminal proceedings (other than the accused) is a 'qualifying witness' if he—

        (i) is not an eligible witness at the time of the hearing (as defined by section 16(3)), but

        (ii) was under the age of 17 when a relevant recording was made;

    (b) a qualifying witness is 'in need of special protection' if the offence (or any of the offences) to which the proceedings relate is—

        (i) an offence falling within section 35(3)(a) (sexual offences etc.), or

        (ii) an offence falling within section 35(3)(b), (c) or (d) (kidnapping, assaults etc.); and

    (c) a 'relevant recording', in relation to a witness, is a video recording of an interview of the witness made with a view to its admission as evidence in chief of the witness.

(2) Subsections (2) to (7) of section 21 shall apply as follows in relation to a qualifying witness—

    (a) subsections (2) to (4), so far as relating to the giving of a direction complying with the requirement contained in subsection (3)(a), shall apply to a qualifying witness in respect of the relevant recording as they apply to a child witness (within the meaning of that section);

    (b) subsection (5), so far as relating to the giving of such a direction, shall apply to a qualifying witness in need of special protection as it applies to a child witness in need of special protection (within the meaning of that section); and

    (c) subsections (6) and (7) shall apply to a qualifying witness in need of special protection by virtue of subsection (1)(b)(i) above as they apply to such a child witness as is mentioned in subsection (6).

23   Screening witness from accused

(1) A special measures direction may provide for the witness, while giving testimony or being sworn in court, to be prevented by means of a screen or other arrangement from seeing the accused.

(2) But the screen or other arrangement must not prevent the witness from being able to see, and to be seen by—

    (a) the judge or justices (or both) and the jury (if there is one);

    (b) legal representatives acting in the proceedings; and

    (c) any interpreter or other person appointed (in pursuance of the direction or otherwise) to assist the witness.

(3) Where two or more legal representatives are acting for a party to the proceedings, subsection (2)(b) is to be regarded as satisfied in relation to those representatives if the witness is able at all material times to see and be seen by at least one of them.

24   Evidence by live link

(1) A special measures direction may provide for the witness to give evidence by means of a live link.

(2) Where a direction provides for the witness to give evidence by means of a live link, the witness may not give evidence in any other way without the permission of the court.

(3) The court may give permission for the purposes of subsection (2) if it appears to the court to be in the interests of justice to do so, and may do so either—

(a) on an application by a party to the proceedings, if there has been a material change of circumstances since the relevant time, or

(b) of its own motion.

(4) In subsection (3) 'the relevant time' means—

(a) the time when the direction was given, or

(b) if a previous application has been made under that subsection, the time when the application (or last application) was made.

(8) In this Chapter 'live link' means a live television link or other arrangement whereby a witness, while absent from the courtroom or other place where the proceedings are being held, is able to see and hear a person there and to be seen and heard by the persons specified in section 23(2)(a) to (c).

25   Evidence given in private

(1) A special measures direction may provide for the exclusion from the court, during the giving of the witness's evidence, of persons of any description specified in the direction.

(2) The persons who may be so excluded do not include—

(a) the accused,

(b) legal representatives acting in the proceedings, or

(c) any interpreter or other person appointed (in pursuance of the direction or otherwise) to assist the witness.

(3) A special measures direction providing for representatives of news gathering or reporting organisations to be so excluded shall be expressed not to apply to one named person who—

(a) is a representative of such an organisation, and

(b) has been nominated for the purpose by one or more such organisations,

unless it appears to the court that no such nomination has been made.

(4) A special measures direction may only provide for the exclusion of persons under this section where—

(a) the proceedings relate to a sexual offence; or

(b) it appears to the court that there are reasonable grounds for believing that any person other than the accused has sought, or will seek, to intimidate the witness in connection with testifying in the proceedings.

(5) Any proceedings from which persons are excluded under this section (whether or not those persons include representatives of news gathering or reporting organisations) shall nevertheless be taken to be held in public for the purposes of any privilege or exemption from liability available in respect of fair, accurate and contemporaneous reports of legal proceedings held in public.

26   Removal of wigs and gowns

A special measures direction may provide for the wearing of wigs or gowns to be dispensed with during the giving of the witness's evidence.

27   Video recorded evidence in chief

(1) A special measures direction may provide for a video recording of an interview of the witness to be admitted as evidence in chief of the witness.

(2) A special measures direction may, however, not provide for a video recording, or a part of such a recording, to be admitted under this section if the court is of the opinion,

having regard to all the circumstances of the case, that in the interests of justice the recording, or that part of it, should not be so admitted.

(3) In considering for the purposes of subsection (2) whether any part of a recording should not be admitted under this section, the court must consider whether any prejudice to the accused which might result from that part being so admitted is outweighed by the desirability of showing the whole, or substantially the whole, of the recorded interview.

(4) Where a special measures direction provides for a recording to be admitted under this section, the court may nevertheless subsequently direct that it is not to be so admitted if—

    (a) it appears to the court that—

        (i) the witness will not be available for cross-examination (whether conducted in the ordinary way or in accordance with any such direction), and

        (ii) the parties to the proceedings have not agreed that there is no need for the witness to be so available; or

    (b) any Criminal Procedure Rules requiring disclosure of the circumstances in which the recording was made have not been complied with to the satisfaction of the court.

(5) Where a recording is admitted under this section—

    (a) the witness must be called by the party tendering it in evidence, unless—

        (i) a special measures direction provides for the witness's evidence on cross-examination to be given otherwise than by testimony in court, or

        (ii) the parties to the proceedings have agreed as mentioned in subsection (4)(a)(ii); and

    (b) the witness may not give evidence in chief otherwise than by means of the recording—

        (i) as to any matter which, in the opinion of the court, has been dealt with adequately in the witness's recorded testimony, or

        (ii) without the permission of the court, as to any other matter which, in the opinion of the court, is dealt with in that testimony.

(6) Where in accordance with subsection (2) a special measures direction provides for part only of a recording to be admitted under this section, references in subsections (4) and (5) to the recording or to the witness's recorded testimony are references to the part of the recording or testimony which is to be so admitted.

(7) The court may give permission for the purposes of subsection (5)(b)(ii) if it appears to the court to be in the interests of justice to do so, and may do so either—

    (a) on an application by a party to the proceedings, if there has been a material change of circumstances since the relevant time, or

    (b) of its own motion.

(8) In subsection (7) 'the relevant time' means—

    (a) the time when the direction was given, or

    (b) if a previous application has been made under that subsection, the time when the application (or last application) was made.

(9) The court may, in giving permission for the purposes of subsection (5)(b)(ii), direct that the evidence in question is to be given by the witness by means of a live link; and, if the court so directs, subsections (5) to (7) of section 24 shall apply in relation to that evidence as they apply in relation to evidence which is to be given in accordance with a special measures direction.

(10)[1] A magistrates' court inquiring into an offence as examining justices under section 6 of the Magistrates' Courts Act 1980 may consider any video recording in relation to which it is proposed to apply for a special measures direction providing for it to be admitted at the trial in accordance with this section.

---

[1] Subsection (10) is due to be repealed by Schedule 3, para 73(2) and Schedule 37, Part IV of the Criminal Justice Act 2003.

(11) Nothing in this section affects the admissibility of any video recording which would be admissible apart from this section.

28 Video recorded cross-examination or re-examination

(1) Where a special measures direction provides for a video recording to be admitted under section 27 as evidence in chief of the witness, the direction may also provide—

  (a) for any cross-examination of the witness, and any re-examination, to be recorded by means of a video recording; and

  (b) for such a recording to be admitted, so far as it relates to any such cross-examination or re-examination, as evidence of the witness under cross-examination or on re-examination, as the case may be.

(2) Such a recording must be made in the presence of such persons as rules of court or the direction may provide and in the absence of the accused, but in circumstances in which—

  (a) the judge or justices (or both) and legal representatives acting in the proceedings are able to see and hear the examination of the witness and to communicate with the persons in whose presence the recording is being made, and

  (b) the accused is able to see and hear any such examination and to communicate with any legal representative acting for him.

(3) Where two or more legal representatives are acting for a party to the proceedings, subsection (2)(a) and (b) are to be regarded as satisfied in relation to those representatives if at all material times they are satisfied in relation to at least one of them.

(4) Where a special measures direction provides for a recording to be admitted under this section, the court may nevertheless subsequently direct that it is not to be so admitted if any requirement of subsection (2) or Criminal Procedure Rules the direction has not been complied with to the satisfaction of the court.

(5) Where in pursuance of subsection (1) a recording has been made of any examination of the witness, the witness may not be subsequently cross-examined or re-examined in respect of any evidence given by the witness in the proceedings (whether in any recording admissible under section 27 or this section or otherwise than in such a recording) unless the court gives a further special measures direction making such provision as is mentioned in subsection (1)(a) and (b) in relation to any subsequent cross-examination, and re-examination, of the witness.

(6) The court may only give such a further direction if it appears to the court—

  (a) that the proposed cross-examination is sought by a party to the proceedings as a result of that party having become aware, since the time when the original recording was made in pursuance of subsection (1), of a matter which that party could not with reasonable diligence have ascertained by then, or

  (b) that for any other reason it is in the interests of justice to give the further direction.

(7) Nothing in this section shall be read as applying in relation to any cross-examination of the witness by the accused in person (in a case where the accused is to be able to conduct any such cross-examination).

29 Examination of witness through intermediary

(1) A special measures direction may provide for any examination of the witness (however and wherever conducted) to be conducted through an interpreter or other person approved by the court for the purposes of this section ('an intermediary').

(2) The function of an intermediary is to communicate—

  (a) to the witness, questions put to the witness, and

  (b) to any person asking such questions, the answers given by the witness in reply to them.

and to explain such question or answers so far as necessary to enable them to be understood by the witness or person in question.

(3) Any examination of the witness in pursuance of subsection (1) must take place in the presence of such persons as rules of court or the direction may provide, but in circumstances in which—

    (a) the judge or justices (or both) and legal representatives acting in the proceedings are able to see and hear the examination of the witness and to communicate with the intermediary, and

    (b) (except in the case of a video recorded examination) the jury (if there is one) are able to see and hear the examination of the witness.

(4) Where two or more legal representatives are acting for a party to the proceedings, subsection (3)(a) is to be regarded as satisfied in relation to those representatives if at all material times it is satisfied in relation to at least one of them.

(5) A person may not act as an intermediary in a particular case except after making a declaration, in such form as may be prescribed by Criminal Procedure Rules that he will faithfully perform his function as intermediary.

(6) Subsection (1) does not apply to an interview of the witness which is recorded by means of a video recording with a view to its admission as evidence in chief of the witness; but a special measures direction may provide for such a recording to be admitted under section 27 if the interview was conducted through an intermediary and—

    (a) that person complied with subsection (5) before the interview began, and

    (b) the court's approval for the purposes of this section is given before the direction is given.

(7) Section 1 of the Perjury Act 1911 (perjury) shall apply in relation to a person acting as an intermediary as it applies in relation to a person lawfully sworn as an interpreter in a judicial proceeding; and for this purpose, where a person acts as an intermediary in any proceeding which is not a judicial proceeding for the purposes of that section, that proceeding shall be taken to be part of the judicial proceeding in which the witness's evidence is given.

30

A special measures direction may provide for the witness, while giving evidence (whether by testimony in court or otherwise), to be provided with such device as the court considers appropriate with a view to enabling questions or answers to be communicated to or by the witness despite any disability or disorder or other impairment which the witness has or suffers from.

CHAPTER II   PROTECTION OF WITNESSES FROM CROSS-EXAMINATION BY ACCUSED IN PERSON

34   Complainants in proceedings for sexual offences

No person charged with a sexual offence may in any criminal proceedings cross-examine in person a witness who is the complainant, either—

    (a) in connection with that offence, or

    (b) in connection with any other offence (of whatever nature) with which that person is charged in the proceedings.

35   Child complainants and other child witnesses

(1) No person charged with an offence to which this section applies may in any criminal proceedings cross-examine in person a protected witness, either—

    (a) in connection with that offence, or

    (b) in connection with any other offence (of whatever nature) with which that person is charged in the proceedings.

(2) For the purposes of subsection (1) a 'protected witness' is a witness who—
    (a) either is the complainant or is alleged to have been a witness to the commission of the offence to which this section applies, and
    (b) either is a child or falls to be cross-examined after giving evidence in chief (whether wholly or in part)—
        (i) by means of a video recording made (for the purposes of section 27) at a time when the witness was a child, or
        (ii) in any other way at any such time.
(3) The offences to which this section applies are—
    (a) any offence under—
        (v) the Protection of Children Act 1978, or
        (vi) Part 1 of the Sexual Offences Act 2003;
    (b) kidnapping, false imprisonment or an offence under section 1 or 2 of the Child Abduction Act 1984;
    (c) any offence under section 1 of the Children and Young Persons Act 1933;
    (d) any offence (not within any of the preceding paragraphs) which involves an assault on, or injury or a threat of injury to, any person.
(4) In this section 'child' means—
    (a) where the offence falls within subsection (3)(a), a person under the age of 17; or
    (b) where the offence falls within subsection (3)(b), (c) or (d), a person under the age of 14.
(5) For the purposes of this section 'witness' includes a witness who is charged with an offence in the proceedings.

36 Direction prohibiting accused from cross-examining particular witness

(1) This section applies where, in a case where neither of sections 34 and 35 operates to prevent an accused in any criminal proceedings from cross-examining a witness in person—
    (a) the prosecutor makes an application for the court to give a direction under this section in relation to the witness, or
    (b) the court of its own motion raises the issue whether such a direction should be given.
(2) If it appears to the court—
    (a) that the quality of evidence given by the witness on cross-examination—
        (i) is likely to be diminished if the cross-examination (or further cross-examination) is conducted by the accused in person, and
        (ii) would be likely to be improved if a direction were given under this section, and
    (b) that it would not be contrary to the interests of justice to give such a direction,
the court may give a direction prohibiting the accused from cross-examining (or further cross-examining) the witness in person.
(3) In determining whether subsection (2)(a) applies in the case of a witness the court must have regard, in particular, to—
    (a) any views expressed by the witness as to whether or not the witness is content to be cross-examined by the accused in person;
    (b) the nature of the questions likely to be asked, having regard to the issues in the proceedings and the defence case advanced so far (if any);
    (c) any behaviour on the part of the accused at any stage of the proceedings, both generally and in relation to the witness;
    (d) any relationship (of whatever nature) between the witness and the accused;
    (e) whether any person (other than the accused) is or has at any time been charged in the proceedings with a sexual offence or an offence to which section 35 applies, and (if so) whether section 34 or 35 operates or would have operated to prevent that person from cross-examining the witness in person;

(f) any direction under section 19 which the court has given, or proposes to give, in relation to the witness.

(4) For the purposes of this section—

(a) 'witness', in relation to an accused, does not include any other person who is charged with an offence in the proceedings; and

(b) any reference to the quality of a witness's evidence shall be construed in accordance with section 16(5).

37   Further provisions about directions under section 36

(1) Subject to subsection (2), a direction has binding effect from the time it is made until the witness to whom it applies is discharged.
In this section 'direction' means a direction under section 36.

(2) The court may discharge a direction if it appears to the court to be in the interests of justice to do so, and may do so either—

(a) on an application made by a party to the proceedings, if there has been a material change of circumstances since the relevant time, or

(b) of its own motion.

(3) In subsection (2) 'the relevant time' means—

(a) the time when the direction was given, or

(b) if a previous application has been made under that subsection, the time when the application (or last application) was made.

(4) The court must state in open court its reasons for—

(a) giving, or

(b) refusing an application for, or for the discharge of, or

(c) discharging,

a direction and, if it is a magistrates' court, must cause them to be entered in the register of its proceedings.

(5) Criminal Procedure Rules may make provision—

(a) for uncontested applications to be determined by the court without a hearing;

(b) for preventing the renewal of an unsuccessful application for a direction except where there has been a material change of circumstances;

(c) for expert evidence to be given in connection with an application for, or for discharging, a direction;

(d) for the manner in which confidential or sensitive information is to be treated in connection with such an application and in particular as to its being disclosed to, or withheld from, a party to the proceedings.

38   Defence representation for purposes of cross-examination

(1) This section applies where an accused is prevented from cross-examining a witness in person by virtue of section 34, 35 or 36.

(2) Where it appears to the court that this section applies, it must—

(a) invite the accused to arrange for a legal representative to act for him for the purpose of cross-examining the witness; and

(b) require the accused to notify the court; by the end of such period as it may specify, whether a legal representative is to act for him for that purpose.

(3) If by the end of the period mentioned in subsection (2)(b) either—

(a) the accused has notified the court that no legal representative is to act for him for the purpose of cross-examining the witness, or

(b) no notification has been received by the court and it appears to the court that no legal representative is to so act,

the court must consider whether it is necessary in the interests of justice for the witness to be cross-examined by a legal representative appointed to represent the interests of the accused.

(4) If the court decides that it is necessary in the interests of justice for the witness to be so cross-examined, the court must appoint a qualified legal representative (chosen by the court) to cross-examine the witness in the interests of the accused.

(5) A person so appointed shall not be responsible to the accused.

(6) Criminal Procedure Rules may make provision—

    (a) as to the time when, and the manner in which, subsection (2) is to be complied with;

    (b) in connection with the appointment of a legal representative under subsection (4), and in particular for securing that a person so appointed is provided with evidence or other material relating to the proceedings.

(7) Criminal Procedure Rules made in pursuance of subsection (6)(b) may make provision for the application, with such modifications as are specified in the rules, of any of the provisions of—

    (a) Part I of the Criminal Procedure and Investigations Act 1996 (disclosure of material in connection with criminal proceedings), or

    (b) the Sexual Offences (Protected Material) Act 1997.

(8) For the purposes of this section—

    (a) any reference to cross-examination includes (in a case where a direction is given under section 36 after the accused has begun cross-examining the witness) a reference to further cross-examination; and

    (b) 'qualified legal representative' means a legal representative who has a right of audience (within the meaning of the Courts and Legal Services Act 1990) in relation to the proceedings before the court.

39   Warning to jury

(1)[2] Where on a trial on indictment an accused is prevented from cross-examining a witness in person by virtue of section 34, 35 or 36, the judge must give the jury such warning (if any) as the judge considers necessary to ensure that the accused is not prejudiced—

    (a) by any inferences that might be drawn from the fact that the accused has been prevented from cross-examining the witness in person;

    (b) where the witness has been cross-examined by a legal representative appointed under section 38(4), by the fact that the cross-examination was carried out by such a legal representative and not by a person acting as the accused's own legal representative.

(2) Subsection (8)(a) of section 38 applies for the purposes of this section as it applies for the purposes of section 38.

40   Funding of defence representation

(1) In section 19(3) of the Prosecution of Offences Act 1985 (regulations authorising payments out of central funds), after paragraph (d) there shall be inserted—

'(e) to cover the proper fee or costs of a legal representative appointed under section 38(4) of the Youth Justice and Criminal Evidence Act 1999 (defence representation for purposes of cross-examination) and any expenses properly incurred in providing such a person with evidence or other material in connection with his appointment.'

CHAPTER III   PROTECTION OF COMPLAINANTS
IN PROCEEDINGS FOR SEXUAL OFFENCES

41   Restriction on evidence or questions about complainant's sexual history

(1) If at a trial a person is charged with a sexual offence, then, except with the leave of the court—

    (a) no evidence may be adduced, and

    (b) no question may be asked in cross-examination,

by or on behalf of any accused at the trial, about any sexual behaviour of the complainant.

---

[2] A minor amendment to subsection (1) will be made when Schedule 36, para 76 of the Criminal Justice Act 2003 comes into force.

(2) The court may give leave in relation to any evidence or question only on an application made by or on behalf of an accused, and may not give such leave unless it is satisfied—

(a) that subsection (3) or (5) applies, and

(b) that a refusal of leave might have the result of rendering unsafe a conclusion of the jury or (as the case may be) the court on any relevant issue in the case.

(3) This subsection applies if the evidence or question relates to a relevant issue in the case and either—

(a) that issue is not an issue of consent; or

(b) it is an issue of consent and the sexual behaviour of the complainant to which the evidence or question relates is alleged to have taken place at or about the same time as the event which is the subject matter of the charge against the accused; or

(c) it is an issue of consent and the sexual behaviour of the complainant to which the evidence or question relates is alleged to have been, in any respect, so similar—

(i)   to any sexual behaviour of the complainant which (according to evidence adduced or to be adduced by or on behalf of the accused) took place as part of the event which is the subject matter of the charge against the accused, or

(ii) to any other sexual behaviour of the complainant which (according to such evidence) took place at or about the same time as that event,

that the similarity cannot reasonably be explained as a coincidence.

(4) For the purposes of subsection (3) no evidence or question shall be regarded as relating to a relevant issue in the case if it appears to the court to be reasonable to assume that the purpose (or main purpose) for which it would be adduced or asked is to establish or elicit material for impugning the credibility of the complainant as a witness.

(5) This subsection applies if the evidence or question—

(a) relates to any evidence adduced by the prosecution about any sexual behaviour of the complainant; and

(b) in the opinion of the court, would go no further than is necessary to enable the evidence adduced by the prosecution to be rebutted or explained by or on behalf of the accused.

(6) For the purposes of subsections (3) and (5) the evidence or question must relate to a specific instance (or specific instances) of alleged sexual behaviour on the part of the complainant (and accordingly nothing in those subsections is capable of applying in relation to the evidence or question to the extent that it does not so relate).

(7) Where this section applies in relation to a trial by virtue of the fact that one or more of a number of persons charged in the proceedings is or are charged with a sexual offence—

(a) it shall cease to apply in relation to the trial if the prosecutor decides not to proceed with the case against that person or those persons in respect of that charge; but

(b) it shall not cease to do so in the event of that person or those persons pleading guilty to, or being convicted of, that charge.

(8) Nothing in this section authorises any evidence to be adduced or any question to be asked which cannot be adduced or asked apart from this section.

42 Interpretation and application of section 41

(1) In section 41—

(a) 'relevant issue in the case' means any issue falling to be proved by the prosecution or defence in the trial of the accused;

(b) 'issue of consent' means any issue whether the complainant in fact consented to the conduct constituting the offence with which the accused is charged (and accordingly does not include any issue as to the belief of the accused that the complainant so consented);

(c) 'sexual behaviour' means any sexual behaviour or other sexual experience, whether or not involving any accused or other person, but excluding (except in section 41(3)(c)(i) and (5)(a)) anything alleged to have taken place as part of the event which is the subject matter of the charge against the accused; and

(d) subject to any order made under subsection (2), 'sexual offence' shall be construed in accordance with section 62.

(2) The Secretary of State may by order make such provision as he considers appropriate for adding or removing, for the purposes of section 41, any offence to or from the offences which are sexual offences for the purposes of this Act by virtue of section 62.

(3)[3] Section 41 applies in relation to the following proceedings as it applies to a trial, namely—

(a) proceedings before a magistrates' court inquiring into an offence as examining justices,

(b) the hearing of an application under paragraph 5(1) of Schedule 6 to the Criminal Justice Act 1991 (application to dismiss charge following notice of transfer of case to Crown Court),

(c) the hearing of an application under paragraph 2(1) of Schedule 3 to the Crime and Disorder Act 1998 (application to dismiss charge by person sent for trial under section 51 or 51A of that Act),

(d) any hearing held, between conviction and sentencing, for the purpose of determining matters relevant to the court's decision as to how the accused is to be dealt with, and

(e) the hearing of an appeal,

and references (in section 41 or this section) to a person charged with an offence accordingly include a person convicted of an offence.

43 Procedure on applications under section 41

(1) An application for leave shall be heard in private and in the absence of the complainant.

In this section 'leave' means leave under section 41.

(2) Where such an application has been determined, the court must state in open court (but in the absence of the jury, if there is one)—

(a) its reasons for giving, or refusing, leave, and

(b) if it gives leave, the extent to which evidence may be adduced or questions asked in pursuance of the leave,

and, if it is a magistrates' court, must cause those matters to be entered in the register of its proceedings.

(3) Criminal Procedure Rules may make provision—

(a) requiring applications for leave to specify, in relation to each item of evidence or question to which they relate, particulars of the grounds on which it is asserted that leave should be given by virtue of subsection (3) or (5) of section 41;

(b) enabling the court to request a party to the proceedings to provide the court with information which it considers would assist it in determining an application for leave;

(c) for the manner in which confidential or sensitive information is to be treated in connection with such an application, and in particular as to its being disclosed to, or withheld from, parties to the proceedings.

---

[3] Paragraphs (a) and (b) are to be repealed when Schedule 3, para 73(3)(a) and Schedule 37, Part IV of the Criminal Justice Act 2003 come into force. The wording of paragraph (c) will be amended when Schedule 3, para 73(3)(b) takes effect.

Criminal Justice and Public Order Act 1994

Inferences from accused's silence

34   Effect of accused's failure to mention facts when questioned or charged

(1) Where, in any proceedings against a person for an offence, evidence is given that the accused—

(a) at any time before he was charged with the offence, on being questioned under caution by a constable trying to discover whether or by whom the offence had been committed, failed to mention any fact relied on in his defence in those proceedings; or

(b) on being charged with the offence or officially informed that he might be prosecuted for it, failed to mention any such fact,

being a fact which in the circumstances existing at the time the accused could reasonably have been expected to mention when so questioned, charged or informed, as the case may be, subsection (2) below applies.

(2) Where this subsection applies—

(a) a magistrates' court inquiring into the offence as examining justices;

(b) a judge, in deciding whether to grant an application made by the accused under paragraph 2 of Schedule 3 to the Crime and Disorder Act 1998;

(c) the court, in determining whether there is a case to answer; and

(d) the court or jury, in determining whether the accused is guilty of the offence charged,

may draw such inferences from the failure as appear proper.

(2A) Where the accused was at an authorised place of detention at the time of the failure, subsections (1) and (2) above do not apply if he had not been allowed an opportunity to consult a solicitor prior to being questioned, charged or informed as mentioned in subsection (1) above.

(3) Subject to any directions by the court, evidence tending to establish the failure may be given before or after evidence tending to establish the fact which the accused is alleged to have failed to mention.

(4) This section applies in relation to questioning by persons (other than constables) charged with the duty of investigating offences or charging offenders as it applies in relation to questioning by constables; and in subsection (1) above 'officially informed' means informed by a constable or any such person.

(5) This section does not—

(a) prejudice the admissibility in evidence of the silence or other reaction of the accused in the face of anything said in his presence relating to the conduct in respect of which he is charged, in so far as evidence thereof would be admissible apart from this section; or

(b) preclude the drawing of any inference from any such silence or other reaction of the accused which could properly be drawn apart from this section.

(6) This section does not apply in relation to a failure to mention a fact if the failure occurred before the commencement of this section.

35   Effect of accused's silence at trial

(1) At the trial of any person for an offence, subsections (2) and (3) below apply unless—

(a) the accused's guilt is not in issue; or

(b) it appears to the court that the physical or mental condition of the accused makes it undesirable for him to give evidence;

but subsection (2) below does not apply if, at the conclusion of the evidence for the prosecution, his legal representative informs the court that the accused will give evidence or, where he is unrepresented, the court ascertains from him that he will give evidence.

(2)[4] Where this subsection applies, the court shall, at the conclusion of the evidence for the prosecution, satisfy itself (in the case of proceedings on indictment, in the presence of the jury) that the accused is aware that the stage has been reached at which evidence can be given for the defence and that he can, if he wishes, give evidence and that, if he chooses not to give evidence, or having been sworn, without good cause refuses to answer any question, it will be permissible for the court or jury to draw such inferences as appear proper from his failure to give evidence or his refusal, without good cause, to answer any question.

(3) Where this subsection applies, the court or jury, in determining whether the accused is guilty of the offence charged, may draw such inferences as appear proper from the failure of the accused to give evidence or his refusal, without good cause, to answer any question.

(4) This section does not render the accused compellable to give evidence on his own behalf, and he shall accordingly not be guilty of contempt of court by reason of a failure to do so.

(5) For the purposes of this section a person who, having been sworn, refuses to answer any question shall be taken to do so without good cause unless—

(a) he is entitled to refuse to answer the question by virtue of any enactment, whenever passed or made, or on the ground of privilege; or

(b) the court in the exercise of its general discretion excuses him from answering it.

(7) This section applies—

(a) in relation to proceedings on indictment for an offence, only if the person charged with the offence is arraigned on or after the commencement of this section;

(b) in relation to proceedings in a magistrates' court, only if the time when the court begins to receive evidence in the proceedings falls after the commencement of this section.

36 Effect of accused's failure or refusal to account for objects, substances or marks

(1) Where—

(a) a person is arrested by a constable, and there is—

(i) on his person; or

(ii) in or on his clothing or footwear; or

(iii) otherwise in his possession; or

(iv) in any place in which he is at the time of his arrest,

any object, substance or mark, or there is any mark on any such object; and

(b) that or another constable investigating the case reasonably believes that the presence of the object, substance or mark may be attributable to the participation of the person arrested in the commission of an offence specified by the constable; and

(c) the constable informs the person arrested that he so believes, and requests him to account for the presence of the object, substance or mark; and

(d) the person fails or refuses to do so,

then if, in any proceedings against the person for the offence so specified, evidence of those matters is given, subsection (2) below applies.

(2) Where this subsection applies—

(a) a magistrates' court, inquiring into the offence as examining justices;

(b) a judge, in deciding whether to grant an application made by the accused under paragraph 2 of Schedule 3 to the Crime and Disorder Act 1998;

(c) the court, in determining whether there is a case to answer; and

---

[4] A minor amendment to subsection (2) is to be made when Schedule 36, para 63 of the Criminal Justice Act 2003 comes into force.

(d) the court or jury, in determining whether the accused is guilty of the offence charged,

may draw such inferences from the failure or refusal as appear proper.

(3) Subsections (1) and (2) above apply to the condition of clothing or footwear as they apply to a substance or mark thereon.

(4) Subsections (1) and (2) above do not apply unless the accused was told in ordinary language by the constable when making the request mentioned in subsection (1)(c) above what the effect of this section would be if he failed or refused to comply with the request.

(4A) Where the accused was at an authorised place of detention at the time of the failure or refusal, subsections (1) and (2) above do not apply if he had not been allowed an opportunity to consult a solicitor prior to the request being made.

(5) This section applies in relation to officers of customs and excise as it applies in relation to constables.

(6) This section does not preclude the drawing of any inference from a failure or refusal of the accused to account for the presence of an object, substance or mark or from the condition of clothing or footwear which could properly be drawn apart from this section.

(7) This section does not apply in relation to a failure or refusal which occurred before the commencement of this section.

37   Effect of accused's failure or refusal to account for presence at a particular place

(1) Where—
    (a) a person arrested by a constable was found by him at a place at or about the time the offence for which he was arrested is alleged to have been committed; and
    (b) that or another constable investigating the offence reasonably believes that the presence of the person at that place and at that time may be attributable to his participation in the commission of the offence; and
    (c) the constable informs the person that he so believes, and requests him to account for that presence; and
    (d) the person fails or refuses to do so,

then if, in any proceedings against the person for the offence, evidence of those matters is given, subsection (2) below applies.

(2) Where this subsection applies—
    (a) a magistrates' court, inquiring into the offence as examining justices;
    (b) a judge, in deciding whether to grant an application made by the accused under paragraph 2 of Schedule 3 to the Crime and Disorder Act 1998;
    (c) the court, in determining whether there is a case to answer; and
    (d) the court or jury, in determining whether the accused is guilty of the offence charged,

may draw such inferences from the failure or refusal as appear proper.

(3) Subsections (1) and (2) do not apply unless the accused was told in ordinary language by the constable when making the request mentioned in subsection (1)(c) above what the effect of this section would be if he failed or refused to comply with the request.

(3A) Where the accused was at an authorised place of detention at the time of the failure or refusal, subsections (1) and (2) do not apply if he had not been allowed an opportunity to consult a solicitor prior to the request being made.

(4) This section applies in relation to officers of customs and excise as it applies in relation to constables.

(5) This section does not preclude the drawing of any inference from a failure or refusal of the accused to account for his presence at a place which could properly be drawn apart from this section.

(6) This section does not apply in relation to a failure or refusal which occurred before the commencement of this section.

Youth Justice and Criminal Evidence Act 1999

59   Restriction on use of answers etc. obtained under compulsion

Schedule 3, which amends enactments providing for the use of answers and statements given under compulsion so as to restrict in criminal proceedings their use in evidence against the persons giving them, shall have effect.

Confessions

Police and Criminal Evidence Act 1984

76   Confessions

(1) In any proceedings a confession made by an accused person may be given in evidence against him in so far as it is relevant to any matter in issue in the proceedings and is not excluded by the court in pursuance of this section.

(2) If, in any proceedings where the prosecution proposes to give in evidence a confession made by an accused person, it is represented to the court that the confession was or may have been obtained—

(a) by oppression of the person who made it; or

(b) in consequence of anything said or done which was likely, in the circumstances existing at the time, to render unreliable any confession which might be made by him in consequence thereof,

the court shall not allow the confession to be given in evidence against him except in so far as the prosecution proves to the court beyond reasonable doubt that the confession (notwithstanding that it may be true) was not obtained as aforesaid.

(3) In any proceedings where the prosecution proposes to give in evidence a confession made by an accused person, the court may of its own motion require the prosecution, as a condition of allowing it to do so, to prove that the confession was not obtained as mentioned in subsection (2) above.

(4) The fact that a confession is wholly or partly excluded in pursuance of this section shall not affect the admissibility in evidence—

(a) of any facts discovered as a result of the confession; or

(b) where the confession is relevant as showing that the accused speaks, writes or expresses himself in a particular way, of so much of the confession as is necessary to show that he does so.

(5) Evidence that a fact to which this subsection applies was discovered as a result of a statement made by an accused person shall not be admissible unless evidence of how it was discovered is given by him or on his behalf.

(6) Subsection (5) above applies—

(a) to any fact discovered as a result of a confession which is wholly excluded in pursuance of this section; and

(b) to any fact discovered as a result of a confession which is partly so excluded, if the fact is discovered as a result of the excluded part of the confession.

(7) Nothing in Part VII of this Act shall prejudice the admissibility of a confession made by an accused person.

(8) In this section 'oppression' includes torture, inhuman or degrading treatment, and the use or threat of violence (whether or not amounting to torture).

(9)[1] Where the proceedings mentioned in subsection (1) above are proceedings before a magistrates' court inquiring into an offence as examining justices this section shall have effect with the omission of—

---

[1] Subsection (9) is due to be repealed when Schedule 3, para 56(4) and Schedule 37, Part IV of the Criminal Justice Act 2003 come into force.

(a) in subsection (1) the words 'and is not excluded by the court in pursuance of this section', and

(b) subsections (2) to (6) and (8).

76A Confessions may be given in evidence for co-accused

(1) In any proceedings a confession made by an accused person may be given in evidence for another person charged in the same proceedings (a co-accused) in so far as it is relevant to any matter in issue in the proceedings and is not excluded by the court in pursuance of this section.

(2) If, in any proceedings where a co-accused proposes to give in evidence a confession made by an accused person, it is represented to the court that the confession was or may have been obtained—

(a) by oppression of the person who made it; or

(b) in consequence of anything said or done which was likely, in the circumstances existing at the time, to render unreliable any confession which might be made by him in consequence thereof,

the court shall not allow the confession to be given in evidence for the co-accused except in so far as it is proved to the court on the balance of probabilities that the confession (notwithstanding that it may be true) was not so obtained.

(3) Before allowing a confession made by an accused person to be given in evidence for a co-accused in any proceedings, the court may of its own motion require the fact that the confession was not obtained as mentioned in subsection (2) above to be proved in the proceedings on the balance of probabilities.

(4) The fact that a confession is wholly or partly excluded in pursuance of this section shall not affect the admissibility in evidence—

(a) of any facts discovered as a result of the confession; or

(b) where the confession is relevant as showing that the accused speaks, writes or expresses himself in a particular way, of so much of the confession as is necessary to show that he does so.

(5) Evidence that a fact to which this subsection applies was discovered as a result of a statement made by an accused person shall not be admissible unless evidence of how it was discovered is given by him or on his behalf.

(6) Subsection (5) above applies—

(a) to any fact discovered as a result of a confession which is wholly excluded in pursuance of this section; and

(b) to any fact discovered as a result of a confession which is partly so excluded, if the fact is discovered as a result of the excluded part of the confession.

(7) In this section 'oppression' includes torture, inhuman or degrading treatment, and the use or threat of violence (whether or not amounting to torture).

77[2] Confessions by mentally handicapped persons

(1) Without prejudice to the general duty of the court at a trial on indictment to direct the jury on any matter on which it appears to the court appropriate to do so, where at such a trial—

(a) the case against the accused depends wholly or substantially on a confession by him; and

(b) the court is satisfied—

(i) that he is mentally handicapped; and

(ii) that the confession was not made in the presence of an independent person,

the court shall warn the jury that there is special need for caution before convicting the accused in reliance on the confession, and shall explain that the need arises because of the circumstances mentioned in paragraphs (a) and (b) above.

(2) In any case where at the summary trial of a person for an offence it appears to the court that a warning under subsection (1) above would be required if the trial were on

---

[2] Subsections (1) and (2) are to be amended and subsection (2A) inserted when Schedule 36, para 48 of the Criminal Justice Act 2003 comes into force.

indictment, the court shall treat the case as one in which there is a special need for caution before convicting the accused on his confession.

(3) In this section—

'independent person' does not include a police officer or a person employed for, or engaged on, police purposes;

'mentally handicapped', in relation to a person, means that he is in a state of arrested or incomplete development of mind which includes significant impairment of intelligence and social functioning; and

'police purposes' has the meaning assigned to it by section 101(2) of the Police Act 1996.

78 Exclusion of unfair evidence

(1) In any proceedings the court may refuse to allow evidence on which the prosecution proposes to rely to be given if it appears to the court that, having regard to all the circumstances, including the circumstances in which the evidence was obtained, the admission of the evidence would have such an adverse effect on the fairness of the proceedings that the court ought not to admit it.

(2) Nothing in this section shall prejudice any rule of law requiring a court to exclude evidence.

(3)[3] This section shall not apply in the case of proceedings before a magistrates' court inquiring into an offences as examining justices.

PART VIII   SUPPLEMENTARY

82 Part VIII—interpretation

(1) In this Part of this Act—

'confession', includes any statement wholly or partly adverse to the person who made it, whether made to a person in authority or not and whether made in words or otherwise; . . . .

(3) Nothing in this Part of this Act shall prejudice any power of a court to exclude evidence (whether by preventing questions from being put or otherwise) at its discretion.

Bad character evidence

Criminal Justice Act 2003

98 'Bad character'

References in this Chapter to evidence of a person's 'bad character' are to evidence of, or of a disposition towards, misconduct on his part, other than evidence which—

(a) has to do with the alleged facts of the offence with which the defendant is charged, or

(b) is evidence of misconduct in connection with the investigation or prosecution of that offence.

99 Abolition of common law rules

(1) The common law rules governing the admissibility of evidence of bad character in criminal proceedings are abolished.

(2) Subsection (1) is subject to section 118(1) in so far as it preserves the rule under which in criminal proceedings a person's reputation is admissible for the purposes of proving his bad character.

---

[3] Subsection (3) is to be repealed when Schedule 3, para 56(5) and Schedule 37, Part IV of the Criminal Justice Act 2003 come into force.

100 Non-defendant's bad character

(1) In criminal proceedings evidence of the bad character of a person other than the defendant is admissible if and only if—

    (a) it is important explanatory evidence,

    (b) it has substantial probative value in relation to a matter which—

        (i) is a matter in issue in the proceedings, and

        (ii) is of substantial importance in the context of the case as a whole,

        or

    (c) all parties to the proceedings agree to the evidence being admissible.

(2) For the purposes of subsection (1)(a) evidence is important explanatory evidence if—

    (a) without it, the court or jury would find it impossible or difficult properly to understand other evidence in the case, and

    (b) its value for understanding the case as a whole is substantial.

(3) In assessing the probative value of evidence for the purposes of subsection (1)(b) the court must have regard to the following factors (and to any others it considers relevant)—

    (a) the nature and number of the events, or other things, to which the evidence relates;

    (b) when those events or things are alleged to have happened or existed;

    (c) where—

        (i) the evidence is evidence of a person's misconduct, and

        (ii) it is suggested that the evidence has probative value by reason of similarity between that misconduct and other alleged misconduct,

        the nature and extent of the similarities and the dissimilarities between each of the alleged instances of misconduct;

    (d) where—

        (i) the evidence is evidence of a person's misconduct,

        (ii) it is suggested that that person is also responsible for the misconduct charged, and

        (iii) the identity of the person responsible for the misconduct charged is disputed,

        the extent to which the evidence shows or tends to show that the same person was responsible each time.

(4) Except where subsection (1)(c) applies, evidence of the bad character of a person other than the defendant must not be given without leave of the court.

101 Defendant's bad character

(1) In criminal proceedings evidence of the defendant's bad character is admissible if, but only if—

    (a) all parties to the proceedings agree to the evidence being admissible,

    (b) the evidence is adduced by the defendant himself or is given in answer to a question asked by him in cross-examination and intended to elicit it,

    (c) it is important explanatory evidence,

    (d) it is relevant to an important matter in issue between the defendant and the prosecution,

    (e) it has substantial probative value in relation to an important matter in issue between the defendant and a co-defendant,

    (f) it is evidence to correct a false impression given by the defendant, or

    (g) the defendant has made an attack on another person's character.

(2) Sections 102 to 106 contain provision supplementing subsection (1).

(3) The court must not admit evidence under subsection (1)(d) or (g) if, on an application by the defendant to exclude it, it appears to the court that the admission of the evidence would have such an adverse effect on the fairness of the proceedings that the court ought not to admit it.

(4) On an application to exclude evidence under subsection (3) the court must have regard, in particular, to the length of time between the matters to which that evidence relates and the matters which form the subject of the offence charged.

102 'Important explanatory evidence'

For the purposes of section 101(1)(c) evidence is important explanatory evidence if—
>   (a) without it, the court or jury would find it impossible or difficult properly to understand other evidence in the case, and
>   (b) its value for understanding the case as a whole is substantial.

103 'Matter in issue between the defendant and the prosecution'

(1) For the purposes of section 101(1)(d) the matters in issue between the defendant and the prosecution include—
>   (a) the question whether the defendant has a propensity to commit offences of the kind with which he is charged, except where his having such a propensity makes it no more likely that he is guilty of the offence;
>   (b) the question whether the defendant has a propensity to be untruthful, except where it is not suggested that the defendant's case is untruthful in any respect.

(2) Where subsection (1)(a) applies, a defendant's propensity to commit offences of the kind with which he is charged may (without prejudice to any other way of doing so) be established by evidence that he has been convicted of—
>   (a) an offence of the same description as the one with which he is charged, or
>   (b) an offence of the same category as the one with which he is charged.

(3) Subsection (2) does not apply in the case of a particular defendant if the court is satisfied, by reason of the length of time since the conviction or for any other reason, that it would be unjust for it to apply in his case.

(4) For the purposes of subsection (2)—
>   (a) two offences are of the same description as each other if the statement of the offence in a written charge or indictment would, in each case, be in the same terms;
>   (b) two offences are of the same category as each other if they belong to the same category of offences prescribed for the purposes of this section by an order made by the Secretary of State.

(5) A category prescribed by an order under subsection (4)(b) must consist of offences of the same type.

(6) Only prosecution evidence is admissible under section 101(1)(d).

104 'Matter in issue between the defendant and a co-defendant'

(1) Evidence which is relevant to the question whether the defendant has a propensity to be untruthful is admissible on that basis under section 101(1)(e) only if the nature or conduct of his defence is such as to undermine the codefendant's defence.

(2) Only evidence—
>   (a) which is to be (or has been) adduced by the co-defendant, or
>   (b) which a witness is to be invited to give (or has given) in cross-examination by the co-defendant,

is admissible under section 101(1)(e).

105 'Evidence to correct a false impression'

(1) For the purposes of section 101(1)(f)—
>   (a) the defendant gives a false impression if he is responsible for the making of an express or implied assertion which is apt to give the court or jury a false or mis-leading impression about the defendant;
>   (b) evidence to correct such an impression is evidence which has probative value in correcting it.

(2) A defendant is treated as being responsible for the making of an assertion if—

    (a) the assertion is made by the defendant in the proceedings (whether or not in evidence given by him),

    (b) the assertion was made by the defendant—

        (i) on being questioned under caution, before charge, about the offence with which he is charged, or

        (ii) on being charged with the offence or officially informed that he might be prosecuted for it,

    and evidence of the assertion is given in the proceedings,

    (c) the assertion is made by a witness called by the defendant,

    (d) the assertion is made by any witness in cross-examination in response to a question asked by the defendant that is intended to elicit it, or is likely to do so, or

    (e) the assertion was made by any person out of court, and the defendant adduces evidence of it in the proceedings.

(3) A defendant who would otherwise be treated as responsible for the making of an assertion shall not be so treated if, or to the extent that, he withdraws it or disassociates himself from it.

(4) Where it appears to the court that a defendant, by means of his conduct (other than the giving of evidence) in the proceedings, is seeking to give the court or jury an impression about himself that is false or misleading, the court may if it appears just to do so treat the defendant as being responsible for the making of an assertion which is apt to give that impression.

(5) In subsection (4) 'conduct' includes appearance or dress.

(6) Evidence is admissible under section 101(1)(f) only if it goes no further than is necessary to correct the false impression.

(7) Only prosecution evidence is admissible under section 101(1)(f).

106   **'Attack on another person's character'**

(1) For the purposes of section 101(1)(g) a defendant makes an attack on another person's character if—

    (a) he adduces evidence attacking the other person's character,

    (b) he (or any legal representative appointed under section 38(4) of the Youth Justice and Criminal Evidence Act 1999 (c. 23) to cross-examine a witness in his interests) asks questions in cross-examination that are intended to elicit such evidence, or are likely to do so, or

    (c) evidence is given of an imputation about the other person made by the defendant—

        (i) on being questioned under caution, before charge, about the offence with which he is charged, or

        (ii) on being charged with the offence or officially informed that he might be prosecuted for it.

(2) In subsection (1) 'evidence attacking the other person's character' means evidence to the effect that the other person—

    (a) has committed an offence (whether a different offence from the one with which the defendant is charged or the same one), or

    (b) has behaved, or is disposed to behave, in a reprehensible way;

and 'imputation about the other person' means an assertion to that effect.

(3) Only prosecution evidence is admissible under section 101(1)(g).

107   **Stopping the case where evidence contaminated**

(1) If on a defendant's trial before a judge and jury for an offence—

    (a) evidence of his bad character has been admitted under any of paragraphs (c) to (g) of section 101(1), and

(b) the court is satisfied at any time after the close of the case for the prosecution that—
    (i)   the evidence is contaminated, and
    (ii) the contamination is such that, considering the importance of the evidence to the case against the defendant, his conviction of the offence would be unsafe,

the court must either direct the jury to acquit the defendant of the offence or, if it considers that there ought to be a retrial, discharge the jury.

(2) Where—
    (a) a jury is directed under subsection (1) to acquit a defendant of an offence, and
    (b) the circumstances are such that, apart from this subsection, the defendant could if acquitted of that offence be found guilty of another offence,

the defendant may not be found guilty of that other offence if the court is satisfied as mentioned in subsection (1)(b) in respect of it.

(3) If—
    (a) a jury is required to determine under section 4A(2) of the Criminal Procedure (Insanity) Act 1964 (c. 84) whether a person charged on an indictment with an offence did the act or made the omission charged,
    (b) evidence of the person's bad character has been admitted under any of paragraphs (c) to (g) of section 101(1), and
    (c) the court is satisfied at any time after the close of the case for the prosecution that—
        (i)   the evidence is contaminated, and
        (ii) the contamination is such that, considering the importance of the evidence to the case against the person, a finding that he did the act or made the omission would be unsafe,

the court must either direct the jury to acquit the defendant of the offence or, if it considers that there ought to be a rehearing, discharge the jury.

(4) This section does not prejudice any other power a court may have to direct a jury to acquit a person of an offence or to discharge a jury.

(5) For the purposes of this section a person's evidence is contaminated where—
    (a) as a result of an agreement or understanding between the person and one or more others, or
    (b) as a result of the person being aware of anything alleged by one or more others whose evidence may be, or has been, given in the proceedings,

the evidence is false or misleading in any respect, or is different from what it would otherwise have been.

108   Offences committed by defendant when a child

(1) Section 16(2) and (3) of the Children and Young Persons Act 1963 (c. 37) (offences committed by person under 14 disregarded for purposes of evidence relating to previous convictions) shall cease to have effect.

(2) In proceedings for an offence committed or alleged to have been committed by the defendant when aged 21 or over, evidence of his conviction for an offence when under the age of 14 is not admissible unless—
    (a) both of the offences are triable only on indictment, and
    (b) the court is satisfied that the interests of justice require the evidence to be admissible.

(3) Subsection (2) applies in addition to section 101.

109   Assumption of truth in assessment of relevance or probative value

(1) Subject to subsection (2), a reference in this Chapter to the relevance or probative value of evidence is a reference to its relevance or probative value on the assumption that it is true.

(2) In assessing the relevance or probative value of an item of evidence for any purpose of this Chapter, a court need not assume that the evidence is true if it appears, on the basis of any material before the court (including any evidence it decides to hear on the matter), that no court or jury could reasonably find it to be true.

110   Court's duty to give reasons for rulings

(1) Where the court makes a relevant ruling—

   (a) it must state in open court (but in the absence of the jury, if there is one) its reasons for the ruling;

   (b) if it is a magistrates' court, it must cause the ruling and the reasons for it to be entered in the register of the court's proceedings.

(2) In this section 'relevant ruling' means—

   (a) a ruling on whether an item of evidence is evidence of a person's bad character;

   (b) a ruling on whether an item of such evidence is admissible under section 100 or 101 (including a ruling on an application under section 101(3));

   (c) a ruling under section 107.

118   Preservation of certain common law categories of admissibility

(1) The following rules of law are preserved.

Public information etc

1   Any rule of law under which in criminal proceedings—

   (a) published works dealing with matters of a public nature (such as histories, scientific works, dictionaries and maps) are admissible as evidence of facts of a public nature stated in them,

   (b) public documents (such as public registers, and returns made under public authority with respect to matters of public interest) are admissible as evidence of facts stated in them,

   (c) records (such as the records of certain courts, treaties, Crown grants, pardons and commissions) are admissible as evidence of facts stated in them, or

   (d) evidence relating to a person's age or date or place of birth may be given by a person without personal knowledge of the matter.

Reputation as to character

2   Any rule of law under which in criminal proceedings evidence of a person's reputation is admissible for the purpose of proving his good or bad character.

Note

The rule is preserved only so far as it allows the court to treat such evidence as proving the matter concerned.

Reputation or family tradition

3   Any rule of law under which in criminal proceedings evidence of reputation or family tradition is admissible for the purpose of proving or disproving—

   (a) pedigree or the existence of a marriage,

   (b) the existence of any public or general right, or

   (c) the identity of any person or thing.

Note

The rule is preserved only so far as it allows the court to treat such evidence as proving or disproving the matter concerned.

Res gestae

4   Any rule of law under which in criminal proceedings a statement is admissible as evidence of any matter stated if—

(a) the statement was made by a person so emotionally overpowered by an event that the possibility of concoction or distortion can be disregarded,

(b) the statement accompanied an act which can be properly evaluated as evidence only if considered in conjunction with the statement, or

(c) the statement relates to a physical sensation or a mental state (such as intention or emotion).

Confessions etc

5   Any rule of law relating to the admissibility of confessions or mixed statements in criminal proceedings.

Admissions by agents etc

6   Any rule of law under which in criminal proceedings—

(a) an admission made by an agent of a defendant is admissible against the defendant as evidence of any matter stated, or

(b) a statement made by a person to whom a defendant refers a person for information is admissible against the defendant as evidence of any matter stated.

Common enterprise

7   Any rule of law under which in criminal proceedings a statement made by a party to a common enterprise is admissible against another party to the enterprise as evidence of any matter stated.

Expert evidence

8   Any rule of law under which in criminal proceedings an expert witness may draw on the body of expertise relevant to his field.

(2)   With the exception of the rules preserved by this section, the common law rules governing the admissibility of hearsay evidence in criminal proceedings are abolished.

Theft Act 1968

27   Evidence and procedure on charge of theft or handling stolen goods

(3)   Where a person is being proceeded against for handling stolen goods (but not for any offence other than handling stolen goods), then at any stage of the proceedings, if evidence has been given of his having or arranging to have in his possession the goods the subject of the charge, or of his undertaking or assisting in, or arranging to undertake or assist in, their retention, removal, disposal or realisation, the following evidence shall be admissible for the purpose of proving that he knew or believed the goods to be stolen goods:—

(a) evidence that he has had in his possession, or has undertaken or assisted in the retention, removal, disposal or realisation of, stolen goods from any theft taking place not earlier than twelve months before the offence charged; and

(b) (provided that seven days' notice in writing has been given to him of the intention to prove the conviction) evidence that he has within the five years preceding the date of the offence charged been convicted of theft or of handling stolen goods.

Appeals and reviews

Magistrates' Courts Act 1980

108   Right of appeal to the Crown Court

(1) A person convicted by a magistrates' court may appeal to the Crown Court—

    (a) if he pleaded guilty, against his sentence;

    (b) if he did not, against the conviction or sentence.

(1A) Section 14 of the Powers of Criminal Courts (Sentencing) Act 2000] (under which a conviction of an offence for which an order for conditional or absolute discharge is made is deemed not to be a conviction except for certain purposes) shall not prevent an appeal under this Act, whether against conviction or otherwise.

(2) A person sentenced by a magistrates' court for an offence in respect of which a probation order or an order for conditional discharge has been previously made may appeal to the Crown Court against the sentence.

(3) In this section 'sentence' includes any order made on conviction by a magistrates' court, not being—

    (b) an order for the payment of costs;

    (c) an order under section 2 of the Protection of Animals Act 1911 (which enables a court to order the destruction of an animal); or

    (d) an order made in pursuance of any enactment under which the court has no discretion as to the making of the order or its terms, and also includes a declaration under the Football Spectators Act 1989.

111   Statement of case by magistrates' court

(1) Any person who was a party to any proceeding before a magistrates' court or is aggrieved by the conviction, order, determination or other proceeding of the court may question the proceeding on the ground that it is wrong in law or is in excess of jurisdiction by applying to the justices composing the court to state a case for the opinion of the High Court on the question of law or jurisdiction involved; but a person shall not make an application under this section in respect of a decision against which he has a right of appeal to the High Court or which by virtue of any enactment passed after 31st December 1879 is final.

(2) An application under subsection (1) above shall be made within 21 days after the day on which the decision of the magistrates' court was given.

(3) For the purpose of subsection (2) above, the day on which the decision of the magistrates' court is given shall, where the court has adjourned the trial of an information after conviction, be the day on which the court sentences or otherwise deals with the offender.

(4) On the making of an application under this section in respect of a decision any right of the applicant to appeal against the decision to the Crown Court shall cease.

(5) If the justices are of opinion that an application under this section is frivolous, they may refuse to state a case, and, if the applicant so requires, shall give him a certificate stating that the application has been refused; but the justices shall not refuse to state a case if the application is made by or under the direction of the Attorney General.

(6) Where justices refuse to state a case, the High Court may, on the application of the person who applied for the case to be stated, make an order of mandamus requiring the justices to state a case.

Supreme Court Act 1981

48   Appeals to Crown Court

(1) The Crown Court may, in the course of hearing any appeal, correct any error or mistake in the order or judgment incorporating the decision which is the subject of the appeal.

(2) On the termination of the hearing of an appeal the Crown Court—

    (a) may confirm, reverse or vary the decision appealed against; or

    (b) may remit the matter with its opinion thereon to the authority whose decision is appealed against; or

    (c) may make such other order in the matter as the court thinks just, and by such order exercise any power which the said authority might have exercised.

(3) Subsection (2) has effect subject to any enactment relating to any such appeal which expressly limits or restricts the powers of the court on the appeal.

(4) Subject to section 11(6) of the Criminal Appeal Act 1995, if the appeal is against a conviction or a sentence, the preceding provisions of this section shall be construed as including power to award any punishment, whether more or less severe than that awarded by the magistrates' court whose decision is appealed against, if that is a punishment which that magistrates' court might have awarded.

(5) This section applies whether or not the appeal is against the whole of the decision.

(6) In this section 'sentence' includes any order made by a court when dealing with an offender, including—

    (a) a hospital order under Part V of the Mental Health 1959 c. 72. Act 1959, with or without an order restricting discharge; and

    (b) a recommendation for deportation made when dealing with an offender.

(7) The fact that an appeal is pending against an interim hospital order under the said Act of 1983 shall not affect the power of the magistrates' court that made it to renew or terminate the order or to deal with the appellant on its termination; and where the Crown Court quashes such an order but does not pass any sentence or make any other order in its place the Court may direct the appellant to be kept in custody or released on bail pending his being dealt with by that magistrates' court.

(8) Where the Crown Court makes an interim hospital order by virtue of subsection (2)—

    (a) the power of renewing or terminating the order and of dealing with the appellant on its termination shall be exercisable by the magistrates' court whose decision is appealed against and not by the Crown Court; and

    (b) that magistrates' court shall be treated for the purposes of section 38(7) of the said Act of 1983 (absconding offenders) as the court that made the order.

Criminal Appeal Act 1968

2   Grounds for allowing an appeal under s 1

[(1) Subject to the provisions of this Act, the Court of Appeal—

    (a) shall allow an appeal against conviction if they think that the conviction is unsafe; and

    (b) shall dismiss such an appeal in any other case.]

(2) In the case of an appeal against conviction the Court shall, if they allow the appeal, quash the conviction.

(3) An order of the Court of Appeal quashing a conviction shall, except when under section 7 below the appellant is ordered to be retired, operate as a direction to the court of trial to enter, instead of the record of conviction, a judgment and verdict of acquittal.

7   Power to order retrial

(1) Where the Court of Appeal allow an appeal against conviction . . . and it appears to the Court that the interests of justice so require, they may order the appellant to be retried.

23   Evidence

(1) For [the purposes of an appeal under] this Part of this Act the Court of Appeal may, if they think it necessary or expedient in the interests of justice—

(a) order the production of any document, exhibit or other thing connected with the proceedings, the production of which appears to them necessary for the determination of the case;

(b) order any witness who would have been a compellable witness in the proceedings from which the appeal lies to attend for examination and be examined before the Court, whether or not he was called in those proceedings; and

[(c) receive any evidence which was not adduced in the proceedings from which the appeal lies.]

[(2) The Court of Appeal shall, in considering whether to receive any evidence, have regard in particular to—

(a) whether the evidence appears to the Court to be capable of belief;

(b) whether it appears to the Court that the evidence may afford any ground for allowing the appeal;

(c) whether the evidence would have been admissible in the proceedings from which the appeal lies on an issue which is the subject of the appeal; and

(d) whether there is a reasonable explanation for the failure to adduce the evidence in those proceedings.]

(3) Subsection (1)(c) above applies to any [evidence of a] witness (including the appellant) who is competent but not compellable...

(4) For [the purposes of an appeal under] this Part of this Act, the Court of Appeal may, if they think it necessary or expedient in the interests of justice, order the examination of any witness whose attendance might be required under subsection (1)(b) above to be conducted, in manner provided by rules of court, before any judge or officer of the Court or other person appointed by the Court for the purpose, and allow the admission of any depositions so taken as evidence before the Court.

[23A   Power to order investigations

(1) On an appeal against conviction the Court of Appeal may direct the Criminal Cases Review Commission to investigate and report to the Court on any matter if it appears to the Court that—

(a) the matter is relevant to the determination of the case and ought, if possible, to be resolved before the case is determined;

(b) an investigation of the matter by the Commission is likely to result in the Court being able to resolve it; and

(c) the matter cannot be resolved by the Court without an investigation by the Commission.

(1A) A direction under subsection (1) above may not be given by a single judge, notwithstanding that, in the case of an application for leave to appeal, the application may be determined by a single judge as provided for by section 31 of this Act.

(2) A direction by the Court of Appeal under subsection (1) above shall be given in writing and shall specify the matter to be investigated.

(3) Copies of such a direction shall be made available to the appellant and the respondent.

(4) Where the Commission have reported to the Court of Appeal on any matter which they have been directed under subsection (1) above to investigate, the Court—

(a) shall notify the appellant and the respondent that the Commission have reported; and

(b) may make available to the appellant and the respondent the report of the Commission and any statements, opinions and reports which accompanied it.

(5) In this section 'respondent' includes a person who will be a respondent if leave to appeal is granted.]

33   Right of appeal to House of Lords

(1) An appeal lies to the House of Lords, at the instance of the defendant or the prosecutor, from any decision of the Court of Appeal on an appeal to that court under Part I of this Act or

Part 9 of the Criminal Justice Act 2003 or section 9 (preparatory hearings) of the Criminal Justice Act 1987 [or section 35 of the Criminal Procedure and Investigations Act 1996].

(1A) In subsection (1) above the reference to the prosecutor includes a reference to the Director of the Assets Recovery Agency in a case where (and to the extent that) he is a party to the appeal to the Court of Appeal.

(1B) An appeal lies to the House of Lords, at the instance of the acquitted person or the prosecutor, from any decision of the Court of Appeal on an application under section 76(1) or (2) of the Criminal Justice Act 2003 (retrial for serious offences).

(2) The appeal lies only with the leave of the Court of Appeal or the House of Lords; and leave shall not be granted unless it is certified by the Court of Appeal that a point of law of general public importance is involved in the decision and it appears to the Court of Appeal or the House of Lords (as the case may be) that the point is one which ought to be considered by that House.

[(3) Except as provided by this Part of this Act and section 13 of the Administration of Justice Act 1960 (appeal in cases of contempt of court), no appeal shall lie from any decision of the criminal division of the Court of Appeal.]

(4) In relation to an appeal under subsection (1B), references in this Part to a defendant are references to the acquitted person.

Criminal Appeal Act 1995

8   The Commission

(1) There shall be a body corporate to be known as the Criminal Cases Commission.

(2) The Commission shall not be regarded as the servant or agent of the Crown or as enjoying any status, immunity or privilege of the Crown; and the Commission's property shall not be regarded as property of, or held on behalf of, the Crown.

(3) The Commission shall consist of not fewer than eleven members.

(4) The members of the Commission shall be appointed by Her Majesty on the recommendation of the Prime Minister.

(5) At least one third of the members of the Commission shall be persons who are legally qualified; and for this purpose a person is legally qualified if—

    (a) he has a ten year general qualification, within the meaning of section 71 of the Courts and Legal Services Act 1990, or

    (b) he is a member of the Bar of Northern Ireland, or solicitor of the Supreme Court of Northern Ireland, of at least ten years' standing.

(6) At least two thirds of the members of the Commission shall be persons who appear to the Prime Minister to have knowledge or experience of any aspect of the criminal justice system and of them at least one shall be a person who appears to him to have knowledge or experience of any aspect of the criminal justice system in Northern Ireland; and for the purposes of this subsection the criminal justice system includes, in particular, the investigation of offences and the treatment of offenders.

(7) Schedule 1 (further provisions with respect to the Commission) shall have effect.

13   Conditions for making of references

(1) A reference of a conviction, verdict, finding or sentence shall not be made under any of sections 9 to 12 unless—

    (a) the Commission consider that there is a real possibility that the conviction, verdict, finding or sentence would not be upheld were the reference to be made,

    (b) the Commission so consider—

        (i)   in the case of a conviction, verdict or finding, because of an argument, or evidence, not raised in the proceedings which led to it or on any appeal or application for leave to appeal against it, or

(ii) in the case of a sentence, because of an argument on a point of law, or information, not so raised, and

(b) an appeal against the conviction, verdict, finding or sentence has been determined or leave to appeal against it has been refused.

(2) Nothing in subsection (1)(b)(i) or (c) shall prevent the making of a reference if it appears to the Commission that there are exceptional circumstances which justify making it.

The prosecution's right to appeal

Criminal Justice Act 2003

57   Introduction

(1) In relation to a trial on indictment, the prosecution is to have the rights of appeal for which provision is made by this Part.

(2) But the prosecution is to have no right of appeal under this Part in respect of—

(a) a ruling that a jury be discharged, or

(b) a ruling from which an appeal lies to the Court of Appeal by virtue of any other enactment.

(3) An appeal under this Part is to lie to the Court of Appeal.

(4) Such an appeal may be brought only with the leave of the judge or the Court of Appeal.

58   General right of appeal in respect of rulings

(1) This section applies where a judge makes a ruling in relation to a trial on indictment at an applicable time and the ruling relates to one or more offences included in the indictment.

(2) The prosecution may appeal in respect of the ruling in accordance with this section.

(3) The ruling is to have no effect whilst the prosecution is able to take any steps under subsection (4).

(4) The prosecution may not appeal in respect of the ruling unless—

(a) following the making of the ruling, it—

(i)   informs the court that it intends to appeal, or

(ii) requests an adjournment to consider whether to appeal, and

(b) if such an adjournment is granted, it informs the court following the adjournment that it intends to appeal.

(5) If the prosecution requests an adjournment under subsection (4)(a)(ii), the judge may grant such an adjournment.

(6) Where the ruling relates to two or more offences—

(a) any one or more of those offences may be the subject of the appeal, and

(b) if the prosecution informs the court in accordance with subsection (4) that it intends to appeal, it must at the same time inform the court of the offence or offences which are the subject of the appeal.

(7) Where—

(a) the ruling is a ruling that there is no case to answer, and

(b) the prosecution, at the same time that it informs the court in accordance with subsection (4) that it intends to appeal, nominates one or more other rulings which have been made by a judge in relation to the trial on indictment at an applicable time and which relate to the offence or offences which are the subject of the appeal,

that other ruling, or those other rulings, are also to be treated as the subject of the appeal.

(8) The prosecution may not inform the court in accordance with subsection (4) that it intends to appeal, unless, at or before that time, it informs the court that it agrees that, in respect of the offence or each offence which is the subject of the appeal, the defendant in relation to that offence should be acquitted of that offence if either of the conditions mentioned in subsection (9) is fulfilled.

(9) Those conditions are—

    (a) that leave to appeal to the Court of Appeal is not obtained, and

    (b) that the appeal is abandoned before it is determined by the Court of Appeal.

(10) If the prosecution informs the court in accordance with subsection (4) that it intends to appeal, the ruling mentioned in subsection (1) is to continue to have no effect in relation to the offence or offences which are the subject of the appeal whilst the appeal is pursued.

(11) If and to the extent that a ruling has no effect in accordance with this section—

    (a) any consequences of the ruling are also to have no effect,

    (b) the judge may not take any steps in consequence of the ruling, and

    (c) if he does so, any such steps are also to have no effect.

(12) Where the prosecution has informed the court of its agreement under subsection (8) and either of the conditions mentioned in subsection (9) is fulfilled, the judge or the Court of Appeal must order that the defendant in relation to the offence or each offence concerned be acquitted of that offence.

(13) In this section 'applicable time', in relation to a trial on indictment, means any time (whether before or after the commencement of the trial) before the start of the judge's summing-up to the jury.

59 Expedited and non-expedited appeals

(1) Where the prosecution informs the court in accordance with section 58(4) that it intends to appeal, the judge must decide whether or not the appeal should be expedited.

(2) If the judge decides that the appeal should be expedited, he may order an adjournment.

(3) If the judge decides that the appeal should not be expedited, he may—

    (a) order an adjournment, or

    (b) discharge the jury (if one has been sworn).

(4) If he decides that the appeal should be expedited, he or the Court of Appeal may subsequently reverse that decision and, if it is reversed, the judge may act as mentioned in subsection (3)(a) or (b).

60 Continuation of proceedings for offences not affected by ruling

(1) This section applies where the prosecution informs the court in accordance with section 58(4) that it intends to appeal.

(2) Proceedings may be continued in respect of any offence which is not the subject of the appeal.

61 Determination of appeal by Court of Appeal

(1) On an appeal under section 58, the Court of Appeal may confirm, reverse or vary any ruling to which the appeal relates.

(2) Subsections (3) to (5) apply where the appeal relates to a single ruling.

(3) Where the Court of Appeal confirms the ruling, it must, in respect of the offence or each offence which is the subject of the appeal, order that the defendant in relation to that offence be acquitted of that offence.

(4) Where the Court of Appeal reverses or varies the ruling, it must, in respect of the offence or each offence which is the subject of the appeal, do any of the following—

    (a) order that proceedings for that offence may be resumed in the Crown Court,

    (b) order that a fresh trial may take place in the Crown Court for that offence,

    (c) order that the defendant in relation to that offence be acquitted of that offence.

(5) But the Court of Appeal may not make an order under subsection (4)(a) or (b) in respect of an offence unless it considers it necessary in the interests of justice to do so.

(6) Subsections (7) and (8) apply where the appeal relates to a ruling that there is no case to answer and one or more other rulings.

(7) Where the Court of Appeal confirms the ruling that there is no case to answer, it must, in respect of the offence or each offence which is the subject of the appeal, order that the defendant in relation to that offence be acquitted of that offence.

(8) Where the Court of Appeal reverses or varies the ruling that there is no case to answer, it must in respect of the offence or each offence which is the subject of the appeal, make any of the orders mentioned in subsection (4)(a) to (c) (but subject to subsection (5)).

67 Reversal of rulings

The Court of Appeal may not reverse a ruling on an appeal under this Part unless it is satisfied—
>   (a) that the ruling was wrong in law,
>   (b) that the ruling involved an error of law or principle, or
>   (c) that the ruling was a ruling that it was not reasonable for the judge to have made.

Re-trials

Criminal Justice Act 2003

75 Cases that may be retried

(1) This Part applies where a person has been acquitted of a qualifying offence in proceedings—
>   (a) on indictment in England and Wales,
>   (b) on appeal against a conviction, verdict or finding in proceedings on indictment in England and Wales, or
>   (c) on appeal from a decision on such an appeal.

(2) A person acquitted of an offence in proceedings mentioned in subsection (1) is treated for the purposes of that subsection as also acquitted of any qualifying offence of which he could have been convicted in the proceedings because of the first-mentioned offence being charged in the indictment, except an offence—
>   (a) of which he has been convicted,
>   (b) of which he has been found not guilty by reason of insanity, or
>   (c) in respect of which, in proceedings where he has been found to be under a disability (as defined by section 4 of the Criminal Procedure (Insanity) Act 1964 (c. 84)), a finding has been made that he did the act or made the omission charged against him.

(3) References in subsections (1) and (2) to a qualifying offence do not include references to an offence which, at the time of the acquittal, was the subject of an order under section 77(1) or (3).

(4) This Part also applies where a person has been acquitted, in proceedings elsewhere than in the United Kingdom, of an offence under the law of the place where the proceedings were held, if the commission of the offence as alleged would have amounted to or included the commission (in the United Kingdom or elsewhere) of a qualifying offence.

(5) Conduct punishable under the law in force elsewhere than in the United Kingdom is an offence under that law for the purposes of subsection (4), however it is described in that law.

(6) This Part applies whether the acquittal was before or after the passing of this Act.

(7) References in this Part to acquittal are to acquittal in circumstances within subsection (1) or (4).

(8) In this Part 'qualifying offence' means an offence listed in Part 1 of Schedule 5.

76   Application to Court of Appeal

(1) A prosecutor may apply to the Court of Appeal for an order—

(a) quashing a person's acquittal in proceedings within section 75(1), and

(b) ordering him to be retried for the qualifying offence.

(2) A prosecutor may apply to the Court of Appeal, in the case of a person acquitted elsewhere than in the United Kingdom, for—

(a) a determination whether the acquittal is a bar to the person being tried in England and Wales for the qualifying offence, and

(b) if it is, an order that the acquittal is not to be a bar.

(3) A prosecutor may make an application under subsection (1) or (2) only with the written consent of the Director of Public Prosecutions.

(4) The Director of Public Prosecutions may give his consent only if satisfied that—

(a) there is evidence as respects which the requirements of section 78 appear to be met,

(b) it is in the public interest for the application to proceed, and

(c) any trial pursuant to an order on the application would not be inconsistent with obligations of the United Kingdom under Article 31 or 34 of the Treaty on European Union relating to the principle of *ne bis in idem*.

(5) Not more than one application may be made under subsection (1) or (2) in relation to an acquittal.

77   Determination by Court of Appeal

(1) On an application under section 76(1), the Court of Appeal—

(a) if satisfied that the requirements of sections 78 and 79 are met, must make the order applied for;

(b) otherwise, must dismiss the application.

(2) Subsections (3) and (4) apply to an application under section 76(2).

(3) Where the Court of Appeal determines that the acquittal is a bar to the person being tried for the qualifying offence, the court—

(a) if satisfied that the requirements of sections 78 and 79 are met, must make the order applied for;

(b) otherwise, must make a declaration to the effect that the acquittal is a bar to the person being tried for the offence.

(4) Where the Court of Appeal determines that the acquittal is not a bar to the person being tried for the qualifying offence, it must make a declaration to that effect.

78   New and compelling evidence

(1) The requirements of this section are met if there is new and compelling evidence against the acquitted person in relation to the qualifying offence.

(2) Evidence is new if it was not adduced in the proceedings in which the person was acquitted (nor, if those were appeal proceedings, in earlier proceedings to which the appeal related).

(3) Evidence is compelling if—

(a) it is reliable,

(b) it is substantial, and

(c) in the context of the outstanding issues, it appears highly probative of the case against the acquitted person.

(4) The outstanding issues are the issues in dispute in the proceedings in which the person was acquitted and, if those were appeal proceedings, any other issues remaining in dispute from earlier proceedings to which the appeal related.

(5) For the purposes of this section, it is irrelevant whether any evidence would have been admissible in earlier proceedings against the acquitted person.

79 Interests of justice

(1) The requirements of this section are met if in all the circumstances it is in the interests of justice for the court to make the order under section 77.

(2) That question is to be determined having regard in particular to—

(a) whether existing circumstances make a fair trial unlikely;

(b) for the purposes of that question and otherwise, the length of time since the qualifying offence was allegedly committed;

(c) whether it is likely that the new evidence would have been adduced in the earlier proceedings against the acquitted person but for a failure by an officer or by a prosecutor to act with due diligence or expedition;

(d) whether, since those proceedings or, if later, since the commencement of this Part, any officer or prosecutor has failed to act with due diligence or expedition.

(3) In subsection (2) references to an officer or prosecutor include references to a person charged with corresponding duties under the law in force elsewhere than in England and Wales.

(4) Where the earlier prosecution was conducted by a person other than a prosecutor, subsection (2)(c) applies in relation to that person as well as in relation to a prosecutor.

82 Restrictions on publication in the interests of justice

(1) Where it appears to the Court of Appeal that the inclusion of any matter in a publication would give rise to a substantial risk of prejudice to the administration of justice in a retrial, the court may order that the matter is not to be included in any publication while the order has effect.

(2) In subsection (1) 'retrial' means the trial of an acquitted person for a qualifying offence pursuant to any order made or that may be made under section 77.

(3) The court may make an order under this section only if it appears to it necessary in the interests of justice to do so.

(4) An order under this section may apply to a matter which has been included in a publication published before the order takes effect, but such an order—

(a) applies only to the later inclusion of the matter in a publication (whether directly or by inclusion of the earlier publication), and

(b) does not otherwise affect the earlier publication.

(5) After notice of an application has been given under section 80(1) relating to the acquitted person and the qualifying offence, the court may make an order under this section only—

(a) of its own motion, or

(b) on the application of the Director of Public Prosecutions.

(6) Before such notice has been given, an order under this section—

(a) may be made only on the application of the Director of Public Prosecutions, and

(b) may not be made unless, since the acquittal concerned, an investigation of the commission by the acquitted person of the qualifying offence has been commenced by officers.

(7) The court may at any time, of its own motion or on an application made by the Director of Public Prosecutions or the acquitted person, vary or revoke an order under this section.

(8) Any order made under this section before notice of an application has been given under section 80(1) relating to the acquitted person and the qualifying offence must specify the time when it ceases to have effect.

(9) An order under this section which is made or has effect after such notice has been given ceases to have effect, unless it specifies an earlier time—

(a) when there is no longer any step that could be taken which would lead to the acquitted person being tried pursuant to an order made on the application, or

(b) if he is tried pursuant to such an order, at the conclusion of the trial.

(10) Nothing in this section affects any prohibition or restriction by virtue of any other enactment on the inclusion of any matter in a publication or any power, under an enactment or otherwise, to impose such a prohibition or restriction.

(11) In this section—

'programme service' has the same meaning as in the Broadcasting Act 1990 (c. 42),

'publication' includes any speech, writing, relevant programme or other communication in whatever form, which is addressed to the public at large or any section of the public (and for this purpose every relevant programme is to be taken to be so addressed), but does not include an indictment or other document prepared for use in particular legal proceedings,

'relevant programme' means a programme included in a programme service.

84 Retrial

(1) Where a person—

    (a) is tried pursuant to an order under section 77(1), or

    (b) is tried on indictment pursuant to an order under section 77(3),

the trial must be on an indictment preferred by direction of the Court of Appeal.

(2) After the end of 2 months after the date of the order, the person may not be arraigned on an indictment preferred in pursuance of such a direction unless the Court of Appeal gives leave.

(3) The Court of Appeal must not give leave unless satisfied that—

    (a) the prosecutor has acted with due expedition, and

    (b) there is a good and sufficient cause for trial despite the lapse of time since the order under section 77.

(4) Where the person may not be arraigned without leave, he may apply to the Court of Appeal to set aside the order and—

    (a) for any direction required for restoring an earlier judgment and verdict of acquittal of the qualifying offence, or

    (b) in the case of a person acquitted elsewhere than in the United Kingdom, for a declaration to the effect that the acquittal is a bar to his being tried for the qualifying offence.

(5) An indictment under subsection (1) may relate to more than one offence, or more than one person, and may relate to an offence which, or a person who, is not the subject of an order or declaration under section 77.

(6) Evidence given at a trial pursuant to an order under section 77(1) or (3) must be given orally if it was given orally at the original trial, unless—

    (a) all the parties to the trial agree otherwise,

    (b) section 116 applies, or

    (c) the witness is unavailable to give evidence, otherwise than as mentioned in subsection (2) of that section, and section 114(1)(d) applies.

(7) At a trial pursuant to an order under section 77(1), paragraph 5 of Schedule 3 to the Crime and Disorder Act 1998 (c. 37) (use of depositions) does not apply to a deposition read as evidence at the original trial.

PART II

....

Sentencing

(a) DEFERMENT AND POSTPONEMENT OF SENTENCING

Powers of Criminal Courts (Sentencing) Act 2000 (as amended)

DEFERMENT OF SENTENCE

1   Deferment of sentence

(1) The Crown Court or a magistrates' court may defer passing sentence on an offender for the purpose of enabling the court, or any other court to which it falls to deal with him, to have regard in dealing with him to—

    (a) his conduct after conviction (including, where appropriate, the making by him of reparation for his offence); or

    (b) any change in his circumstances;

but this is subject to subsections (3) and (4) below.

(2) Without prejudice to the generality of subsection (1) above, the matters to which the court to which it falls to deal with the offender may have regard by virtue of paragraph (a) of that subsection include the extent to which the offender has complied with any requirements imposed under subsection (3)(b) below.

(3) The power conferred by subsection (1) above shall be exercisable only if—

    (a) the offender consents;

    (b) the offender undertakes to comply with any requirements as to his conduct during the period of the deferment that the court considers it appropriate to impose; and

    (c) the court is satisfied, having regard to the nature of the offence and the character and circumstances of the offender, that it would be in the interests of justice to exercise the power.

(4) Any deferment under this section shall be until such date as may be specified by the court, not being more than six months after the date on which the deferment is announced by the court; and, subject to section 1D(3) below, where the passing of sentence has been deferred under this section it shall not be further so deferred.

(8) Nothing in this section or sections 1A to 1D below shall affect—

    (a) the power of the Crown Court to bind over an offender to come up for judgment when called upon; or

    (b) the power of any court to defer passing sentence for any purpose for which it may lawfully do so apart from this section.

1A   Further provision about undertakings

(1) Without prejudice to the generality of paragraph (b) of section 1(3) above, the requirements that may be imposed by virtue of that paragraph include requirements as to the residence of the offender during the whole or any part of the period of deferment.

(2) Where an offender has undertaken to comply with any requirements imposed under section 1(3)(b) above the court may appoint—

(a) an officer of a local probation board, or

(b) any other person whom the court thinks appropriate, to act as a supervisor in relation to him.

(3) A person shall not be appointed under subsection (2)(b) above without his consent.

(4) It shall be the duty of a supervisor appointed under subsection (2) above—

(a) to monitor the offender's compliance with the requirements; and

(b) to provide the court to which it falls to deal with the offender in respect of the offence in question with such information as the court may require relating to the offender's compliance with the requirements.

1B Breach of undertakings

(1) A court which under section 1 above has deferred passing sentence on an offender may deal with him before the end of the period of deferment if—

(a) he appears or is brought before the court under subsection (3) below; and

(b) the court is satisfied that he has failed to comply with one or more requirements imposed under section 1(3)(b) above in connection with the deferment.

(2) Subsection (3) below applies where—

(a) a court has under section 1 above deferred passing sentence on an offender;

(b) the offender undertook to comply with one or more requirements imposed under section 1(3)(b) above in connection with the deferment; and

(c) a person appointed under section 1A(2) above to act as a supervisor in relation to the offender has reported to the court that the offender has failed to comply with one or more of those requirements.

(3) Where this subsection applies, the court may issue—

(a) a summons requiring the offender to appear before the court at a time and place specified in the summons; or

(b) a warrant to arrest him and bring him before the court at a time and place specified in the warrant.

1C Conviction of offence during period of deferment

(1) A court which under section 1 above has deferred passing sentence on an offender may deal with him before the end of the period of deferment if during that period he is convicted in Great Britain of any offence.

(2) Subsection (3) below applies where a court has under section 1 above deferred passing sentence on an offender in respect of one or more offences and during the period of deferment the offender is convicted in England and Wales of any offence ('the later offence').

(3) Where this subsection applies, then (without prejudice to subsection (1) above and whether or not the offender is sentenced for the later offence during the period of deferment), the court which passes sentence on him for the later offence may also, if this has not already been done, deal with him for the offence or offences for which passing of sentence has been deferred, except that—

(a) the power conferred by this subsection shall not be exercised by a magistrates' court if the court which deferred passing sentence was the Crown Court; and

(b) the Crown Court, in exercising that power in a case in which the court which deferred passing sentence was a magistrates' court, shall not pass any sentence which could not have been passed by a magistrates' court in exercising that power.

(4) Where a court which under section 1 above has deferred passing sentence on an offender proposes to deal with him by virtue of subsection (1) above before the end of the period of deferment, the court may issue—

(a) a summons requiring him to appear before the court at a time and place specified in the summons; or

(b) a warrant to arrest him and bring him before the court at a time and place specified in the warrant.

1D Deferment of sentence: supplementary

(1) In deferring the passing of sentence under section 1 above a magistrates' court shall be regarded as exercising the power of adjourning the trial conferred by section 10(1) of the Magistrates' Courts Act 1980, and accordingly sections 11(1) and 13(1) to (3A) and (5) of that Act (non-appearance of the accused) apply (without prejudice to section 1(7) above) if the offender does not appear on the date specified under section 1(4) above.

(2) Where the passing of sentence on an offender has been deferred by a court ('the original court') under section 1 above, the power of that court under that section to deal with the offender at the end of the period of deferment and any power of that court under section 1B(1) or 1C(1) above, or of any court under section 1C(3) above, to deal with the offender—

(a) is power to deal with him, in respect of the offence for which passing of sentence has been deferred, in any way in which the original court could have dealt with him if it had not deferred passing sentence; and

(b) without prejudice to the generality of paragraph (a) above, in the case of a magistrates' court, includes the power conferred by section 3 below to commit him to the Crown Court for sentence.

(3) Where—

(a) the passing of sentence on an offender in respect of one or more offences has been deferred under section 1 above, and

(b) a magistrates' court deals with him in respect of the offence or any of the offences by committing him to the Crown Court under section 3 below,

the power of the Crown Court to deal with him includes the same power to defer passing sentence on him as if he had just been convicted of the offence or offences on indictment before the court.

COMMITTAL TO CROWN COURT FOR SENTENCE

3 Committal for sentence on indication of guilty plea to serious offence triable either way

(1) Subject to subsection (4) below, this section applies where—

(a) a person aged 18 or over appears or is brought before a magistrates' court ('the court') on an information charging him with an offence triable either way ('the offence');

(b) he or his representative indicates under section 17A or (as the case may be) 17B of the Magistrates' Courts Act 1980 (initial procedure: accused to indicate intention as to plea), but not section 20(7) of that Act, that he would plead guilty if the offence were to proceed to trial; and

(c) proceeding as if section 9(1) of that Act were complied with and he pleaded guilty under it, the court convicts him of the offence.

(2) If the court is of the opinion that—

(a) the offence; or

(b) the combination of the offence and one or more offences associated with it,

was so serious that the Crown Court should, in the court's opinion, have the power to deal with the offender in any way it could deal with him if he had been convicted on indictment, the court may commit him in custody or on bail to the Crown Court for sentence in accordance with section 5(1) below.

(3) Where the court commits a person under subsection (2) above, section 6 below (which enables a magistrates' court, where it commits a person under this section in respect

of an offence, also to commit him to the Crown Court to be dealt with in respect of certain other offences) shall apply accordingly.

3A Committal for sentence of dangerous adult offenders
(1) This section applies where on the summary trial of a specified offence triable either way a person aged 18 or over is convicted of the offence.

(2) If, in relation to the offence, it appears to the court that the criteria for the imposition of a sentence under section 225(3) or 227(2) of the Criminal Justice Act 2003 would be met, the court must commit the offender in custody or on bail to the Crown Court for sentence in accordance with section 5(1) below.

(3) Where the court commits a person under subsection (2) above, section 6 below (which enables a magistrates' court, where it commits a person under this section in respect of an offence, also to commit him to the Crown Court to be dealt with in respect of certain other offences) shall apply accordingly.

(4) In reaching any decision under or taking any step contemplated by this section—
  (a) the court shall not be bound by any indication of sentence given in respect of the offence under section 20 of the Magistrates' Courts Act 1980 (procedure where summary trial appears more suitable); and
  (b) nothing the court does under this section may be challenged or be the subject of any appeal in any court on the ground that it is not consistent with an indication of sentence.

(5) Nothing in this section shall prevent the court from committing a specified offence to the Crown Court for sentence under section 3 above if the provisions of that section are satisfied.

(6) In this section, references to a specified offence are to a specified offence within the meaning of section 224 of the Criminal Justice Act 2003.

3B Committal for sentence on indication of guilty plea by child or young person
(1) This section applies where—
  (a) a person aged under 18 appears or is brought before a magistrates' court ('the court') on an information charging him with an offence mentioned in subsection (1) of section 91 below ('the offence');
  (b) he or his representative indicates under section 24A or (as the case may be) 24B of the Magistrates' Courts Act 1980 (child or young person to indicate intention as to plea in certain cases) that he would plead guilty if the offence were to proceed to trial; and
  (c) proceeding as if section 9(1) of that Act were complied with and he pleaded guilty under it, the court convicts him of the offence.

(2) If the court is of the opinion that—
  (a) the offence; or
  (b) the combination of the offence and one or more offences associated with it,
was such that the Crown Court should, in the court's opinion, have power to deal with the offender as if the provisions of section 91(3) below applied, the court may commit him in custody or on bail to the Crown Court for sentence in accordance with section 5A(1) below.

(3) Where the court commits a person under subsection (2) above, section 6 below (which enables a magistrates' court, where it commits a person under this section in respect of an offence, also to commit him to the Crown Court to be dealt with in respect of certain other offences) shall apply accordingly.

3C Committal for sentence of dangerous young offenders
(1) This section applies where on the summary trial of a specified offence a person aged under 18 is convicted of the offence.

(2) If, in relation to the offence, it appears to the court that the criteria for the imposition of a sentence under section 226(3) or 228(2) of the Criminal Justice Act 2003 would be met,

the court must commit the offender in custody or on bail to the Crown Court for sentence in accordance with section 5A(1) below.

(3) Where the court commits a person under subsection (2) above, section 6 below (which enables a magistrates' court, where it commits a person under this section in respect of an offence, also to commit him to the Crown Court to be dealt with in respect of certain other offences) shall apply accordingly.

4   Committal for sentence on indication of guilty plea to offence triable either way
  (1) This section applies where—
  (a) a person aged 18 or over appears or is brought before a magistrates' court ('the court') on an information charging him with an offence triable either way ('the offence');
  (b) he or (where applicable) his representative indicates under section 17A, 17B or 20(7) of the Magistrates' Courts Act 1980 that he would plead guilty if the offence were to proceed to trial; and
  (c) proceeding as if section 9(1) of that Act were complied with and he pleaded guilty under it, the court convicts him of the offence.

(1A) But this section does not apply to an offence as regards which this section is excluded by section 17D of that Act (certain offences where value involved is small).

(2) If the court has committed the offender to the Crown Court for trial for one or more related offences, that is to say, one or more offences which, in its opinion, are related to the offence, it may commit him in custody or on bail to the Crown Court to be dealt with in respect of the offence in accordance with section 5(1) below.

(3) If the power conferred by subsection (2) above is not exercisable but the court is still to determine to, or to determine whether to, send the offender to the Crown Court for trial under section 51 or 51A of the Crime and Disorder Act 1998 for one or more related offences—
  (a) it shall adjourn the proceedings relating to the offence until after it has made those determinations; and
  (b) if it sends the offender to the Crown Court for trial for one or more related offences, it may then exercise that power.'
  (4) Where the court—
  (a) under subsection (2) above commits the offender to the Crown Court to be dealt with in respect of the offence, and
  (b) does not state that, in its opinion, it also has power so to commit him under section 3(2) or, as the case may be, section 3A(2),
section 5(1) below shall not apply unless he is convicted before the Crown Court of one or more of the related offences.

(5) Where section 5(1) below does not apply, the Crown Court may deal with the offender in respect of the offence in any way in which the magistrates' court could deal with him if it had just convicted him of the offence.

(6) Where the court commits a person under subsection (2) above, section 6 below (which enables a magistrates' court, where it commits a person under this section in respect of an offence, also to commit him to the Crown Court to be dealt with in respect of certain other offences) shall apply accordingly.

(7) For the purposes of this section one offence is related to another if, were they both to be prosecuted on indictment, the charges for them could be joined in the same indictment.
Section 4A is to be inserted when Schedule 3, para 23 of the Criminal Justice Act 2003 comes into force.
  (8) In reaching any decision under or taking any step contemplated by this section—
  (a) the court shall not be bound by any indication of sentence given in respect of the offence under section 20 of the Magistrates' Courts Act 1980 (procedure where summary trial appears more suitable); and
  (b) nothing the court does under this section may be challenged or be the subject of any appeal in any court on the ground that it is not consistent with an indication of sentence.

4A   Committal for sentence on indication of guilty plea by child or young person with related offences

(1) This section applies where—

(a) a person aged under 18 appears or brought before a magistrates' court ('the court') on an information charging him with an offence mentioned in subsection (1) of section 91 below ('the offence');

(b) he or his representative indicates under section 24A or (as the case may be) 24B of the Magistrates' Courts Act 1980 (child or young person to indicate intention as to plea in certain cases) that he would plead guilty if the offence were to proceed to trial; and

(c) proceeding as if section 9(1) of that Act were complied with and he pleaded guilty under it, the court convicts him of the offence.

(2) If the court has sent the offender to the Crown Court for trial for one or more related offences, that is to say one or more offences which, in its opinion, are related to the offence, it may commit him in custody or on bail to the Crown Court to be dealt with in respect of the offence in accordance with section 5A(1) below.

(3) If the power conferred by subsection (2) above is not exercisable but the court is still to determine to, or to determine whether to, send the offender to the Crown Court for trial under section 51 or 51A of the Crime and Disorder Act 1998 for one or more related offences—

(a) it shall adjourn the proceedings relating to the offence until after it has made those determinations; and

(b) if it sends the offender to the Crown Court for trial for one or more related offences, it may then exercise that power.

(4) Where the court—

(a) under subsection (2) above commits the offender to the Crown Court to be dealt with in respect of the offence; and

(b) does not state that, in its opinion, it also has power so to commit him under section 3B(2) or, as the case may be, section 3C(2) above,

section 5A(1) below shall not apply unless he is convicted before the Crown Court of one or more of the related offences.

5   Power of Crown Court on committal for sentence under sections 3, 3A and 4

(1) Where an offender is committed by a magistrates' court for sentence under section 3, 3A or 4 above, the Crown Court shall inquire into the circumstances of the case and may deal with the offender in any way in which it could deal with him if he had just been convicted of the offence on indictment before the court.

(2) In relation to committals under section 4 above, subsection (1) above has effect subject to section 4(4) and (5) above.

(3) Section 20A(1) of the Magistrates' Courts Act 1980 (which relates to the effect of an indication of sentence under section 20 of that Act) shall not apply in respect of any specified offence (within the meaning of section 224 of the Criminal Justice Act 2003)—

(a) in respect of which the offender is committed under section 3A(2) above; or

(b) in respect of which—

(i)   the offender is committed under section 4(2) above; and

(ii) the court states under section 4(4) above that, in its opinion, it also has power to commit the offender under section 3A(2) above.

5A   Power of Crown Court on committal for sentence under sections 3B, 3C and 4A

(1) Where an offender is committed by a magistrates' court for sentence under section 3B, 3C or 4A above, the Crown Court shall inquire into the circumstances of the case and may deal with the offender in any way in which it could deal with him if he had just been convicted of the offence on indictment before the court.

(2) In relation to committals under section 4A above, subsection (1) above has effect subject to section 4A(4) and (5) above.

6 Committal for sentence in certain cases where offender committed in respect of another offence

(1) This section applies where a magistrates' court ('the committing court') commits a person in custody or on bail to the Crown Court under any enactment mentioned in subsection (4) below to be sentenced or otherwise dealt with in respect of an offence ('the relevant offence').

(2) Where this section applies and the relevant offence is an indictable offence, the committing court may also commit the offender, in custody or on bail as the case may require, to the Crown Court to be dealt with in respect of any other offence whatsoever in respect of which the committing court has power to deal with him (being an offence of which he has been convicted by that or any other court).

(3) Where this section applies and the relevant offence is a summary offence, the committing court may commit the offender, in custody or on bail as the case may require, to the Crown Court to be dealt with in respect of—

    (a) any other offence of which the committing court has convicted him, being either—

        (i)   an offence punishable with imprisonment; or

        (ii) an offence in respect of which the committing court has a power or duty to order him to be disqualified under section 34, 35 or 36 of the Road Traffic Offenders Act 1988 (disqualification for certain motoring offences); or

    (b) any suspended sentence in respect of which the committing court has under paragraph 11(1) of Schedule 12 to the Criminal Justice Act 2003 power to deal with him.

(4) The enactments referred to in subsection (1) above are—

    (a) the Vagrancy Act 1824 (incorrigible rogues);

    (b) sections 3 to 4A above (committal for sentence for offences triable either way);

    (c) section 13(5) below (conditionally discharged person convicted of further offence);

    (d) section 116(3)(b) below (offender convicted of offence committed during currency of original sentence); and

    (e) paragraph 11(2) of Schedule 12 to the Criminal Justice Act 2003 (committal to Crown Court when offender convicted during operational period of suspended sentence).

7 Power of Crown Court on committal for sentence under section 6

(1) Where under section 6 above a magistrates' court commits a person to be dealt with by the Crown Court in respect of an offence, the Crown Court may after inquiring into the circumstances of the case deal with him in any way in which the magistrates' court could deal with him if it had just convicted him of the offence.

(2) Subsection (1) above does not apply where under section 6 above a magistrates' court commits a person to be dealt with by the Crown Court in respect of a suspended sentence, but in such a case the powers under paragraphs 8 and 9 of Schedule 12 to the Criminal Justice Act 2003 (power of court to deal with suspended sentence) shall be exercisable by the Crown Court.

(3) Without prejudice to subsections (1) and (2) above, where under section 6 above or any enactment mentioned in subsection (4) of that section a magistrates' court commits a person to be dealt with by the Crown Court, any duty or power which, apart from this subsection, would fall to be discharged or exercised by the magistrates' court shall not be discharged or exercised by that court but shall instead be discharged or may instead be exercised by the Crown Court.

(4) Where under section 6 above a magistrates' court commits a person to be dealt with by the Crown Court in respect of an offence triable only on indictment in the case of an adult (being an offence which was tried summarily because of the offender's being under 18 years

of age), the Crown Court's powers under subsection (1) above in respect of the offender after he attains the age of 18 shall be powers to do either or both of the following—

    (a) to impose a fine not exceeding £5,000;

    (b) to deal with the offender in respect of the offence in any way in which the magistrates' court could deal with him if it had just convicted him of an offence punishable with imprisonment for a term not exceeding six months.

REMISSION FOR SENTENCE: YOUNG OFFENDERS ETC.

8 Power and duty to remit young offenders to youth courts for sentence

    (1) Subsection (2) below applies where a child or young person (that is to say, any person aged under 18) is convicted by or before any court of an offence other than homicide.

    (2) The court may and, if it is not a youth court, shall unless satisfied that it would be undesirable to do so, remit the case—

    (a)[1] if the offender was committed for trial or sent to the Crown Court for trial under section 51 of the Crime and Disorder Act 1998, to a youth court acting for the place where he was committed for trial or sent to the Crown Court for trial;

    (b) in any other case, to a youth court acting either for the same place as the remitting court or for the place where the offender habitually resides;

but in relation to a magistrates' court other than a youth court this subsection has effect subject to subsection (6) below.

    (3) Where a case is remitted under subsection (2) above, the offender shall be brought before a youth court accordingly, and that court may deal with him in any way in which it might have dealt with him if he had been tried and convicted by that court.

    (4) A court by which an order remitting a case to a youth court is made under subsection (2) above—

    (a) may, subject to section 25 of the Criminal Justice and Public Order Act 1994 (restrictions on granting bail), give such directions as appear to be necessary with respect to the custody of the offender or for his release on bail until he can be brought before the youth court; and

    (b) shall cause to be transmitted to the designated officer for the youth court a certificate setting out the nature of the offence and stating—

      (i) that the offender has been convicted of the offence; and

      (ii) that the case has been remitted for the purpose of being dealt with under the preceding provisions of this section.

    (5) Where a case is remitted under subsection (2) above, the offender shall have no right of appeal against the order of remission, but shall have the same right of appeal against any order of the court to which the case is remitted as if he had been convicted by that court.

    (6) Without prejudice to the power to remit any case to a youth court which is conferred on a magistrates' court other than a youth court by subsections (1) and (2) above, where such a magistrates' court convicts a child or young person of an offence it must exercise that power unless the case falls within subsection (7) or (8) below.

    (7) The case falls within this subsection if the court would, were it not so to remit the case, be required by section 16(2) below to refer the offender to a youth offender panel (in which event the court may, but need not, so remit the case).

    (8) The case falls within this subsection if it does not fall within subsection (7) above but the court is of the opinion that the case is one which can properly be dealt with by means of—

    (a) an order discharging the offender absolutely or conditionally, or

    (b) an order for the payment of a fine, or

---

[1] Paragraph (a) is to be substituted when Schedule 3, para 74(2) of the Criminal Justice Act 2003 comes into force.

(c) an order (under section 150 below) requiring the offender's parent or guardian to enter into a recognizance to take proper care of him and exercise proper control over him,

with or without any other order that the court has power to make when absolutely or conditionally discharging an offender.

(9) In subsection (8) above 'care' and 'control' shall be construed in accordance with section 150(11) below.

(10) A document purporting to be a copy of an order made by a court under this section shall, if it purports to be certified as a true copy by the designated officer for the court, be evidence of the order.

9 Power of youth court to remit offender who attains age of 18 to magistrates' court other than youth court for sentence

(1) Where a person who appears or is brought before a youth court charged with an offence subsequently attains the age of 18, the youth court may, at any time after conviction and before sentence, remit him for sentence to a magistrates' court (other than a youth court).

(2) Where an offender is remitted under subsection (1) above, the youth court shall adjourn proceedings in relation to the offence, and—

(a) section 128 of the Magistrates' Courts Act 1980 (remand in custody or on bail) and all other enactments, whenever passed, relating to remand or the granting of bail in criminal proceedings shall have effect, in relation to the youth court's power or duty to remand the offender on that adjournment, as if any reference to the court to or before which the person remanded is to be brought or appear after remand were a reference to the court to which he is being remitted; and

(b) subject to subsection (3) below, the court to which the offender is remitted ('the other court') may deal with the case in any way in which it would have power to deal with it if all proceedings relating to the offence which took place before the youth court had taken place before the other court.

(3) Where an offender is remitted under subsection (1) above, section 8(6) above (duty of adult magistrates' court to remit young offenders to youth court for sentence) shall not apply to the court to which he is remitted.

(4) Where an offender is remitted under subsection (1) above he shall have no right of appeal against the order of remission (but without prejudice to any right of appeal against an order made in respect of the offence by the court to which he is remitted).

10 Power of magistrates' court to remit case to another magistrates' court for sentence

(1) Where a person aged 18 or over ('the offender') has been convicted by a magistrates' court ('the convicting court') of an offence to which this section applies ('the instant offence') and—

(a) it appears to the convicting court that some other magistrates' court ('the other court') has convicted him of another such offence in respect of which the other court has neither passed sentence on him nor committed him to the Crown Court for sentence nor dealt with him in any other way, and

(b) the other court consents to his being remitted under this section to the other court,

the convicting court may remit him to the other court to be dealt with in respect of the instant offence by the other court instead of by the convicting court.

(2) This section applies to—

(a) any offence punishable with imprisonment; and

(b) any offence in respect of which the convicting court has a power or duty to order the offender to be disqualified under section 34, 35 or 36 of the Road Traffic Offenders Act 1988 (disqualification for certain motoring offences).

(3) Where the convicting court remits the offender to the other court under this section, it shall adjourn the trial of the information charging him with the instant offence, and—

(a) section 128 of the Magistrates' Courts Act 1980 (remand in custody or on bail) and all other enactments, whenever passed, relating to remand or the granting of bail in criminal proceedings shall have effect, in relation to the convicting court's power or duty to remand the offender on that adjournment, as if any reference to the court to or before which the person remanded is to be brought or appear after remand were a reference to the court to which he is being remitted; and

(b) subject to subsection (7) below, the other court may deal with the case in any way in which it would have power to deal with it if all proceedings relating to the instant offence which took place before the convicting court had taken place before the other court.

(4) The power conferred on the other court by subsection (3)(b) above includes, where applicable, the power to remit the offender under this section to another magistrates' court in respect of the instant offence.

REMAND BY MAGISTRATES' COURT FOR
MEDICAL EXAMINATION

11 Remand by magistrates' court for medical examination

(1) If, on the trial by a magistrates' court of an offence punishable on summary conviction with imprisonment, the court—

(a) is satisfied that the accused did the act or made the omission charged, but

(b) is of the opinion that an inquiry ought to be made into his physical or mental condition before the method of dealing with him is determined,

the court shall adjourn the case to enable a medical examination and report to be made, and shall remand him.

(2) An adjournment under subsection (1) above shall not be for more than three weeks at a time where the court remands the accused in custody, nor for more than four weeks at a time where it remands him on bail.

(3) Where on an adjournment under subsection (1) above the accused is remanded on bail, the court shall impose conditions under paragraph (d) of section 3(6) of the Bail Act 1976 and the requirements imposed as conditions under that paragraph shall be or shall include requirements that the accused—

(a) undergo medical examination by a registered medical practitioner or, where the inquiry is into his mental condition and the court so directs, two such practitioners; and

(b) for that purpose attend such an institution or place, or on such practitioner, as the court directs and, where the inquiry is into his mental condition, comply with any other directions which may be given to him for that purpose by any person specified by the court or by a person of any class so specified.

(b) GENERAL PROVISIONS ABOUT SENTENCING

Criminal Justice Act 2003

Matters to be taken into account in sentencing

142 Purposes of sentencing

(1) Any court dealing with an offender in respect of his offence must have regard to the following purposes of sentencing—

(a) the punishment of offenders,

(b) the reduction of crime (including its reduction by deterrence),

(c) the reform and rehabilitation of offenders,

(d) the protection of the public, and

(e) the making of reparation by offenders to persons affected by their offences.

(2) Subsection (1) does not apply—

(a) in relation to an offender who is aged under 18 at the time of conviction,

(b) to an offence the sentence for which is fixed by law,

(c) to an offence the sentence for which falls to be imposed under section 51A(2) of the Firearms Act 1968 (c. 27) (minimum sentence for certain firearms offences), under subsection (2) of section 110 or 111 of the Sentencing Act (required custodial sentences) or under any of sections 225 to 228 of this Act (dangerous offenders), or

(d) in relation to the making under Part 3 of the Mental Health Act 1983 (c. 20) of a hospital order (with or without a restriction order), an interim hospital order, a hospital direction or a limitation direction.

(3) In this Chapter 'sentence', in relation to an offence, includes any order made by a court when dealing with the offender in respect of his offence; and 'sentencing' is to be construed accordingly.

143 Determining the seriousness of an offence

(1) In considering the seriousness of any offence, the court must consider the offender's culpability in committing the offence and any harm which the offence caused, was intended to cause or might foreseeably have caused.

(2) In considering the seriousness of an offence ('the current offence') committed by an offender who has one or more previous convictions, the court must treat each previous conviction as an aggravating factor if (in the case of that conviction) the court considers that it can reasonably be so treated having regard, in particular, to—

(a) the nature of the offence to which the conviction relates and its relevance to the current offence, and

(b) the time that has elapsed since the conviction.

(3) In considering the seriousness of any offence committed while the offender was on bail, the court must treat the fact that it was committed in those circumstances as an aggravating factor.

144 Reduction in sentences for guilty pleas

(1) In determining what sentence to pass on an offender who has pleaded guilty to an offence in proceedings before that or another court, a court must take into account—

(a) the stage in the proceedings for the offence at which the offender indicated his intention to plead guilty, and

(b) the circumstances in which this indication was given.

(2) In the case of an offence the sentence for which falls to be imposed under subsection (2) of section 110 or 111 of the Sentencing Act, nothing in that subsection prevents the court, after taking into account any matter referred to in subsection (1) of this section, from imposing any sentence which is not less than 80 per cent of that specified in that subsection.

145 Increase in sentences for racial or religious aggravation

(1) This section applies where a court is considering the seriousness of an offence other than one under sections 29 to 32 of the Crime and Disorder Act 1998 (c. 37) (racially or religiously aggravated assaults, criminal damage, public order offences and harassment etc).

(2) If the offence was racially or religiously aggravated, the court—

(a) must treat that fact as an aggravating factor, and

(b) must state in open court that the offence was so aggravated.

146 Increase in sentences for aggravation related to disability or sexual orientation

(1) This section applies where the court is considering the seriousness of an offence committed in any of the circumstances mentioned in subsection (2).

(2) Those circumstances are—
  (a) that, at the time of committing the offence, or immediately before or after doing so, the offender demonstrated towards the victim of the offence hostility based on—
    (i)   the sexual orientation (or presumed sexual orientation) of the victim, or
    (ii) a disability (or presumed disability) of the victim, or
  (b) that the offence is motivated (wholly or partly)—
    (i)   by hostility towards persons who are of a particular sexual orientation, or
    (ii) by hostility towards persons who have a disability or a particular disability.
(3) The court—
  (a) must treat the fact that the offence was committed in any of those circumstances as an aggravating factor, and
  (b) must state in open court that the offence was committed in such circumstances.

174   Duty to give reasons for, and explain effect of, sentence
(1) Subject to subsections (3) and (4), any court passing sentence on an offender—
  (a) must state in open court, in ordinary language and in general terms, its reasons for deciding on the sentence passed, and
  (b) must explain to the offender in ordinary language—
    (i)   the effect of the sentence,
    (ii) where the offender is required to comply with any order of the court forming part of the sentence, the effects of non-compliance with the order,
    (iii) any power of the court, on the application of the offender or any other person, to vary or review any order of the court forming part of the sentence, and
    (iv) where the sentence consists of or includes a fine, the effects of failure to pay the fine.
(2) In complying with subsection (1)(a), the court must—
  (a) where guidelines indicate that a sentence of a particular kind, or within a particular range, would normally be appropriate for the offence and the sentence is of a different kind, or is outside that range, state the court's reasons for deciding on a sentence of a different kind or outside that range,
  (b) where the sentence is a custodial sentence and the duty in subsection (2) of section 152 is not excluded by subsection (1)(a) or (b) or (3) of that section, state that it is of the opinion referred to in section 152(2) and why it is of that opinion,
  (c) where the sentence is a community sentence and the case does not fall within section 151(2), state that it is of the opinion that section 148(1) applies and why it is of that opinion,
  (d) where as a result of taking into account any matter referred to in section 144(1), the court imposes a punishment on the offender which is less severe than the punishment it would otherwise have imposed, state that fact, and
  (e) in any case, mention any aggravating or mitigating factors which the court has regarded as being of particular importance.
(3) Subsection (1)(a) does not apply—
  (a) to an offence the sentence for which is fixed by law (provision relating to sentencing for such an offence being made by section 270), or
  (b) to an offence the sentence for which falls to be imposed under section 51A(2) of the Firearms Act 1968 (c. 27) or under subsection (2) of section 110 or 111 of the Sentencing Act (required custodial sentences).
(4) The Secretary of State may by order—
  (a) prescribe cases in which subsection (1)(a) or (b) does not apply, and
  (b) prescribe cases in which the statement referred to in subsection (1)(a) or the explanation referred to in subsection (1)(b) may be made in the absence of the offender, or may be provided in written form.

Community sentences and discretionary custodial sentences

Criminal Justice Act 2003

147 Meaning of 'community sentence' etc.

(1) In this Part 'community sentence' means a sentence which consists of or includes—
  (a) a community order (as defined by section 177), or
  (b) one or more youth community orders.

(2) In this Chapter 'youth community order' means—
  (a) a curfew order as defined by section 163 of the Sentencing Act,
  (b) an exclusion order under section 40A(1) of that Act,
  (c) an attendance centre order as defined by section 163 of that Act,
  (d) a supervision order under section 63(1) of that Act, or
  (e) an action plan order under section 69(1) of that Act.

148 Restrictions on imposing community sentences

(1) A court must not pass a community sentence on an offender unless it is of the opinion that the offence, or the combination of the offence and one or more offences associated with it, was serious enough to warrant such a sentence.

(2) Where a court passes a community sentence which consists of or includes a community order—
  (a) the particular requirement or requirements forming part of the community order must be such as, in the opinion of the court, is, or taken together are, the most suitable for the offender, and
  (b) the restrictions on liberty imposed by the order must be such as in the opinion of the court are commensurate with the seriousness of the offence, or the combination of the offence and one or more offences associated with it.

(3) Where a court passes a community sentence which consists of or includes one or more youth community orders—
  (a) the particular order or orders forming part of the sentence must be such as, in the opinion of the court, is, or taken together are, the most suitable for the offender, and
  (b) the restrictions on liberty imposed by the order or orders must be such as in the opinion of the court are commensurate with the seriousness of the offence, or the combination of the offence and one or more offences associated with it.

149 Passing of community sentence on offender remanded in custody

(1) In determining the restrictions on liberty to be imposed by a community order or youth community order in respect of an offence, the court may have regard to any period for which the offender has been remanded in custody in connection with the offence or any other offence the charge for which was founded on the same facts or evidence.

150 Community sentence not available where sentence fixed by law etc.

The power to make a community order or youth community order is not exercisable in respect of an offence for which the sentence—
  (a) is fixed by law,
  (b) falls to be imposed under section 51A(2) of the Firearms Act 1968 (c. 27) (required custodial sentence for certain firearms offences),
  (c) falls to be imposed under section 110(2) or 111(2) of the Sentencing Act (requirement to impose custodial sentences for certain repeated offences committed by offenders aged 18 or over), or
  (d) falls to be imposed under any of sections 225 to 228 of this Act (requirement to impose custodial sentences for certain offences committed by offenders posing risk to public).

156 Pre-sentence reports and other requirements

(1) In forming any such opinion as is mentioned in section 148(1), (2)(b) or (3)(b), section 152(2) or section 153(2), a court must take into account all such information as is available to it about the circumstances of the offence or (as the case may be) of the offence and the offence or offences associated with it, including any aggravating or mitigating factors.

(2) In forming any such opinion as is mentioned in section 148(2)(a) or (3)(a), the court may take into account any information about the offender which is before it.

(3) Subject to subsection (4), a court must obtain and consider a pre-sentence report before—

(a) in the case of a custodial sentence, forming any such opinion as is mentioned in section 152(2), section 153(2), section 225(1)(b), section 226(1)(b), section 227(1)(b) or section 228(1)(b)(i), or

(b) in the case of a community sentence, forming any such opinion as is mentioned in section 148(1), (2)(b) or (3)(b) or any opinion as to the suitability for the offender of the particular requirement or requirements to be imposed by the community order.

(4) Subsection (3) does not apply if, in the circumstances of the case, the court is of the opinion that it is unnecessary to obtain a pre-sentence report.

(5) In a case where the offender is aged under 18, the court must not form the opinion mentioned in subsection (4) unless—

(a) there exists a previous pre-sentence report obtained in respect of the offender, and

(b) the court has had regard to the information contained in that report, or, if there is more than one such report, the most recent report.

(6) No custodial sentence or community sentence is invalidated by the failure of a court to obtain and consider a pre-sentence report before forming an opinion referred to in sub-section (3), but any court on an appeal against such a sentence—

(a) must, subject to subsection (7), obtain a pre-sentence report if none was obtained by the court below, and

(b) must consider any such report obtained by it or by that court.

(7) Subsection (6)(a) does not apply if the court is of the opinion—

(a) that the court below was justified in forming an opinion that it was unnecessary to obtain a pre-sentence report, or

(b) that, although the court below was not justified in forming that opinion, in the circumstances of the case at the time it is before the court, it is unnecessary to obtain a pre-sentence report.

(8) In a case where the offender is aged under 18, the court must not form the opinion mentioned in subsection (7) unless—

(a) there exists a previous pre-sentence report obtained in respect of the offender, and

(b) the court has had regard to the information contained in that report, or, if there is more than one such report, the most recent report.

157 Additional requirements in case of mentally disordered offender

(1) Subject to subsection (2), in any case where the offender is or appears to be mentally disordered, the court must obtain and consider a medical report before passing a custodial sentence other than one fixed by law.

(2) Subsection (1) does not apply if, in the circumstances of the case, the court is of the opinion that it is unnecessary to obtain a medical report.

(3) Before passing a custodial sentence other than one fixed by law on an offender who is or appears to be mentally disordered, a court must consider—

(a) any information before it which relates to his mental condition (whether given in a medical report, a pre-sentence report or otherwise), and

(b) the likely effect of such a sentence on that condition and on any treatment which may be available for it.

(4) No custodial sentence which is passed in a case to which subsection (1) applies is invalidated by the failure of a court to comply with that subsection, but any court on an appeal against such a sentence—

(a) must obtain a medical report if none was obtained by the court below, and

(b) must consider any such report obtained by it or by that court.

(5) In this section 'mentally disordered', in relation to any person, means suffering from a mental disorder within the meaning of the Mental Health Act 1983 (c. 20).

158   Meaning of 'pre-sentence report'

(1) In this Part 'pre-sentence report' means a report which—

(a) with a view to assisting the court in determining the most suitable method of dealing with an offender, is made or submitted by an appropriate officer, and

(b) contains information as to such matters, presented in such manner, as may be prescribed by rules made by the Secretary of State.

(2) In subsection (1) 'an appropriate officer' means—

(a) where the offender is aged 18 or over, an officer of a local probation board, and

(b) where the offender is aged under 18, an officer of a local probation board, a social worker of a local authority or a member of a youth offending team.

159   Disclosure of pre-sentence reports

(1) This section applies where the court obtains a pre-sentence report, other than a report given orally in open court.

(2) Subject to subsections (3) and (4), the court must give a copy of the report—

(a) to the offender or his counsel or solicitor,

(b) if the offender is aged under 18, to any parent or guardian of his who is present in court, and

(c) to the prosecutor, that is to say, the person having the conduct of the proceedings in respect of the offence.

(3) If the offender is aged under 18 and it appears to the court that the disclosure to the offender or to any parent or guardian of his of any information contained in the report would be likely to create a risk of significant harm to the offender, a complete copy of the report need not be given to the offender or, as the case may be, to that parent or guardian.

(4) If the prosecutor is not of a description prescribed by order made by the Secretary of State, a copy of the report need not be given to the prosecutor if the court considers that it would be inappropriate for him to be given it.

(5) No information obtained by virtue of subsection (2)(c) may be used or disclosed otherwise than for the purpose of—

(a) determining whether representations as to matters contained in the report need to be made to the court, or

(b) making such representations to the court.

More general provisions[1]

Criminal Justice Act 2003

196   Meaning of 'relevant order'

(1) In this Chapter 'relevant order' means—

(a) a community order,

---

[1] In this Section, sections 196, 204, 213 and 216 were only partially commenced at the time of editing.

(b) a custody plus order,

(c) a suspended sentence order, or

(d) an intermittent custody order.

197 Meaning of 'the responsible officer'

(1) For the purposes of this Part, 'the responsible officer', in relation to an offender to whom a relevant order relates, means—

    (a) in a case where the order—

        (i) imposes a curfew requirement or an exclusion requirement but no other requirement mentioned in section 177(1) or, as the case requires, section 182(1) or 190(1), and

        (ii) imposes an electronic monitoring requirement,

        the person who under section 215(3) is responsible for the electronic monitoring required by the order;

    (b) in a case where the offender is aged 18 or over and the only requirement imposed by the order is an attendance centre requirement, the officer in charge of the attendance centre in question;

    (c) in any other case, the qualifying officer who, as respects the offender, is for the time being responsible for discharging the functions conferred by this Part on the responsible officer.

(2) The following are qualifying officers for the purposes of subsection (1)(c)—

    (a) in a case where the offender is aged under 18 at the time when the relevant order is made, an officer of a local probation board appointed for or assigned to the local justice area for the time being specified in the order or a member of a youth offending team established by a local authority for the time being specified in the order;

    (b) in any other case, an officer of a local probation board appointed for or assigned to the local justice area for the time being specified in the order.

198 Duties of responsible officer

(1) Where a relevant order has effect, it is the duty of the responsible officer—

    (a) to make any arrangements that are necessary in connection with the requirements imposed by the order,

    (b) to promote the offender's compliance with those requirements, and

    (c) where appropriate, to take steps to enforce those requirements.

Requirements available in case of all offenders

199 Unpaid work requirement

(1) In this Part 'unpaid work requirement', in relation to a relevant order, means a requirement that the offender must perform unpaid work in accordance with section 200.

(2) The number of hours which a person may be required to work under an unpaid work requirement must be specified in the relevant order and must be in the aggregate—

    (a) not less than 40, and

    (b) not more than 300.

(3) A court may not impose an unpaid work requirement in respect of an offender unless after hearing (if the courts thinks necessary) an appropriate officer, the court is satisfied that the offender is a suitable person to perform work under such a requirement.

(4) In subsection (3) 'an appropriate officer' means—

    (a) in the case of an offender aged 18 or over, an officer of a local probation board, and

    (b) in the case of an offender aged under 18, an officer of a local probation board, a social worker of a local authority or a member of a youth offending team.

(5) Where the court makes relevant orders in respect of two or more offences of which the offender has been convicted on the same occasion and includes unpaid work requirements in each of them, the court may direct that the hours of work specified in any of those

requirements is to be concurrent with or additional to those specified in any other of those orders, but so that the total number of hours which are not concurrent does not exceed the maximum specified in subsection (2)(b).

200 Obligations of person subject to unpaid work requirement

(1) An offender in respect of whom an unpaid work requirement of a relevant order is in force must perform for the number of hours specified in the order such work at such times as he may be instructed by the responsible officer.

(2) Subject to paragraph 20 of Schedule 8 and paragraph 18 of Schedule 12 (power to extend order), the work required to be performed under an unpaid work requirement of a community order or a suspended sentence order must be performed during a period of twelve months.

201 Activity requirement

(1) In this Part 'activity requirement', in relation to a relevant order, means a requirement that the offender must do either or both of the following—
  (a) present himself to a person or persons specified in the relevant order at a place or places so specified on such number of days as may be so specified;
  (b) participate in activities specified in the order on such number of days as may be so specified.

(2) The specified activities may consist of or include activities whose purpose is that of reparation, such as activities involving contact between offenders and persons affected by their offences.

(3) A court may not include an activity requirement in a relevant order unless—
  (a) it has consulted—
    (i) in the case of an offender aged 18 or over, an officer of a local probation board,
    (ii) in the case of an offender aged under 18, either an officer of a local probation board or a member of a youth offending team, and
  (b) it is satisfied that it is feasible to secure compliance with the requirement.

(4) A court may not include an activity requirement in a relevant order if compliance with that requirement would involve the co-operation of a person other than the offender and the offender's responsible officer, unless that other person consents to its inclusion.

(5) The aggregate of the number of days specified under subsection (1)(a) and (b) must not exceed 60.

(6) A requirement such as is mentioned in subsection (1)(a) operates to require the offender—
  (a) in accordance with instructions given by his responsible officer, to present himself at a place or places on the number of days specified in the order, and
  (b) while at any place, to comply with instructions given by, or under the authority of, the person in charge of that place.

(7) A place specified under subsection (1)(a) must be—
  (a) a community rehabilitation centre, or
  (b) a place that has been approved by the local probation board for the area in which the premises are situated as providing facilities suitable for persons subject to activity requirements.

202 Programme requirement

(1) In this Part 'programme requirement', in relation to a relevant order, means a requirement that the offender must participate in an accredited programme specified in the order at a place so specified on such number of days as may be so specified.

(2) In this Part 'accredited programme' means a programme that is for the time being accredited by the accreditation body.

(3) In this section—
  (a) 'programme' means a systematic set of activities, and
  (b) 'the accreditation body' means such body as the Secretary of State may designate for the purposes of this section by order.

(4) A court may not include a programme requirement in a relevant order unless—

(a) the accredited programme which the court proposes to specify in the order has been recommended to the court as being suitable for the offender—

(i) in the case of an offender aged 18 or over, by an officer of a local probation board, or

(ii) in the case of an offender aged under 18, either by an officer of a local probation board or by a member of a youth offending team, and

(b) the court is satisfied that the programme is (or, where the relevant order is a custody plus order or an intermittent custody order, will be) available at the place proposed to be specified.

(5) A court may not include a programme requirement in a relevant order if compliance with that requirement would involve the co-operation of a person other than the offender and the offender's responsible officer, unless that other person consents to its inclusion.

203 Prohibited activity requirement

(1) In this Part 'prohibited activity requirement', in relation to a relevant order, means a requirement that the offender must refrain from participating in activities specified in the order—

(a) on a day or days so specified, or

(b) during a period so specified.

(2) A court may not include a prohibited activity requirement in a relevant order unless it has consulted—

(a) in the case of an offender aged 18 or over, an officer of a local probation board;

(b) in the case of an offender aged under 18, either an officer of a local probation board or a member of a youth offending team.

204 Curfew requirement

(1) In this Part 'curfew requirement', in relation to a relevant order, means a requirement that the offender must remain, for periods specified in the relevant order, at a place so specified.

(2) A relevant order imposing a curfew requirement may specify different places or different periods for different days, but may not specify periods which amount to less than two hours or more than twelve hours in any day.

(3) A community order or suspended sentence order which imposes a curfew requirement may not specify periods which fall outside the period of six months beginning with the day on which it is made.

(4) A custody plus order which imposes a curfew requirement may not specify a period which falls outside the period of six months beginning with the first day of the licence period as defined by section 181(3)(b).

(5) An intermittent custody order which imposes a curfew requirement must not specify a period if to do so would cause the aggregate number of days on which the offender is subject to the requirement for any part of the day to exceed 182.

(6) Before making a relevant order imposing a curfew requirement, the court must obtain and consider information about the place proposed to be specified in the order (including information as to the attitude of persons likely to be affected by the enforced presence there of the offender).

205 Exclusion requirement

(1) In this Part 'exclusion requirement', in relation to a relevant order, means a provision prohibiting the offender from entering a place specified in the order for a period so specified.

(2) Where the relevant order is a community order, the period specified must not be more than two years.

(3) An exclusion requirement—

(a) may provide for the prohibition to operate only during the periods specified in the order, and

(b) may specify different places for different periods or days.

206 Residence requirement

(1) In this Part, 'residence requirement', in relation to a community order or a suspended sentence order, means a requirement that, during a period specified in the relevant order, the offender must reside at a place specified in the order.

(2) If the order so provides, a residence requirement does not prohibit the offender from residing, with the prior approval of the responsible officer, at a place other than that specified in the order.

207 Mental health treatment requirement

(1) In this Part, 'mental health treatment requirement', in relation to a community order or suspended sentence order, means a requirement that the offender must submit, during a period or periods specified in the order, to treatment by or under the direction of a registered medical practitioner or a chartered psychologist (or both, for different periods) with a view to the improvement of the offender's mental condition.

(2) The treatment required must be such one of the following kinds of treatment as may be specified in the relevant order—

> (a) treatment as a resident patient in an independent hospital or care home within the meaning of the Care Standards Act 2000 (c. 14) or a hospital within the meaning of the Mental Health Act 1983 (c. 20), but not in hospital premises where high security psychiatric services within the meaning of that Act are provided;
>
> (b) treatment as a non-resident patient at such institution or place as may be specified in the order;
>
> (c) treatment by or under the direction of such registered medical practitioner or chartered psychologist (or both) as may be so specified;

but the nature of the treatment is not to be specified in the order except as mentioned in paragraph (a), (b) or (c).

(3) A court may not by virtue of this section include a mental health treatment requirement in a relevant order unless—

> (a) the court is satisfied, on the evidence of a registered medical practitioner approved for the purposes of section 12 of the Mental Health Act 1983, that the mental condition of the offender—
>
> > (i)   is such as requires and may be susceptible to treatment, but
> >
> > (ii) is not such as to warrant the making of a hospital order or guardianship order within the meaning of that Act;
>
> (b) the court is also satisfied that arrangements have been or can be made for the treatment intended to be specified in the order (including arrangements for the reception of the offender where he is to be required to submit to treatment as a resident patient); and
>
> (c) the offender has expressed his willingness to comply with such a requirement.

208 Mental health treatment at place other than that specified in order

(1) Where the medical practitioner or chartered psychologist by whom or under whose direction an offender is being treated for his mental condition in pursuance of a mental health treatment requirement is of the opinion that part of the treatment can be better or more conveniently given in or at an institution or place which—

> (a) is not specified in the relevant order, and
>
> (b) is one in or at which the treatment of the offender will be given by or under the direction of a registered medical practitioner or chartered psychologist,

he may, with the consent of the offender, make arrangements for him to be treated accordingly.

(2) Such arrangements as are mentioned in subsection (1) may provide for the offender to receive part of his treatment as a resident patient in an institution or place notwithstanding that the institution or place is not one which could have been specified for that purpose in the relevant order.

209   Drug rehabilitation requirement

(1) In this Part 'drug rehabilitation requirement', in relation to a community order or suspended sentence order, means a requirement that during a period specified in the order ('the treatment and testing period') the offender—

(a) must submit to treatment by or under the direction of a specified person having the necessary qualifications or experience with a view to the reduction or elimination of the offender's dependency on or propensity to misuse drugs, and

(b) for the purpose of ascertaining whether he has any drug in his body during that period, must provide samples of such description as may be so determined, at such times or in such circumstances as may (subject to the provisions of the order) be determined by the responsible officer or by the person specified as the person by or under whose direction the treatment is to be provided.

(2) A court may not impose a drug rehabilitation requirement unless—

(a) it is satisfied—

(i) that the offender is dependent on, or has a propensity to misuse, drugs, and

(ii) that his dependency or propensity is such as requires and may be susceptible to treatment,

(b) it is also satisfied that arrangements have been or can be made for the treatment intended to be specified in the order (including arrangements for the reception of the offender where he is to be required to submit to treatment as a resident),

(c) the requirement has been recommended to the court as being suitable for the offender—

(i) in the case of an offender aged 18 or over, by an officer of a local probation board, or

(ii) in the case of an offender aged under 18, either by an officer of a local probation board or by a member of a youth offending team, and

(d) the offender expresses his willingness to comply with the requirement.

(3) The treatment and testing period must be at least six months.

(4) The required treatment for any particular period must be—

(a) treatment as a resident in such institution or place as may be specified in the order, or

(b) treatment as a non-resident in or at such institution or place, and at such intervals, as may be so specified;

but the nature of the treatment is not to be specified in the order except as mentioned in paragraph (a) or (b) above.

210   Drug rehabilitation requirement: provision for review by court

(1) A community order or suspended sentence order imposing a drug rehabilitation requirement may (and must if the treatment and testing period is more than 12 months)—

(a) provide for the requirement to be reviewed periodically at intervals of not less than one month,

(b) provide for each review of the requirement to be made, subject to section 211(6), at a hearing held for the purpose by the court responsible for the order (a 'review hearing'),

(c) require the offender to attend each review hearing,

(d) provide for the responsible officer to make to the court responsible for the order, before each review, a report in writing on the offender's progress under the requirement, and

(e) provide for each such report to include the test results communicated to the responsible officer under section 209(6) or otherwise and the views of the treatment provider as to the treatment and testing of the offender.

211   Periodic review of drug rehabilitation requirement

(1) At a review hearing (within the meaning given by subsection (1) of section 210) the court may, after considering the responsible officer's report referred to in that subsection,

amend the community order or suspended sentence order, so far as it relates to the drug rehabilitation requirement.

(2) The court—

(a) may not amend the drug rehabilitation requirement unless the offender expresses his willingness to comply with the requirement as amended,

(b) may not amend any provision of the order so as to reduce the period for which the drug rehabilitation requirement has effect below the minimum specified in section 209(3), and

(c) except with the consent of the offender, may not amend any requirement or provision of the order while an appeal against the order is pending.

(3) If the offender fails to express his willingness to comply with the drug rehabilitation requirement as proposed to be amended by the court, the court may—

(a) revoke the community order, or the suspended sentence order and the suspended sentence to which it relates, and

(b) deal with him, for the offence in respect of which the order was made, in any way in which he could have been dealt with for that offence by the court which made the order if the order had not been made.

(4) In dealing with the offender under subsection (3)(b), the court—

(a) shall take into account the extent to which the offender has complied with the requirements of the order, and

(b) may impose a custodial sentence (where the order was made in respect of an offence punishable with such a sentence) notwithstanding anything in section 152(2).

(5) Where the order is a community order made by a magistrates' court in the case of an offender under 18 years of age in respect of an offence triable only on indictment in the case of an adult, any powers exercisable under subsection (3)(b) in respect of the offender after he attains the age of 18 are powers to do either or both of the following—

(a) to impose a fine not exceeding £5,000 for the offence in respect of which the order was made;

(b) to deal with the offender for that offence in any way in which the court could deal with him if it had just convicted him of an offence punishable with imprisonment for a term not exceeding twelve months.

212   Alcohol treatment requirement

(1) In this Part 'alcohol treatment requirement', in relation to a community order or suspended sentence order, means a requirement that the offender must submit during a period specified in the order to treatment by or under the direction of a specified person having the necessary qualifications or experience with a view to the reduction or elimination of the offender's dependency on alcohol.

(2) A court may not impose an alcohol treatment requirement in respect of an offender unless it is satisfied—

(a) that he is dependent on alcohol,

(b) that his dependency is such as requires and may be susceptible to treatment, and

(c) that arrangements have been or can be made for the treatment intended to be specified in the order (including arrangements for the reception of the offender where he is to be required to submit to treatment as a resident).

(3) A court may not impose an alcohol treatment requirement unless the offender expresses his willingness to comply with its requirements.

(4) The period for which the alcohol treatment requirement has effect must be not less than six months.

(5) The treatment required by an alcohol treatment requirement for any particular period must be—

(a) treatment as a resident in such institution or place as may be specified in the order,

(b) treatment as a non-resident in or at such institution or place, and at such intervals, as may be so specified, or

(c) treatment by or under the direction of such person having the necessary qualification or experience as may be so specified;

but the nature of the treatment shall not be specified in the order except as mentioned in
paragraph (a), (b) or (c) above.

213 Supervision requirement

(1) In this Part 'supervision requirement', in relation to a relevant order, means a
requirement that, during the relevant period, the offender must attend appointments with
the responsible officer or another person determined by the responsible officer, at such time
and place as may be determined by the officer.

(2) The purpose for which a supervision requirement may be imposed is that of
promoting the offender's rehabilitation.

(c) SENTENCING GUIDELINES

Criminal Justice Act 2003

167 The Sentencing Guidelines Council

(1) There shall be a Sentencing Guidelines Council (in this Chapter referred to as the
Council) consisting of—

(a) the Lord Chief Justice, who is to be chairman of the Council,

(b) seven members (in this section and section 168 referred to as 'judicial members')
appointed by the Lord Chancellor after consultation with the Secretary of State
and the Lord Chief Justice, and

(c) four members (in this section and section 168 referred to as 'non-judicial members') appointed by the Secretary of State after consultation with the Lord
Chancellor and the Lord Chief Justice.

169 The Sentencing Advisory Panel

(1) There shall continue to be a Sentencing Advisory Panel (in this Chapter referred to as
'the Panel') constituted by the Lord Chancellor after consultation with the Secretary of State
and the Lord Chief Justice.

170 Guidelines relating to sentencing and allocation

(1) In this Chapter—

(a) 'sentencing guidelines' means guidelines relating to the sentencing of offenders,
which may be general in nature or limited to a particular category of offence or
offender, and

(b) 'allocation guidelines' means guidelines relating to decisions by a magistrates'
court under section 19 of the Magistrates' Courts Act 1980 (c. 43) as to whether an
offence is more suitable for summary trial or trial on indictment.

(2) The Secretary of State may at any time propose to the Council—

(a) that sentencing guidelines be framed or revised by the Council—

(i)   in respect of offences or offenders of a particular category, or

(ii) in respect of a particular matter affecting sentencing, or

(b) that allocation guidelines be framed or revised by the Council.

(3) The Council may from time to time consider whether to frame sentencing guidelines
or allocation guidelines and, if it receives—

(a) a proposal under section 171(2) from the Panel, or

(b) a proposal under subsection (2) from the Secretary of State,

must consider whether to do so.

(4) Where sentencing guidelines or allocation guidelines have been issued by the
Council as definitive guidelines, the Council must from time to time (and, in particular, if it

receives a proposal under section 171(2) from the Panel or under subsection (2) from the Secretary of State) consider whether to revise them.

(5) Where the Council decides to frame or revise sentencing guidelines, the matters to which the Council must have regard include—

(a) the need to promote consistency in sentencing,

(b) the sentences imposed by courts in England and Wales for offences to which the guidelines relate,

(c) the cost of different sentences and their relative effectiveness in preventing re-offending,

(d) the need to promote public confidence in the criminal justice system, and

(e) the views communicated to the Council, in accordance with section 171(3)(b), by the Panel.

(6) Where the Council decides to frame or revise allocation guidelines, the matters to which the Council must have regard include—

(a) the need to promote consistency in decisions under section 19 of the Magistrates' Courts Act 1980 (c. 43), and

(b) the views communicated to the Council, in accordance with section 171(3)(b), by the Panel.

(7) Sentencing guidelines in respect of an offence or category of offences must include criteria for determining the seriousness of the offence or offences, including (where appropriate) criteria for determining the weight to be given to any previous convictions of offenders.

(8) Where the Council has prepared or revised any sentencing guidelines or allocation guidelines, it must—

(a) publish them as draft guidelines, and

(b) consult about the draft guidelines—

(i)   the Secretary of State,

(ii) such persons as the Lord Chancellor, after consultation with the Secretary of State, may direct, and

(iii) such other persons as the Council considers appropriate.

171   Functions of Sentencing Advisory Panel in relation to guidelines

(1) Where the Council decides to frame or revise any sentencing guidelines or allocation guidelines, otherwise than in response to a proposal from the Panel under subsection (2), the Council must notify the Panel.

(2) The Panel may at any time propose to the Council—

(a) that sentencing guidelines be framed or revised by the Council—

(i)   in respect of offences or offenders of a particular category, or

(ii) in respect of a particular matter affecting sentencing, or

(b) that allocation guidelines be framed or revised by the Council.

(3) Where the Panel receives a notification under subsection (1) or makes a proposal under subsection (2), the Panel must—

(a) obtain and consider the views on the matters in issue of such persons or bodies as may be determined, after consultation with the Secretary of State and the Lord Chancellor, by the Council, and

(b) formulate its own views on those matters and communicate them to the Council.

172   Duty of court to have regard to sentencing guidelines

(1) Every court must—

(a) in sentencing an offender, have regard to any guidelines which are relevant to the offender's case, and

(b) in exercising any other function relating to the sentencing of offenders, have regard to any guidelines which are relevant to the exercise of the function.

(d) CUSTODIAL SENTENCING

General provisions

Powers of Criminal Courts (Sentencing) Act 2000

76 Meaning of 'custodial sentence'

(1) In this Act 'custodial sentence' means—

    (a) a sentence of imprisonment (as to which, see section 89(1)(a) below);

    (b) a sentence of detention under section 90 or 91 below;

    (bb) a sentence of detention for public protection under section 226 of the Criminal Justice Act 2003;

    (bc) a sentence of detention under section 228 of that Act;

    (e) a detention and training order (under section 100 below).

(2) In subsection (1) above 'sentence of imprisonment' does not include a committal for contempt of court or any kindred offence.

77 Liability to imprisonment on conviction on indictment

Where a person is convicted on indictment of an offence against any enactment and is for that offence liable to be sentenced to imprisonment, but the sentence is not by any enactment either limited to a specified term or expressed to extend to imprisonment for life, the person so convicted shall be liable to imprisonment for not more than two years.

Criminal Justice Act 2003

152 General restrictions on imposing discretionary custodial sentences

(1) This section applies where a person is convicted of an offence punishable with a custodial sentence other than one—

    (a) fixed by law, or

    (b) falling to be imposed under section 51A(2) of the Firearms Act 1968 (c. 27), under 110(2) or 111(2) of the Sentencing Act or under any of sections 225 to 228 of this Act.

(2) The court must not pass a custodial sentence unless it is of the opinion that the offence, or the combination of the offence and one or more offences associated with it, was so serious that neither a fine alone nor a community sentence can be justified for the offence.

(3) Nothing in subsection (2) prevents the court from passing a custodial sentence on the offender if—

    (a) he fails to express his willingness to comply with a requirement which is proposed by the court to be included in a community order and which requires an expression of such willingness, or

    (b) he fails to comply with an order under section 161(2) (pre-sentence drug testing).

153 Length of discretionary custodial sentences: general provision

(1) This section applies where a court passes a custodial sentence other than one fixed by law or falling to be imposed under section 225 or 226.

(2) Subject to section 51A(2) of the Firearms Act 1968 (c. 27), sections 110(2) and 111(2) of the Sentencing Act and sections 227(2) and 228(2) of this Act, the custodial sentence must be for the shortest term (not exceeding the permitted maximum) that in the opinion of the court is commensurate with the seriousness of the offence, or the combination of the offence and one or more offences associated with it.

Powers of Criminal Courts (Sentencing) Act 2000

83 Restriction on imposing custodial sentences on persons not legally represented

(1) A magistrates' court on summary conviction, or the Crown Court on committal for sentence or on conviction on indictment, shall not pass a sentence of imprisonment on a person who—

    (a) is not legally represented in that court, and

    (b) has not been previously sentenced to that punishment by a court in any part of the United Kingdom,

unless he is a person to whom subsection (3) below applies.

(2) A magistrates' court on summary conviction, or the Crown Court on committal for sentence or on conviction on indictment, shall not—

    (a) pass a sentence of detention under section 90 or 91 below,

    (aa) pass a sentence of imprisonment on a person who, when convicted, was at least 18 but under 21, or

    (d) make a detention and training order,

on or in respect of a person who is not legally represented in that court unless he is a person to whom subsection (3) below applies.

(3) This subsection applies to a person if either—

    (a) he was granted a right to representation funded by the Legal Services Commission as part of the Criminal Defence Service but the right was withdrawn because of his conduct or because it appeared that his financial resources were such that he was not eligible to be granted such a right;

    (aa) he applied for such representation and the application was refused because it appeared that his financial resources were such that he was not eligible to be granted a right to it; or

    (b) having been informed of his right to apply for such representation and having had the opportunity to do so, he refused or failed to apply.

(4) For the purposes of this section a person is to be treated as legally represented in a court, if but only if, he has the assistance of counsel or a solicitor to represent him in the proceedings in that court at some time after he is found guilty and before he is sentenced.

(5) For the purposes of subsection (1)(b) above a previous sentence of imprisonment which has been suspended and which has not taken effect under section 119 below or under section 19 of the Treatment of Offenders Act (Northern Ireland) 1968 shall be disregarded.

(6) In this section 'sentence of imprisonment' does not include a committal for contempt of court or any kindred offence.

89 Restriction on imposing imprisonment on persons under 18

(1) Subject to subsection (2) below, no court shall—

    (a) pass a sentence of imprisonment on a person for an offence if he is aged under 18 when convicted of the offence; or

    (b) commit a person aged under 18 to prison for any reason.

(2) Nothing in subsection (1) above shall prevent the committal to prison of a person aged under 18 who is—

    (a) remanded in custody;

    (b) committed in custody for sentence; or

    (c) sent in custody for trial under section 51 or 51A of the Crime and Disorder Act 1998.

90 Offenders who commit murder etc. when under 18: duty to detain at Her Majesty's pleasure

Where a person convicted of murder or any other offence the sentence for which is fixed by law as life imprisonment appears to the court to have been aged under 18 at the time the offence was committed, the court shall (notwithstanding anything in this or any other Act) sentence him to be detained during Her Majesty's pleasure.

91   Offenders under 18 convicted of certain serious offences: power to detain for specified period

(1) Subsection (3) below applies where a person aged under 18 is convicted on indictment of—

   (a) an offence punishable in the case of a person aged 18 or over with imprisonment for 14 years or more, not being an offence the sentence for which is fixed by law; or

   (b) an offence under section 3 of the Sexual Offences Act 2003 (in this section, 'the 2003 Act') (sexual assault); or

   (c) an offence under section 13 of the 2003 Act (child sex offences committed by children or young persons); or

   (d) an offence under section 25 of the 2003 Act (sexual activity with a child family member); or

   (e) an offence under section 26 of the 2003 Act (inciting a child family member to engage in sexual activity).

(1A) Subsection (3) below also applies where—

   (a) a person aged under 18 is convicted on indictment of an offence—

     (i)   under subsection (1)(a), (ab), (aba), (ac), (ad), (ae), (af) or (c) of section 5 of the Firearms Act 1968 (prohibited weapons), or

     (ii) under subsection (1A)(a) of that section,

   (b) the offence was committed after the commencement of section 51A of that Act and at a time when he was aged 16 or over, and

   (c) the court is of the opinion mentioned in section 51A(2) of that Act (exceptional circumstances which justify its not imposing required custodial sentence).

(3) If the court is of the opinion that neither a community sentence nor a detention and training order is suitable, the court may sentence the offender to be detained for such period, not exceeding the maximum term of imprisonment with which the offence is punishable in the case of a person aged 18 or over, as may be specified in the sentence.

(5) Where subsection (2) of section 51A of the Firearms Act 1968 requires the imposition of a sentence of detention under this section for a term of at least the required minimum term (within the meaning of that section), the court shall sentence the offender to be detained for such period, of at least that term but not exceeding the maximum term of imprisonment with which the offence is punishable in the case of a person aged 18 or over, as may be specified in the sentence.

92   Detention under sections 90 and 91: place of detention etc

(1) A person sentenced to be detained under section 90 or 91 above shall be liable to be detained in such place and under such conditions—

   (a) as the Secretary of State may direct; or

   (b) as the Secretary of State may arrange with any person.

(2) A person detained pursuant to the directions or arrangements made by the Secretary of State under this section shall be deemed to be in legal custody.

99   Conversion of sentence of detention to sentence of imprisonment

(1) Subject to the following provisions of this section, where an offender has been sentenced by a relevant sentence of detention to a term of detention and either—

   (a) he has attained the age of 21, or

   (b) he has attained the age of 18 and has been reported to the Secretary of State by the board of visitors of the institution in which he is detained as exercising a bad

influence on the other inmates of the institution or as behaving in a disruptive manner to the detriment of those inmates,
the Secretary of State may direct that he shall be treated as if he had been sentenced to imprisonment for the same term.

(2) Where the Secretary of State gives a direction under subsection (1) above in relation to an offender, the portion of the term of detention imposed under the relevant sentence of detention which he has already served shall be deemed to have been a portion of a term of imprisonment.

(3) Where the Secretary of State gives a direction under subsection (1) above in relation to an offender serving a sentence of detention for public protection under section 226 of the Criminal Justice Act 2003 the offender shall be treated as if he had been sentenced under section 225 of that Act; and where the Secretary of State gives such a direction in relation to an offender serving an extended sentence of detention under section 228 of that Act the offender shall be treated as if he had been sentenced under section 227 of that Act.

100   Offenders under 18: detention and training orders

(1) Subject to sections 90 and 91 above, sections 226 and 228 of the Criminal Justice Act 2003, and subsection (2) below, where—

   (a) a child or young person (that is to say, any person aged under 18) is convicted of an offence which is punishable with imprisonment in the case of a person aged 18 or over, and

   (b) the court is of the opinion that subsection (2) of section 152 of the Criminal Justice Act 2003 applies or the case falls within subsection (3) of that section,
the sentence that the court is to pass is a detention and training order.

(2) A court shall not make a detention and training order—

   (a) in the case of an offender under the age of 15 at the time of the conviction, unless it is of the opinion that he is a persistent offender;

   (b) in the case of an offender under the age of 12 at that time, unless—

      (i)   it is of the opinion that only a custodial sentence would be adequate to protect the public from further offending by him; and

      (ii) the offence was committed on or after such date as the Secretary of State may be order appoint.

101   Term of order, consecutive terms and taking account of remands

(1) Subject to subsection (2) and (2A) below, the term of a detention and training order made in respect of an offence (whether by a magistrates' court or otherwise) shall be 4, 6, 8, 10, 12, 18 or 24 months.

(2) The term of a detention and training order may not exceed the maximum term of imprisonment that the Crown Court could (in the case of an offender aged 18 or over) impose for the offence.

(2A) Where—

   (a) the offence is a summary offence,

   (b) the maximum term of imprisonment that a court could (in the case of an offender aged 18 or over) impose for the offence is 51 weeks,
the term of a detention and training order may not exceed 6 months.

(3) Subject to subsections (4) and (6) below, a court making a detention and training order may order that its term shall commence on the expiry of the term of any other detention and training order made by that or any other court.

(4) A court shall not make in respect of an offender a detention and training order the effect of which would be that he would be subject to detention and training orders for a term which exceeds 24 months.

(5) Where the term of the detention and training orders to which an offender would otherwise be subject exceeds 24 months, the excess shall be treated as remitted.

(6) A court making a detention and training order shall not order that its term shall commence on the expiry of the term of a detention and training order under which the period of supervision has already begun (under section 103(1) below).

(7) Where a detention and training order ('the new order') is made in respect of an offender who is subject to a detention and training order under which the period of supervision has begun ('the old order'), the old order shall be disregarded in determining—

    (a) for the purposes of subsection (4) above whether the effect of the new order would be that the offender would be subject to detention and training orders for a term which exceeds 24 months; and

    (b) for the purposes of subsection (5) above whether the term of the detention and training orders to which the offender would (apart from that subsection) be subject exceeds 24 months.

(8) In determining the term of a detention and training order for an offence, the court shall take account of any period for which the offender has been remanded in custody in connection with the offence, or any other offence the charge for which was founded on the same facts or evidence.

(9) Where a court proposes to make detention and training orders in respect of an offender for two or more offences—

    (a) subsection (8) above shall not apply; but

    (b) in determining the total term of the detention and training orders it proposes to make in respect of the offender, the court shall take account of the total period (if any) for which he has been remanded in custody in connection with any of those offences, or any other offence the charge for which was founded on the same facts or evidence.

102   The period of detention and training

(1) An offender shall serve the period of detention and training under a detention and training order in such secure accommodation as may be determined by the Secretary of State or by such other person as may be authorised by him for that purpose.

(2) Subject to subsections (3) to (5) below, the period of detention and training under a detention and training order shall be one-half of the term of the order.

(3) The Secretary of State may at any time release the offender if he is satisfied that exceptional circumstances exist which justify the offender's release on compassionate grounds.

(4) The Secretary of State may release the offender—

    (a) in the case of an order for a term of 8 months or more but less than 18 months, one month before the half-way point of the term of the order; and

    (b) in the case of an order for a term of 18 months or more, one month or two months before that point.

(5) If a youth court so orders on an application made by the Secretary of State for the purpose, the Secretary of State shall release the offender—

    (a) in the case of an order for a term of 8 months or more but less than 18 months, one month after the half-way point of the term of the order; and

    (b) in the case of an order for a term of 18 months or more, one month or two months after that point.

103   The period of supervision

(1) The period of supervision of an offender who is subject to a detention and training order—

    (a) shall begin with the offender's release, whether at the half-way point of the term of the order or otherwise; and

    (b) subject to subsection (2) below, shall end when the term of the order ends.

(2) The Secretary of State may by order provide that the period of supervision shall end at such point during the term of a detention and training order as may be specified in the order under this subsection.

(3) During the period of supervision, the offender shall be under the supervision of—

(a) an officer of a local probation board;

(b) a social worker of a local authority social services department; or

(c) a member of a youth offending team;

and the category of person to supervise the offender shall be determined from time to time by the Secretary of State.

104 Breach of supervision requirements

(1) Where a detention and training order is in force in respect of an offender and it appears on information to a justice of the peace acting in a relevant local justice area that the offender has failed to comply with requirements under section 103(6)(b) above, the justice—

(a) may issue a summons requiring the offender to appear at the place and time specified in the summons before a youth court acting in the area; or

(b) if the information is in writing and on oath, may issue a warrant for the offender's arrest requiring him to be brought before such a court.

(3) If it is proved to the satisfaction of the youth court before which an offender appears or is brought under this section that he has failed to comply with requirements under section 103(6)(b) above, that court may—

(a) order the offender to be detained, in such secure accommodation as the Secretary of State may determine, for such period, not exceeding the shorter of three months or the remainder of the term of the detention and training order, as the court may specify; or

(b) impose on the offender a fine not exceeding level 3 on the standard scale.

105 Offences during currency of order

(1) This section applies to a person subject to a detention and training order if—

(a) after his release and before the date on which the term of the order ends, he commits an offence punishable with imprisonment in the case of a person aged 18 or over ('the new offence'); and

(b) whether before or after that date, he is convicted of the new offence.

(2) Subject to section 8(6) above (duty of adult magistrates' court to remit young offenders to youth court for sentence), the court by or before which a person to whom this section applies is convicted of the new offence may, whether or not it passes any other sentence on him, order him to be detained in such secure accommodation as the Secretary of State may determine for the whole or any part of the period which—

(a) begins with the date of the court's order; and

(b) is equal in length to the period between the date on which the new offence was committed and the date mentioned in subsection (1) above.

(3) The period for which a person to whom this section applies is ordered under subsection (2) above to be detained in secure accommodation—

(a) shall, as the court may direct, either be served before and be followed by, or be served concurrently with, any sentence imposed for the new offence; and

(b) in either case, shall be disregarded in determining the appropriate length of that sentence.

106A Interaction with sentences of detention

(1) In this section—

'the 2003 Act' means the Criminal Justice Act 2003;

'sentence of detention' means—

(a) a sentence of detention under section 91 above, or

(b) a sentence of detention under section 228 of the 2003 Act (extended sentence for certain violent or sexual offences: persons under 18).

(2) Where a court passes a sentence of detention in the case of an offender who is subject to a detention and training order, the sentence shall take effect as follows—

    (a) if the offender has at any time been released by virtue of subsection (2), (3), (4) or (5) of section 102 above, at the beginning of the day on which the sentence is passed, and

    (b) if not, either as mentioned in paragraph (a) above or, if the court so orders, at the time when the offender would otherwise be released by virtue of subsection (2), (3), (4) or (5) of section 102.

(3) Where a court makes a detention and training order in the case of an offender who is subject to a sentence of detention, the order shall take effect as follows—

    (a) if the offender has at any time been released under Chapter 6 of Part 12 of the 2003 Act (release on licence of fixed-term prisoners), at the beginning of the day on which the order is made, and

    (b) if not, either as mentioned in paragraph (a) above or, if the court so orders, at the time when the offender would otherwise be released under that Chapter.

(4) Where an order under section 102(5) above is made in the case of a person in respect of whom a sentence of detention is to take effect as mentioned in subsection (2)(b) above, the order is to be expressed as an order that the period of detention attributable to the detention and training order is to end at the time determined under section 102(5)(a) or (b) above.

107 Meaning of 'secure accommodation' and references to terms

(1) In sections 102, 104 and 105 above 'secure accommodation' means—

    (a) a secure training centre;

    (b) a young offender institution;

    (c) accommodation provided by a local authority for the purpose of restricting the liberty of children and young persons;

    (d) accommodation provided for that purpose under subsection (5) of section 82 of the Children Act 1989 (financial support by the Secretary of State); or

    (e) such other accommodation provided for the purpose of restricting liberty as the Secretary of State may direct.

110 Minimum of seven years for third class A drug trafficking offence

(1) This section applies where—

    (a) a person is convicted of a class A drug trafficking offence committed after 30th September 1997;

    (b) at the time when that offence was committed, he was 18 or over and had been convicted in any part of the United Kingdom of two other class A drug trafficking offences; and

    (c) one of those other offences was committed after he had been convicted of the other.

(2) The court shall impose a sentence of imprisonment for a term of at least seven years except where the court is of the opinion that there are particular circumstances which—

    (a) relate to any of the offences or to the offender; and

    (b) would make it unjust to do so in all the circumstances.

(4) Where—

    (a) a person is charged with a class A drug trafficking offence (which, apart from this subsection, would be triable either way), and

    (b) the circumstances are such that, if he were convicted of the offence, he could be sentenced for it under subsection (2) above,

the offence shall be triable only on indictment.

(5) In this section 'class A drug trafficking offence' means a drug trafficking offence committed in respect of a class A drug; and for this purpose—

'class A drug' has the same meaning as in the Misuse of Drugs Act 1971;

'drug trafficking offence' means an offence which is specified in—

(a) paragraph 1 of Schedule 2 to the Proceeds of Crime Act 2002 (drug trafficking offences), or

(b) so far as it relates to that paragraph, paragraph 10 of that Schedule.

111 Minimum of three years for third domestic burglary

(1) This section applies where—

(a) a person is convicted of a domestic burglary committed after 30th November 1999;

(b) at the time when that burglary was committed, he was 18 or over and had been convicted in England and Wales of two other domestic burglaries; and

(c) one of those other burglaries was committed after he had been convicted of the other, and both of them were committed after 30th November 1999.

(2) The court shall impose a sentence of imprisonment for a term of at least three years except where the court is of the opinion that there are particular circumstances which—

(a) relate to any of the offences or to the offender; and

(b) would make it unjust to do so in all the circumstances.

(4) Where—

(a) a person is charged with a domestic burglary which, apart from this subsection, would be triable either way, and

(b) the circumstances are such that, if he were convicted of the burglary, he could be sentenced for it under subsection (2) above,

the burglary shall be triable only on indictment.

Magistrates' Courts Act 1980

32 Penalties on summary conviction for offences triable either way

(1) On summary conviction of any of the offences triable either way listed in Schedule 1 to this Act a person shall be liable to imprisonment for a term not exceeding 6 months or to a fine not exceeding the prescribed sum or both, except that—

(a) a magistrates' court shall not have power to impose imprisonment for an offence so listed if the Crown Court would not have that power in the case of an adult convicted of it on indictment;

(b) on summary conviction of an offence consisting in the incitement to commit an offence triable either way a person shall not be liable to on summary conviction of the last-mentioned offence; and

(c) on summary conviction of attempting to commit an offence triable either way a person shall not be liable to any greater penalty than he would be liable to on summary conviction of the completed offence.

(2) For any offence triable either way which is not listed in Schedule 1 to this Act, being an offence under a relevant enactment, the maximum fine which may be imposed on summary conviction shall by virtue of this subsection be the prescribed sum unless the offence is one for which by virtue of an enactment other than this subsection a larger fine may be imposed on summary conviction.

(3) Where, by virtue of any relevant enactment, a person summarily convicted of an offence triable either way would, apart from this section, be liable to a maximum fine of one amount in the case of a first conviction and of a different amount in the case of a second or subsequent conviction, subsection (2) above shall apply irrespective of whether the conviction is a first, second or subsequent one.

(4) Subsection (2) above shall not affect so much of any enactment as (in whatever words) makes a person liable on summary conviction to a fine not exceeding a specified

amount for each day on which a continuing offence is continued after conviction or the occurrence of any other specified event.

(5) Subsection (2) above shall not apply on summary conviction of any of the following offences:—

(a) offences under section 5 (2) of the Misuse of Drugs Act 1971 (having possession of a controlled drug) where the controlled drug in relation to which the offence was committed was a Class B or Class C drug;

(b) offences under the following provisions of that Act, where the controlled drug in relation to which the offence was committed was a Class C drug, namely—

(i) section 4 (2) (production, or being concerned in the production, of a controlled drug);

(ii) section 4 (3) (supplying or offering a controlled drug or being concerned in the doing of either activity by another);

(iii) section 5 (3) (having possession of a controlled drug with intent to supply it to another);

(iv) section 8 (being the occupier, or concerned in the management, of premises and permitting or suffering certain activities to take place there);

(v) section 12 (6) (contravention of direction prohibiting practitioner etc. from possessing, supplying etc. controlled drugs); or

(vi) section 13 (3) (contravention of direction prohibiting practitioner etc. from prescribing, supplying etc. controlled drugs).

(9) In this section—

'fine' includes a pecuniary penalty but does not include a pecuniary forfeiture or pecuniary compensation;

'the prescribed sum' means £5,000 or such sum as is for the time being substituted in this definition by an order in force under section 143 (1) below;

'relevant enactment' means an enactment contained in the Criminal Law Act 1977 or in any Act passed before, or in the same Session as, that Act.

Murder (Abolition of Death Penalty) Act 1965 (as amended)

1   Abolition of death penalty for murder

(1) No person shall suffer death for murder, and a person convicted of murder shall be sentenced to imprisonment for life.

Prison sentences of less than 12 months[1]

Criminal Justice Act 2003

181   Prison sentences of less than 12 months

(1) Any power of a court to impose a sentence of imprisonment for a term of less than 12 months on an offender may be exercised only in accordance with the following provisions of this section unless the court makes an intermittent custody order (as defined by section 183).

(2) The term of the sentence—

(a) must be expressed in weeks,

(b) must be at least 28 weeks,

(c) must not be more than 51 weeks in respect of any one offence, and

(d) must not exceed the maximum term permitted for the offence.

---

[1] None of s 181 of the Criminal Justice Act 2003 had been commenced at the time of editing this book, and the other sections had been only partly implemented.

(3) The court, when passing sentence, must—
  (a) specify a period (in this Chapter referred to as 'the custodial period') at the end of which the offender is to be released on a licence, and
  (b) by order require the licence to be granted subject to conditions requiring the offender's compliance during the remainder of the term (in this Chapter referred to as 'the licence period') or any part of it with one or more requirements falling within section 182(1) and specified in the order.

(4) In this Part 'custody plus order' means an order under subsection (3)(b).

(5) The custodial period—
  (a) must be at least 2 weeks, and
  (b) in respect of any one offence, must not be more than 13 weeks.

(6) In determining the term of the sentence and the length of the custodial period, the court must ensure that the licence period is at least 26 weeks in length.

(7) Where a court imposes two or more terms of imprisonment in accordance with this section to be served consecutively—
  (a) the aggregate length of the terms of imprisonment must not be more than 65 weeks, and
  (b) the aggregate length of the custodial periods must not be more than 26 weeks.

182   Licence conditions

(1) The requirements falling within this subsection are—
  (a) an unpaid work requirement (as defined by section 199),
  (b) an activity requirement (as defined by section 201),
  (c) a programme requirement (as defined by section 202),
  (d) a prohibited activity requirement (as defined by section 203),
  (e) a curfew requirement (as defined by section 204),
  (f) an exclusion requirement (as defined by section 205),
  (g) a supervision requirement (as defined by section 213), and
  (h) in a case where the offender is aged under 25, an attendance centre requirement (as defined by section 214).

(2) The power under section 181(3)(b) to determine the conditions of the licence has effect subject to section 218 and to the following provisions of Chapter 4 relating to particular requirements—
  (a) section 199(3) (unpaid work requirement),
  (b) section 201(3) and (4) (activity requirement),
  (c) section 202(4) and (5) (programme requirement), and
  (d) section 203(2) (prohibited activity requirement).

(3) Where the court makes a custody plus order requiring a licence to contain a curfew requirement or an exclusion requirement, the court must also require the licence to contain an electronic monitoring requirement (as defined by section 215) unless—
  (a) the court is prevented from doing so by section 215(2) or 218(4), or
  (b) in the particular circumstances of the case, it considers it inappropriate to do so.

(4) Where the court makes a custody plus order requiring a licence to contain an unpaid work requirement, an activity requirement, a programme requirement, a prohibited activity requirement, a supervision requirement or an attendance centre requirement, the court may also require the licence to contain an electronic monitoring requirement unless the court is prevented from doing so by section 215(2) or 218(4).

Intermittent custody

183   Intermittent custody

(1) A court may, when passing a sentence of imprisonment for a term complying with subsection (4)—
  (a) specify the number of days that the offender must serve in prison under the sentence before being released on licence for the remainder of the term, and

    (b) by order—
        (i) specify periods during which the offender is to be released temporarily on licence before he has served that number of days in prison, and
        (ii) require any licence to be granted subject to conditions requiring the offender's compliance during the licence periods with one or more requirements falling within section 182(1) and specified in the order.

(2) In this Part 'intermittent custody order' means an order under subsection (1)(b).

(3) In this Chapter—

'licence period', in relation to a term of imprisonment to which an intermittent custody order relates, means any period during which the offender is released on licence by virtue of subsection (1)(a) or (b)(i);

'the number of custodial days', in relation to a term of imprisonment to which an intermittent custody order relates, means the number of days specified under subsection (1)(a).

(4) The term of the sentence—
    (a) must be expressed in weeks,
    (b) must be at least 28 weeks,
    (c) must not be more than 51 weeks in respect of any one offence, and
    (d) must not exceed the maximum term permitted for the offence.

(5) The number of custodial days—
    (a) must be at least 14, and
    (b) in respect of any one offence, must not be more than 90.

(6) A court may not exercise its powers under subsection (1) unless the offender has expressed his willingness to serve the custodial part of the proposed sentence intermittently, during the parts of the sentence that are not to be licence periods.

(7) Where a court exercises its powers under subsection (1) in respect of two or more terms of imprisonment that are to be served consecutively—
    (a) the aggregate length of the terms of imprisonment must not be more than 65 weeks, and
    (b) the aggregate of the numbers of custodial days must not be more than 180.

184   Restrictions on power to make intermittent custody order

(1) A court may not make an intermittent custody order unless it has been notified by the Secretary of State that arrangements for implementing such orders are available in the area proposed to be specified in the intermittent custody order and the notice has not been withdrawn.

(2) The court may not make an intermittent custody order in respect of any offender unless—
    (a) it has consulted an officer of a local probation board,
    (b) it has received from the Secretary of State notification that suitable prison accommodation is available for the offender during the custodial periods, and
    (c) it appears to the court that the offender will have suitable accommodation available to him during the licence periods.

185   Intermittent custody: licence conditions

(1) Section 183(1)(b) has effect subject to section 218 and to the following provisions of Chapter 4 limiting the power to require the licence to contain particular requirements—
    (a) section 199(3) (unpaid work requirement),
    (b) section 201(3) and (4) (activity requirement),
    (c) section 202(4) and (5) (programme requirement), and
    (d) section 203(2) (prohibited activity requirement).

186   Further provisions relating to intermittent custody

(2) The Secretary of State may pay to any offender to whom an intermittent custody order relates the whole or part of any expenses incurred by the offender in travelling to and from prison during licence periods.

Suspended sentences

189 Suspended sentences of imprisonment

(1) A court which passes a sentence of imprisonment for a term of at least 28 weeks but not more than 51 weeks in accordance with section 181 may—

(a) order the offender to comply during a period specified for the purposes of this paragraph in the order (in this Chapter referred to as 'the supervision period') with one or more requirements falling within section 190(1) and specified in the order, and

(b) order that the sentence of imprisonment is not to take effect unless either—

(i) during the supervision period the offender fails to comply with a requirement imposed under paragraph (a), or

(ii) during a period specified in the order for the purposes of this sub-paragraph (in this Chapter referred to as 'the operational period') the offender commits in the United Kingdom another offence (whether or not punishable with imprisonment),

and (in either case) a court having power to do so subsequently orders under paragraph 8 of Schedule 12 that the original sentence is to take effect.

(2) Where two or more sentences imposed on the same occasion are to be served consecutively, the power conferred by subsection (1) is not exercisable in relation to any of them unless the aggregate of the terms of the sentences does not exceed 65 weeks.

(3) The supervision period and the operational period must each be a period of not less than six months and not more than two years beginning with the date of the order.

(4) The supervision period must not end later than the operational period.

(5) A court which passes a suspended sentence on any person for an offence may not impose a community sentence in his case in respect of that offence or any other offence of which he is convicted by or before the court or for which he is dealt with by the court.

190 Imposition of requirements by suspended sentence order

(1) The requirements falling within this subsection are—

(a) an unpaid work requirement (as defined by section 199),

(b) an activity requirement (as defined by section 201),

(c) a programme requirement (as defined by section 202),

(d) a prohibited activity requirement (as defined by section 203),

(e) a curfew requirement (as defined by section 204),

(f) an exclusion requirement (as defined by section 205),

(g) a residence requirement (as defined by section 206),

(h) a mental health treatment requirement (as defined by section 207),

(i) a drug rehabilitation requirement (as defined by section 209),

(j) an alcohol treatment requirement (as defined by section 212),

(k) a supervision requirement (as defined by section 213), and

(l) in a case where the offender is aged under 25, an attendance centre requirement (as defined by section 214).

(2) Section 189(1)(a) has effect subject to section 218 and to the following provisions of Chapter 4 relating to particular requirements—

(a) section 199(3) (unpaid work requirement),

(b) section 201(3) and (4) (activity requirement),

(c) section 202(4) and (5) (programme requirement),

(d) section 203(2) (prohibited activity requirement),

(e) section 207(3) (mental health treatment requirement),

(f) section 209(2) (drug rehabilitation requirement), and

(g) section 212(2) and (3) (alcohol treatment requirement).

(3) Where the court makes a suspended sentence order imposing a curfew requirement or an exclusion requirement, it must also impose an electronic monitoring requirement (as

defined by section 215) unless—

(a) the court is prevented from doing so by section 215(2) or 218(4), or

(b) in the particular circumstances of the case, it considers it inappropriate to do so.

(4) Where the court makes a suspended sentence order imposing an unpaid work requirement, an activity requirement, a programme requirement, a prohibited activity requirement, a residence requirement, a mental health treatment requirement, a drug rehabilitation requirement, an alcohol treatment requirement, a supervision requirement or an attendance centre requirement, the court may also impose an electronic monitoring requirement unless the court is prevented from doing so by section 215(2) or 218(4).

191   Power to provide for review of suspended sentence order

(1) A suspended sentence order may—

(a) provide for the order to be reviewed periodically at specified intervals,

(b) provide for each review to be made, subject to section 192(4), at a hearing held for the purpose by the court responsible for the order (a 'review hearing'),

(c) require the offender to attend each review hearing, and

(d) provide for the responsible officer to make to the court responsible for the order, before each review, a report on the offender's progress in complying with the community requirements of the order.

(2) Subsection (1) does not apply in the case of an order imposing a drug rehabilitation requirement (provision for such a requirement to be subject to review being made by section 210).

192   Periodic reviews of suspended sentence order

(1) At a review hearing (within the meaning of subsection (1) of section 191) the court may, after considering the responsible officer's report referred to in that subsection, amend the community requirements of the suspended sentence order, or any provision of the order which relates to those requirements.

(2) The court—

(a) may not amend the community requirements of the order so as to impose a requirement of a different kind unless the offender expresses his willingness to comply with that requirement,

(b) may not amend a mental health treatment requirement, a drug rehabilitation requirement or an alcohol treatment requirement unless the offender expresses his willingness to comply with the requirement as amended,

(c) may amend the supervision period only if the period as amended complies with section 189(3) and (4),

(d) may not amend the operational period of the suspended sentence, and

(e) except with the consent of the offender, may not amend the order while an appeal against the order is pending.

(3) For the purposes of subsection (2)(a)—

(a) a community requirement falling within any paragraph of section 190(1) is of the same kind as any other community requirement falling within that paragraph, and

(b) an electronic monitoring requirement is a community requirement of the same kind as any requirement falling within section 190(1) to which it relates.

(4) If before a review hearing is held at any review the court, after considering the responsible officer's report, is of the opinion that the offender's progress in complying with the community requirements of the order is satisfactory, it may order that no review hearing is to be held at that review; and if before a review hearing is held at any review, or at a review hearing, the court, after considering that report, is of that opinion, it may amend the suspended sentence order so as to provide for each subsequent review to be held without a hearing.

(5) If at a review held without a hearing the court, after considering the responsible officer's report, is of the opinion that the offender's progress under the order is no longer satisfactory, the court may require the offender to attend a hearing of the court at a specified time and place.

(6) If at a review hearing the court is of the opinion that the offender has without reasonable excuse failed to comply with any of the community requirements of the order, the court may adjourn the hearing for the purpose of dealing with the case under paragraph 8 of Schedule 12.

(7) At a review hearing the court may amend the suspended sentence order so as to vary the intervals specified under section 191(1).

Consecutive or concurrent terms

---

263 Concurrent terms

(1) This section applies where—
   (a) a person ('the offender') has been sentenced by any court to two or more terms of imprisonment which are wholly or partly concurrent, and
   (b) the sentences were passed on the same occasion or, where they were passed on different occasions, the person has not been released under this Chapter at any time during the period beginning with the first and ending with the last of those occasions.

(2) Where this section applies—
   (a) nothing in this Chapter requires the Secretary of State to release the offender in respect of any of the terms unless and until he is required to release him in respect of each of the others,
   (b) section 244 does not authorise the Secretary of State to release him on licence under that section in respect of any of the terms unless and until that section authorises the Secretary of State to do so in respect of each of the others,
   (c) on and after his release under this Chapter the offender is to be on licence for so long, and subject to such conditions, as is required by this Chapter in respect of any of the sentences.

(3) Where the sentences include one or more sentences of twelve months or more and one or more sentences of less than twelve months, the terms of the licence may be determined by the Secretary of State in accordance with section 250(4)(b), without regard to the requirements of any custody plus order or intermittent custody order.

264[2] Consecutive terms

(1) This section applies where—
   (a) a person ('the offender') has been sentenced to two or more terms of imprisonment which are to be served consecutively on each other
   (b) the sentences were passed on the same occasion or, where they were passed on different occasions, the person has not been released under this Chapter at any time during the period beginning with the first and ending with the last of those occasions, and
   (c) none of those terms is a term to which an intermittent custody order relates.

(2) Nothing in this Chapter requires the Secretary of State to release the offender on licence until he has served a period equal in length to the aggregate of the length of the custodial periods in relation to each of the terms of imprisonment.

(3) Where any of the terms of imprisonment is a term of twelve months or more, the offender is, on and after his release under this Chapter, to be on licence—
   (a) until he would, but for his release, have served a term equal in length to the aggregate length of the terms of imprisonment, and

---

[2] Section 264 has only been partially commenced at the time of editing this book.

(b) subject to such conditions as are required by this Chapter in respect of each of those terms of imprisonment.

(4) Where each of the terms of imprisonment is a term of less than twelve months, the offender is, on and after his release under this Chapter, to be on licence until the relevant time, and subject to such conditions as are required by this Chapter in respect of any of the terms of imprisonment, and none of the terms is to be regarded for any purpose as continuing after the relevant time.

(5) In subsection (4) 'the relevant time' means the time when the offender would, but for his release, have served a term equal in length to the aggregate of—

(a) all the custodial periods in relation to the terms of imprisonment, and

(b) the longest of the licence periods in relation to those terms.

(6) In this section—

(a) 'custodial period'—

(i) in relation to an extended sentence imposed under section 227 or 228, means the appropriate custodial term determined under that section,

(ii) in relation to a term of twelve months or more, means one-half of the term, and

(iii) in relation to a term of less than twelve months complying with section 181, means the custodial period as defined by subsection (3)(a) of that section;

(b) 'licence period', in relation to a term of less than twelve months complying with section 181, has the meaning given by subsection (3)(b) of that section.

(7) This section applies to a determinate sentence of detention under section 91 of the Sentencing Act or under section 228 of this Act as it applies to a term of imprisonment of 12 months or more.

264A Consecutive terms: intermittent custody

(1) This section applies where—

(a) a person ('the offender') has been sentenced to two or more terms of imprisonment which are to be served consecutively on each other,

(b) the sentences were passed on the same occasion or, where they were passed on different occasions, the person has not been released under this Chapter at any time during the period beginning with the first and ending with the last of those occasions, and

(c) each of the terms is a term to which an intermittent custody order relates.

(2) The offender is not to be treated as having served all the required custodial days in relation to any of the terms of imprisonment until he has served the aggregate of all the required custodial days in relation to each of them.

(3) After the number of days served by the offender in prison is equal to the aggregate of the required custodial days in relation to each of the terms of imprisonment, the offender is to be on licence until the relevant time and subject to such conditions as are required by this Chapter in respect of any of the terms of imprisonment, and none of the terms is to be regarded for any purpose as continuing after the relevant time.

(4) In subsection (3) 'the relevant time' means the time when the offender would, but for his release, have served a term equal in length to the aggregate of—

(a) all the required custodial days in relation to the terms of imprisonment, and

(b) the longest of the total licence periods in relation to those terms.

265[3] Restriction on consecutive sentences for released prisoners

(1) A court sentencing a person to a term of imprisonment may not order or direct that the term is to commence on the expiry of any other sentence of imprisonment from which he had been released early under this Chapter.

---

[3] Section 265 is only partially commenced at the time of editing.

Release on licence

Criminal Justice Act 2003

237 Meaning of 'fixed-term prisoner'
(1) In this Chapter 'fixed-term prisoner' means—
   (a) a person serving a sentence of imprisonment for a determinate term, or
   (b) a person serving a determinate sentence of detention under section 91 of the Sentencing Act or under section 228 of this Act.

(2) In this Chapter, unless the context otherwise requires, 'prisoner' includes a person serving a sentence falling within subsection (1)(b); and 'prison' includes any place where a person serving such a sentence is liable to be detained.

238 Power of court to recommend licence conditions for certain prisoners
(1) A court which sentences an offender to a term of imprisonment of twelve months or more in respect of any offence may, when passing sentence, recommend to the Secretary of State particular conditions which in its view should be included in any licence granted to the offender under this Chapter on his release from prison.

(2) In exercising his powers under section 250(4)(b) in respect of an offender, the Secretary of State must have regard to any recommendation.

239 The Parole Board
(1) The Parole Board is to continue to be, by that name, a body corporate and as such is—
   (a) to be constituted in accordance with this Chapter, and
   (b) to have the functions conferred on it by this Chapter in respect of fixed-term prisoners and by Chapter 2 of Part 2 of the Crime (Sentences) Act 1997 (c. 43) (in this Chapter referred to as 'the 1997 Act') in respect of life prisoners within the meaning of that Chapter.

(2) It is the duty of the Board to advise the Secretary of State with respect to any matter referred to it by him which is to do with the early release or recall of prisoners.

(3) The Board must, in dealing with cases as respects which it makes recommendations under this Chapter or under Chapter 2 of Part 2 of the 1997 Act, consider—
   (a) any documents given to it by the Secretary of State, and
   (b) any other oral or written information obtained by it;
and if in any particular case the Board thinks it necessary to interview the person to whom the case relates before reaching a decision, the Board may authorise one of its members to interview him and must consider the report of the interview made by that member.

240 Crediting of periods of remand in custody: terms of imprisonment and detention
(1) This section applies where—
   (a) a court sentences an offender to imprisonment for a term in respect of an offence committed after the commencement of this section, and
   (b) the offender has been remanded in custody (within the meaning given by section 242) in connection with the offence or a related offence, that is to say, any other offence the charge for which was founded on the same facts or evidence.

(2) It is immaterial for that purpose whether the offender—
   (a) has also been remanded in custody in connection with other offences; or
   (b) has also been detained in connection with other matters.

(3) Subject to subsection (4), the court must direct that the number of days for which the offender was remanded in custody in connection with the offence or a related offence is to count as time served by him as part of the sentence.

(4) Subsection (3) does not apply if and to the extent that—
  (a) rules made by the Secretary of State so provide in the case of—
    (i) a remand in custody which is wholly or partly concurrent with a sentence of imprisonment, or
    (ii) sentences of imprisonment for consecutive terms or for terms which are wholly or partly concurrent, or
  (b) it is in the opinion of the court just in all the circumstances not to give a direction under that subsection.
(5) Where the court gives a direction under subsection (3), it shall state in open court—
  (a) the number of days for which the offender was remanded in custody, and
  (b) the number of days in relation to which the direction is given.

Release on licence[1]

244 Duty to release prisoners

(1) As soon as a fixed-term prisoner, other than a prisoner to whom section 247 applies, has served the requisite custodial period, it is the duty of the Secretary of State to release him on licence under this section.
(2) Subsection (1) is subject to section 245.
(3) In this section 'the requisite custodial period' means—
  (a) in relation to a person serving a sentence of imprisonment for a term of twelve months or more or any determinate sentence of detention under section 91 of the Sentencing Act, one-half of his sentence,
  (b) in relation to a person serving a sentence of imprisonment for a term of less than twelve months (other than one to which an intermittent custody order relates), the custodial period within the meaning of section 181,
  (c) in relation to a person serving a sentence of imprisonment to which an intermittent custody order relates, any part of the term which for the purposes of section 183 (as read with section 263(2) or 264A(2) in the case of concurrent or consecutive sentences) is not a licence period, and
  (d) in relation to a person serving two or more concurrent or consecutive sentences, none of which falls within paragraph (c), the period determined under sections 263(2) and 264(2).

246 Power to release prisoners on licence before required to do so

(1) Subject to subsections (2) to (4), the Secretary of State may—
  (a) release on licence under this section a fixed-term prisoner, other than an intermittent custody prisoner, at any time during the period of 135 days ending with the day on which the prisoner will have served the requisite custodial period, and
  (b) release on licence under this section an intermittent custody prisoner when 135 or less of the required custodial days remain to be served.
(2) Subsection (1)(a) does not apply in relation to a prisoner unless—
  (a) the length of the requisite custodial period is at least 6 weeks,
  (b) he has served—
    (i) at least 4 weeks of his sentence, and
    (ii) at least one-half of the requisite custodial period.
(3) Subsection (1)(b) does not apply in relation to a prisoner unless—
  (a) the number of required custodial days is at least 42, and
  (b) the prisoner has served—
    (i) at least 28 of those days, and
    (ii) at least one-half of the total number of those days.

---

[1] Sections 244, 250 and 251 have only been partially commenced at the time of editing this book.

(4) Subsection (1) does not apply where—
    (a) the sentence is imposed under section 227 or 228,
    (b) the sentence is for an offence under section 1 of the Prisoners (Return to Custody) Act 1995 (c. 16),
    (c) the prisoner is subject to a hospital order, hospital direction or transfer direction under section 37, 45A or 47 of the Mental Health Act 1983 (c. 20),
    (d) the sentence was imposed by virtue of paragraph 9(1)(b) or (c) or 10(1)(b) or (c) of Schedule 8 in a case where the prisoner has failed to comply with a curfew requirement of a community order,
    (e) the prisoner is subject to the notification requirements of Part 2 of the Sexual Offences Act 2003 (c. 42),
    (f) the prisoner is liable to removal from the United Kingdom,
    (g) the prisoner has been released on licence under this section during the currency of the sentence, and has been recalled to prison under section 255(1)(a),
    (h) the prisoner has been released on licence under section 248 during the currency of the sentence, and has been recalled to prison under section 254, or
    (i) in the case of a prisoner to whom a direction under section 240 relates, the interval between the date on which the sentence was passed and the date on which the prisoner will have served the requisite custodial period is less than 14 days or, where the sentence is one of intermittent custody, the number of the required custodial days remaining to be served is less than 14.

247 Release on licence of prisoner serving extended sentence under section 227 or 228

    (1) This section applies to a prisoner who is serving an extended sentence imposed under section 227 or 228.
    (2) As soon as—
    (a) a prisoner to whom this section applies has served one-half of the appropriate custodial term, and
    (b) the Parole Board has directed his release under this section,
it is the duty of the Secretary of State to release him on licence.
    (3) The Parole Board may not give a direction under subsection (2) unless the Board is satisfied that it is no longer necessary for the protection of the public that the prisoner should be confined.
    (4) As soon as a prisoner to whom this section applies has served the appropriate custodial term, it is the duty of the Secretary of State to release him on licence unless the prisoner has previously been recalled under section 254.

248 Power to release prisoners on compassionate grounds

    (1) The Secretary of State may at any time release a fixed-term prisoner on licence if he is satisfied that exceptional circumstances exist which justify the prisoner's release on compassionate grounds.
    (2) Before releasing under this section a prisoner to whom section 247 applies, the Secretary of State must consult the Board, unless the circumstances are such as to render such consultation impracticable.

249 Duration of licence

    (1) Subject to subsections (2) and (3), where a fixed-term prisoner is released on licence, the licence shall, subject to any revocation under section 254 or 255, remain in force for the remainder of his sentence.
    (2) Where an intermittent custody prisoner is released on licence under section 244, the licence shall, subject to any revocation under section 254, remain in force—
    (a) until the time when he is required to return to prison at the beginning of the next custodial period of the sentence, or

(b) where it is granted at the end of the last custodial period, for the remainder of his sentence.

(3) Subsection (1) has effect subject to sections 263(2) (concurrent terms) and 264(3) and (4) (consecutive terms) and section 264A(3) (consecutive terms: intermittent custody).

250 Licence conditions

(1) In this section—

(a) 'the standard conditions' means such conditions as may be prescribed for the purposes of this section as standard conditions, and

(b) 'prescribed' means prescribed by the Secretary of State by order.

(2) Subject to subsection (6) and section 251, any licence under this Chapter in respect of a prisoner serving one or more sentences of imprisonment of less than twelve months and no sentence of twelve months or more—

(a) must include—

(i) the conditions required by the relevant court order, and

(ii) so far as not inconsistent with them, the standard conditions, and

(b) may also include—

(i) any condition which is authorised by section 62 of the Criminal Justice and Court Services Act 2000 (c. 43) (electronic monitoring) or section 64 of that Act (drug testing requirements) and which is compatible with the conditions required by the relevant court order, and

(ii) such other conditions of a kind prescribed for the purposes of this paragraph as the Secretary of State may for the time being consider to be necessary for the protection of the public and specify in the licence.

(4) Any licence under this Chapter in respect of a prisoner serving a sentence of imprisonment for a term of twelve months or more (including such a sentence imposed under section 227) or any sentence of detention under section 91 of the Sentencing Act or section 228 of this Act—

(a) must include the standard conditions, and

(b) may include—

(i) any condition authorised by section 62 or 64 of the Criminal Justice and Court Services Act 2000, and

(ii) such other conditions of a kind prescribed by the Secretary of State for the purposes of this paragraph as the Secretary of State may for the time being specify in the licence.

(5) A licence under section 246 must also include a curfew condition complying with section 253.

(7) The preceding provisions of this section have effect subject to section 263(3) (concurrent terms) and section 264(3) and (4) (consecutive terms) and section 264A(3) (consecutive terms: intermittent custody).

(8) In exercising his powers to prescribe standard conditions or the other conditions referred to in subsection (4)(b)(ii), the Secretary of State must have regard to the following purposes of the supervision of offenders while on licence under this Chapter—

(a) the protection of the public,

(b) the prevention of re-offending, and

(c) securing the successful re-integration of the prisoner into the community.

251 Licence conditions on re-release of prisoner serving sentence of less than 12 months

(1) In relation to any licence under this Chapter which is granted to a prisoner serving one or more sentences of imprisonment of less than twelve months and no sentence of twelve months or more on his release in pursuance of a decision of the Board under section 254 or 256, subsections (2) and (3) apply instead of section 250(2).

(2) The licence—

    (a) must include the standard conditions, and

    (b) may include—

        (i) any condition authorised by section 62 or 64 of the Criminal Justice and Court Services Act 2000 (c. 43), and

        (ii) such other conditions of a kind prescribed by the Secretary of State for the purposes of section 250(4)(b)(ii) as the Secretary of State may for the time being specify in the licence.

252   Duty to comply with licence conditions

A person subject to a licence under this Chapter must comply with such conditions as may for the time being be specified in the licence.

253   Curfew condition to be included in licence under section 246

(1) For the purposes of this Chapter, a curfew condition is a condition which—

    (a) requires the released person to remain, for periods for the time being specified in the condition, at a place for the time being so specified (which may be premises approved by the Secretary of State under section 9 of the Criminal Justice and Court Services Act 2000 (c. 43)), and

    (b) includes requirements for securing the electronic monitoring of his whereabouts during the periods for the time being so specified.

(2) The curfew condition may specify different places or different periods for different days, but may not specify periods which amount to less than 9 hours in any one day (excluding for this purpose the first and last days of the period for which the condition is in force).

(3) The curfew condition is to remain in force until the date when the released person would (but for his release) fall to be released on licence under section 244.

(4) Subsection (3) does not apply in relation to a released person to whom an intermittent custody order relates; and in relation to such a person the curfew condition is to remain in force until the number of days during which it has been in force is equal to the number of the required custodial days, as defined in section 246(6), that remained to be served at the time when he was released under section 246.

(5) The curfew condition must include provision for making a person responsible for monitoring the released person's whereabouts during the periods for the time being specified in the condition; and a person who is made so responsible shall be of a description specified in an order made by the Secretary of State.

Recall after release

254   Recall of prisoners while on licence

(1) The Secretary of State may, in the case of any prisoner who has been released on licence under this Chapter, revoke his licence and recall him to prison.

(2) A person recalled to prison under subsection (1)—

    (a) may make representations in writing with respect to his recall, and

    (b) on his return to prison, must be informed of the reasons for his recall and of his right to make representations.

(3) The Secretary of State must refer to the Board the case of a person recalled under subsection (1).

(4) Where on a reference under subsection (3) relating to any person the Board recommends his immediate release on licence under this Chapter, the Secretary of State must give effect to the recommendation.

(5) In the case of an intermittent custody prisoner who has not yet served in prison the number of custodial days specified in the intermittent custody order, any recommendation by the Board as to immediate release on licence is to be a recommendation as to his release on licence until the end of one of the licence periods specified by virtue of section 183(1)(b) in the intermittent custody order.

255   Recall of prisoners released early under section 246

(1) If it appears to the Secretary of State, as regards a person released on licence under section 246—

(a) that he has failed to comply with any condition included in his licence, or

(b) that his whereabouts can no longer be electronically monitored at the place for the time being specified in the curfew condition included in his licence,

the Secretary of State may, if the curfew condition is still in force, revoke the licence and recall the person to prison under this section.

(2) A person whose licence under section 246 is revoked under this section—

(a) may make representations in writing with respect to the revocation, and

(b) on his return to prison, must be informed of the reasons for the revocation and of his right to make representations.

256   Further release after recall

(1) Where on a reference under section 254(3) in relation to any person, the Board does not recommend his immediate release on licence under this Chapter, the Board must either—

(a) fix a date for the person's release on licence, or

(b) fix a date as the date for the next review of the person's case by the Board.

(2) Any date fixed under subsection (1)(a) or (b) must not be later than the first anniversary of the date on which the decision is taken.

(3) The Board need not fix a date under subsection (1)(a) or (b) if the prisoner will fall to be released unconditionally at any time within the next 12 months.

(4) Where the Board has fixed a date under subsection (1)(a), it is the duty of the Secretary of State to release him on licence on that date.

(5) On a review required by subsection (1)(b) in relation to any person, the Board may—

(a) recommend his immediate release on licence, or

(b) fix a date under subsection (1)(a) or (b).

Additional days

257   Additional days for disciplinary offences

(1) Prison rules, that is to say, rules made under section 47 of the Prison Act 1952 (c. 52), may include provision for the award of additional days—

(a) to fixed-term prisoners, or

(b) conditionally on their subsequently becoming such prisoners, to persons on remand,

who (in either case) are guilty of disciplinary offences.

(2) Where additional days are awarded to a fixed-term prisoner, or to a person on remand who subsequently becomes such a prisoner, and are not remitted in accordance with prison rules—

(a) any period which he must serve before becoming entitled to or eligible for release under this Chapter,

(b) any period which he must serve before he can be removed from prison under section 260, and

(c) any period for which a licence granted to him under this Chapter remains in force,

is extended by the aggregate of those additional days.

Fine defaulters and contemnors

258   Early release of fine defaulters and contemnors

(1) This section applies in relation to a person committed to prison—

(a) in default of payment of a sum adjudged to be paid by a conviction, or

(b) for contempt of court or any kindred offence.

(2) As soon as a person to whom this section applies has served one-half of the term for which he was committed, it is the duty of the Secretary of State to release him unconditionally.

(4) The Secretary of State may at any time release unconditionally a person to whom this section applies if he is satisfied that exceptional circumstances exist which justify the person's release on compassionate grounds.

(e) DANGEROUS OFFENDERS

Criminal Justice Act 2003

224   Meaning of 'specified offence' etc.

(1) An offence is a 'specified offence' for the purposes of this Chapter if it is a specified violent offence or a specified sexual offence.

(2) An offence is a 'serious offence' for the purposes of this Chapter if and only if—

(a) it is a specified offence, and

(b) it is, apart from section 225, punishable in the case of a person aged 18 or over by—

(i)   imprisonment for life, or

(ii) imprisonment for a determinate period of ten years or more.

(3) In this Chapter—

'relevant offence' has the meaning given by section 229(4);

'serious harm' means death or serious personal injury, whether physical or psychological;

'specified violent offence' means an offence specified in Part 1 of Schedule 15;

'specified sexual offence' means an offence specified in Part 2 of that Schedule.

225   Life sentence or imprisonment for public protection for serious offences

(1) This section applies where—

(a) a person aged 18 or over is convicted of a serious offence committed after the commencement of this section, and

(b) the court is of the opinion that there is a significant risk to members of the public of serious harm occasioned by the commission by him of further specified offences.

(2) If—

(a) the offence is one in respect of which the offender would apart from this section be liable to imprisonment for life, and

(b) the court considers that the seriousness of the offence, or of the offence and one or more offences associated with it, is such as to justify the imposition of a sentence of imprisonment for life,

the court must impose a sentence of imprisonment for life.

(3) In a case not falling within subsection (2), the court must impose a sentence of imprisonment for public protection.

(4) A sentence of imprisonment for public protection is a sentence of imprisonment for an indeterminate period, subject to the provisions of Chapter 2 of Part 2 of the Crime (Sentences) Act 1997 (c. 43) as to the release of prisoners and duration of licences.

(5) An offence the sentence for which is imposed under this section is not to be regarded as an offence the sentence for which is fixed by law.

226   Detention for life or detention for public protection for serious offences committed by those under 18

(1) This section applies where—

(a) a person aged under 18 is convicted of a serious offence committed after the commencement of this section, and

(b) the court is of the opinion that there is a significant risk to members of the public of serious harm occasioned by the commission by him of further specified offences.

(2) If—

(a) the offence is one in respect of which the offender would apart from this section be liable to a sentence of detention for life under section 91 of the Sentencing Act, and

(b) the court considers that the seriousness of the offence, or of the offence and one or more offences associated with it, is such as to justify the imposition of a sentence of detention for life,

the court must impose a sentence of detention for life under that section.

(3) If, in a case not falling within subsection (2), the court considers that an extended sentence under section 228 would not be adequate for the purpose of protecting the public from serious harm occasioned by the commission by the offender of further specified offences, the court must impose a sentence of detention for public protection.

227 Extended sentence for certain violent or sexual offences: persons 18 or over

(1) This section applies where—

(a) a person aged 18 or over is convicted of a specified offence, other than a serious offence, committed after the commencement of this section, and

(b) the court considers that there is a significant risk to members of the public of serious harm occasioned by the commission by the offender of further specified offences.

(2) The court must impose on the offender an extended sentence of imprisonment, that is to say, a sentence of imprisonment the term of which is equal to the aggregate of—

(a) the appropriate custodial term, and

(b) a further period ('the extension period') for which the offender is to be subject to a licence and which is of such length as the court considers necessary for the purpose of protecting members of the public from serious harm occasioned by the commission by him of further specified offences.

(3) In subsection (2) 'the appropriate custodial term' means a term of imprisonment (not exceeding the maximum term permitted for the offence) which—

(a) is the term that would (apart from this section) be imposed in compliance with section 153(2), or

(b) where the term that would be so imposed is a term of less than 12 months, is a term of 12 months.

(4) The extension period must not exceed—

(a) five years in the case of a specified violent offence, and

(b) eight years in the case of a specified sexual offence.

(5) The term of an extended sentence of imprisonment passed under this section in respect of an offence must not exceed the maximum term permitted for the offence.

228 Extended sentence for certain violent or sexual offences: persons under 18

(1) This section applies where—

(a) a person aged under 18 is convicted of a specified offence committed after the commencement of this section, and

(b) the court considers—

  (i) that there is a significant risk to members of the public of serious harm occasioned by the commission by the offender of further specified offences, and

  (ii) where the specified offence is a serious offence, that the case is not one in which the court is required by section 226(2) to impose a sentence of detention for life under section 91 of the Sentencing Act or by section 226(3) to impose a sentence of detention for public protection.

(2) The court must impose on the offender an extended sentence of detention, that is to say, a sentence of detention the term of which is equal to the aggregate of—

  (a) the appropriate custodial term, and

  (b) a further period ('the extension period') for which the offender is to be subject to a licence and which is of such length as the court considers necessary for the purpose of protecting members of the public from serious harm occasioned by the commission by him of further specified offences.

(3) In subsection (2) 'the appropriate custodial term' means such term as the court considers appropriate, which—

  (a) must be at least 12 months, and

  (b) must not exceed the maximum term of imprisonment permitted for the offence.

(4) The extension period must not exceed—

  (a) five years in the case of a specified violent offence, and

  (b) eight years in the case of a specified sexual offence.

(5) The term of an extended sentence of detention passed under this section in respect of an offence must not exceed the maximum term of imprisonment permitted for the offence.

229   The assessment of dangerousness

(1) This section applies where—

  (a) a person has been convicted of a specified offence, and

  (b) it falls to a court to assess under any of sections 225 to 228 whether there is a significant risk to members of the public of serious harm occasioned by the commission by him of further such offences.

(2) If at the time when that offence was committed the offender had not been convicted in any part of the United Kingdom of any relevant offence or was aged under 18, the court in making the assessment referred to in subsection (1)(b)—

  (a) must take into account all such information as is available to it about the nature and circumstances of the offence,

  (b) may take into account any information which is before it about any pattern of behaviour of which the offence forms part, and

  (c) may take into account any information about the offender which is before it.

(3) If at the time when that offence was committed the offender was aged 18 or over and had been convicted in any part of the United Kingdom of one or more relevant offences, the court must assume that there is such a risk as is mentioned in subsection (1)(b) unless, after taking into account—

  (a) all such information as is available to it about the nature and circumstances of each of the offences,

  (b) where appropriate, any information which is before it about any pattern of behaviour of which any of the offences forms part, and

  (c) any information about the offender which is before it,

the court considers that it would be unreasonable to conclude that there is such a risk.

231   Appeals where previous convictions set aside

(1) This section applies where—

  (a) a sentence has been imposed on any person under section 225 or 227, and

  (b) any previous conviction of his without which the court would not have been required to make the assumption mentioned in section 229(3) has been subsequently set aside on appeal.

(2) Notwithstanding anything in section 18 of the Criminal Appeal Act 1968 (c. 19), notice of appeal against the sentence may be given at any time within 28 days from the date on which the previous conviction was set aside.

232   Certificates of convictions for purposes of section 229

Where—

  (a) on any date after the commencement of this section a person is convicted in England and Wales of a relevant offence, and

(b) the court by or before which he is so convicted states in open court that he has been convicted of such an offence on that date, and

(c) that court subsequently certifies that fact,

that certificate shall be evidence, for the purposes of section 229, that he was convicted of such an offence on that date.

233 Offences under service law
Where—
(a) a person has at any time been convicted of an offence under section 70 of the Army Act 1955 (3 & 4 Eliz. 2 c. 18), section 70 of the Air Force Act 1955 (3 & 4 Eliz. 2 c. 19) or section 42 of the Naval Discipline Act 1957 (c. 53), and
(b) the corresponding civil offence (within the meaning of that Act) was a relevant offence,

section 229 shall have effect as if he had at that time been convicted in England and Wales of the corresponding civil offence.

234 Determination of day when offence committed
Where an offence is found to have been committed over a period of two or more days, or at some time during a period of two or more days, it shall be taken for the purposes of section 229 to have been committed on the last of those days.

235 Detention under sections 226 and 228
A person sentenced to be detained under section 226 or 228 is liable to be detained in such place, and under such conditions, as may be determined by the Secretary of State or by such other person as may be authorised by him for the purpose.

(f) SEX OFFENDERS

Notification requirements for sex offenders

Sexual Offences Act 2003

80 Persons becoming subject to notification requirements
(1) A person is subject to the notification requirements of this Part for the period set out in section 82 ('the notification period') if—
(a) he is convicted of an offence listed in Schedule 3;
(b) he is found not guilty of such an offence by reason of insanity;
(c) he is found to be under a disability and to have done the act charged against him in respect of such an offence; or
(d) in England and Wales or Northern Ireland, he is cautioned in respect of such an offence.
(2) A person for the time being subject to the notification requirements of this Part is referred to in this Part as a 'relevant offender'.

81 Persons formerly subject to Part 1 of the Sex Offenders Act 1997
(1) A person is, from the commencement of this Part until the end of the notification period, subject to the notification requirements of this Part if, before the commencement of this Part—
(a) he was convicted of an offence listed in Schedule 3;
(b) he was found not guilty of such an offence by reason of insanity;
(c) he was found to be under a disability and to have done the act charged against him in respect of such an offence; or

(d) in England and Wales or Northern Ireland, he was cautioned in respect of such an offence.

(2) Subsection (1) does not apply if the notification period ended before the commencement of this Part.

(3) Subsection (1)(a) does not apply to a conviction before 1st September 1997 unless, at the beginning of that day, the person—

(a) had not been dealt with in respect of the offence;

(b) was serving a sentence of imprisonment or a term of service detention, or was subject to a community order, in respect of the offence;

(c) was subject to supervision, having been released from prison after serving the whole or part of a sentence of imprisonment in respect of the offence; or

(d) was detained in a hospital or was subject to a guardianship order, following the conviction.

(4) Paragraphs (b) and (c) of subsection (1) do not apply to a finding made before 1st September 1997 unless, at the beginning of that day, the person—

(a) had not been dealt with in respect of the finding; or

(b) was detained in a hospital, following the finding.

(5) Subsection (1)(d) does not apply to a caution given before 1st September 1997.

(6) A person who would have been within subsection (3)(b) or (d) or (4)(b) but for the fact that at the beginning of 1st September 1997 he was unlawfully at large or absent without leave, on temporary release or leave of absence, or on bail pending an appeal, is to be treated as being within that provision.

(7) Where, immediately before the commencement of this Part, an order under a provision within subsection (8) wasin force in respect of a person, the person is subject to the notification requirements of this Part from that commencement until the order is discharged or otherwise ceases to have effect.

(8) The provisions are—

(a) section 5A of the Sex Offenders Act 1997 (c. 51) (restraining orders);

(b) section 2 of the Crime and Disorder Act 1998 (c. 37) (sex offender orders made in England and Wales);

(c) section 2A of the Crime and Disorder Act 1998 (interim orders made in England and Wales);

(d) section 20 of the Crime and Disorder Act 1998 (sex offender orders and interim orders made in Scotland);

(e) Article 6 of the Criminal Justice (Northern Ireland) Order 1998 (SI 1998/2839 (NI 20)) (sex offender orders made in Northern Ireland);

(f) Article 6A of the Criminal Justice (Northern Ireland) Order 1998 (interim orders made in Northern Ireland).

82   The notification period

(1) The notification period for a person within section 80(1) or 81(1) is the period in the second column of the following Table the description that applies to him.

Table

Description of relevant offender	Notification period
A person who, in respect of the offence, is or has been sentenced to imprisonment for life or for a term of 30 months or more	An indefinite period beginning with the relevant date
A person who, in respect of the offence, has been made the subject of an order under section 210F(1) of the Criminal Procedure (Scotland) Act 1995 (order for lifelong restriction)	An indefinite period beginning with that date

Table (*cont.*)

Description of relevant offender	Notification period
A person who, in respect of the offence or finding, is or has been admitted to a hospital subject to a restriction order	An indefinite period beginning with that date
A person who, in respect of the offence, is or has been sentenced to imprisonment for a term of more than 6 months but less than 30 months	10 years beginning with that date
A person who, in respect of the offence, is or has been sentenced to imprisonment for a term of 6 months or less	7 years beginning with that date
A person who, in respect of the offence or finding, is or has been admitted to a hospital without being subject to a restriction order	7 years beginning with that date
A person within section 80(1)(d)	2 years beginning with that date
A person in whose case an order for conditional discharge or, in Scotland, a probation order, is made in respect of the offence	The period of conditional discharge or, in Scotland, the probation period
A person of any other description	5 years beginning with the relevant date

(2) Where a person is under 18 on the relevant date, subsection (1) has effect as if for any reference to a period of 10 years, 7 years, 5 years or 2 years there were substituted a reference to one-half of that period.

(3) Subsection (4) applies where a relevant offender within section 80(1)(a) or 81(1)(a) is or has been sentenced, in respect of two or more offences listed in Schedule 3—
    (a) to consecutive terms of imprisonment; or
    (b) to terms of imprisonment which are partly concurrent.

(4) Where this subsection applies, subsection (1) has effect as if the relevant offender were or had been sentenced, in respect of each of the offences, to a term of imprisonment which—
    (a) in the case of consecutive terms, is equal to the aggregate of those terms;
    (b) in the case of partly concurrent terms (X and Y, which overlap for a period Z), is equal to X plus Y minus Z.

(5) Where a relevant offender the subject of a finding within section 80(1)(c) or 81(1)(c) is subsequently tried for the offence, the notification period relating to the finding ends at the conclusion of the trial.

(6) In this Part, 'relevant date' means—
    (a) in the case of a person within section 80(1)(a) or 81(1)(a), the date of the conviction;
    (b) in the case of a person within section 80(1)(b) or (c) or 81(1)(b) or (c), the date of the finding;
    (c) in the case of a person within section 80(1)(d) or 81(1)(d), the date of the caution;
    (d) in the case of a person within section 81(7), the date which, for the purposes of Part 1 of the Sex Offenders Act 1997 (c. 51), was the relevant date in relation to that person.

83 Notification requirements: initial notification
(1) A relevant offender must, within the period of 3 days beginning with the relevant date (or, if later, the commencement of this Part), notify to the police the information set out in subsection (5).

(2) Subsection (1) does not apply to a relevant offender in respect of a conviction, finding or caution within section 80(1) if—

  (a) immediately before the conviction, finding or caution, he was subject to the notification requirements of this Part as a result of another conviction, finding or caution or an order of a court ('the earlier event'),

  (b) at that time, he had made a notification under subsection (1) in respect of the earlier event, and

  (c) throughout the period referred to in subsection (1), he remains subject to the notification requirements as a result of the earlier event.

(3) Subsection (1) does not apply to a relevant offender in respect of a conviction, finding or caution within section 81(1) or an order within section 81(7) if the offender complied with section 2(1) of the Sex Offenders Act 1997 in respect of the conviction, finding, caution or order.

(4) Where a notification order is made in respect of a conviction, finding or caution, subsection (1) does not apply to the relevant offender in respect of the conviction, finding or caution if—

  (a) immediately before the order was made, he was subject to the notification requirements of this Part as a result of another conviction, finding or caution or an order of a court ('the earlier event'),

  (b) at that time, he had made a notification under subsection (1) in respect of the earlier event, and

  (c) throughout the period referred to in subsection (1), he remains subject to the notification requirements as a result of the earlier event.

(5) The information is—

  (a) the relevant offender's date of birth;

  (b) his national insurance number;

  (c) his name on the relevant date and, where he used one or more other names on that date, each of those names;

  (d) his home address on the relevant date;

  (e) his name on the date on which notification is given and, where he uses one or more other names on that date, each of those names;

  (f) his home address on the date on which notification is given;

  (g) the address of any other premises in the United Kingdom at which, at the time the notification is given, he regularly resides or stays.

(6) When determining the period for the purpose of subsection (1), there is to be disregarded any time when the relevant offender is—

  (a) remanded in or committed to custody by an order of a court;

  (b) serving a sentence of imprisonment or a term of service detention;

  (c) detained in a hospital; or

  (d) outside the United Kingdom.

(7) In this Part, 'home address' means, in relation to any person—

  (a) the address of his sole or main residence in the United Kingdom, or

  (b) where he has no such residence, the address or location of a place in the United Kingdom where he can regularly be found and, if there is more than one such place, such one of those places as the person may select.

84 Notification requirements: changes

(1) A relevant offender must, within the period of 3 days beginning with—

  (a) his using a name which has not been notified to the police under section 83(1), this subsection, or section 2 of the Sex Offenders Act 1997 (c. 51),

  (b) any change of his home address,

  (c) his having resided or stayed, for a qualifying period, at any premises in the United Kingdom the address of which has not been notified to the police under section 83(1), this subsection, or section 2 of the Sex Offenders Act 1997, or

(d) his release from custody pursuant to an order of a court or from imprisonment, service detention or detention in a hospital,

notify to the police that name, the new home address, the address of those premises or (as the case may be) the fact that he has been released, and (in addition) the information set out in section 83(5).

(2) A notification under subsection (1) may be given before the name is used, the change of home address occurs or the qualifying period ends, but in that case the relevant offender must also specify the date when the event is expected to occur.

(3) If a notification is given in accordance with subsection (2) and the event to which it relates occurs more than 2 days before the date specified, the notification does not affect the duty imposed by subsection (1).

(4) If a notification is given in accordance with subsection (2) and the event to which it relates has not occurred by the end of the period of 3 days beginning with the date specified—

(a) the notification does not affect the duty imposed by subsection (1), and

(b) the relevant offender must, within the period of 6 days beginning with the date specified, notify to the police the fact that the event did not occur within the period of 3 days beginning with the date specified.

(5) Section 83(6) applies to the determination of the period of 3 days mentioned in subsection (1) and the period of 6 days mentioned in subsection (4)(b), as it applies to the determination of the period mentioned in section 83(1).

(6) In this section, 'qualifying period' means—

(a) a period of 7 days, or

(b) two or more periods, in any period of 12 months, which taken together amount to 7 days.

85 Notification requirements: periodic notification

(1) A relevant offender must, within the period of one year after each event within subsection (2), notify to the police the information set out in section 83(5), unless within that period he has given a notification under section 84(1).

(2) The events are—

(a) the commencement of this Part (but only in the case of a person who is a relevant offender from that commencement);

(b) any notification given by the relevant offender under section 83(1) or 84(1); and

(c) any notification given by him under subsection (1).

(3) Where the period referred to in subsection (1) would (apart from this subsection) end whilst subsection (4) applies to the relevant offender, that period is to be treated as continuing until the end of the period of 3 days beginning when subsection (4) first ceases to apply to him.

(4) This subsection applies to the relevant offender if he is—

(a) remanded in or committed to custody by an order of a court,

(b) serving a sentence of imprisonment or a term of service detention,

(c) detained in a hospital, or

(d) outside the United Kingdom.

86 Notification requirements: travel outside the United Kingdom

(1) The Secretary of State may by regulations make provision requiring relevant offenders who leave the United Kingdom, or any description of such offenders—

(a) to give in accordance with the regulations, before they leave, a notification under subsection (2);

(b) if they subsequently return to the United Kingdom, to give in accordance with the regulations a notification under subsection (3).

(2) A notification under this subsection must disclose—

(a) the date on which the offender will leave the United Kingdom;

(b) the country (or, if there is more than one, the first country) to which he will travel and his point of arrival (determined in accordance with the regulations) in that country;

(c) any other information prescribed by the regulations which the offender holds about his departure from or return to the United Kingdom or his movements while outside the United Kingdom.

(3) A notification under this subsection must disclose any information prescribed by the regulations about the offender's return to the United Kingdom.

(4) Regulations under subsection (1) may make different provision for different categories of person.

87   Method of notification and related matters

(1) A person gives a notification under section 83(1), 84(1) or 85(1) by—

(a) attending at such police station in his local police area as the Secretary of State may by regulations prescribe or, if there is more than one, at any of them, and

(b) giving an oral notification to any police officer, or to any person authorised for the purpose by the officer in charge of the station.

(2) A person giving a notification under section 84(1)—

(a) in relation to a prospective change of home address, or

(b) in relation to premises referred to in subsection (1)(c) of that section,

may give the notification at a police station that would fall within subsection (1) above if the change in home address had already occurred or (as the case may be) if the address of those premises were his home address.

(3) Any notification under this section must be acknowledged; and an acknowledgment under this subsection must be in writing, and in such form as the Secretary of State may direct.

(4) Where a notification is given under section 83(1), 84(1) or 85(1), the relevant offender must, if requested to do so by the police officer or person referred to in subsection (1)(b), allow the officer or person to—

(a) take his fingerprints,

(b) photograph any part of him, or

(c) do both these things.

(5) The power in subsection (4) is exercisable for the purpose of verifying the identity of the relevant offender.

(6) Regulations under subsection (1) may make different provision for different categories of person.

88   Section 87: interpretation

(1) Subsections (2) to (4) apply for the purposes of section 87.

(2) 'Photograph' includes any process by means of which an image may be produced.

(3) 'Local police area' means, in relation to a person—

(a) the police area in which his home address is situated;

(b) in the absence of a home address, the police area in which the home address last notified is situated;

(c) in the absence of a home address and of any such notification, the police area in which the court which last dealt with the person in a way mentioned in subsection (4) is situated.

(4) The ways are—

(a) dealing with a person in respect of an offence listed in Schedule 3 or a finding in relation to such an offence;

(b) dealing with a person in respect of an offence under section 128 or a finding in relation to such an offence;

(c) making, in respect of a person, a notification order, interim notification order, sexual offences preventionorder or interim sexual offences prevention order;

(d) making, in respect of a person, an order under section 2, 2A or 20 of the Crime and Disorder Act 1998 (c. 37) (sex offender orders and interim orders made in England and Wales or Scotland) or Article 6 or 6A of the Criminal Justice (Northern Ireland) Order 1998 (SI 1998/2839 (NI 20)) (sex offender orders and interim orders made in Northern Ireland);

and in paragraphs (a) and (b), 'finding' in relation to an offence means a finding of not guilty of the offence by reason of insanity or a finding that the person was under a disability and did the act or omission charged against him in respect of the offence.

(5) Subsection (3) applies as if Northern Ireland were a police area.

89 Young offenders: parental directions

(1) Where a person within the first column of the following Table ('the young offender') is under 18 (or, in Scotland, 16) when he is before the court referred to in the second column of the Table opposite the description that applies to him, that court may direct that subsection (2) applies in respect of an individual ('the parent') having parental responsibility for (or, in Scotland, parental responsibilities in relation to) the young offender.

Table

Description of person	Court which may make the direction
A relevant offender within section 80(1)(a) to (c) or 81(1)(a) to (c)	The court which deals with the offender in respect of the offence or finding
A relevant offender within section 129(1)(a) to (c)	The court which deals with the offender in respect of the offence or finding
A person who is the subject of a notification order, interim notification order, sexual offences prevention order or interim sexual offences prevention order	The court which makes the order
A relevant offender who is the defendant to an application under subsection (4) (or, in Scotland, the subject of an application under subsection (5))	The court which hears the application

(2) Where this subsection applies—
(a) the obligations that would (apart from this subsection) be imposed by or under sections 83 to 86 on the young offender are to be treated instead as obligations on the parent, and
(b) the parent must ensure that the young offender attends at the police station with him, when a notification is being given.
(3) A direction under subsection (1) takes immediate effect and applies—
(a) until the young offender attains the age of 18 (or, where a court in Scotland gives the direction, 16); or
(b) for such shorter period as the court may, at the time the direction is given, direct.
(4) A chief officer of police may, by complaint to any magistrates' court whose commission area includes any part of his police area, apply for a direction under subsection (1) in respect of a relevant offender ('the defendant')—
(a) who resides in his police area, or who the chief officer believes is in or is intending to come to his police area, and
(b) who the chief officer believes is under 18.
(5) In Scotland, a chief constable may, by summary application to any sheriff within whose sheriffdom lies any part of the area of his police force, apply for a direction under subsection (1) in respect of a relevant offender ('the subject')—

    (a) who resides in that area, or who the chief constable believes is in or is intending to come to that area, and

    (b) who the chief constable believes is under 16.

90   Parental directions: variations, renewals and discharges

(1) A person within subsection (2) may apply to the appropriate court for an order varying, renewing or discharging a direction under section 89(1).

(2) The persons are—

    (a) the young offender;

    (b) the parent;

    (c) the chief officer of police for the area in which the young offender resides;

    (d) a chief officer of police who believes that the young offender is in, or is intending to come to, his police area;

    (e) in Scotland, where the appropriate court is a civil court—

        (i) the chief constable of the police force within the area of which the young offender resides;

        (ii) a chief constable who believes that the young offender is in, or is intending to come to, the area of his police force,

    and in any other case, the prosecutor;

    (f) where the direction was made on an application under section 89(4), the chief officer of police who made the application;

    (g) where the direction was made on an application under section 89(5), the chief constable who made the application.

(3) An application under subsection (1) may be made—

    (a) where the appropriate court is the Crown Court (or in Scotland a criminal court), in accordance with rules of court;

    (b) in any other case, by complaint (or, in Scotland, by summary application).

(4) On the application the court, after hearing the person making the application and (if they wish to be heard) the other persons mentioned in subsection (2), may make any order, varying, renewing or discharging the direction, that the court considers appropriate.

(5) In this section, the 'appropriate court' means—

    (a) where the Court of Appeal made the order, the Crown Court;

    (b) in any other case, the court that made the direction under section 89(1).

91   Offences relating to notification

(1) A person commits an offence if he—

    (a) fails, without reasonable excuse, to comply with section 83(1), 84(1), 84(4)(b), 85(1), 87(4) or 89(2)(b) or any requirement imposed by regulations made under section 86(1); or

    (b) notifies to the police, in purported compliance with section 83(1), 84(1) or 85(1) or any requirement imposed by regulations made under section 86(1), any information which he knows to be false.

(2) A person guilty of an offence under this section is liable—

    (a) on summary conviction, to imprisonment for a term not exceeding 6 months or a fine not exceeding the statutory maximum or both;

    (b) on conviction on indictment, to imprisonment for a term not exceeding 5 years.

(3) A person commits an offence under paragraph (a) of subsection (1) on the day on which he first fails, without reasonable excuse, to comply with section 83(1), 84(1) or 85(1) or a requirement imposed by regulations made under section 86(1), and continues to commit it throughout any period during which the failure continues; but a person must not be prosecuted under subsection (1) more than once in respect of the same failure.

(4) Proceedings for an offence under this section may be commenced in any court—

    (a) having jurisdiction in any place where the accused—

        (i) resides;

      (ii) is last known to have resided; or

      (iii) is found;

  (b) which has convicted the accused of an offence if the accused is subject to the notification requirements of this Part by virtue of that conviction; or

  (c) which has made an order under section 104(1)(b) in respect of the accused if the accused is subject to those requirements by virtue of that order.

92 Certificates for purposes of Part 2

  (1) Subsection (2) applies where on any date a person is—

    (a) convicted of an offence listed in Schedule 3;

    (b) found not guilty of such an offence by reason of insanity; or

    (c) found to be under a disability and to have done the act charged against him in respect of such an offence.

  (2) If the court by or before which the person is so convicted or found—

    (a) states in open court—

      (i)   that on that date he has been convicted, found not guilty by reason of insanity or found to be under a disability and to have done the act charged against him, and

      (ii) that the offence in question is an offence listed in Schedule 3, and

    (b) certifies those facts, whether at the time or subsequently,

the certificate is, for the purposes of this Part, evidence (or, in Scotland, sufficient evidence) of those facts.

  (3) Subsection (4) applies where on any date a person is, in England and Wales or Northern Ireland, cautioned in respect of an offence listed in Schedule 3.

  (4) If the constable—

    (a) informs the person that he has been cautioned on that date and that the offence in question is an offence listed in Schedule 3, and

    (b) certifies those facts, whether at the time or subsequently, in such form as the Secretary of State may by order prescribe,

the certificate is, for the purposes of this Part, evidence (or, in Scotland, sufficient evidence) of those facts.

(g) LIFE SENTENCES

Powers of Criminal Courts (Sentencing) Act 2000

82A Life sentences

  (1) This section applies if a court passes a life sentence in circumstances where the sentence is not fixed by law.

  (2) The court shall, unless it makes an order under subsection (4) below, order that the provisions of section 28(5) to (8) of the Crime (Sentences) Act 1997 (referred to in this section as the 'early release provisions') shall apply to the offender as soon as he has served the part of his sentence which is specified in the order.

  (3) The part of his sentence shall be such as the court considers appropriate taking into account—

    (a) the seriousness of the offence, or of the combination of the offence and one or more offences associated with it;

    (b) the effect of any direction which it would have given under section 240 of the Criminal Justice Act 2003 (crediting periods of remand in custody) if it had sentenced him to a term of imprisonment; and

    (c) the early release provisions as compared with section 244(1) of the Criminal Justice Act 2003.

(4) If the offender was aged 21 or over when he committed the offence and the court is of the opinion that, because of the seriousness of the offence or of the combination of the offence and one or more offences associated with it, no order should be made under subsection (2) above, the court shall order that the early release provisions shall not apply to the offender.

(4A) No order under subsection (4) above may be made where the life sentence is—

(a) a sentence of imprisonment for public protection under section 225 of the Criminal Justice Act 2003, or

(b) a sentence of detention for public protection under section 226 of that Act.

(7) In this section—

'court' includes a court-martial;

'life sentence' has the same meaning as in Chapter II of Part II of the Crime (Sentences) Act 1997.

Criminal Justice Act 2003

EFFECT OF LIFE SENTENCE

269   Determination of minimum term in relation to mandatory life sentence

(1) This section applies where after the commencement of this section a court passes a life sentence in circumstances where the sentence is fixed by law.

(2) The court must, unless it makes an order under subsection (4), order that the provisions of section 28(5) to (8) of the Crime (Sentences) Act 1997 (referred to in this Chapter as 'the early release provisions') are to apply to the offender as soon as he has served the part of his sentence which is specified in the order.

(3) The part of his sentence is to be such as the court considers appropriate taking into account—

(a) the seriousness of the offence, or of the combination of the offence and any one or more offences associated with it, and

(b) the effect of any direction which it would have given under section 240 (crediting periods of remand in custody) if it had sentenced him to a term of imprisonment.

(4) If the offender was 21 or over when he committed the offence and the court is of the opinion that, because of the seriousness of the offence, or of the combination of the offence and one or more offences associated with it, no order should be made under subsection (2), the court must order that the early release provisions are not to apply to the offender.

(5) In considering under subsection (3) or (4) the seriousness of an offence (or of the combination of an offence and one or more offences associated with it), the court must have regard to—

(a) the general principles set out in Schedule 21, and

(b) any guidelines relating to offences in general which are relevant to the case and are not incompatible with the provisions of Schedule 21.

270   Duty to give reasons

(1) Any court making an order under subsection (2) or (4) of section 269 must state in open court, in ordinary language, its reasons for deciding on the order made.

(2) In stating its reasons the court must, in particular—

(a) state which of the starting points in Schedule 21 it has chosen and its reasons for doing so, and

(b) state its reasons for any departure from that starting point.

SCHEDULE 21   DETERMINATION OF MINIMUM TERM
IN RELATION TO MANDATORY LIFE SENTENCE

Interpretation

1 In this Schedule—

'child' means a person under 18 years;

'mandatory life sentence' means a life sentence passed in circumstances where the sentence is fixed by law;

'minimum term', in relation to a mandatory life sentence, means the part of the sentence to be specified in an order under section 269(2);

'whole life order' means an order under subsection (4) of section 269.

2 Section 28 of the Crime and Disorder Act 1998 (c. 37) (meaning of 'racially or religiously aggravated') applies for the purposes of this Schedule as it applies for the purposes of sections 29 to 32 of that Act.

3 For the purposes of this Schedule an offence is aggravated by sexual orientation if it is committed in circumstances falling within subsection (2)(a)(i) or (b)(i) of section 146.

Starting points

4 (1) If—

    (a) the court considers that the seriousness of the offence (or the combination of the offence and one or more offences associated with it) is exceptionally high, and

    (b) the offender was aged 21 or over when he committed the offence,

the appropriate starting point is a whole life order.

    (2) Cases that would normally fall within sub-paragraph (1)(a) include—

    (a) the murder of two or more persons, where each murder involves any of the following—

        (i)   a substantial degree of premeditation or planning,

        (ii) the abduction of the victim, or

        (iii) sexual or sadistic conduct,

    (b) the murder of a child if involving the abduction of the child or sexual or sadistic motivation,

    (c) a murder done for the purpose of advancing a political, religious or ideological cause, or

    (d) a murder by an offender previously convicted of murder.

5 (1) If—

    (a) the case does not fall within paragraph 4(1) but the court considers that the seriousness of the offence (or the combination of the offence and one or more offences associated with it) is particularly high, and

    (b) the offender was aged 18 or over when he committed the offence,

the appropriate starting point, in determining the minimum term, is 30 years.

    (2) Cases that (if not falling within paragraph 4(1)) would normally fall within sub-paragraph (1)(a) include—

    (a) the murder of a police officer or prison officer in the course of his duty,

    (b) a murder involving the use of a firearm or explosive,

    (c) a murder done for gain (such as a murder done in the course or furtherance of robbery or burglary, done for payment or done in the expectation of gain as a result of the death),

    (d) a murder intended to obstruct or interfere with the course of justice,

    (e) a murder involving sexual or sadistic conduct,

    (f) the murder of two or more persons,

    (g) a murder that is racially or religiously aggravated or aggravated by sexual orientation, or

  (h) a murder falling within paragraph 4(2) committed by an offender who was aged
    under 21 when he committed the offence.
6 If the offender was aged 18 or over when he committed the offence and the case does not
fall within paragraph 4(1) or 5(1), the appropriate starting point, in determining the minimum term, is 15 years.
7 If the offender was aged under 18 when he committed the offence, the appropriate
starting point, in determining the minimum term, is 12 years.

Aggravating and mitigating factors

8 Having chosen a starting point, the court should take into account any aggravating or
mitigating factors, to the extent that it has not allowed for them in its choice of starting point.
9 Detailed consideration of aggravating or mitigating factors may result in a minimum term
of any length (whatever the starting point), or in the making of a whole life order.
10 Aggravating factors (additional to those mentioned in paragraph 4(2) and 5(2)) that may
be relevant to the offence of murder include—
  (a) a significant degree of planning or premeditation,
  (b) the fact that the victim was particularly vulnerable because of age or disability,
  (c) mental or physical suffering inflicted on the victim before death,
  (d) the abuse of a position of trust,
  (e) the use of duress or threats against another person to facilitate the commission of
    the offence,
  (f) the fact that the victim was providing a public service or performing a public
    duty, and
  (g) concealment, destruction or dismemberment of the body.
11 Mitigating factors that may be relevant to the offence of murder include—
  (a) an intention to cause serious bodily harm rather than to kill,
  (b) lack of premeditation,
  (c) the fact that the offender suffered from any mental disorder or mental disability
    which (although not falling within section 2(1) of the Homicide Act 1957 (c. 11)),
    lowered his degree of culpability,
  (d) the fact that the offender was provoked (for example, by prolonged stress) in a
    way not amounting to a defence of provocation,
  (e) the fact that the offender acted to any extent in self-defence,
  (f) a belief by the offender that the murder was an act of mercy, and
  (g) the age of the offender.
12 Nothing in this Schedule restricts the application of—
  (a) section 143(2) (previous convictions),
  (b) section 143(3) (bail), or
  (c) section 144 (guilty plea).

(h) COMMUNITY ORDERS

Powers of Criminal Courts (Sentencing)
Act 2000 (as amended)

GENERAL PROVISIONS

33 **Meaning of 'youth community order' and 'community sentence'**
 (1) In this Act 'youth community order' means any of the following orders—
  (a) a curfew order;
  (b) an exclusion order;

(c) an attendance centre order;

(d) a supervision order;

(e) an action plan order.

(2) In this Act 'community sentence' means a sentence which consists of or includes—

(a) a community order under section 177 of the Criminal Justice Act 2003, or

(b) one or more youth community orders.

Criminal Justice Act 2003

177   Community orders

(1) Where a person aged 16 or over is convicted of an offence, the court by or before which he is convicted may make an order (in this Part referred to as a 'community order') imposing on him any one or more of the following requirements—

(a) an unpaid work requirement (as defined by section 199),

(b) an activity requirement (as defined by section 201),

(c) a programme requirement (as defined by section 202),

(d) a prohibited activity requirement (as defined by section 203),

(e) a curfew requirement (as defined by section 204),

(f) an exclusion requirement (as defined by section 205),

(g) a residence requirement (as defined by section 206),

(h) a mental health treatment requirement (as defined by section 207),

(i) a drug rehabilitation requirement (as defined by section 209),

(j) an alcohol treatment requirement (as defined by section 212),

(k) a supervision requirement (as defined by section 213), and

(l) in a case where the offender is aged under 25, an attendance centre requirement (as defined by ection 214).

(2) Subsection (1) has effect subject to sections 150 and 218 and to the following provisions of Chapter 4 relating to particular requirements—

(a) section 199(3) (unpaid work requirement),

(b) section 201(3) and (4) (activity requirement),

(c) section 202(4) and (5) (programme requirement),

(d) section 203(2) (prohibited activity requirement),

(e) section 207(3) (mental health treatment requirement),

(f) section 209(2) (drug rehabilitation requirement), and

(g) section 212(2) and (3) (alcohol treatment requirement).

(3) Where the court makes a community order imposing a curfew requirement or an exclusion requirement, the court must also impose an electronic monitoring requirement (as defined by section 215) unless—

(a) it is prevented from doing so by section 215(2) or 218(4), or

(b) in the particular circumstances of the case, it considers it inappropriate to do so.

(4) Where the court makes a community order imposing an unpaid work requirement, an activity requirement, a programme requirement, a prohibited activity requirement, a residence requirement, a mental health treatment requirement, a drug rehabilitation requirement, an alcohol treatment requirement, a supervision requirement or an attendance centre requirement, the court may also impose an electronic monitoring requirement unless prevented from doing so by section 215(2) or 218(4).

(5) A community order must specify a date, not more than three years after the date of the order, by which all the requirements in it must have been complied with; and a community order which imposes two or more different requirements falling within subsection (1) may also specify an earlier date or dates in relation to compliance with any one or more of them.

178   Power to provide for court review of community orders

(1) The Secretary of State may by order—

    (a) enable or require a court making a community order to provide for the community order to be reviewed periodically by that or another court,

    (b) enable a court to amend a community order so as to include or remove a provision for review by a court, and

    (c) make provision as to the timing and conduct of reviews and as to the powers of the court on a review.

179   Breach, revocation or amendment of community order

Schedule 8 (which relates to failures to comply with the requirements of community orders and to the revocation or amendment of such orders) shall have effect.

Powers of Criminal Courts (Sentencing) Act 2000 (as amended)

36B   Electronic monitoring of requirements in youth community orders

(1) Subject to subsections (2) and (3) below, a youth community order may include requirements for securing the electronic monitoring of the offender's compliance with any other requirements imposed by the order.

(2) A court shall not include in a youth community order a requirement under subsection (1) above unless the court—

    (a) has been notified by the Secretary of State that electronic monitoring arrangements are available in the relevant areas specified in subsections (7) to (10) below; and

    (b) is satisfied that the necessary provision can be made under those arrangements.

(3) Where—

    (a) it is proposed to include in an exclusion order a requirement for securing electronic monitoring in accordance with this section; but

    (b) there is a person (other than the offender) without whose co-operation it will not be practicable to secure the monitoring,

the requirement shall not be included in the order without that person's consent.

(5) An order which includes requirements under subsection (1) above shall include provision for making a person responsible for the monitoring; and a person who is made so responsible shall be of a description specified in an order made by the Secretary of State.

(6) The Secretary of State may make rules for regulating—

    (a) the electronic monitoring of compliance with requirements included in a youth community order; and

    (b) without prejudice to the generality of paragraph (a) above, the functions of persons made responsible for securing the electronic monitoring of compliance with requirements included in the order.

(7) In the case of a curfew order or an exclusion order, the relevant area is the area in which the place proposed to be specified in the order is situated.

In this subsection, 'place', in relation to an exclusion order, has the same meaning as in section 40A below.

(9) In the case of a supervision order or an action plan order, the relevant area is the local justice area proposed to be specified in the order.

(10) In the case of an attendance centre order, the relevant area is the local justice area in which the attendance centre proposed to be specified in the order is situated.

CURFEW ORDERS

37   Curfew orders

(1) Where a person age under 16 is convicted of an offence, the court by or before which he is convicted may (subject to sections 148, 150 and 156 of the Criminal Justice Act 2003)

make an order requiring him to remain, for periods specified in the order, at a place so specified.

(3) A curfew order may specify different places or different periods for different days, but shall not specify—

> (a) periods which fall outside the period of six months beginning with the day on which it is made; or
> (b) periods which amount to less than two hours or more than twelve hours in any one day.

(5) The requirements in a curfew order shall, as far as practicable, be such as to avoid—

> (a) any conflict with the offender's religious beliefs or with the requirements of any other youth community order to which he may be subject; and
> (b) any interference with the times, if any, at which he normally works or attends school or any other educational establishment.

(6) A curfew order shall include provision for making a person responsible for monitoring the offender's whereabouts during the curfew periods specified in the order; and a person who is made so responsible shall be of a description specified in an order made by the Secretary of State.

(7) A court shall not make a curfew order unless the court has been notified by the Secretary of State that arrangements for monitoring the offender's whereabouts are available in the area in which the place proposed to be specified in the order is situated and the notice has not been withdrawn.

(8) Before making a curfew order, the court shall obtain and consider information about the place proposed to be specified in the order (including information as to the attitude of persons likely to be affected by the enforced presence there of the offender).

(9) Before making a curfew order in respect of an offender, the court shall obtain and consider information about his family circumstances and the likely effect of such an order on those circumstances.

39 Breach, revocation and amendment of curfew orders

Schedule 3 to this Act (which makes provision for dealing with failures to comply with the requirements of certain youth community orders, for revoking such orders with or without the substitution of other sentences and for amending such orders) shall have effect so far as relating to curfew orders.

40 Curfew orders: supplementary

(1) The Secretary of State may make rules for regulating—

> (a) the monitoring of the whereabouts of persons who are subject to curfew orders; and
> (b) without prejudice to the generality of paragraph (a) above, the functions of the responsible officers of persons who are subject to curfew orders.

(2) The Secretary of State may by order direct—

> (a) that subsection (3) of section 37 above shall have effect with the substitution, for any period there specified, of such period as may be specified in the order; or
> (b) that subsection (5) of that section shall have effect with such additional restrictions as may be so specified.

ATTENDANCE CENTRE ORDERS

60 Attendance centre orders

(1) Where—

> (a) (subject to sections 148, 150 and 156 of the Criminal Justice Act 2003) a person aged under 16 is convicted by or before a court of an offence punishable with imprisonment, or

(b) a court has power or would have power, but for section 89 below (restrictions on imprisonment of young offenders and defaulters), to commit a person aged under 16 to prison in default of payment of any sum of money or for failing to do or abstain from doing anything required to be done or left undone,

the court may, if it has been notified by the Secretary of State that an attendance centre is available for the reception of persons of his description, order him to attend at such a centre, to be specified in the order, for such number of hours as may be so specified.

(3) The aggregate number of hours for which an attendance centre order may require a person to attend at an attendance centre shall not be less than 12 except where—

(a) he is aged under 14; and

(b) the court is of the opinion that 12 hours would be excessive, having regard to his age or any other circumstances.

(4) The aggregate number of hours shall not exceed 12 except where the court is of the opinion, having regard to all the circumstances, that 12 hours would be inadequate, and in that case shall not exceed 24.

(5) A court may make an attendance centre order in respect of a person before a previous attendance centre order made in respect of him has ceased to have effect, and may determine the number of hours to be specified in the order without regard—

(a) to the number specified in the previous order; or

(b) to the fact that that order is still in effect.

(6) An attendance centre order shall not be made unless the court is satisfied that the attendance centre to be specified in it is reasonably accessible to the person concerned, having regard to his age, the means of access available to him and any other circumstances.

(7) The times at which a person is required to attend at an attendance centre shall, as far as practicable, be such as to avoid—

(a) any conflict with his religious beliefs or with the requirements of any other youth community order to which he may be subject; and

(b) any interference with the times, if any, at which he normally works or attends school or any other educational establishment.

(10) A person shall not be required under this section to attend at an attendance centre on more than one occasion on any day, or for more than three hours on any occasion.

SCHEDULE 5

BREACH, REVOCATION AND AMENDMENT OF ATTENDANCE CENTRE ORDERS

1. *Breach of order or attendance centre rules*

(1) Where an attendance centre order is in force and it appears on information to a justice that the offender—

(a) has failed to attend in accordance with the order, or

(b) while attending has committed a breach of rules made under section 222(1)(d) or (e) of the Criminal Justice Act 2003 which cannot be adequately dealt with under those rules,

the justice may issue a summons requiring the offender to appear at the place and time specified in the summons or, if the information is in writing and on oath, may issue a warrant for the offender's arrest.

2—(1) If it is proved to the satisfaction of the magistrates' court before which an offender appears or is brought under paragraph 1 above that he has failed without reasonable excuse to attend as mentioned in sub-paragraph (1)(a) of that paragraph or has committed such a breach of rules as is mentioned in sub-paragraph (1)(b) of that paragraph, that court may deal with him in any one of the following ways—

(a) it may impose on him a fine not exceeding £1,000;

(b) where the attendance centre order was made by a magistrates' court, it may deal with him, for the offence in respect of which the order was made, in any way in which he could have been dealt with for that offence by the court which made the order if the order had not been made; or

(c) where the order was made by the Crown Court, it may commit him to custody or release him on bail until he can be brought or appear before the Crown Court.

(3) A fine imposed under sub-paragraph (1)(a) above shall be deemed, for the purposes of any enactment, to be a sum adjudged to be paid by a conviction.

(4) Where a magistrates' court deals with an offender under sub-paragraph (1)(b) above, it shall revoke the attendance centre order if it is still in force.

(5) In dealing with an offender under sub-paragraph (1)(b) above, a magistrates' court—

(a) shall take into account the extent to which the offender has complied with the requirements of the attendance centre order; and

(b) in the case of an offender who has wilfully and persistently failed to comply with those requirements, may impose a custodial sentence notwithstanding anything in section 152(2) of the Criminal Justice Act 2003.

(5A) Where a magistrates' court dealing with an offender under sub-paragraph (1)(a) above would not otherwise have the power to amend the order under paragraph 5(1)(b) below (substitution of different attendance centre), that paragraph has effect as if references to an appropriate magistrates' court were references to the court dealing with the offender.

3—(1) Where by virtue of paragraph 2(1)(c) above the offender is brought or appears before the Crown Court and it is proved to the satisfaction of the court—

(a) that he has failed without reasonable excuse to attend as mentioned in paragraph 1(1)(a) above, or

(b) that he has committed such a breach of rules as is mentioned in paragraph 1(1)(b) above,

that court may deal with him, for the offence in respect of which the order was made, in any way in which it could have dealt with him for that offence if it had not made the order.

(2) Where the Crown Court deals with an offender under sub-paragraph (1) above, it shall revoke the attendance centre order if it is still in force.

(3) In dealing with an offender under sub-paragraph (1) above, the Crown Court—

(a) shall take into account the extent to which the offender has complied with the requirements of the attendance centre order; and

(b) in the case of an offender who has wilfully and persistently failed to comply with those requirements, may impose a custodial sentence notwithstanding anything in section 152(2) of the Criminal Justice Act 2003.

4. *Revocation of order with or without re-sentencing*

(1) Where an attendance centre order is in force in respect of an offender, an appropriate court may, on an application made by the offender or by the officer in charge of the relevant attendance centre, revoke the order.

(2) In sub-paragraph (1) above 'an appropriate court' means—

(a) where the court which made the order was the Crown Court and there is included in the order a direction that the power to revoke the order is reserved to that court, the Crown Court;

(b) in any other case, either of the following—

(i) a magistrates' court acting for the petty sessions area in which the relevant attendance centre is situated;

(ii) the court which made the order.

(3) Any power conferred by this paragraph—

(a) on a magistrates' court to revoke an attendance centre order made by such a court, or

(b) on the Crown Court to revoke an attendance centre order made by the Crown Court,

includes power to deal with the offender, for the offence in respect of which the order was made, in any way in which he could have been dealt with for that offence by the court which made the order if the order had not been made.

5. *Amendment of order*

(1) Where an attendance centre order is in force in respect of an offender, an appropriate magistrates' court may, on an application made by the offender or by the officer in charge of the relevant attendance centre, by order—

(a) vary the day or hour specified in the order for the offender's first attendance at the relevant attendance centre; or

(b) substitute for the relevant attendance centre an attendance centre which the court is satisfied is reasonably accessible to the offender, having regard to his age, the means of access available to him and any other circumstances.

SUPERVISION ORDERS

63 Supervision orders

(1) Where a child or young person (that is to say, any person aged under 18) is convicted of an offence, the court by or before which he is convicted may (subject to sections 148, 150 and 156 of the Criminal Justice Act 2003) make an order placing him under the supervision of—

(a) a local authority designated by the order;

(b) an officer of a local probation board; or

(c) a member of a youth offending team.

(5) A court shall not make a supervision order unless it is satisfied that the offender resides or will reside in the area of a local authority; and a court shall be entitled to be satisfied that the offender will so reside if he is to be required so to reside by a provision to be included in the order in pursuance of paragraph 1 of Schedule 6 to this Act.

(6) A supervision order—

(a) shall name the area of the local authority and the local justice area in which it appears to the court making the order (or to the court amending under Schedule 7 to this Act any provision included in the order in pursuance of this paragraph) that the offender resides or will reside; and

(b) may contain such prescribed provisions as the court making the order (or amending it under that Schedule) considers appropriate for facilitating the performance by the supervisor of his functions under section 64(4) below, including any prescribed provisions for requiring visits to be made by the offender to the supervisor;

and in paragraph (b) above 'prescribed' means prescribed by Criminal Procedure Rules.

(7) A supervision order shall, unless it has previously been revoked, cease to have effect at the end of the period of three years, or such shorter period as may be specified in the order, beginning with the date on which the order was originally made.

64 Selection and duty of supervisor and certain expenditure of his

(1) A court shall not designate a local authority as the supervisor by a provision of a supervision order unless—

(a) the authority agree; or

(b) it appears to the court that the offender resides or will reside in the area of the authority.

(2) Where a provision of a supervision order places the offender under the supervision of an officer of a local probation board, the supervisor shall be an officer of a local probation

board appointed for or assigned to the local justice area named in the order in pursuance of section 63(6) above.

(3) Where a provision of a supervision order places the offender under the supervision of a member of a youth offending team, the supervisor shall be a member of a team established by the local authority within whose area it appears to the court that the offender resides or will reside.

(4) While a supervision order is in force, the supervisor shall advise, assist and befriend the offender.

64A Supervision orders and curfew orders

Nothing in this Chapter prevents a court which makes a supervision order in respect of an offender from also making a curfew order in respect of him.

SCHEDULE 6

REQUIREMENTS WHICH MAY BE INCLUDED IN SUPERVISION ORDERS

1. Requirement to reside with named individual

A supervision order may require the offender to reside with an individual named in the order who agrees to the requirement, but a requirement imposed by a supervision order in pursuance of this paragraph shall be subject to any such requirement of the order as is authorised by paragraph 2, 3, 6 or 7 below.

2. Requirement to comply with directions of supervisor

(1) Subject to sub-paragraph (2) below, a supervision order may require the offender to comply with any directions given from time to time by the supervisor and requiring him to do all or any of the following things—

(a) to live at a place or places specified in the directions for a period or periods so specified;
(b) to present himself to a person or persons specified in the directions at a place or places and on a day or days so specified;
(c) to participate in activities specified in the directions on a day or days so specified.

(2) A supervision order shall not require compliance with directions given by virtue of sub-paragraph (1) above unless the court making it is satisfied that a scheme under section 66 of this Act (local authority schemes) is in force for the area where the offender resides or will reside; and no such directions may involve the use of facilities which are not for the time being specified in a scheme in force under that section for that area.

(3) A requirement imposed by a supervision order in pursuance of sub-paragraph (1) above shall be subject to any such requirement of the order as is authorised by paragraph 6 below (treatment for offender's mental condition).

(4) It shall be for the supervisor to decide—

(a) whether and to what extent he exercises any power to give directions conferred on him by virtue of sub-paragraph (1) above; and
(b) the form of any directions.

(5) The total number of days in respect of which an offender may be required to comply with directions given by virtue of paragraph (a), (b) or (c) of sub-paragraph (1) above shall not exceed 180 or such lesser number, if any, as the order may specify for the purposes of this sub-paragraph.

(6) For the purpose of calculating the total number of days in respect of which such directions may be given, the supervisor shall be entitled to disregard any day in respect of which directions were previously given in pursuance of the order and on which the directions were not complied with.

(7) Directions given by the supervisor by virtue of sub-paragraph (1)(b) or (c) above shall, as far as practicable, be such as to avoid—

(a) any conflict with the offender's religious beliefs or with the requirements of any other youth community order or any community order to which he may be subject; and

(b) any interference with the times, if any, at which he normally works or attends school or any other educational establishment.

3. *Requirements as to activities, reparation, night restrictions etc.*

(1) This paragraph applies to a supervision order unless the order requires the offender to comply with directions given by the supervisor under paragraph 2(1) above.

(2) Subject to the following provisions of this paragraph and paragraph 4 below, a supervision order to which this paragraph applies may require the offender—

(a) to live at a place or places specified in the order for a period or periods so specified;

(b) to present himself to a person or persons specified in the order at a place or places and on a day or days so specified;

(c) to participate in activities specified in the order on a day or days so specified;

(d) to make reparation specified in the order to a person or persons so specified or to the community at large;

(f) to refrain from participating in activities specified in the order—

(i) on a specified day or days during the period for which the supervision order is in force; or

(ii) during the whole of that period or a specified portion of it;

and in this paragraph 'make reparation' means make reparation for the offence otherwise than by the payment of compensation.

(3) The total number of days in respect of which an offender may be subject to requirements imposed by virtue of paragraph (a), (b), (c) or (d) of sub-paragraph (2) above shall not exceed 180.

(4) The court may not include requirements under sub-paragraph (2) above in a supervision order unless—

(a) it has first consulted the supervisor as to—

(i) the offender's circumstances, and

(ii) the feasibility of securing compliance with the requirements,

and is satisfied, having regard to the supervisor's report, that it is feasible to secure compliance with them;

(b) having regard to the circumstances of the case, it considers the requirements necessary for securing the good conduct of the offender or for preventing a repetition by him of the same offence or the commission of other offences; and

(c) if the offender is aged under 16, it has obtained and considered information about his family circumstances and the likely effect of the requirements on those circumstances.

(5) The court shall not by virtue of sub-paragraph (2) above include in a supervision order—

(a) any requirement that would involve the co-operation of a person other than the supervisor and the offender, unless that other person consents to its inclusion;

(b) any requirement to make reparation to any person unless that person—

(i) is identified by the court as a victim of the offence or a person otherwise affected by it; and

(ii) consents to the inclusion of the requirement;

(c) any requirement requiring the offender to reside with a specified individual; or

(d) any such requirement as is mentioned in paragraph 6(2) below (treatment for offender's mental condition).

(6) Requirements included in a supervision order by virtue of sub-paragraph (2)(b) or (c) above shall, as far as practicable, be such as to avoid—
- (a) any conflict with the offender's religious beliefs or with the requirements of any other youth community order to which he may be subject; and
- (b) any interference with the times, if any, at which he normally works or attends school or any other educational establishment;

and sub-paragraph (7) and (8) below are without prejudice to this sub-paragraph.

(7) Subject to sub-paragraph (8) below, a supervision order may not by virtue of sub-paragraph (2) above include—
- (a) any requirement that would involve the offender in absence from home—
  - (i) for more than two consecutive nights, or
  - (ii) for more than two nights in any one week, or
- (b) if the offender is of compulsory school age, any requirement to participate in activities during normal school hours,

unless the court making the order is satisfied that the facilities whose use would be involved are for the time being specified in a scheme in force under section 66 of this Act for the area in which the offender resides or will reside.

(8) Sub-paragraph (7)(b) above does not apply to activities carried out in accordance with arrangements made or approved by the local education authority in whose area the offender resides or will reside.

5. *Requirement to live for specified period in local authority accommodation*

(1) Where the conditions mentioned in sub-paragraph (2) below are satisfied, a supervision order may impose a requirement ('a local authority residence requirement') that the offender shall live for a specified period in local authority accommodation (as defined by section 163 of this Act).

(2) The conditions are that—
- (a) a supervision order has previously been made in respect of the offender;
- (b) that order imposed—
  - (i) a requirement under paragraph 1, 2, 3 or 7 of this Schedule; or
  - (ii) a local authority residence requirement;
- (c) the offender fails to comply with that requirement, or is convicted of an offence committed while that order was in force; and
- (d) the court is satisfied that—
  - (i) the failure to comply with the requirement, or the behaviour which constituted the offence, was due to a significant extent to the circumstances in which the offender was living; and
  - (ii) the imposition of a local authority residence requirement will assist in his rehabilitation;

except that sub-paragraph (i) of paragraph (d) above does not apply where the condition in paragraph (b)(ii) above is satisfied.

(3) A local authority residence requirement shall designate the local authority who are to receive the offender, and that authority shall be the authority in whose area the offender resides.

(4) The court shall not impose a local authority residence requirement without first consulting the designated authority.

(5) A local authority residence requirement may stipulate that the offender shall not live with a named person.

(6) The maximum period which may be specified in a local authority residence requirement is six months.

5A *Requirement to live for specified period with local authority foster parent*

(1) Where the conditions mentioned in sub-paragraph (2) below are satisfied, a supervision order may impose a requirement ('a foster parent residence requirement') that the offender shall live for a specified period with a local authority foster parent.

(2) The conditions are that—

    (a) the offence is punishable with imprisonment in the case of an offender aged 18 or over;

    (b) the offence, or the combination of the offence and one or more offences associated with it, was so serious that a custodial sentence would normally be appropriate (or, where the offender is aged 10 or 11, would normally be appropriate if the offender were aged 12 or over); and

    (c) the court is satisfied that—

        (i) the behaviour which constituted the offence was due to a significant extent to the circumstances in which the offender was living, and

        (ii) the imposition of a foster parent residence requirement will assist in his rehabilitation.

6. Requirements as to treatment for mental condition

(1) This paragraph applies where a court which proposes to make a supervision order is satisfied, on the evidence of a registered medical practitioner approved for the purposes of section 12 of the Mental Health Act 1983, that the mental condition of the offender—

    (a) is such as requires and may be susceptible to treatment; but

    (b) is not such as to warrant the making of a hospital order or guardianship order within the meaning of that Act.

(2) Where this paragraph applies, the court may include in the supervision order a requirement that the offender shall, for a period specified in the order, submit to treatment of one of the following descriptions so specified, that is to say—

    (a) treatment as a resident patient in an independent hospital or care home within the meaning of the Care Standard Act 2000 or in a hospital within the meaning of the Mental Health Act 1983, but not a hospital at which high security psychiatric services within the meaning of that Act are provided;

    (b) treatment as a non-resident patient at an institution or place specified in the order;

    (c) treatment by or under the direction of a registered medical practitioner specified in the order; or

    (d) treatment by or under the direction of a chartered psychologist specified in the order.

(3) A requirement shall not be included in a supervision order by virtue of sub-paragraph (2) above—

    (a) in any case, unless the court is satisfied that arrangements have been or can be made for the treatment in question and, in the case of treatment as a resident patient, for the reception of the patient;

    (b) in the case of an order made or to be made in respect of a person aged 14 or over, unless he consents to its inclusion;

and a requirement so included shall not in any case continue in force after the offender attains the age of 18.

7. Requirements as to education

(1) This paragraph applies to a supervision order unless the order requires the offender to comply with directions given by the supervisor under paragraph 2(1) above.

(2) Subject to the following provisions of this paragraph, a supervision order to which this paragraph applies may require the offender, if he is of compulsory school age, to comply, for as long as he is of that age and the order remains in force, with such arrangements for his education as may from time to time be made by his parent, being arrangements for the time being approved by the local education authority.

(3) The court shall not include such a requirement in a supervision order unless—

    (a) it has consulted the local education authority with regard to its proposal to include the requirement; and

(b) it is satisfied that in the view of the local education authority arrangements exist for the offender to receive efficient full-time education suitable to his age, ability and aptitude and to any special educational need he may have.

(5) The court may not include a requirement under sub-paragraph (2) above unless it has first consulted the supervisor as to the offender's circumstances and, having regard to the circumstances of the case, it considers the requirement necessary for securing the good conduct of the offender or for preventing a repetition by him of the same offence or the commission of other offences.

SCHEDULE 7

BREACH, REVOCATION AND AMENDMENT OF SUPERVISION ORDERS

2. Breach of requirement of supervision order

(1) This paragraph applies if while a supervision order is in force in respect of an offender it is proved to the satisfaction of a relevant court, on the application of the supervisor, that the offender has failed to comply with any requirement included in the supervision order in pursuance of paragraph 1, 2, 3, 5, 5A, 6A or 7 of Schedule 6 to this Act or section 63(6)(b) of this Act.

(2) Where this paragraph applies, the court—

(a) whether or not it also makes an order under paragraph 5(1) below (revocation or amendment of supervision order)—

(i)   may order the offender to pay a fine of an amount not exceeding £1,000; or

(ii) subject to sub-paragraph (2A) below and paragraph 3 below, may make a curfew order in respect of him; or

(iii) subject to paragraph 4 below, may make an attendance centre order in respect of him; or

(b) if the supervision order was made by a magistrates' court, may revoke the supervision order and deal with the offender, for the offence in respect of which the order was made, in any way in which he could have been dealt with for that offence by the court which made the order if the order had not been made; or

(c) if the supervision order was made by the Crown Court, may commit him in custody or release him on bail until he can be brought or appear before the Crown Court.

(2A) The court may not make a curfew order under sub-paragraph (2)(a)(ii) above in respect of an offender who is already subject to a curfew order.

(3) Where a court deals with an offender under sub-paragraph (2)(c) above, it shall send to the Crown Court a certificate signed by a justice of the peace giving—

(a) particulars of the offender's failure to comply with the requirement in question; and

(b) such other particulars of the case as may be desirable;

and a certificate purporting to be so signed shall be admissible as evidence of the failure before the Crown Court.

(4) Where—

(a) by virtue of sub-paragraph (2)(c) above the offender is brought or appears before the Crown Court, and

(b) it is proved to the satisfaction of the court that he has failed to comply with the requirement in question,

that court may deal with him, for the offence in respect of which the supervision order was made, in any way in which it could have dealt with him for that offence if it had not made the order.

(5) Where the Crown Court deals with an offender under sub-paragraph (4) above, it shall revoke the supervision order if it is still in force.

(6) A fine imposed under this paragraph shall be deemed, for the purposes of any enactment, to be a sum adjudged to be paid by a conviction.

(7) In dealing with an offender under this paragraph, a court shall take into account the extent to which he has complied with the requirements of the supervision order.

5. *Revocation and amendment of supervision order*

(1) If while a supervision order is in force in respect of an offender it appears to a relevant court, on the application of the supervisor or the offender, that it is appropriate to make an order under this sub-paragraph, the court may—

    (a) make an order revoking the supervision order; or

    (b) make an order amending it—

        (i) by cancelling any requirement included in it in pursuance of Schedule 6 to, or section 63(6)(b) of, this Act; or

        (ii) by inserting in it (either in addition to or in substitution for any of its provisions) any provision which could have been included in the order if the court had then had power to make it and were exercising the power.

(3) The powers of amendment conferred by sub-paragraph (1) above do not include power—

    (a) to insert in the supervision order, after the end of three months beginning with the date when the order was originally made, a requirement in pursuance of paragraph 6 of Schedule 6 to this Act (treatment for mental condition), unless it is in substitution for such a requirement already included in the order; or

    (b) to insert in the supervision order a requirement in pursuance of paragraph 3(2)(e) of that Schedule (night restrictions) in respect of any day which falls outside the period of three months beginning with the date when the order was originally made.

6. *Amendment of order on report of medical practitioner*

(1) If a medical practitioner by whom or under whose direction an offender is being treated for his mental condition in pursuance of a requirement included in a supervision order by virtue of paragraph 6 of Schedule 6 to this Act—

    (a) is unwilling to continue to treat or direct the treatment of the offender, or

    (b) is of the opinion mentioned in sub-paragraph (2) below, the practitioner shall make a report in writing to that effect to the supervisor.

(2) The opinion referred to in sub-paragraph (1) above is—

    (a) that the treatment of the offender should be continued beyond the period specified in that behalf in the order;

    (b) that the offender needs different treatment;

    (c) that the offender is not susceptible to treatment; or

    (d) that the offender does not require further treatment.

ACTION PLAN ORDERS

69 Action plan orders

(1) Where a child or young person (that is to say, any person aged under 18) is convicted of an offence and the court by or before which he is convicted is of the opinion mentioned in subsection (3) below, the court may (subject to sections 148, 150 and 156 of the Criminal Justice Act 2003) make an order which—

    (a) requires the offender, for a period of three months beginning with the date of the order, to comply with an action plan, that is to say, a series of requirements with respect to his actions and whereabouts during that period;

(b) places the offender for that period under the supervision of the responsible officer; and

(c) requires the offender to comply with any directions given by the responsible officer with a view to the implementation of that plan;

and the requirements included in the order, and any directions given by the responsible officer, may include requirements authorised by section 70 below.

(3) The opinion referred to in subsection (1) above is that the making of an action plan order is desirable in the interests of—

(a) securing the rehabilitation of the offender; or

(b) preventing the commission by him of further offences.

(4) In this Act 'responsible officer', in relation to an offender subject to an action plan order, means one of the following who is specified in the order, namely—

(a) an officer of a local probation board;

(b) a social worker of a local authority;

(c) a member of a youth offending team.

(5) The court shall not make an action plan order in respect of the offender if—

(a) he is already the subject of such an order; or

(b) the court proposes to pass on him a custodial sentence or to make in respect of him a community order under section 177 of the Criminal Justice Act 2003, an attendance centre order, a supervision order or a referral order.

(6) Before making an action plan order, the court shall obtain and consider—

(a) a written report by an officer of a local probation board, a social worker of a local authority or a member of a youth offending team indicating—

(i) the requirements proposed by that person to be included in the order;

(ii) the benefits to the offender that the proposed requirements are designed to achieve; and

(iii) the attitude of a parent or guardian of the offender to the proposed requirements; and

(b) where the offender is aged under 16, information about the offender's family circumstances and the likely effect of the order on those circumstances.

(7) The court shall not make an action plan order unless it has been notified by the Secretary of State that arrangements for implementing such orders are available in the area proposed to be named in the order under subsection (8) below and the notice has not been withdrawn.

(10) Where an action plan order specifies under that subsection—

(a) a social worker of a local authority, or

(b) a member of a youth offending team,

the social worker or member specified must be a social worker of, or a member of a youth offending team established by, the local authority within whose area it appears to the court that the offender resides or will reside.

70 Requirements which may be included in action plan orders and directions

(1) Requirements included in an action plan order, or directions given by a responsible officer, may require the offender to do all or any of the following things, namely—

(a) to participate in activities specified in the requirements or directions at a time or times so specified;

(b) to present himself to a person or persons specified in the requirements or directions at a place or places and at a time or times so specified;

(c) subject to subsection (2) below, to attend at an attendance centre specified in the requirements or directions for a number of hours so specified;

(d) to stay away from a place or places specified in the requirements or directions;

(e) to comply with any arrangements for his education specified in the requirements or directions;

(f) to make reparation specified in the requirements or directions to a person or persons so specified or to the community at large; and

(g) to attend any hearing fixed by the court under section 71 below.

(2) Subsection (1)(c) above applies only where the offence committed by the offender is an offence punishable with imprisonment.

(3) In subsection (1)(f) above 'make reparation', in relation to an offender, means make reparation for the offence otherwise than by the payment of compensation.

(4A) Subsection (4B) below applies where a court proposing to make an action plan order is satisfied—

(a) that the offender is dependent on, or has a propensity to misuse, drugs, and

(b) that his dependency or propensity is such as requires and may be susceptible to treatment.

(4B) Where this subsection applies, requirements included in an action plan order may require the offender for a period specified in the order ('the treatment period') to submit to treatment by or under the direction of a specified person having the necessary qualifications and experience ('the treatment provider') with a view to the reduction or elimination of the offender's dependency on or propensity to misuse drugs.

(4C) The required treatment shall be—

(a) treatment as a resident in such institution or place as may be specified in the order, or

(b) treatment as a non-resident at such institution or place, and at such intervals, as may be so specified;

but the nature of the treatment shall not be specified in the order except as mentioned in paragraph (a) or (b) above.

(4D) A requirement shall not be included in an action plan order by virtue of subsection (4B) above—

(a) in any case, unless—

(i) the court is satisfied that arrangements have been or can be made for the treatment intended to be specified in the order (including arrangements for the reception of the offender where he is to be required to submit to treatment as a resident), and

(ii) the requirement has been recommended to the court as suitable for the offender by an officer of a local probation board or by a member of a youth offending team; and

(b) in the case of an order made or to be made in respect of a person aged 14 or over, unless he consents to its inclusion.

(4E) Subject to subsection (4F), an action plan order which includes a requirement by virtue of subsection (4B) above may, if the offender is aged 14 or over, also include a requirement ('a testing requirement') that, for the purpose of ascertaining whether he has any drug in his body during the treatment period, the offender shall during that period, at such times or in such circumstances as may (subject to the provisions of the order) be determined by the responsible officer or the treatment provider, provide samples of such description as may be so determined.

(4F) A testing requirement shall not be included in an action plan order by virtue of subsection (4E) above unless—

(a) the offender is aged 14 or over and consents to its inclusion, and

(b) the court has been notified by the Secretary of State that arrangements for implementing such requirements are in force in the area proposed to be specified in the order

(4G) A testing requirement shall specify for each month the minimum number of occasions on which samples are to be provided.

(5) Requirements included in an action plan order and directions given by a responsible officer shall, as far as practicable, be such as to avoid—

(a) any conflict with the offender's religious beliefs or with the requirements of any other youth community order or any community order to which he may be subject; and

(b) any interference with the times, if any, at which he normally works or attends school or any other educational establishment.

71 Action plan orders: power to fix further hearings

(1) Immediately after making an action plan order, a court may—

(a) fix a further hearing for a date not more than 21 days after the making of the order; and

(b) direct the responsible officer to make, at that hearing, a report as to the effectiveness of the order and the extent to which it has been implemented.

(2) At a hearing fixed under subsection (1) above, the court—

(a) shall consider the responsible officer's report; and

(b) may, on the application of the responsible officer or the offender, amend the order—

(i) by cancelling any provision included in it; or

(ii) by inserting in it (either in addition to or in substitution for any of its provisions) any provision that the court could originally have included in it.

(i) FINANCIAL PENALTIES AND ORDERS

Criminal Justice Act 2003

Fines

162 Powers to order statement as to offender's financial circumstances

(1) Where an individual has been convicted of an offence, the court may, before sentencing him, make a financial circumstances order with respect to him.

(2) Where a magistrates' court has been notified in accordance with section 12(4) of the Magistrates' Courts Act 1980 (c. 43) that an individual desires to plead guilty without appearing before the court, the court may make a financial circumstances order with respect to him.

(3) In this section 'a financial circumstances order' means, in relation to any individual, an order requiring him to give to the court, within such period as may be specified in the order, such a statement of his financial circumstances as the court may require.

(4) An individual who without reasonable excuse fails to comply with a financial circumstances order is liable on summary conviction to a fine not exceeding level 3 on the standard scale.

(5) If an individual, in furnishing any statement in pursuance of a financial circumstances order—

(a) makes a statement which he knows to be false in a material particular,

(b) recklessly furnishes a statement which is false in a material particular, or

(c) knowingly fails to disclose any material fact,

he is liable on summary conviction to a fine not exceeding level 4 on the standard scale.

163 General power of Crown Court to fine offender convicted on indictment

Where a person is convicted on indictment of any offence, other than an offence for which the sentence is fixed by law or falls to be imposed under section 110(2) or 111(2) of the Sentencing Act or under any of sections 225 to 228 of this Act, the court, if not precluded from sentencing an offender by its exercise of some other power, may impose a fine instead of or in addition to dealing with him in any other way in which the court has power to deal with him, subject however to any enactment requiring the offender to be dealt with in a particular way.

164   Fixing of fines

(1) Before fixing the amount of any fine to be imposed on an offender who is an individual, a court must inquire into his financial circumstances.

(2) The amount of any fine fixed by a court must be such as, in the opinion of the court, reflects the seriousness of the offence.

(3) In fixing the amount of any fine to be imposed on an offender (whether an individual or other person), a court must take into account the circumstances of the case including, among other things, the financial circumstances of the offender so far as they are known, or appear, to the court.

(4) Subsection (3) applies whether taking into account the financial circumstances of the offender has the effect of increasing or reducing the amount of the fine.

(5) Where—

    (a) an offender has been convicted in his absence in pursuance of section 11 or 12 of the Magistrates' Courts Act 1980 (c. 43) (non-appearance of accused), or

    (b) an offender—

        (i)   has failed to furnish a statement of his financial circumstances in response to a request which is an official request for the purposes of section 20A of the Criminal Justice Act 1991 (c.53) (offence of making false statement as to financial circumstances),

        (ii) has failed to comply with an order under section 162(1), or

        (iii) has otherwise failed to co-operate with the court in its inquiry into his financial circumstances,

and the court considers that it has insufficient information to make a proper determination of the financial circumstances of the offender, it may make such determination as it thinks fit.

165   Remission of fines

(1) This section applies where a court has, in fixing the amount of a fine, determined the offender's financial circumstances under section 164(5).

(2) If, on subsequently inquiring into the offender's financial circumstances, the court is satisfied that had it had the results of that inquiry when sentencing the offender it would—

    (a) have fixed a smaller amount, or

    (b) not have fined him,

it may remit the whole or part of the fine.

(3) Where under this section the court remits the whole or part of a fine after a term of imprisonment has been fixed under section 139 of the Sentencing Act (powers of Crown Court in relation to fines) or section 82(5) of the Magistrates' Courts Act 1980 (magistrates' powers in relation to default) it must reduce the term by the corresponding proportion.

(4) In calculating any reduction required by subsection (3), any fraction of a day is to be ignored.

Powers of Criminal Courts (Sentencing) Act 2000

COMPENSATION ORDERS

130   Compensation orders against convicted persons

(1) A court by or before which a person is convicted of an offence, instead of or in addition to dealing with him in any other way, may, on application or otherwise, make an order (in this Act referred to as a 'compensation order') requiring him—

    (a) to pay compensation for any personal injury, loss or damage resulting from that offence or any other offence which is taken into consideration by the court in determining sentence; or

(b) to make payments for funeral expenses or bereavement in respect of a death resulting from any such offence, other than a death due to an accident arising out of the presence of a motor vehicle on a road;

but this is subject to the following provisions of this section and to section 131 below.

(3) A court shall give reasons, on passing sentence, if it does not make a compensation order in a case where this section empowers it to do so.

(4) Compensation under subsection (1) above shall be of such amount as the court considers appropriate, having regard to any evidence and to any representations that are made by or on behalf of the accused or the prosecutor.

(5) In the case of an offence under the Theft Act 1968, where the property in question is recovered, any damage to the property occurring while it was out of the owner's possession shall be treated for the purposes of subsection (1) above as having resulted from the offence, however and by whomever the damage was caused.

(6) A compensation order may only be made in respect of injury, loss or damage (other than loss suffered by a person's dependants in consequence of his death) which was due to an accident arising out of the presence of a motor vehicle on a road, if—

(a) it is in respect of damage which is treated by subsection (5) above as resulting from an offence under the Theft Act 1968; or

(b) it is in respect of injury, loss or damage as respects which—

(i) the offender is uninsured in relation to the use of the vehicle; and

(ii) compensation is not payable under any arrangements to which the Secretary of State is a party.

(7) Where a compensation order is made in respect of injury, loss or damage due to an accident arising out of the presence of a motor vehicle on a road, the amount to be paid may include an amount representing the whole or part of any loss of or reduction in preferential rates of insurance attributable to the accident.

(11) In determining whether to make a compensation order against any person, and in determining the amount to be paid by any person under such an order, the court shall have regard to his means so far as they appear or are known to the court.

(12) Where the court considers—

(a) that it would be appropriate both to impose a fine and to make a compensation order, but

(b) that the offender has insufficient means to pay both an appropriate fine and appropriate compensation,

the court shall give preference to compensation (though it may impose a fine as well).

131 Limit on amount payable under compensation order of magistrates' court

(1) The compensation to be paid under a compensation order made by a magistrates' court in respect of any offence of which the court has convicted the offender shall not exceed £5,000.

(2) The compensation or total compensation to be paid under a compensation order or compensation orders made by a magistrates' court in respect of any offence or offences taken into consideration in determining sentence shall not exceed the difference (if any) between—

(a) the amount or total amount which under subsection (1) above is the maximum for the offence or offences of which the offender has been convicted; and

(b) the amount or total amounts (if any) which are in fact ordered to be paid in respect of that offence or those offences.

133 Review of compensation orders

(1) The magistrates' court for the time being having functions in relation to the enforcement of a compensation order (in this section referred to as 'the appropriate court') may, on the application of the person against whom the compensation order was made, discharge

the order or reduce the amount which remains to be paid; but this is subject to subsections (2) to (4) below.

(2) The appropriate court may exercise a power conferred by subsection (1) above only—

(a) at a time when (disregarding any power of a court to grant leave to appeal out of time) there is no further possibility of an appeal on which the compensation order could be varied or set aside; and

(b) at a time before the person against whom the compensation order was made has paid into court the whole of the compensation which the order requires him to pay.

(3) The appropriate court may exercise a power conferred by subsection (1) above only if it appears to the court—

(a) that the injury, loss or damage in respect of which the compensation order was made has been held in civil proceedings to be less than it was taken to be for the purposes of the order; or

(b) in the case of a compensation order in respect of the loss of any property, that the property has been recovered by the person in whose favour the order was made; or

(c) that the means of the person against whom the compensation order was made are insufficient to satisfy in full both the order and a confiscation order under Part VI of the Criminal Justice Act 1988 or Part 2 of the Proceeds of Crime Act 2002 made against him in the same proceedings; or

(d) that the person against whom the compensation order was made has suffered a substantial reduction in his means which was unexpected at the time when the order was made, and that his means seem unlikely to increase for a considerable period.

YOUNG OFFENDERS

135 Limit on fines imposed by magistrates' courts in respect of young offenders

(1) Where a person aged under 18 is found guilty by a magistrates' court of an offence for which, apart from this section, the court would have power to impose a fine of an amount exceeding £1,000, the amount of any fine imposed by the court shall not exceed £1,000.

(2) In relation to a person aged under 14, subsection (1) above shall have effect as if for '£1,000', in both places where it occurs, there were substituted '£250'.

136 Power to order statement as to financial circumstances of parent or guardian

(1) Before exercising its powers under section 137 below (power to order parent or guardian to pay fine, costs, compensation or surcharge) against the parent or guardian of an individual who has been convicted of an offence, the court may make a financial circumstances order with respect to the parent or (as the case may be) guardian.

(2) In this section 'financial circumstances order' has the meaning given by subsection (3) of section 162 of the Criminal Justice Act 2003, and subsections (4) to (6) of that section shall apply in relation to a financial circumstances order made under this section as they apply in relation to such an order made under that section.

137 Power to order parent or guardian to pay fine, costs, compensation or surcharge

(1) Where—

(a) a child or young person (that is to say, any person aged under 18) is convicted of any offence for the commission of which a fine or costs may be imposed or a compensation order may be made, and

(b) the court is of the opinion that the case would best be met by the imposition of a fine or costs or the making of such an order, whether with or without any other punishment, the court shall order that the fine, compensation or costs awarded be paid by the parent or guardian of the child or young person instead of by the child or young person himself, unless the court is satisfied—

(i)   that the parent or guardian cannot be found; or

(ii) that it would be unreasonable to make an order for payment, having regard to the circumstances of the case.

(1A) Where but for this subsection a court would order a child or young person to pay a surcharge under section 161A of the Criminal Justice Act 2003, the court shall order that the surcharge be paid by the parent or guardian of the child or young person instead of by the child or young person himself, unless the court is satisfied—

(a) that the parent or guardian cannot be found; or

(b) that it would be unreasonable to make an order for payment, having regard to the circumstances of the case.

(2) Where but for this subsection a court would impose a fine on a child or young person under—

(b) paragraph 2(1)(a) of Schedule 5 to this Act (breach of attendance centre order or attendance centre rules),

(c) paragraph 2(2)(a) of Schedule 7 to this Act (breach of supervision order),

(d) paragraph 2(2)(a) of Schedule 8 to this Act (breach of action plan order or reparation order),

(e) section 104(3)(b) above (breach of requirements of supervision under a detention and training order), or

(f) section 4(3)(b) of the Criminal Justice and Public Order Act 1994 (breach of requirements of supervision under a secure training order),

the court shall order that the fine be paid by the parent or guardian of the child or young person instead of by the child or young person himself, unless the court is satisfied—

(i)   that the parent or guardian cannot be found; or

(ii) that it would be unreasonable to make an order for payment, having regard to the circumstances of the case.

138   Fixing of fine, compensation or surcharge to be paid by parent or guardian

(1) For the purposes of any order under section 137 above made against the parent or guardian of a child or young person—

(za) subsection (3) of section 161A of the Criminal Justice Act 2003 (surcharges) and subsection (4A) of section 164 of that Act (fixing of fines) shall have effect as if any reference in those subsections to the offender's means were a reference to those of the parent or guardian;

(a) section 164 of the Criminal Justice Act 2003 (fixing of fines) shall have effect as if any reference in subsections (1) to (4) to the financial circumstances of the offender were a reference to the financial circumstances of the parent or guardian, and as if subsection (5) were omitted;

(b) section 130(11) above (determination of compensation order) shall have effect as if any reference to the means of the person against whom the compensation order is made were a reference to the financial circumstances of the parent or guardian; and

(c) section 130(12) above (preference to be given to compensation if insufficient means to pay both compensation and a fine) shall have effect as if the reference to the offender were a reference to the parent or guardian;

but in relation to an order under section 137 made against a local authority this subsection has effect subject to subsection (2) below.

(2) For the purposes of any order under section 137 above made against a local authority, section 164(1) of the Criminal Justice Act 2003 and section 130(11) above shall not apply.

(3) For the purposes of any order under section 137 above, where the parent or guardian

of an offender who is a child or young person—
> (a) has failed to comply with an order under section 136 above, or
> (b) has otherwise failed to co-operate with the court in its inquiry into his financial circumstances,

and the court considers that it has insufficient information to make a proper determination of the parent's or guardian's financial circumstances, it may make such determination as it thinks fit.

MISCELLANEOUS POWERS

139 Powers and duties of Crown Court in relation to fines and forfeited recognizances

(1) Subject to the provisions of this section, if the Crown Court imposes a fine on any person or forfeits his recognizance, the court may make an order—
> (a) allowing time for the payment of the amount of the fine or the amount due under the recognizance;
> (b) directing payment of that amount by instalments of such amounts and on such dates as may be specified in the order;
> (c) in the case of a recognizance, discharging the recognizance or reducing the amount due under it.

(2) Subject to the provisions of this section, if the Crown Court imposes a fine on any person or forfeits his recognizance, the court shall make an order fixing a term of imprisonment which he is to undergo if any sum which he is liable to pay is not duly paid or recovered.

(3) No person shall on the occasion when a fine is imposed on him or his recognizance is forfeited by the Crown Court be committed to prison in pursuance of an order under subsection (2) above unless—
> (a) in the case of an offence punishable with imprisonment, he appears to the court to have sufficient means to pay the sum forthwith;
> (b) it appears to the court that he is unlikely to remain long enough at a place of abode in the United Kingdom to enable payment of the sum to be enforced by other methods; or

Table

An amount not exceeding £200	7 days
An amount exceeding £200 but not exceeding £500	14 days
An amount exceeding £500 but not exceeding £1,000	28 days
An amount exceeding £1,000 but not exceeding £2,500	45 days
An amount exceeding £2,500 but not exceeding £5,000	3 months
An amount exceeding £5,000 but not exceeding £10,000	6 months
An amount exceeding £10,000 but not exceeding £20,000	12 months
An amount exceeding £20,000 but not exceeding £50,000	18 months
An amount exceeding £50,000 but not exceeding £100,000	2 years
An amount exceeding £100,000 but not exceeding £250,000	3 years
An amount exceeding £250,000 but not exceeding £1 million	5 years
An amount exceeding £1 million	10 years

> (c) on the occasion when the order is made the court sentences him to immediate imprisonment for that or another offence, or so sentences him for an offence in addition to forfeiting his recognizance, or he is already serving a sentence of custody for life or a term—
> > (i)   of imprisonment;
> > (ii) of detention in a young offender institution; or
> > (iii) of detention under section 108 above.

(4) The periods set out in the second column of the Table shall be the maximum periods of imprisonment under subsection (2) above applicable respectively to the amounts set out opposite them.

(5) Where any person liable for the payment of a fine or a sum due under a recognizance to which this section applies is sentenced by the court to, or is serving or otherwise liable to serve, a term of imprisonment or detention in a young offender institution or a term of detention under section 108 above, the court may order that any term of imprisonment fixed under subsection (2) above shall not begin to run until after the end of the first-mentioned term.

(7) Subject to subsection (8) below, the powers conferred by this section shall not be taken as restricted by any enactment which authorises the Crown Court to deal with an offender in any way in which a magistrates' court might have dealt with him or could deal with him.

(8) Any term fixed under subsection (2) above as respects a fine imposed in pursuance of such an enactment, that is to say a fine which the magistrates' court could have imposed, shall not exceed the period applicable to that fine (if imposed by the magistrates' court) under section 149(1) of the Customs and Excise Management Act 1979 (maximum periods of imprisonment in default of payment of certain fines).

140 Enforcement of fines imposed and recognizances forfeited by Crown Court
(1) Subject to subsection (5) below, a fine imposed or a recognizance forfeited by the Crown Court shall be treated for the purposes of collection, enforcement and remission of the fine or other sum as having been imposed or forfeited—
    (a) by a magistrates' court specified in an order made by the Crown Court, or
    (b) if no such order is made, by the magistrates' court by which the offender was sent to the Crown Court for trial under section 51 or 51A of the Crime and Disorder Act 1998,
and, in the case of a fine, as having been so imposed on conviction by the magistrates' court in question.

(2) Subsection (3) below applies where a magistrates' court issues a warrant of commitment on a default in the payment of—
    (a) a fine imposed by the Crown Court; or
    (b) a sum due under a recognizance forfeited by the Crown Court.

(3) In such a case, the term of imprisonment specified in the warrant of commitment as the term which the offender is liable to serve shall be—
    (a) the term fixed by the Crown Court under section 139(2) above, or
    (b) if that term has been reduced under section 79(2) of the Magistrates' Courts Act 1980 (part payment) or section 85(2) of that Act (remission), that term as so reduced,
notwithstanding that that term exceeds the period applicable to the case under section 149(1) of the Customs and Excise Management Act 1979 (maximum periods of imprisonment in default of payment of certain fines).

(5) A magistrates' court shall not, under section 85(1) or 120 of the Magistrates' Courts Act 1980 as applied by subsection (1) above, remit the whole or any part of a fine imposed by, or sum due under a recognizance forfeited by—
    (a) the Crown Court,
    (b) the criminal division of the Court of Appeal, or
    (c) the Supreme Court on appeal from that division,
without the consent of the Crown Court.

141 Power of Crown Court to allow time for payment, or payment by instalments, of costs and compensation
Where the Crown Court makes any such order as is mentioned in Part I of Schedule 9 to the Administration of Justice Act 1970 (orders against accused for the payment of costs or compensation), the court may—

(a) allow time for the payment of the sum due under the order;

(b) direct payment of that sum by instalments of such amounts and on such dates as the court may specify.

Deprivation orders

Powers of Criminal Courts (Sentencing) Act 2000

143 Powers to deprive offender of property used etc for purposes of crime

(1) Where a person is convicted of an offence and the court by or before which he is convicted is satisfied that any property which has been lawfully seized from him, or which was in his possession or under his control at the time when he was apprehended for the offence or when a summons in respect of it was issued—

(a) has been used for the purpose of committing, or facilitating the commission of, any offence, or

(b) was intended by him to be used for that purpose,

the court may (subject to subsection (5) below) make an order under this section in respect of that property.

(2) Where a person is convicted of an offence and the offence, or an offence which the court has taken into consideration in determining his sentence, consists of unlawful possession of property which—

(a) has been lawfully seized from him, or

(b) was in his possession or under his control at the time when he was apprehended for the offence of which he has been convicted or when a summons in respect of that offence was issued,

the court may (subject to subsection (5) below) make an order under this section in respect of that property.

(3) An order under this section shall operate to deprive the offender of his rights, if any, in the property to which it relates, and the property shall (if not already in their possession) be taken into the possession of the police.

(4) Any power conferred on a court by subsection (1) or (2) above may be exercised—

(a) whether or not the court also deals with the offender in any other way in respect of the offence of which he has been convicted; and

(b) without regard to any restrictions on forfeiture in any enactment contained in an Act passed before 29th July 1988.

(5) In considering whether to make an order under this section in respect of any property, a court shall have regard—

(a) to the value of the property; and

(b) to the likely financial and other effects on the offender of the making of the order (taken together with any other order that the court contemplates making).

144 Property which is in possession of police by virtue of section 143

(1) The Police (Property) Act 1897 shall apply, with the following modifications, to property which is in the possession of the police by virtue of section 143 above—

(a) no application shall be made under section 1(1) of that Act by any claimant of the property after the end of six months from the date on which the order in respect of the property was made under section 143 above; and

(b) no such application shall succeed unless the claimant satisfies the court either—
  (i) that he had not consented to the offender having possession of the property; or
  (ii) where an order is made under subsection (1) of section 143 above, that he did not know, and had no reason to suspect, that the property was likely to be used for the purpose mentioned in that subsection.

145 Application of proceeds of forfeited property
  (1) Where a court makes an order under section 143 above in a case where—
    (a) the offender has been convicted of an offence which has resulted in a person suffering personal injury, loss or damage, or
    (b) any such offence is taken into consideration by the court in determining sentence,
the court may also make an order that any proceeds which arise from the disposal of the property and which do not exceed a sum specified by the court shall be paid to that person.

  (2) The court may make an order under this section only if it is satisfied that but for the inadequacy of the offender's means it would have made a compensation order under which the offender would have been required to pay compensation of an amount not less than the specified amount.

Misuse of Drugs Act 1971

27 Forfeiture
  (1) Subject to subsection (2) below, the court by or before which a person is convicted of an offence under this Act or an offence falling within subsection (3) below ... or an offence to which section 1 of the Proceeds of Crime (Scotland) Act 1995 relates may order anything shown to the satisfaction of the court to relate to the offence, to be forfeited and either destroyed or dealt with in such other manner as the court may order.

  (2) The court shall not order anything to be forfeited under this section, where a person claiming to be the owner of or otherwise interested in it applies to be heard by the court, unless an opportunity has been given to him to show cause why the order should not be made.

Firearms Act 1968

52 Forfeiture and disposal of firearms; cancellation of certificate by convicting court
  (1) Where a person—
    (a) is convicted of an offence under this Act (other than an offence under section 22 (3) or an offence relating specifically to air weapons) or is convicted of a crime for which he is sentenced to imprisonment, preventive detention, corrective training, borstal training or detention in a detention centre or in a young offenders' institution in Scotland; or
    (b) has been ordered to enter into a recognizance to keep the peace or to be of good behaviour, a condition of which is that he shall not possess, use or carry a firearm; or
    (c) is subject to a probation order containing a requirement that he shall not possess, use or carry a firearm; or
    (d) has, in Scotland, been ordained to find caution a condition of which is that he shall not possess, use or carry a firearm,
the court by or before which he is convicted, or by which the order is made, may make such order as to the forfeiture or disposal of any firearm or ammunition found in his possession as the court thinks fit and may cancel any firearm certificate or shot gun certificate held by him.

Prevention of Crime Act 1953

1 Prohibition of the carrying of offensive weapons without lawful authority or reasonable excuse

(1) Any person who without lawful authority or reasonable excuse, the proof whereof shall lie on him, has with him in any public place any offensive weapon shall be guilty of an offence, and shall be liable—

  (a) on summary conviction, to imprisonment for a term not exceeding six months or a fine not exceeding £200 pounds, or both;

  (b) on conviction on indictment, to imprisonment for a term not exceeding four years or a fine not exceeding one hundred pounds, or both.

(2) Where any person is convicted of an offence under subsection (1) of this section the court may make an order for the forfeiture or disposal of any weapon in respect of which the offence was committed.

(j) RESTITUTION ORDERS

Powers of Criminal Courts (Sentencing) Act 2000

148 Restitution orders

(1) This section applies where goods have been stolen, and either—

  (a) a person is convicted of any offence with reference to the theft (whether or not the stealing is the gist of his offence); or

  (b) a person is convicted of any other offence, but such an offence as is mentioned in paragraph (a) above is taken into consideration in determining his sentence.

(2) Where this section applies, the court by or before which the offender is convicted may on the conviction (whether or not the passing of sentence is in other respects deferred) exercise any of the following powers—

  (a) the court may order anyone having possession or control of the stolen goods to restore them to any person entitled to recover them from him; or

  (b) on the application of a person entitled to recover from the person convicted any other goods directly or indirectly representing the stolen goods (as being the proceeds of any disposal or realisation of the whole or part of them or of goods so representing them), the court may order those other goods to be delivered or transferred to the applicant; or

  (c) the court may order that a sum not exceeding the value of the stolen goods shall be paid, out of any money of the person convicted which was taken out of his possession on his apprehension, to any person who, if those goods were in the possession of the person convicted, would be entitled to recover them from him;

and in this subsection 'the stolen goods' means the goods referred to in subsection (1) above.

(3) Where the court has power on a person's conviction to make an order against him both under paragraph (b) and under paragraph (c) of subsection (2) above with reference to the stealing of the same goods, the court may make orders under both paragraphs provided that the person in whose favour the orders are made does not thereby recover more than the value of those goods.

(4) Where the court on a person's conviction makes an order under subsection (2)(a) above for the restoration of any goods, and it appears to the court that the person convicted—

  (a) has sold the goods to a person acting in good faith, or

  (b) has borrowed money on the security of them from a person so acting, the court may order that there shall be paid to the purchaser or lender, out of any money of the person convicted which was taken out of his possession on his apprehension, a sum not exceeding the amount paid for the purchase by the purchaser or, as the case may be, the amount owed to the lender in respect of the loan.

(5) The court shall not exercise the powers conferred by this section unless in the opinion of the court the relevant facts sufficiently appear from evidence given at the trial or the available documents, together with admissions made by or on behalf of any person in connection with any proposed exercise of the powers.

(6) In subsection (5) above 'the available documents' means—

> (a) any written statements or admissions which were made for use, and would have been admissible, as evidence at the trial; and
>
> (b) such documents as were served on the offender in pursuance of regulations made under paragraph 1 of Schedule 3 to the Crime and Disorder Act 1998.

149 Restitution orders: supplementary

(1) The following provisions of this section shall have effect with respect to section 148 above.

(2) The powers conferred by subsections (2)(c) and (4) of that section shall be exercisable without any application being made in that behalf or on the application of any person appearing to the court to be interested in the property concerned.

(3) Where an order is made under that section against any person in respect of an offence taken into consideration in determining his sentence—

> (a) the order shall cease to have effect if he successfully appeals against his conviction of the offence or, if more than one, all the offences, of which he was convicted in the proceedings in which the order was made;
>
> (b) he may appeal against the order as if it were part of the sentence imposed in respect of the offence or, if more than one, any of the offences, of which he was so convicted.

(4) Any order under that section made by a magistrates' court shall be suspended—

> (a) in any case until the end of the period for the time being prescribed by law for the giving of notice of appeal against a decision of a magistrates' court;
>
> (b) where notice of appeal is given within the period so prescribed, until the determination of the appeal;

but this subsection shall not apply where the order is made under section 148(2)(a) or (b) and the court so directs, being of the opinion that the title to the goods to be restored or, as the case may be, delivered or transferred under the order is not in dispute.

(k) REPARATION ORDERS ETC.

Reparation orders

Powers of Criminal Courts (Sentencing) Act 2000

73 Reparation orders

(1) Where a child or young person (that is to say, any person aged under 18) is convicted of an offence other than one for which the sentence is fixed by law, the court by or before which he is convicted may make an order requiring him to make reparation specified in the order—

> (a) to a person or persons so specified; or
>
> (b) to the community at large;

and any person so specified must be a person identified by the court as a victim of the offence or a person otherwise affected by it.

(3) In this section and section 74 below 'make reparation', in relation to an offender, means make reparation for the offence otherwise than by the payment of compensation; and the requirements that may be specified in a reparation order are subject to section 74(1) to (3).

(4) The court shall not make a reparation order in respect of the offender if it proposes—

(a) to pass on him a custodial sentence; or

(b) to make in respect of him a community order under section 177 of the Criminal Justice Act 2003, a supervision order which includes requirements authorised by Schedule 6 to this Act, an action plan order or a referral order.

(5) Before making a reparation order, a court shall obtain and consider a written report by an officer of a local probation board, a social worker of a local authority or a member of a youth offending team indicating—

(a) the type of work that is suitable for the offender; and

(b) the attitude of the victim or victims to the requirements proposed to be included in the order.

(6) The court shall not make a reparation order unless it has been notified by the Secretary of State that arrangements for implementing such orders are available in the area proposed to be named in the order under section 74(4) below and the notice has not been withdrawn.

74 Requirements and provisions of reparation order, and obligations of person subject to it

(1) A reparation order shall not require the offender—

(a) to work for more than 24 hours in aggregate; or

(b) to make reparation to any person without the consent of that person.

(2) Subject to subsection (1) above, requirements specified in a reparation order shall be such as in the opinion of the court are commensurate with the seriousness of the offence, or the combination of the offence and one or more offences associated with it.

(3) Requirements so specified shall, as far as practicable, be such as to avoid—

(a) any conflict with the offender's religious beliefs or with the requirements of any community order or any youth community order to which he may be subject; and

(b) any interference with the times, if any, at which he normally works or attends school or any other educational establishment.

SCHEDULE 8

BREACH, REVOCATION AND AMENDMENT OF ACTION PLAN ORDERS AND REPARATION ORDERS

2. Breach of requirement of action plan order or reparation order

(1) This paragraph applies if while an action plan order or reparation order is in force in respect of an offender it is proved to the satisfaction of the appropriate court, on the application of the responsible officer, that the offender has failed to comply with any requirement included in the order.

(2) Where this paragraph applies, the court—

(a) whether or not it also makes an order under paragraph 5(1) below (revocation or amendment of order)—

(i) may order the offender to pay a fine of an amount not exceeding £1,000; or

(ii) subject to paragraph 3 below, may make a curfew order in respect of him; or

(iii) subject to paragraph 4 below, may make an attendance centre order in respect of him; or

(b) if the action plan order or reparation order was made by a magistrates' court, may revoke the order and deal with the offender, for the offence in respect of which the order was made, in any way in which he could have been dealt with for that offence by the court which made the order if the order had not been made; or

(c) if the action plan order or reparation order was made by the Crown Court, may commit him in custody or release him on bail until he can be brought or appear before the Crown Court

(4) Where—

(a) by virtue of sub-paragraph (2)(c) above the offender is brought or appears before the Crown Court, and

(b) it is proved to the satisfaction of the court that he has failed to comply with the requirement in question,

that court may deal with him, for the offence in respect of which the order was made, in any way in which it could have dealt with him for that offence if it had not made the order.

(5) Where the Crown Court deals with an offender under sub-paragraph (4) above, it shall revoke the action plan order or reparation order if it is still in force.

(6) A fine imposed under this paragraph shall be deemed, for the purposes of any enactment, to be a sum adjudged to be paid by a conviction.

(7) In dealing with an offender under this paragraph, a court shall take into account the extent to which he has complied with the requirements of the action plan order or reparation order.

5. *Revocation and amendment of action plan order or reparation order*

(1) If while an action plan order or reparation order is in force in respect of an offender it appears to the appropriate court, on the application of the responsible officer or the offender, that it is appropriate to make an order under this sub-paragraph, the court may—

(a) make an order revoking the action plan order or reparation order; or

(b) make an order amending it—

(i) by cancelling any provision included in it; or

(ii) by inserting in it (either in addition to or in substitution for any of its provisions) any provision which could have been included in the order if the court had then had power to make it and were exercising the power.

6. *Presence of offender in court, remands etc.*

(9) A court may make an order under paragraph 5(1) above in the absence of the offender if the effect of the order is confined to one or more of the following, that is to say—

(a) revoking the action plan order or reparation order;

(b) cancelling a requirement included in the action plan order or reparation order;

(c) altering in the action plan order or reparation order the name of any area;

(d) changing the responsible officer.

Referral of young offenders

Powers of Criminal Courts (Sentencing) Act 2000

16 Duty and power to refer certain young offenders to youth offender panels

(1) This section applies where a youth court or other magistrates' court is dealing with a person aged under 18 for an offence and—

(a) neither the offence nor any connected offence is one for which the sentence is fixed by law;

(b) the court is not, in respect of the offence or any connected offence, proposing to impose a custodial sentence on the offender or make a hospital order (within the meaning of the Mental Health Act 1983) in his case; and

(c) the court is not proposing to discharge him absolutely in respect of the offence.

(2) If—

(a) the compulsory referral conditions are satisfied in accordance with section 17 below, and

(b) referral is available to the court,

the court shall sentence the offender for the offence by ordering him to be referred to a youth offender panel.

(3) If—

(a) the discretionary referral conditions are satisfied in accordance with section 17 below, and

(b) referral is available to the court,

the court may sentence the offender for the offence by ordering him to be referred to a youth offender panel.

(4) For the purposes of this Part an offence is connected with another if the offender falls to be dealt with for it at the same time as he is dealt with for the other offence (whether or not he is convicted of the offences at the same time or by or before the same court).

(5) For the purposes of this section referral is available to a court if—

(a) the court has been notified by the Secretary of State that arrangements for the implementation of referral orders are available in the area in which it appears to the court that the offender resides or will reside; and

(b) the notice has not been withdrawn.

(7) No referral order may be made in respect of any offence committed before the commencement of section 1 of the Youth Justice and Criminal Evidence Act 1999.

17   The referral conditions

(1) For the purposes of section 16(2) above the compulsory referral conditions are satisfied in relation to an offence if the offence is an offence punishable with imprisonment and the offender—

(a) pleaded guilty to the offence and to any connected offence;

(b) has never been convicted by or before a court in the United Kingdom of any offence other than the offence and any connected offence; and

(c) has never been bound over in criminal proceedings in England and Wales or Northern Ireland to keep the peace or to be of good behaviour.

(1A) For the purpose of section 16(3) above, the discretionary referral conditions are satisfied in relation to an offence if the offence is not an offence punishable with imprisonment but the offender meets the conditions in paragraphs (a) to (c) of subsection (1) above.

(2) For the purposes of section 16(3) above the discretionary referral conditions are also satisfied in relation to an offence if—

(a) the offender is being dealt with by the court for the offence and one or more connected offences (whether or not any of them is an offence punishable with imprisonment);

(b) although he pleaded guilty to at least one of the offences mentioned in paragraph (a) above, he also pleaded not guilty to at least one of them;

(c) he has never been convicted by or before a court in the United Kingdom of any offence other than the offences mentioned in paragraph (a) above; and

(d) he has never been bound over in criminal proceedings in England and Wales or Northern Ireland to keep the peace or to be of good behaviour.

(3) The Secretary of State may by regulations make such amendments of this section as he considers appropriate for altering in any way the descriptions of offenders in the case of which the compulsory referral conditions or the discretionary referral conditions fall to be satisfied for the purposes of section 16(2) or (3) above (as the case may be).

(4) Any description of offender having effect for those purposes by virtue of such regulations may be framed by reference to such matters as the Secretary of State considers appropriate, including (in particular) one or more of the following—

  (a) the offender's age;
  (b) how the offender has pleaded;
  (c) the offence (or offences) of which the offender has been convicted;
  (d) the offender's previous convictions (if any);
  (e) how (if at all) the offender has been previously punished or otherwise dealt with by any court; and
  (f) any characteristics or behaviour of, or circumstances relating to, any person who has at any time been charged in the same proceedings as the offender (whether or not in respect of the same offence).

(5) For the purposes of this section an offender who has been convicted of an offence in respect of which he was conditionally discharged (whether by a court in England and Wales or in Northern Ireland) shall be treated, despite—

  (a) section 14(1) above (conviction of offence for which offender so discharged deemed not a conviction), or
  (b) Article 6(1) of the Criminal Justice (Northern Ireland) Order 1996 (corresponding provision for Northern Ireland),

as having been convicted of that offence.

18 Making of referral orders: general

(1) A referral order shall—

  (a) specify the youth offending team responsible for implementing the order;
  (b) require the offender to attend each of the meetings of a youth offender panel to be established by the team for the offender; and
  (c) specify the period for which any youth offender contract taking effect between the offender and the panel under section 23 below is to have effect (which must not be less than three nor more than twelve months).

(2) The youth offending team specified under subsection (1)(a) above shall be the team having the function of implementing referral orders in the area in which it appears to the court that the offender resides or will reside.

(3) On making a referral order the court shall explain to the offender in ordinary language—

  (a) the effect of the order; and
  (b) the consequences which may follow—
    (i) if no youth offender contract takes effect between the offender and the panel under section 23 below; or
    (ii) if the offender breaches any of the terms of any such contract.

(4) Subsections (5) to (7) below apply where, in dealing with an offender for two or more connected offences, a court makes a referral order in respect of each, or each of two or more, of the offences.

(5) The orders shall have the effect of referring the offender to a single youth offender panel; and the provision made by them under subsection (1) above shall accordingly be the same in each case, except that the periods specified under subsection (1)(c) may be different.

(6) The court may direct that the period so specified in either or any of the orders is to run concurrently with or be additional to that specified in the other or any of the others; but in exercising its power under this subsection the court must ensure that the total period for which such a contract as is mentioned in subsection (1)(c) above is to have effect does not exceed twelve months.

(7) Each of the orders mentioned in subsection (4) above shall, for the purposes of this Part, be treated as associated with the other or each of the others.

19   Making of referral orders: effect on court's other sentencing powers

(1) Subsections (2) to (5) below apply where a court makes a referral order in respect of an offence.

(2) The court may not deal with the offender for the offence in any of the prohibited ways.

(3) The court—

(a) shall, in respect of any connected offence, either sentence the offender by making a referral order or make an order discharging him absolutely; and

(b) may not deal with the offender for any such offence in any of the prohibited ways.

(4) For the purposes of subsections (2) and (3) above the prohibited ways are—

(a) imposing a community sentence on the offender;

(b) ordering him to pay a fine;

(c) making a reparation order in respect of him; and

(d) making an order discharging him conditionally.

(5) The court may not make, in connection with the conviction of the offender for the offence or any connected offence—

(a) an order binding him over to keep the peace or to be of good behaviour; or

(b) an order under section 150 below (binding over of parent or guardian).

20   Making of referral orders: attendance of parents etc

(1) A court making a referral order may make an order requiring—

(a) the appropriate person, or

(b) in a case where there are two or more appropriate persons, any one or more of them,

to attend the meetings of the youth offender panel.

(2) Where an offender is aged under 16 when a court makes a referral order in his case—

(a) the court shall exercise its power under subsection (1) above so as to require at least one appropriate person to attend meetings of the youth offender panel; and

(b) if the offender falls within subsection (6) below, the person or persons so required to attend those meetings shall be or include a representative of the local authority mentioned in that subsection.

(3) The court shall not under this section make an order requiring a person to attend meetings of the youth offender panel—

(a) if the court is satisfied that it would be unreasonable to do so; or

(b) to an extent which the court is satisfied would be unreasonable.

(5) Where the offender falls within subsection (6) below, each of the following is an 'appropriate person' for the purposes of this section—

(a) a representative of the local authority mentioned in that subsection; and

(b) each person who is a parent or guardian of the offender with whom the offender is allowed to live.

(7) If, at the time when a court makes an order under this section—

(a) a person who is required by the order to attend meetings of a youth offender panel is not present in court, or

(b) a local authority whose representative is so required to attend such meetings is not represented in court,

the court must send him or (as the case may be) the authority a copy of the order forthwith.

Youth offender panels

21   Establishment of panels

(1) Where a referral order has been made in respect of an offender (or two or more associated referral orders have been so made), it is the duty of the youth offending team specified in the order (or orders)—

(a) to establish a youth offender panel for the offender;

(b) to arrange for the first meeting of the panel to be held for the purposes of section 23 below; and

    (c) subsequently to arrange for the holding of any further meetings of the panel required by virtue of section 25 below (in addition to those required by virtue of any other provision of this Part).

(2) A youth offender panel shall—

    (a) be constituted,

    (b) conduct its proceedings, and

    (c) discharge its functions under this Part (and in particular those arising under section 23 below),

in accordance with guidance given from time to time by the Secretary of State.

(3) At each of its meetings a panel shall, however, consist of at least—

    (a) one member appointed by the youth offending team from among its members; and

    (b) two members so appointed who are not members of the team.

22 Attendance at panel meetings

(1) The specified team shall, in the case of each meeting of the panel established for the offender, notify—

    (a) the offender, and

    (b) any person to whom an order under section 20 above applies,

of the time and place at which he is required to attend that meeting.

(2) If the offender fails to attend any part of such a meeting the panel may—

    (a) adjourn the meeting to such time and place as it may specify; or

    (b) end the meeting and refer the offender back to the appropriate court;

and subsection (1) above shall apply in relation to any such adjourned meeting.

(2A) If—

    (a) a parent or guardian of the offender fails to comply with an order under section 20 above (requirement to attend the meetings of the panel), and

    (b) the offender is aged under 18 at the time of the failure,

the panel may refer that parent or guardian to a youth court acting in the local justice area in which it appears to the panel that the offender resides or will reside.

(3) One person aged 18 or over chosen by the offender, with the agreement of the panel, shall be entitled to accompany the offender to any meeting of the panel (and it need not be the same person who accompanies him to every meeting).

(4) The panel may allow to attend any such meeting—

    (a) any person who appears to the panel to be a victim of, or otherwise affected by, the offence, or any of the offences, in respect of which the offender was referred to the panel;

    (b) any person who appears to the panel to be someone capable of having a good influence on the offender.

(5) Where the panel allows any such person as is mentioned in subsection (4)(a) above ('the victim') to attend a meeting of the panel, the panel may allow the victim to be accompanied to the meeting by one person chosen by the victim with the agreement of the panel.

Youth offender contracts

23 First meeting: agreement of contract with offender

(1) At the first meeting of the youth offender panel established for an offender the panel shall seek to reach agreement with the offender on a programme of behaviour the aim (or principal aim) of which is the prevention of re-offending by the offender.

(2) The terms of the programme may, in particular, include provision for any of the following—

    (a) the offender to make financial or other reparation to any person who appears to the panel to be a victim of, or otherwise affected by, the offence, or any of the offences, for which the offender was referred to the panel;

324 Powers of Criminal Courts (Sentencing) Act 2000

(b) the offender to attend mediation sessions with any such victim or other person;

(c) the offender to carry out unpaid work or service in or for the community;

(d) the offender to be at home at times specified in or determined under the programme;

(e) attendance by the offender at a school or other educational establishment or at a place of work;

(f) the offender to participate in specified activities (such as those designed to address offending behaviour, those offering education or training or those assisting with the rehabilitation of persons dependent on, or having a propensity to misuse, alcohol or drugs);

(g) the offender to present himself to specified persons at times and places specified in or determined under the programme;

(h) the offender to stay away from specified places or persons (or both);

(i) enabling the offender's compliance with the programme to be supervised and recorded.

(3) The programme may not, however, provide—

(a) for the electronic monitoring of the offender's whereabouts; or

(b) for the offender to have imposed on him any physical restriction on his movements.

(4) No term which provides for anything to be done to or with any such victim or other affected person as is mentioned in subsection (2)(a) above may be included in the programme without the consent of that person.

24 First meeting: duration of contract

(1) This section applies where a youth offender contract has taken effect under section 23 above between an offender and a youth offender panel.

(2) The day on which the contract so takes effect shall be the first day of the period for which it has effect.

25 First meeting: failure to agree contract

(1) Where it appears to a youth offender panel to be appropriate to do so, the panel may—

(a) end the first meeting (or any further meeting held in pursuance of paragraph (b) below) without having reached agreement with the offender on a programme of behaviour of the kind mentioned in section 23(1) above; and

(b) resume consideration of the offender's case at a further meeting of the panel.

(2) If, however, it appears to the panel at the first meeting or any such further meeting that there is no prospect of agreement being reached with the offender within a reasonable period after the making of the referral order (or orders)—

(a) subsection (1)(b) above shall not apply; and

(b) instead the panel shall refer the offender back to the appropriate court.

(3) If at a meeting of the panel—

(a) agreement is reached with the offender but he does not sign the record produced in pursuance of section 23(5) above, and

(b) his failure to do so appears to the panel to be unreasonable,

the panel shall end the meeting and refer the offender back to the appropriate court.

26 Progress meetings

(1) At any time—

(a) after a youth offender contract has taken effect under section 23 above, but

(b) before the end of the period for which the contract has effect,

the specified team shall, if so requested by the panel, arrange for the holding of a meeting of the panel under this section ('a progress meeting').

(2) The panel may make a request under subsection (1) above if it appears to the panel to be expedient to review—

    (a) the offender's progress in implementing the programme of behaviour contained in the contract; or

    (b) any other matter arising in connection with the contract.

(3) The panel shall make such a request if—

    (a) the offender has notified the panel that—

        (i) he wishes to seek the panel's agreement to a variation in the terms of the contract; or

        (ii) he wishes the panel to refer him back to the appropriate court with a view to the referral order (or orders) being revoked on account of a significant change in his circumstances (such as his being taken to live abroad) making compliance with any youth offender contract impractical; or

    (b) it appears to the panel that the offender is in breach of any of the terms of the contract.

(4) At a progress meeting the panel shall do such one or more of the following things as it considers appropriate in the circumstances, namely—

    (a) review the offender's progress or any such other matter as is mentioned in subsection (2) above;

    (b) discuss with the offender any breach of the terms of the contract which it appears to the panel that he has committed;

    (c) consider any variation in the terms of the contract sought by the offender or which it appears to the panel to be expedient to make in the light of any such review or discussion;

    (d) consider whether to accede to any request by the offender that he be referred back to the appropriate court.

(5) Where the panel has discussed with the offender such a breach as is mentioned in subsection (4)(b) above—

    (a) the panel and the offender may agree that the offender is to continue to be required to comply with the contract (either in its original form or with any agreed variation in its terms) without being referred back to the appropriate court; or

    (b) the panel may decide to end the meeting and refer the offender back to that court.

(6) Where a variation in the terms of the contract is agreed between the offender and the panel, the panel shall cause a written record of the variation to be produced forthwith—

    (a) in language capable of being readily understood by, or explained to, the offender; and

    (b) for signature by him.

(7) Any such variation shall take effect once the record has been signed—

    (a) by the offender; and

    (b) by a member of the panel on behalf of the panel;

and the panel shall cause a copy of the record to be given or sent to the offender.

(8) If at a progress meeting—

    (a) any such variation is agreed but the offender does not sign the record produced in pursuance of subsection (6) above, and

    (b) his failure to do so appears to the panel to be unreasonable,

the panel may end the meeting and refer the offender back to the appropriate court.

27 Final meeting

(1) Where the compliance period in the case of a youth offender contract is due to expire, the specified team shall arrange for the holding, before the end of that period, of a meeting of the panel under this section ('the final meeting').

(2) At the final meeting the panel shall—

    (a) review the extent of the offender's compliance to date with the terms of the contract; and

(b) decide, in the light of that review, whether his compliance with those terms has been such as to justify the conclusion that, by the time the compliance period expires, he will have satisfactorily completed the contract;

and the panel shall give the offender written confirmation of its decision.

(3) Where the panel decides that the offender's compliance with the terms of the contract has been such as to justify that conclusion, the panel's decision shall have the effect of discharging the referral order (or orders) as from the end of the compliance period.

(4) Otherwise the panel shall refer the offender back to the appropriate court.

Supplementary

29   Functions of youth offending teams

(1) The functions of a youth offending team responsible for implementing a referral order include, in particular, arranging for the provision of such administrative staff, accommodation or other facilities as are required by the youth offender panel established in pursuance of the order.

(2) During the period for which a youth offender contract between a youth offender panel and an offender has effect—

(a) the specified team shall make arrangements for supervising the offender's compliance with the terms of the contract; and

(b) the person who is the member of the panel referred to in section 21(3)(a) above shall ensure that records are kept of the offender's compliance (or non-compliance) with those terms.

SCHEDULE 1

PART I   REFERRAL BACK TO APPROPRIATE COURT

1. *Introductory*

(2) For the purposes of this Part of this Schedule and the provisions mentioned in sub-paragraph (1) above the appropriate court is—

(a) in the case of an offender aged under 18 at the time when (in pursuance of the referral back) he first appears before the court, a youth court acting in the local justice area in which it appears to the youth offender panel that the offender resides or will reside; and

(b) otherwise, a magistrates' court (other than a youth court) acting in that area.

2. *Mode of referral back to court*

The panel shall make the referral by sending a report to the appropriate court explaining why the offender is being referred back to it.

4. *Detention and remand of arrested offender*

(1) Where the offender is arrested in pursuance of a warrant under paragraph 3(2) above and cannot be brought immediately before the appropriate court—

(a) the person in whose custody he is may make arrangements for his detention in a place of safety (within the meaning given by section 107(1) of the Children and Young Persons Act 1933) for a period of not more than 72 hours from the time of the arrest (and it shall be lawful for him to be detained in pursuance of the arrangements); and

(b) that person shall within that period bring him before a court which—

(i)   if he is under the age of 18 when he is brought before the court, shall be a youth court; and

(ii) if he has then attained that age, shall be a magistrates' court other than a youth court.

5. *Power of court where it upholds panel's decision*

(1) If it is proved to the satisfaction of the appropriate court as regards any decision of the panel which resulted in the offender being referred back to the court—

(a) that, so far as the decision relied on any finding of fact by the panel, the panel was entitled to make that finding in the circumstances, and

(b) that, so far as the decision involved any exercise of discretion by the panel, the panel reasonably exercised that discretion in the circumstances,

the court may exercise the power conferred by sub-paragraph (2) below.

(2) That power is a power to revoke the referral order (or each of the referral orders).

(3) The revocation under sub-paragraph (2) above of a referral order has the effect of revoking any related order under paragraph 11 or 12 below.

(4) Where any order is revoked under sub-paragraph (2) above or by virtue of sub-paragraph (3) above, the appropriate court may deal with the offender in accordance with sub-paragraph (5) below for the offence in respect of which the revoked order was made.

(5) In so dealing with the offender for such an offence, the appropriate court—

(a) may deal with him in any way in which (assuming section 16 of this Act had not applied) he could have been dealt with for that offence by the court which made the order; and

(b) shall have regard to—

(i) the circumstances of his referral back to the court; and

(ii) where a contract has taken effect under section 23 of this Act between the offender and the panel, the extent of his compliance with the terms of the contract.

PART IA   REFERRAL OF PARENT OR GUARDIAN FOR BREACH OF SECTION 20 ORDER

Introductory

9A—(1) This Part of this Schedule applies where, under section 22(2A) of this Act, a youth offender panel refers an offender's parent or guardian to a youth court.

(2) In this Part of this Schedule—

(a) 'the offender' means the offender whose parent or guardian is referred under section 22(2A);

(b) 'the parent' means the parent or guardian so referred; and

(c) 'the youth court' means a youth court as mentioned in section 22(2A).

Mode of referral to court

9B The panel shall make the referral by sending a report to the youth court explaining why the parent is being referred to it.

Bringing the parent before the court

9C—(1) Where the youth court receives such a report it shall cause the parent to appear before it.

(2) For the purpose of securing the attendance of the parent before the court, a justice acting in the local justice area in which the court acts may—

(a) issue a summons requiring the parent to appear at the place and time specified in it; or

(b) if the report is substantiated on oath, issue a warrant for the parent's arrest.

(3) Any summons or warrant issued under sub-paragraph (2) above shall direct the parent to appear or be brought before the youth court.

Power of court to make parenting order: application of supplemental provisions

9D—(1) Where the parent appears or is brought before the youth court under paragraph 9C above, the court may make a parenting order in respect of the parent if—
  (a) it is proved to the satisfaction of the court that the parent has failed without reasonable excuse to comply with the order under section 20 of this Act; and
  (b) the court is satisfied that the parenting order would be desirable in the interests of preventing the commission of any further offence by the offender.

(2) A parenting order is an order which requires the parent—
  (a) to comply, for a period not exceeding twelve months, with such requirements as are specified in the order, and
  (b) subject to sub-paragraph (4) below, to attend, for a concurrent period not exceeding three months, such counselling or guidance programme as may be specified in directions given by the responsible officer.

(3) The requirements that may be specified under sub-paragraph (2)(a) above are those which the court considers desirable in the interests of preventing the commission of any further offence by the offender.

(4) A parenting order under this paragraph may, but need not, include a requirement mentioned in subsection (2)(b) above in any case where a parenting order under this paragraph or any other enactment has been made in respect of the parent on a previous occasion.

(5) A counselling or guidance programme which a parent is required to attend by virtue of subsection (2)(b) above may be or include a residential course but only if the court is satisfied—
  (a) that the attendance of the parent at a residential course is likely to be more effective than his attendance at a non-residential course in preventing the commission of any further offence by the offender, and
  (b) that any interference with family life which is likely to result from the attendance of the parent at a residential course is proportionate in all the circumstances.

(6) Before making a parenting order under this paragraph where the offender is aged under 16, the court shall obtain and consider information about his family circumstances and the likely effect of the order on those circumstances.

(7) Sections 8(3) and (8), 9(3) to (7) and 18(3) and (4) of the Crime and Disorder Act 1998 apply in relation to a parenting order made under this paragraph as they apply in relation to any other parenting order.

Appeal

9E—(1) An appeal shall lie to the Crown Court against the making of a parenting order under paragraph 9D above.

(2) Subsections (2) and (3) of section 10 of the Crime and Disorder Act 1998 (appeals against parenting orders) apply in relation to an appeal under this paragraph as they apply in relation to an appeal under subsection (1)(b) of that section.

Effect on section 20 order

9F—(1) The making of a parenting order under paragraph 9D above is without prejudice to the continuance of the order under section 20 of this Act.

(2) Section 63(1) to (4) of the Magistrates' Courts Act 1980 (power of magistrates' court to deal with person for breach of order, etc) apply (as well as section 22(2A) of this Act and this Part of this Schedule) in relation to an order under section 20 of this Act.

PART II   FURTHER CONVICTIONS DURING REFERRAL

10. *Extension of referral for further offences*

(1) Paragraphs 11 and 12 below apply where, at a time when an offender aged under 18 is subject to referral, a youth court or other magistrates' court ('the relevant court') is dealing with him for an offence in relation to which paragraphs (a) to (c) of section 16(1) of this Act are applicable.

(2) But paragraphs 11 and 12 do not apply unless the offender's compliance period is less than twelve months.

11. *Extension where further offences committed pre-referral*

If—
  (a) the occasion on which the offender was referred to the panel is the only other occasion on which it has fallen to a court in the United Kingdom to deal with the offender for any offence or offences, and
  (b) the offender committed the offence mentioned in paragraph 10 above, and any connected offence, before he was referred to the panel,
the relevant court may sentence the offender for the offence by making an order extending his compliance period.

12. *Extension where further offence committed after referral*

(1) If—
  (a) paragraph 11(a) above applies, but
  (b) the offender committed the offence mentioned in paragraph 10 above, or any connected offence, after he was referred to the panel,
the relevant court may sentence the offender for the offence by making an order extending his compliance period, but only if the requirements of sub-paragraph (2) below are complied with.

(2) Those requirements are that the court must—
  (a) be satisfied, on the basis of a report made to it by the relevant body, that there are exceptional circumstances which indicate that, even though the offender has re-offended since being referred to the panel, extending his compliance period is likely to help prevent further re-offending by him; and
  (b) state in open court that it is so satisfied and why it is.

(3) In sub-paragraph (2) above 'the relevant body' means the panel to which the offender has been referred or, if no contract has yet taken effect between the offender and the panel under section 23 of this Act, the specified team.

13. *Provisions supplementary to paragraphs 11 and 12*

(1) An order under paragraph 11 or 12 above, or two or more orders under one or other of those paragraphs made in respect of connected offences, must not so extend the offender's compliance period as to cause it to exceed twelve months.

14. *Further convictions which lead to revocation of referral*

(1) This paragraph applies where, at a time when an offender is subject to referral, a court in England and Wales deals with him for an offence (whether committed before or after he was referred to the panel) by making an order other than—
  (a) an order under paragraph 11 or 12 above; or
  (b) an order discharging him absolutely.

(2) In such a case the order of the court shall have the effect of revoking—
- (a) the referral order (or orders); and
- (b) any related order or orders under paragraph 11 or 12 above.

(3) Where any order is revoked by virtue of sub-paragraph (2) above, the court may, if appears to the court that it would be in the interests of justice to do so, deal with the offender for the offence in respect of which the revoked order was made in any way in which (assuming section 16 of this Act had not applied) he could have been dealt with for that offence by the court which made the order.

(4) When dealing with the offender under sub-paragraph (3) above the court shall, where a contract has taken effect between the offender and the panel under section 23 of this Act, have regard to the extent of his compliance with the terms of the contract.

Parenting orders

Crime and Disorder Act 1998

8   Crime and Disorder Act 1998

(1) This section applies where, in any court proceedings—
- (a)   a child safety order is made in respect of a child or the court determines on an application under section 12(6) below that a child has failed to comply with any requirement included in such an order;
- (aa)   a parental compensation order is made in relation to a child's behaviour;
- (b)   an anti-social behaviour order or sex offender order is made in respect of a child or young person;
- (c)   a child or young person is convicted of an offence; or
- (d)   a person is convicted of an offence under section 443 (failure to comply with school attendance order) or section 444 (failure to secure regular attendance at school of registered pupil) of the Education Act 1996.

(2) Subject to subsection (3) and section 9(1) below, if in the proceedings the court is satisfied that the relevant condition is fulfilled, it may make a parenting order in respect of a person who is a parent or guardian of the child or young person or, as the case may be, the person convicted of the offence under section 443 or 444 ('the parent').

(3) A court shall not make a parenting order unless it has been notified by the Secretary of State that arrangements for implementing such orders are available in the area in which it appears to the court that the parent resides or will reside and the notice has not been withdrawn.

(4) A parenting order is an order which requires the parent—
- (a)   to comply, for a period not exceeding twelve months, with such requirements as are specified in the order; and
- (b)   subject to subsection (5) below, to attend, for a concurrent period not exceeding three months, such counselling or guidance programme as may be specified in directions given by the responsible officer.

(5) A parenting order may, but need not, include such a requirement as is mentioned in subsection (4)(b) above in any case where a parenting order under this section or any other enactment has been made in respect of the parent on a previous occasion.

(6) The relevant condition is that the parenting order would be desirable in the interests of preventing—
- (a)   in a case falling within paragraph (a), (aa) or (b) of subsection (1) above, any repetition of the kind of behaviour which led to the child safety order, parental

compensation order, anti-social behaviour order or sex offender order being made;

    (b) in a case falling within paragraph (c) of that subsection, the commission of any further offence by the child or young person;

    (c) in a case falling within paragraph (d) of that subsection, the commission of any further offence under section 443 or 444 of the Education Act 1996.

(7) The requirements that may be specified under subsection (4)(a) above are those which the court considers desirable in the interests of preventing any such repetition or, as the case may be, the commission of any such further offence.

(7A) A counselling or guidance programme which a parent is required to attend by virtue of subsection (4)(b) above may be or include a residential course but only if the court is satisfied—

    (a) that the attendance of the parent at a residential course is likely to be more effective than his attendance at a non-residential course in preventing any such repetition or, as the case may be, the commission of any such further offence, and

    (b) that any interference with family life which is likely to result from the attendance of the parent at a residential course is proportionate in all the circumstances.

9 Parenting orders: supplemental

(1) Where a person under the age of 16 is convicted of an offence, the court by or before which he is so convicted—

    (a) if it is satisfied that the relevant condition is fulfilled, shall make a parenting order; and

    (b) if it is not so satisfied, shall state in open court that it is not and why it is not.

(1A) The requirements of subsection (1) do not apply where the court makes a referral order in respect of the offence.

(1B) If an anti-social behaviour order is made in respect of a person under the age of 16 the court which makes the order—

    (a) must make a parenting order if it is satisfied that the relevant condition is fulfilled;

    (b) if it is not so satisfied, must state in open court that it is not and why it is not.

(2) Before making a parenting order—

    (a) in a case falling within paragraph (a) of subsection (1) of section 8 above;

    (b) in a case falling within paragraph (b) or (c) of that subsection, where the person concerned is under the age of 16; or

    (c) in a case falling within paragraph (d) of that subsection, where the person to whom the offence related is under that age,

a court shall obtain and consider information about the person's family circumstances and the likely effect of the order on those circumstances.

(2A) In a case where a court proposes to make both a referral order in respect of a child or young person convicted of an offence and a parenting order, before making the parenting order the court shall obtain and consider a report by an appropriate officer—

    (a) indicating the requirements proposed by that officer to be included in the parenting order;

    (b) indicating the reasons why he considers those requirements would be desirable in the interests of preventing the commission of any further offence by the child or young person; and

    (c) if the child or young person is aged under 16, containing the information required by subsection (2) above.

(2B) In subsection (2A) above 'an appropriate officer' means—

    (a) an officer of a local probation board;

    (b) a social worker of a local authority; or

    (c) a member of a youth offending team.

(3) Before making a parenting order, a court shall explain to the parent in ordinary language—

    (a) the effect of the order and of the requirements proposed to be included in it;

    (b) the consequences which may follow (under subsection (7) below) if he fails to comply with any of those requirements; and

    (c) that the court has power (under subsection (5) below) to review the order on the application either of the parent or of the responsible officer.

(4) Requirements specified in, and directions given under, a parenting order shall, as far as practicable, be such as to avoid—

    (a) any conflict with the parent's religious beliefs; and

    (b) any interference with the times, if any, at which he normally works or attends an educational establishment.

(5) If while a parenting order is in force it appears to the court which made it, on the application of the responsible officer or the parent, that it is appropriate to make an order under this subsection, the court may make an order discharging the parenting order or varying it—

    (a) by cancelling any provision included in it; or

    (b) by inserting in it (either in addition to or in substitution for any of its provisions) any provision that could have been included in the order if the court had then had power to make it and were exercising the power.

(7) If while a parenting order is in force the parent without reasonable excuse fails to comply with any requirement included in the order, or specified in directions given by the responsible officer, he shall be liable on summary conviction to a fine not exceeding level 3 on the standard scale.

(7A) In this section 'referral order' means an order under section 16(2) or (3) of the Powers of Criminal Courts (Sentencing) Act 2000 (referral of offender to youth offender panel).

Binding over to keep the peace

Justices of the Peace Act 1968

1   Appointment of justices, oaths of office, etc

(7) It is hereby declared that any court of record having a criminal jurisdiction has, as ancillary to that jurisdiction, the power to bind over to keep the peace, and power to bind over to be of good behaviour, a person who or whose case is before the court, by requiring him to enter into his own recognizances or to find sureties or both, and committing him to prison if he does not comply.

Magistrates' Courts Act 1980

115   Binding over to keep the peace or be of good behaviour

(1) The power of a magistrates' court on the complaint of any person to adjudge any other person to enter into a recognizance, with or without sureties, to keep the peace or to be of good behaviour towards the complainant shall be exercised by order on complaint.

(2) Where a complaint is made under this section, the power of the court to remand the defendant under subsection (5) of section 55 above shall not be subject to the restrictions imposed by subsection (6) of that section.

(3) If any person ordered by a magistrates' court under subsection (1) above to enter into a recognizance, with or without sureties, to keep the peace or to be of good behaviour fails to comply with the order, the court may commit him to custody for a period not exceeding 6 months or until he sooner complies with the order.

Binding over of parent or guardian

Powers of Criminal Courts (Sentencing) Act 2000

150 Binding over of parent or guardian

(1) Where a child or young person (that is to say, any person aged under 18) is convicted of an offence, the powers conferred by this section shall be exercisable by the court by which he is sentenced for that offence, and where the offender is aged under 16 when sentenced it shall be the duty of that court—

> (a) to exercise those powers if it is satisfied, having regard to the circumstances of the case, that their exercise would be desirable in the interests of preventing the commission by him of further offences; and
>
> (b) if it does not exercise them, to state in open court that it is not satisfied as mentioned in paragraph (a) above and why it is not so satisfied;

but this subsection has effect subject to section 19(5) above and paragraph 13(5) of Schedule 1 to this Act (cases where referral orders made or extended).

(2) The powers conferred by this section are as follows—

> (a) with the consent of the offender's parent or guardian, to order the parent or guardian to enter into a recognizance to take proper care of him and exercise proper control over him; and
>
> (b) if the parent or guardian refuses consent and the court considers the refusal unreasonable, to order the parent or guardian to pay a fine not exceeding £1,000;

and where the court has passed a community sentence on the offender, it may include in the recognizance a provision that the offender's parent or guardian ensure that the offender complies with the requirements of that sentence.

(3) An order under this section shall not require the parent or guardian to enter into a recognizance for an amount exceeding £1,000.

(4) An order under this section shall not require the parent or guardian to enter into a recognizance—

> (a) for a period exceeding three years; or
>
> (b) where the offender will attain the age of 18 in a period shorter than three years, for a period exceeding that shorter period.

(7) In fixing the amount of a recognizance under this section, the court shall take into account among other things the means of the parent or guardian so far as they appear or are known to the court; and this subsection applies whether taking into account the means of the parent or guardian has the effect of increasing or reducing the amount of the recognizance.

Discharge

Powers of Criminal Courts (Sentencing) Act 2000

12 Absolute and conditional discharge

(1) Where a court by or before which a person is convicted of an offence (not being an offence the sentence for which is fixed by law or falls to be imposed under section 110(2) or

111(2) below, section 51A(2) of the Firearms Act 1968 or section 225, 226, 227 or 228 of the Criminal Justice Act 2003 is of the opinion, having regard to the circumstances including the nature of the offence and the character of the offender, that it is inexpedient to inflict punishment, the court may make an order either—

(a) discharging him absolutely; or

(b) if the court thinks fit, discharging him subject to the condition that he commits no offence during such period, not exceeding three years from the date of the order, as may be specified in the order.

(2) Subsection (1)(b) above has effect subject to section 66(4) of the Crime and Disorder Act 1998 (as amended by Sch. 9, para 198 Powers of Criminal Courts (Sentencing) Act 2000) (effect of reprimands and warnings).

(3) An order discharging a person subject to such a condition as is mentioned in sub-section (1)(b) above is in this Act referred to as an 'order for conditional discharge'; and the period specified in any such order is in this Act referred to as 'the period of conditional discharge'.

(5) If (by virtue of section 13 below) a person conditionally discharged under this section is sentenced for the offence in respect of which the order for conditional discharge was made, that order shall cease to have effect.

(6) On making an order for conditional discharge, the court may, if it thinks it expedient for the purpose of the offender's reformation, allow any person who consents to do so to give security for the good behaviour of the offender.

(7) Nothing in this section shall be construed as preventing a court, on discharging an offender absolutely or conditionally in respect of any offence, from making an order for costs against the offender or imposing any disqualification on him or from making in respect of the offence an order under section 130, 143 or 148 below (compensation orders, deprivation orders and restitution orders).

13 Commission of further offence by person conditionally discharged

(1) If it appears to the Crown Court, where that court has jurisdiction in accordance with subsection (2) below, or to a justice of the peace having jurisdiction in accordance with that subsection, that a person in whose case an order for conditional discharge has been made—

(a) has been convicted by a court in Great Britain of an offence committed during the period of conditional discharge, and

(b) has been dealt with in respect of that offence,

that court or justice may, subject to subsection (3) below, issue a summons requiring that person to appear at the place and time specified in it or a warrant for his arrest.

(2) Jurisdiction for the purposes of subsection (1) above may be exercised—

(a) if the order for conditional discharge was made by the Crown Court, by that court;

(b) if the order was made by a magistrates' court, by a justice of the peace.

(5) If a person in whose case an order for conditional discharge has been made by the Crown Court is convicted by a magistrates' court of an offence committed during the period of conditional discharge, the magistrates' court—

(a) may commit him to custody or release him on bail until he can be brought or appear before the Crown Court; and

(b) if it does so, shall send to the Crown Court a copy of the minute or memorandum of the conviction entered in the register, signed by the designated officer by whom the register is kept.

(6) Where it is proved to the satisfaction of the court by which an order for conditional discharge was made that the person in whose case the order was made has been convicted of an offence committed during the period of conditional discharge, the court may deal with him, for the offence for which the order was made, in any way in which it could deal with him if he had just been convicted by or before that court of that offence.

(7) If a person in whose case an order for conditional discharge has been made by a magistrates' court—
- (a) is convicted before the Crown Court of an offence committed during the period of conditional discharge, or
- (b) is dealt with by the Crown Court for any such offence in respect of which he was committed for sentence to the Crown Court,

the Crown Court may deal with him, for the offence for which the order was made, in any way in which the magistrates' court could deal with him if it had just convicted him of that offence.

(8) If a person in whose case an order for conditional discharge has been made by a magistrates' court is convicted by another magistrates' court of any offence committed during the period of conditional discharge, that other court may, with the consent of the court which made the order, deal with him, for the offence for which the order was made, in any way in which the court could deal with him if it had just convicted him of that offence.

(9) Where an order for conditional discharge has been made by a magistrates' court in the case of an offender under 18 years of age in respect of an offence triable only on indictment in the case of an adult, any powers exercisable under subsection (6), (7) or (8) above by that or any other court in respect of the offender after he attains the age of 18 shall be powers to do either or both of the following—
- (a) to impose a fine not exceeding £5,000 for the offence in respect of which the order was made;
- (b) to deal with the offender for that offence in any way in which a magistrates' court could deal with him if it had just convicted him of an offence punishable with imprisonment for a term not exceeding six months.

(10) The reference in subsection (6) above to a person's having been convicted of an offence committed during the period of conditional discharge is a reference to his having been so convicted by a court in Great Britain.

14 Effect of discharge

(1) Subject to subsection (2) below, a conviction of an offence for which an order is made under section 12 above discharging the offender absolutely or conditionally shall be deemed not to be a conviction for any purpose other than the purposes of the proceedings in which the order is made and of any subsequent proceedings which may be taken against the offender under section 13 above.

(2) Where the offender was aged 18 or over at the time of his conviction of the offence in question and is subsequently sentenced (under section 13 above) for that offence, subsection (1) above shall cease to apply to the conviction.

(3) Without prejudice to subsections (1) and (2) above, the conviction of an offender who is discharged absolutely or conditionally under section 12 above shall in any event be disregarded for the purposes of any enactment or instrument which—
- (a) imposes any disqualification or disability upon convicted persons; or
- (b) authorises or requires the imposition of any such disqualification or disability.

(4) Subsections (1) to (3) above shall not affect—
- (a) any right of an offender discharged absolutely or conditionally under section 12 above to rely on his conviction in bar of any subsequent proceedings for the same offence;
- (b) the restoration of any property in consequence of the conviction of any such offender; or
- (c) the operation, in relation to any such offender, of any enactment or instrument in force on 1st July 1974 which is expressed to extend to persons dealt with under section 1(1) of the Probation of Offenders Act 1907 as well as to convicted persons.

(5) In subsections (3) and (4) above—
'enactment' includes an enactment contained in a local Act; and
'instrument' means an instrument having effect by virtue of an Act.

15 Discharge: supplementary

(1) The Secretary of State may by order direct that subsection (1) of section 12 above shall be amended by substituting, for the maximum period specified in that subsection as originally enacted or as previously amended under this subsection, such period as may be specified in the order.

(2) Where an order for conditional discharge has been made on appeal, for the purposes of section 13 above it shall be deemed—

(a) if it was made on an appeal brought from a magistrates' court, to have been made by that magistrates' court;

(b) if it was made on an appeal brought from the Crown Court or from the criminal division of the Court of Appeal, to have been made by the Crown Court.

(I) CONFISCATION ORDERS

Proceeds of Crime Act 2002

6 Making of order

(1) The Crown Court must proceed under this section if the following two conditions are satisfied.

(2) The first condition is that a defendant falls within any of the following paragraphs—

(a) he is convicted of an offence or offences in proceedings before the Crown Court;

(b) he is committed to the Crown Court for sentence in respect of an offence or offences under section 3, 3A, 3B, 3C, 4, 4A or 6 of the Sentencing Act;

(c) he is committed to the Crown Court in respect of an offence or offences under section 70 below (committal with a view to a confiscation order being considered).

(3) The second condition is that—

(a) the prosecutor or the Director asks the court to proceed under this section, or

(b) the court believes it is appropriate for it to do so.

(4) The court must proceed as follows—

(a) it must decide whether the defendant has a criminal lifestyle;

(b) if it decides that he has a criminal lifestyle it must decide whether he has benefited from his general criminal conduct;

(c) if it decides that he does not have a criminal lifestyle it must decide whether he has benefited from his particular criminal conduct.

(5) If the court decides under subsection (4)(b) or (c) that the defendant has benefited from the conduct referred to it must—

(a) decide the recoverable amount, and

(b) make an order (a confiscation order) requiring him to pay that amount.

(6) But the court must treat the duty in subsection (5) as a power if it believes that any victim of the conduct has at any time started or intends to start proceedings against the defendant in respect of loss, injury or damage sustained in connection with the conduct.

(7) The court must decide any question arising under subsection (4) or (5) on a balance of probabilities.

(8) The first condition is not satisfied if the defendant absconds (but section 27 may apply).

(9) References in this Part to the offence (or offences) concerned are to the offence (or offences) mentioned in subsection (2).

7 Recoverable amount

(1) The recoverable amount for the purposes of section 6 is an amount equal to the defendant's benefit from the conduct concerned.

(2) But if the defendant shows that the available amount is less than that benefit the recoverable amount is—

    (a) the available amount, or

    (b) a nominal amount, if the available amount is nil.

(3) But if section 6(6) applies the recoverable amount is such amount as—

    (a) the court believes is just, but

    (b) does not exceed the amount found under subsection (1) or (2) (as the case may be).

(4) In calculating the defendant's benefit from the conduct concerned for the purposes of subsection (1), any property in respect of which—

    (a) a recovery order is in force under section 266, or

    (b) a forfeiture order is in force under section 298(2),

must be ignored.

(5) If the court decides the available amount, it must include in the confiscation order a statement of its findings as to the matters relevant for deciding that amount.

8 Defendant's benefit

(1) If the court is proceeding under section 6 this section applies for the purpose of—

    (a) deciding whether the defendant has benefited from conduct, and

    (b) deciding his benefit from the conduct.

(2) The court must—

    (a) take account of conduct occurring up to the time it makes its decision;

    (b) take account of property obtained up to that time.

(3) Subsection (4) applies if—

    (a) the conduct concerned is general criminal conduct,

    (b) a confiscation order mentioned in subsection (5) has at an earlier time been made against the defendant, and

    (c) his benefit for the purposes of that order was benefit from his general criminal conduct.

(4) His benefit found at the time the last confiscation order mentioned in subsection (3)(c) was made against him must be taken for the purposes of this section to be his benefit from his general criminal conduct at that time.

(5) If the conduct concerned is general criminal conduct the court must deduct the aggregate of the following amounts—

    (a) the amount ordered to be paid under each confiscation order previously made against the defendant;

    (b) the amount ordered to be paid under each confiscation order previously made against him under any of the provisions listed in subsection (7).

(6) But subsection (5) does not apply to an amount which has been taken into account for the purposes of a deduction under that subsection on any earlier occasion.

(7) These are the provisions—

    (a) the Drug Trafficking Offences Act 1986 (c. 32);

    (b) Part 1 of the Criminal Justice (Scotland) Act 1987 (c. 41);

    (c) Part 6 of the Criminal Justice Act 1988 (c. 33);

    (d) the Criminal Justice (Confiscation) (Northern Ireland) Order 1990 (SI 1990/2588 (NI 17));

    (e) Part 1 of the Drug Trafficking Act 1994 (c. 37);

    (f) Part 1 of the Proceeds of Crime (Scotland) Act 1995 (c. 43);

    (g) the Proceeds of Crime (Northern Ireland) Order 1996 (SI 1996/1299 (NI 9));

    (h) Part 3 or 4 of this Act.

(8) The reference to general criminal conduct in the case of a confiscation order made under any of the provisions listed in subsection (7) is a reference to conduct in respect of which a court is required or entitled to make one or more assumptions for the purpose of assessing a person's benefit from the conduct.

9   Available amount

(1) For the purposes of deciding the recoverable amount, the available amount is the aggregate of—

> (a) the total of the values (at the time the confiscation order is made) of all the free property then held by the defendant minus the total amount payable in pursuance of obligations which then have priority, and
>
> (b) the total of the values (at that time) of all tainted gifts.

(2) An obligation has priority if it is an obligation of the defendant—

> (a) to pay an amount due in respect of a fine or other order of a court which was imposed or made on conviction of an offence and at any time before the time the confiscation order is made, or
>
> (b) to pay a sum which would be included among the preferential debts if the defendant's bankruptcy had commenced on the date of the confiscation order or his winding up had been ordered on that date.

(3) 'Preferential debts' has the meaning given by section 386 of the Insolvency Act 1986 (c. 45).

10   Assumptions to be made in case of criminal lifestyle

(1) If the court decides under section 6 that the defendant has a criminal lifestyle it must make the following four assumptions for the purpose of—

> (a) deciding whether he has benefited from his general criminal conduct, and
>
> (b) deciding his benefit from the conduct.

(2) The first assumption is that any property transferred to the defendant at any time after the relevant day was obtained by him—

> (a) as a result of his general criminal conduct, and
>
> (b) at the earliest time he appears to have held it.

(3) The second assumption is that any property held by the defendant at any time after the date of conviction was obtained by him—

> (a) as a result of his general criminal conduct, and
>
> (b) at the earliest time he appears to have held it.

(4) The third assumption is that any expenditure incurred by the defendant at any time after the relevant day was met from property obtained by him as a result of his general criminal conduct.

(5) The fourth assumption is that, for the purpose of valuing any property obtained (or assumed to have been obtained) by the defendant, he obtained it free of any other interests in it.

(6) But the court must not make a required assumption in relation to particular property or expenditure if—

> (a) the assumption is shown to be incorrect, or
>
> (b) there would be a serious risk of injustice if the assumption were made.

(7) If the court does not make one or more of the required assumptions it must state its reasons.

(8) The relevant day is the first day of the period of six years ending with—

> (a) the day when proceedings for the offence concerned were started against the defendant, or
>
> (b) if there are two or more offences and proceedings for them were started on different days, the earliest of those days.

(9) But if a confiscation order mentioned in section 8(3)(c) has been made against the defendant at any time during the period mentioned in subsection (8)—

> (a) the relevant day is the day when the defendant's benefit was calculated for the purposes of the last such confiscation order;
>
> (b) the second assumption does not apply to any property which was held by him on or before the relevant day.

(10) The date of conviction is—

    (a) the date on which the defendant was convicted of the offence concerned, or

    (b) if there are two or more offences and the convictions were on different dates, the date of the latest.

11 Time for payment

(1) The amount ordered to be paid under a confiscation order must be paid on the making of the order; but this is subject to the following provisions of this section.

(2) If the defendant shows that he needs time to pay the amount ordered to be paid, the court making the confiscation order may make an order allowing payment to be made in a specified period.

(3) The specified period—

    (a) must start with the day on which the confiscation order is made, and

    (b) must not exceed six months.

(4) If within the specified period the defendant applies to the Crown Court for the period to be extended and the court believes there are exceptional circumstances, it may make an order extending the period.

(5) The extended period—

    (a) must start with the day on which the confiscation order is made, and

    (b) must not exceed 12 months.

(6) An order under subsection (4)—

    (a) may be made after the end of the specified period, but

    (b) must not be made after the end of the period of 12 months starting with the day on which the confiscation order is made.

(7) The court must not make an order under subsection (2) or (4) unless it gives—

    (a) the prosecutor, or

    (b) if the Director was appointed as the enforcement authority for the order under section 34, the Director,

an opportunity to make representations.

12 Interest on unpaid sums

(1) If the amount required to be paid by a person under a confiscation order is not paid when it is required to be paid, he must pay interest on the amount for the period for which it remains unpaid.

(2) The rate of interest is the same rate as that for the time being specified in section 17 of the Judgments Act 1838 (c. 110) (interest on civil judgment debts).

(3) For the purposes of this section no amount is required to be paid under a confiscation order if—

    (a) an application has been made under section 11(4),

    (b) the application has not been determined by the court, and

    (c) the period of 12 months starting with the day on which the confiscation order was made has not ended.

(4) In applying this Part the amount of the interest must be treated as part of the amount to be paid under the confiscation order.

13 Effect of order on court's other powers

(1) If the court makes a confiscation order it must proceed as mentioned in subsections (2) and (4) in respect of the offence or offences concerned.

(2) The court must take account of the confiscation order before—

    (a) it imposes a fine on the defendant, or

    (b) it makes an order falling within subsection (3).

(3) These orders fall within this subsection—

    (a) an order involving payment by the defendant, other than an order under section 130 of the Sentencing Act (compensation orders);

(b) an order under section 27 of the Misuse of Drugs Act 1971 (c. 38) (forfeiture orders);

(c) an order under section 143 of the Sentencing Act (deprivation orders);

(d) an order under section 23 of the Terrorism Act 2000 (c. 11) (forfeiture orders).

(4) Subject to subsection (2), the court must leave the confiscation order out of account in deciding the appropriate sentence for the defendant.

(5) Subsection (6) applies if—

(a) the Crown Court makes both a confiscation order and an order for the payment of compensation under section 130 of the Sentencing Act against the same person in the same proceedings, and

(b) the court believes he will not have sufficient means to satisfy both the orders in full.

(6) In such a case the court must direct that so much of the compensation as it specifies is to be paid out of any sums recovered under the confiscation order; and the amount it specifies must be the amount it believes will not be recoverable because of the insufficiency of the person's means.

Procedural matters

14   Postponement

(1) The court may—

(a) proceed under section 6 before it sentences the defendant for the offence (or any of the offences) concerned, or

(b) postpone proceedings under section 6 for a specified period.

(2) A period of postponement may be extended.

(3) A period of postponement (including one as extended) must not end after the permitted period ends.

(m) DISQUALIFICATION AND EXCLUSION ETC.

Recommendation for deportation

Immigration Act 1971

6   Recommendations by court for deportation

(1) Where under section 3(6) above a person convicted of an offence is liable to deportation on the recommendation of a court, he may be recommended for deportation by any court having power to sentence him for the offence unless the court commits him to be sentenced or further dealt with for that offence by another court:

Provided that in Scotland the power to recommend a person for deportation shall be exercisable only by the sheriff or the High Court of Justiciary, and shall not be exercisable by the latter on an appeal unless the appeal is against a conviction on indictment or against a sentence upon such a conviction.

(2) A court shall not recommend a person for deportation unless he has been given not less than seven days' notice in writing stating that a person is not liable to deportation if he is partial, describing the persons who are partial and stating (so far as material) the effect of section 3(8) above and section 7 below; but the powers of adjournment conferred by section 10(3) of the Magistrates' Courts Act 1980, section 179 or 380 of the Criminal Procedure (Scotland) Act 1975 or any corresponding enactment for the time being in force in Northern

Ireland shall include power to adjourn, after convicting an offender, for the purpose of enabling a notice to be given to him under this subsection or, if a notice was so given to him less than seven days previously, for the purpose of enabling the necessary seven days to elapse.

7 Exemption from deportation for certain existing residents

(1) Notwithstanding anything in section 3(5) or (6) above but subject to the provisions of this section, a Commonwealth citizen or citizen of the Republic of Ireland who was such a citizen at the coming into force of this Act and was then ordinarily resident in the United Kingdom—

   (a) shall not be liable to deportation under section 3(5)(b) if at the time of the Secretary of State's decision he had at all times since the coming into force of this Act been ordinarily resident in the United Kingdom and Islands; and

   (b) shall not be liable to deportation under section 3(5)(a), (b) or (c) if at the time of the Secretary of State's decision he had for the last five years been ordinarily resident in the United Kingdom and Islands; and

   (c) shall not on conviction of an offence be recommended for deportation under section 3 (6) if at the time of the conviction he had for the last five years been ordinarily resident in the United Kingdom and Islands.

(2) A person who has at any time become ordinarily resident in the United Kingdom or in any of the Islands shall not be treated for the purposes of this section as having ceased to be so by reason only of his having remained there in breach of the immigration laws.

(3) The 'last five years' before the material time under subsection (1)(b) or (c) above is to be taken as a period amounting in total to five years exclusive of any time during which the person claiming exemption under this section was undergoing imprisonment or detention by virtue of a sentence passed for an offence on a conviction in the United Kingdom and Islands, and the period for which he was imprisoned or detained by virtue of the sentence amounted to six months or more.

SCHEDULE 3

SUPPLEMENTARY PROVISIONS AS TO DEPORTATION

1. *Removal of persons liable to deportation*

(1) Where a deportation order is in force against any person, the Secretary of State may give directions for his removal to a country or territory specified in the directions being either—

   (a) a country of which he is a national or citizen; or

   (b) a country or territory to which there is reason to believe that he will be admitted.

2. *Detention or control pending deportation*

(1) Where a recommendation for deportation made by a court is in force in respect of any person, and that person is neither detained in pursuance of the sentence or order of any court nor for the time being released on bail by any court having power so to release him, he shall, unless the court by which the recommendation is made otherwise directs or a direction is given under sub-paragraph (1A) below, be detained pending the making of a deportation order in pursuance of the recommendation, unless the Secretary of State directs him to be released pending further consideration of his case or he is released on bail.

   (1A) Where—

   (a) a recommendation for deportation made by a court on conviction of a person is in force in respect of him; and

   (b) he appeals against his conviction or against that recommendation, the powers that the court determining the appeal may exercise include power to direct him to be released without setting aside the recommendation.

(2) Where notice has been given to a person in accordance with regulations under [section 105 of the Nationality, Immigration and Asylum Act 2002 (notice of decision)] of a decision to make a deportation order against him, and he is neither detained in pursuance of the sentence or order of a court nor for the time being released on bail by a court having power so to release him, he may be detained under the authority of the Secretary of State pending the making of the deportation order.

(3) Where a deportation order is in force against any person, he may be detained under the authority of the Secretary of State pending his removal or departure from the United Kingdom (and if already detained by virtue of sub-paragraph (1) or (2) above when the order is made, shall continue to be detained unless he is released on bail or the Secretary of State directs otherwise).

Exclusion from licensed premises

Licensed Premises (Exclusion of Certain Persons) Act 1980

1   Exclusion orders

(1) Where a court by or before which a person is convicted of an offence committed on licensed premises is satisfied that in committing that offence he resorted to violence or offered or threatened to resort to violence, the court may, subject to subsection (2) below, make an order (in this Act referred to as an 'exclusion order') prohibiting him from entering those premises or any other specified premises, without the express consent of the licensee of the premises or his servant or agent.

(2) An exclusion order may be made either—

    (a) in addition to any sentence which is imposed in respect of the offence of which the person is convicted; or

    (b) where the offence was committed in England or Wales, notwithstanding the provisions of sections 12 and 14 of the Powers of Criminal Courts (Sentencing) Act 2000 (cases in which community rehabilitation orders and absolute and conditional discharges may be made, and their effect), in addition to a community rehabilitation order or an order discharging him absolutely or conditionally; or

    (c) where the offence was committed in Scotland, notwithstanding the provisions of sections 228, 246(2) and (3) and 247 of the Criminal Procedure (Scotland) Act 1995 (cases in which community rehabilitation orders and absolute discharges may be made, and their effect), in addition to a community rehabilitation order or an order discharging him absolutely;

but not otherwise.

(3) An exclusion order shall have effect for such period, not less than three months or more than two years, as is specified in the order, unless it is terminated under section 2 (2) below.

2   Penalty for non-compliance with exclusion order

(1) A person who enters any premises in breach of an exclusion order shall be guilty of an offence and shall be liable on summary conviction or, in Scotland, on conviction in a court of summary jurisdiction to a fine not exceeding level 4 on the standard scale or to imprisonment for a term not exceeding one month or both.

(2) The court by which a person is convicted of an offence under subsection (1) above shall consider whether or not the exclusion order should continue in force, and may, if it

thinks fit, by order terminate the exclusion order or vary it by deleting the name of any specified premises, but an exclusion order shall not otherwise be affected by a person's conviction for such an offence.

Football banning orders

Football Spectators Act 1989 (as amended)

14 Main definitions

(1) This section applies for the purposes of this Part.

(2) 'Regulated football match' means an association football match (whether in England and Wales or elsewhere) which is a prescribed match or a match of a prescribed description.

(3) 'External tournament' means a football competition which includes regulated football matches outside England and Wales.

(4) 'Banning order' means an order made by the court under this Part which—

(a) in relation to regulated football matches in England and Wales, prohibits the person who is subject to the order from entering any premises for the purpose of attending such matches, and

(b) in relation to regulated football matches outside England and Wales, requires that person to report at a police station in accordance with this Part.

(5) 'Control period', in relation to a regulated football match outside England and Wales, means the period—

(a) beginning five days before the day of the match, and

(b) ending when the match is finished or cancelled.

(6) 'Control period', in relation to an external tournament, means any period described in an order made by the Secretary of State—

(a) beginning five days before the day of the first football match outside England and Wales which is included in the tournament, and

(b) ending when the last football match outside England and Wales which is included in the tournament is finished or cancelled,

but, for the purposes of paragraph (a), any football match included in the qualifying or pre-qualifying stages of the tournament is to be left out of account.

14A   Banning orders made on conviction of an offence

(1) This section applies where a person (the 'offender') is convicted of a relevant offence.

(2) If the court is satisfied that there are reasonable grounds to believe that making a banning order would help to prevent violence or disorder at or in connection with any regulated football matches, it must make such an order in respect of the offender.

(3) If the court is not so satisfied, it must in open court state that fact and give its reasons.

(3A) For the purpose of deciding whether to make an order under this section the court may consider evidence led by the prosecution and the defence.

(3B) It is immaterial whether evidence led in pursuance of subsection (3A) would have been admissible in the proceedings in which the offender was convicted.

(4) A banning order may only be made under this section—

(a) in addition to a sentence imposed in respect of the relevant offence, or

(b) in addition to an order discharging him conditionally.

(4A) The court may adjourn any proceedings in relation to an order under this section even after sentencing the offender.

(4B) If the offender does not appear for any adjourned proceedings, the court may further adjourn the proceedings or may issue a warrant for his arrest.

(4C) But the court may not issue a warrant for the offender's arrest unless it is satisfied that he has had adequate notice of the time and place of the adjourned proceedings.

(5) A banning order may be made as mentioned in subsection (4)(b) above in spite of anything in sections 12 and 14 of the Powers of Criminal Courts (Sentencing) Act 2000 (which relate to orders discharging a person absolutely or conditionally and their effect).

(6) In this section, 'the court' in relation to an offender means—

    (a) the court by or before which he is convicted of the relevant offence, or

    (b) if he is committed to the Crown Court to be dealt with for that offence, the Crown Court.

14B Banning orders made on a complaint

(1) An application for a banning order in respect of any person may be made by the chief officer of police for the area in which the person resides or appears to reside, if it appears to the officer that the condition in subsection (2) below is met.

(2) That condition is that the respondent has at any time caused or contributed to any violence or disorder in the United Kingdom or elsewhere.

(3) The application is to be made by complaint to a magistrates' court.

(4) If—

    (a) it is proved on the application that the condition in subsection (2) above is met, and

    (b) the court is satisfied that there are reasonable grounds to believe that making a banning order would help to prevent violence or disorder at or in connection with any regulated football matches,

the court must make a banning order in respect of the respondent.

14C Banning orders: supplementary

(1) In this Part, 'violence' means violence against persons or property and includes threatening violence and doing anything which endangers the life of any person.

(2) In this Part, 'disorder' includes—

    (a) stirring up hatred against a group of persons defined by reference to colour, race, nationality (including citizenship) or ethnic or national origins, or against an individual as a member of such a group,

    (b) using threatening, abusive or insulting words or behaviour or disorderly behaviour,

    (c) displaying any writing or other thing which is threatening, abusive or insulting.

(3) In this Part, 'violence' and 'disorder' are not limited to violence or disorder in connection with football.

(4) The magistrates' court may take into account the following matters (among others), so far as they consider it appropriate to do so, in determining whether to make an order under section 14B above—

    (a) any decision of a court or tribunal outside the United Kingdom,

    (b) deportation or exclusion from a country outside the United Kingdom,

    (c) removal or exclusion from premises used for playing football matches, whether in the United Kingdom or elsewhere,

    (d) conduct recorded on video or by any other means.

(5) In determining whether to make such an order—

    (a) the magistrates' court may not take into account anything done by the respondent before the beginning of the period of ten years ending with the application under section 14B(1) above, except circumstances ancillary to a conviction,

    (b) before taking into account any conviction for a relevant offence, where a court made a statement under section 14A(3) above (or section 15(2A) below or section 30(3) of the Public Order Act 1986), the magistrates' court must consider the reasons given in the statement, and in this subsection 'circumstances ancillary to a conviction' has the same meaning as it has for the purposes of section 4 of the Rehabilitation of Offenders Act 1974 (effect of rehabilitation).

(6) Subsection (5) does not prejudice anything in the Rehabilitation of Offenders Act 1974.

14E   Banning orders: general

(1) On making a banning order, a court must in ordinary language explain its effect to the person subject to the order.

(2) A banning order must require the person subject to the order to report initially at a police station in England and Wales specified in the order within the period of five days beginning with the day on which the order is made.

(3) A banning order must, unless it appears to the court that there are exceptional circumstances, impose a requirement as to the surrender in accordance with this Part, in connection with regulated football matches outside the United Kingdom, of the travel authorisation of the person subject to the order.

(4) If it appears to the court that there are such circumstances, it must in open court state what they are.

(5) In the case of a person detained in legal custody—

(a) the requirement under this section to report at a police station, and

(b) any requirement imposed under section 19 below,

is suspended until his release from custody.

(6) If—

(a) he is released from custody more than five days before the expiry of the period for which the order has effect, and

(b) he was precluded by his being in custody from reporting initially,

the order is to have effect as if it required him to report initially at the police station specified in the order within the period of five days beginning with the date of his release.

(7) A person serving a sentence of imprisonment to which an intermittent custody order under section 183 of the Criminal Justice Act 2003 relates is to be treated for the purposes of this section as having been detained in legal custody until his final release, and accordingly any reference in this section to release is, in relation to a person serving such a sentence, a reference to his final release.

14F   Period of banning orders

(1) Subject to the following provisions of this Part, a banning order has effect for a period beginning with the day on which the order is made.

(2) The period must not be longer than the maximum or shorter than the minimum.

(3) Where the order is made under section 14A above in addition to a sentence of imprisonment taking immediate effect, the maximum is ten years and the minimum is six years; and in this subsection 'imprisonment' includes any form of detention.

(4) In any other case where the order is made under section 14A above, the maximum is five years and the minimum is three years.

(5) Where the order is made under section 14B above, the maximum is three years and the minimum is two years.

14G   Additional requirements of orders

(1) A banning order may, if the court making the order thinks fit, impose additional requirements on the person subject to the order in relation to any regulated football matches.

(2) The court by which a banning order was made may, on an application made by—

(a) the person subject to the order, or

(b) the person who applied for the order or who was the prosecutor in relation to the order,

vary the order so as to impose, replace or omit any such requirements.

(3) In the case of a banning order made by a magistrates' court, the reference in sub-section (2) above to the court by which it was made includes a reference to any magistrates' court acting for the same petty sessions area as that court.

14H Termination of orders

(1) If a banning order has had effect for at least two-thirds of the period determined under section 14F above, the person subject to the order may apply to the court by which it was made to terminate it.

(2) On the application, the court may by order terminate the banning order as from a specified date or refuse the application.

(3) In exercising its powers under subsection (2) above, the court must have regard to the person's character, his conduct since the banning order was made, the nature of the offence or conduct which led to it and any other circumstances which appear to it to be relevant.

(4) Where an application under subsection (1) above in respect of a banning order is refused, no further application in respect of the order may be made within the period of six months beginning with the day of the refusal.

(5) The court may order the applicant to pay all or any part of the costs of an application under this section.

(6) In the case of a banning order made by a magistrates' court, the reference in sub-section (1) above to the court by which it was made includes a reference to any magistrates' court acting for the same petty sessions area as that court.

14J Offences

(1) A person subject to a banning order who fails to comply with—

    (a) any requirement imposed by the order, or

    (b) any requirement imposed under section 19(2B) or (2C) below,

is guilty of an offence.

(2) A person guilty of an offence under this section is liable on summary conviction to imprisonment for a term not exceeding six months, or a fine not exceeding level 5 on the standard scale, or both.

Disqualification of company directors

Company Directors Disqualification Act 1986

1 Disqualification orders: general

(1) In the circumstances specified below in this Act a court may, and under sections 6 and 9A shall, make against a person a disqualification order, that is to say an order that he shall not, without leave of the court—

    (a) be a director of a company, or

    (b) be a liquidator or administrator of a company, or

    (c) be a receiver or manager of a company's property, or

    (d) in any way, whether directly or indirectly, be concerned or take part in the promotion, formation or management of a company,

for a specified period beginning with the date of the order.

(2) In each section of this Act which gives to a court power or, as the case may be, imposes on it the duty to make a disqualification order there is specified the maximum (and, in section 6, the minimum) period of disqualification which may or (as the case may be) must be imposed by means of the order.

(3) Where a disqualification order is made against a person who is already subject to such an order or to a disqualification undertaking, the periods specified in those orders shall run concurrently.

(4) A disqualification order may be made on grounds which are or include matters other than criminal convictions, notwithstanding that the person in respect of whom it is to be made may be criminally liable in respect of those matters.

2   Disqualification on conviction of indictable offence

(1) The court may make a disqualification order against a person where he is convicted of an indictable offence (whether on indictment or summarily) in connection with the promotion, formation, management or liquidation of a company, or with the receivership of a company's property or with his being an administrative receiver of a company.

(2) 'The court' for this purpose means—

(a) any court having jurisdiction to wind up the company in relation to which the offence was committed, or

(b) the court by or before which the person is convicted of the offence, or

(c) in the case of a summary conviction in England and Wales, any other magistrates' court acting in the same local justice area;

and for the purposes of this section the definition of 'indictable offence' in Schedule 1 to the Interpretation Act 1978 applies for Scotland as it does for England and Wales.

(3) The maximum period of disqualification under this section is—

(a) where the disqualification order is made by a court of summary jurisdiction, 5 years, and

(b) in any other case, 15 years.

11   Undischarged bankrupts

(1) It is an offence for a person who is an undischarged bankrupt to act as director of, or directly or indirectly to take part in or be concerned in the promotion, formation or management of, a company, except with the leave of the court.

13   Criminal penalties

(1) If a person acts in contravention of a disqualification order or disqualification undertaking or in contravention of section 12(2) or 12A, or is guilty of an offence under section 11, he is liable—

(a) on conviction on indictment, to imprisonment for not more than 2 years or a fine, or both; and

(b) on summary conviction, to imprisonment for not more than 6 months or a fine not exceeding the statutory maximum, or both.

Disqualification from driving

Road Traffic Offenders Act 1988 (as amended)

34   Disqualification for certain offences

(1) Where a person is convicted of an offence involving obligatory disqualification, the court must order him to be disqualified for such period not less than twelve months as the court thinks fit unless the court for special reasons thinks fit to order him to be disqualified for a shorter period or not to order him to be disqualified.

(1A) Where a person is convicted of an offence under section 12A of the Theft Act 1968 (aggravated vehicle-taking), the fact that he did not drive the vehicle in question at any particular time or at all shall not be regarded as a special reason for the purposes of subsection (1) above.

(2) Where a person is convicted of an offence involving discretionary disqualification, and either—

(a) the penalty points to be taken into account on that occasion number fewer than twelve, or

(b) the offence is not one involving obligatory endorsement,
the court may order him to be disqualified for such period as the court thinks fit.

(3) Where a person convicted of an offence under any of the following provisions of the Road Traffic Act 1988, that is—

    (aa) section 3A (causing death by careless driving when under the influence of drink or drugs;

    (a) section 4(1) (driving or attempting to drive while unfit),

    (b) section 5(1)(a) (driving or attempting to drive with excess alcohol),

    (c) section 7(6) (failing to provide a specimen) where that is an offence involving obligatory disqualification,

    (d) Section 7A(6) (failing to allow a specimen to be subjected to laboratory test) where that is an offence involving obligatory disqualification.

has within the ten years immediately preceding the commission of the offence been convicted of any such offence, subsection (1) above shall apply in relation to him as if the reference to twelve months were a reference to three years.

(4) Subject to subsection (3) above, subsection (1) above shall apply as if the reference to twelve months were a reference to two years—

    (a) in relation to a person convicted of—

        (i) manslaughter, or in Scotland culpable homicide, or

        (ii) an offence under section 1 of the Road Traffic Act 1988 (causing death by dangerous driving), or

        (iii) an offence under section 3A of that Act (causing death by careless driving while under the influence of drink or drugs), and

    (b) in relation to a person on whom more than one disqualification for a fixed period of 56 days or more has been imposed within the three years immediately preceding the commission of the offence.

(4A) For the purposes of subsection (4)(b) above there shall be disregarded any disqualification imposed under section 26 of this Act or section 147 of the Powers of Criminal Courts (Sentencing) Act 2000 or section 223A or 436A of the Criminal Procedure (Scotland) Act 1975 (offences committed by using vehicles) and any disqualification imposed in respect of an offence of stealing a motor vehicle, an offence under section 12 or 25 of the Theft Act 1968, an offence under section 178 of the Road Traffic Act 1988, or an attempt to commit such an offence.

(5) The preceding provisions of this section shall apply in relation to a conviction of an offence committed by aiding, abetting, counselling or procuring, or inciting to the commission of, an offence involving obligatory disqualification as if the offence were an offence involving discretionary disqualification.

34A   Reduced disqualification period for attendance on courses

(1) This section applies where—

    (a) a person is convicted of an offence under section 3A (causing death by careless driving when under influence of drink or drugs), 4 (driving or being in charge when under influence of drink or drugs), 5 (driving or being in charge with excess alcohol) or 7 (failing to provide a specimen) of the Road Traffic Act 1988, and

    (b) the court makes an order under section 34 of this Act disqualifying him for a period of not less than twelve months.

(2) Where this section applies, the court may make an order that the period of disqualification imposed under section 34 shall be reduced if, by a date specified in the order under this section, the offender satisfactorily completes a course approved by the Secretary of State for the purposes of this section and specified in the order.

(3) The reduction made by an order under this section in a period of disqualification imposed under section 34 shall be a period specified in the order of not less than three months and not more than one quarter of the unreduced period (and accordingly where

the period imposed under section 34 is twelve months, the reduced period shall be nine months).

(4) The court shall not make an order under this section unless—

    (a) it is satisfied that a place on the course specified in the order will be available for the offender,

    (b) the offender appears to the court to be of or over the age of 17,

    (c) the court has explained the effect of the order to the offender in ordinary language, and has informed him of the amount of the fees for the course and of the requirement that he must pay them before beginning the course, and

    (d) the offender has agreed that the order should be made.

(5) The date specified in an order under this section as the latest date for completion of a course must be at least two months before the last day of the period of disqualification as reduced by the order.

(6) An order under this section shall name the petty sessions area (or in Scotland the sheriff court district or, where an order has been made under this section by a stipendiary magistrate, the commission area) in which the offender resides or will reside.

34B   Certificates of completion of courses

(1) An offender shall be regarded for the purposes of section 34A of this Act as having completed a course satisfactorily if (and only if) a certificate that he has done so is received by the proper officer of the supervising court before the end of the period of disqualification imposed under section 34.

(2) If the certificate referred to in subsection (1) above is received by the proper officer of the supervising court before the end of the period of disqualification imposed under section 34 but after the end of the period as it would have been reduced by the order, the order shall have effect as if the reduced period ended with the day on which the certificate is received by the proper officer.

(3) The certificate referred to in subsection (1) above shall be a certificate in such form, containing such particulars, and given by such person, as may be prescribed by, or determined in accordance with, regulations made by the Secretary of State.

(4) A course organiser shall give the certificate mentioned in subsection (1) above to the offender not later than fourteen days after the date specified in the order as the latest date for completion of the course, unless the offender fails to make due payment of the fees for the course, fails to attend the course in accordance with the organiser's reasonable instructions, or fails to comply with any other reasonable requirements of the organiser.

(5) Where a course organiser decides not to give the certificate mentioned in subsection (1) above, he shall give written notice of his decision to the offender as soon as possible, and in any event not later than fourteen days after the date specified in the order as the latest date for completion of the course.

(6) An offender to whom a notice is given under subsection (5) above may, within such period as may be prescribed by rules of court, apply to the supervising court for a declaration that the course organiser's decision not to give a certificate was contrary to subsection (4) above; and if the court grants the application section 34A of this Act shall have effect as if the certificate had been duly received by the proper officer of the court.

(7) If fourteen days after the date specified in the order as the latest date for completion of the course the course organiser has given neither the certificate mentioned in subsection (1) above nor a notice under subsection (5) above, the offender may, within such period as may be prescribed by rules of court, apply to the supervising court for a declaration that the course organiser is in default; and if the court grants the application section 34A of this Act shall have effect as if the certificate had been duly received by the proper officer of the court.

(8) A notice under subsection (5) above shall specify the ground on which it is given, and the Secretary of State may by regulations make provision as to the form of notices under that subsection and as to the circumstances in which they are to be treated as given.

(9) Where the proper officer of a court receives a certificate of the kind referred to in subsection (1) above, or a court grants an application under subsection (6) or (7) above, the officer or court must send notice of that fact to the Secretary of State; and the notice must be sent in such manner and to such address, and must contain such particulars, as the Secretary of State may determine.

34C Provisions supplementary to sections 34A and 34B.

(1) The Secretary of State may issue guidance to course organisers, or to any category of course organiser as to the conduct of courses approved for the purposes of section 34A of this Act; and—

(a) course organisers shall have regard to any guidance given to them under this subsection, and

(b) in determining for the purposes of section 34B(6) whether any instructions or requirements of an organiser were reasonable, a court shall have regard to any guidance given to him under this subsection.

(2) In sections 34A and 34B and this section—

'course organiser', in relation to a course, means the person who, in accordance with regulations made by the Secretary of State, is responsible for giving the certificates mentioned in section 34B(1) in respect of the completion of the course;

'petty sessions area' has the same meaning as in the Magistrates' Courts Act 1980;

'proper officer' means—

(a) in relation to a magistrates' court in England and Wales, the justices' chief executive for the court, and

(b) in relation to a sheriff court in Scotland, the clerk of the court.

'supervising court', in relation to an order under section 34A, means—

(a) in England and Wales, a magistrates' court acting for the petty sessions area named in the order as the area where the offender resides or will reside;

(b) in Scotland, the sheriff court for the district where the offender resides or will reside or, where the order is made by a stipendiary magistrate and the offender resides or will reside within his commission area, the district court for that area,

and any reference to the clerk of a magistrates' court is a reference to the clerk to the justices for the petty sessions area for which the court acts.

(3) Any power to make regulations under section 34B or this section—

(a) includes power to make different provision for different cases, and to make such incidental or supplemental provision as appears to the Secretary of State to be necessary or expedient;

(b) shall be exercisable by statutory instrument, which shall be subject to annulment in pursuance of a resolution of either House of Parliament.'

35 Disqualification for repeated offences

(1) Where—

(a) a person is convicted of an offence to which this subsection applies, and

(b) the penalty points to be taken into account on that occasion number twelve or more,

the court must order him to be disqualified for not less than the minimum period unless the court is satisfied, having regard to all the circumstances, that there are grounds for mitigating the normal consequences of the conviction and thinks fit to order him to be disqualified for a shorter period or not to order him to be disqualified.

(1A) Subsection (1) above applies to—

(a) an offence involving discretionary disqualification and obligatory endorsement, and

(b) an offence involving obligatory disqualification in respect of which no order is made under section 34 of this Act.

(2) The minimum period referred to in subsection (1) above is—

(a) six months if no previous disqualification imposed on the offender is to be taken into account, and

(b) one year if one, and two years if more than one, such disqualification is to be taken into account;

and a previous disqualification imposed on an offender is to be taken into account if it was for a period of 56 days or more and was imposed within the three years immediately preceding the commission of the latest offence in respect of which penalty points are taken into account under section 29 of this Act.

(3) Where an offender is convicted on the same occasion of more than one offence to which subsection (1) above applies—

(a) not more than one disqualification shall be imposed on him under subsection (1) above,

(b) in determining the period of the disqualification the court must take into account all the offences, and

(c) for the purposes of any appeal any disqualification imposed under subsection (1) above shall be treated as an order made on the conviction of each of the offences.

(4) No account is to be taken under subsection (1) above of any of the following circumstances—

(a) any circumstances that are alleged to make the offence or any of the offences not a serious one,

(b) hardship, other than exceptional hardship, or

(c) any circumstances which, within the three years immediately preceding the conviction, have been taken into account under that subsection in ordering the offender to be disqualified for a shorter period or not ordering him to be disqualified.

36   Disqualification until test is passed

(1) Where this subsection applies to a person the court must order him to be disqualified until he passes the appropriate driving test.

(2) Subsection (1) above applies to a person who is disqualified under section 34 of this Act on conviction of—

(a) manslaughter, or in Scotland culpable homicide, by the driver of a motor vehicle, or

(b) an offence under section 1 (causing death by dangerous driving) or section 2 (dangerous driving) of the Road Traffic Act 1988.

(3) Subsection (1) above also applies—

(a) to a person who is disqualified under section 34 or 35 of this Act in such circumstances or for such period as the Secretary of State may by order prescribe, or

(b) to such other persons convicted of such offences involving obligatory endorsement as may be so prescribed.

(4) Where a person to whom subsection (1) above does not apply is convicted of an offence involving obligatory endorsement, the court may order him to be disqualified until he passes the appropriate driving test (whether or not he has previously passed any test).

(5) In this section—

'appropriate driving test' means—

(a) an extended driving test, where a person is convicted of an offence involving obligatory disqualification or is disqualified under section 35 of this Act,

(b) a test of competence to drive, other than an extended driving test, in any other case,

'extended driving test' means a test of competence to drive prescribed for the purposes of this section, and 'test of competence to drive' means a test prescribed by virtue of section 89(3) of the Road Traffic Act 1988.

(6) In determining whether to make an order under subsection (4) above, the court shall have regard to the safety of road users.

(7) Where a person is disqualified until he passes the extended driving test—

(a) any earlier order under this section shall cease to have effect, and

(b) a court shall not make a further order under this section while he is so disqualified.

(8) Subject to subsection (9) below, a disqualification by virtue of an order under this section shall be deemed to have expired on production to the Secretary of State of evidence, in such form as may be prescribed by regulations under section 105 of the Road Traffic Act 1988, that the person disqualified has passed the test in question since the order was made.

(9) A disqualification shall be deemed to have expired only in relation to vehicles of such classes as may be prescribed in relation to the test passed by regulations under that section.

(10) Where there is issued to a person a licence on the counterpart of which are endorsed particulars of a disqualification under this section, there shall also be endorsed the particulars of any test of competence to drive that he has passed since the order of disqualification was made.

(11) For the purposes of an order under this section, a person shall be treated as having passed a test of competence to drive other than an extended driving test if he passes a corresponding test conducted—

(a) under the law of Northern Ireland, the Isle of Man, any of the Channel Islands, another member State, Gibraltar or a designated country or territory (as defined by section 89(11) of the Road Traffic Act 1988), or

(b) for the purposes of obtaining a British Forces licence (as defined by section 88(8) of that Act);

and accordingly subsections (8) to (10) above shall apply in relation to such a test as they apply in relation to a test prescribed by virtue of section 89(3) of that Act.

(12) This section is subject to section 48 of this Act.

(13) The power to make an order under subsection (3) above shall be exercisable by statutory instrument; and no such order shall be made unless a draft of it has been laid before and approved by resolution of each House of Parliament.

(14) The Secretary of State shall not make an order under subsection (3) above after the end of 2001 if he has not previously made such an order.

37   Effect of order of disqualification

(1) Where the holder of a licence is disqualified by an order of a court, the licence be treated as being revoked with effect from the beginning of the period of disqualification.

(1A) Where—

(a) the disqualification is for a fixed period shorter than 56 days in respect of an offence involving obligatory endorsement or

(b) the order is made under section 26 of this Act,

Subsection (1) above shall not prevent the licence from again having effect at the end of the period of disqualification.

(2) Where the holder of the licence appeals against the order and the disqualification is suspended under section 39 of this Act, the period of disqualification shall be treated for the purpose of subsection (1) above as beginning on the day on which the disqualification ceases to be suspended.

(3) Notwithstanding anything in Part III of the Road Traffic Act 1988, a person disqualified by an order of a court under section 36 of this Act is (unless he is also disqualified otherwise than by virtue of such an order) entitled to obtain and to hold a provisional licence and to drive a motor vehicle in accordance with the conditions subject to which the provisional licence as granted.

38   Appeal against disqualification

(1) A person disqualified by an order of a magistrates' court under section 34 or 35 of this Act may appeal against the order in the same manner as against a conviction.

39   Suspension of disqualification pending appeal

(1) Any court in England and Wales (whether a magistrates' court or another) which makes an order disqualifying a person may, if it thinks fit, suspend the disqualification pending an appeal against the order.

(2) The court by or before which a person disqualified by an order of a court in Scotland was convicted may, if it thinks fit, suspend the disqualification pending an appeal against the order.

40   Power of appellate courts in England and Wales to suspend disqualification

(1) This section applies where a person has been convicted by or before a court in England and Wales of an offence involving obligatory or discretionary disqualification and has been ordered to be disqualified; and in the following provisions of this section—

(a) any reference to a person ordered to be disqualified is to be construed as a reference to a person so convicted and so ordered to be disqualified, and

(b) any reference to his sentence includes a reference to the order of disqualification and to any other order made on his conviction and, accordingly, any reference to an appeal against his sentence includes a reference to an appeal against any order forming part of his sentence.

(2) Where a person ordered to be disqualified—

(a) appeals to the Crown Court, or

(b) appeals or applies for leave to appeal to the Court of Appeal,

against his conviction or his sentence, the Crown Court or, as the case may require, the Court of Appeal may, if it thinks fit, suspend the disqualification.

(3) Where a person ordered to be disqualified has appealed or applied for leave to appeal to the Supreme Court—

(a) under section 1 of the Administration of Justice Act 1960 from any decision of a Divisional Court of the Queen's Bench Division which is material to his conviction or sentence, or

(b) under section 33 of the Criminal Appeal Act 1968 from any decision of the Court of Appeal which is material to his conviction or sentence,

the Divisional Court or, as the case may require, the Court of Appeal may, if it thinks fit, suspend the disqualification.

(4) Where a person ordered to be disqualified makes an application in respect of the decision of the court in question under section 111 of the Magistrates' Courts Act 1980 (statement of case by magistrates' court) or section 28 of the Supreme Court Act 1981 (statement of case by Crown Court) the High Court may, if it thinks fit, suspend the disqualification.

(5) Where a person ordered to be disqualified—

(a) applies to the High Court for an order of certiorari to remove into the High Court any proceedings of a magistrates' court or of the Crown Court, being proceedings in or in consequence of which he was convicted or his sentence was passed, or

(b) applies to the High Court for leave to make such an application,

the High Court may, if it thinks fit, suspend the disqualification.

(6) Any power of a court under the preceding provisions of this section to suspend the disqualification of any person is a power to do so on such terms as the court thinks fit.

42   Removal of disqualification

(1) Subject to the provisions of this section, a person who by an order of a court is disqualified may apply to the court by which the order was made to remove the disqualification.

(2) On any such application the court may, as it thinks proper having regard to—

(a) the character of the person disqualified and his conduct subsequent to the order,

(b) the nature of the offence, and

(c) any other circumstances of the case,

either by order remove the disqualification as from such date as may be specified in the order or refuse the application.

(3) No application shall be made under subsection (1) above for the removal of a disqualification before the expiration of whichever is relevant of the following periods from the date of the order by which the disqualification was imposed, that is—

(a) two years, if the disqualification is for less than four years,

(b) one half of the period of disqualification, if it is for less than ten years but not less than four years,

(c) five years in any other case;

and in determining the expiration of the period after which under this subsection a person may apply for the removal of a disqualification, any time after the conviction during which the disqualification was suspended or he was not disqualified shall be disregarded.

43   Rule for determining end of period of disqualification

In determining the expiration of the period for which a person is disqualified by an order of a court made in consequence of a conviction, any time after the conviction during which the disqualification was suspended or he was not disqualified shall be disregarded.

Powers of Criminal Courts (Sentencing) Act 2000

146   Driving disqualification for any offence

(1) The court by or before which a person is convicted of an offence committed after 31st December 1997 may, instead of or in addition to dealing with him in any other way, order him to be disqualified, for such period as it thinks fit, for holding or obtaining a driving licence.

(3) A court shall not make an order under subsection (1) above unless the court has been notified by the Secretary of State that the power to make such orders is exercisable by the court and the notice has not been withdrawn.

(4) A court which makes an order under this section disqualifying a person for holding or obtaining a driving licence shall require him to produce—

(a)   any such licence held by him together with its counterpart;

(aa) in the case where he holds a Northern Ireland licence (within the meaning of Part 3 of the Road Traffic Act 1988), his Northern Ireland licence and its counterpart (if any); or

(b)   in the case where he holds a Community licence (within the meaning of Part III of the Road Traffic Act 1988), his Community licence and its counterpart (if any).

147   Driving disqualification where vehicle used for purposes of crime

(1) This section applies where a person—

(a) is convicted before the Crown Court of an offence punishable on indictment with imprisonment for a term of two years or more; or

(b) having been convicted by a magistrates' court of such an offence, is committed under section 3 above to the Crown Court for sentence.

(2) This section also applies where a person is convicted by or before any court of common assault or of any other offence involving an assault (including an offence of aiding, abetting, counselling or procuring, or inciting to the commission of, an offence).

(3) If, in a case to which this section applies by virtue of subsection (1) above, the Crown Court is satisfied that a motor vehicle was used (by the person convicted or by anyone else) for the purpose of committing, or facilitating the commission of, the offence in question, the

court may order the person convicted to be disqualified, for such period as the court thinks fit, for holding or obtaining a driving licence.

(4) If, in a case to which this section applies by virtue of subsection (2) above, the court is satisfied that the assault was committed by driving a motor vehicle, the court may order the person convicted to be disqualified, for such period as the court thinks fit, for holding or obtaining a driving licence.

(5) A court which makes an order under this section disqualifying a person for holding or obtaining a driving licence shall require him to produce—

    (a) any such licence held by him together with its counterpart;

    (aa) in the case where he holds a Northern Ireland licence (within the meaning of Part 3 of the Road Traffic Act 1988), his Northern Ireland licence and its counterpart (if any); or

    (b) in the case where he holds a Community licence (within the meaning of Part III of the Road Traffic Act 1988), his Community licence and its counterpart (if any).

(6) Facilitating the commission of an offence shall be taken for the purposes of this section to include the taking of any steps after it has been committed for the purpose of disposing of any property to which it relates or of avoiding apprehension or detection.

(n) MENTALLY DISORDERED OFFENDERS

Powers of Criminal Courts (Sentencing) Act 2000

SUPERVISION ORDERS

SCHEDULE 6

6. Requirements as to treatment for mental condition

(1) This paragraph applies where a court which proposes to make a supervision order is satisfied, on the evidence of a registered medical practitioner approved for the purposes of section 12 of the Mental Health Act 1983, that the mental condition of the offender—

    (a) is such as requires and may be susceptible to treatment; but

    (b) is not such as to warrant the making of a hospital order or guardianship order within the meaning of that Act.

(2) Where this paragraph applies, the court may include in the supervision order a requirement that the offender shall, for a period specified in the order, submit to treatment of one of the following descriptions so specified, that is to say—

    (a) treatment as a resident patient in an independent hospital or care home within the meaning of the Care Standards Act 2000 or a hospital within the meaning of the Mental Health Act 1983, but not a hospital at which high security psychiatric services within the meaning of that Act are provided;

    (b) treatment as a non-resident patient at an institution or place specified in the order;

    (c) treatment by or under the direction of a registered medical practitioner specified in the order; or

    (d) treatment by or under the direction of a chartered psychologist specified in the order.

(3) A requirement shall not be included in a supervision order by virtue of sub-paragraph (2) above—

    (a) in any case, unless the court is satisfied that arrangements have been or can be made for the treatment in question and, in the case of treatment as a resident patient, for the reception of the patient;

(b) in the case of an order made or to be made in respect of a person aged 14 or over, unless he consents to its inclusion;

and a requirement so included shall not in any case continue in force after the offender attains the age of 18.

Mental Health Act 1983 (as amended)

HOSPITAL AND GUARDIANSHIP ORDERS

37   Powers of courts to order hospital admission or guardianship

(1) Where a person is convicted before the Crown Court of an offence punishable with imprisonment other than an offence the sentence for which is fixed by law or falls to be imposed under section 109(2) of the Powers of Criminal Courts (Sentencing) Act 2000, or is convicted by a magistrates' court of an offence punishable on summary conviction with imprisonment, and the conditions mentioned in subsection (2) below are satisfied, the court may by order authorise his admission to and detention in such hospital as may be specified in the order or, as the case may be, place him under the guardianship of a local social services authority or of such other person approved by a local social services authority as may be so specified.

(1A) In the case of an offence the sentence for which would otherwise fall to be imposed under subsection (2) of section 110 or 111 of the Powers of Criminal Courts (Sentencing) Act 2000, nothing in that subsection shall prevent a court from making an order under subsection (1) above for the admission of the offender to a hospital.

(1B) For the purposes of subsection (1) and (1A) above, a sentence falls to be imposed under section 109(2), 110(2) or 111(2) of the Powers of Criminal Courts (Sentencing) Act 2000 if it is required by that provision and the court is not of the opinion there mentioned.

(2) The conditions referred to in subsection (1) above are that—

(a) the court is satisfied, on the written or oral evidence of two registered medical practitioners, that the offender is suffering from mental illness, psychopathic disorder, severe mental impairment or mental impairment and that either—

(i)   the mental disorder from which the offender is suffering is of a nature or degree which makes it appropriate for him to be detained in a hospital for medical treatment and, in the case of psychopathic disorder or mental impairment, that such treatment is likely to alleviate or prevent a deterioration of his condition; or

(ii) in the case of an offender who has attained the age of 16 years, the mental disorder is of a nature or degree which warrants his reception into guardianship under this Act; and

(b) the court is of the opinion, having regard to all the circumstances including the nature of the offence and the character and antecedents of the offender, and to the other available methods of dealing with him, that the most suitable method of disposing of the case is by means of an order under this section.

(3) Where a person is charged before a magistrates' court with any act or omission as an offence and the court would have power, on convicting him of that offence, to make an order under subsection (1) above in his case as being a person suffering from mental illness or severe mental impairment, then, if the court is satisfied that the accused did the act or made the omission charged, the court may, if it thinks fit, make such an order without convicting him.

(4) An order for the admission of an offender to a hospital (in this Act referred to as 'a hospital order') shall not be made under this section unless the court is satisfied on the

written or oral evidence of the registered medical practitioner who would be in charge of his treatment or of some other person representing the managers of the hospital that arrangements have been made for his admission to that hospital, and for his admission to it within the period of 28 days beginning with the date of the making of such an order; and the court may, pending his admission within that period, given such directions as it thinks fit for his conveyance to and detention in a place of safety.

(5) If within the said period of 28 days it appears to the Secretary of State that by reason of an emergency or other special circumstances it is not practicable for the patient to be received into the hospital specified in the order, he may give directions for the admission of the patient to such other hospital as appears to be appropriate instead of the hospital so specified; and where such directions are given—

    (a) the Secretary of State shall cause the person having the custody of the patient to be informed, and

    (b) the hospital order shall have effect as if the hospital specified in the directions were substituted for the hospital specified in the order.

(6) An order placing an offender under the guardianship of a local social services authority or of any other person (in this Act referred to as 'a guardianship order') shall not be made under this section unless the court is satisfied that that authority or person is willing to receive the offender into guardianship.

(7) A hospital order or guardianship order shall specify the form or forms of mental disorder referred to in subsection (2)(a) above from which, upon the evidence taken into account under that subsection, the offender is found by the court to be suffering; and no such order shall be made unless the offender is described by each of the practitioners whose evidence is taken into account under that subsection as suffering from the same one of those forms of mental disorder, whether or not he is also described by either of them as suffering from another of them.

(8) Where an order is made under this section, the court shall not—

    (a) pass sentence of imprisonment or impose a fine or make a probation order in respect of the offence,

    (b) if the order under this section is a hospital order, make a referral order (within the meaning of [the Powers of Criminal Courts (Sentencing) Act 2000]) in respect of the offence, or

    (c) make in respect of the offender [a supervision order (within the meaning of that Act) or an order under section 150 of that Act (binding over of parent or guardian)]

but the court may make any other order which it has power to make apart from this section; and for the purposes of this subsection 'sentence of imprisonment' includes any sentence or order for detention.

38 Interim hospital orders

(1) Where a person is convicted before the Crown Court of an offence punishable with imprisonment (other than an offence the sentence for which is fixed by law) or is convicted by a magistrates' court of an offence punishable on summary conviction with imprisonment and the court before or by which he is convicted is satisfied, on the written or oral evidence of two registered medical practitioners—

    (a) that the offender is suffering from mental illness, psychopathic disorder, severe mental impairment or mental impairment; and

    (b) that there is reason to suppose that the mental disorder from which the offender is suffering is such that it may be appropriate for a hospital order to be made in his case,

the court may, before making a hospital order or dealing with him in some other way, make an order (in this Act referred to as 'an interim hospital order') authorising his admission to such hospital as may be specified in the order and his detention there in accordance with this section.

(2) In the case of an offender who is subject to an interim hospital order the court may make a hospital order without his being brought before the court if he is represented by counsel or a solicitor and his counsel or solicitor is given an opportunity of being heard.

(3) At least one of the registered medical practitioners whose evidence is taken into account under subsection (1) above shall be employed at the hospital which is to be specified in the order.

(4) An interim hospital order shall not be made for admission of an offender to a hospital unless the court is satisfied, on the written or oral evidence of the registered medical practitioner who would be in charge of his treatment or of some other person representing the managers of the hospital, that arrangements have been made for his admission to that hospital and for his admission to it within the period of 28 days beginning with the date of the order; and if the court is so satisfied the court may, pending his admission, give directions for his conveyance to and detention in a place of safety.

(5) An interim hospital order—

(a) shall be in force for such period, not exceeding 12 weeks, as the court may specify when making the order; but

(b) may be renewed for further periods of not more than 28 days at a time if it appears to the court, on the written or oral evidence of the responsible medical officer, that the continuation of the order is warranted;

but no such order shall continue in force for more than six months in all and the court shall terminate the order if it makes a hospital order in respect of the offender or decides after considering the written or oral evidence of the responsible medical officer to deal with the offender in some other way.

(6) The power of renewing an interim hospital order may be exercised without the offender being brought before the court if he is represented by counsel or a solicitor and his counsel or solicitor is given an opportunity of being heard.

(7) If an offender absconds from a hospital in which he is detained in pursuance of an interim hospital order, or while being conveyed to or from such a hospital, he may be arrested without warrant by a constable and shall, after being arrested, be brought as soon as practicable before the court that made the order; and the court may thereupon terminate the order and deal with him in any way in which it could have dealt with him if no such order had been made.

39 Information as to hospitals

(1) Where a court is minded to make a hospital order or interim hospital order in respect of any person it may request—

(a) the Primary Care Trust or Health Authority for the area in which that person resides or last resided; or

(b) any other Primary Care Trust or Health Authority that appears to the court to be appropriate,

to furnish the court with such information as that Primary Care Trust or Health Authority has or can reasonably obtain with respect to the hospital or hospitals (if any) in their area or elsewhere at which arrangements could be made for the admission of that person in pursuance of the order, and that Primary Care Trust or Health Authority shall comply with any such request.

39A Information to facilitate guardianship orders

Where a court is minded to make a guardianship order in respect of any offender, it may request the local social services authority for the area in which the offender resides or last resided, or any other local social services authority that appears to the court to be appropriate—

(a) to inform the court whether it or any other person approved by it is willing to receive the offender into guardianship; and

(b) if so, to give such information as it reasonably can about how it or the other person could be expected to exercise in relation to the offender the powers conferred by section 40(2) below;

and that authority shall comply with any such request.

40 Effect of hospital orders, guardianship orders and interim hospital orders

(1) A hospital order shall be sufficient authority—

(a) for a constable, an approved social worker or any other person directed to do so by the court to convey the patient to the hospital specified in the order within a period of 28 days; and

(b) for the managers of the hospital to admit him at any time within that period and thereafter detain him in accordance with the provisions of this Act.

(2) A guardianship order shall confer on the authority or person named in the order as guardian the same powers as a guardianship application made and accepted under Part II of this Act.

(3) Where an interim hospital order is made in respect of an offender—

(a) a constable or any other person directed to do so by the court shall convey the offender to the hospital specified in the order within the period mentioned in section 38(4) above; and

(b) the managers of the hospital shall admit him within that period and thereafter detain him in accordance with the provisions of section 38 above.

(4) A patient who is admitted to a hospital in pursuance of a hospital order, or placed under guardianship by a guardianship order, shall, subject to the provisions of this subsection, be treated for the purposes of the provisions of this Act mentioned in Part I of Schedule 1 to this Act as if he had been so admitted or placed on the date of the order in pursuance of an application for admission for treatment or a guardianship application, as the case may be, duly made under Part II of this Act, but subject to any modifications of those provisions specified in that Part of that Schedule.

(5) Where a patient is admitted to a hospital in pursuance of a hospital order, or placed under guardianship by a guardianship order, any previous application, hospital order or guardianship order by virtue of which he was liable to be detained in a hospital or subject to guardianship shall cease to have effect; but if the first-mentioned order, or the conviction on which it was made, is quashed on appeal, this subsection shall not apply and section 22 above shall have effect as if during any period for which the patient was liable to be detained or subject to guardianship under the order, he had been detained in custody as mentioned in that section.

RESTRICTION ORDERS

41 Power of higher courts to restrict discharge from hospital

(1) Where a hospital order is made in respect of an offender by the Crown Court, and it appears to the court, having regard to the nature of the offence, the antecedents of the offender and the risk of his committing further offences if set at large, that it is necessary for the protection of the public from serious harm so to do, the court may, subject to the provisions of this section, further order that the offender shall be subject to the special restrictions set out in this section, either without limit of time or during such period as may be specified in the order; and an order under this section shall be known as 'a restriction order'.

(2) A restriction order shall not be made in the case of any person unless at least one of the registered medical practitioners whose evidence is taken into account by the court under section 37(2)(a) above has given evidence orally before the court.

(3) The special restrictions applicable to a patient in respect of whom a restriction order is in force are as follows—

(a) none of the provisions of Part II of this Act relating to the duration, renewal and expiration of authority for the detention of patients shall apply, and the patient shall continue to be liable to be detained by virtue of the relevant hospital order until he is duly discharged under the said Part II or absolutely discharged under section 42, 73, 74 or 75 below;

(b) no application shall be made to a Mental Health Review Tribunal in respect of a patient under section 66 or 69(1) below;

(c) the following powers shall be exercisable only with the consent of the Secretary of State, namely—

    (i) power to grant leave of absence to the patient under section 17 above;

    (ii) power to transfer the patient in pursuance of regulations under section 19 above (or in pursuance of subsection (3) of that section); and

    (iii) power to order the discharge of the patient under section 23 above;

and if leave of absence is granted under the said section 17 power to recall the patient under that section shall vest in the Secretary of State as well as the responsible medical officer; and

(d) the power of the Secretary of State to recall the patient under the said section 17 and power to take the patient into custody and return him under section 18 above may be exercised at any time;

and in relation to any such patient section 40(4) above shall have effect as if it referred to Part II of Schedule 1 to this Act instead of Part I of that Schedule.

(4) A hospital order shall not cease to have effect under section 40(5) above if a restriction order in respect of the patient is in force at the material time.

(5) Where a restriction order in respect of a patient ceases to have effect while the relevant hospital order continues in force, the provisions of section 40 above and Part I of Schedule 1 to this Act shall apply to the patient as if he had been admitted to the hospital in pursuance of a hospital order (without a restriction order) made on the date on which the restriction order ceased to have effect.

42 **Powers of Secretary of State in respect of patients subject to restriction orders**

(1) If the Secretary of State is satisfied that in the case of any patient a restriction order is no longer required for the protection of the public from serious harm, he may direct that the patient shall cease to be subject to the special restrictions set out in section 41(3) above; and where the Secretary of State so directs, the restriction order shall cease to have effect, and section 41(5) above shall apply accordingly.

(2) At any time while a restriction order is in force in respect of a patient, the Secretary of State may, if he thinks fit, by warrant discharge the patient from hospital, either absolutely or subject to conditions; and where a person is absolutely discharged under this subsection, he shall thereupon cease to be liable to be detained by virtue of the relevant hospital order, and the restriction order shall cease to have effect accordingly.

(3) The Secretary of State may at any time during the continuance in force of a restriction order in respect of a patient who has been conditionally discharged under subsection (2) above by warrant recall the patient to such hospital as may be specified in the warrant.

(4) Where a patient is recalled as mentioned in subsection (3) above—

(a) if the hospital specified in the warrant is not the hospital from which the patient was conditionally discharged, the hospital order and the restriction order shall have effect as if the hospital specified in the warrant were substituted for the hospital specified in the hospital order;

(b) in any case, the patient shall be treated for the purposes of section 18 above as if he had absented himself without leave from the hospital specified in the warrant, and, if the restriction order was made for a specified period, that period shall not in any event expire until the patient returns to the hospital or is returned to the hospital under that section.

(5) If a restriction order in respect of a patient ceases to have effect after the patient has been conditionally discharged under this section, the patient shall, unless previously recalled

under subsection (3) above, be deemed to be absolutely discharged on the date when the order ceases to have effect, and shall cease to be liable to be detained by virtue of the relevant hospital order accordingly.

(6) The Secretary of State may, if satisfied that the attendance at any place in Great Britain of a patient who is subject to a restriction order is desirable in the interests of justice or for the purposes of any public inquiry, direct him to be taken to that place; and where a patient is directed under this subsection to be taken to any place he shall, unless the Secretary of State otherwise directs, be kept in custody while being so taken, while at that place and while being taken back to the hospital in which he is liable to be detained.

43 Power of magistrates' courts to commit for restriction order

(1) If in the case of a person of or over the age of 14 years who is convicted by a magistrates' court of an offence punishable on summary conviction with imprisonment—

    (a) the conditions which under section 37(1) above are required to be satisfied for the making of a hospital order are satisfied in respect of the offender; but

    (b) it appears to the court, having regard to the nature of the offence, the antecedents of the offender and the risk of his committing further offences if set at large, that if a hospital order is made a restriction order should also be made,

the court may, instead of making a hospital order or dealing with him in any other manner, commit him in custody to the Crown Court to be dealt with in respect of the offence.

(2) Where an offender is committed to the Crown Court under this section, the Crown Court shall inquire into the circumstances of the case and may—

    (a) if that court would have power so to do under the foregoing provisions of this Part of this Act upon the conviction of the offender before that court of such an offence as is described in section 37(1) above, make a hospital order in his case, with or without a restriction order;

    (b) if the court does not make such an order, deal with the offender in any other manner in which the magistrates' court might have dealt with him.

(3) The Crown Court shall have the same power to make orders under sections 35, 36 and 38 above in the case of a person committed to the court under this section as the Crown Court has under those sections in the case of an accused person within the meaning of section 35 or 36 above or of a person convicted before that court as mentioned in section 38 above.

(4) The power of a magistrates' court under section 3 of the Powers of Criminal Courts (Sentencing) Act 2000 (which enables such a court to commit an offender to the Crown Court where the court is of the opinion that greater punishment should be inflicted for the offence than the court has power to inflict) shall also be exercisable by a magistrates' court where it is of the opinion that greater punishment should be inflicted as aforesaid on the offender unless a hospital order is made in his case with a restriction order.

(5) The power of the Crown Court to make a hospital order, with or without a restriction order, in the case of a person convicted before that court of an offence may, in the same circumstances and subject to the same conditions, be exercised by such a court in the case of a person committed to the court under section 5 of the Vagrancy Act 1824 (which provides for the committal to the Crown Court of persons who are incorrigible rogues within the meaning of that section).

45 Appeals from magistrates' courts

(1) Where on the trial of an information charging a person with an offence a magistrates' court makes a hospital order or guardianship order in respect of him without convicting him, he shall have the same right of appeal against the order as if it had been made on his conviction; and on any such appeal the Crown Court shall have the same powers as if the appeal had been against both conviction and sentence.

(2) An appeal by a child or young person with respect to whom any such order has been made, whether the appeal is against the order or against the finding upon which the order was made, may be brought by him or by his parent or guardian on his behalf.

45A   Power of higher courts to direct hospital admission

(1) This section applies where, in the case of a person convicted before the Crown Court of an offence the sentence for which is not fixed by law—

    (a) the conditions mentioned in subsection (2) below are fulfilled; and

    (b) except where the offence is one the sentence for which falls to be imposed under section 109 of the Powers of Criminal Courts (Sentencing) Act 2000, the court considers making a hospital order in respect of him before deciding to impose a sentence of imprisonment ('the relevant sentence') in respect of the offence.

(2) The conditions referred to in subsection (1) above are that the court is satisfied, on the written or oral evidence of two registered medical practitioners—

    (a) that the offender is suffering from psychopathic disorder;

    (b) that the mental disorder from which the offender is suffering is of a nature or degree which makes it appropriate for him to be detained in a hospital for medical treatment; and

    (c) that such treatment is likely to alleviate or prevent a deterioration of his condition.

(3) The court may give both of the following directions, namely—

    (a) a direction that, instead of being removed to and detained in a prison, the offender be removed to and detained in such hospital as may be specified in the direction (in this Act referred to as a 'hospital direction'); and

    (b) a direction that the offender be subject to the special restrictions set out in section 41 above (in this Act referred to as a 'limitation direction').

(4) A hospital direction and a limitation direction shall not be given in relation to an offender unless at least one of the medical practitioners whose evidence is taken into account by the court under subsection (2) above has given evidence orally before the court.

(5) A hospital direction and a limitation direction shall not be given in relation to an offender unless the court is satisfied on the written or oral evidence of the registered medical practitioner who would be in charge of his treatment, or of some other person representing the managers of the hospital that arrangements have been made—

    (a) for his admission to that hospital; and

    (b) for his admission to it within the period of 28 days beginning with the day of the giving of such directions;

and the court may, pending his admission within that period, give such directions as it thinks fit for his conveyance to and detention in a place of safety.

(6) If within the said period of 28 days it appears to the Secretary of State that by reason of an emergency or other special circumstances it is not practicable for the patient to be received into the hospital specified in the hospital direction, he may give instructions for the admission of the patient to such other hospital as appears to be appropriate instead of the hospital so specified.

(7) Where such instructions are given—

    (a) the Secretary of State shall cause the person having the custody of the patient to be informed, and

    (b) the hospital direction shall have effect as if the hospital specified in the instructions were substituted for the hospital specified in the hospital direction.

45B   Effect of hospital and limitation directions

(1) A hospital direction and a limitation direction shall be sufficient authority—

    (a) for a constable or any other person directed to do so by the court to convey the patient to the hospital specified in the hospital direction within a period of 28 days; and

    (b) for the managers of the hospital to admit him at any time within that period and thereafter detain him in accordance with the provisions of this Act.

(2) With respect to any person—

    (a) a hospital direction shall have effect as a transfer direction; and

    (b) a limitation direction shall have effect as a restriction direction.

(3) While a person is subject to a hospital direction and a limitation direction the responsible medical officer shall at such intervals (not exceeding one year) as the Secretary of State may direct examine and report to the Secretary of State on that person; and every report shall contain such particulars as the Secretary of State may require.

47   Removal to hospital of persons serving sentences of imprisonment, etc

(1) If in the case of a person serving a sentence of imprisonment the Secretary of State is satisfied, by reports from at least two registered medical practitioners—

    (a) that the said person is suffering from mental illness, psychopathic disorder, severe mental impairment or mental impairment; and

    (b) that the mental disorder from which that person is suffering is of a nature or degree which makes it appropriate for him to be detained in a hospital for medical treatment and, in the case of psychopathic disorder or mental impairment, that such treatment is likely to alleviate or prevent a deterioration of his condition;

the Secretary of State may, if he is of the opinion having regard to the public interest and all the circumstances that it is expedient so to do, by warrant direct that that person be removed to and detained in such hospital as may be specified in the direction; and a direction under this section shall be known as 'a transfer direction'.

(2) A transfer direction shall cease to have effect at the expiration of the period of 14 days beginning with the date on which it is given unless within that period the person with respect to whom it was given has been received into the hospital specified in the direction.

(3) A transfer direction with respect to any person shall have the same effect as a hospital order made in his case.

(4) A transfer direction shall specify the form or forms of mental disorder referred to in paragraph (a) of subsection (1) above from which, upon the reports taken into account under that subsection, the patient is found by the Secretary of State to be suffering; and no such direction shall be given unless the patient is described in each of those reports as suffering from the same form of disorder, whether or not he is also described in either of them as suffering from another form.

54   Requirements as to medical evidence

(1) The registered medical practitioner whose evidence is taken into account under section 35(3)(a) above and at least one of the registered medical practitioners whose evidence is taken into account under sections 36(1), 37(2)(a), 38(1), 45A(2) and 51(6)(a) above and whose reports are taken into account under sections 47(1) and 48(1) above shall be a practitioner approved for the purposes of section 12 above by the Secretary of State as having special experience in the diagnosis or treatment of mental disorder.

(2) For the purposes of any provision of this Part of this Act under which a court may act on the written evidence of—

    (a) a registered medical practitioner or a registered medical practitioner of any description; or

    (b) a person representing the managers of a hospital,

a report in writing purporting to be signed by a registered medical practitioner or a registered medical practitioner of such a description or by a person representing the managers of a hospital may, subject to the provisions of this section, be received in evidence without proof of the signature of the practitioner or that person and without proof that he has the requisite qualifications or authority or is of the requisite description: but the court may require the signatory of any such report to be called to give oral evidence.

Criminal Procedure (Insanity) Act 1964 (as amended)

5   Powers to deal with persons not guilty by reason of insanity or unfit to plead etc

    (1) This section applies where—

(a) a special verdict is returned that the accused is not guilty by reason of insanity; or

(b) findings have been made that the accused is under a disability and that he did the act or made the omission charged against him.

(2) The court shall make in respect of the accused—

(a) a hospital order (with or without a restriction order);

(b) a supervision order; or

(c) an order for his absolute discharge.

(3) Where—

(a) the offence to which the special verdict or the findings relate is an offence the sentence for which is fixed by law, and

(b) the court have power to make a hospital order,

the court shall make a hospital order with a restriction order (whether or not they would have power to make a restriction order apart from this subsection).

(4) In this section—

'hospital order' has the meaning given in section 37 of the Mental Health Act 1983;

'restriction order' has the meaning given to it by section 41 of that Act;

'supervision order' has the meaning given in Part 1 of Schedule 1A to this Act.

(O) HUMAN RIGHTS

Human Rights Act 1998

Introduction

1   The Convention Rights

(1) In this Act 'the Convention rights' means the rights and fundamental freedoms set out in—

(a) Articles 2 to 12 and 14 of the Convention,

(b) Articles 1 to 3 of the First Protocol, and

(c) Article 1 of the Thirteenth Protocol,

as read with Articles 16 to 18 of the Convention.

(2) Those Articles are to have effect for the purposes of this Act subject to any designated derogation or reservation(as to which see sections 14 and 15).

(3) The Articles are set out in Schedule 1.

(4) The Lord Chancellor may by order make such amendments to this Act as he considers appropriate to reflect the effect, in relation to the United Kingdom, of a protocol.

(5) In subsection(4) 'protocol' means a protocol to the Convention—

(a) which the United Kingdom has ratified; or

(b) which the United Kingdom has signed with a view to ratification.

(6) No amendment may be made by an order under subsection(4) so as to come into force before the protocol concerned is in force in relation to the United Kingdom.

2   Interpretation of Convention rights

(1) A court or tribunal determining a question which has arisen in connection with a Convention right must take into account any—

(a) judgment, decision, declaration or advisory opinion of the European Court of Human Rights,

(b) opinion of the Commission given in a report adopted under Article 31 of the Convention,

(c) decision of the Commission in connection with Article 26 or 27(2) of the Convention, or

(d) decision of the Committee of Ministers taken under Article 46 of the Convention, whenever made or given, so far as, in the opinion of the court or tribunal, it is relevant to the proceedings in which that question has arisen.

(2) Evidence of any judgment, decision, declaration or opinion of which account may have to be taken under this section is to be given in proceedings before any court or tribunal in such manner as may be provided by rules.

(3) In this section 'rules' means rules of court or, in the case of proceedings before a tribunal, rules made for the purposes of this section—

(a) by the Lord Chancellor or Secretary of State, in relation to any proceedings outside Scotland;

(b) by the Secretary of State, in relation to proceedings in Scotland; or

(c) by a Northern Ireland department, in relation to proceedings before a tribunal in Northern Ireland—

(i) which deals with transferred matters; and

(ii) for which no rules made under paragraph(a) are in force.

3 Interpretation of legislation

(1) So far as it is possible to do so, primary legislation and subordinate legislation must be read and given effect in a way which is compatible with the Convention rights.

(2) This section—

(a) applies to primary legislation and subordinate legislation whenever enacted;

(b) does not affect the validity, continuing operation or enforcement of any incompatible primary legislation; and

(c) does not affect the validity, continuing operation or enforcement of any incompatible subordinate legislation if (disregarding any possibility of revocation) primary legislation prevents removal of the incompatibility.

4 Declaration of incompatibility

(1) Subsection (2) applies in any proceedings in which a court determines whether a provision of primary legislation is compatible with a Convention right.

(2) If the court is satisfied that the provision is incompatible with a Convention right, it may make a declaration of that incompatibility.

(3) Subsection(4) applies in any proceedings in which a court determines whether a provision of subordinate legislation, made in the exercise of a power conferred by primary legislation, is compatible with a Convention right.

(4) If the court is satisfied—

(a) that the provision is incompatible with a Convention right, and

(b) that (disregarding any possibility of revocation) the primary legislation concerned prevents removal of the incompatibility,

it may make a declaration of that incompatibility.

(5) In this section 'court' means—

(a) the Supreme Court;

(b) the Judicial Committee of the Privy Council;

(c) the Courts-Martial Appeal Court;

(d) in Scotland, the High Court of Justiciary sitting otherwise than as a trial court or the Court of Session;

(e) in England and Wales or Northern Ireland, the High Court or the Court of Appeal;

(f) the Court of Protection, in any matter being dealt with by the President of the Family Division, the Vice-Chancellor or a puisne judge of the High Court.

(6) A declaration under this section ('a declaration of

(a) does not affect the validity, continuing operation or enforcement of the provision in respect of which it is given; and

(b) is not binding on the parties to the proceedings in which it is made.

5 Right of Crown to intervene

(1) Where a court is considering whether to make a declaration of incompatibility, the Crown is entitled to notice in accordance with rules of court.

(2) In any case to which subsection (1) applies—

(a) a Minister of the Crown(or a person nominated by him),

(b) a member of the Scottish Executive,

(c) a Northern Ireland Minister,

(d) a Northern Ireland department,

is entitled, on giving notice in accordance with rules of court, to be joined as a party to the proceedings.

(3) Notice under subsection (2) may be given at any time during the proceedings.

(4) A person who has been made a party to criminal proceedings(other than in Scotland) as the result of a notice under subsection (2) may, with leave, appeal to the Supreme Court against any declaration of incompatibility made in the proceedings.

(5) In subsection (4)—

'criminal proceedings' includes all proceedings before the Courts-Martial Appeal Court; and

'leave' means leave granted by the court making the declaration of incompatibility or by the Supreme Court.

6 Acts of public authorities

(1) It is unlawful for a public authority to act in a way which is incompatible with a Convention right.

(2) Subsection (1) does not apply to an act if—

(a) as the result of one or more provisions of primary legislation, the authority could not have acted differently; or

(b) in the case of one or more provisions of, or made under, primary legislation which cannot be read or given effect in a way which is compatible with the Convention rights, the authority was acting so as to give effect to or enforce those provisions.

(3) In this section 'public authority' includes—

(a) a court or tribunal, and

(b) any person certain of whose functions are functions of a public nature,

but does not include either House of Parliament or a person exercising functions in connection with proceedings in Parliament.

(5) In relation to a particular act, a person is not a public authority by virtue only of subsection (3)(b) if the nature of the act is private.

(6) 'An act' includes a failure to act but does not include a failure to—

(a) introduce in, or lay before, Parliament a proposal for legislation; or

(b) make any primary legislation or remedial order.

7 Proceedings

(1) A person who claims that a public authority has acted(or proposes to act) in a way which is made unlawful by section 6(1) may—

(a) bring proceedings against the authority under this Act in the appropriate court or tribunal, or

(b) rely on the Convention right or rights concerned in any legal proceedings,

but only if he is (or would be) a victim of the unlawful act.

(2) In subsection (1)(a) 'appropriate court or tribunal' means such court or tribunal as may be determined in accordance with rules; and proceedings against an authority include a counterclaim or similar proceeding.

(3) If the proceedings are brought on an application for judicial review, the applicant is to be taken to have a sufficient interest in relation to the unlawful act only if he is, or would be, a victim of that act.

(4) If the proceedings are made by way of a petition for judicial review in Scotland, the applicant shall be taken to have title and interest to sue in relation to the unlawful act only if he is, or would be, a victim of that act.

(5) Proceedings under subsection (1)(a) must be brought before the end of—

    (a) the period of one year beginning with the date on which the act complained of took place; or

    (b) such longer period as the court or tribunal considers equitable having regard to all the circumstances,

but that is subject to any rule imposing a stricter time limit in relation to the procedure in question.

(6) In subsection (1)(b) 'legal proceedings' includes—

    (a) proceedings brought by or at the instigation of a public authority; and

    (b) an appeal against the decision of a court or tribunal.

(7) For the purposes of this section, a person is a victim of an unlawful act only if he would be a victim for the purposes of Article 34 of the Convention if proceedings were brought in the European Court of Human Rights in respect of that act.

(8) Nothing in this Act creates a criminal offence.

(9) In this section 'rules' means—

    (a) in relation to proceedings before a court or tribunal outside Scotland, rules made by the Secretary of State for the purposes of this section or rules of court,

    (b) in relation to proceedings before a court or tribunal in Scotland, rules made by the Secretary of State for those purposes,

    (c) in relation to proceedings before a tribunal in Northern Ireland—

        (i)   which deals with transferred matters; and

        (ii) for which no rules made under paragraph(a) are in force,

rules made by a Northern Ireland department for those purposes,

and includes provision made by order under section 1 of the Courts and Legal Services Act 1990.

(10) In making rules, regard must be had to section 9.

(11) The Minister who has power to make rules in relation to a particular tribunal may, to the extent he considers it necessary to ensure that the tribunal can provide an appropriate remedy in relation to an act (or proposed act) of a public authority which is(or would be) unlawful as a result of section 6(i), by order add to—

    (a) the relief or remedies which the tribunal may grant; or

    (b) the grounds on which it may grant any of them.

(12) An order made under subsection(11) may contain such incidental, supplemental, consequential or transitional provision as the Minister making it considers appropriate.

(13) 'The Minister' includes the Northern Ireland department concerned.

8 Judicial remedies

(1) In relation to any act (or proposed act) of a public authority which the court finds is (or would be) unlawful, it may grant such relief or remedy, or make such order, within its powers as it considers just and appropriate.

(2) But damages may be awarded only by a court which has power to award damages, or to order the payment of compensation, in civil proceedings.

(3) No award of damages is to be made unless, taking account of all the circumstances of the case, including—

    (a) any other relief or remedy granted, or order made, in relation to the act in question(by that or any other court), and

    (b) the consequences of any decision (of that or any other court) in respect of that act,

the court is satisfied that the award is necessary to afford just satisfaction to the person in whose favour it is made.

(4) In determining—
    (a) whether to award damages, or
    (b) the amount of an award,
the court must take into account the principles applied by the European Court of Human Rights in relation to the award of
    (5) A public authority against which damages are awarded is to be treated—
        (a) in Scotland, for the purposes of section 3 of the Law Reform(Miscellaneous Provisions)(Scotland) Act 1940 as if the award were made in an action of damages in which the authority has been found liable in respect of loss or damage to the person to whom the award is made;
        (b) for the purposes of the Civil Liability(Contribution) Act 1978 as liable in respect of damage suffered by the person to whom the award is made.
    (6) In this section—
'court' includes a tribunal;
'damages' means damages for an unlawful act of a public authority; and
'unlawful' means unlawful under section 6(1).

SCHEDULE 1   THE ARTICLES

PART 1   THE CONVENTION

Article 3   Prohibition of torture
No one shall be subjected to torture or to inhuman or degrading treatment or punishment.

Article 5   Right to liberty and security
    1. Everyone has the right to liberty and security of person. No one shall be deprived of his liberty save in the following cases and in accordance with a procedure prescribed by law:
        (a) the lawful detention of a person after conviction by a competent court;
        (b) the lawful arrest or detention of a person for non-compliance with the lawful order of a court or in order to secure the fulfilment of any obligation prescribed by law;
        (c) the lawful arrest or detention of a person effected for the purpose of bringing him before the competent legal authority on reasonable suspicion of having committed an offence or when it is reasonably considered necessary to prevent his committing an offence or fleeing after having done so;
        (d) the detention of a minor by lawful order for the purpose of educational supervision or his lawful detention for the purpose of bringing him before the competent legal authority;
        (e) the lawful detention of persons for the prevention of the spreading of infectious diseases, of persons of unsound mind, alcoholics or drug addicts or vagrants;
        (f) the lawful arrest or detention of a person to prevent his effecting an unauthorised entry into the country or of a person against whom action is being taken with a view to deportation or extradition.
    2. Everyone who is arrested shall be informed promptly, in a language which he understands, of the reasons for his arrest and of any charge against him.
    3. Everyone arrested or detained in accordance with the provisions of paragraph 1(c) of this Article shall be brought promptly before a judge or other officer authorised by law to exercise judicial power and shall be entitled to trial within a reasonable time or to release pending trial. Release may be conditioned by guarantees to appear for trial.
    4. Everyone who is deprived of his liberty by arrest or detention shall be entitled to take proceedings by which the lawfulness of his detention shall be decided speedily by a court and his release ordered if the detention is not lawful.

5. Everyone who has been the victim of arrest or detention in contravention of the provisions of this Article shall have an enforceable right to compensation.

Article 7   No punishment without law

1. No one shall be held guilty of any criminal offence on account of any act or omission which did not constitute a criminal offence under national or international law at the time when it was committed. Nor shall a heavier penalty be imposed than the one that was applicable at the time the criminal offence was committed.

2. This Article shall not prejudice the trial and punishment of any person for any act or omission which, at the time when it was committed, was criminal according to the general principles of law recognised by civilised nations.

(p) REHABILITATION

Rehabilitation of Offenders Act 1974 (as amended)

1   Rehabilitated persons and spent convictions

(1) Subject to subsection (2) below, where an individual has been convicted, whether before or after the commencement of this Act, of any offence or offences, and the following conditions are satisfied, that is to say—

   (a) he did not have imposed on him in respect of that conviction a sentence which is excluded from rehabilitation under this Act; and

   (b) he has not had imposed on him in respect of a subsequent conviction during the rehabilitation period applicable to the first-mentioned conviction in accordance with section 6 below a sentence which is excluded from rehabilitation under this Act;

then, after the end of the rehabilitation period so applicable (including, where appropriate, any extension under section 6 (4) below of the period originally applicable to the first-mentioned conviction) or, where that rehabilitation period ended before the commencement of this Act, after the commencement of this Act, that individual shall for the purposes of this Act be treated as a rehabilitated person in respect of the first-mentioned conviction and that conviction shall for those purposes be treated as spent.

(2) A person shall not become a rehabilitated person for the purposes of this Act in respect of a conviction unless he has served or otherwise undergone or complied with any sentence imposed on him in respect of that conviction; but the following shall not, by virtue of this subsection, prevent a person from becoming a rehabilitated person for those purposes—

   (a) failure to pay a fine or other sum adjudged to be paid by or imposed on a conviction, or breach of a condition of a recognizance or of a bond of caution to keep the peace or be of good behaviour;

   (b) breach of any condition or requirement applicable in relation to a sentence which renders the person to whom it applies liable to be dealt with for the offence for which the sentence was imposed, or, where the sentence was a suspended sentence of imprisonment, liable to be dealt with in respect of that sentence (whether or not, in any case, he is in fact so dealt with);

   (c) failure to comply with any requirement of a suspended sentence supervision order.

(2A) Where in respect of a conviction a person has been sentenced to imprisonment with an order under section 47(1) of the Criminal Law Act 1977, he is to be treated for the purposes of subsection (2) above as having served the sentence as soon as he completes service of so much of the sentence as was by that order required to be served in prison.

(2B) In subsection (2)(A) above the reference to a fine or other sum adjudged to be paid by or imposed on a conviction does not include a reference to an amount payable under a confiscation order made under Part 2 or 3 of the Proceeds of Crime Act 2002.

(3) In this Act 'sentence' includes any order made by a court in dealing with a person in respect of his conviction of any offence or offences, other than—

(a) an order for committal or any other order made in default of payment of any fine or other sum adjudged to be paid by or imposed on a conviction, or for want of sufficient distress to satisfy any such fine or other sum;

(b) an order dealing with a person in respect of a suspended sentence of imprisonment.

(4) In this Act, references to a conviction, however expressed, include references—

(a) to a conviction by or before a court outside Great Britain; and

(b) to any finding (other than a finding linked with a finding of insanity) in any criminal proceedings or in care proceedings under section 1 of the Children and Young Persons Act 1969 that a person has committed an offence or done the act or made the omission charged;

and notwithstanding anything in section 9 of the Criminal Justice (Scotland) Act 1949 or section 14 of the Powers of Criminal Courts (Sentencing) Act 2000 (conviction of a person discharged to be deemed not to be a conviction) a conviction in respect of which an order is made discharging him absolutely or conditionally shall be treated as a conviction for the purposes of this Act and the person in question may become a rehabilitated person in respect of that conviction and the conviction a spent conviction for those purposes accordingly.

4   Effect of rehabilitation

(1) Subject to sections 7 and 8 below, a person who has become a rehabilitated person for the purposes of this Act in respect of a conviction shall be treated for all purposes in law as a person who has not committed or been charged with or prosecuted for or convicted of or sentenced for the offence or offences which were the subject of that conviction; and, notwithstanding the provisions of any other enactment or rule of law to the contrary, but subject as aforesaid—

(a) no evidence shall be admissible in any proceedings before a judicial authority exercising its jurisdiction or functions in Great Britain to prove that any such person has committed or been charged with or prosecuted for or convicted of or sentenced for any offence which was the subject of a spent conviction; and

(b) a person shall not, in any such proceedings, be asked, and, if asked, shall not be required to answer, any question relating to his past which cannot be answered without acknowledging or referring to a spent conviction or spent convictions or any circumstances ancillary thereto.

(2) Subject to the provisions of any order made under subsection (4) below, where a question seeking information with respect to a person's previous convictions, offences, conduct or circumstances is put to him or to any other person otherwise than in proceedings before a judicial authority—

(a) the question shall be treated as not relating to spent convictions or to any circumstances ancillary to spent convictions, and the answer thereto may be framed accordingly; and

(b) the person questioned shall not be subjected to any liability or otherwise prejudiced in law by reason of any failure to acknowledge or disclose a spent conviction or any circumstances ancilary to a spent conviction in his answer to the question.

(5) For the purposes of this section and section 7 below any of the following are circumstances ancillary to a conviction, that is to say—

(a) the offence or offences which were the subject of that conviction;

(b) the conduct constituting that offence or those offences; and

(c) any process or proceedings preliminary to that conviction, any sentence imposed in respect of that conviction, any proceedings (whether by way of appeal or otherwise) for reviewing that conviction or any such sentence, and anything done in pursuance of or undergone in compliance with any such sentence.

(6) For the purposes of this section and section 7 below 'proceedings before a judicial authority' includes, in addition to proceedings before any of the ordinary courts of law, proceedings before any tribunal, body or person having power—

(a) by virtue of any enactment, law, custom or practice;

(b) under the rules governing any association, institution, profession, occupation or employment; or

(c) under any provision of any agreement providing for arbitration with respect to questions arising thereunder;

to determine any question affecting the rights, privileges, obligations or liabilities of any person, or to receive evidence affecting the determination of any such question.

5 Rehabilitation periods for particular sentences

(1) The sentences excluded from rehabilitation under this Act are—

(a) a sentence of Imprisonment for life;

(b) a sentence of imprisonment, youth custody detention in a young offender institution or corrective training for a term exceeding thirty months;

(c) a sentence of preventive detention;

(d) a sentence of detention during Her Majesty's pleasure or for life, under section 90 or 91 of the Powers of Criminal Courts (Sentencing) Act 2000, or under section 205(2) or (3) of the Criminal Procedure (Scotland) Act 1975 or a sentence of detention for a term exceeding thirty months passed under section 91 of the said Act of 2000 (young offenders convicted of grave crimes) or under section 206 of the said Act of 1975 (detention of children convicted on indictment), or a corresponding court-martial punishment;

(e) a sentence of custody for life; and

(f) a sentence of imprisonment for public protection under section 225 of the Criminal Justice Act 2003, a sentence of detention for public protection under section 226 of that Act or an extended sentence under section 227 or 228 of that Act.

and any other sentence is a sentence subject to rehabilitation under this Act.

(1A) In subsection (1)(d) above 'corresponding court-martial punishment' means a punishment awarded under section 71A(3) or (4) of the Army Act 1955, section 71A(9) or (4) of the Air Force Act 1955 or section 43A(3) or (4) of the Naval Discipline Act 1957.

(2) For the purposes of this Act—

(a) the rehabilitation period applicable to a sentence specified in the first column of Table A below is the period specified in the second column of that Table in relation to that sentence, or, where the sentence was imposed on a person who was under eighteen years of age at the date of his conviction, half that period; and

(b) the rehabilitation period applicable to a sentence specified in the first column of Table B below is the period specified in the second column of that Table in relation to that sentence;

reckoned in either case from the date of the conviction in respect of which the sentence was imposed.

Table A Rehabilitation periods subject to reduction by half for persons under18

Sentence	Rehabilitation period
A sentence of imprisonment, detention in a young offender institution or youth custody or corrective training for a term exceeding six months but not exceeding thirty months.	Ten years
A sentence of cashiering, discharge with ignominy or dismissal with disgrace from Her Majesty's service.	Ten years
A sentence of imprisonment, detention in a young offender institution or youth custody for a term not exceeding six months.	Seven years
A sentence of dismissal from Her Majesty's service.	Seven year
Any sentence of detention in respect of a conviction in service disciplinary proceedings.	Five years
A fine or any other sentence subject to rehabilitation under this Act, not being a sentence to which Table B below or any of subsections (3) to (8) below applies.	Five years

Table B Rehabilitation periods for certain sentences confined to young offenders

Sentence	Rehabilitation period
A sentence of Borstal training.	Seven years
A custodial order under Schedule 5A to the Army Act 1955 or the Air Force Act 1955, or under Schedule 4A to the Naval Discipline Act 1957, where the maximum period of detention specified in the order is more than six months.	Seven years
A custodial order under section 71AA of the Army Act 1955 or the Air Force Act 1955, or under section 43AA of the Naval Discipline Act 1957, where the maximum period of detention specified in the order is more than six months.	Seven years
A sentence of detention for a term exceeding six months but not exceeding thirty months passed under section 91 of the Powers of Criminal Courts (Sentencing) Act 2000 or under section 206 of the Criminal Procedure (Scotland) Act 1975.	Five years
Any sentence of detention for a term not exceeding six months passed under either of those provisions.	Three years
An order for detention in a detention centre made under section 4 of the Criminal Justice Act 1982 or section 4 of the Criminal Justice Act 1961.	Three years
A custodial order under any of the Schedules to the said Acts of 1955 and 1957 mentioned above, where the maximum period of detention specified in the order is six months or less.	Three years
A custodial order under section 71AA of the said Acts of 1955, or section 43AA of the said Act of 1957, where the maximum period of detention specified in the order is six months or less.	Three years

(3) The rehabilitation period applicable—

 (a) to an order discharging a person absolutely for an offence; and

 (b) to the discharge by a children's hearing under section 69(1)(b) and (12) of the Children (Scotland) Act 1995 of the referral of a child's case;

shall be six months from the date of conviction.

(4) Where in respect of a conviction a person was conditionally discharged, bound over to keep the peace or he of good behaviour... the rehabilitation period applicable to the sentence shall be one year from the date of conviction or a period beginning with that date and ending when the order for conditional discharge... or (as the case may be) the recognizance or bond of caution to keep the peace or be of good behaviour ceases or ceased to have effect, whichever is the longer.

(4A) Where in respect of a conviction a probation order or a community order under section 177 of the Criminal Justice Act 2003, the rehabilitation period applicable to the sentence shall be—

 (a) in the case of a person aged eighteen years or over at the date of his conviction. five years from the date of his conviction.

 (b) in the case of a person aged under the age of eighteen years at the date of his conviction, two and a half years from the date of conviction or a period beginning with the date of conviction and ending when the order in question ceases or ceased to have effect whichever is the longer.

(4B) Where is respect of a conviction a referral order (within the meaning of the Powers of Criminal Courts (Sentencing) Act 2000) is made in respect of the person convicted, the rehabilitation period applicable to the sentence shall be—

 (a) if a youth offender contract takes effect under section 23 of that Act between him and a youth offender panel, the period beginning with the date of conviction and ending on the date when (in accordance with section 24 of the Act) the contract ceases to have effect;

 (b) if no such contract so takes effect, the period beginning with the date of conviction and having the same length as the period for which such a contract would ignoring any order under paragraph 11 or 12 of Schedule 1 to that Act have had effect had one so taken effect.

(4C) Where in respect of a conviction an order is made in respect of the person convicted under paragraph 11 or 12 of Schedule 1 to the Powers of Criminal Court (Sentencing) Act 2000 (extension of period for which youth offender contract has effects the rehabilitation period applicable to the sentence shall be—

 (a) if a youth offender contract takes effect under section 23 of that Act between the offender and a youth offender panel, the period beginning with the date of conviction and ending on the date when (in accordance with section 24 of that Act) the contract ceases to have effect

 (b) if no such contract so takes effect, the period beginning with the date of conviction and having the same length as the period for which, in accordance with the order, such a contract would have had effect had one no taken effect.

6   The rehabilitation period applicable to a conviction

(1) Where only one sentence is imposed in respect of a conviction (not being a sentence excluded from rehabilitation under this Act) the rehabilitation period applicable to the conviction is, subject to the following provisions of this section, the period applicable to the sentence in accordance with section 5 above.

(2) Where more than one sentence is imposed in respect of a conviction (whether or not in the same proceedings) and none of the sentences imposed is excluded from rehabilitation under this Act, then, subject to the following provisions of this section, if the periods applicable to those sentences in accordance with section 5 above differ, the rehabilitation

period applicable to the conviction shall be the longer or the longest (as the case may be) of those periods.

(4) Subject to subsection (5) below, where during the rehabilitation period applicable to a conviction—

(a) the person convicted is convicted of a further offence; and

(b) no sentence excluded from rehabilitation under this Act is imposed on him in respect of the later conviction;

if the rehabilitation period applicable in accordance with this section to either of the convictions would end earlier than the period so applicable in relation to the other, the rehabilitation period which would (apart from this subsection) end the earlier shall be extended so as to end at the same time as the other rehabilitation period.

(5) Where the rehabilitation period applicable to a conviction is the rehabilitation period applicable in accordance with section 5 (8) above to an order imposing on a person any disqualification, disability, prohibition or other penalty, the rehabilitation period applicable to another conviction shall not by virtue of subsection (4) above be extended by reference to that period; but if any other sentence is imposed in respect of the first-mentioned conviction for which a rehabilitation period is prescribed by any other provision of section 5 above, the rehabilitation period applicable to another conviction shall, where appropriate, be extended under subsection (4) above by reference to the rehabilitation period applicable in accordance with that section to that sentence or, where more than one such sentence is imposed, by reference to the longer or longest of the periods so applicable to those sentences, as if the period in question were the rehabilitation period applicable to the first-mentioned conviction.

7 Limitations on rehabilitation under this Act, etc.

(1) Nothing in section 4 (1) above shall affect—

(a) any right of Her Majesty, by virtue of Her Royal prerogative or otherwise, to grant a free pardon, to quash any conviction or sentence, or to commute any sentence;

(b) the enforcement by any process or proceedings of any fine or other sum adjudged to be paid by or imposed on a spent conviction;

(c) the issue of any process for the purpose of proceedings in respect of any breach of a condition or requirement applicable to a sentence imposed in respect of a spent conviction; or

(d) the operation of any enactment by virtue of which, in consequence of any conviction, a person is subject, otherwise than by way of sentence, to any disqualification, disability, prohibition or other penalty the period of which extends beyond the rehabilitation period applicable in accordance with section 6 above to the conviction.

(2) Nothing in section 4 (1) above shall affect the determination of any issue, or prevent the admission or requirement of any evidence, relating to a person's previous convictions or to circumstances ancillary thereto—

(a) in any criminal proceedings before a court in Great Britain (including any appeal or reference in a criminal matter);

(b) in any service disciplinary proceedings or in any proceedings on appeal from any service disciplinary proceedings;

(bb) in any proceedings under Part 2 of the Sexual Offences Act 2003, or on appeal from any such proceedings;

(c) in any proceedings relating to parental responsibilities or parental rights (within the meaning of section 1(3) and section 2(4) respectively of the Children (Scotland) Act 1995), guardianship, adoption or the provision by any person of accommodation, care or schooling for children under the age of 18 years;

(cc) in any proceedings under Part II of the Children (Scotland) Act 1995;

(d) in any care proceedings under section 1 of the Powers of Criminal Courts (Sentencing) Act 2000 or on appeal from any such proceedings, or in any proceedings relating to the variation or discharge of a care order or supervision order under that Act;

(f) in any proceedings in which he is a party or a witness, provided that, on the occasion when the issue or the admission or requirement of the evidence falls to be determined, he consents to the determination of the issue or, as the case may be, the admission or requirement of the evidence notwithstanding the provisions of section 4(1).

INDEX

Access to Justice Act 1999
ss. 12–18   *1–5*

Bail Act 1976 (as amended)
ss. 3–7, Sched. 1   *157–68*
Bail (Amendment) Act 1993
s. 1   *171–2*

Children and Young Persons Act 1969
ss. 23–23AA   *172–75*
Codes of Practice
Stop and Search (A)   *9–23*
Detention (C)   *48–52, 69–86, 116–25*
Identification (D)   *86–115*
Tape Recorded Interviews (E)   *125–9*
Visually Recorded Interviews (F)   *130–6*
Arrest (G)   *52–5*
Company Directors Disqualification
Act 1986
ss. 1, 2, 13   *346–7*
Contempt of Court Act 1981
s. 8   *187*
Crime and Disorder Act 1998
ss. 8, 9   *330–2*
Criminal Appeal Act 1968
ss. 2, 7(1), 23, 23A, 33   *225–7*
Criminal Appeal Act 1995
ss. 8, 13   *227–8*
Criminal Evidence (Amendment) Act 1997
ss. 1, 2   *42–4*
Criminal Justice Act 1988
ss. 32, 34   *197*
Criminal Justice Act 2003
ss. 22–24   *116*
ss. 57–61, 67   *228–30*
ss. 75–79, 82, 84   *230–3*
ss. 98–110, 118   *217–23*
ss. 162–165   *307–8*
ss. 177–179   *293–4*
ss. 181–186 *265–7*
ss. 189–192 *268–70*
ss. 224–229, 231–235   *278–81*
ss. 237–240, 244, 246–258   *272–8*
ss. 263–265   *270–1*
ss. 269, 270, Sched. 21   *290–2*
Criminal Justice and Public Order Act 1994
s. 25   *168–9*
ss. 34–37   *212–14*
s. 60   *23–5*

Criminal Procedure and Investigations
Act 1996
ss. 1, 3–8, 10–18   *187–97*
Criminal Procedure (Insanity) Act 1964
s. 5   *363–4*

European Convention on Human Rights (1950)
Art. 6(1)   *176*
Art. 6(3)(b), (c)   *1*
Arts   5, 8   *5–6*

Firearms Act 1968
s. 52   *315*
Football Spectators Act 1989
ss. 14–14J   *343–6*

Human Rights Act 1998
ss. 1–8, Sched. 1 (Articles 3, 5, 7)   *364–9*

Immigration Act 1971
ss. 6, 7, Sched. 3   *340–2*

Juries Act 1974
ss. 1, 3, 8, 9, 9A, 17, Sched. 1   *183–7*
Justices of the Peace Act 1968
s. 1   *332*

Licensed Premises (Exclusion of Certain
Persons) Act 1980
ss. 1, 2   *342–3*

Magistrates' Courts Act 1980
ss. 17–23, 25, 26, Sched. 1   *177–83*
s. 32   *264–5*
s. 115   *332–3*
ss. 108, 111   *224*
Mental Health Act 1983 (as amended)
ss. 37–43, 45–45B, 47, 54   *356–63*
Misuse of Drugs Act 1971
s. 27   *315*
Murder (Abolition of Death Penalty) Act 1965
s. 1   *265*

Police and Criminal Evidence Act 1984
ss. 1–3   *6–9*
ss. 24–30, 56   *44–8*
ss. 37–46A   *55–69*
ss. 46A–47A   *169–71*

s. 55   *25–8*
ss. 61–65   *29–42*
ss. 76–78, 82(1), (3)   *215–17*
Police Reform Act (2002)
    ss. 9–24, 26–29   *136–54*
Powers of Criminal Courts (Sentencing)
    Act 2000
    ss. 1–11   *234–43*
    ss. 12–15   *333–6*
    ss. 16–27, 29, Sched. 1   *319–30*
    s. 33   *292–3*
    ss. 36B, 37, 39, 40   *294–5*
    s. 60, Scheds 5, 6, 7   *295–307*
    ss. 73, 74, Sched. 8   *317–19*
    ss. 76, 77   *257*
    s. 82A   *289–90*
    ss. 83, 89, 90–92, 99–107, 110,
        111   *258–64*
    ss. 130, 131, 133, 135–141,
        143–145   *308–15*
    ss. 142–146, 174   *243–5*
    ss.146, 147   *354–5*
    ss. 147–150, 156–159   *246–8*
    ss. 148, 149   *316–17*
    s. 150   *333*
    ss. 152, 153   *257*
    ss. 167–172   *255–6*
    ss. 196–213   *248–55*

Sched. 6   *355–6*
Prevention of Crime Act 1953
    s. 1   *316*
Proceeds of Crime Act 2002
    ss. 6–14   *336–40*
Prosecution of Offences Act 1985
    ss. 1–3, 10   *154–6*

Rehabilitation of Offenders Act 1974
    ss. 1, 4–7   *369–75*
Road Traffic Offenders Act 1988
    ss. 34–40, 42, 43   *347–54*

Serious Organised Crime and
        Police Act 2005
    s. 112   *28*
Sexual Offences Act 2003
    ss. 80–92   *281–9*
Supreme Court Act 1981
    s. 48   *224–5*

Theft Act 1968
    s. 27(3)   *223*

Youth Justice and Criminal Evidence Act 1999
    ss. 16–30, 34–43   *197–212*
    s. 59   *215*